*Second Edition*
*Revised and Expanded*

# Classics of
# Public Personnel Policy

**Frank J. Thompson**
*State University of New York at Albany*

*Brooks/Cole Publishing Company*
*Pacific Grove, California*

**Brooks/Cole Publishing Company**
A Division of Wadsworth, Inc.

© 1991, 1979 by Wadsworth, Inc., Belmont, California
94002. All rights reserved. No part of this book may be
reproduced, stored in a retrieval system, or transcribed,
in any form or by any means—electronic, mechanical,
photocopying, recording, or otherwise—without the prior
written permission of the publisher, Brooks/Cole
Publishing Company, Pacific Grove, California 93950,
a division of Wadsworth, Inc.

Printed in the United States of America
10  9  8  7  6  5  4  3  2  1

**Library of Congress Cataloging-in-Publication Data**
Classics of public policy / [edited by] Frank J. Thompson—
2nd ed., rev. and expanded.
    p.    cm.
  ISBN 0-534-13938-8
  1.Civil service—United States—Personnel management.
I.  Thompson, Frank J.
JK765.C57  1990
353.001—dc20                        90-30767
                                        CIP

Sponsoring Editor: *Cynthia C. Stormer*
Editorial Assistant: *Cathleen Sue Collins*
Production Editor: *Ben Greensfelder*
Manuscript Editor: *Robert E. Baker*
Permissions Editor: *Carline Haga*
Interior and Cover Design: *Katherine Minerva*
Art Coordinator: *Lisa Torri*
Typesetting: *Execustaff*
Printing and Binding: *Malloy Lithographing, Inc.*

*For my Parents*

# Preface

Public personnel policy penetrates government operations in myriad ways. It can energize human-resource management in public programs; it can vitiate such management. Personnel policies lay the ground rules for position determination—the creation and allocation of formal roles within agencies (e.g., job design and classification). They shape human-resource flows—recruitment, promotion, transfer, demotion, removal. They specify an approach to performance appraisal—processes through which managers acquire and interpret information concerning the activities of subordinates. They seek to motivate subordinates to behave in certain ways through regulation, the establishment of incentive systems (e.g., merit pay), and socialization that instills certain knowledge, perceptions, skills, and values.

Policy, as used here, refers to formal mandates or statements of intent that purport to guide behavior in personnel arenas. Laws and court opinions serve as obvious examples. These mandates usually specify goals and procedures (at times institutions) to be used in human-resource management. The way in which officials implement (or do nothing to implement) these policies determines their ultimate implications. In this regard students of policy have long understood that there's many a slip between the cup and the lip. The best laid plans often yield unanticipated outcomes, at times benign and at times malignant.

Given a focus on personnel policy, its implementation, and its consequences, what qualifies as a classic? A classic is above all a work of enduring value. Destined not to become obsolete tomorrow, it commands the attention of any serious student of public personnel policy. Usually the work becomes enduring via a breakthrough. This can occur in at least two major ways. First, the work may represent a contribution to empirical theory in that it facilitates in notable ways the conceptualization, description, and explanation of behavior in the public personnel arena. For instance, the work may set the pace in uncovering and explaining fundamental transformations in the hiring practices of government. Second, a classic may earn its status for its normative contribution. In one fashion or another, the work judges whether what *is* ought to be; in light of implicitly held or explicitly stated values, it prescribes remedies. To the degree that these normative assessments leave their mark on the scholarship of the field or on the behavior of participants in the personnel arena, they become contenders for classic status. Scholarly articles and books at times do this. In other cases, court opinions, public laws, and other policies have a particularly pronounced impact. No book of classics could, for instance, ignore the Pendleton Act of 1883, which galvanized the development of merit systems.

Picking classics is, of course, an invitation to debate. Although I doubt that observers will challenge the significance of most of this book's contents, some will naturally question why certain materials fail to appear. Those authors whose work appears in this volume may wonder whether I have ferreted out the truly classic portion of their writing. It deserves note that, in selecting contributions of enduring value, other secondary criteria influenced my choices. Several current texts and readers contain insights likely to endure. Their contents do not appear here, however, because they are readily available to students and often assigned in courses where this book might be used. I also excluded my own published work from consideration, since I cannot even pretend to be objective about it. The need to cover a spectrum of topics in limited space also led me to pick certain materials over others. Finally, readability counted. I sought selections that people without extensive backgrounds in public personnel administration or methodology could readily absorb. This concern led me to avoid certain materials featuring complex statistical manipulations.

Those familiar with the first edition of *Classics of Public Personnel Policy* will note some changes in the selections. With the exception of the Supreme Court's *Bakke* decision, I believe that the selections present in the earlier edition, but absent from this one, rank as classics. Competition for space, the discovery of a few new works from the past, the quest for balance, and the need to cover an extra decade led to their displacement.

Some readers, of course, will care less about whether I have selected *the* classics than about the value of a classics volume, period. Why read classics? For serious students of public administration, the answer is open and shut. Respectable grasp of a subject matter requires some appreciation of historical origins and trends—of the evolution of ideas. For the "here-and-now" MPA student eager to practice the latest techniques of human resource management in government, however, the answer may seem less obvious. Can books of classics be "relevant" to this group? I think so.

First, and least important, many of the selections printed in this book are relatively recent. For instance, the Supreme Court decisions that appear continue to shape the behavior of human-resource practitioners as the 1990s commence. Second, the introductions to each section of this book supplement the material in the classics with more contemporary analysis. Third, and most important, classics broach *enduring* questions. Should strikes be permitted in the public sector? What institutional arrangements best serve the interests of effective and accountable personnel administration in government? What factors undermined the pervasive practice of patronage? Historical works have much of intelligence to say about these questions. Frequently, they say it much

better than contemporary analyses of the same issues. Fourth, practitioners can hone their capacity to evaluate current reform proposals by studying the waves of reform in the past. Historical appreciation can alert these practitioners to possible and probable consequences of reform initiatives. It can inhibit them from running after every fad or nostrum pushed by the latest collection of human-resource consultants or policy entrepreneurs. Thus, I think the case for reading classics is very strong.

The selections in this volume appear under six major headings. The first section provides the historical foundation of public personnel policy. It examines the Pendleton Act and the thesis that politics could be exorcised from personnel administration.

The second section focuses on a particularly enduring issue in the personnel arena—the question of the proper relationship between human-resource management and executive or political leadership.

The third section deals with the triumph of public personnel policy—its success in greatly reducing political patronage. It recognizes, however, that each policy "solution" tends to generate a new set of problems. In this regard, it surveys the legacy of discontent with many features of contemporary civil-service systems in general and specific terms. It plumbs the meanings and origins of this discontent.

Sections four and five focus on two arenas that, more than others, have given rise to ferment in the public personnel arena over the last thirty years—equal employment opportunity, and labor relations and employee rights issues.

The sixth section looks to the future. It assesses two major challenges that public personnel policy faces as the United States moves toward the year 2000—privatization and the threat of a "crisis" of competence.

As usual, able colleagues and associates stood ready to assist me as I assembled this book. Carolyn Ban, Phil Cooper, Helen Desfosses, Martin Edelman, Jim Perry, Norma Riccucci, David Rosenbloom, Jay Shafritz, Lana Stein, and Paul Thompson provided sage advice. The comments of the following reviewers were most helpful in the preparation of the manuscript: N. Joseph Cayer, Arizona State University; Dennis Daley, North Carolina State University; Mary E. Guy, University of Alabama at Birmingham; and George Sulzner, University of Massachusetts, Amherst. Dave Smith did yeoman's work in helping me track down materials. Of course, errors of omission and commission remain my responsibility alone. Finally, Sam, Aliza, and, especially, Elizabeth helped by not letting me forget the human dimension of everyday living. As in the past, Benna provided an environment supportive of a scholar in more ways than one.

Frank J. Thompson

# Topical Contents

# Chronological Contents

*Second Edition*
*Revised and Expanded*

# Classics of
# Public Personnel Policy

# I

# Beginnings:
# Politics and Personnel Policy

The story is by now familiar. George Washington and his immediate successors strove to place the competent in public office. "Fitness of character" became the key selection criterion as indicated by family background, educational attainment, social status, and the like. With the election of Andrew Jackson in 1828, an egalitarian movement to ensure rotation in the public bureaucracy ascended. Looking at the top levels of the Jackson Administration, one observer noted: "No previous administration could boast such a uniform deficiency in on-the-job training."[1] Although he had a reputation for pursuing spoils with a vengeance, Jackson actually hired and promoted many competent people. He probably dismissed from office less than 1,000 civil servants who had served under his predecessor, John Quincy Adams—about 10 percent of the government's total personnel at the time.[2]

Subsequent presidents pursued patronage with more vigor than Jackson. In this regard, one history of the period notes that "the American Civil War has the distinction of being the most extensive modern conflict won with the aid of public service built up primarily by means of the spoils system. . . ." (One wag claimed that the Union Army's disorderly retreat at the first battle of Bull Run stemmed from a rumor of three vacancies in the New York customs house.)[3] The spoils system reached heretofore unknown heights under Abraham Lincoln; it grew even more pervasive in the decade after the war.

By the 1880s, political elites and much of the public sought reform. With the passage of the Pendleton Act in 1883, the contemporary era in public personnel policy in the United States commenced. A selection from Paul Van Riper's seminal *History of the United States Civil Service* captures the political origins of the act. The statute, which survived in essential form for almost a century, also appears.

The importance of the Pendleton Act stemmed from its capacity not only to shape personnel practices in the federal government, but also to serve as a model for state and local agencies. In addition the legislation reinforced certain intellectual currents in public administration. Above all, it helped buttress a paradigm in pubic administration that distinguished between politics and administration. Writing in 1887, Woodrow Wilson helped lay the groundwork for this dichotomy. Praising civil service reform for cleansing "the moral atmosphere" of public life, Wilson went on to note, "Most important to be observed is the truth already so much and so fortunately insisted upon by

*1*

our civil-service reformers; namely, that administration lies outside of the proper sphere of politics."[4]

If Wilson gave impetus to these ideas, Frank Goodnow, a professor of administrative law at Columbia University, hammered them home in his book *Politics and Administration*. Published in 1900, the selection from Goodnow's work not only illustrates a commitment to the politics–administration dichotomy, it also conveys the moralistic flavor of much of the early writing on personnel administration. Contemporary public-administration students learn to speak dispassionately of the costs and benefits of some reform. Goodnow and his contemporaries addressed reform issues as contests between good and evil. The politics–administration distinction dominated much of the public-administration literature for roughly half a century. In the case of the personnel field, its impact lasted even longer. Socialized into a specialty hostile to politics, personnel students were reluctant to acknowledge the political character of merit systems.

A critical reawakening of the field to the role of politics in public personnel administration did not fully emerge until the 1960s. In this regard Frederick Mosher's *Democracy and the Public Service* stands out. As the excerpt from this book indicates, Mosher firmly grasped that so-called merit institutions often failed to realize merit objectives. Moreover, he observed that social trends, such as the growth of professionalism, collective bargaining, and affirmative action increasingly called into question the value of traditional merit practices. Above all, however, Mosher noted that efforts to segregate administration and politics in the personnel field could hardly satisfy any but the "blind."

Mosher's work helped to heighten awareness of the political character of personnel processes. In a broad sense, virtually all of public personnel administration possesses political ramifications. It cannot be "neutral" or value free; ultimately it affects who gets what from government. For instance, one of the most vaunted components of merit systems, written examinations, in effect shape who gets a very valued resource in society—reasonably secure and adequately paying jobs. These tests lead to choices that ultimately affect government's ability to deliver services efficiently and effectively. They have affected the degree to which political machines and political parties can survive.

But if all public personnel administration is political in that it shapes the authoritative allocation of values in society, one must guard against throwing the baby out with the bath water in rejecting a simple politics–administration distinction.[5] When people talk about some aspect of personnel management in a public agency as being "very political" or "politicized" and some other aspect in a different agency as being relatively free of "politics," they should not be automatically dismissed as know-nothings. Instead, one needs to probe the meanings attached to these terms.[6] Such an exercise quickly indicates that "politics" carries many connotations, some of which commend themselves for analytic purposes.

While an exhaustive taxonomy of the different connotations of politics in the personnel arena lies beyond the scope of this volume, two prominent types deserve mention: elective and generic. Early reformers fought against *elective personnel politics,* that is, intervention by elected officials and their partisan allies in personnel decision making. As will become evident later, reformers succeeded in reducing one form of elective politics—spoils involving the massive allocation of public jobs to the party faithful. Other brands of this form of personnel politics have flourished, however. In particular top elected executives (presidents, governors, mayors) have increasingly attempted to shape certain personnel decisions in the name of keeping the bureaucracy responsive to them. President Reagan, for instance, strove to ensure that top appointments as well as many jobs in the middle levels of the bureaucracy went to those ideologically sympathetic to his policies. Some jurisdictions, however, feature little participation by elected officials in public personnel administration. Thus in one sense, personnel administration can be thought of as "depoliticized" or not being involved much in "politics."

A second useful concept, *generic personnel politics,* derives from organization theory.[7] This concept denotes activities within the personnel arena aimed at acquiring and using resources to exert power (obtain some desired outcome) where disagreement about appropriate action exists. The notion of "office politics" or "bureaucratic politics" captures part of what this concept conveys. The conscious plotting of strategy, mobilizing coalitions, bargaining and compromise comprise the key ingredients of generic personnel politics. The list of players in such politics need not (although may) include elected officials and their immediate appointees. Often the struggle involves different factions within public agencies with little or no involvement by top elected officials.

Generic personnel politics usually requires the presence of at least five major conditions: heterogeneous preferences, interdependence, a measure of scarcity, issue importance, and some dispersal of power resources. Variations in preferences deserve particular attention. Players in the personnel game may disagree about ends, means, or both. While recognizing the protean forms disagreement can assume, it deserves note that much of generic personnel politics reflects a tension among five basic values that compete for emphasis in civil-service systems.

*Agency competence* refers to a concern that personnel policy and its implementation serve the interests of economy, efficiency, and effectiveness. *Merit* emphasizes that the rewards ought to go to the most competent—those individuals with the best record of, or potential for, achievement. A sense of society as a market where individuals compete and the prize goes to the most adroit undergirds this view. Hence, the rhetoric of civil-service testing justifies the practice on grounds that it isolates the most competent applicants available. The value of *political responsiveness* asserts that the preferences of elected officials and their appointees, as reflected in law and in other actions, should weigh heavily in personnel management. The civil-service reform movement of the late nineteenth century was an effort to reduce the weight assigned to one type of political responsiveness—that associated with spoils systems. *Social equity* concerns the use of government employment practices to help "worthy" societal groups deemed disadvantaged or potentially disadvantaged (e.g., women and racial minorities). *Employee rights and well-being* refers to a pervasive norm, buttressed in many instances by law and regulation, that individuals enjoy certain substantive and procedural rights as employees of some organization. Moreover, many believe that employers (whether government or private sector) ought to sustain conditions that allow employees to reap psychological gratification from work (e.g., self-actualization).

These core values do not always conflict with one another, but often they do. Consider one example. In the mid-1980s, top officials in the federal Customs Service sought to require employees seeking promotion to certain jobs to submit to drug-use testing. The jobs in question involved drug enforcement, the use of fire arms, or access to classified materials. Officials in the Customs Service saw drug testing as serving the agency's broad goals of competence and merit. The National Treasury Employees Union, however, viewed the move as a violation of employee rights and sued. In March, 1989, the Supreme Court ruled by a five to four margin that the Customs Service could test workers who applied for drug enforcement jobs (*National Treasury Employees Union v. Von Raab*). The court did not, however, address the constitutionality of random-testing programs for public employees.[8]

Interdependence, scarcity, and issue importance also galvanize generic politics. Interdependence means that participants are "in it together." The activities of one directly affect the fortunes of another. Otherwise, heterogeneous preferences matter less because each participant can pursue a certain value independent of the others. They do not need to fight each other or negotiate to get what they want. Scarcity is an important factor for similar reasons. If participants confront a huge pie, they may see little reason to contest outcomes vigorously because everyone can easily get a piece. Issue importance simply refers to the fact that participants must care enough about a matter to participate. People disagree on countless things but they lack the time, energy, and other resources to fight about them all. Matters deemed less important relative to others often fail to spark generic politics even though the other conditions apply (disagreement, interdependence, scarcity, power dispersal).

Finally, politicization tends to increase when (up to some threshold) power resources become dispersed among more participants in the personnel arena. The movement toward a dispersal of power, more than any other single factor, accounts for the greater generic politicization of personnel issues over the last quarter of a century. If one set of players holds all the cards, opponents, no matter how much they strongly disagree, may decline to fight. Why, barring extraordinary circumstances, sacrifice time and effort to a lost cause? Since the 1960s, changes in the law and other factors have improved the power position of such groups as racial minorities, women, and the unions. A greater willingness by the courts to strike a blow for employee rights has also contributed. Groups that once stood little chance of getting their way in the personnel arena came to enjoy a measure of empowerment that allowed them to contest more issues and heighten conflict.[9]

To recapitulate, the early reformers sought to eradicate "politics" from public personnel administration. Subsequently, others pounded home the point that human-resource management in government is inescapably political. And in a fundamental sense—that public personnel administration cannot be value neutral and neatly separated from issues of who gets what in the political system—this view is correct. But rejection of the politics–administration dichotomy takes students of public personnel policy a limited distance. When one analyzes decision making in various personnel arenas, it is probably not very useful to view choice processes as equally politicized. Some personnel arenas feature more politics than others. Hence, scholars need to distinguish among different connotations of politics in the personnel arena and fashion research that will contribute to a more sophisticated theory of the phenomena in their myriad forms. Developments here can in turn enlighten the discussion and pursuit of changes in public personnel policy.

# Notes

1. Matthew A. Crenson, *The Federal Machine* (Baltimore: Johns Hopkins University Press, 1975), p. 51.
2. *Ibid.*, p. 55.
3. Paul P. Van Riper, *History of the United States Civil Service* (Evanston, Ill.: Row, Peterson, 1958), pp. 43, 60.
4. Woodrow Wilson, "The Study of Administration," *Political Science Quarterly* 2 (1987). Reprinted in Jay M. Shafritz and Albert C. Hyde (eds.), *Classics of Public Administration* (Oak Park, Ill.: Moore Publishing, 1978), p. 10.
5. For more detailed discussion, see Frank J. Thompson, "The Politics of Public Personnel Administration," in Steven W. Hays and Richard C. Kearney, eds., *Public Personnel Administration: Problems and Prospects* (Englewood Cliffs, N.J.: Prentice-Hall, 1983), pp. 3–16.
6. This is an approach recommended by ordinary language philosophers. See Hannah Pitkin, *The Concept of Representation* (Berkeley: University of California Press, 1967).
7. See Jeffrey Pfeffer, *Power in Organizations* (Marshfield, Mass.: Pitman, 1981).
8. *Federal Times* (October 24, 1988); p. 14; *Albany Times Union* (March 22, 1989); p. A-1.
9. At some point, power dispersal becomes so great as to depress the level of generic politics. If everyone has a piece of power, the sheer costs of organizing a coalition for change can grow to a point that participants accept the status quo rather than launch new initiatives. One can make a similar point about scarcity.

# 1

# Americanizing a Foreign Invention: The Pendleton Act of 1883

*Paul P. Van Riper*
*Cornell University*

There seems to be a general impression both at home and abroad that the civil service in the United States has, as Americans sometimes put it, "just growed" without much conscious direction. To a limited extent this is true. Certainly civil service reform was not adopted as fully in as short a period of time as was the case in Great Britain.

However, a fairly complete and firm legislative foundation for the development of a civil service based on examinations and merit in the English manner has existed in the United States since the passage of the Pendleton Act of 1883.[1] It is important, therefore, that we consider this fundamental piece of legislation in some detail, not only because it was the first legislation of its kind in this country, but also because it to-day enjoys the unusual distinction of remaining on the statute books without fundamental change since its passage three-quarters of a century ago. Essentially a modification of a British political invention in terms of the constitutional and administrative inclinations of this country, the Pendleton Act becomes even more intriguing as a case study in cross-cultural adaptation, a topic of increasing interest and concern in the modern political world.

SOURCE: From *History of the United States Civil Service,* by Paul P. Van Riper. Copyright © 1958 by Harper & Row, Publishers, Inc. Reprinted by permission of the publisher.

What kind of law, then, was this new civil service reform act of 1883, passed so precipitately by a Republican Congress hitherto apathetic at best toward governmental reform of any sort?

## The Legislative Debate

The legislative debate which preceded the passage of the Pendleton Act was limited almost exclusively to the Senate. When the bill came before the House nearly all attempts to discuss it were literally shouted down, and it was overwhelmingly approved. The most likely explanation for the difference in legislative attitude lies in the fact that the members of the House knew they would be affected by the next election far more than the members of the Senate. The House was taking no chances. Reform was too important an issue at this time.

Fortunately for any analysis of congressional intent, the Senate debate was detailed and exhaustive.[2] Nearly all the major problems involved in the legislation were discussed at length. A sizable number of amendments—with only a few deliberately obstructionist—were considered and many adopted. The likely effects of the proposed legislation upon the constitutional position of the President and Congress, upon the party system, upon the civil service, and upon the public in general were thoroughly explored. Political assessments, the corruption of the previous twenty years, and the history of the reform before 1883 both in the United States and Great Britain were presented in detail. All in all the debate fills nearly 200 pages in the *Congressional Record.* That the argument frequently revolved around a strictly partisan quarrel over responsibility for the system which was to be reformed is quite true. But the major portion of the debate, occupying by far the greater part of the Senate's time for two weeks, was to the point.

This debate, plus the reports of two Senate committees, together with a consideration of the implications of certain events of the preceding twenty years or so, make possible a fairly clear analysis of the thinking involved in the new legislation.[3] An analysis of the voting shows that the later claims of both parties for credit for passage of the act are not entirely justified.[4] The Democrats by no means fully supported Senator Pendleton. If anything, the law must be considered primarily a Republican measure, spurred somewhat by the assassination of Garfield. However, this event has been overrated as an immediate cause of the enactment of the Pendleton Act. After all, Garfield had been shot a year and a half before its passage. More important as a motivating force for Republican action in late 1883 were the Republican reverses in the election of 1882. The Republicans were apprehensive about the 1884 election, while the Democrats were hopeful. Nevertheless, the sponsor of the new law was a prominent Democrat and the legislation profited from the careful attention of representatives of both parties.

## Fundamentals of the Act

The Pendleton bill as reported to the Senate provided, basically, for the adoption of the British civil service system in the United States. A commission was to administer competitive examinations; entrance into the public service would be possible only at the bottom; a full-scale career service was implied; and the offices were not to be used for political purposes. Throughout the Senate debate, reference was constantly made to European experience, and especially that of the British. However, the act as finally approved followed the British reform pattern only in a very general way.

In America, as in England, the central concept was that of *competitive examinations* for entrance into the public service. The Senate Committee on Civil Service and Retrenchment, in reporting the Pendleton measure, said:

The single, simple, fundamental, pivotal idea of the whole bill is, that whenever, hereafter, a new appointment or a promotion shall be made in the subordinate civil service in the departments or larger offices, such appointment or promotion shall be given to the man who is best fitted to discharge the duties of the position, and that such fitness shall be ascertained by open, fair, honest, impartial, competitive examination.[5]

Though the old idea of pass-examinations was occasionally referred to in the Senate committee reports and the debate to follow, Congress showed no inclination to challenge the fundamental idea of entrance into the public service via a really serious competition.

Congress also accepted the idea of relative *security of tenure* for employees entering the service through the examination system. The whole idea of entrance by examination meant, in itself, a considerable guarantee of tenure, because it tended to eliminate the incentive for removals. Beyond this, under the new law appointing officers could not discharge classified employees[6] for refusal to be politically active. To be sure, this prohibition was not reenforced by any criminal penalty and its execution was entirely up to the pleasure of the executive branch of the government. There was little the Civil Service Commission could do by itself about political removals, other than investigate and publicize the facts. But as long as Congress favored the elimination of politics from the competitive service, President Arthur's support was assured.[7]

The final concept for which any debt is owed to the British is that of the *neutrality* of the civil service. Congress forbade any employees covered by the new act "to coerce the political action of any person," and the new Commission was directed to prepare rules to implement this prohibition as well as that directed against political removals of competitive employees. Further, the Senate amended the act to provide substantial penalties for political assessments of or by competitive employees, or by any other federal officials.[8] However, only in the case of assessments was any criminal penalty attached to the provisions designed to insure neutrality. Again, the constitutional authority as well as the inclination of the chief executive was to be relied upon. It would take a President Cleveland and a President Theodore Roosevelt to turn this possibility of developing a nonpartisan civil service into something approaching reality. In effect, the Pendleton Act *demanded* nonpartisanship in initial selection procedures (for a limited number of positions) but only *encouraged* nonpartisanship in other matters.

We can conclude, then, that the American legislation of 1883 stimulated the development in the United States of a *merit system* founded on British precedents: that is, a system of civil service recruitment and organization based on (1) competitive examinations, (2) relative security of tenure, and (3) political neutrality. On the other hand, the new act also reflected peculiarly American patterns of thought and action. If we appropriated the main outlines of the foreign device, we were anything but abject copyists. We thoroughly adapted it to the American political and social climate.

As early as December 6, 1881, President Arthur had referred to the Pendleton bill, even then before the Senate, in his first message to Congress and had noted its "conformity with the existing civil-service system of Great Britain." But he had also noted with prophetic insight that "there are certain features of the English system which have not generally been received with favor in this country, even among the foremost advocates of civil-service reform."[9] The problem was to reconcile British ideas with American experience and inclination.

## The Power to Hire

First of all, the American conception of a proper competitive examination for public office differed radically from that of the British. Even the relatively down-to-earth examinations used by the Grant Commission had been criticized as too theoretical. Therefore, the Senate, by an amendment to the original legislation, instructed the new commission to make its tests "practical in character" and related to the duties that would be performed. The Senate and the public were averse to the academic essay-type of civil service testing then—and frequently still—current in Great Britain. Ever since 1883 testing development in this country has consistently reflected this basic American idea of the desirability of the "practical."

Many senators were especially incensed over the proposal of the Pendleton bill to permit entrance into the public service *only* "at the lowest grade." Finally, Senator Pendleton himself proposed an amendment to strike out the offending provision. It was overwhelmingly accepted without even the formality of a roll call. Another amendment opened up promotional examinations to more general competition than had been originally envisioned. We had no desire to develop an entirely ingrown civil establishment.

While the British civil service was normally closed to outsiders except at the bottom, the American federal service was to continue to be infiltrated by new talents at all levels. From 1883 to this day, one may enter the American public service at almost any level and at almost any age. Indeed, the adoption of age and other restrictions tending to prevent this mobility have been on many occasions, and often still are, bitterly attacked as "undemocratic."

Throughout the entire history of the public service the federal offices have never been permitted to form any kind of closed bureaucratic system on the European pattern. Such a mobile system, approaching the mobility of private employment, is unique among modern national public services. Its foundation was firmly embedded in the legislation of 1883. It has been responsible for the continuance of the representative type of bureaucracy which the Jacksonian Democrats had first declared to be a fundamental requisite of the democratic state.

In details of recruitment procedure the act also paid its respects to the Jacksonian theories of democracy in public office, and especially to the idea of rotation in office. No more than two members of the same family were declared to be eligible for public office. The majority of the clerical offices in the city of Washington were to be filled according to an "apportionment" of offices among the states, based upon population. Later in 1883, this last provision was interpreted to mean "as nearly as may be practicable." Its inclusion in the act undoubtedly secured much political support for the reform which otherwise might have been withheld. The authors of the legislation of 1883 and their political supporters, knowingly or unknowingly, were taking as few chances as possible that the American civil service might not be representative of the nation as a whole, in terms of geography, mobility, ideals, and outlook.

## The Power to Fire

Americans also refused to accept the almost absolute security of tenure that has often been guaranteed to European civil servants, and which reflects the veneration by Europeans of the mechanism of the state. Both the original civil service reformers and many subsequent American legislators have consistently fought against an overly absolute tenure as undesirable and unnecessary for civil service reform. Life tenure in office had been repudiated in 1829 and there was no desire to revive the idea in 1883. Besides, the removal power was a potent political tool which could not be lightly discarded.

Since 1829, the principal American controversy about tenure had been over whether the power to remove should be left primarily in the hands of the President or in the hands of Congress. That the removal power of the President was left largely untouched was the outstanding difference between pre-Civil War attempts at reform and the Act of 1883. Under the new legislation there was no bar to opening the so-called "back-door" to the classified service, as long as removals were not for partisan reasons. Undoubtedly the failure of the principal effort to limit the executive removal power, the attempted impeachment of President Johnson, helped force political minds to think in other terms. Senator George F. Hoar, a Massachusetts Republican, represented a fairly typical opinion when, during the course of the Senate debate on the Pendleton Act, he said:

The measure commends itself to me also because. . . . It does not assert any disputed legislative control over the tenure of office. The great debate as to the President's power of removal, . . .which began in the first Congress, . . .does not in the least become important under the skillful and admirable provisions of this bill.

It does not even. . .deal directly with the question of removals, but it takes away every possible temptation to improper removals.[10]

Nonetheless, a portion of the credit for this innovation must be given to the reformers, who consistently emphasized that, if the *front-door* were properly tended, the *back-door* would take care of itself. The supervision of the one would remove the incentive for the abuse of the other. George William Curtis, for instance, felt in 1876 that any system of "removal by lawsuit" would completely demoralize the service:

Having annulled all reason for the improper exercise of the power of dismissal, we hold that it is better to take the risk of occasional injustice from passion and prejudice, which no law or regulation can control, than to seal up incompetency, negligence, insubordination, insolence, and every other mischief in the service, by requiring a virtual trial at law before an unfit or incapable clerk can be removed.[11]

Senator Pendleton accepted the reformers' view of the proper way to regulate dismissals, and it was not successfully challenged in the debates that followed. The Act of 1883 left the President in control of his own household as far as the power to fire was concerned. Once more the "decision of 1789" was reaffirmed.

## Administrative Details

From an administrative point of view, the act was based firmly upon the experience gained from the ill-fated Grant Commission of 1871–75. In fact, the new law provided that the President should have all the powers of the 1871 legislation not inconsistent with the Pendleton Act. Similarly, the simple clerical classification acts of the eighteen fifties and an already existing military preference statute of a mild, exhortatory character were specifically integrated into the bill. Senator Pendleton, in answering the first question put to him after concluding his initial speech in favor of the bill, replied:

> This system is not entirely new, but . . .to a very large extent in certain offices in New York, in Philadelphia, and in Boston it has been put into practical operation under the heads of the offices there, and . . .they have devised, with the assistance of the commission originally appointed by General Grant, but largely upon their own motion, a system which I suppose would, to some extent, be followed under this bill.[12]

The careful statement of a careful legislator, his remarks indicate where indebtedness was due.

The agent of the executive branch in the establishment of the new personnel system was to be a bipartisan Civil Service Commission of three full-time members appointed for indefinite terms by the President with the advice and consent of the Senate.[13] The administration of the system was to be directed by a chief examiner.[14] He was to coordinate the work of the local examination boards, composed of government employees in local areas. The members of these local boards remained attached to their departments and were only to be loaned to the Commission for examination purposes. Just a very few permanent employees were expected to work full-time for the Commission itself. As the work became more and more complex and less a part-time operation, the dependence upon other departments for "details" of working personnel, full-time as well as part-time, caused the Commission many headaches. Full-time details ended in the nineteen twenties, but the "local board system" still remains very much alive today. However, it now supplements the activity of a greatly expanded body of full-time Commission employees numbering more than 4,000 since 1950.

The new agency was required to keep the necessary records, conduct investigations, and make reports to Congress through the President. As soon as possible, it was to publish its rules implementing the act, subject of course to the approval of the President. For housekeeping purposes the Secretary of the Interior was designated to provide quarters and essential supplies for the new organization. He had, however, no other jurisdiction over the Commission. This arrangement was not entirely satisfactory and was completely terminated by 1925.

Turning to minor details, the act provided for a probationary period of six months. Applicants were forbidden to present recommendations from senators and representatives which referred to matters other than character and residence. Drunkards were made ineligible for governmental positions. Appointments were to be made from "among those graded highest." This latter phrase was then used for constitutional rather than administrative reasons as a result of an important opinion of the Attorney General, discussed in detail shortly. In effect, this provided that the regulations must offer some discretion for the appointing officer. That the "rule of three" (a rule of "four" was adopted from 1883 to 1888), followed still today, was originally based upon constitutional necessity, rather than upon administrative desirability or upon any occult power of the word "three," is often forgotten. The act also provided that any commissioner or other public employee who might be found guilty of any collusion or corruption in the administration of the examinations should be open to punishment by a fine of up to $1,000 or imprisonment up to a year or both.

## Constitutional Questions

In yet another important respect the Pendleton Act reflected the peculiarities of the American Constitution as well as those of the political tendencies of the times. The new legislation, for the most part, was *permissive* rather than mandatory. The act itself placed only slightly over 10 percent of the positions in the federal public service—mainly clerical positions in Washington and in post offices and custom houses employing fifty or more persons—under the merit system to form the *classified civil service.* The remainder of the civil service was left *unclassified,* to be brought under the new regulations by Executive Order when and if the President saw fit. The only public officials exempted from the authority of the President under the act were laborers and those whose appointments were subject to the advice and consent of the Senate. These exemptions accounted for roughly 20 to 30 percent of the federal civil service, which in the eighteen eighties averaged over 140,000.

The permissive nature of the act—a relatively unusual characteristic in American legislation —stemmed from two somewhat different but temporarily compatible sets of circumstances. It was both politically and administratively impossible in 1883 to apply the merit system to the entire federal civil service. Administratively, the Civil Service Commission simply was not ready to do a complete job as yet. It takes time to develop examinations, to organize boards to administer the examinations, and to obtain the cooperation of the departmental agencies and the general public.[15] Permissiveness also had its political advantages. The politicians were able to announce that they had accomplished the desired reform—the rest being up to the President—knowing full well that they would not be hurt through a too sudden or drastic curtailing of their patronage. If the act permitted an orderly retreat of parties from their prerogatives of plunder, it made possible as well the gradual administrative development of the merit system.[16] Had the merit system been forced to wait for precise formulation and expansion by successive Congresses, no one knows what the result might have been. Under the law of 1883, the President was free to move as fast or as slowly as political circumstances might permit, under the broad, general rules laid down by Congress. The permissive feature was thus a recognition of practical political as well as administrative realities.

It probably was also necessary from a constitutional point of view. From the very beginning of the civil service reform movement, a large number of congressmen and politicians questioned the constitutionality of the new political device. Lionel Murphy, in his history of the first Civil Service Commission appointed by President Grant, has described how the new plan for centralized control of public personnel administration in the hands of a commission was attacked as an unconstitutional invasion of the powers both of Congress and of the President over personnel matters. The members of this Commission felt they had to defer any plans for a merit system until they first received an opinion by Attorney General Akerman on the constitutionality of the proposed arrangement.[17]

Akerman's opinion, however, did not fully resolve the conflict. One cannot join what is deliberately put asunder. He insisted that it was not constitutional for Congress by law to give to the Commission power which the Constitution places in the President, the department heads, and the courts of law. Congress "has no power to vest appointments elsewhere, directly or indirectly." However, in support of the Commission, Akerman went about as far as he could go. He concluded that "the test of a competitive examination may be resorted to in order to inform the conscience of the appointing power, but cannot be made legally conclusive upon that power against its own judgment and will." And further:

> Though the appointing power alone can designate an individual for an office, either Congress, by direct legislation, or the President, by authority derived from Congress, can prescribe qualifications, and require that the designation shall be made out of a class of persons ascertained by proper tests to have those qualifications.[18]

The ultimate constitutional dilemma involved in the regulation of the powers of appointment and removal within the American framework of government is well put in the unusually forthright conclusion to Akerman's opinion:

The act under which the present civil-service commission has been organized gives the President authority "to prescribe such rules and regulations for the admission of persons into the civil service of the United States as will best promote the efficiency thereof," and this very ample authority will certainly embrace the right to require that the persons admitted into the service shall have been found qualified by competent examiners.

It has been argued that a right in Congress to limit in the least the field of selection, implies a right to carry on the contracting process to the designation of a particular individual. But I do not think this a fair conclusion. Congress could require that officers shall be of American citizenship of a certain age, that judges should be of the legal profession and of a certain standing in the profession, and still leave room to the appointing power for the exercise of its own judgment and will; and I am not prepared to affirm that to go further, and require that the selection shall be made from persons found by an examining board to be qualified in such particulars as diligence, scholarship, integrity, good manners, and attachment to the Government, would impose an unconstitutional limitation on the appointing power. It would still have a reasonable scope for its own judgment and will. But it may be asked, at what point must the contracting process stop? I confess my inability to answer. But the difficulty of drawing a line between such limitations as are, and such as are not, allowed by the Constitution, is no proof that both classes do not exist. In constitutional and legal inquiries, right or wrong is often a question of degree. Yet it is impossible to tell precisely where in the scale right ceases and wrong begins. Questions of excessive bail, cruel punishments, excessive damages, and reasonable doubts are familiar instances. In the matter now in question, it is not supposable that Congress or the President would require of candidates for office qualifications unattainable by a sufficient number to afford ample room for choice.

Very respectfully, your obedient servant,

A. T. AKERMAN[19]

There was little else that Akerman could say under our existing constitutional arrangement, and the principles of his opinion still govern today. No wonder Oliver Field, nearly seventy years later, considered the legal basis of our federal merit system to be somewhat uncertain and concluded that in the states, all of which also operate under the separation-of-powers doctrine, as well as in the federal government:

> The theory upon which civil service laws have been upheld as constitutional, in so far as they affect the appointing power itself, is that the officer to whom the appointing power is given retains that discretion which it was intended he should exercise in making appointments, but that as an aid to his exercise of the power, another body may be given the power to determine the qualifications necessary for the position under consideration.[20]

After Akerman's opinion and much discussion of the problem, Congress did not feel that it should—it is questionable if it legally could—go too far in making the provisions of the Pendleton Act mandatory upon the President. Indicative of current thinking on the subject was the testimony of George William Curtis before the Senate Committee on Civil Service and Retrenchment on February 26, 1882. Curtis was speaking here of two bills then before the Committee—that of Pendleton and another temporarily proposed by Senator Henry L. Dawes of Massachusetts—and in reply to questions by two senators concerning the effect of the bills upon the relationship of the President to the proposed Commission:

> Of course the bills in no sense change the President's constitutional power. The Pendleton bill simply recognizes that the President appoints, and substantially they both provide for the same exercise of power, so far as that is concerned, although the

exercise is different in its details. If the President chose to disregard it, he would take no action, and there would be no remedy except in public opinion. *The whole thing presupposes a friendly President.*[21]

During the entire legislative debate and in the two major committee reports there was no attempt to change the presidential relationship described by Curtis.

There were, however, those like Senator Charles H. Van Wyck of Nebraska and Senator Wilkinson Call of Florida, who felt that the Pendleton bill—because it affected the power of the President so little—was unnecessary in light of the legislation of 1871. If the bill only outlined what the President already had authority to do, then why bother? But in 1882 the Senate accepted the proposition that, without congressional approval and encouragement, it was impossible for the executive branch to carry out the reform alone. Moreover, the portions of the bill which provided for criminal sanctions for several types of offenses were clearly beyond the power of the executive branch acting alone.

As a result, this act—and others like it, such as the more recent Ramspeck Act of 1940—for the most part merely authorizes, but does not require, the President to place offices in the classified civil service and under the merit system. This means that the great bulk of the federal employees under the merit system are there by Executive Order. Thus it would probably be legal for the President today to return to the processes of spoils politics a great many of the public offices now under the merit system. All the President needs do to accomplish this is to issue another executive order. Actually several presidents have returned positions to the unclassified service, McKinley, for instance, returning several thousand during his first term in office.

To put the whole problem another way: the constitutional realities of a separation of powers made it impossible for the American Congress to make the competitive system mandatory in the way that it had been made mandatory in Great Britain. From a superficial examination it might seem as if both countries had faced a similar problem, one to be solved in a similar fashion. British constitutional opinion, like American, agreed that the executive branch could be advised, but not directed, in its selection of personnel.

But the similarity ends there. The British Crown is not, nor was it in mid-nineteenth century, an executive comparable to the American Presidency. The one is shadow; the other is real. There has never been any great conflict in modern England arising from the separation of powers. That the British competitive system was the result of a series of Orders in Council is well known, but those Orders in Council actually represented the Cabinet which in turn represented the legislative branch of the government. British reform was therefore the result of legislative requirement and legislative mandate.

In the United States the legislative branch had attempted to coerce the executive branch in a similar fashion in the eighteen sixties and failed. The Pendleton Act recognized that failure and attempted to avoid another such impasse. American constitutional realities simply are not British constitutional realities and the American version of British civil service reform has reflected, and will continue to reflect, such fundamental differences in governmental systems.

## Safeguards

Since the Pendleton Act left the President's power to hire and fire relatively unimpeded, what safeguards were planned by a Congress which had not long before threatened a president with impeachment in an effort to control his relationship to public office-holders?

In the first place, the development of the merit system was considered as effective a check against the President as against Congress. Further, no more than two members of the agency administering the new law were to represent the same political party. Finally, the Civil Service

Commission was to be outside the traditional administrative hierarchy. The new agency was to be as nonpolitical as possible and as free from interference from either the executive or the legislative branches as feasible under the American Constitution.[22] The Civil Service Commission thus became the first of the separate commissions, devised to remove controversial issues from the hands of the usual administrative and political channels and thus to avoid some of the most acrimonious of the presidential–congressional conflicts. The emergence of a new[23] administrative pattern on the federal scene was undoubtedly related to a perception by Congress—whether consciously verbalized or merely sensed does not matter— that the relatively novel idea of political neutrality in civil service selection methods deserved a relatively novel administrative solution if it was to survive.

Nevertheless, the Civil Service Commission differs in several important respects from later regulatory boards such as the Interstate Commerce Commission. The members of the Civil Service Commission may be removed by the President without restriction. While it is their duty to advise the President on matters of policy affecting the public service, the Pendleton Act specifies that the regulations made by them derive their authority from and will be promulgated by the President. Hence, the Commission cannot properly be classed as an *independent* commission, though it represents a political innovation of some importance.

## The End of Two Eras

Just as 1829 marked the end of the bureaucracy of the Founding Fathers, 1883 marked the first great inroad into the spoils system of the mid-nineteenth century. Twice within a hundred years the American public service had been "reformed." What fundamental contrasts can be drawn between the two movements?

The Jacksonian movement can best be described as a class bursting of bonds. As the new democracy received the ballot—its ticket of admission to participation in government— it insisted on a show to its pleasure. And the cast of characters was adjusted accordingly. American democracy moved by the logic implicit in its premises to a recognition—practical this time, not theoretical—of the implications of both liberty and equality. Public office was to become almost a perquisite of citizenship and "rotation" the watchword. The spoils system provided a system of recruitment for public office very little at odds with the individualism of the day. May the best man win! The whole mechanism reflected the ideals and attitudes of American nineteenth century agrarian democracy.

In the decades immediately after the Civil War, however, individualism seemed to be producing inequality. The "best" men were winning by more of a margin than many people liked to see. And not a few questioned whether those who were winning were actually the "best." What had once been intended as an opening up of public office to the mass of citizens had all the earmarks of becoming the opening up of office to plundering by the politically privileged.

In 1883, contrasted to 1829, there was no new class to turn to, nor any particular desire to turn the clock back to 1829. If democracy was not satisfied with its own product, then it would have to reform itself. There was no one else to do it.

The invention of the merit system of recruitment for public office by examination made possible a new reformation of a different sort. Essentially a foreign idea, imported from a Europe which had faced similar problems earlier, civil service reform, suitably modified to conform to American ideas of a mobile, classless society, was a scheme brilliantly devised to meet the needs of our version of the modern democratic state.

First, the Civil Service Commission could distribute offices more systematically and rationally than the spoils system had ever been able to do. While the new scheme did not guarantee a partisan apportionment of offices to the party in power, it certainly did not guarantee offices to the opposition. If a compromise had to be reached, political neutrality in the distribution of public office was reasonably acceptable to all concerned.

Second, the merit system provided a remedy for those who objected to the obvious corruption and the oligarchical tendencies of the combination of business and politics into which the spoils system had developed. Civil service reform did again open up many of the public offices to all on a new kind of equal basis;[24] and it provided through a new measure of merit, the examination system, the rewards for individual effort so prized in American life.

Finally, the new reform laid the foundation for the development of that technical expertise crucial to the operation of the modern state. And it reached this goal without offending the democratic sensibilities of the great mass of American citizens. Posing no overt threat to the overpowering individualism of the day, it nevertheless gave implicit promise of other reforms to come. Once again a form of latent antagonism between liberty and equality—potentially so explosive in a democracy—was temporarily pacified.

# Notes

1. We may even push this back to 1871, in terms of precedent though not of effective action, if we consider the short-lived Grant Commission.

2. Carl Fish describes the debate as "entirely unworthy of the occasion, hardly touching any of the serious considerations involved." *The Civil Service and the Patronage* (New York: Longmans, Green and Co., 1905), p. 218. The writer does not accept this judgment for the reasons indicated in the text.

3. For the debate see the *Congressional Record,* which records almost daily discussion in the Senate from December 12, 1882, through December 27, 1882, the date of the passage of the bill by the Senate. For the only important hearings on the legislation see U.S. Congress, Senate, *The Regulation and Improvement of the Civil Service,* 46th Cong., 3d Sess., Senate Report 872, 1881 (Washington: Government Printing Office, 1881); and U.S. Congress, Senate, *Report of the Committee on Civil Service and Retrenchment,* 47th Cong., 1st Sess., Senate Report 576, 1882 (Washington: Government Printing Office, 1882). In the House there were no committee reports of even minor importance. The House approved the bill on January 4, 1883, and President Arthur signed it on January 16. For a more detailed chronology, see USCSC, *Civil Service Act: Legislative History,* a currently updated copy of which is maintained in the Commission's library. For another type of analysis of the Act of 1883, done more in terms of a chronological consideration of amendments and counter-amendments, see A. Bower Sageser's important study of *The First Two Decades of the Pendleton Act* (Lincoln: University of Nebraska, 1935), ch. ii.

4. As tabulated by Sageser, as cited in footnote 3, pp. 57 and 59, the final votes in the two houses were as follows: In the Senate the bill was passed by 38 to 5, with 33 absent. The affirmative vote included 23 Republicans, 14 Democrats and 1 Independent; the negative vote, 5 Democrats; and those absent, 14 Republicans, 18 Democrats, and 1 Readjuster (Independent). In the House the bill was approved by a vote of 155 to 47, with 87 not voting. The affirmative vote was cast by 102 Republicans, 49 Democrats, and 4 Nationals (Independents); the negative vote, by 7 Republicans, 39 Democrats, and 1 National, with those not voting, 39 Republicans, 41 Democrats, and 7 Nationals. In its partial crisscross of party lines, the vote was fairly typical of our national legislative practice.

5. U.S. Congress, Senate Report 576, as cited in footnote 3, pp. IX–X.

6. The term "classified service" has always been interpreted to cover positions where political removal is forbidden. Until about 1895 the terms "classified service," "classified employees," "competitive employees," "positions under the merit system," and "permanent service," while not exactly synonymous, were reasonably interchangeable; and they have been so used through this chapter and the next two to follow. However, after this date, the term "classified service" became sufficiently ambiguous, for reasons explained in the supplementary notes to ch. viii, that it has been used with much more care in the chapters covering the period from McKinley's administration to the present.

7. See President Arthur's messages to Congress on December 6, 1881, and December 4, 1882. Moreover, everyone understood that the trouble was with the legislative rather than the executive branch. The former, not the latter, had forced the dissolution of the competitive system as first established under President Grant.

8. The inclusion of other federal officials was designed to preclude a repetition of the Hubbell case, mentioned in the previous chapter. The law of 1876 against assessments was substantially reinforced.

9. James D. Richardson (ed.), *Messages and Papers of the Presidents* (New York: Bureau of National Literature and Art, 1905), VIII, 60.

10. *Congressional Record,* 47th Cong., 2nd Sess., 1882, XIV, Part I, 274.

11. As quoted in Ruth M. Berens, "Blueprint for Reform: Curtis, Eaton, and Schurz" (unpublished Master's thesis, Department of Political Science, University of Chicago, 1943), p. 50. As we have become more security minded with respect to employment, both public and private, recent legislation and custom have tended to close the back door; but, compared to European practice, it is still ajar.

12. *Congressional Record,* 47th Cong., 2nd Sess., 1882, XIV, Part I, 207. The New York, Philadelphia, and Boston references were to experimental postal and custom house competitive examination systems established in these cities under the authority of the rider of 1871 and continued, with some success, until they were incorporated in the larger program fostered by the Pendleton Act.

13. In 1883 it was anticipated that the commissioners would serve perhaps indefinitely. However, within a decade or so it became customary for the commissioners to offer their resignations on the occasion of a change in administration. To provide more continuity, Congress directed in 1956 that the commissioners serve for six-year, staggered terms. They may be reappointed. Most commissioners have served for less than six years, and this new legislation could in fact provide more continuity than that of 1883. However, the 1956 law did not place any barrier in the way of removal by the President other than that suggested by the six-year term; and the resignation custom may, of course, still continue.

14. In the nineteen thirties the "Chief Examiner" was retitled "Executive Director and Chief Examiner," and in the late nineteen forties "Executive Director." Under Reorganization Plan No. 5 of 1949, effective in August of that year, the administrative direction of the work of the Commission was placed officially under the authority of the Chairman (formerly known as the "President") of the Commission. There is, however, still an Executive Director who is in fact the day-by-day chief administrative officer.

15. In testifying before the Senate Select Committee to Examine the various Branches of the Civil Service on January 13, 1881, concerning the Pendleton proposal, Dorman B. Eaton said, "Another observation I want to make is, that I think no law should be passed which would require the application of this system of examinations to the whole civil service of the government at once, or even to all that part to which it is legitimately applicable, as I have defined it. It would be too large altogether.... We have got to create the machinery.... In bringing new men together and entering for the first time upon a new system, you would be utterly overslaughed and broken down if you were to be required to carry it all on at once." U.S. Congress, Senate Report 872, as cited in footnote 3, pp. 19–20.

16. In his study of civil service law, Oliver P. Field regards this permissiveness as a defect in the federal personnel legislation. *Civil Service Law* (Minneapolis: University of Minnesota Press, 1939), p. 4.

17. 13 Op. Att. Gen. 516 (31 Aug. 1871). This was well before the Curtis case of 1882, discussed in the previous chapter, in which the Supreme Court implied the constitutionality of civil service reform.

18. For this and the quotations above, see same, pp. 521 and 524.

19. Same, pp. 524–25.

20. As cited in footnote 16, p. 13.

21. U.S. Congress, Senate Report 576, as cited in footnote 3, p. 178. The italics are added.

22. The Senate Committee on Civil Service and Retrenchment, on reporting the Pendleton bill in 1882, said: "Such a board is necessary to secure the coherence, the authority, the uniformity, the assurance of freedom from partiality or influence which are vital to the system." U.S. Congress, Senate Report 576, as cited in footnote 3, p. X. Earlier, in reporting the same bill to a previous Congress, the Senate Select Committee on the Civil Service also concluded, "The commission needs a firm tenure, and should be as far as practicable removed from partisan influences. It needs to have knowledge of the practical methods of the departments, without falling under mere official control." U.S. Congress, Senate Report 872, as cited in footnote 3, p. 12.

23. The word "new" is justified in so far as the Civil Service Commission was the first federal agency of considerable importance and permanence to be organized as a semi-independent, bipartisan agency for what, in the days of its formation, was considered a kind of policing function.

24. As Dorman B. Eaton said in testifying before the Senate Committee considering the Pendleton bill, "This bill assumes that every citizen has an equal claim to be appointed if he has equal capacity." U.S. Congress, Senate Report 576, as cited in footnote 3, p. 6.

# 2

# The Pendleton Act

*U.S. Congress*

*Be it enacted by the Senate and House of Representatives of the United States of America in Congress assembled,* That the President is authorized to appoint, by and with the advice and consent of the Senate, three persons, not more than two of whom shall be adherents of the same party, as Civil Service Commissioners, and said three commissioners shall constitute the United States Civil Service Commission. Said commissioners shall hold no other official place under the United States.

The President may remove any commissioner; and any vacancy in the position of commissioner shall be so filled by the President, by and with the advice and consent of the Senate, as to conform to said conditions for the first selection of commissioners.

The commissioners shall each receive a salary of three thousand five hundred dollars a year. And each of said commissioners shall be paid his necessary traveling expenses incurred in the discharge of his duty as a commissioner.

SEC. 2. That it shall be the duty of said commissioners:

FIRST. To aid the President, as he may request, in preparing suitable rules for carrying this act into effect, and when said rules shall have been promulgated it shall be the duty of all officers of the United States in the departments and offices to which any such rules may relate to aid, in all proper ways, in carrying said rules, and any modifications thereof, into effect.

SECOND. And, among other things, said rules shall provide and declare, as nearly as the conditions of good administration will warrant, as follows:

First, for open, competitive examinations for testing the fitness of applicants for the public service now classified or to be classified hereunder. Such examinations shall be practical in their character, and so far as may be shall relate to those matters which will fairly test the relative capacity and fitness of the persons examined to discharge the duties of the service into which they seek to be appointed.

Second, that all the offices, places, and employments so arranged or to be arranged in classes shall be filled by selections according to grade from among those graded highest as the results of such competitive examinations.

Third, appointments to the public service aforesaid in the departments at Washington shall be apportioned among the several States and Territories and the District of Columbia upon the basis of population as ascertained at the last preceding census. Every application for an examination shall contain, among other things, a statement, under oath, setting forth his or her actual bona fide residence at the time of making the application, as well as how long he or she has been a resident of such place.

Fourth, that there shall be a period of probation before any absolute appointment or employment aforesaid.

Fifth, that no person in the public service is for that reason under any obligations to contribute to any political fund, or to render any political service, and that he will not be removed or otherwise prejudiced for refusing to do so.

Sixth, that no person in said service has any right to use his official authority or influence to coerce the political action of any person or body.

Seventh, there shall be non-competitive examinations in all proper cases before the commission, when competent persons do not compete, after notice has been given of the existence of the vacancy, under such rules as may be prescribed by the commissioners as to the manner of giving notice.

SOURCE: 22 Stat. 27 (1883). Formal title: "An Act to Regulate and Improve the Civil Service at the United States."

Eighth, that notice shall be given in writing by the appointing power to said commission of the persons selected for appointment or employment from among those who have been examined, of the place of residence of such persons, of the rejection of any such persons after probation, of transfers, resignations, and removals, and of the date thereof, and a record of the same shall be kept by said commission. And any necessary exceptions from said eight fundamental provisions of the rules shall be set forth in connection with such rules, and the reasons therefor shall be stated in the annual reports of the commission.

THIRD. Said commission shall, subject to the rules that may be made by the President, make regulations for, and have control of, such examinations, and, through its members or the examiners, it shall supervise and preserve the records of the same; and said commission shall keep minutes of its own proceedings.

FOURTH. Said commission may make investigations concerning the facts, and may report upon all matters touching the enforcement and effects of said rules and regulations, and concerning the action of any examiner or board of examiners hereinafter provided for, and its own subordinates, and those in the public service, in respect to the execution of this act.

FIFTH. Said commission shall make an annual report to the President for transmission to Congress, showing its own action, the rules and regulations and the exceptions thereto in force, the practical effects thereof, and any suggestions it may approve for the more effectual accomplishment of the purposes of this act.

SEC. 3. That said commission is authorized to employ a chief examiner, a part of whose duty it shall be, under its direction, to act with the examining boards, so far as practicable, whether at Washington or elsewhere, and to secure accuracy, uniformity, and justice in all their proceedings, which shall be at all times open to him. The chief examiner shall be entitled to receive a salary at the rate of three thousand dollars a year, and he shall be paid his necessary traveling expenses incurred in the discharge of his duty. The commission shall have a secretary,

to be appointed by the President, who shall receive a salary of one thousand six hundred dollars per annum. It may, when necessary, employ a stenographer, and a messenger, who shall be paid, when employed, the former at the rate of one thousand six hundred dollars a year, and the latter at the rate of six hundred dollars a year. The commission shall, at Washington, and in one or more places in each State and Territory where examinations are to take place, designate and select a suitable number of persons, not less than three, in the official service of the United States, residing in said State or Territory, after consulting the head of the department or office in which such persons serve, to be members of boards of examiners, and may at any time substitute any other person in said service living in such State or Territory in the place of any one so selected. Such boards of examiners shall be so located as to make it reasonably convenient and inexpensive for applicants to attend before them; and where there are persons to be examined in any State or Territory, examinations shall be held therein at least twice in each year. It shall be the duty of the collector, postmaster, and other officers of the United States, at any place outside of the District of Columbia where examinations are directed by the President or by said board to be held, to allow the reasonable use of the public buildings for holding such examinations, and in all proper ways to facilitate the same.

SEC. 4. That it shall be the duty of the Secretary of the Interior to cause suitable and convenient rooms and accommodations to be assigned or provided, and to be furnished, heated, and lighted, at the city of Washington, for carrying on the work of said commission and said examinations, and to cause the necessary stationery and other articles to be supplied, and the necessary printing to be done for said commission.

SEC. 5. That any said commissioner, examiner, copyist, or messenger, or any person in the public service who shall willfully and corruptly, by himself or in co-operation with one or more other persons, defeat, deceive, or obstruct any person in respect of his or her right of examination according to any such rules or regulations, or who shall willfully, corruptly, and falsely mark, grade, estimate, or report upon the examination or proper standing of any person examined hereunder, or aid in so doing, or who shall willfully and corruptly make any false representations concerning the same or concerning the person examined, or who shall willfully and corruptly furnish to any person any special or secret information for the purpose of either improving or injuring the prospects or chances of any person so examined, or to be examined, being appointed, employed, or promoted, shall for each such offense be deemed guilty of a misdemeanor, and upon conviction thereof, shall be punished by a fine of not less than one hundred dollars, nor more than one thousand dollars, or by imprisonment not less than ten days, nor more than one year, or by both such fine and imprisonment.

SEC. 6. That within sixty days after the passage of this act it shall be the duty of the Secretary of the Treasury, in as near conformity as may be to the classification of certain clerks now existing under the one hundred and sixty-third section of the Revised Statutes, to arrange in classes the several clerks and persons employed by the collector, naval officer, surveyor, and appraisers, or either of them, or being in the public service, at their respective offices in each customs district where the whole number of said clerks and persons shall be all together as many as fifty. And thereafter, from time to time, on the direction of the President, said Secretary shall make the like classification or arrangement of clerks and persons so employed, in connection with any said office or offices, in any other customs district. And, upon like request, and for the purposes of this act, said Secretary shall arrange in one or more of said classes, or of existing classes, any other clerks, agents, or persons employed under his department in any said district not now classified; and every such arrangement and classification upon being made shall be reported to the President.

Second. Within said sixty days it shall be the duty of the Postmaster-General, in general conformity to said one hundred and sixty-third section, to separately arrange in classes the several clerks and persons employed, or in the public service, at each post-office, or under any postmaster of the United States, where the whole number of said clerks and persons shall together amount to as many as fifty. And thereafter, from time to time, on the direction of the President, it shall be the duty of the Postmaster-General to arrange in like classes the clerks and persons so employed in the postal service in connection with any other post-office; and every such arrangement and classification upon being made shall be reported to the President.

Third. That from time to time said Secretary, the Postmaster-General, and each of the heads of departments mentioned in the one hundred and fifty-eighth section of the Revised Statutes, and each head of an office, shall, on the direction of the President, and for facilitating the execution of this act, respectively revise any then existing classification or arrangement of those in their respective departments and offices, and shall, for the purposes of the examination herein provided for, include in one or more of such classes, so far as practicable, subordinate places, clerks, and officers in the public service pertaining to their respective departments not before classified for examination.

SEC. 7. That after the expiration of six months from the passage of this act no officer or clerk shall be appointed, and no person shall be employed to enter or be promoted in either of the said classes now existing, or that may be arranged hereunder pursuant to said rules, until he has passed an examination, or is shown to be specially exempted from such examination in conformity herewith. But nothing herein contained shall be construed to take from those honorably discharged from the military or naval service any preference conferred by the seventeen hundred and fifty-fourth section of the Revised Statutes, nor to take from the President any authority not inconsistent with this act conferred by the seventeen hundred and fifty-third section of said statutes; nor shall any officer not in the executive branch of the government, or any person merely employed as a laborer or workman, be required to be classified hereunder; nor, unless by direction of the Senate, shall any person who has been nominated for confirmation by the Senate be required to be classified or to pass an examination.

SEC. 8. That no person habitually using intoxicating beverages to excess shall be appointed to, or retained in, any office, appointment, or employment to which the provisions of this act are applicable.

SEC. 9. That whenever there are already two or more members of a family in the public service in the grades covered by this act, no other member of such family shall be eligible to appointment to any of said grades.

SEC. 10. That no recommendation of any person who shall apply for office or place under the provisions of this act which may be given by any Senator or member of the House of Representatives, except as to the character or residence of the applicant, shall be received or considered by any person concerned in making any examination or appointment under this act.

SEC. 11. That no Senator, or Representative, or Territorial Delegate of the Congress, or Senator, Representative, or Delegate elect, or any officer or employee of either of said houses, and no executive, judicial, military, or naval officer of the United States, and no clerk or employee of any department, branch or bureau of the executive, judicial, or military or naval service of the United States, shall, directly or indirectly, solicit or receive, or be in any manner concerned in soliciting or receiving, any assessment, subscription, or contribution for any political purpose whatever, from any officer, clerk, or employee of the United States, or any

department, branch, or bureau thereof, or from any person receiving any salary or compensation from moneys derived from the Treasury of the United States.

SEC. 12. That no person shall, in any room or building occupied in the discharge of official duties by any officer or employee of the United States mentioned in this act, or in any navy-yard, fort, or arsenal, solicit in any manner whatever, or receive any contribution of money or any other thing of value for any political purpose whatever.

SEC. 13. No officer or employee of the United States mentioned in this act shall discharge, or promote, or degrade, or in manner change the official rank or compensation of any other officer or employee, or promise or threaten so to do, for giving or withholding or neglecting to make any contribution of money or other valuable thing for any political purpose.

SEC. 14. That no officer, clerk, or other person in the service of the United States shall, directly or indirectly, give or hand over to any other officer, clerk, or person in the service of the United States, or to any Senator or Member of the House of Representatives, or Territorial Delegate, any money or other valuable thing on account of or to be applied to the promotion of any political object whatever.

SEC. 15. That any person who shall be guilty of violating any provision of the four foregoing sections shall be deemed guilty of a misdemeanor, and shall, on conviction thereof, be punished by a fine not exceeding five thousand dollars, or by imprisonment for a term not exceeding three years, or by such fine and imprisonment both, in the discretion of the court.

Approved, January sixteenth, 1883.

# 3

# Merit Systems and Politics

*Frank J. Goodnow*
*Columbia University*

The adoption of the "spoils system," as it was called, was possible because of the failure to distinguish administration from politics, promoted by the character of the administrative system. Seeing a great body of elected officials changed frequently, the people naturally did not protest when the principle of "rotation in office," as it was called, was applied as well to appointed ministerial officers. It is true, of course, that certain of the most prominent statesmen of the time called attention to the evils which would result from the adoption of the principle of rotation in office of these appointed officers.[1] But it is to be remembered that at the time the spoils system got its hold on American public life, the distinctly administrative functions were not so important as they later became. This was due to the fact that, our civilization being comparatively simple, the work of the government was not nearly so extensive or complicated as it is now.

The spoils system was first introduced in the state of New York, whose politics, even in colonial times, were probably more bitter than elsewhere. It was taken from New York into the national administration at about the time when, owing to the democratic movement beginning with 1820, and the slavery question, the political struggles of the nation began to assume somewhat the same bitterness which had characterized the politics of New York. Thence it spread

SOURCE: From *Politics and Administration: A Study in Government,* by Frank J. Goodnow. New York: Macmillan, 1900.

through the entire Union, and soon began to be regarded as an essential part of the American political system.

The spoils system, considered from the point of view of political theory, consisted in subjecting all officers, discretionary or ministerial, appointive or elective, who were intrusted with the execution of the law, to the control of the political party, the body which in the American political system had the task of coordinating the functions of politics and administration.

The spoils system had, however, two great faults. In the first place, when applied to ministerial appointive officers, it seriously impaired administrative efficiency. In the second place, even where applied to elective officers, and much more so when applied to appointive officers, where it had no theoretical justification except that to be found in the necessity of keeping up the party organization, it tended to aid in the formation of political party machines, organized not so much for facilitating the expression of the will of the state as for keeping the party in power. It thus aided in making the party an end rather than a means. The party, largely owing to the spoils system, gradually ceased to discharge, as fully as it should, the function of facilitating the expression of the will of the state, and indeed in many instances came to be a hindrance rather than an aid.

The evil of decreased administrative efficiency first became noticeable. It naturally attracted attention in the national administration sooner than in that of the states. This was so because the formal administrative system of the national government did not lend itself so readily as did the state administrative system to the idea which it has been pointed out was at the bottom of the spoils system. The national administrative system differed at the time of its formation considerably from that obtaining in the states. It embodied, much more than did that of the states, the principles of the English system which have promoted the development in England during the present century of considerable centralization in administration. Thus the principle of popular election, which, even at the time the national government was formed, had begun to win popular approval in the states, received no recognition in the national Constitution. Practically all national officers were, by the Constitution, to be appointed by the chief executive or by his appointees. . . .

The enormous increase in the administrative work of the national government, much of which was of a semi-scientific character,—*e.g.* the patent office administration, the geological survey, the work of various statistical bureaus,—made the loss of administrative efficiency, due to the adoption of the spoils idea, very prominent. The demand was made as early as 1841 that some means should be adopted which should make the administration more efficient. A committee of the House of Representatives appointed in that year, reported that "the habit of applying mere political tests to the mass of appointments is believed to be injurious to the public service, by often filling important offices with incompetent men," and proposed the adoption of preliminary examinations for those desiring to enter the civil service.[2] In 1853, pass examinations were provided, in the hope that absolute incompetence might be denied entrance into the civil service.[3] This method was not effective, and in 1872, in imitation of English precedents adopted to remedy evils similar to those which had appeared here, open competitive examinations were introduced.[4] Since 1883, when the present civil service law was passed, these examinations have been steadily made necessary for more and more ministerial appointive positions whose incumbents could not exercise an appreciable influence on the general policy of the government, until now nearly eighty-seven thousand positions are subject to the Civil Service Rules.[5]

The last step that has been taken is the attempt to prevent removals for political reasons. The recent order of the President[6] on this subject thus recognizes that a vast body of ministerial administrative officers shall be taken out of the control of the parties.[7]

Open competitive examinations for entrance into the civil service, although they embody in the minds of most people all the purposes of civil service reform, are really but a small part of this reform. Its ultimate object is the recognition of a function of government whose discharge, like that of the administration of justice, shall be free from the influences of politics. This ultimate object is made evident in the recent order of the President relative to removals. Competitive examinations can, in the nature of things, be applied successfully only to comparatively unimportant positions in the service. They will, however, have amply justified their adoption if, in addition to relieving the lower branches of the service from the influence of politics, they succeed in impressing on the public mind the feeling that it is not necessary either in the national government, nor, for that matter, in many cases in the present state governments, to accord the political parties the great powers they have possessed in the past over governmental officers whose only duty is to aid in the execution of the laws. Once that idea is possessed by the public, it will be a comparatively easy matter to insist that officers of greater importance, such as chiefs of divisions, collectors of customs and internal revenue, postmasters, even, in many cases, commissioners of bureaus, shall be selected on account of fitness for their positions, and shall, so long as they give evidence of such fitness, be retained in office. That this can be accomplished by any changes in the law may, perhaps, be doubted. That it will be accomplished, as soon as an educated and intelligent public opinion demands it, is a moral certainty.

## Notes

1. See Fifteenth Report of the United States Civil Service Commission, Part VI., p. 443, which contains an excellent history of the development of the spoils system. See also Ford, *op. cit.*, Chap. XI.

2. Fifteenth Report, United States Civil Service Commission, p. 466.

3. *Ibid.*, p. 474.

4. See United States Revised Statutes, § 1753.

5. Fifteenth Report, United States Civil Service Commission, p. 141.

6. Civil Service Rule II., Sect. 8.

7. It has been held by the Supreme Court that this order cannot be enforced by injunction. White *v.* Berry, 171 U.S. 366.

# 4

# Merit, Morality and Democracy

*Frederick C. Mosher*
*The University of California at Berkeley*

My focus in this volume is upon the public service itself, and particularly upon the appointive public service, in its relation to democracy both as an idea and as a way of governance. For this purpose it seems unnecessary to dwell upon disputable definitions of polyarchy or consensual elite or similar intellectual constructs. My premises are relatively clear and limited; that

1. governmental decisions and behavior have tremendous influence upon the nature and development of our society, our economy, and our policy;
2. the great bulk of decisions and actions taken by governments are determined or heavily influenced by administrative officials, most of whom are appointed, not elected;
3. the kinds of decisions and actions these officials take depend upon their capabilities, their orientations, and their values; and
4. these attributes depend heavily upon their backgrounds, their training and education, and their current associations.

Only recently have we had many studies about public executives—about who they are, where they came from, what kinds of preparation and experience they bring to their jobs; and what kinds of objectives they pursue. Many political scientists prefer to deal with the concepts and ideas of old thinkers, of whom few were concerned with administration; or with

SOURCE: From *Democracy and the Public Service, Second Edition,* by Frederick C. Mosher (pp. 1–7, 101–110, and 216–219). Copyright © 1968, 1982 by Oxford University Press. Reprinted by permission.

items they can count—citizen votes, legislative votes, or attitudes as measured through surveys. They have given rather little attention to administration and administrators as a significant element in government.

Perhaps the most concise, simplest, most widely accepted definitions of democracy were those implicit in the Gettysburg Address of Abraham Lincoln. Our nation was one "conceived in liberty and dedicated to the proposition that all men are created equal." And our Civil War was to ensure the survival of government "of the people, by the people, for the people." Clearly the one phrase of the triad which is distinctive for democracy is the second one, "by the people." The first would apply to government of any stripe, and the third to any of paternalistic flavor. But what does "by the people" mean? By *all* the people? If not, by which people? The early, hopeful answer was the former—*all the people,* deciding matters through discussion and debate and vote as exemplified by the Greek city-state and the New England town meeting.[1] Even this elementary pattern could not by itself be fully effective in the community because meetings could not be assembled on the hour every day to handle the continuing problems of government. So was devised the method, once removed from the people, of governance by individuals elected by the people, answerable to them and removable by them—i.e. representatives. Preferably, such officers would serve short terms within narrowly circumscribed zones of discretion and would be forbidden to serve more than one or two terms in office. Although we commonly associate the elected representative officer with legislatures and chief executives, the basic concept has applied widely in this country to administrative and judicial officers as well.

Reliance upon popularly elected representatives is one step removed from direct participative democracy. A second step occurs when officers so chosen select and delegate powers to other officers, appointed and removable by them. As the dimensions of the administrative tasks of government grew these came greatly to outnumber the elective officers; and for a period in U.S. history, a substantial part of the public service were politically appointive and removable officers and employees. A third step away from direct democracy is taken with the designation of personnel who are neither elected nor politically appointive and removable, but rather are chosen on bases of stated criteria—social class or caste, family, general competence, specialization in given tasks and skills, etc.—and, once appointed, are protected from removal on political grounds. It is now of course clear that in every developed country in the world the vast majority of public officers and employees are in this category; that many of them command specialized knowledges and skills which give them unique competence in some subject-matter fields—competence that neither the people nor their elected or appointed political officers possess. It is also obvious that they influence—or make—decisions of great significance for the people, though within an environment of constraints, controls, and pressures which itself varies widely from one jurisdiction to another, from one field or subject to another, and from one time to another.

The accretion of specialization and of technological and social complexity seems to be an irreversible trend, one that leads to increasing dependence upon the protected, appointive public service, thrice removed from direct democracy. Herein lies the central and underlying problem to which this volume is addressed: how can a public service so constituted be made to operate in a manner compatible with democracy? How can we be assured that a highly differentiated body of public employees will act in the interests of all the people, will be an instrument of all the people? My focus in the pages that follow is upon the appointive administrative services, those sectors that are twice and thrice removed from direct democracy. My primary concern is with our experience, our practices, and our directions in the United States; but I include some references to other countries for purposes of contrast and comparison.

In the paragraphs that follow in this chapter, I should like to state some of the principal themes and sub-issues which have underlain the basic problem as it has evolved in American thinking. My purpose is to define and to establish a terminology. All the topics suggested here are treated later on in various connections. They include: policy-politics and administration; responsibility; representation and representativeness; mobility; participation; elitism; the rights of public servants.

## Policy-Politics and Administration

The concept that policy should be determined by politically responsible officials, institutionally separated from the execution of policy—i.e. administration—and the arguments attendant upon it are relatively recent in political and intellectual history. One finds little reference to them in the writings of the great political thinkers, and this perhaps reflects the general lack of concern about administration anyway. In much of this writing, there seems to have been an implicit assumption that administration is the obedient and willing pawn of whoever controls it; the primary issue then is the locus of control. The separation of policy from administration has been equated with the separation of the legislative from the executive power, but the identification in both theory and practice has been a very rough one. In our own Constitutional debates and early political history, it was hardly contemplated that the executive would be or should be powerless on matters of national policy, and in fact certain specific powers with respect to policy were granted him in the Constitution itself. The emergence of the doctrine of institutional dichotomy between policy and administration seems both logically and historically to have followed two basic developments. First was the rise of representative democracy in the Western countries during the eighteenth and nineteenth centuries, expressed primarily through legislative bodies and the emergence of political parties. One of the chief objects of contest became the control of administration—of its positions, its powers, and its policy influence. Second was the recognition of the need for a permanent, protected, and specialized civil service. This recognition arose in some places (as in the United States) primarily from moral indignation at the corruption and excesses of political patronage, and in others primarily from the obvious necessity for adequate skills, knowledge, and experience within administration. How does one square a permanent civil service—which neither the people by their vote nor their representatives by their appointments can replace—with the principle of government "by the people"?

The responses to the problem took somewhat different forms and emphases in different countries, though all were essentially compatible. On the Continent and stemming principally from Germany and Austria, the principal emphasis was upon law—natural law and civil law. Administration is essentially the business of carrying out the affairs of state in accordance with law and due process. The laws expressing public policies are made by the people's representatives in Parliament. In Britain, the Parliament, consisting again of elected representatives of the people, is supreme; the cabinet is a committee of Parliament, removable by the latter. The permanent civil service consists of neutral, impartial individuals who can and will serve any cabinet with equal loyalty and devotion. In the United States, we have taken something from both camps. Our government too is conceived as one of laws rather than of men, and lawyers have long been the largest single occupational group in the top echelons of the public service. Our permanent, protected civil service, which, interestingly, does not yet include lawyers, would be impartial and neutral like its British counterpart. It would carry out policies determined elsewhere, either by the people directly (through initiative and referendum) or by their elected representatives in legislative bodies. In short, there would be a clean division between those responsible for determining policy (the people and their elected representatives) and those responsible for carrying it out (the appointive public service).

The developments in recent decades in the "real world" of government have brought to the policy-administration dichotomy strains which have grown almost beyond the point of toleration.[2] In fact, on the theoretical plane, the finding of a viable substitute may well be the number one problem of public administration today. But this concept, like most others, dies hard. There are built-in obstacles of motivation in favor of perpetuating it. By and large, legislators prefer not to derogate their importance by advertising that it is smaller than it appears to be, and when they do it is usually to denounce administrative (or judicial) "usurpation" of legislative power. Likewise, administrators—especially those in specialized professions—prefer not to advertise, or even to recognize, that they are significantly influencing policy for fear of provoking such charges. Finally, many students of government—as I have already suggested—prefer to study those subjects which are amenable to scientific, objective, and quantifiable treatment. A declaration that these topics are somewhat less important than they seem would be self-defeating. For all three groups—elected officers, appointed administrators, and political scientists—the policy-administration dichotomy is a convenient crutch—or myth—to support and justify their current interests...(Pages 1-7).

## The Professional State

The characteristic of the public service—and indeed of a great part of the rest of society—which seems to me most significant today is *professionalism*. If it is defined broadly, as it is here, it relates to all of the types of emphasis suggested above, and encompasses a substantial part of some of them. Daniel Bell,[3] like Don K. Price before him,[4] recently wrote of an emerging new society in which old values and social power associated with property, wealth, production, and industry are giving way to knowledge, education, and intellect.

To speak rashly: if the dominant figures of the past hundred years have been the entrepreneur, the businessman, and the industrial executive, the "new men" are the scientists, the mathematicians, the economists, and the engineers of the new computer technology. And the dominant institutions of the new society—in the sense that they will provide the most creative challenges and enlist the richest talents—will be the intellectual institutions. The leadership of the new society will rest, not with businessmen or corporations as we know them..., but with the research corporation, the industrial laboratories, the experimental stations, and the universities.[5]

If Bell and Price are near the mark, as I think they are, the importance of the professions, among which I would include the applied scientists in virtually all disciplines, is increasing rapidly and will continue to do so. Viewed broadly, the professions are social mechanisms whereby knowledge, including particularly new knowledge, is translated into action and service. They provide the means whereby intellectual achievement becomes operational.

The extent to which the professions have become dominant in American society has been noted by a number of commentators. In a recent issue of *Daedalus* which was entirely devoted to the professions, Kenneth S. Lynn maintained that: "Everywhere in American life, the professions are triumphant."[6] And Everett C. Hughes wrote in the same issue: "Professions are more numerous than ever before. Professional people are a larger proportion of the labor force. The professional attitude, or mood, is likewise more widespread; professional status more sought after."[7]

In statistical terms the U.S. Census reflects the accelerating growth of what it terms "professional, technical, and kindred" workers, who grew from 4 to 11 percent of the American labor force between 1920 and 1960. The fastest growth has been since World War II; it continues today and certainly will do so well into the future.

## The Professional Public Services

The prominent role of American governments in the development and utilization of professions seems to have gone largely unnoticed. They are the principal employers of professionals. According to the 1960 Census, 36 percent of all the "professional, technical, and kindred" workers in the United States were employed by governments, and this of course did not include a multitude of scientists, engineers and others indirectly employed through government contracts, subsidies, and grants. Looked at another way, about one-third of all government employees were engaged in professional and technical pursuits. This was more than three times the comparable proportion in the private sector. The governmental proportion is heavily inflated by school teachers, who are classified as professional. Even if they are omitted, however, the proportion of professionals in total public employment was nearly one-fifth, more than double the comparable proportion in the private sector.

Leaving aside the political appointees at or near the top of our public agencies and jurisdictions, the administrative leadership of government is increasingly professional in terms of educational and experiential backgrounds. This is not to say that public leadership as such is an administrative profession, rather that it consists of a very wide variety of professions and professionals in diverse fields, most of them related to the missions of the organizations in which they lead.

In government, the professions are the conveyor belts between knowledge and theory on one hand and public purpose on the other. The interdependencies between the professions and government are many. Governments are, or have been:

the creators of many professions
the legitimizers of all those which have been
    legitimized
protectors of the autonomy, integrity, monopoly, and standards of those which have
    such protections
the principal supporters of their research
    and of that of the sciences upon which
    they depend
subsidizers of much of their education
among their principal employers and the
    nearly exclusive employers of some of
    them, which means also

among the principal utilizers of their knowledge and skills

For their part, the professions:

contribute to government a very substantial proportion of public servants

provide most of the leadership in a considerable number of public agencies

through their educational programs, examinations, accreditation, and licensing, very largely determine what the content of each profession is in terms of knowledge, skills, and work

influence public policy and the definition of public purpose in those many fields within which they operate

in varying degree and in different ways provide or control the recruitment, selection, and other personnel actions for their members

shape the structure as well as the social organization of many public agencies

It may accurately be argued that there is nothing very new about professionalism in government. The principal spawning period for educational programs for the professions, as indicated in Chapter 2 above, was the first quarter of this century, and the U.S. Classification Act of 1923 established a professional and scientific service. In all probability the number of professionally educated personnel in all governments has been rising for the past half-century. Yet there appears to have been very little recognition of or concern about the significance of professionalism in the public service and its leadership until quite recently. For example, the Brownlow report and those of the two Hoover commissions, for all of their concern about administrative management, paid scant attention to professionals in fields other than management as such. Contrast the emphasis of recent studies. The Municipal Manpower Commission in its 1962 study of *Governmental Manpower for Tomorrow's Cities*[8] focused its entire report on what it called APT personnel, the abbreviations standing for administrative, professional and technical. Investigation of Federal personnel

problems, such as that of the Herter Committee on Foreign Affairs Personnel[9] and the study of personnel problems of the Public Health Service, similarly have concentrated on professional and administrative positions. The same is true of various studies at the state and local levels, of which David T. Stanley's recent report on *Professional Personnel for the City of New York*[10] is a notable example. All of these inquiries have either taken for granted or have clearly indicated that a large part of the administrative leadership is now and will continue to be drawn from professional fields considered appropriate for the programs of particular agencies.

The degree to which individual professional specialisms have come to dominate public agencies is suggested by the small sample below. The right hand column indicates both the primary professional field in the agency and the normal professional source of its career leadership.

### Federal

| | |
|---|---|
| All the military agencies | Military officers |
| Department of State | Foreign Service officers |
| Public Health Service | Public health doctors |
| Forest Service | Foresters |
| Bureau of Reclamation | Civil engineers |
| Geological Survey | Geologists |
| Department of Justice | Lawyers |
| Office of Education | Educators |
| Bureau of Standards | Natural scientists |

### State and Local

| | |
|---|---|
| Highways and other public works agencies | Civil engineers |
| Welfare agencies | Social workers |
| Mental hygiene agencies | Psychiatrists |
| Public health agencies | Public health doctors |

| Elementary and secondary education offices and schools | Educators |
| Higher education institutions | Professors |
| Attorneys general, district attorneys, legal counsel | Lawyers |

I define the word "profession" liberally as (1) a reasonably clear-cut occupational field, (2) which ordinarily requires higher education at least through the bachelor's level, and (3) which offers a lifetime career to its members.[11] The professions in government may conveniently be divided in two classes: first, those in fields employed in the public *and* the private sectors and for whom the government must compete in both recruitment and retention. This category, which I shall call "general professions," includes most of the callings commonly understood as professions: law, medicine, engineering, architecture, to illustrate. I also include among them applied scientists in general and college professors. Second are those employed predominantly and sometimes exclusively by governmental agencies, which I shall call "public service professions." Most of these were generated within government in response to the needs of public programs, and although there has been a tendency in the direction of increased private employment for many of them, governments are still the predominant employers. They fall in two classes: first, those which are employed exclusively by a single agency such as military officers, Foreign Service officers, and Coast Guard officers; and second, those employed by a number of different governmental jurisdictions, such as school teachers, educational administrators, social workers, public health officers, foresters, agricultural scientists, and librarians.

Most of those listed above in both categories may be described as "established professions" in the sense that they are widely recognized *qua* professions and, with only a few exceptions, their status has been legitimized by formal state action

through licensing, credentialing, commissioning, or recognizing educational accreditation.

In addition to these, there are many "emergent professions" which have not been so recognized and legitimized but which are valiantly and hopefully pulling themselves up by their vocational bootstraps to full professional status. In the "emergent" and "general" group are included, for example, specialists in personnel, public relations, computer technology, recreation, financial management, purchasing. "Emergent" in the "public service" category are governmental sub-divisions of all of these and some which are more exclusively governmental: assessors, police, penologists, employment security officers, air pollution specialists, etc.

The professions—whether general or public service, whether established or emergent—display some common characteristics which are significant for democracy and the public service. One of these is the continuing drive of each of them to elevate its stature and strengthen its public image as a profession. In a very few highly esteemed fields, such as law and medicine, the word "maintain" is perhaps more appropriate than "elevate." A prominent device for furthering this goal is the establishment of the clear and (where possible) expanding boundaries of work within which members of the profession have exclusive prerogatives to operate. Other means include the assurance and protection of career opportunities for professionals; the establishment and continuous elevation of standards of education and entrance into the profession; the upgrading of rewards (pay) for professionals; and the improvement of their prestige before their associates and, if possible, the public in general.

A second common denominator of the professions is their concentration upon the *work substance* of their field, both in preparatory education and in journeyman activities, and the differentiation of that field from other kinds of work (including other professions) and from work at a lower or subprofessional level in the same field. Accompanying this emphasis upon work substance has been a growing concentration, particularly in preprofessional education, upon the sciences which are considered foundational for the profession in question, whether they be natural or biological or social (behavioral). This emphasis is an inevitable consequence of the explosive developments of science in the last two decades, and unquestionably it has contributed to the betterment of professional performance.

Partially in consequence of the concentration upon science and work substance there has been a much less than parallel treatment of the *ecology* of the profession in the total social milieu: of the consequences and purposes of the profession and of the constraints within which it operates. There are signs in a good many fields today that attention to these topics is increasing, particularly in the public service professions. Yet much of professional education and practice is so focused on substance and science as to obscure the larger meaning of the profession in the society. Except for those professionals who grow beyond their field, the real world is seen as by a submariner through a periscope whose direction is fixed and immutable.

One of the most obscure sectors of the real world in professional education and much of its practice is the realm of government and politics. There is a built-in aversion between the professions and politics. Its origin is historical: most of the professions, and particularly those in the public service category, won their professional spurs over many arduous years to the extent they could escape the infiltration, the domination, and the influence of politicians (who, to most professionals, are by definition amateurs at best and corrupt ones at worst). Compare, for example, the evolution of the military, diplomatic, social welfare, city manager, and like fields. The aversion to politics has contemporary supports. Professionalism rests upon specialized knowledge, science, and rationality. There are *correct* ways of solving problems and doing things. Politics is seen as constituting negotiation, elections, votes, compromises—all carried on by subject-matter amateurs. Politics is to the professions as ambiguity to truth, expediency to rightness, heresy to true belief.

Government as a whole comes off not much better than politics in the eyes of most professions, particulary the "general" ones. In the first place, it carries the political taint by definition. Secondly, it violates or threatens some of the treasured attributes and myths of true professionalism: individual and professional autonomy and freedom from "bureaucratic" control; service to, and fees from, individual clients; vocational self-government. Among those general professions with large numbers of members employed privately, pre-service education usually treats government (insofar as it is considered at all) as an outside agency with or against which one must deal. This seems to be true of most education in law, engineering, accounting, and some other business fields, upon all of which government is heavily dependent. It is also true of medicine and most of its sub-specialties. Even in many public service professions—public school education provides an excellent example—there is a considerable aversion to government *in general* and to politics—which may be another word for the same thing. Government is all right in those particular areas in which the specified profession has dominant control; but beyond those perimeters, it is equated with "politics" and "bureaucracy" in their more invidious senses.

I doubt that it is appropriate to speak of "strategies" of the professions in government because some of their consequences seem to have "just growed" rather than to have been consciously planned. Yet those consequences are fairly consistent, particularly among the established professions, whether of the public service or the general category. And the emergent professions are varying distances down the road. The pattern has these features:

(1) the given profession has staked its territory within the appropriate governmental agency or agencies, usually with boundaries coterminous with those of the organization itself;
(2) within its organization, it has formed an elite corps with substantial control over the operations of the agency, significant influence on agency policies, and high internal prestige;

(3) to the extent possible, it has assumed control over employment policies and individual personnel actions for its own members in the agency and also over the employment of employees not in the elite profession;

(4) it has provided its members the opportunities, assurances, and protections of a career system of employment. . . [Pages 101–110].

## Democracy and Education

The winds of change, however, bear other straws, straws which promise new and more meaningful definitions of "merit" and also a broader and deeper understanding of administrative responsibility. One of these straws is simply the urgency of public problems. The underdeveloped populations of the world are impatient, as are our own minorities, our own impoverished, our own urban populations. Action will not wait for the completion of data-gathering and analysis or for the negotiation of boundaries between occupational monopolies. A second straw is a product of the knowledge explosion itself, which among other things has taught the interconnection of social conditions and the obstinacy of any social problem to respond to a specific, functionally defined solution. The educators by themselves are unable to cope with the problem of education, because it goes far beyond teaching. The doctors and the health officers are confronted with the same situation in the area of health, as are the police in that of crime, the transportation engineers in transportation, the welfare workers in poverty, and all of these in racial discrimination and hostility. Each profession is learning the hard way of its own inadequacies and its underlying dependence upon the methods and understandings of other disciplines. The interdisciplinary and interprofessional approach is no longer a mere academic curio, an interesting but dilettantish experiment. In today's world it is an absolute necessity, for no discipline, no profession, can handle even its own problems by itself. This lesson was learned a good many years ago

by the natural sciences and the "natural" professions. It is coming later and harder in the social fields, particularly economics; but its ultimate acceptance is inevitable. The interconnection of social problems and the interdependence of disciplines in dealing with them are two sides of the same coin.

Another product of the knowledge explosion has been a growing faith of the society and particularly of its leaders in the value of research to enable us more effectively to deal with our problems. This growth too started in the natural sciences and is least questioned there. It has recently spread rapidly in the life and medical sciences. It is beginning to develop in the social sciences. It is interesting, paradoxical, and indeed tragic that government has so tremendously stimulated and supported the physical sciences while giving the back of its hand to those fields of social knowledge upon which government and the society itself most immediately depend. Who first reaches the moon, and when he does it, are not of overpowering importance. What kind of an earth he returns to is. The problems of Hunter's Point, Selma, Harlem, Lagos, Havana, and Hong Kong are not going to be solved by anti-ballistic missiles or atomic energy or space spectaculars. They are human problems that can respond only to human remedies. We are only beginning to learn how to analyze these problems and to devise means of coping with them. Social policies must be focused on values, tempered by sympathy, grounded in knowledge.

The higher officials in the public service are products of the colleges and universities, and principally their professional departments and schools. This will be increasingly, even exclusively, true in the future. These persons will have a growing influence in the determination of public policy. Ultimately the possibilities of a truly democratic public service will depend upon (1) the mobility whereby intelligent individuals from all walks of life may progress to higher education and (2) the kind of orientation and education they receive in the universities. On the first point there is evidence of progress, though there is a long way to go. On the second, in spite of centripetal, problem-oriented pressures described earlier, there remains a high and perhaps growing degree of specialization in particular fields accompanied by a declining exposure to, and interest in, broader social areas, including the context within which each specialization operates.

Merit as traditionally defined is today an anchronism for a large and important part of the public service. In the future, merit will increasingly be measured by professionals against criteria established by the professions and by the universities which spawn them. It will depend in part upon technical and cognitive qualifications in the fields of specialization. The danger is that these will be too large a part of the criteria. Truly meritorious performance in public administration will depend at least equally upon the values, the objectives, and the moral standards which the administrator brings to his decisions, and upon his ability to weigh the relevant premises judiciously in his approach to the problems at hand. His code can hardly be as simple as the Ten Commandments, the Boy Scout Code, or the code of ethics of any of the professions; his decisions usually will require some kind of interpretation of *public* and *public interest*—explicit, implicit, even unconscious.

Such decisions are difficult, complex, and soul-testing, for the qualities they demand search the depths of both mind and spirit. As Bailey wrote, "Virtue without understanding can be quite as disastrous as understanding without virtue."[12] Understanding entails a degree of knowledge, a sense of relationships among phenomena, an appreciation of both social and private values. Most of the ingredients of understanding can be learned, and many of them can be taught. They go well beyond the mastery of scientific method, of substantive knowledge, of professional technique. They go beyond the boundaries of the typical profession or the curriculum of the standard professional training course. Yet understanding in this sense must become a major ingredient of public service merit in the future. This will require a degree of modesty and even humility on the part of individual professionals (and professors) about

their fields; a curiosity about, and accommodation toward, other fields of study and vocation; a sense of the society and the polity, and of the relationships between them and the field of occupational concentration.

Governmental agencies have for the most part accepted professional and academic definitions and measurements of merit as applied to specific academic and occupational fields. Most of them have, however, minimized the broader understanding discussed in the preceding paragraph as an element in appointment or advancement. The more difficult, less measurable elements of morality in public decision-making have been almost completely ignored in discussions of merit principles, although they may well be the most important criteria of all.

As in our culture in the past and in a good many other civilizations, the nature and quality of the public service depend principally upon the system of education. Almost all of our future public administrators will be college graduates, and within two or three decades a majority of them will have graduate degrees. Rising proportions of public administrators are returning to graduate schools for refresher courses, mid-career training, and higher degrees. These trends suggest that university faculties will have growing responsibility for preparing and for developing public servants both in their technical specialities and in the broader social fields with which their professions interact.

The universities offer the best hope of making the professions safe for democracy. [Pages 216–219]

## Notes

1. Though in neither case was participation open to anywhere near *all* the people.

2. These developments are discussed in subsequent chapters, especially 3 and 4.

3. "Notes on the Post-Industrial Society" I *The Public Interest*, 6 (Winter 1967). pp. 24–35.

4. Don K. Price, *The Scientific Estate* (Cambridge, Harvard University Press, 1965), pp. 15–16.

5. Bell, op. cit. p. 27.

6. *Daedalus*, Vol. 92, No. 4 (Fall 1963), p. 649.

7. Ibid. p. 655.

8. New York, McGraw-Hill Book Company.

9. *Personnel for the New Diplomacy* (New York, Carnegie Endowment for International Peace, December 1962).

10. Washington, D.C., The Brookings Institution, 1963.

11. The definition is unquestionably too loose to satisfy many students of occupations who would like to add other requisites, such as: professional organization; or eleemosynary or service orientation; or legal establishment; or individual autonomy in performance of work; or code of ethics. In terms of governmental consequences, the liberal usage is more appropriate. For example, in terms of their group behavior in government, the officers of the U.S. Navy are at least as "professionalized" as are lawyers.

12. Steven K. Bailey, "Ethics and the Public Service." In Roscoe C. Marrtin (ed.), *Public Administration and Democracy: Essays in Honor of Paul H. Appleby* (Syracuse, N.Y.: Syracuse University Press, 1965).

# II

# Merit Systems and Executive Leadership

The passage of the Pendleton Act and the extension of merit practices to other levels of government did not resolve institutional questions once and for all. As the chapter from Hugh Heclo's *A Government of Strangers* notes, two questions persistently pervaded subsequent discussions of reform. "First, what sort of central authority, if any, should guide the civil service system as a whole? Second, how should the responsibility for protecting the civil service from political partisanship be organized?" In some respects, this discussion embodied a quest to strike the appropriate balance between political responsiveness (especially in terms of deference to a top elected executive) and such values as agency competence, merit, and employee rights. In other guises, the issue centered on whether career executives should have access to a personnel staff more interested in helping them manage than serving as a watchdog eager to sniff out abuse.

The ferment over these and related institutional questions gained momentum in the 1930s. In 1936, William E. Mosher, then director of the School of Citizenship and Public Affairs at Syracuse University, and J. Donald Kingsley of Antioch College published *Public Personnel Administration*. This seminal text and the revised editions that followed dominated the personnel field for nearly two decades. The selection reprinted here conveys the reformist tone of the 1930s. The two authors questioned the traditional role of the civil-service commission and urged that personnel administration be made more responsive to executive leadership. They argued that "like other important staff agencies, the personnel agency must be closely associated with the administrative head and must continuously enjoy the prestige, the understanding, and support of his office." In their view the typical civil-service commission had not proven adequate in this regard. While they endorsed the establishment of a "judicial" body for handling appeals, they urged that another personnel agency also be established and headed by a director who reported to the chief executive, in this case, the President.

The reports of public commissions and governmental advisory groups stressed similar themes. In December 1933, the Social Science Research Council, a body representing seven national professional societies (e.g., anthropology, political science), appointed the Commission of Inquiry on Public Service Personnel. Charged with examining "the broad problems of public personnel within the United States and to outline a program for future action," the commission included three major figures in public administration—Louis Brownlow, Charles E. Merriam, and Luther Gulick. Following extensive hearings across the country, the preparation of monographs on the operation of certain European civil service systems, and other research, the Commission reported its findings in 1935. Consistent with a general theme of the 1930s, it advocated the development "in each of the larger governmental units an agency for personnel administration, to render constructive personnel service instead of devoting its entire attention to the policing of appointments, as has been all too common under civil service."[1]

The Report of the President's Committee on Administrative Management of 1937 (often called the Brownlow Committee) achieved even greater prominence. As the selection reprinted here indicates, the report argued that "federal personnel management. . . needs fundamental revision." It recommended that the Civil Service Commission be reorganized into a Civil Service Administration, which would be headed by a single executive responsible to the President. A separate Civil Service Board would be created to perform the watchdog functions designed to protect the system from excessive partisan influence.[2]

In considering the reports dominant in the 1930s, it deserves emphasis that the call for change in personnel institutions did not march hand in hand with a desire to give elected executives unrestricted discretion over appointments to top posts. Thus, the Commission of Inquiry on the Public Service emphasized the importance of staffing "posts of real eminence and honor" with career civil servants. It noted: "All the evidence presented shows clearly that the top posts are of supreme importance, and that chief administrative officers who are spoilsmen can demoralize the rank and file and wreck the service. . . ."[3] So, too, Mosher and Kingsley argued for the "elimination of the spoils policy as it affects the upper tier of executives and sub-executives." That these positions "have been filled in so many jurisdictions by birds of passage unfamiliar with the characteristics of public administration constitutes one of the severest handicaps under which the government has labored." Despite these exhortations, however, elected executives frequently demonstrated little interest in this aspect of the reform proposals.

Many of the reforms espoused by the President's Committee on Administrative Management garnered the support of President Roosevelt. Ultimately, however, Congress defeated the proposals by a narrow margin. As the selection from Heclo indicates, reform initiatives sporadically surfaced over the next forty years. In the meantime, however, executives frequently used more informal means to influence personnel decisions. In Washington, for instance, presidents understood that they could forge significant changes in policy outputs and outcomes by acquiring more control over various personnel levers. The Nixon Administration took particular interest in them. Upon assuming office in 1969, President Nixon sensed that opponents to his programs existed in many quarters of the higher civil service. (Although Nixon exaggerated the presence of "enemies" in the bureaucracy, the evidence suggests that this perception had some basis in fact.)[4] In an effort to ensure greater loyalty to the President's programs—to help the President rule rather than reign—the staff of the White House Personnel Office drafted a political personnel manual. Since Fred Malek headed the office during the early years of the Nixon Administration, the document became known as the *Malek Manual*. As the selection presented here indicates, the manual not only suggested strategies for manipulating personnel rules, it also vividly described how certain personnel processes actually worked in the federal bureaucracy. In some respects the *Malek Manual* is to personnel administration what Machiavelli's *The Prince* is to the broader field of political science.

The Watergate scandal brought down the curtain on Nixon's administrative initiatives and triggered congressional hearings on abuses in federal personnel practices. But it did not block the quest to make civil-service systems more responsive to executive leadership. With the coming of the Carter Administration, civil-service reform moved to the front burner. Jimmy Carter had inveighed against the sluggishness of the federal bureaucracy during his election campaign. Soon after taking office, he initiated a personnel-system study that helped lay the groundwork for reform proposals submitted to Congress on March 2, 1978. In presenting his reform package to Congress, Carter acknowledged that the institutions established under the Pendleton Act had for nearly a century served the nation well. But he went on to charge that the present system suffered from serious defects. The testimony before Congress by Alan K. Campbell (reprinted here), former Dean of the Maxwell School at Syracuse University and Carter's appointee as chair of the Civil Service Commission, points to these alleged defects and describes the rationale behind the Carter Administration's proposal. As is evident, many of the proposals (e.g., dividing the Civil Service Commission into the Merit System Protection Board and the Office of Personnel Management) reflected ideas very much present in the 1930s. Of particular relevance here, however, Title IV of the act established a Senior Executive Service. Proponents of this provision in part sought to give the president greater flexibility in assigning political appointees and career civil servants to top jobs in the federal government.

Several groups tried to derail the Carter proposal as it moved through Congress. For instance, federal employee unions, who viewed the bill as too management oriented, toiled diligently to defeat it. Filibuster threats also surfaced from time to time. Ultimately, however, the Senate approved the measure by a voice vote and the House endorsed it by a margin of 365 to 8. The final bill contained most of the features Carter had proposed with the glaring exception of those aimed at curtailing veterans preference.

While the Civil Service Reform Act of 1978 sought to bolster the president's authority to shape major personnel decisions, the Supreme Court in *Branti* v. *Finkel* moved in the opposite direction two years later. The designation of this case as a "classic" reflects not only its own significance but its review of another major Supreme Court case decided in the 1970s—*Elrod* v. *Burns*. As the selection indicates, the Court in *Elrod* v. *Burns* (1976) decided that the newly elected sheriff of Cook County, Illinois, Democrat Richard J. Elrod, had violated the constitutional rights of certain lower level (allegedly "nonpolicymaking, nonconfidential") patronage employees by discharging them "because they did not support and were not members of the Democratic Party and had failed to obtain the sponsorship of one of its leaders." This decision gave further impetus to the forces working against low-level spoils politics (see the Sorauf selection in the next section). By so doing, it provided impetus to those who saw a greater need for personnel offices to act less as police officers and more as support staffs. With the Supreme Court dealing a blow to patronage, jurisdictions with merit systems would presumably need to invest less heavily in formal institutions designed to fight such practices.

It was *Branti* v. *Finkel*, however, that pushed restrictions on overt political patronage up the hierarchy to certain top policy jobs. Aaron Finkel had worked as an assistant public defender in Rockland County, New York. In this post he served at the discretion of the public defender who in turn was selected by the majority party of the county legislature. When a new Democratic majority emerged in this legislature, Peter Branti was appointed public defender. Branti promptly attempted to dismiss Finkel and other Republican assistant defenders. Finkel and a colleague challenged the action in court. Subsequently, six members of the Supreme Court held for Finkel. Writing for the majority, Justice Stevens argued that "party affiliation is not necessarily relevant to every policymaking or confidential position. The coach of a state university's football team formulates policy, but no one could seriously claim that Republicans make better coaches than Democrats, or vice versa...." Ultimately, "the question is whether the hiring authority can demonstrate that party affiliation is an appropriate requirement for the effective performance of the public office involved."

Defining and measuring effective performance as well as determining the degree to which party affiliation correlates with such performance poses great difficulties. It remains the subject of educated guesswork rather than finely calibrated judgment. Nonetheless, the Supreme Court gave all the appearances of limiting the discretion of top elected officials and their immediate appointees. What has been the outcome of *Branti* v. *Finkel*? Have elected officials pulled back from applying partisan considerations in hiring and firing for certain top policy jobs? Has the decision, as Justice Powell suggested in a dissenting opinion, weakened the salutary impact of political parties on democratic governance? Given the vast number of governmental jurisdictions and gaps in existing research, definitive answers to these questions remain elusive.

Paradoxically, however, some (admittedly incomplete) evidence indicates that the 1980s witnessed growing interest by elected executives in controlling top appointments. Faced with growing government involvement in many policy spheres and a constitutional system (e.g., federalism, separation of powers) that tends to pulverize the potential for leadership, elected executives have become increasingly conscious of the role that personnel processes can play in helping them shape administrative discretion. The Reagan Administration worked diligently and often successfully to establish an administrative presidency (i.e., acquire influence over policy via administrative levers rather than obtaining changes in the law). In screening candidates for political appointment, the White House staff heavily emphasized ideological compatibility with the president.[5] Political penetration by the Reagan White House went beyond the very highest bureaucratic levels to the Senior Executive Service (SES) and below. In this regard, one study found that from fiscal 1980 to 1986 the number of career SES members declined by about 5 percent while the number of noncareer SES members rose by just over 13 percent. Schedule C employees (those political appointees in the lower ranks) increased by nearly 13 percent over the same period.[6]

Developments in the states and localities also testify to the appeal of control over top positions. One analysis conducted in the mid-1980s found that, since 1970, twenty-eight states had significantly modified policies relating to the proportion of high-level executives exempted from civil-service protection. The study concludes that almost all of these changes moved "in the direction of increasing the number of exempted top managers..., and giving elected and appointed administrative superiors more discretion..."[7] At the local level, elected officials faced with dwindling opportunities for patronage in lower level posts often struggled to ensure that they controlled appointments to top positions. In Chicago, for example, court orders severely constricted the spoils options of the late Mayor Harold Washington. While conceding much with respect to political appointments to lower level jobs, Washington fought tenaciously to preserve leverage over appointments to top posts. When the court proposed 250 exempt positions, Washington asked for 1,200; he eventually obtained approval to exempt 900 top jobs from merit system coverage.[8] In the states as well as in Chicago, little evidence exists that greater numbers of exempt appointments have unleashed wholesale removals of executives from top administrative posts. This may in part reflect deference to *Branti v. Finkel*. But the absence of mass removals should not be construed as implying that the movement toward greater numbers of exempt positions has had no effect on power relationships between elected executives and their top subordinates. Their exempt status may lead these subordinates to be more deferential to the preferences of a president, a governor, or mayor.

As the 1990s approached, observers demonstrated less concern that personnel systems thwarted political responsiveness than that civil service institutions failed to place enough emphasis on other pertinent values. Some blamed the Civil Service Reform Act of 1978 for unleashing an excessive tilt toward political responsiveness at the expense of merit and agency competence.[9] Analysts begin to contemplate institutional changes to remedy the newly perceived imbalance. Echoing reform currents of the 1930s, for instance, the National Academy of Public Administration publicly opposed any increase in the number of senior executive positions filled by presidential appointees.[10] Other reform proposals will undoubtedly surface. The fact that civil-service institutions serve multiple values means reforms that enhance political responsiveness tend to spawn proposals designed to ensure that other core values will not suffer undue neglect.

# Notes

1. Commission of Inquiry on Public Service Personnel, *Better Government Personnel* (New York: Whittlesey House, 1935), pp. vi, 4. See also Herman Finer, "Better Government Personnel: America's Next Frontier," *Political Science Quarterly* LI (December, 1936); pp. 569–599.

2. Reports focused on local governments echoed these sentiments. See Municipal Manpower Commission, *Governmental Manpower for Tomorrow's Cities* (New York: McGraw-Hill, 1962), p. 106.

3. Commission of Inquiry, *Better Government Personnel*, pp. 5, 20.

4. Joel D. Aberbach and Bert A. Rockman, "Clashing Beliefs Within the Executive Branch: The Nixon Administration Bureaucracy," *American Political Science Review* 70 (June, 1976); pp. 456–468.

5. See Richard P. Nathan, *The Administrative Presidency* (New York: John Wiley, 1983), and Chester A. Newland, "A Mid-term Appraisal—The Reagan Presidency: Limited Government and Political Administration," *Public Administration Review* 43 (January/February, 1983); pp. 1–21.

6. U.S. General Accounting Office, *Federal Employees: Trends in Career and Noncareer Employee Appointments in the Executive Branch* (Washington, D.C.: GAO/GGD-87-96FS, 1987).

7. Deborah D. Roberts, "A New Breed of Public Executive: Top Level 'Exempt' Managers in State Government," *Review of Public Personnel Administration* 8 (Spring, 1988); p. 23.

8. Ann Freedman, "Doing Battle with the Patronage Army: Politics, Courts, and Personnel Administration in Chicago," *Public Administration Review* 48 (September/October, 1988); p. 850.

9. See Bernard Rosen, "Crises in the U.S. Civil Service," *Public Administrative Review* 46 (May/June, 1986); pp. 207–214. For a general retrospective on the Civil Service Reform Act by those involved in its creation, see U.S. General Accounting Office, *Civil Service Reform: Development of 1978 Civil Service Reform Proposals* (Washington, D.C.: GAO/GGD-89-18, 1988).

10. National Academy of Public Administration, *The Executive Presidency: Federal Management for the 1990s* (Washington, D.C., 1988).

# 5

# The Idea of Civil Service: A Third Force?

*Hugh Heclo*
*The Brookings Institution*

Political leadership seems problematic and bureaucratic power unavoidable. The Political side (with a capital "P") of people in government evokes an image of changeable personal, party, or philosophical loyalties. Bureaucratic figures may have no less political acumen (i.e., small "p" in the sense of how to get things done), but they also suggest a more institutional commitment to established programs, procedures, and organizations.

There is another force at work in executive politics that is less familiar and somewhat more difficult to visualize. Political leaders in the executive branch deal not simply with bureaucrats but with career officials who are part of a civil service system. The civil service is a personnel structure (or more accurately a collection of structures) manifested in a dozen or more statutory laws, in hundreds of executive orders by the President, and in literally thousands of rules and regulations supervised by the U.S. Civil Service Commission. But the core of the civil service is an idea rather than a body of personnel regulations. This idea is somewhat distinct from notions of either political leadership or bureaucratic power.

In a sense bureaucracies are a "natural" phenomenon in modern society; they have

SOURCE: From *A Government of Strangers: Executive Politics in Washington* by Hugh Heclo, pp. 19–33. Copyright © 1977 by The Brookings Institution. Reprinted by permission. Footnotes renumbered.

occurred and grown without anyone having to decide or plan consciously that they should do so. The civil service, however, has been a kind of social invention. Deliberate planning and struggle for the establishment of a civil service system can be traced back a hundred years or more.[1] Unlike the fact of bureaucracy, the design of the civil service was normative, a statement of what should be.

Throughout its history, the civil service idea has rested on three basic principles: (1) that the selection of subordinate government officials should be based on merit—the ability to perform the work rather than any form of personal or political favoritism; (2) that since jobs are to be filled by weighing the merits of applicants, those hired should have tenure regardless of political changes at the top of organizations; and (3) that the price of job security should be a willing responsiveness to the legitimate political leaders of the day.

Because preconceptions abound, it is worth pointing out that nothing in the basic civil service idea requires that such an official be passive rather than actively responsible for expressing his views, or politically insensitive, or on the right side of some mythical line separating administration and policy. In fact, at the higher levels of nonroutinized work, the merit principle's stress on competent performance may imply just the opposite. Neither does the basic idea suggest that the civil service is created primarily for the sake of providing job security to public employees. Rather, security of tenure was a by-product of assuring the competence of government personnel by an open, competitive examination of merits in hiring.[2]

Potentially at least, the civil service concept adds a third dimension to the interaction between top political executives and officials in the bureaucracy. It may mitigate and soften though it does not entirely eliminate the apparent conflict between purely political and bureaucratic self-interests. Unlike archetypal "bureaucratic man" interested in protecting existing operations and organizations, the civil servant is supposed to be responsive to the legal authority of political heads. Unlike pure "political man," the civil servant has a responsibility that is institutional and enduring, whoever the political figures in charge might be. To institute a civil service system is to accept the idea that competent personnel manning the government machinery should be available for use by—but not at the absolute disposal of—any political group arriving in office through legitimate means. If there is an analogy, it is to be found in the differentiation of a career military service from both the self-contained private armies of the past (one of the earliest forms of bureaucracy) and from the inchoate militia that (much like sets of democratic politicians) were periodically called on to exercise the power of the state. Thus to some extent the civil service idea can be an important fulcrum for trying to balance the demands of political leadership and bureaucratic power. How far it actually does so can only be determined by looking at the actual practices of people in government. The following two sections suggest why the historical and structural context reduces the odds for the civil service performing such a role in Washington.

## A Precarious Idea

Relevant rules and regulations are well ensconced in personnel offices throughout Washington, but the basic idea of a civil service has always had a precarious existence. One reason stems from the original design of American national government. Having settled on a single rather than a plural executive and a sharing of powers among the three branches, the Founders could easily relegate the rest of government administration to a matter of "executive details."[3] The advent of modern bureaucracies, however, added the civil servant as an unexpected and insecurely placed participant to the original grand design of American government. Higher civil service officials are apt to find themselves in the middle—a part of the unitary executive branch under the President's

guidance but also dependent on a Congress sharing important life and death powers over their work. As civil servants, the price of their secure tenure is supposed to be responsiveness to political leadership, but both presidents and congressmen can legitimately claim that role. Thus on the one hand, smart bureaucrats with their own program loyalties can play presidents and congressional committees against each other.[4] On the other hand, even without such intrigue, civil servants can easily make a misstep that destroys the trust and understanding they need from all sides. To protect and advance the aims of their organizations, officials have to deal with large numbers of power centers outside the executive branch. But bureaucratic entrepreneurs who build this needed support can also become visibly identified with special interests and less responsive as civil servants.

In its search for an accepted role the U.S. civil service has been the victim of not only constitutional design but also of its own history. The U.S. civil service system, unlike that in other Western democracies, developed well after democratic political parties and mass political participation but somewhat ahead of industrialization and the accompanying expansion of central government bureaucracies (through business regulations, health and safety requirements, technical standard-setting, and so on). In the last quarter of the nineteenth century, when the first stirrings of modern bureaucratic power associated with industrialization were being felt, civil service reformers were already concentrating on an older American problem: how to reverse the intrusion of political party spoils into the work of government administration.[5] History thus bequeathed a concern that focused somewhat more on negative protections and somewhat less on the positive duties and direction of the U.S. civil service. Many reformers also recognized that without responsibility to political leaders, the protected civil servants could themselves become a threat to democracy. But in general there was little need to pay attention to the problems that would face future political executives who would have to deal with the growing power of the bureaucracy.[6]

The arrangements created by the Civil Service Act of 1883, which remains applicable today, represented an ingenious and necessarily ambiguous attempt to straddle these cross pressures of protecting and directing the civil service.

On the one hand, the act not only accepted but reemphasized the President's constitutional position as the ultimate repository of executive power: rules and regulations for civil service personnel actions in the executive branch derive their authority from and are proclaimed by the President.[7] The Civil Service Commission was created "to aid the President as he may request in preparing suitable rules for carrying this Act into effect," and the same perspective was deliberately expressed by making commissioners serve at the pleasure of the President.

On the other hand, the concern for protection from politics was expressed in the creation of a Civil Service Commission that would be more insulated from political influences than any of the government departments (it was in fact the first attempt to stretch the three-branch constitutional structure by creating a separate regulatory commission). This effort to distance the commission from the regular political apparatus was signified by providing three commissioners, only two of whom would be members of the same party, and by making the commission a separate agency permanently outside the existing hierarchy of government departments. Since 1883 the customary but obscure terminology has been that the commission is a "semi-independent" agency. If it is responsible political leadership that worries people, emphasis can be put on "semi"; if political partisanship seems the threat, one can always accentuate the "independent" side of things.

This ambivalence has received unexpected emphasis in recent years. It is not just that civil servants have quietly become a major component of the ostensible political leadership in the executive branch. Experiences with the Nixon administration have raised doubts once more among many of the public administration experts who had previously sought with moderate success to downplay the negative, protectionist tradition in favor of more flexible and positive approaches to managing the career public service. The mea culpa of a distinguished Civil Service Commission adviser and personnel expert shows how much feelings have changed:

> We, professionally, are very largely responsible for the attitude that gave the Nixon staffers a rationale in their own minds as to what they were doing. That was this business of control. Our profession has constantly preached that a guy can't have responsibility without the requisite authority, that he can't direct a staff of people unless he has selected them.... Our doctrine has been that you have to have this personal, individual administrative control of selection of people in order to direct their activity.... [The Civil Service Commission] did pull in their horns a little bit. They did modify their role of protecting the merit system.[8]

Such complaints reflect not only the misdeeds of one administration but also a feeling that the basic concept of civil service has been lost from view with the passage of time. This historical precariousness of the civil service idea has only been accentuated by uncertainty about the organizational structure for guiding personnel policies in Washington.

## Four Decades of Truncated Reform

Toward the end of every decade since the 1930s efforts have been made to restructure the organizational arrangements inherited from the nineteenth century. Two questions have remained as basic to the reform efforts during this period as they were to the 1883 act. First, what sort of central authority, if any, should guide the civil service system as a whole? Second, how should responsibility for protecting the civil service from political partisanship be organized? Both questions are important to institutionalizing the civil service idea; if anything, both have become more pressing than they were in the days when presidential power was in repose and the federal bureaucracy left the average citizen alone.

Looked at as a whole, none of the reform efforts have succeeded in creating the major change intended, that is, strengthening central institutions for guiding and protecting a governmentwide civil service system. But this has not been for want of proposals. In 1937 President Franklin Roosevelt and his administrative advisers advanced a plan to replace the Civil Service Commission with a single-headed Central Personnel Agency directly under the President and a wholly separate Civil Service Board. The presidential agency would perform the positive work of setting standards and policies for nonpolitical personnel throughout the executive branch, while the independent board would perform the traditional role of protecting the civil service from partisan and personal favoritism. Despite a combination of forces defending the commission and numerous complaints about presidential dictatorship, the plan failed by only eight votes in the House of Representatives.[9]

The 1937 defeat was the closest reformers have ever come to major structural change since 1883. What has occurred instead has been a series of attempts to modify—first this way and then that—central staff for overseeing the career personnel system. In a scaled-down reorganization plan of 1939,[10] FDR used his new discretion to appoint a respected civil servant as Liaison Officer for Personnel Management, who thus became one of the six new personal assistants to the President in the newly created Executive Office of the President. By the end of the 1940s the liaison office was being run by a political aide and was heavily involved in trying to manage the system of political appointments as well as advise the President on civil service policies. In 1949 the first Hoover Commission on government reorganization proposed that the chairman of the three-member Civil Service Commission should become its chief administering officer and also serve as staff adviser to the President on all policies affecting career employees.

This plan was adopted at the outset of the Eisenhower administration,[11] but the "two-hat" arrangement for the Civil Service chairman did not work satisfactorily. By 1956 the top presidential advisers on civil service personnel were themselves dissatisfied with existing arrangements. As both White House aide and Civil Service Commission head, the chairman was strained between divers part-time roles as an advocate for what the commission staff wanted, as a personal adviser trying to look at matters strictly from the President's point of view, and as a nonpartisan commissioner appearing before a Democratic Congress suspicious of Republican raids on the civil service.

Thus in the last half of the 1950s the cycle of reform sentiment swung forward again. Early in 1957 Dwight Eisenhower's advisers on career personnel policies recommended to the Republican President a plan that was basically the same as the one sought unsuccessfully by Franklin Roosevelt twenty years earlier. Reacting against efforts to politicize the civil service in the early Eisenhower years (see discussion of the Willis Plan in chapter 2), a few members of Congress and civic group leaders introduced similar proposals to recast the top structure with a presidential agency for civil service policies and a separate unit to police the civil service rules.[12] But again Congress and public employee groups showed little receptivity, and the President was reluctant to push the issue. In fact, far from wishing to strengthen the President's hand in personnel policies for the executive branch, the Democratic Congress easily and without hearings passed legislation moving the Civil Service Commission somewhat further from direct presidential control.[13] Rather than risk presidential prestige by proposing major structural changes, the Eisenhower administration after 1957 reverted to the earlier pattern and replaced the Civil Service chairman's job in the White House with a special presidential assistant for civil service policies. In 1961 the Kennedy administration abruptly abolished the special assistant's office for civil service policies, in large part because of the last Eisenhower assistant's political activities in the 1960 campaign.

With several important variations, the 1960s repeated what was by then a familiar story of pushing civil service policymaking in and out of the White House advisory system. Increasingly in the Johnson administration, the White House relied directly on the Civil Service chairman for advice on personnel policies. Yet what developed after the 1964 election until the end of the Johnson administration was not, as many observers assumed, simply a return to the "two-hat" model of the first Eisenhower term. In effect there now evolved a tripartite role for the Civil Service chairman—one as administrative head of the commission, a second as presidential adviser on civil service policies, and a third as operational director of the White House office responsible for staff work and advice on political appointments. The first two roles were known to Eisenhower's chairman; the second and third had occupied Harry Truman's liaison aide on personnel, but never before had all three been put together at once. While by all accounts the arrangement worked fairly effectively in the Johnson years, the potential for abuse seemed clear. As one former White House aide put it:

> [The Civil Service chairman] is a man of high integrity. The civil service work was done over in the commission office from 8 A.M. to 2 P.M. and political appointments handled in the White House office from 2 P.M. to 8 P.M.... Still, you had one man in the middle instead of people on both sides. There was no one to see if the civil service side of things or the political side of things were encroaching on each other.

The advantage gained, of course, was access to the President and support for a number of things wanted by the personnel experts in the Civil Service Commission.

The close working relations between commission and White House in the Democratic administrations fueled suspicions in an already distrustful Nixon White House. More than ever after 1968, the Civil Service Commission found itself cut off from personal access to the President but subject to political pressures from the White House in its work. At the same time, management experts advising the President returned to a familiar theme. Surveying the operation of government personnel policies at the end of 1969, they concluded that as part of his management responsibilities the President needed a direct capability in the Executive Office. Against the objections of the Civil Service Commission and several members of Congress, the Bureau of the Budget—now the Office of Management and Budget (OMB)—was "charged with advising the President on the development of new programs to recruit, train, motivate, deploy and evaluate the men and women who make up the top ranks of the civil service, in the broadest sense of that term."[14] One month later, OMB acquired a new Division of Executive Development and Labor Relations to carry out this responsibility.

Hence if the basic overall structure for guiding the civil service system has remained unchanged since 1883, it is also true that the relationship between civil service leadership and the presidency has never been firmly established. That relationship has regularly oscillated between more and less White House proximity, between more and less clarity in distinguishing personal political advisers to the President from civil service policymakers.

Throughout these decades the Civil Service Commission itself has undergone important changes in its approach. By the end of the 1960s the trend was well established—away from the traditional emphasis on negative protections and detailed control of personnel operations and toward what the commission has viewed as a positive approach to allow greater executive flexibility in the agencies for managing career personnel. Gradually in the past forty years, the bulk of routine operations have been decentralized to personnel offices in the agencies, with the commission concentrating instead on setting standards, overseeing the procedural rules it promulgates, and auditing personnel operations. Its desire for a positive approach to civil service employment has been reflected in new programs for training, college recruitment, civil service awards, and manpower planning. And as the "management" side in government labor relations, its policymaking role has been heightened by the growing power of public employee unions. If presidential advisers persisted in recommending the creation of a central capability under the President for leadership in civil service policy, it was not because officials at the Civil Service Commission failed to claim that they were already performing that role.

But experiences in the Nixon years also showed that the commission's emphasis on flexibility and managerial discretion was to some extent purchased at the price of its policing role. In part there was the gradual accumulation over many years of "flexible" arrangements that violated the spirit and occasionally the letter of civil service rules. In part, too, the commission's vigor in protecting the civil service idea was muted by a desire to establish good relations with an especially suspicious Nixon White House. During 1976 a self-evaluation by the Civil Service Commission showed that in the years 1969–73 (1) staffing and examining processes had been subject to manipulation in a way inconsistent with merit principles; (2) commission officials and employees had actively participated in these and other improper acts of favoritism and preferential treatment; (3) the commission had lacked the will to respond to allegations of political intrusion into the civil service system; and (4) once started, its enforcement efforts were ineffective and superficial.[15] Far from being in a position to discipline others, the Civil Service Commission by 1976 had to admit that it had been part of the problem.

None of this is to say that the majority of commission activities have been handled improperly, and procedures have been tightened up since 1973 (see chapter 4). Yet seen in perspective, the commission's recent failings have shown that the question hedged in previous decades is still alive. Can the commission be an agent of presidential leadership in guiding civil service policies and a watchdog for impartially protecting merit system principles? Many reformers have thought not, but none of their efforts to recast the top personnel structures for dealing with the bureaucracy have been realized. The civil service remains a precarious idea in an ambiguous organizational structure.

The same problems have emerged in accentuated form with regard to higher civil servants, the ones who are likely to deal personally with political executives. This, too, is a story of truncated reform inasmuch as organizational arrangements for top careerists have aroused considerable dissatisfaction but little concerted change. The Classification Act of 1949 created a more uniform schedule of job classifications for the many employees bunched at the top civil service grade, then GS 15. The act was primarily intended as a pay and classification reform, however, and in no way attempted to create a higher civil service with distinctive responsibilities.[16] In 1955 the second Hoover Commission on government organization gave an unprecedented amount of attention to problems of the higher civil service and proposed the creation of a senior corps of up to 3,000 civil servants who would carry their high rank with them as they moved throughout government, breaking the tradition of making civil service rank the attribute of a particular classified job.[17] Supported by the Eisenhower White House, the idea encountered strong opposition from top careerists in various agencies and their friends in Congress. Presidential attempts to initiate a scaled-down version of the same plan were defeated when Congress attached an appropriation rider denying any funds to administer such a program.[18]

The first significant reform occurred only in 1966, when the Civil Service Commission was able to use its rapport at the White House to gain support for some modest changes at the top career levels. In 1966 the new Executive Assignment System created a somewhat neater typology of appointment authorities and a computerized inventory with biographical information on 25,000 high-ranking federal employees that could be used by all agency heads in filling vacancies.[19] At the same time, a new Bureau of Executive Manpower was created in the Civil Service Commission to encourage the development of and planning for top career personnel, a mission it began sharing in 1970 with the OMB's new Division of Executive Development.

To date the results of these changes have been meager. Hiring officials often complain that the computerized inventory merely produces lists of names but offers no in-depth evaluation of the people or their qualifications. More important are doubts that an admonition from the commission of the OMB is capable of penetrating the territorial boundaries that separate the bureaucrats' agency-centered careers, much less promote movement toward a governmentwide personnel system for higher civil servants. Far from demonstrating a serious concern for top civil service manpower, the new arrangements have remained undermanned, underfunded, and politically undersupported. With the exception of a few efforts confined to certain agencies, the overall executive development program can be rated a failure in its attempt to generate groups of more broadly experienced and more organizationally mobile career executives.[20] In 1973, for example, a new Federal Executive Development Program was started with high hopes for centrally identifying, training, and assigning a few promising career executives on a governmentwide basis. By 1976 the hopes were gone and the program had retreated to a position of allowing agencies to select their own candidates for executive development; each of these careerists is to be trained to advance slowly within his own agency and to meet its specific needs. One of the officials in charge of executive development in the civil service described it in the following manner in the summer of 1976:

We haven't accomplished much. A number of those selected in the first two years felt they were taken out of the stream for promotions in their old bureaus. And the bureaus resisted because they knew the whole idea of this program was to arrange things so that a good guy didn't necessarily return to spend his entire life in one bureau. I guess I shouldn't have been so surprised at how unwilling and parochial the agencies would be. . . . So now we've trimmed our sails to cope with the reality that the departments are conglomerates and the real management is at the bureau level.

I've got to work with the bureau chiefs, not fight them. Now it's just a program for encouraging them to develop better personnel systems for their own use.

Even less was accomplished when the Nixon administration and the Civil Service Commission proposed creating one common pool of government career executives who could be moved at the discretion of agency heads. By 1972 the intentions of the Nixon White House toward the civil service were already arousing suspicion, and no one was surprised when the House of Representatives rejected the plan.[21]

Meanwhile, Congress has continued to play an important but disorganized part in managing the civil service system. By adding to governmentwide quotas on supergrades, exempting particular bureaus from overall personnel ceilings, creating uncoordinated provisions for ranking and classifying civil service positions—in these and other ways it has become customary in Congress to bypass House and Senate civil service committees and to develop civil service policies through the ad hoc actions of committees that deal with particular agencies and programs. For example, 400 new supergrade positions created in 1949 were established as a single governmentwide quota allocated by the Civil Service Commission acting for the President. In 1951 Congress passed the first of its "special authorizations," and since then new supergrade positions have come to depend on special congressional provisions rather than on a centrally allocated quota.[22]

Likewise, no one appears to have control over personnel totals, for when a bureau's activity appeals to a particular committee, presidential personnel ceilings can make little difference.[23] As a manager of other civil service policies, Congress has been rated by its own analysts in much the way that reformers several years ago described its incoherent control over budget totals and their allocation.

Subject matter committees of the Congress do not coordinate their actions on the classification or ranking of positions with the

Post Office and Civil Service Committees of the Senate and House. This is the basic cause of inconsistencies and inequities among the classification, ranking, and pay systems throughout the Federal Service.[24]

Thus most attempts to plan and coordinate the civil service system as a whole have been accepted only grudgingly, if at all, in Congress; by contrast, detailed administrative interventions on those personnel issues of particular interest to individual congressmen find ready acceptance on Capitol Hill.

THESE FACTORS taken together suggest that while in theory the civil service idea in Washington may be a counterpoint for balancing strictly political and bureaucratic demands, in practice it rests on slippery foundations. Constitutionally, it leads a precarious existence between separated executive and legislative institutions that share important powers over each other's work. Historically, a tradition of party spoils has encouraged more attention to preventing patronage abuses than to building the civil service as an instrument of improved government performance. Structurally, there has been persistent ambivalence about how close or how far from the White House the direction of civil service policies should be. Administratively, attempts to reform the top career levels suggest the ease with which any idea of a governmentwide civil service becomes subordinated to particular bureau and congressional interests. Recent events have only reemphasized the strength of the prevailing crosscurrents: since 1969 it has been possible to have both a lapse in the traditional negative protections of the civil service and a record of continued frustration in reforms trying to create more positive management of the career system.

In general, then, as the search for political leadership has become more demanding, answers to the two basic questions about the bureaucracy's civilian personnel system have remained relatively unchanged since the decision of 1883. What sort of central authority should there be? Never have reformers managed to create a single presidential staff arm for a governmentwide civil service policy. Instead, a bureau-level focus in using civil servants has been coupled with central regulation over procedural techniques for taking personnel actions. This process regulator has remained the Civil Service Commission, which is located ambiguously as more central than the departments but more peripheral than the Executive Office of the President. How should protection be organized? The answer has continued to be reliance on the "semi-independent" status of the same commission—part presidential agency and part policeman against political intrusions. And always in the background has loomed a Congress that is vocal in support for better management but jealous of any rearrangements that might disturb its own diverse lines into each fragment of the bureaucracy.

It is within this historical structure that American national government seeks to cope with the problem of relating political and bureaucratic executives. But the structure itself does not reveal very much about what these relationships of executive politics are like or how they work. For that it is necessary to watch and listen to people in government who have had the actual experiences.

## Notes

1. The best historical treatments of the U.S. civil service are Paul P. Van Riper, *History of the United States Civil Service* (Row, Peterson, 1958); and *History of the Civil Service Merit Systems of the United States and Selected Foreign Countries,* compiled by the Congressional Research Service for the Subcommittee on Manpower and Civil Service of the House Committee on Post Office and Civil Service, Committee Print 94-29, 94 Cong. 2 sess. (GPO, 1976). George A. Graham attempted to distill what is in essence a civil service concept of public administration in "Ethical Guidelines for Public Administration: Observations on Rules of the Game," *Public Administration Review,* vol. 34 (January–February 1974), pp. 90–92.

2. The Civil Service Act of 1883 provided for no restrictions on the removal of civil service employees. At Civil Service Commission urging, President McKinley in 1897 issued the first rules restricting removal. These, together with clarifications issued by President Roosevelt in 1902, are still the applicable basic provisions. See U.S. Civil Service Commission, *14th Report,* 1896–97 (GPO, 1897), p. 24; and *19th Report,* 1901–02 (GPO, 1902), p. 18.

3. Alexander Hamilton, James Madison, and John Jay, *The Federalist,* or, *The New Constitution,* Max Beloff, ed. (Oxford: Basil Blackwell, 1948), no. 72, p. 369.

4. For a discussion based on this perspective, see Richard E. Neustadt, "Politicians and Bureaucrats," in American Assembly, *Congress and America's Future* (2d ed., Prentice-Hall, 1973), pp. 118–40.

5. The reform movement emerged and gathered momentum in the 1860s and 1870s, finally culminating with the Civil Service Act of January 16, 1883 (22 Stat. 403). By contrast, there were almost no statutes of national importance regarding U.S. commerce before the Interstate Commerce Act of 1887.

6. The somewhat divergent aims were described by a leading reformer, William D. Foulke, in his memoirs, *Fighting the Spoilsmen* (Putnam, 1919).

7. The heart of the provision (22 Stat. 403 [1883]) reads as follows:

The President is authorized to prescribe such regulations for the admission of persons into the civil service of the United States as may best promote the efficiency thereof, and ascertain the fitness of each candidate in respect to age, health, character, knowledge, and ability for the branch of service into which he seeks to enter; and for this purpose he may employ suitable persons to conduct such inquiries, and may prescribe their duties, and establish the regulations for the conduct of persons who may receive appointments in the civil service.

8. "Discussion of the Federal Personnel Crisis," *The Bureaucrat,* vol. 4 (January 1976), p. 377.

9. President's Committee on Administrative Management, *Report with Special Studies* (GPO, 1937), pp. 95–101; and Richard Polenberg, *Reorganizing Roosevelt's Government* (Harvard University Press, 1966), pp. 47, 80–84, 93–94, 129.

10. Executive Order 8248, September 8, 1939.

11. *First Report of the Commission on Organization of the Executive Branch of the Government,* H. Doc. 55, 81 Cong. 1 sess. (GPO, 1949), pp. 23–25. The plan was implemented in Executive Order 10452, May 1, 1953.

12. See *Administration of the Civil Service System,* Report to the Senate Committee on Post Office and Civil Service, Committee Print 2, 85 Cong. 1 sess. (GPO, 1957), and *Federal Personnel Administration,* S. Rept. 1545, 86 Cong. 2 sess. (GPO, June 10, 1960).

13. Public Law 854 of 1957 established six-year overlapping terms for the commissioners; it thus subtly modified the reasoning of 1883; i.e., that since personnel policy was part of the President's general responsibility for executive branch management, Civil Service commissioners should serve only at his pleasure.

14. Executive Order 11541, July 1, 1970.

15. *A Self-Inquiry into Merit Staffing,* Report of the Merit Staffing Review Team, U.S. Civil Service Commission, for the House Committee on Post Office and Civil Service, Committee Print 94-14, 94 Cong. 2 sess. (1976), pp. 14, 65, 82. The evidence for an even more damning indictment of the commission's work is contained in *Final Report on Violations and Abuses of Merit Principles in Federal Employment Together with Minority Views,* Subcommittee on Manpower and Civil Service of the House Committee on Post Office and Civil Service, Committee Print 94-28, 94 Cong. 2 sess. (GPO, 1976), pp. 1–138.

16. Ismar Baruch, "The Supergrade Story, 1949–1952" (Ismar Baruch Collection, U.S. Civil Service Commission Library, Washington, D.C., n.d.).

17. See Commission on the Organization of the Executive Branch of the Government, *Task Force Report on Personnel and Civil Service* (GPO, 1955).

18. The events are recounted in George A. Graham, *America's Capacity to Govern: Some Preliminary Thoughts for Prospective Administrators* (University of Alabama Press, 1960).

19. In brief, the system established three types of appointments at the supergrade level: career executive assignments for positions in the career service filled through the competitive staffing process; noncareer executive assignments to replace the old schedule C for supergrade positions involving advocacy or confidential or policy responsibilities; and limited executive assignments, which are career-type assignments for a short duration or to meet emergency needs. In addition there remain appointment authorities under schedules A, B, and C. Noncareer executive assignments and the various schedules are defined and discussed in chapter 2. For a more complete description, see the annual report of the U.S. Civil Service Commission, Bureau of Executive Manpower, *Executive Manpower in the Federal Service,* for January 1972 and following years.

20. William A. Medina offers one assessment in "Factors Which Condition the Responses of Departments and Agencies to Centrally Mandated Management Improvement Approaches" (Ph.D. dissertation, American University, Washington, D.C., 1976), chaps. 4–6. The formal guidelines for executive development are set out in *The Federal Personnel Manual,* chap. 412, app. A. The Internal Revenue Service is generally regarded as having one of the best-established programs of this kind. For a description, see U.S. Department of the Treasury, Internal Revenue Service, *The Executive Selection and Development Program,* Doc. 5659 (rev., GPO, 1974).

21. See *The Federal Executive Service,* Hearings before the Subcommittee on Manpower and Civil Service of the House Committee on Post Office and Civil Service, 92 Cong. 2 sess. (GPO, 1972). Incredibly, a revised version of the same plan was proposed one month before the Nixon resignation. See "Government Executive Development" (White House press release, Office of the White House Press Secretary, San Clemente, Calif., July 17, 1974).

22. From 1963 to 1974 the commission's governmentwide quota increased by only 350 positions, but special congressional authorizations increased by 780, and the so-called nonquota positions (first instituted in 1963) grew by 1,660. See U.S. Civil Service Commission, Bureau of Executive Manpower, *Executive Manpower in the Federal Service* (GPO, September 1975), table 2, p. 2.

23. Frequently, this is apparent in the language of appropriation committee reports. In one recent example the directive to an Interior Department bureau was as follows:

The Committee expects these new 683 positions to be filled without regard to Departmental restrictions imposed under position ceilings fixed by the Office of Management and Budget. These added positions shall not, under any circumstances, be filled at the expense of personnel allocations to other agencies.... Although reluctant to write personnel provisions into the bill itself, the Committee is prepared to take this step if positive directives accompanying this appropriation are not followed.

*Department of the Interior and Related Agencies Appropriation Bill,* 1977, Senate Appropriations Committee Report 94-991, 94 Cong. 2 sess. (GPO, 1976), pp. 13–14.

24. *Report on Job Evaluation and Ranking in the Federal Government,* H. Rept. 91-28, 91 Cong. 1 sess. (GPO, 1969), p. 11. An earlier summary of the role of Congress in dealing with civil service policies is in Joseph P. Harris, *Congressional Control of Administration* (Brookings Institution, 1964), pp. 163–203.

# 6

# The Civil Service Commission and Executive Leadership

*William E. Mosher
and J. Donald Kingsley*

## General Conclusions

Since the foremost task of management is the management of men and since pay-rolls constitute the largest single item in the operating budget of any representative public jurisdiction, the chief test of good management will be the organization's morale. Good morale is the most valuable asset of any large-scale organization. It is something intangible; something of the spirit. It makes for a spiritual kinship binding men together, keeping them in step, as they move toward a common worth-while goal. It breeds enthusiasm, good will, and cooperativeness. Its consequences are measured in terms of personal satisfactions, in the constant development of new ideas leading to improvements in methods and, finally, in more and better output.

To build up morale calls for personal leadership, the kind that through its contagious influence permeates the whole organization. Its original source will be the head of the administration. Its channels will flow through the offices of his assistants and their assistants to those of the section supervisors and foremen. It serves as a substitute for disciplinary measures.

Discipline there must be, but as the tide of leadership rises, the need of appealing to it will

subside. Good leadership will tolerate none of the petty despotism, the fear and subserviency that are bred in many a public office; nor will it be content with the easy-going "routineerism" that characterizes others.

Morale has been defined as a thing of the spirit, but its roots are imbedded in a variety of soils, some tangible and some intangible. They are as varied as are the factors which make for the well-being of the human elements constituting the working force: sound placement procedures, fair wage policies permitting of an appropriate standard of living, assurance of income in periods of sickness, disability, and old age, wholesome working conditions, opportunities for participation and growth, recognition of work well done, and, in all things, justice and fair dealing. If these conditions are realized, the working life will become a way of living, not simply the doing of a job.

Although the most important functions of the supervisory, executive, and administrative staffs are personnel functions, it must be apparent that the various phases of personnel administration, if for no other reason than their technical character, call for a staff agency which will be devoted exclusively to handling either in an administrative or in an advisory capacity the various techniques involved. These range from examinations and training programs to suggestion systems and the leadership necessary for successful employee organizations.

Like other important staff agencies, the personnel agency must be closely associated with the administrative head and must continuously enjoy the prestige, the understanding, and support of his office. This is the justification for the establishment of the office of vice-president in charge of personnel in some of the largest organizations in the field of private enterprise. Like other vice-presidents, such an official has his seat at the council table and his appropriate vote when policies and changes in policies are under consideration because nearly all administrative policies impinge upon personnel in one way or another.

If this conception of the importance of personnel in administration is approved, there can be no doubt but that the typical civil service commission as the standard personnel agency in government has not proved adequate to the execution of those several functions which are appropriate to a personnel agency. The appointment of three or five commissioners whose primary qualification is that they shall represent the two major parties is not conducive to the upbuilding of the merit system and even less conducive to the introduction of progressive employment policies. Available records go to show that most commissioners are lacking in personnel experience which is a *sine qua non* for fruitful cooperation with operating heads. This partially explains the lack of sympathy and misunderstanding, if not real estrangement, between the commission and those responsible for getting out the work of government. It also explains the neglect of many of the duties that normally fall to the lot of the division of personnel.

This indictment must be qualified by a recognition of the ability and devotion of many commissioners who have served at one time or another and are now serving in various jurisdictions of the country. They have contributed materially to the advancement of the merit principle and in scattering instances have overcome the prejudices of operating officials toward the division of authority inherent in the typical civil service law. But even such commissioners have been seriously handicapped by a chronic lack of funds necessary for the proper conduct of their office.

It has been consistently maintained throughout this work that the official personnel agency must become a "part of the works," must have its acknowledged place in the official family. As a staff agency it should become a part of the staff. This can be accomplished under the standard law by insisting that those appointed to the commission both believe in the merit principle and have some understanding and experience in the problems of management. A second and equally important requirement is that a representative of the commission should have his regularly assigned seat in the cabinet of the chief executive. If properly qualified he would soon win the respect and cooperation of his associates by virtue of his substantive contributions to the formulation of policy, particularly as new policies affect the personnel.

Any such innovation will depend on the development of an enlightened public opinion. Up to the present the chief executive has been under little constraint in making appointments to the civil service commission. The public's attitude has been one of indifference. How otherwise can nominations of men and women totally inexperienced in personnel and management and even of political henchmen be explained? The character of the commissioners themselves goes far toward explaining both the general lack of confidence in civil service laws and the prevailing attitude of administrative heads that may be summed up in the phrase that the commission is a necessary evil.

The above suggestions are made in the thought that whether well- or ill-founded the public in many localities retains its confidence in the commission in its present form as a desirable protective device.

But if further amendments are in order it is proposed that the functions of the commission be redistributed in the following manner: (1) assign all administrative duties including that of rule-making to a single executive head employed on a full-time basis, and (2) constitute the commission as such as a judicial body for the handling of appeals and endow it with only advisory responsibility on other matters. As has already been pointed out there is sufficient precedent for this policy to warrant its adoption.

In the opinion of the authors, however, the above are but half-way measures. It is held first of all that the handling of personnel is so largely an administrative matter and so interwoven with every phase of operation that it should be assigned to a single competent individual who has his accepted place as a peer of other administrative heads. Like theirs his responsibility should be directly to the chief executive. The proposed personnel director should be a man of the highest standing and of proved competency, selected through an open competitive examination and appointed for a long term or for an indefinite period and removeable only for cause and after an appropriate public hearing. Such an official should have an adequate staff which would undoubtedly result in much larger appropriations than are now available for the conduct of the civil service commission. In the larger jurisdictions, provision would be made for the more or less permanent assignment of members of the staff to the several departments. By this means administration of personnel would be dealt with on a uniform basis and in close cooperation with those in direct charge of the working force. Transfers, promotions, and demotions would be handled without regard to departmental lines so far as this might be dictated by the interests of those concerned.

In view of the conviction that employees' rights should be safeguarded, it is further proposed that the personnel office be supplemented by a judicial body for the handling of appeals. Such a body should preferably consist of representatives of the administrative staff, the rank and file of employees and the personnel office. But, as was just suggested, the civil service commission might serve in this capacity until such time as it is replaced by a properly constituted administrative court.

The final proposal envisages the elimination of the commission. This recommendation has been carefully argued in the preceding pages. It was specially stressed that the bipartisan commission has been no guarantee of nonpartisanship, that the commissions have been and can be packed, and above all else, that under ordinary circumstances the commission is more or less "on the outside looking in." Finally, it is emphasized that the chief contribution of the civil service reform movement was not the agency of administration so much as the recognition of the principle of merit in the form of competitive examinations given by a competent staff. This principle would be conserved in the proposed reorganization.

Hand in hand with the increased concentration and centralization of responsibility for personnel should go the elimination of the spoils policy as it affects the upper tier of executives and subexecutives, that is, below the level of strictly policy-determining officials. The incumbents of such positions in any large-scale organization determine its tone, its pace, and its progress. That they have been filled in so many jurisdictions by birds of passage unfamiliar with the characteristics of public adminstration constitutes one of the severest handicaps under which government has labored. Furthermore, unless such positions are open on a competitive basis to those already in the service, it means that the top rungs of the promotional ladder are cut off.

Without the above thoroughgoing and fundamental reorganization of personnel management, it is difficult to see how a public-career service can be developed and made attractive to the abler young people who must be recruited into the service of government if government is not to collapse of its own weight.

Finally, it may be pointed out that there is no single economy which will net such savings or promote such efficiency as may be realized through the feasible improvement of the quality of the public personnel. Government today has ceased being an incidental or second-rate business of the people of the United States. From the point of view of the essential character of the services performed, from the point of view of the percentage of the national income spent, the public business has become the foremost business enterprise of the country. Unless history misleads us and quite apart from the future of the New Deal, there is no reason to believe that it will be otherwise as time goes on. And so we would close with the conviction that the most important and fruitful reform challenging the American public is placing public personnel on a new level and securing for the public service men and women of capacities commensurate with the vast responsibilities now vested in modern government.

# 7

# Reorganization and Improvement of Personnel Administration

*President's Committee on Administrative Management*

The extension of the merit system in the federal government requires the reorganization of the Civil Service Commission as a central personnel agency. The Civil Service Commission was established over 50 years ago to meet conditions quite different from those of today. The number of government employees was small and personnel requirements were relatively simple. Set up as an agency to protect the federal executive establishment against the evils of political patronage, it has made many notable advances. The Civil Service Commission and its staff have devoted themselves assiduously to the public business and have endeavored conscientiously to observe the statutes and orders that have been laid down for their guidance. The commission has achieved its greatest success in the administration of open competitive examinations for positions in the lower grades of the service. It has pioneered in personnel research and efficiency ratings. Its new series of general-purpose examinations for recent college graduates to fill positions at the bottom of the career ladder was a marked step forward and has resulted in improved recruitment for positions requiring general ability and capacity for development.

Nevertheless, the existing civil service system is poorly adapted to meet the larger

SOURCE: President's Committee on Administrative Management, *Report with Special Studies* (Washington, D.C.: U.S. Government Printing Office, 1937), pp. 9–12.

responsibilities of serving as a central personnel agency for a vast and complicated governmental administration in which there are over 800,000 civilian employees. Its organization is unsuited to the present needs. The Civil Service Commission has not been appropriately staffed to do the constructive work which modern personnel management presupposes. The absence of an adequate staff has imposed upon the commission a negative, protective, and legalistic role, whereas the need today is for a positive, constructive, and active central personnel agency.

The board form of organization is unsuited to the work of a central personnel agency. This form of organization, as stated elsewhere in this report, has everywhere been found slow, cumbersome, wasteful, and ineffective in the conduct of administrative duties. Board members are customarily laymen not professionally trained or experienced in the activities for which they are responsible. They remain in office for relatively short periods and rarely acquire the degree of expertness necessary to executive direction. The board form of organization also has a serious internal weakness. Conflicts and jealousies frequently develop within a board and extend downward throughout the organization, causing cliques and internal dissensions disrupting to morale and to work. Board administration tends to diffuse responsibility, to produce delays, and to make effective cooperation or vigorous leadership impossible. The history of the Civil Service Commission has been no exception to this general rule.

Federal personnel management, therefore, needs fundamental revision. The Civil Service Commission should be reorganized into a Civil Service Administration, with a single executive officer, to be known as the civil service administrator, and a nonsalaried Civil Service Board of seven members appointed by the president. This board would be charged not with administrative duties but with the protection and development of the merit system in the government. The functions of the administrator and the board are outlined below.

The adoption of the plan of a single-headed executive for the central personnel agency would give it a degree of unity, energy, and responsibility impossible to obtain in an administrative agency headed by a full-time board of several members. The administrator should be selected on a competitive, nonpartisan basis by a special examining board designated by the Civil Service Board and should be appointed by the president, with the advice and consent of the Senate, from the three highest candidates passing the examination conducted to fill the post. In this manner careful attention would be given to the professional and technical qualifications required by the office and the merit principle would be extended to the very top of the civil service administration. The president should be able to remove the head of this managerial agency at any time but would be required to appoint his successor in the manner stated above.

The civil service administrator would take over the functions and activities of the present Civil Service Commission. In addition, he would act as the direct adviser to the president upon all personnel matters and would be responsible to the president for the development of improved personnel policies and practices throughout the service. From time to time he would propose to the president needed amendments to the civil service rules and regulations. He would suggest to the president recommendations for civil service legislation and would assume initiative and leadership in personnel management.

It would be a special responsibility of the civil service administrator to stimulate and aid the departments and bureaus in the establishment and development of able personnel staffs. Personnel management at the departmental and bureau level is exceedingly important. The administrative and professional staffs of the central personnel agency and of the personnel offices of operating establishments should be regarded collectively as a unified career service of personnel administration.

The administrator should strengthen and vitalize the present Council of Personnel Administration as a professional advisory group within the government. He should act as chairman of the council and should develop it as a special instrument for the formulation of constructive personnel policies and standards.

The administrator should give particular attention to a number of important aspects of personnel administration which are now inadequately performed. These include training within the service, the facilities for transfer as a means of utilizing more completely the personnel resources of the government, the development of executives, the promotion system, examinations for higher positions, and cooperation with the personnel agencies of state and local governments.

Personnel management is an essential element of executive management. To set it apart or to organize it in a manner unsuited to serve the needs of the chief executive and the executive establishments is to render it impotent and ineffective. It may be said that a central personnel managerial agency directly under the president, with the primary duty of serving rather than of policing the departments, would be subject to political manipulation and would afford less protection against political spoils than a Civil Service Commission somewhat detached from the administration. This criticism does not take into account the fact that the Civil Service Commission today is directly responsible to the president; its members are appointed by him and serve at his pleasure; they are not independent of the president and could not be made so under the Constitution. The reorganization of the Civil Service Commission as a central personnel managerial agency of the president would greatly advance the merit principle in the government and would lead to the extension of civil service.

The valuable services that can be performed and the contributions that can be made by a lay board representing the public interest in the merit system should not be sacrificed, even though responsibility for actual administration is vested in a single administrator. The placing of large powers of administration in one official makes it essential to preserve the values of vigilance and criticism that, in a large measure, have been afforded by the rotation in office of lay civil service commissioners who have hitherto supervised the staff work.

A fundamental flaw in the present organization of the commission would be removed by the establishment of an administrator and a board. The commission is now obliged both to administer and to appraise and criticize its own administration. These functions are basically incompatible. An effective appraisal, critical and constructive, must be entirely detached from execution.

The usefulness of a lay board is not confined to its function as a watchdog of the merit system. From the more constructive angle of supporting progressive programs in the federal personnel administration, a board of lay advisers properly chosen can be a continual leaven. It can serve to focus the spotlight of public opinion on the human side of government. It can enlist the interest and cooperation of business, agriculture, labor, education, and the professions in improving the government service as a career. It can stimulate the initiation of progressive personnel programs and serve as a critic which will protect the service from the dangers of bureaucracy, spoils, and deadly routine. It can advise the president and the Congress on weaknesses in personnel administration, policies, and practices.

In order to achieve its utmost usefulness, such a board must be entirely divorced from partisan influences and from administrative or operating functions of any kind; it should be nonpartisan instead of bipartisan. Its members should be drawn in, from time to time, from active participation in various fields of endeavor so that they do not become too closely attached to the government establishment or too closely identified with any administration.

## Recommendations

In order to effect the reorganization of the civil service administration of the United States, we recommend that:

1. A United States Civil Service Administration should be established to serve as the central personnel agency of the federal government. The officers of the administration should consist of a single executive officer to be known as the civil service administrator and a nonsalaried Civil Service Board of seven members, with the powers and duties outlined below.

2. The administrator should be highly competent, should possess a broad knowledge of personnel administration, and should be a qualified and experienced executive. He should be appointed by the president, with the advice and consent of the Senate, on the basis of an open competitive examination conducted by a special board of examiners appointed by the Civil Service Board. He should be responsible to and hold office at the pleasure of the president.

3. The duties, powers, functions, and authority now vested in the Civil Service Commission should be transferred to the administrator. Authority should be given to the administrator to develop and perform the additional functions which should be performed by an adequate central personnel agency. He should be authorized to participate in employee training programs; to make, or to cooperate with other groups in making, studies or investigations of personnel policies, practices, procedures, and methods in other governmental jurisdictions and industry; and to cooperate with state and local personnel agencies and with independent agencies and corporations of the federal government. The Civil Service Administration should be authorized to render services to outside governmental units under suitable provision for reimbursement for the actual cost of such services.

4. The Civil Service Board should consist of seven members, appointed by the president, with the advice and consent of the senate, for overlapping terms of seven years. This board should be composed of outstanding men and women drawn from private business, education, labor, agriculture, public administration, and professional life. No person should be eligible for membership if at any time within five years preceding the date of his appointment he has been a member or officer of any local, state, or national political party committee or has held, or been a candidate for, any elective public

office. Members of the board should receive no salaries, but they should be reimbursed for their actual time and expenses, plus the cost of transportation.

5. The board should meet not less than four times a year upon call by the president, the chairman of the board or any four members of the board. It should have authority and funds to employ temporary personnel for special investigations in addition to secretarial, clerical, and other necessary services provided by assignment from the staff of the administrator.

6. The functions of the Civil Service Board should be:

a. To act as watchdog of the merit system and to represent the public interest in the improvement of personnel administration in the federal service.

b. To appoint a special board of qualified examiners whenever there is a vacancy in the office of the Civil Service Administrator in order to conduct a new open competitive examination for the office, and to certify to the president the names of the three highest candidates.

c. To advise the president as to plans and procedures for dealing with federal employment questions which cannot be handled satisfactorily through established channels.

d. To propose to the president or to the administrator amendments to the rules for the administration of the federal civil service and to review and comment upon amendments proposed by the administrator.

e. To make annual and special reports to the president and the Congress on the quality and status of the personnel administration of the federal government and to make recommendations on possible improvements in the laws or the administration of matters affecting federal personnel. In this connection, the board should have powers to undertake special investigations.

f. To act in an advisory capacity upon the request of the president or the administrator on matters concerning personnel administration.

g. To study and report from time to time upon the relations of the federal civil service to the merit system in state and local jurisdictions, particularly with reference to state and local activities in which there is federal participation through grants-in-aid.

h. To advise and assist the administrator in fostering the interest of institutions of learning, civic and professional organizations, and labor and employee organizations in the improvement of personnel standards in the federal service.

# 8

# The Malek Manual

*White House
Personnel Office*

## Introduction

Because of the many appointees that come from the business world into an Administration, there is a great tendency for managers to equate Government with corporate life and to manage accordingly. There are indeed similarities in terms of size and budget, manpower and scope of activities, but there are some very essential differences which must be understood by those with personnel or management responsibilities.

A corporation will have a board of directors elected by a majority of shareholders. That board of directors designates the principal officers of the corporation who in turn can hire and fire subordinate employees. There is no inherent conflict between the board of directors and its principal officers. The success of the corporation can be easily measured; you subtract cost from income and you arrive at a profit which is measured in dollars.

On the other hand, however, Government is not so streamlined. You have one group of majority shareholders that elects the "board of directors" being the Congress. Like a board of directors, the Congress through authorizing legislation determines the programs of the Government, through appropriations allocates the resources of the Government and through tax legislation, bond authorizations, etc. determines the sources and amount of funding for the Federal Government.

SOURCE: From U.S. Senate Select Committee on Presidential Campaign Activities, *Presidential Campaign Activities of 1972, Book 19* (Washington, D.C.: Government Printing Office, 1974).

Meanwhile, another group of majority shareholders elect the President, the principal executive officer of the Government, who in turn appoints the balance of the principal officers of the Government. They form a Cabinet which in many ways acts like another board of directors. As in the case of the last four years, the officers of the Government owe their loyalty to one group of "shareholders," while the majority in Congress owe their loyalty to another group of "shareholders." And of course this creates a constant tension between the officers of the Government and the Congress who appeal to the shareholders to turn out each other in the hope of getting officers and a Congress who are loyal to the same group of "shareholders" and to each other.

This places the career bureaucrat in the unique position of remaining loyal to his "government," while choosing whether he'll be loyal to the officers or to Congress, or to use the fact of tension between the executive and legislative branches to do his own thing.

Further, because of the maze of rules and regulations with regard to the hiring and firing of Federal employees, the executive is more often than not frustrated with its ability to insure a loyal chain of command. Yet the executive is answerable to the electorate, every four years, for its management of the Government.

Further, not only can we disagree on the programs of the Government, but there is constant controversy over what are the measuring devices of success or failure.

In short, in our constitutional form of Government, the Executive Branch is, and always will be, a political institution. This is not to say that the application of good management practices, sound policy formulation, and the highest caliber of program implementation are not of vital importance. The best politics is still good Government. BUT YOU CANNOT ACHIEVE MANAGEMENT, POLICY OR PROGRAM CONTROL UNLESS YOU HAVE ESTABLISHED POLITICAL CONTROL. The record is quite replete with instances of the failures of program, policy and management goals because of sabotage by employees of the Executive Branch who engage in the frustration of those efforts because of their political persuasion and their loyalty to the majority party of Congress rather than the executive that supervises them. And yet, in their own eyes they are sincere and loyal to their Government.

The above facts were not lost on John and Robert Kennedy. Shortly after Kennedy's nomination the Kennedy campaign reportedly hired a management consulting firm which made a survey of the Executive Branch of Government. In that survey they pointed out every position, regardless of grade, regardless of whether it was career or noncareer, which was thought to be an important pressure point in the Executive Branch. They did a thorough research job on the incumbents occupying those positions. After Kennedy's inauguration, they put Larry O'Brien in charge of the effort to "clean out the Executive Branch" all incumbents of those positions whom they felt they could not rely upon politically. Larry O'Brien, with the assistance of the Departments and Agencies, reportedly, boasted that he accomplished the task in 180 days. It is widely believed, and probably true, that we did not come close to meeting Larry O'Brien's record in 180 days. Quite to the contrary, at the end of three times that 180 days in this Administration, Republicans only occupied 61% of the *non-career* positions that were filled below the PAS and PA level, Republicans only filled 1708 out of 3391 Presidential appointments, and this Administration had only bothered to utilize 899 out of 1333 Schedule C (GS-15 and below) authorities granted to the Departments and Agencies, with incumbents of any persuasion.

Lyndon Johnson went a step further. He appointed John Macy to two positions simultaneously. He was the Special Assistant to the President for personnel matters directly in charge of the recruitment of ranking Administration officials, the political clearance system at the White House, and the Johnson White House political control over the personnel in the Executive Branch. He was also appointed Chairman of the Civil Service Commission, the "guardian of the Civil Service and the merit system." Ludwig Andolsek, formerly Administrative Assistant to Rep. John Blatnik (D–Minn), and the staff man in charge of Democratic patronage matters for the House of Representatives Democratic Caucus, was the Vice Chairman of the Civil Service Commission and "vice guardian of the Civil Service and the merit system." Together they formed the two man majority on the three man commission. Naturally, there wasn't a ripple of concern from a Democratic Congress, only the covert clapping of hands and salivation at the opportunities that now were theirs.

Of course, Congress proceeded to more than double the number of supergrade positions and Executive Level positions in the Government. And naturally the White House did a thorough job of insuring that those appointed to those positions were politically reliable. Documents left behind reveal that even nominees for *career* positions at the supergrade level, and the equivalents, were cleared and interviewed at the White House. The documents substantiate that the interview process was conducted by Marvin Watson's office prior to, or simultaneously, with submission of paperwork to the Civil Service Commission. And in many instances a little "insurance" was obtained with respect to the loyal performance of the appointee by appointing him or her under Limited Executive Assignment and converting that person to career status a year later.

A final objective of the Johnson Administration was to insure the continued loyalty of the bureaucracy to the Democratic programs and the Johnson policies after the takeover by the Nixon Administration. They did this by several reorganizational processes in 1968 which allowed them to freeze in both the people and the positions they had created into the career service. They also made some startling last minute appointments.

HEW is a department which serves as a startling example. After Nixon's inauguration there were but 47 excepted positions (including Presidential appointees and confidential secretaries) available to the Administration out of 115,000 positions. In the Social Security Administration there were two excepted positions out of 52,000. In the Office of Education there were only four, and even the Commissioner of Higher Education of the United States was a *career* GS-18. The Office of Education reorganized between November 8, 1968 and January 11, 1969 creating nearly 125 new branch chief positions all filled on a career basis. In the health field the Public Health Service was essentially reorganized out of any meaningful existence in 1968, and in its place the National Institutes of Health in charge of all health research, the Health Services and Mental Health Administration in charge of controversial areas of health delivery and mental health programs and the Consumer Protection and Environmental Health Services in charge of all preventative health programs were created. Though a Public Health Service Officer, carefully selected, was put in charge of CPEHS, new Executive Level IVs were created for the other two. The career appointment to the Directorship of NIH was given to one who had been brought into NIH a few years previously, cleared through Marvin Watson's office at the White House. The head of HSMHA went to a close Kennedy family friend. He was mentioned in "Death of a President" as the close Kennedy family physician present at the autopsy of President John F. Kennedy. He was appointed at the beginning of the Kennedy Administration as a deputy to Sargent Shriver at the Peace Corps. When Sarge Shriver fully moved to the Directorship of OEO, he moved with him as a deputy to Shriver and also held the title of Deputy Assistant to the President. He was appointed to his career Executive Level IV post in January 1969, just eleven days before President Nixon's inauguration.

# Section I—Organization of a Political Personnel Office and Program

## 1. Organization

The ideal organization to plan, implement and operate the political personnel program

necessary is headed by a special assistant to the head of the department, or agency, or to the assistant head of the department, or agency, for administration. Reporting to the special assistant would be an operations section within his immediate office and one or two staff assistants helping him to coordinate and to handle the specialized function of the morale building which will be explained later. In addition there should be four branches: the Area Liaison Branch, the Agency Liaison Branch, the Recruitment Branch, and the Research and Development Branch. (See Appendix 4—Charts.)

### *a. Functions*

The functions of that office broadly defined are: to advise the managers of the department or agency on the suitability of personnel applying for positions; to render their staff assistance by recruiting personnel, and to relieve them of the time consuming burdens involved in the correspondence, evaluation and interviewing of candidates for prospective positions. The overriding goal to be achieved is to insure placement in all key positions of substantively qualified and politically reliable officials with a minimum burden on line managers in achieving that goal. The objective of that goal is firm political control of the Department, or agency, while at the same time effecting good management and good programs.

Another function is to insure that personnel, which is a resource of the government, is utilized in such a way that it not only produces better government, but is utilized in a manner which creates maximum political benefit for the President and the Party.

Toward those ends the critical functions of such an office encompass the following:

***(a-1) Research and development.*** The study and pinpointing of those positions within the Department or Agency which are critical to control of that Department or Agency. That office must then study and know the suitability of whatever incumbents occupy those positions. Where an unsuitable incumbent does occupy one of those positions, that office must effect his removal or devise a plan to organize the critical responsibilities he administers from without his control.

**(a-2) Patronage.** That office would handle the unsolicited requests for the employment of personnel, the appropriate correspondence generated thereto, the evaluation of the candidates both substantively and politically, the interview process, and the placement of those suitable in positions commensurate with their background and ability.

**(a-3) Recruitment.** The affirmative search for candidates for specific positions (both political and non-political) and the handling of the appropriate correspondence, evaluation, and interview process attached thereto.

**(a-4) Clearance.** The screening of candidates and nominees with respect to their suitability based upon substantive criteria, political criteria, and national security criteria.

**(a-5) Research and development.** The constant evaluation of both the substantive and political performance of our appointees and the development of cross-training programs and upward mobility programs for those appointees who show promise and merit.

**(a-6) Morale.** The administration of a program of awards, incentives, and events designed to promote the morale and continued enthusiasm of our Adminstration's appointees.

### b. Location

Location deals with two aspects: a) organizational location and b) physical location.

**(b-1) Organizational location.** The Assistant Secretary, or Assistant Agency Head, for Administration has usually within his control all the operational offices dealing with governmental resources, i.e. personnel, general services and financial management (and through financial management a second guess as to the direction of program dollars). It is always easier

if the man who directs the implementation and procedures of slot allocations, pay levels, space, organization, and personnel operations also directs the political applications of these same resources. This fact was not lost on the Kennedy Administration. During the early 60s most Republicans were swept out of the Assistant Secretaryships for Administration. Kennedy loyalists assumed those positions, and thereafter Congress by statute quickly made most of those positions career. So, if the Assistant Secretary, or Agency Head, for Administration is, or the position can be filled by, someone both fiercely loyal to the President and savvy in the ways of Government bureaucracy, he should supervise and direct the Special Assistant in charge of the Political Personnel Office. In the instance where the office is so located, the Assistant Secretary, or Agency Head, will be the key political contact for the White House with the Special Assistant in charge of the day-to-day operations of the Political Personnel Office functions essentially as an operational deputy.

The other alternative is that the Special Assistant be located in the Office of the Secretary or Agency Head. As a Special Assistant to the Secretary or Agency Head he would be the key political contact for the White House and a Deputy should serve as operational director on a day-to-day basis of the Political Personnel Office. It is essential that the office be located at this high level, in the absence of the authority being vested in an Assistant Secretary or Assistant Agency Head, so that the apparent authority to speak and act in the name of the Secretary, or Agency Head, is recognized throughout the Department. Otherwise that office will be viewed as an undesirable advocate rather than a high level policy and implementing arm of the Secretary, or Agency Head, with respect to personnel matters.

**(b-2) Physical location.** Physical location is of the utmost importance although it is usually not seriously considered. Rightly or wrongly, both the physical location and the majesty of decor of the offices of the Political Personnel Office, which will have constant public contact, will communicate to both the bureaucracy and the public apparent power and authority. For example, if a candidate, or a political sponsor of a candidate, comes to the Secretary's office seeking an audience to discuss an appointment matter, presumably he will be referred to the Political Personnel Office, for presumably one of the functions of that office is to relieve the Secretary as much as possible of the burden of having to hold their hands. If he walks down the hall to another suite of well furnished offices and has his audience, he's going to regard that audience as being meaningful and the next best thing to seeing the Secretary himself. If, however, he is shuffled to offices down a couple of floors with rather bureaucratic and unimpressive surroundings, experience tells us that most likely he's going to feel he received a bureaucratic run-around and will quickly reappear in the Secretary's office demanding once again to see the Secretary or one of his "top aides" presumably located physically close to him.

The same is true when a bureaucrat must be called in for one reason or another. The apparent power communicated by being summoned to the office of an aide close to the Office of the Agency Head or Secretary effects better results than to be summoned to just another office in the building. It's the old political parable that "proximity implies power."

### c. Coordinating and Approval Authorities

*(c-1) Coordination.* There are four areas within an agency that require almost perfect rapport and coordination between those areas and the Political Personnel Office. They are 1) Congressional Liaison 2) the Personnel Office 3) the Budget's Director's office and 4) the Public Information Office.

The Congressional Liaison Office has a responsibility to serve as the link between the agency and Congress. It is an inescapable fact of life that Congressmen and their staffs, sensitive to political power-brokering, will more often than not bypass liaison shops and deal directly with those involved in making decisions

they are interested in. This is especially true in recruitment and patronage matters. When the Congressman who has sponsored a candidate is informed by that candidate that he is going to be interviewed, or has received a communication from a person in a Political Personnel Office, that Congressman will generally begin to communicate and bring direct pressure on the Political Personnel Office. Sensitivities being what they are, coordinating procedures between the Congressional Liaison shop and the Political Personnel Office must be carefully worked out from the beginning in order to avoid the inevitable friction and questions of jurisdiction that will ultimately arise. Some suggestions will be offered in this manual when we come to that part where we deal with the specific procedures and operations of each Branch of the Political Personnel Office.

The Personnel Office of the Department, or Agency, of course, must process the appointments of all officials. They can make that process either very easy or very rough depending on the rapport and coordination the Political Personnel Office establishes with them. Ideally the Personnel Director will be a loyal member of the team (another important pressure point in the agency). That Personnel Director, and his staff, will obviously have to be relied upon to render technical advice, and to implement by processing, personnel decisions made by the Political Personnel Office and the line managers. There is no way to really exclude them from whatever it is that you're doing.

Again, the Budget Director is a key man with respect to resources, including personnel. Since the Budget Director usually has control over the allocation of positions and the allocation of money for salaries, he is a necessary "team member" when using those resources to accomplish personnel objectives. This is especially true when extra positions, for political reasons, must be created with the accompaniment of salary dollars. Or another example of where his cooperation is indispensable is when reorganizing for political and/or personal objectives.

One other area of coordination and rapport that is important is between the Political

Personnel Office and the Public Information Office. Premature announcements of appointments can be both legally and politically detrimental. While on the other hand, maximum publicity for an appointment in certain instances might be desired for certain political purposes. It is therefore very important that at the very beginning the Political Personnel Office and the Public Information Office work out a very well outlined announcement procedure. Again, suggestions will be made later in this manual in the part where we deal with the special procedures and operations of each branch of the Political Personnel Office.

*(c-2) Approval authorities.* It is obviously important that the Political Personnel Office serve in more than an advisory role if it is to have any teeth at all. It must play a role in the formal authorizations for hiring and firing.

There are two types of authorities that have been used with respect to hiring. The most common, and least desirable, is the *approval* authority role. The least used, but most successful and desirable, is the *nominating* authority role.

1) *Approval Authority*

Most Departments and Agencies require the submission of appointments to excepted positions, all supergrade positions, and in some instances all GS-13 through GS-15 positions to the Office of the Secretary (or Assistant Secretary, if the Political Personnel Office is located there) for approval. The rationale, of course, is quality control. The Political Personnel Office upon receiving the submission then usually makes the appropriate inquiries and/or clearances and then recommends to the approving authority that he approve or disapprove the submission. This procedure has caused great problems. For what you have here is a candidate who has been interviewed and probably told he has been selected subject only to the approval of the "man upstairs" and/or the White House. If he is disapproved, the "man upstairs" and/or the White House frequently will be pressured to explain why and must grope for non-political rationale. Aside from politics, this has also caused problems in the security area. Where a candidate is submitted and his background investigation provides unfavorable information sufficient that you would not want to proceed with his appointment, but insufficient to meet the legal test the courts have set for denial of a security clearance, the agency is placed on the horns of a dilemma. Either you proceed with the appointment against your better instincts or according to the law, you must notify the nominee that he is being denied the position on the basis of a security check. The nominee can then take you to court challenging the security determination and if he wins the court will order him to be placed in that position.

In addition the approval process rubs against the grain of even our appointees causing friction and dissention within our own ranks. No office head, or line manager, likes to be placed in the position of having made a selection and become committed to the appointment of an individual only to have his judgement challenged by a disapproval upon the recommendation of "an aide" to the approving authority. A confidence crisis usually erupts.

Further all of the above has the effect of placing the burden and the heat generated by a personnel decision on the shoulders of the Agency Head and/or the White House. Instead of subordinates taking the heat on behalf of their superiors, you have the superiors taking the heat for their subordinates.

2) *Nomination Authority*

The nomination authority grants to the person to whom the Political Personnel Office reports the authority to nominate a register of candidates from among whom the line managers and the Office Heads can select. In short, it's a political equivalent of the Civil Service Commission certification process. Under this authority what happens is that all candidate applications and recommendations on behalf of candidates from both inside and outside the agency are funnelled to a central office, that office being the Political Personnel Office. That office then combines the in-house recommendations, the outside applications and recommendations, and the results of their own recruitment efforts into a single group of possible nominees for a particular position. That office then provides the following "services" for the eventual benefit of the line manager or office head.

1. It makes a reference check of previous employers to determine the accuracy of the application and to get a reading on the person's past performance and abilities.
2. It initiates a security check to determine the suitability of the various prospective nominees
3. Where applicable a preliminary political check is made of the prospective nominee.

Those that have an unfavorable reading as a result of the three types of inquires made are eliminated. And from the rest the five best qualified are then nominated and submitted to the Office Head or line manager who is then free to interview and make any selection he wishes. In this way the deck is essentially stacked before the cards are dealt and rarely is a selection ever disapproved. Rather the disappointed candidate is simply informed *in the affirmative* that *someone else was simply selected.*

The Office Heads and line managers, especially if your recruitment operation functions effectively to produce quality candidates, will prefer this system. Even though the field from which he may select is imposed, in exchange he is rendered the services and relieved of the burden of recruiting, reference checks, and the uncertainty as to the political and security considerations that will be a factor later on. He is emancipated from the prospect that once he has selected a candidate and is committed to a person that he will be embarrassed in front of his staff and that person by having his decision overturned. Rather, he begins to build the reputation for having his decisions in personnel matters almost always approved. This, of course, builds his own apparent proximity to the Agency Head or Secretary which, in turn, gives him more clout. And finally, it is he who in the end interviews, tests personnel chemistry, and finally selects his own subordinates—reaffirming faith in his judgment.

As is apparent, this system reduces to a minimum the probabilities of the buck being passed up and the Secretary or Agency Head and/or the White House taking the heat for the personnel decision.

### d. Operations Section

The Operations Section is the eye of the hurricane. It serves both as the distribution point through which all paperwork entering and leaving the Political Personnel Office flows, and serves a necessary recording and tracking function which will allow the Special Assistant in charge of the Political Personnel Office to be able to locate and find the status of any activity in progress.

As mentioned, all paperwork addressed to the Political Personnel Office, or members of its staff, comes into the Operations Section. This section then proceeds to do the following:

*(d-1).* If it is an unsolicited application, recommendation or endorsement from a political source, they put routing/evaluation and correspondence forms on the correspondence and route it to the Area Liaison Branch, maintaining a file copy. (See Appendix 1.)

*(d-2).* If it is an unsolicited application, recommendation or endorsement from a non-political source, they put a routing/evaluation and correspondence form on the correspondence and route it to the Recruiting Branch, maintaining a file copy. (See Appendix 2.)

*(d-3).* If the paperwork is for an approval and/or clearance, the Operations Section attaches the appropriate routing sheet and forwards it to the Agency Liaison Branch. (See Appendix 3.)

*(d-4).* If the correspondence is an inquiry from a political source as to the status of a candidate or appointment in process, they will refer the request to the area Liaison Branch.

*(d-5).* If the correspondence is an inquiry from a non-political source as to the status of a candidate or appointment in process, they will

refer the request to the recruitment Branch. In both instances a suspense file is maintained to insure that a timely reply is made.

*(d-6).* If the request or inquiry is from an agency within the Department or office within an agency, the Operations Section will route it to the Agency Liaison Branch.

*(d-7).* The Operations Section maintains a suspense file on all reports to be submitted by the Political Personnel Office and insures the Research and Development Branch issues said reports.

*(d-8).* The operations Section serves as the Special Assistant's coordinating arm to insure the proper operation of the procedures and systems of the office.

The importance of the Operations Section cannot be underestimated. Because of the volume of correspondence, projects, requests for information and reports that deluge a Political Personnel Office in the year following a Presidential election, the greatest pitfall a Political Personnel Office can fall into is the inability to quickly, expediently, and efficiently route, deal with and reply to the demands placed on it. The Operations Section replaces the "scramble-around-the-office-and-find-out-who-has-what" system that can often take as much time and manpower as the positive functions of the office. The Operations Section is like the hub of the wheel, joining all the spokes and insuring that the wheel turns quickly and smoothly.

### e. Area Liaison Branch

Experience has shown that it is best to have a single source contact for all political officials when dealing with political personnel matters. Comity of interests suggest that the best approach to liaison with political officials is by geographical location. Four Area Liaison Officers are suggested: one for New England and the Middle Atlantic States, one for the Southern States, one for the Midwestern States and one for the Western States.

For all political officials in that geographical location (Republican local and state party officials, Republicans local and state office holders, appointed Federal officials from that geographical location, and all Congressmen and Senators from that geographical location—either directly or through Congressional Liaison—and candidates whose political impact comes from that geographical location), the Area Liaison Officer is their contact and he has the following responsibilities with respect to dealing with political personnel matters for his geographical location.

*(e-1) Patronage.* He receives the applications of candidates with political backgrounds and/or recommendations or endorsements from that geographical location. He then proceeds to make a political evaluation with respect to the importance of placement of the individual to the political constituency, and the political benefit or disadvantage therefore to the Administration and the President. He does this by making inquiries and/or simply evaluating the language of the correspondence and/or endorsement(s) that accompanies or follows the application. A suggested rating system is as follows:

*I—Must Placement.* The candidate because of his own past political activities and/or the importance of his placement to his political sponsor(s) leads the evaluator to believe that his *placement in a position commensurate with his ability and background* will bring great political credit to the party and/or the President, while conversely, failure to place the individual will cause severe political damage to the party and/or the President.

*II—Priority Placement.* The placement of the individual *in a position commensurate with his ability and background* will bring political benefit to the party and/or the President, while, conversely, failure to place the candidate will cause some political adversity to the party and/or the President.

*III—Courtesy Referral.* The individual is to be judged on his own merits but should receive a massaging as a political courtesy, and if he is placed some small political benefit to the party and/or the President will be derived, while failure to place him will cause little or no political adversity to the party and/or the President.

*IV—Politically Undesirable.* The placement of the individual will create strong political adversity to the party and/or the President, while, conversely, the failure to place the individual will be politically beneficial to the party and/or the President.

*V—Political Problem.* This category is a holding category until a determination can be made whether or not to place the individual in one of the above four categories. For example:

The Republican Senator from a state says a candidate is a must placement and is essential because the candidate's father is the Senator's largest contributor and finance chairman and crucial to the Senator's re-election. Meanwhile, the Republican Governor of that same state and a Republican Congressman from that same state who sits as a ranking Republican on your agency's appropriations committee strongly object to the individual's placement because he has traditionally and vocally backed their Democratic opponents in past campaigns. It is evident that some additional political research and decision making is going to have to take place before you can make him a Category I or a Category IV.

Having rated the individual, the Area Liaison Officer is then responsible for drafting the response to the candidate and sponsors, and finalizing such correspondence for his own signature, the signature of the Special Assistant or the signature of the Agency Head depending on the candidate and/or sponsor and to whom the initial correspondence was addressed. The ALO will then forward a copy of the application with the routing/evaluation form to the Agency Liaison Branch while retaining a copy of the application and the correspondence for his files where it should be filed by sponsor or sponsors. He should also maintain a cross-file suspense file to insure his follow-up on the placement of those candidates rated I and II.

*(e-2) Recruitment.* The Area Liaison Officer is responsible for making the appropriate political officials within his geographical location aware of existing vacancies within the Department or Agency and the substantive qualifications the agency is seeking in a candidate to fill that position. This provides the political sector an opportunity to specifically respond with candidates for specific positions. Whether or not qualified candidates ever emerge from the political recruitment, that step is a very beneficial one. It often eliminates delays later in the clearance process that can be caused by political officials objecting to an appointment on the basis that they were never given an opportunity to have some of their candidates considered. It also creates the feeling of involvement which is beneficial to the President. HEW used this concept extensively, and Clarke Reed, Southern GOP Conference Chairman, was known to remark that though he could rarely find qualified candidates for the positions he was solicited for, by HEW, it meant a great deal to him that he was asked and could use that fact to demonstrate the President's interest in the party when he dealt with state and local party leaders in the South.

*(e-3) Clearance and pre-checks.* The Area Liaison Officer, upon receiving a request for a pre-check on a candidate or nominee, is responsible for contacting the appropriate political officials within his area to determine the political registration, loyalties and activities of the individual. The Area Liaison Officer is also responsible in the formal clearance procedure for making the necessary contacts to obtain the approval or objections of those from within his geographical location who have a role in the formal clearance process. (See Appendix 5.) Toward that end he has a dual advocate role, that of representing the political point of view obtained from his area to the Department and the White House, and to achieve the affirmative political maneuvering necessary to obtain the clearance of a candidate desired by the Department and/or the White House. In short, he's a wholesaler who must sell and bargain in both directions.

Experience has found that a single source contact with the Area Liaison Officer being the political face of the Department, or Agency, to the political sector in a given area is very important. For by handling all the political aspects of recruitment, patronage and clearance with political officials, the ALO is better equipped than would be three separate individuals to become firmly grounded in the political problems and needs of a given political area. He is equipped to make tradeoffs to accomplish what mission he has as a priority. And there is a time saving factor to the office in view of the fact that in one telephone conversation with a political official the Area Liaison Officer can obtain clearances, answer status requests, recruit for specific positions and listen to patronage requests. This also simplifies the line of communication for the political officials and creates a feeling that he has a "representative" within the Department or Agency.

### f. Recruitment

The Recruiters are the agency's face with the outside world of business, labor and the community aside from the political world. It is suggested that you have a recruiter covering the business world and the Chambers of Commerce, a recruiter covering the academic world (universities, colleges, research think-tanks) and foundations, one covering labor and like organizations, and one recruiter who would cover other special interest groups and general recruiting assignments. Variations on these groupings will, of course, occur from department to department.

The recruiters perform for the non-political sector the same functions the Area Liaison Officers perform for the political sector. The Recruitment Branch differs in the clearance process in as much as their reference checks will be to previous employers and non-political references of the nominee.

**(f-1) Patronage.** The Recruitment Branch receives applications of candidates from that particular area which each recruiter covers. Having rated the individual, the recruitment officer is then responsible for drafting a response to the candidate and sponsors, and finalizing such correspondence for his own signature, the signature of the Special Assistant or the signature of the Agency Head depending on the candidate and/or sponsors and to whom the initial correspondence was addressed. The recruiter will then forward a copy of the application with the routing/evaluation slip to the Agency Liaison Branch while retaining a copy of the application and the correspondence for his files.

**(f-2) Recruitment.** The Recruiters are responsible for making the appropriate personnel in their jurisdiction aware of existing vacancies within the Department or Agency and the substantive qualifications the agency is seeking in a candidate to fill that position. This provides the appropriate sources and contacts with an opportunity to specifically respond with candidates for specific positions.

**(f-3) Clearance and pre-checks.** The Recruiters upon receiving a request for a pre-check on a candidate or nominee are responsible for contacting the appropriate references and past employers. (See Appendix 6.)

### g. Agency Liaison Officers

Just as the political and non-political sectors all have a single source contact, and thus a person with whom mutual confidence, credibility, and rapport is established, so the Agency Liaison Officers become the single source contact and your salesmen to an area of your department or agency. Your Agency Liaison Officers should be well credentialized to, and become both well versed and well known, within the bureaucracy of that part of the department, or agency, for which they have responsibilities. They will serve as your eyes and ears within the department, your salesman for placement, the balancing factor representing the substantive needs of your agency's component parts, and will serve as the judge to a great extent of the substantive qualifications in candidates.

**(g-1) Patronage.** Upon receiving a copy of an application for employment along with the routing/evaluation sheet from both the Area Liaison Branch and the Recruitment Branch, the Agency Liaison Branch then does three things:

a) They make a substantive evaluation of the candidate's background and experience and give him a quality rating, and
b) they then determine the level and appropriate place(s) in which the candidate might be considered for a position, and
c) they channel to the appropriate location the applications of the candidates to be considered as part of a general referral, and monitor the placement activities. (See Appendix 7.)

*(g-2) Recruitment.* The Agency Liaison Officers are responsible for being thoroughly familiar with the organizations for which they have jurisdiction and for forecasting in advance vacancies. It is then their responsibility to draw up a "request for recruitment" (see Appendix 8) stating the grade and salary range for the position, its title and organizational location and the substantive qualifications sought in a candidate for that position. The Agency Liaison Branch then sends the request to the Research and Development Branch which then searches the Talent Bank and sends back the candidates that fulfill the qualifications by screening all existing candidates on file as a result of unsolicited applications (patronage), previous recruitment, and names suggested from within the agency itself. If there are not sufficient numbers of candidates in the files that meet the necessary qualifications for the position, the Agency Liaison Branch then sends the "Request for Recruitment" to the Recruitment Branch. *In all cases*, they send the "Request for Recruitment" to the Research and Development and Area Liaison Branches.

On a set closing date, the Agency Liaison Branch looks at the accumulated files of in-house candidates, candidates on file as a result of unsolicited applications (patronage) and the applications received as a result of the recruitment efforts of both the Recruitment Branch and the Area Liaison Branch. It will then narrow the field down on the basis of substantive qualifications to a group of "semi-finalists."

*(g-3) Clearance.* The names of the semi-finalists are submitted then to the Operations Section which will then trigger the Area Liaison Branch to make its inquiries, the Recruitment Branch to make its reference checks and the Departmental Security Office to make its inquiries.

A Committee consisting of a member of the Agency Liaison Branch, the Area Liaison Branch, and the Recruitment Branch will, upon receipt of the results of the appropriate inquiries, narrow the field down to the "finalists" who will then be nominated for the vacant position by the Agency Liaison Officer to the appropriate area of which he has jurisdiction.

### h. Research and Development Branch

The Research and Development Branch serves as the in-house management consultants, operates, updates and programs the talent bank, operates and programs the "personnel evaluation" activities, and through these devices monitors the progress made toward the goal of political control over the Department or Agency. As the repository for all critical data, the Research and Development Branch also is responsible for issuing the appropriate reports required by the White House and other governmental officials.

*(h-1) Management consulting role.* One of the first tasks to be performed by the Research and Development Branch, with the cooperation of the Agency Liaison Branch, is to conduct an overall personnel management study of the Department, or Agency, to determine those positions in which a "loyal" competent incumbent is necessary to effect control. Those areas (the pressure points) include the following:

a) Those positions which necessitate and give easy, frequent access to the media, such as the Public Information Office—controlling your image to the public.
b) Those positions which necessitate frequent contact with the Legislative Branch, such as

Congressional Liaison—thus controlling your relations with the Congress.

c) Those positions which control governmental resources (or at the very least must process the disbursement of govenment resources) such as the personnel director, budget director, director of general services (whose responsibilities include the letting of contracts) and legal personnel (which pass on the legality of almost everything).

d) Those in sensitive policy-making roles.

e) Those whose approval, or disapproval, in fact effectuates the disbursement of discretionary grants and loans or loan guarantees.

Some helpful tools to establishing the foregoing are as follows:

a) The Departmental organization chart.

b) The organizational listings in the Departmental telephone book. This is perhaps a better guide to the way the organizations within a Department or Agency really operate than the organization chart. Experience has demonstrated that while bureaucrats will often hide their importance and authority on an organization chart which you might acquire (in order to hide and disclaim responsibility), they tend to step forward when listing themselves in the organizational portion of the telephone directory in order to enhance their status and standing with their colleagues who more often refer to the directory than to the organizational charts.

c) The Catalog of Federal Domestic Assistance. There is a many-volume set of this catalog that can be obtained from the Government Printing Office for the Federal Government, and many departments have such a catalog (also obtainable from the Government Printing Office) which tend to be more accurate and updated. These catalogs, designed for public information, list categorically the Federal assistance programs, their legislative basis, their current and past funding levels, method of application for such funds or assistance, *and the person responsible* for the disbursement of such Federal assistance.

*(h-2) "Personnel evaluation."* With the assistance of the Agency Liaison Branch and the Area Liaison Branch, the Research and Development Branch is then responsible for compiling the necessary data to establish whether any incumbent of a "target" position meets the required qualifications for that post. A recommended evaluation system might be:

K = Keep    A substantially qualified, dependable member of the team.

O = Out    Either unqualified or lacking in dependability as a member of the team, or both.

L = Let's Watch This Fellow.

A person whose qualifications and/or dependability have raised questions but there is not sufficient data to make a decision.

N = Neuter    A qualified individual who can ordinarily be depended on to follow instructions but cannot be regarded as personally, on his own volition, a member of the team.

*(h-3) Organizational planning.* The Research and Development Branch, with the cooperation of the personnel office, the budget office and the Department's management planning office, if any, will then design any organizational or reorganizational plans necessary in aid of personnel objectives. This group would also be consulted by other parts of the Department when planning organizational, or reorganizational, plans for management reasons to assure that "personnel objectives" are also considered.

*(h-4) Talent bank.* The Research and Development Branch will be the repository for the Talent Bank which will include all candidates collected as a matter of patronage (unsolicited applications and recommendations once processed), recruitment and, very importantly, personnel already appointed within the Department with an eye to upward mobility.

*(h-5) Data bank.* The Research and Development Branch will keep a special roster,

with appropriate data, concerning those about whom periodic reports are required by the White House and other Federal officials. In addition the Research and Development Branch is responsible for the collection, through the Agency Liaison Branch and the Personnel Office, to maintain personnel statistics often called for by the White House, Civil Service Commission, and other Federal officials.

*(h-6) Technical training and advice.* The Research and Development Branch will also maintain an active file of the current rules and regulations promulgated by the White House, the Civil Service Commission, and the Office of Management and Budget concerning personnel matters and will be responsible for insuring the orientation, training and currency of the personnel in the Political Personnel Office with regard to the same.

*(h-7) Upward mobility roster.* And last, but certainly not least, the Research and Development Branch with the cooperation of the Agency Liaison Branch will maintain a special roster of Administration appointees with a view toward upward mobility and cross-training. To this end the Research and Development Office should preplan transfers and upward mobility ladders for Administration appointees.

### I. Morale

Of all the functions of a Political Personnel Office, perhaps the area that has been given the least attention has been that of maintaining and enhancing the morale of our Administration appointees. It is true that they receive a salary for their work and the possibility of promotion always is present. We also must assume that the morale will generally be affirmative because of the outstanding leadership in this Administration. However, good personnel management experience has shown the advantages of a system of awards and incentives and morale building activities in both corporate life and among government employees. Our Administration appointees deserve no less.

Most Departments and Agencies have a pretty fine system of awards and incentives. For some reason the general myth that seems to be maintained by our loyal bureaucracy is that they are only available for career employees. This is not true. Most regulations and programs contain the language "any employee of the Department," or to appear more restrictive the language may contain the words "permanent employee." As shall be discussed later, the word *permanent* specifies a type of appointment which is not to be equated with a career appointment. And a person appointed to an excepted appointment of any nature, other than that specifically entitled temporary appointment, is a permanent employee though he lacks any tenure. Thus, our excepted appointees are as eligible for most of the system of awards and incentives now provided by Departments and Agencies as career employees. Further, they are just as often deserving.

There is also a tendency for the high ranking officials of the Department or Agency to take Administration appointees for granted while pandering to the career service for purposes of loyalty, credibility, and morale. And yet, most Administration appointees come into office with the expectation that they will have a special place alongside the high ranking officials of the Department or Agency. Because of this "gap" between high expectations and low fulfillment, low morale among the Administration's appointees can set in very fast. Too often it is heard that Schedule C appointees within a Department, or Agency, have never even had the opportunity to meet the agency head....

### 3. Appointment, Tenure, Promotions, Demotions, Reassignments (By Type of Appointment)

It is important to understand the appointment, tenure and other factors affecting positions in the Federal Government. In this section we briefly describe the tenure of each type of appointment, and the possibilities of promotions, demotions, reassignments and removals of each type of appointment. Generally speaking the tenure of an appointment is granted and governed by the type of appointment under which an employee is currently serving, without regard to whether he has competitive status or whether his appointment is to a competitive position or an excepted position.

Believe it or not the Civil Service rules and regulations, as complex and restrictive as we think they are, do not cause most of the problems. The bureaucrats, not satisfied with the unprecedented protection and job security given them by the Civil Service Commission have, in various Departments and agencies, piled a maze of departmental regulations on top of the CSC regulations. The Civil Service Commission will require an agency to follow its own regulations even though they may be far more restrictive and far more excessive than the CSC regulations. Some examples: In HEW career rights were extended to all attorneys though by CSC rules they are excepted employees. Some departments have extended the notification procedures of the Veterans Preference Act to all employees. A few agencies allowed formal hearings and appeals if a person was transferred to a post outside a fifty mile radius from his present geographical location. Our best advice is to revoke them all and write departmental regulations narrowly in line with the Civil Service Commission regulations. But in any case before relying alone on this Manual and the Civil Service regulations, CHECK YOUR DEPARTMENT OR AGENCY REGULATIONS CAREFULLY.

### a. Career Appointments

***Career and career-conditional.*** In the last section we defined a career appointment as an appointment in the competitive service at any level where the incumbent has completed three years of substantially continuous service in the Government. A career-conditional appointment was defined as a position at any level where the incumbent has completed less than three years of substantially continuous service in the government. We also noted that the first year of a career or career-conditional appointment is usually, although not always, a probationary period during which an employee whose performance is determined to be unsatisfactory may, in the words of the Civil Service Commission, "be separated from the service without undue formality." During the probationary period only very limited protections are available to the employee who is being removed.

Once past the completion of the probationary period, however, persons serving in career or career-conditional appointments have certain protections which are spelled out in the CSC rules and regulations. With few exceptions, the tenure of employees serving in such positions is referred to as *career tenure* and is practically forever.

***(a-1) Appointment.*** Appointment to career positions must be made from a listing of three individuals certified to the Department or Agency from the Civil Service Commission. It might be of value to digress and explain the CSC system of rating candidates to determine their eligibility and the certification process.

***The rating process.*** For entry level positions at GS-1 through GS-8, a person to be placed on the register must apply for a written examination, for the type of jobs for which he wishes to receive an eligibility rating, to the Civil Service Commission. He is then given an objective score. If he passes the examination with the minimum required score of 70, they will then give him an eligibility rating (such as eligible for GS-5 and GS-7) for the appropriate types of positions for which he applied. Those who have received an eligibility rating are then placed on the register for the type of position applied for at the grade levels for which they have received the eligibility rating in order of the numerical scores attained on the examination. For mid-level (GS-9 through GS-12) and Senior level positions (GS-13 through GS-15) the candidate submits his "Application for Federal Employment" (Form 171) to the Civil Service Commission. The Civil Service examiners then conduct an "examination" by evaluating his education and employment experience. Based on this evaluation the candidate receives an eligibility rating for the types of positions applied for. *Note:* A candidate might receive different eligibility ratings for different types of jobs. If a candidate has extensive experience as a financial manager and limited experience in the field of public relations, he might receive an eligibility rating of GS-13-14-15 for positions in the financial management field while receiving an eligibility rating of only GS-11 for public information positions.

Those candidates rated as eligible for mid-level and senior level positions are then placed on the register for the areas and grades in which they have been rated as eligible. *Another important note:* Just because a candidate shows you a letter from the Civil Service Commission notifying him that he has been rated eligible for the grade and type of position you are seeking to fill *does not* entitle your department or the candidate to have him hired in that position. He must still be *certified* to the agency, according to the "merit" system through the certification process which we shall discuss shortly.

In the case of veterans, five points is automatically added to whatever score they make for whatever examination they have taken. This is called 5 point veterans preference. Disabled veterans are similarly given a 10 point preference.

***The certification process.*** The certification process begins when your Department or Agency submits to the Civil Service Commission a job description, and a form outlining the selective criteria you are seeking in a candidate, for a specific position.

In the case of entry level positions, they simply take the top three candidates in order of numerical score, which meet your selection criteria, and certify them to your Department or Agency. The Department or Agency must then select from among those three. It can, however, reject all three and ask for a new certification of the next three on the list. However, when so doing the Department or Agency must explain to the CSC's satisfaction some very cogent reasons why none of the first three were selected.

For mid-level positions and senior level positions the Commission "spins" the register. What this means is that they take the list of eligibles

on a given register which is appropriate to the position you seek to fill, and using this selective criteria determine the three "most qualified" that meet that criteria. They do so by having a panel of three persons give a rating to each eligible with respect to each of the selective criteria you have specified. Those with the three top scores (which will include those who have attained that score by veterans preference) will then be certified to your Department or Agency. Again, you must select from among the three certified candidates. It can, however, reject all three eligibles and ask for a new certification of the next three on the list. However, when doing so the Department or Agency must explain to the Commission some very cogent reasons why none of the first three were selected.

*Very important note:* Because of the subjectiveness of the certification process with respect to mid-level and senior level positions there is really no "merit" in the "merit system" save the minimum qualifications that a candidate be eligible. First of all the panel which "spins the register" is usually made up of one member of the Commission staff and two persons selected by your personnel office from your Department or Agency. Secondly, you'll remember the panel rates the eligibles on the register on the basis of the job description and selective criteria that your personnel office has submitted to the Commission. Together this has the effect of simply turning the "career merit system" into a device by which the bureaucrats operate their own patronage system while telling the politicians to "keep their hands off" so as not to interfere with the "merit system." The best way to explain why we state it's the bureaucratic patronage system —they can really insure the certification of someone they have pre-selected, *and so can you*—is by taking you through an example of the rape of the "merit system."

Let us assume that you have a career opening in your Department's personnel office for a Staff Recruitment Officer. Sitting in front of you is your college roommate from Stanford University in California who was born and raised in San Francisco. He received his law degree from Boalt Hall at the University of

California. While studying for the bar he worked at an advertising agency handling newspaper accounts. He also worked as a reporter on the college newspaper. Your personnel experts judge that he could receive an eligibility rating for a GS-11.

The first thing you do is tear up the old job description that goes with that job. You then have a new one written, to be classified at GS-11, describing the duties of that specific Staff Recruitment Officer as directed toward the recruitment of recent law graduates for entry level attorney positions, entry level public information officers for the creative arts and college new liaison sections of your public information shop, and to be responsible for general recruiting for entry level candidates on the West Coast. You follow that by listing your selective criteria as follows: Education: BA and LLB, stating that the candidate should have extensive experience and knowledge by reason of employment or residence of the West Coast. Candidate should have attended or be familiar with law schools, and institutes of higher education, preferably on the West Coast. The candidate should also possess some knowledge by reasons of education or experience of the fields of college journalism, advertising, and law.

You then trot this candidate's Application for Federal Employment over to the Civil Service Commission, and shortly thereafter he receives an eligibility rating for a GS-11. Your personnel office then sends over the job description (GS-11) along with the selective criteria which was based on the duties of the job description. When the moment arrives for the panel to "spin the register" you insure that your personnel office sends over two "friendly" bureaucrats. The register is then spun and your candidate will certainly be among the only three who even meet the selective criteria, must less be rated by your two "friendly" panel members as among the "highest qualified" that meet the selection criteria. In short, you write the job description and selective criteria around your candidate's Form 171.

There is no merit in the merit system! The fact is that the Civil Service Commission and the bureaucrats in the personnel system recognize this truth, for the Civil Service Commission, brazenly, even allows the Departments and Agencies to *name request* a particular candidate when asking for a certification from the register.

***Removal.*** Due to the maze of Civil Service rules and regulations, it is very difficult to remove an employee serving in a career appointment once he has completed the probationary period. The only real grounds for removal is "for such cause and will promote the efficiency of the service..." (FPM Section 752.104) Agencies are generally responsible for removing, demoting or reassigning any employee whose conduct or capacity is such that one of these actions will "promote the efficiency of the service." Conduct which may allow the department or agency to remove, demote, or reassign an employee for this reason are listed as follows:

1. Removal from employment for misconduct or delinquency.
2. Criminal, infamous, dishonest, immoral, or notoriously disgraceful conduct.
3. Intentional false statements or deception or fraud in examination or appointment.
4. Refusal to furnish testimony as required by Section 5.3 of Rule V.
5. Habitual use of intoxicating beverages to excess.
6. Reasonable doubt of the loyalty of the person involved to the Government of the United States.
7. A person who seeks the overthrow of the Government by force, violence or other unlawful means.
8. Membership in an organization that he knows seeks the overthrow of the Government by force or violence.
9. Participation in a strike against the Government.
10. Membership in the Communist Party of the United States.

Unfortunately the vast majority of bureaucrats you may wish to remove will not fall into any of these categories, and generally any action taken to *involuntarily* remove an employee, other than under the circumstances listed above, will be considered an adverse action against the employee. The adverse action proceedings are extremely lengthy and time consuming and are outlined briefly as follows.

Civil Service rules and regulations require that the employee, against whom adverse action is sought, is entitled to at least 30 days advance written notice stating all the reasons for the proposed action. The action proposed must be just that, a proposal, and the notice should not indicate that a decision has already been made. The employee must be given a reasonable time to prepare and submit a reply to this notice and the amount of time given must be contained in the employee's advance notice. He must also have the right to reply in writing, or personally, to a superior.

Once a decision has been made to either proceed or not with the adverse action, the employee has the right to a written, dated notice informing him of the decision and his appeal rights. This notice must be given to him at the earliest possible date at, or before, the time the action will be made effective. The employee must be fully informed of his appeal rights to the agency, if any, and to the Civil Service Commission. This same procedure applies to any action taken against an employee serving in a career appointment which could be considered an adversity (such as suspension for more than 30 days, and reduction in rank or compensation).

Because this procedure is lengthy, and due to the fact that the resulting publicity can do great harm to the Department, it is suggested that you study the techniques outlined in Section III, Chapter 3 of this Manual.

It is, however, important to keep in mind that the adverse action procedure does not apply to *voluntary* separations such as resignations, mandatory retirement, disability retirement and military separations. It is not considered improper by the Civil Service Commission for an agency to "initiate a discussion with an employee in which he is given an election between leaving his position voluntarily or

facing charges looking towards an adverse action. Neither is it improper for the agency to attempt to influence the employee's decision by pointing out how one of the possible alternatives will be in his best interests, as long as this does not appear to be duress, intimidation or deception."

**(a-3) Demotions.** A demotion in either pay or rank (status), as stated later in Section III, Chapter 3 of this Manual, is considered to be an adverse action against the employee if it is based on a decision of an administrative officer and is not part of a reduction in force procedure. A reduction in rank (Demotion) does not refer to the employee's grade but rather to his relative status or standing in the agency's organizational structure (status). As explained later in Section III, Chapter 3 of this Manual, the movement of an employee from one position to another with less status than the one previously held is grounds for an adverse action.

A reduction in pay (demotion) is also considered an adverse action if it is a result of a decision of an administrative officer and not the result of a reduction in force procedure. It should be noted that the term *pay* refers to the employee's basic pay and does not include differentials for hazardous work, overtime and holiday work.

**(a-4) Reassignments.** A reassignment is the movement of an employee, while serving continuously within an agency, from one position to another without promotion or demotion. In this Manual we have used the terms *reassignment* and *transfer* interchangeably although they are not defined as the same by the Civil Service Commission.

An employee serving in a career appointment may be reassigned to another position for which he qualifies on a noncompetitive basis. Geographical reassignments are frequently used as a hopeful removal technique and these are outlined in Section III, Chapter 3 of this Manual. . . .

# Section III Organizational and Reorganizational Techniques in Aid of the Personnel Process

## 1. Budget and Slots

In order to understand the techniques used in organizing and reorganizing component parts of a Department, or Agency, in order to achieve personnel objectives, one must understand three fundamental areas. One would be the rules and regulations covering the government personnel and pay systems. These have been treated in Section II of this Manual. The other two pieces of the puzzle are the personnel ceiling (slots) available, and the funds (salaries and expenses) available.

### a. Slots

The personnel ceiling for a Department or Agency is set by the Office of Management and Budget, usually during the budget process. Because slots are so closely tied to the money necessary to pay incumbents filling them, the two are usually equated. This is a fundamental mistake. There is a common misconception that Congress, by law through the appropriation process, sets the incremental ceilings for the component parts of a Department or Agency. Though budget examinations and committee reports often use the personnel ceilings, their grades, and accompanying expenses as backup information justifying an appropriation, the appropriations acts themselves (and thus the law) simply gives to a Department, or Agency, sums of money for a given program or, in some cases, program dollars and salary and expense money.

The Office of Management and Budget (OMB), however, has imposed an Administration-side ceiling on the number of persons to be employed in the Executive Branch, and thus rations out ceilings to each Department and Agency. In turn, each Department or Agency then rations out personnel ceilings to its component parts.

It is important to keep in mind that the allocation of a personnel ceiling (slots) is that and no more. A personnel ceiling (slots) is the authorization to the Department, or Agency, and its component parts thereafter, with respect to the total number of people that can be employed without regard to the type of appointment, pay schedule or level.

Once having received the slots, it is through the personnel process (classification and determining whether or not to fill a position on a career or noncareer basis) that a position acquires its status, pay level, and pay system. (See Chapter II).

*NOTE:* The personnel ceiling (slots) system is a hangover from the Johnson Administration. Upon assuming the Presidency in 1964, the Johnson Administration presided over a dramatic increase in Federal employment— layering into the bureaus the faithful. In 1966 Johnson offered legislation, which Congress passed, called the Revenue Expenditure Control Act. It required the Executive Branch of Government to reduce itself in size to the level of employment in fact existing in 1964. The cosmetic public theory behind the Act was that the reduction of and stabilization of, a personnel ceiling for the Executive Branch would first cut, and then stabilize, Federal expenditures connected with personnel costs. The real motive, however, was that having layered in the faithful for a period of two years, he could use that Act to reduce the personnel in the Federal Government. Not being a non-political President, I think we can be certain that those who exited generally, were as carefully selected as those who entered. The Act, of course, was repealed by Congress in 1969.

In fact, the Revenue Expenditure Control Act saved no money at all, but rather *increased* Federal expenditures. For what the Johnson Administration simply did after passage of that Act was to see to it that "friendly" consulting firms began to spring up, founded and staffed by many former Johnson and Kennedy Administration employees. They then received fat contracts to perform functions previously performed within the Government by Federal employees. The commerical costs, naturally, exceeded the personnel costs they replaced.

Examples of such firms might be TransCentury Corporation formed on behalf of the Peace Corps, and Volt Tech formed on behalf of the Office of Economic Opportunity.

The OMB, none-the-less, persists with the personnel ceiling (slots) system ever faithful to the Democratic majority in Congress with whom the bureaucrats of the OMB (and its predecessors) have worked for 36 of the past 40 years. Its only effect is to impose on the Departments and Agencies an artificial restraint, beyond the budgetary restraints, that need not exist.

Most Departments or Agencies continue to get around the system anyway. The ceilings are counted by the OMB annually, by looking at the Department's employment during the last pay period in the fiscal year (June). Departments have been known to have employees resign as of the first pay period in June only to be rehired in the first pay period in July. Another technique is to hire full-time consultants, for whom a time card is not submitted in the last pay period in June, with a time card being submitted again beginning with the first pay period in July. The OMB has tried to clamp down on this practice by reducing the amount of money available to the Department from that appropriated by Congress (freezing funds) commensurate with the ceilings they have allocated to the Department, as opposed to the number of persons employed that the appropriation from Congress might support. But most agencies have gotten around that by listing the employment of certain persons, and more generally consultants, as program expenses rather than as a salary expense and find the necessary funds from program dollars instead of that appropriated for salaries and expenses. And then the Departments, out of program funds, continue to contract out to consulting firms work which can be more economically done in-house because of the manpower restraints. Unfortunately many of the contracts still go to the same firm that sprang up during the 1960s. . . .

### 3. Techniques for Removal Through Organizational or Management Procedures

The Civil Service system creates many hardships in trying to remove undesirable employees from their positions. Because of the rape of the career service by the Kennedy and Johnson Administrations, as described in the Introduction, this Administration has been left a legacy of finding disloyalty and obstruction at high levels while those incumbents rest comfortably on career civil service status. Political disloyalty and insimpatico relationships with the Administration, unfortunately, are not grounds for the removal or suspension of an employee. Career employees, as discussed in Chapter 2, can only be dismissed or otherwise punished for direct disobedience of lawful orders, actions which are tantamount to the commission of a crime, and well documented and provable incompetence. (See FPM Section 752.) Even if you follow the time consuming process of documenting a case to proceed with an adverse action, the administration and legal process is slow and lengthy and great damage can accrue to the Department prior to your successful conclusion of your case. However, there are several techniques which can be designed carefully, to skirt around the adverse action proceedings. One must always bear in mind the following rules. The reduction of a person to a position of lower status and/or grade is considered an adverse action which necessitates formal proceedings. Secondly, an administrative or management decision cannot be based on the political background or persuasion of an individual, his race, sex, religion, or national origin.

### a. Individual Techniques

**(a-1) Frontal assault.** You simply call an individual in and tell him he is no longer wanted, that you'll assist him in finding another job and will keep him around until such time as he finds other employment. But you do expect him to immediately relinquish his duties, accept reassignment to a make-shift position at his current grade and then quietly resign for the good of the service. Of course, you promise him that he will leave with honor and with the finest recommendations, a farewell luncheon, and perhaps even a Departmental award. You, naturally, point out that should he not accept such an offer, and he later is forced to resign or retire through regular process or on his own volition, that his employment references from the Department and his permanent personnel record may not look the same as if he accepted your offer. There should be no witnesses in the room at the time. *Caution:* This technique should only be used for the timid at heart with a giant ego. This is an extremely dangerous technique and the very fact of your conversation can be used against the Department in any subsequent adverse action proceedings. It should never be used with that fervent, zealous employee committed to Democratic policies and programs, or to the bureaucracy, who might relish the opportunity to be martyred on the cross of his cause.

*(a-2) Transfer technique.* By carefully researching the background of the proposed employee–victim, one can always establish that geographical part of the country and/or organizational unit to which the employee would rather resign than obey and accept transfer orders. For example, if you have an employee who was born and raised in New England and is currently serving in your Boston Regional Office, and his record shows reluctance to move far from that location (he may have family and financial commitments not easily severed), a transfer accompanied by a promotion to an existing or newly created position in Dallas, Texas might just fill the bill. It is always suggested that a transfer be accompanied with a promotion, if possible. Since a promotion is *per se* beneficial to the employee, it immediately forecloses any claim that the transfer is an adverse action. It also reduces the possibility of a claim that the transfer was motivated for prohibited purposes since, again, the transfer resulted in a beneficial action for the employee and the word *discrimination* implies some adversity to have been suffered. It is also important that you carefully check your organizational charts to insure that not only is there no reduction in grade, but no reduction in status. For instance, if a person is a Deputy Regional Director at GS-14, the promotion to a position of State Director in another region

(who reports to a Deputy Regional Director) even at a grade increase to GS-15 will be a demotion in status and thus an adverse action. Transfers must also be presented as necessary for "the efficiency of the service." It is, therefore, necessary that the position to which the person is being transferred fits in with his current job experience or his past responsibilities. The technical assistance of your personnel office is indispensable in prosecuting such transfers. But there is no reason why they cannot artfully find, or create, the necessary position that will satisfy the transfer requirements necessary to cause the prospective transferee to be confronted with the choice of being transferred to a position he does not want or resigning. Of course, one can sweeten the potion by privately assuring the proposed transferee, upon delivery of his transfer notification, that should he refuse the transfer, and resign, that his resignation will be accepted without prejudice. Further, he may remain for a period until he finds other employment and leave with the highest honors and references.

*(a-3) Special assignment technique (the traveling salesman).* This technique is especially useful for the family man and those who do not enjoy traveling. What you do is to suddenly recognize the outstanding abilities of your employee–victim and immediately seize upon his competence and talent to assign him to a special research and evaluation project. This is best explained by way of example. Let us assume that our employee is a program analyst with the Department of Transportation. You immediately discover the high level interest and policy requirements for creating a program to meet the transportation needs of all U. S. cities and towns with a population of 20,000 and under. Nothing is more revealing than first hand inspections and consultations with town officials. And so you hand your expert a promotion and his new assignment. (Again, a promotion is desirable to diminish any possible claim of adversity.) Along with his promotion and assignment your expert is given extensive travel orders criss-crossing him across the

country to towns (hopefully with the worst accommodations possible) of a population of 20,000 or under. Until his wife threatens him with divorce unless he quits, you have him out of town and out of the way. When he finally asks for relief you tearfully reiterate the importance of the project and state that he must continue to obey travel orders or resign. Failure to obey travel orders is a ground for immediate separation.

### b. The Layering Technique

The layering technique, as its full name implies, is an organization technique to "layer" over insubordinate/subordinates, managers who are loyal and faithful. This technique, however, requires at least the temporary need for additional slots and may, in some cases, require supergrade authorities. Again, the best way to explain the layering technique is to depict its application in an example. Let us assume you have two branches whose chiefs are GS-14s and report directly to your deputy, who is a GS-15, who in turn reports to you (you are a GS-16). The object is to remove from critical responsibilities your deputy and the two GS-14 branch chiefs. All three positions you find were cosily frozen into the career service when you assumed your noncareer office head post.

A slot saving can be realized if you have any vacancies within your office no matter what type of job they were previously utilized for, such as secretarial vacancies. (Remember your ceiling does not address itself to how you are going to use your positions. Don't ever let the bureaucrats tell you it is automatically a such-and-such slot. By budget adjustment you can use existing vacancies to create any new positions and functions you desire.) Utilizing vacant positions, or new postions, and acquiring the appropriate budget adjustment, you get your position upgraded to a GS-17 NEA. You then create a new position of Deputy Office Director, at a noncareer GS-16. Because that position is noncareer, your former deputy has no rights to it. (*Note of caution*: The question may be asked why you don't simply convert those positions from career to noncareer and then fire the incumbents. The Civil Service rules and regulations

contain a "grandfather clause" which provides that if a position which is filled by a career incumbent is converted from career to non-career, the incumbent still maintains his career status in the job. Operationally, therefore, the position does not become noncareer until the career incumbent vacates that position. If you convert it to noncareer before he vacates the position, you run the risk that if you take some administrative action to transfer him out of the position later he can claim political discrimination pointing to the very fact that you converted his position to excepted status as evidence.) To make sure that the reorganization does not result in a reduction of status for your former deputy, you appoint him as a GS-15 Special Assistant to yourself so that he retains both his grade and his direct reporting relationship. You then create two Staff Assistant positions for your Branch Chiefs reporting to your new Special Assistant. They also retain their GS-14 grades. You upgrade the Branch Chief positions to GS-15 and create two Deputy Branch Chief positions at GS-14. To your new deputy position, the two upgraded branch chief positions and the two new deputy branch chief positions you then effect the appointment of persons of unquestioned loyalty. You have thus layered into the organization into key positions your own people, still isolating your road-blocks into powerless make-shift positions. In all likelihood the three will probably end up resigning out of disgust and boredom. You can then return the three slots from wherever you borrowed them. If this does not occur, you can have a reduction in force which will cause certain job abolitions and thus the elimination of selected employees. As mentioned in the Introduction, this layering technique followed by a reduction in force, after a respectable waiting period, was the technique used extensively by Lyndon Johnson's Administration.

A variation of the layering technique is called the *Bypass Layering Technique* which may be utilized in the event the two GS-14 branch chiefs should be eligible for promotion and placement in the upgraded GS-15 branch chief positions. That will frequently be the case, especially if these upgraded branch chief positions cannot be made noncareer. In that case the scenario for the creation of a new upgraded deputy to yourself remains the same. Your former deputy is likewise made a Special Assistant to yourself at GS-15 having no rights to the noncareer GS-16 position. The two GS-14 branch chiefs are promoted to GS-15 making way for the creation of two deputy branch chief positions at GS-14. You then layer in your own people to the deputy branch chief positions. From then on all business is conducted between the deputy branch chiefs, your deputy and yourself. You rudely bypass your branch chiefs on all office matters. You also totally ignore your special assistant. If all three don't at least quit in disgust, at least you have removed them from the mainstream of office operations.

### c. Shifting Responsibilities and Isolation Techniques

This is a classic organizational technique first introduced by Franklin D. Roosevelt. It does involve a sizeable investment of budget and slots. Its purpose is to isolate and bypass an entire organization which is so hopeless that there is an immediate desire to deal with nobody in the organization at all. The shifting responsibilities and isolation technique entails the setting up of a parallel organization to one already in existence, and giving that new organization most of the real authorities previously vested in the old organization it parallels. The alphabet agencies created by FDR to usurp existing functions of existing departments and to assume new functions that ordinarily would have gone to those existing departments is an example of the wholesale uses of the shifting functions technique. Let's use another example. Perhaps you're unhappy with your whole budget office. You inform the budget office that the tail will no longer wag the dog. From now on they will exercise what are supposed to be the functions of the budget office which are the technical accounting procedures and documenting procedures necessary for promulgating a budget. You create a new Office of Financial Policy Review which will have the responsibility for examining the proposed budgets of the component parts

of your organization and then recommend the "policy decisions" necessary to put together your organization's budget. Because of the policy content, the positions in the new office will be largely noncareer and thus unavailable as a matter of right to those bureaucrats in your existing budget office. You then impose unbearable ceilings on your budget office specifically in the area of accounting. This renders that budget office increasingly incapable of producing adequate accounting data to the new Financial Policy Review Office. As a result, the Financial Policy Review Office must of a necessity create its own accounting area (hopefully from slots you have squeezed out of the budget office. *Note:* It is important that you do not create *career* positions in the new office comparable to those in the old budget office at the same time you reduce the personnel ceilings in the old budget office creating a RIF. Whereas the civil service rules do not allow careerists being RIF'd to exercise claims to like positions in the non-career service, they do grant careerists the right to claim placement into like *career* positions that are created.) Slowly but surely the new Financial Policy Review Office accrues all of the meaningful functions of the budget office isolating those bureaucrats who have not quit in disgust into meaningless technical positions out of the mainstream of the Department's operations.

### d. New Activity Technique

Another organizational technique for the wholesale isolation and disposition of undesirable employee–victims is the creation of an apparently meaningful, but essentially meaningless, new activity to which they are all transferred. This technique, unlike the shifting responsibilities and isolation technique designed to immobilize a group of people in a single organizational entity, is designed to provide a single barrel into which you can dump a large number of widely located bad apples. Again let us use an example to illustrate this technique. Let us apply this to the Department of Health, Education, and Welfare. A startling new trust to HEW's participation in the Model Cities

Program might be a new research and development Model Cities Laboratory. With the concurrence of the Governor of Alabama, one might choose Alabama, or a region thereof, to be a "model state" or "model region" like we now have sections of cities designated as "model cities." For office facilities the Department of the Army might be prevailed upon to provide surplus buildings at Fort Rucker, Alabama. The Alabama State Department of Education would, I am sure, be more than happy to provide school buses to bus HEW employees between their offices and the nearest town where they would live. Naturally, to such a high priority and high visibility project as a "model state" lab you would want to assign some of the most "qualified" employees and administrators you could find throughout the Department, both in Washington and in the field. By carefully looking at the personnel jackets of your selected employee–victims, you can easily design an organization chart for the project that would create positions to which these employee–victims can be transferred that meet the necessary job description requirements, offer promotional opportunities in grade, and by having the project report directly into the Secretary's office provide for promotions in status.

### e. Additional Notes
### (Bureaucratic Countermeasures)

The techniques proffered above are not unknown to our loyal civil servants. Since extensive use of the layering techniques and the shifting responsibilities techniques were made by the previous Administration, between November of 1968 and January 20, 1969, tremendous reorganizations occurred within the Federal Government designed to make those techniques difficult to apply by our new Administration. With the help of the OMB, following the policies of the Revenue Expenditure Control Act, many positions not filled in the spring of 1969 were eliminated from the personnel ceilings of the Departments, or Agencies, and their funding for salaries was commensurately reduced. With the OMB continuing to reduce personnel ceilings, the availability of extra slots and salary funds

for purposes of both layering and shifting responsibilities all but do not exist. Had the OMB acted in the President's best interests to help him obtain control over his Administration, and rule rather than reign, it would have recommended an expansion of personnel ceilings and funding for salaries for the first two years. This would have enabled the Departments and Agencies to conduct the necessary layering and shifting responsibility functions during those first two years. During the last two years of the Administration, we could have enjoyed a reduction in personnel ceilings and funds and conducted a selected reduction in force. As it is, by and large, the personnel ceilings and funding policies of the OMB have only frustrated this Administration from any meaningful program for bringing in substantial numbers of loyal team members into the bureaucracy.

Likewise the OMB cooperated with the Johnson Administration during 1963 in the distribution to the Departments and Agencies of all but a few of the Executive Levels in the President's pool which were promptly filled, mostly on a career basis. This deprived this Administration of a flexible resource of Executive Level positions from which new positions for layering and shifting responsibilities at a high level could have been accomplished. The Administration was left with the alternative of seeking additional Executive Level positions from a Congress not likely to be cooperative.

Furthermore, as mentioned in the Introduction, the Departments and Agencies absorbed and filled on a career basis most of the outstanding supergrade quota allocations given to the Executive Branch by Congress. This again makes the creation of additional supergrade positions for the purposes of layering, shifting responsibilities, or setting up a new activity extremely difficult. It is to an uncooperative Congress that the Administration must look for additional supergrade quota allocations.

Further, between November 7, 1968 and January 20, 1969, most Government departments and agencies experienced a rapid increase in the classification of positions to their optimum level, followed by the promotion to and filling of those positions with those who had been loyal to that Administration. Again, this "counter-layering" activity had made it difficult for this Administration.

## Conclusion

There is no substitute in the beginning of any Administration for a very active political personnel operation. Whatever investment is made in positions, salaries, systems, training and intelligent work in this area, will yield a return ten-fold. Conversely, the failure to invest what is necessary to a political personnel program, will cost the Administration and the Department or Agency fifty-fold what they might otherwise have invested. These estimates are borne out by experience. Where Departments and Agencies, and Administrations, have failed to invest the manpower and other necessary aforementioned items into an effective political personnel program—blindly paying lip service to such a function and proceeding immediately to invest heavily in the management and program functions—they have only been plagued by such folly. The time consumed of high level Administration appointees, and the manpower and expenses involved in the creation of fire fighting forces, caused by acts in attempt to frustrate the Administration's policies, program objectives and management objectives, as well as to embarrass the Administration, engaged in by unloyal employees of the Executive Branch, have far exceeded the investment a political personnel operation would have required. In those few organizations where an effective political personnel office was the forerunner of "new directions" in policy, program objectives, and management objectives, the ease and low visibility with which they were accomplished was markedly contrasted to the rest of the Administration. There is no question that the effective activities of a political personnel office will invoke a one-shot furor in the hostile press and Congress. But there is no question that these costs are far less than the costs of the frequent crescendos of bad publicity that are sure to occur frequently and indefinitely if you do not. In short, it is far better and healthier to swallow a large bitter pill in the beginning, and then run rigorously toward your objectives, than to run toward your objectives stopping so frequently for small bitter pills that you become drained of the endurance, the will and the ability to ever reach your objectives. As one of the ranking members of this Administration once put it: "You cannot hope to achieve policy, program or management control until you have achieved political control. That is the difference between ruling and reigning."

# 9

# Testimony on Civil Service Reform and Organization

*Alan K. Campbell*

## Introduction

Mr. Chairman, I am grateful for this opportunity to testify on behalf of the Administration about civil service reform and reorganization of the Civil Service Commission and the Federal Labor Relations Council. My colleagues on the Commission, Jule Sugarman and Ersa Poston, are here with me today. My remarks today are addressed principally to H.R. 11280, the Civil Service Reform Act of 1978. However, I will also comment on Reorganization Plan No. 2 of 1978, which will shortly be considered by the Government Operations Committee. That Plan provides the framework for carrying out several provisions in this Reform Bill.

The Federal civil service system is in trouble. Most people view the Federal Government as a greater source of problems and red tape than of solutions to the needs of this Nation. This lack of public confidence has sapped the strength of many Government programs and depressed the morale of civil service employees and managers alike.

Many factors account for the current crisis in the civil service, but the most important relate to the accumulation of laws, regulations, and policies which have grown up over the last 95 years. Complaints about the civil service system

are shared by managers and employees as well as the general public.

Managers in charge of Government programs claim that personnel management procedures seriously impede their efforts to be good managers. Employees believe they are not adequately protected from partisan pressures, will not get much recognition if they do good work, and can not get a fair shake if they register legitimate complaints. Much of the public believes that Federal employees are overpaid and underworked and have too much tenure.

Some of these beliefs—particularly those of the public—are exaggerated. But the complaints about the civil service system are held widely enough, and sufficiently based in fact, as to demand immediate attention.

Soon after our confirmation last year, the other two Commissioners and I, in cooperation with the Office of Management and Budget, began a serious study of the charges being made by managers, employees, and the public. We found that some of these compliants could be traced to the layers of controls and procedures that have been added over the years to correct problems as they developed in the civil service system. While each such control may be defensible, their aggregation has produced a semi-paralysis in administration. Thus, it now may take six to eight months to fill many important jobs; nearly two years to resolve a discrimination complaint rather than the statutorily mandated 180 days; and many months to resolve an adverse action appeal. Other complaints are related to the present organizational structure for Federal personnel management. The central personnel agency—the Civil Service Commission—has had major new functions and responsibilities heaped on it that have caused serious stresses in its structure.

Our early analyses convinced us that the problems go back to the fundamental laws, rules, regulations, and organization that govern Federal personnel management. We further concluded that these problems are so pervasive and

SOURCE: From U.S. House Committee on Post Office and Civil Service, *Civil Service Reform* (Washington, D.C.: Government Printing Office, 1978).

fundamental that merely patching the existing system will not solve them.

## The Federal Personnel Management Project

We decided it was time to step back, look at the whole picture, see what the problems really are, and then try to devise lasting, systemwide solutions. To this end, the president set up the Federal Personnel Management Project in May, 1977 as part of his reorganization effort. This was a full-scale review of Federal personnel management laws, principles, policies, processes, and organization.

Leadership for the Project was drawn jointly from the Civil Service Commission and the Office of Management and Budget. I served as Chairman of the Project and Wayne Granquist of the Office of Management and Budget served as Vice Chairman. The Project was advised by a Working Group made up of the Assistant Secretaries for Administration of the Federal departments and their counterparts in major independent agencies. The co-chairmen of the Working Group were Jule Sugarman, Vice Chairman of the Commission, and Howard Messner, Assistant Director of the Office of Management and Budget.

The Project had nine subject-matter task forces which worked under the day-to-day management of Dwight Ink and Thomas Murphy, the Project's Executive Director and Deputy Executive Director. The task forces were staffed primarily by experienced careerists drawn from many Federal agencies. The task force managers were selected from among highly-respected Federal executives, from industry, and from the academic world.

The Project scoured the Government for ideas about personnel management problems and what could be done to solve them. The Civil Service Commissioners, together with representatives of the Office of Management and Budget, personally went to all regions of the country and listened to the views of managers, unions, individual employees, personnel officials, equal employment opportunity officials, and State and local government officials.

We held hearings in Washington, D.C. and in nearby Virginia and Maryland to get the views of the large Federal employee populations in this area. Some members of Congress participated in those hearings. In all, we heard from over seven thousand people who had ideas about the civil service system.

The Project then developed option papers on seven broad topics and sent them out for comments to some 800 organizations and individuals. Typically we received 150 to 200 replies on each paper. By this means, the Project obtained the views of an enormous range of knowledgeable people with widely varing concerns about the system.

This outpouring of ideas confirmed our earlier hypothesis: the problems of the civil service system will not yield to patchwork repairs. Some of the problems can be solved by administrative action within the context of the present personnel laws, and we will move to deal with those. Other major problems need changes in the fundamental laws governing the civil service. Still others need changes in the organizational structure for personnel management.

## Problems in Personnel Management

And that is why we are here today. The need for reform may be illustrated by outlining ten of the most salient problems confronting the Federal civil service system.

1. Supervisors, employees, political leaders, and others are confused about what they may and may not do without violating essential merit principles.

2. Employees feel they cannot get a fair hearing when they believe political, arbitrary, discriminatory, or illegal personnel actions have taken place.

3. The dangers of exposing wrongdoing in Government may deter employees from "blowing the whistle," although it would be in the public interest for them to do so.

4. Excessive centralization of personnel authorities takes many types of day-to-day personnel decisions out of the hands of line

managers who nonetheless are held responsible for accomplishment in major program areas. Managers must go through extensive paperwork justifications to obtain Civil Service Commission approval of relatively minor decisions.

5. Over-centralized and restrictive systems for examining and selecting employees make it hard for managers to hire expeditiously the best qualified people and to meet their equal employment opportunity responsibilities.

6. Managers find a confusing array of regulations and procedures standing in their way when they seek to reward good work performance, to discipline employees, or to remove employees whose performance is clearly inadequate and cannot be improved.

7. The jumble of laws, regulations, and special provisions affecting executive positions makes it very difficult for agency heads to utilize their top staff most effectively, to hold managers accountable for program accomplishment, and to reward or remove them on the basis of performance. There is virtually no mobility of senior executives among Federal agencies.

8. Present laws provide pay increases primarily based on length of service and do not allow adequately for granting extra pay for better performance or for withholding pay increases when performance is less effective.

9. Research in civilian personnel management is completely inadequate, and statutory restraints prevent experimentation in new management approaches. Therefore, new ideas are not encouraged and, when developed, are often ignored, or are installed on a large scale without adequate testing.

10. The Federal agencies involved in grant-in-aid programs impose conflicting personnel requirements on State and local agencies, thereby unreasonably complicating their work.

Analysis of these problems reveals two central challenges to Federal personnel management. One is to build a stronger foundation for the protection of employee rights and the application of the merit concept. The other is to develop new approaches to personnel operations and administration, so that they may become aids rather than obstacles to effective management of the Government workforce.

At first glance these challenges appear contradictory, because we are accustomed to equating merit and employee protection with complex procedural requirements, centralized review and approval processes, and intricate checks and balances. Too often, however, these measures have become the refuge of the unsatisfactory employee or the excuse for managerial failure to act.

The fundamental reforms proposed in the reorganization plan and Civil Service Reform Bill attempt to stake out the foundation points of a sound public merit system and the rights and manner of fair treatment of individuals in the system, while also providing those tools that are essential for public managers who are responsible for the efficient and effective accomplishment of the missions of the Federal Government.

## Overview of the Reform Proposals

Before beginning my discussion of the proposed Civil Service Reform Act of 1978, let me mention a related matter.

The proposed Reform Act is the centerpiece of the civil service reform legislation that we will be proposing. It encompasses many of the basic features of civil service that are of central importance to the system.

The President will formally submit the reorganization plan for the Civil Service Commission, a draft of which he has sent to Congress for information, at a time convenient to the Government Operations Committee. We believe that early approval by the Congress of the reorganization plan will enable us to put the new organizational structures in place in time to carry out the substantive reforms embodied in the Civil Service Reform Act.

Since the legislative proposal to reform the civil service is closely related to the reorganization plan, I would like to comment briefly on the contents of the plan.

# Reorganization Plan No. 2 of 1978

The reorganization plan will divide the present functions and responsibilities of the Civil Service Commission between two new agencies, an Office of Personnel Management and a Merit Systems Protection Board. In addition, it will create a Federal Labor Relations Authority to replace the Federal Labor Relations Council and other organizational components of the Government's labor relations program.

The plan transfers to the Office of Personnel Management all the personnel policy making, operating, advisory, assistance, and evaluation functions previously assigned to the Commission, except those expressly retained by the Merit Systems Protection Board. Remaining with the Board are almost all of the adjudication and appellate functions now vested in the Commission by law. The plan establishes an Office of Special Counsel within the Board to investigate and prosecute officials who engage in prohibited personnel practices.

## Problems in the Organizational Structure for Personnel Management

The basic problems in the present structure for Federal personnel management are worth specifying here, because the proposed Civil Service Reform Act has been framed in the context of a new structure.

First, the Civil Service Commission currently has so many conflicting roles that it is unable to perform all of them adequately. At one and the same time it is expected to serve the President in providing managerial leadership for the positive personnel management functions in the Executive Branch—that is, establishing personnel policies and advising and assisting agencies on personnel management functions—while also serving as a "watchdog" over the integrity of the merit system, protecting employee rights, and performing a variety of adjudicatory functions. As a direct result, the Commission lacks credibility in performing its merit protection functions with both employees and managers who recognize the inherent conflicts among these functions.

Second, the President lacks an appropriate staff organization for directing the positive personnel management responsibilities inherent in his position as Chief Executive. Whereas an industrial manager, a military commander, or subordinate Federal executive normally assigns personnel management responsibility to a key member of his executive staff, the President must rely on a semi-independent body separated by structure and tradition from the Chief Executive. As a consequence, Presidential effectiveness in directing Federal personnel management is weakened and problems do not receive the attention they should.

Third, as made painfully evident in recent years, The Civil Service Commission, despite its presumed political neutrality, has not been an effective deterrent to partisan political or other abuses of the merit system. Further, there is insufficient protection for employees—so-called "whistle-blowers"—who are harassed for calling attention to violations of laws and regulations within their agencies.

Fourth, the existing machinery for administering the Federal labor-management relations program is not fully integrated nor fully acceptable to employee organizations. The functions are fragmented among the Federal Labor Relations Council, the Federal Service Impasses Panel, the Department of Labor, and the Civil Service Commission, which has a special third-party role. The Council—which consists of the Chairman of the Civil Service Commission, the Director of the Office of Management and Budget, and the Secretary of Labor—is criticized by some as "management-dominated." The resolution of unfair labor practices also is criticized as relatively ineffective due to the current lack of independent enforcement authority within the third-party machinery.

Fifth, control over personnel management functions is so centralized as to unreasonably increase paperwork, create system inflexibility, and cause excessive delays. This centralization requires the Commission to be deeply involved in processing a multitude of individual personnel actions and reviewing operational details. This prevents the Commission from giving sufficient attention to policy, oversight, and systemic improvements in Federal personnel management. Excessive centralization produces long delays in hiring and other job placement matters, and erodes the authority and accountability of line supervisors and managers. Employees' dissatisfaction with the Commission's performance in the protection of their rights is matched by managers' view of the Commission as an administrative bottleneck and source of excessive procedural obstacles.

### The Merit Systems Protection Board

The reorganization plan and companion Civil Service Reform Act will go a long way towards solving these fundamental problems. The Merit Systems Protection Board will be an independent agency to adjudicate employee appeals and to investigate allegations of prohibited personnel practices and to prosecute offenders. Based on Reorganization Plan No. 2 of 1978 and implementing Executive orders and regulations, the Board will have jurisdiction over the following twenty-three different types of appeals:

1. Withholding of within-grade salary increase (5 USC 5335)
2. Removal of a hearing examiner (5 USC 7521)
3. Adverse actions against preference eligibles (5 USC 7701)
4. Adverse actions against non-preference eligibles in the competitive service (EO 11491, as amended)
5. Determinations by the Bureau of Retirement, Insurance, and Occupational Health concerning retirement applications and annuities (5 USC 8347(d) and 5 CFR 831.107, 831.1101-12, and 831.1205)
6. Restoration to duty following military service or following recovery or partial recovery from a compensable injury (38 USC 2023 and 5 CFR 302.501-03, 353.401)
7. Complaints of discrimination based on race, color, religion, national origin, age, or sex (29 USC 633a and 42 USC 2000e-16)

(Under Reorganization Plan No. 1 of 1978, these complaints would go to the Equal Employment Opportunity Commission)
8. Employment practices administered or required by the Civil Service Commission (5 CFR 300.104(a) )
9. Terminations during probationary periods (5 CFR 315.806)
10. Reemployment priority lists (5 CFR 330.202)
11. Reduction in force (5 CFR 351.901)
12. Reemployment rights based on movement between Executive agencies during emergencies (5 CFR 352.209)
13. Reemployment rights following details or transfers to international organizations (5 CFR 352.313)
14. Reinstatement rights after service under the Foreign Assistance Act of 1961 (5 CFR 352.508)
15. Reemployment rights after service in the Economic Stabilization Program (5 CFR 352.607)
16. Reemployment rights after service under the Indian Self-Determination Act (5 CFR 352.707)
17. Retention of salaries of employees demoted to General Schedule positions without personal cause, not at their own request, and not in a reduction in force due to lack of funds or curtailment of work (5 CFR 531.517)
18. Disqualification of employees or applicants by the Commission based on suitability determinations (5 CFR 731.401 and 754.105)
19. Denials by employing agencies of regular or optional life insurance coverage (5 CFR 870.205 and 871.206)
20. Refusal by employing agencies to permit employees to enroll, or to change their enrollment, in a health benefits plan (5 CFR 890.103)
21. Determination by the Commission's Bureau of Retirement, Insurance, and Occupational Health that annuitants are not eligible to elect health benefits plans or to receive Government contributions related to such plans (5 CFR 891.105)

22. Complaints of agency non-compliance with Fair Labor Standards Act (FPM Letter No. 551-9)
23. Appeals from an examination rating or the rejection of an application in connection with an administrative law judge position (CSC Minute Number 5 of April 29, 1974).

The Merit Systems Protection Board will also designate individuals to serve as chairmen of performance rating boards established pursuant to 5 USC 4305, and the Chairman of the Board will designate a representative who shall serve as chairman of all boards of review established pursuant to 5 USC 3383(b).

The Board will not have the authority to adjudicate appeals from examination ratings or rejection of applications (other than those pertaining to administrative law judge positions), from position classification or job grading determinations (other than those related to adverse actions), or from decisions of insurance carriers denying claims of employees, annuitants, or family members. These matters have been determined to be more suitable for administrative review to determine accuracy and consistency with the intentions of the administrative authority.

The appellate function will also be affected by Reorganization Plan No. 1 of 1978, which would transfer discrimination complaints to the Equal Employment Opportunity Commission. If a matter appealable to the Board covers both civil service and discrimination issues, both issues will first be decided by the Merit Systems Protection Board, and then the Equal Employment Opportunity Commission will have the option to review the discrimination issue.

The Merit Systems Protection Board will also have authority to conduct special studies to determine whether Federal personnel systems are operating in accordance with merit principles.

Redesignation of the Civil Service Commission as the Merit Systems Protection Board and excluding management assistance functions from that Board will provide employees a greater sense of impartial action on their appeals. The streamlining of appellate procedures provided in title II of the Civil Service Reform Bill will give employees speedy resolution of their appeals.

Establishment of the Special Counsel with investigative and prosecutorial authority will provide employees increased protection from improper managerial actions and increase the accountability of managers for the exercise of discretionary authorities. (Enactment of titles I and II of the Civil Service Reform Bill will further strengthen these safeguards.)

## The Office of Personnel Management

Establishment of the Office of Personnel Management will provide the President with the personnel management staff arm that he needs. The Office will be in a better position to provide more constructive advice to agency managers on personnel management matters than is possible in the existing organizational framework. Greater delegations of personnel authorities by the Office of Personnel Management will provide agency managers with authority that is commensurate with their responsibility for mission accomplishment. It will also permit the Office to shift a greater portion of its resources toward an expansion of technical assistance services to agencies aimed at improving the productivity, management, and quality of the Federal workforce.

## The Federal Labor Relations Authority

The Federal Labor Relations Authority will integrate the third-party functions in the labor relations program under an independent and neutral body. The Authority will assume the functions of the Federal Labor Relations Council and Assistant Secretary of Labor for Labor-Management Relations (except standards of conduct for labor organizations). The Federal Service Impasses Panel will remain a distinct organizational entity within the Authority.

Improvement in the delivery of services to the public is dependent upon both stronger protection for the merit concept and improved management of the personnel functions of the Federal Government. I believe that the structural changes embodied in Reorganization Plan No. 2 of 1978 achieve this vital balance.

The Merit Systems Protection Board will provide protection against improper personnel actions and will ensure due process for employees affected by adverse personnel actions. The Federal Labor Relations Authority will provide the credible and effective organization that is necessary for resolving disputes between Federal management and recognized employee organizations and for ensuring that such disputes are settled quickly and fairly. The Office of Personnel Management will provide the President the means to carry out the personnel management functions inherent in his role as Chief Executive.

## The Civil Service Reform Act of 1978

### Title I—Merit System Principles

I would now like to discuss H.R. 11280, the Civil Service Reform Act of 1978. Title I of the Reform Bill establishes in law both the basic merit principles of the Federal personnel system and the specific personnel practices that are prohibited in this system. Title I expresses the responsibility and authority of the President and agency heads for assuring that personnel management in the Executive Branch is carried out in accordance with these merit principles. Specifically, it states that not only agency heads, but also those to whom agency heads delegate personnel management authority, are responsible for preventing prohibited personnel practices and for the proper execution of all civil service laws and regulations. Finally, title I recognizes the authority of the General Accounting Office to audit personnel programs for conformance with law and also for overall management effectiveness.

Personnel management in the Federal Government is based on the principle that the Government and the Nation are best served by safeguarding its career employees against improper political influences and personal favoritism and by recruiting, hiring, advancing, and retaining them on the basis of individual ability and performance without regard to political affiliation, race, color, national origin, sex, marital status, age or handicapping condition. A corollary principle is that employees who do not adequately perform, and who cannot or will not improve, will be separated. These tenets are among those commonly referred to as the "merit principles."

While these principles are implicit in the laws, Executive orders, rules, and regulations for administration of the Federal personnel system, and while Congress defined basic merit principles with regard to State and local governments in the Intergovernmental Personnel Act of 1970, no clear expression of the merit principles that apply to Federal personnel management exists in current law. Therefore, the merit principles which shall provide the foundation for Federal personnel management are identified at the outset of this Reform Bill in section 2301 (p. 5 of H.R. 11280).

However, codification of merit system principles alone will not by itself prevent abuse of these principles. Experience has shown that existing legal authority is not sufficient to effectively prosecute those who abuse the principles. Moreover, currently articulated prohibitions do not make clear against which culpable officials and employees disciplinary action may be taken; nor is the authority for investigating allegations of prohibited personnel practices and initiating disciplinary action as clear as it should be in all cases. This ambiguity has hindered past efforts to protect merit systems from abuse and to discipline those who have consciously acted contrary to merit principles. Therefore, H.R. 11280 specifies and prohibits eight types of actions and practices which violate the basic merit principles.

The prohibited personnel practices enumerated in title I are not all new; but in some instances they are the first expression of Congressional policy. Most may be traced to existing laws, Executive orders, rules or regulations of the Civil Service Commission. However, for the first time employee whistle-blowers are given express protection against reprisal actions for lawful disclosures of agency violations of laws or regulations.

Title I does not change the responsibility of agency heads for personnel management. They are still primarily responsible for the conduct of personnel management in their agencies. But the language makes clear that there is a responsibility on the part of all managers and those in a position to take or influence personnel actions to assure that their decisions and actions are consistent with merit principles. Clarification of the responsibilities of managers and enumeration of proscribed actions gives employees increased protection against arbitrary and capricious personnel actions and decisions.

## Title II—Civil Service Functions; Performance Appraisal; Adverse Actions

This title strengthens the Merit Systems Protection Board and offers new protections to Federal employees, establishes new and revised adverse action procedures and appeal rights, provides for new systems of appraising employee performance, and establishes new procedures for removal or demotion based on unacceptable performance and for appeals based on such actions. It also provides for greater delegations of personnel authorities to Federal departments and agencies.

### Protection of Employee Rights

Title II increases the safeguards for employee rights and merit principles without infringing on the legitimate prerogatives or authority of managers. Sections 1201 (p. 17) and 1202 (p. 18) increase the independence of the Merit Systems Protection Board beyond that affordable under the reorganization plan by lengthening terms of Board members from six to seven years, by prohibiting appointment to more than one full seven year term, and by providing for removal by the President only for misconduct, inefficiency, neglect of duty, or malfeasance in office, after notice and hearing. The present Civil Service Commissioners may be removed at the will of the President. Section 1204 (p. 19) establishes the term of the Special Counsel at seven years, but without the non-renewability

clause. Because of constitutional restrictions, no conditions may be specified for removal of the Special Counsel.

H.R. 11280 authorizes any Board member, the Special Counsel, or hearing examiner or any employee of the Board so designated to subpoena witnesses and documents, to seek a court order enforcing the subpoena, and to take or order the taking of depositions. The lack of such authority has sometimes prevented the Civil Service Commission from conducting fair hearings in the past.

Section 1206 (p. 20) establishes the responsibility and authority of the Special Counsel to investigate and act up on allegations of agency reprisals against "whistle-blowers." Specifically, the Special Counsel is authorized: (1) to stay a personnel action (such as reassignment to another geographic area) which could have a substantial economic impact on the employee if the status quo were not maintained during the Counsel's investigation—except in those cases in which the action is appealable to the Board; (2) to report a finding of reprisal to the agency head and to require appropriate action; and (3) to file disciplinary charges before the Board against those responsible for the reprisal. Title II authorizes the board to impose disciplinary actions, ranging from reprimand to dismissal and fines of up to $1,000.

The protection of whistle-blowers is, in our judgment, essential to the improvement of the public service. Too often in the past such employees have experienced reprisals in the form of transfers to remote locations, demotions, removel of duties and responsibilities, or discharges from the agency. These employees have found agency grievance procedures unavailable or unsatisfactory in protecting their rights.

H.R. 11280 provides protection to those employees who give lawfully available information to Congress, the media, or the public showing that agency officials have broken a law, rule, or regulation. Inquiry into such circumstances may be initiated by a Federal employee or any member of the public, and the inquiry will be handled in confidence during the investigative phase, to the extent possible.

It should be clear that H.R. 11280 does *not* authorize the Special Counsel to determine the truth of an employee's charges. That is the responsibility of the agency head or, as appropriate, the Department of Justice or the President. It is intended that the Special Counsel shall have a duty to act only in those cases involving significant retaliation. His office should not become the recipient of complaints of every real or imagined slight or injury. Similarly, the Special Counsel may not act to protect the employee where there is a right of appeal available to the employee. The Special Counsel is required to maintain and make public a list of all non-criminal matters referred to the agencies together with the agency responses.

H.R. 11280 also authorizes the Special Counsel to report prohibited personnel practices and suggest methods of correction to the agency head and to the Office of Personnel Management.

### Improvements in Adverse Action Procedures and Appeal Rights

Title II improves employee rights in the area of adverse actions and appeals. These changes will afford employees due process and prompt resolution of their appeals. I will address six of the most important changes. First, section 7511 (p. 36) extends statutory due process rights in adverse actions—now provided by statute only to veteran preference eligibles—to all competitive service employees. Employees in the competitive service who are not eligible for veterans preference now have the same rights as veterans in adverse actions and appeals only because of administrative action through Executive order. These rights cover actions such as removals, suspensions for more than 30 days, furloughs without pay, and reductions in grade or pay.

Second, the Office of Personnel Management is authorized to extend adverse action and appeals coverage to positions administratively excepted from the competitive service. Presently, employees in the excepted service (other than those entitled to veteran preference) are entitled to only those rights which may be provided by agency regulations, without the right of appeal to the Civil Service Commission. Yet many of these administratively excepted employees are careerists within their agencies.

The rights extended to competitive service employees by Executive order are now established as basic employee rights. Consideration of equity and fairness—which is at the very heart of the merit concept—dictates that all employees with Federal career expectations should be accorded equal rights, rather than making their rights dependent upon their entitlement to veterans preference or upon an administrative determination that a competitive examination can or cannot be administered.

Third, section 7512 (p. 38) eliminates "reduction in rank" as an appealable adverse action. When reduction in rank was originally defined as an adverse action, many employees were not under uniform position classification, grading, and pay systems, and including reduction in rank within the adverse action coverage had meaning and served to protect employees. Under present circumstances, however, it is difficult to determine whether a reduction in rank will occur when an employee is reassigned to a different position without loss of pay or grade level. Thus, reduction in rank as an appealable adverse action now serves no useful purpose. It does cause pointless misunderstandings between employees and managers about what constitutes rank and is an unnecessary impediment to reassignments to meet the needs of the agency.

Elimination of "reduction in rank" as an appealable adverse action may reduce the rights of employees in certain circumstances, but does not have a significant impact on any substantive rights. An employee whose reassignment is found to be a reduction in rank generally gains little or nothing by his appeal, since no back pay can be awarded and the agency is free to effect the reassignment again under adverse action procedures which can have a stigmatizing effect on the appellant's employment record. Employees will still be able to appeal a reduction in grade or pay.

Fourth, section 7701(h) (p. 44) authorizes the Merit Systems Protection Board to require agencies to pay reasonable attorney's fees for employees who prevail in their appeals and show that the action was wholly without basis in law or fact. These costs are sometimes very high, and represent a difficult burden for an employee who has been subjected to such an action.

Fifth, the Board will be able to issue decisions expeditiously, by the provision of section 7701(b) (p. 42) which permits a hearing only where genuine issues of material fact are raised. If such issues are not involved, a decision will be made based on the written record, including the representation of the parties. This will eliminate hearings in cases where hearings would make no difference in the outcome, and will leave more time for work on other cases.

Section 7701(c) (p. 42) introduces new criteria for judging appeals from employees who have been affected by an adverse action. At present, the only standard against which an adverse action may be taken is that it "promotes the efficiency of the service." The burden of proof is on the agency to meet that standard. Over the years a series of court and administrative interpretations has developed which Government managers see as tipping the scales of justice too strongly in favor of employees. As a result, managers are not acting in situations which clearly require discipline.

We have prepared an analysis of case decisions which illustrate a variety of situations where minor deficiencies in the agency's procedures or non-relevant substantive matters were used to overcome a clear case against an employee. In section 7701(c) we have sought to rebalance the scales to provide both a fair consideration of the employee's arguments and of the manager's judgment.

Under the new criteria the employee is required to show one of three things: that there was a procedural error of sufficient gravity that it substantially impaired the employee's rights; that there had been an act of unlawful discrimination which influenced the agency's decision; or that the agency's action had been arbitrary or capricious—that is to say, that there were no facts on which a reasonable person *could* conclude that the action was justified. It is intended that these three matters will be the only ones which will be taken into account by the appellate body. This provision will preserve the due process rights of employees and avoid unwarranted reversal of an agency's action.

## New Systems of Performance Appraisal and Actions Based on Performance

Title II provides for new systems of appraising employee performance that will make it possible for agencies to do a better job of recognizing and rewarding good employees and of identifying and helping those who are just getting by or are not performing at the level required. Also, it establishes new procedures for removals or demotions based on unacceptable performance and for appeals of these actions. These procedures will make it possible to act against ineffective employees with reasonable dispatch, while still providing them with due process rights.

The present performance appraisal requirements are based on the Performance Rating Act of 1950. The purposes of that Act were to recognize the merits of employees and their contributions to efficiency and economy, to provide fair appraisals of employee performance, to improve employee performance, to strengthen supervisor–employee relationships, and to remove employees whose performance is unsatisfactory from their positions. These purposes have not been achieved. In part, this failure is attributable to inadequacies in the state-of-the-art for appraising employee performance. In other respects, the constraints and complexities of the present statutory provisions have made it impossible to administer a workable program that provides managers and employees the information they both need about employee performance.

Of the existing statutory provisions, one of the weakest is the requirement to assign summary adjective performance ratings. Such ratings are useless as a basis for rewarding superior performance, encouraging improved performance, withholding pay step-increases of employees whose performance is marginal or substandard, or removing employees for unsatisfactory performance because they do not provide enough information to make any of these decisions. The inadequacy of summary adjective ratings as a management tool stems from the excessively restrictive statutory criterion for assigning an "outstanding" rating, from subsequent changes in the General Schedule pay statutes governing the determination of entitlement to within-grade pay increases, and from the requirement to use adverse action procedures to demote or remove an employee for "unsatisfactory" performance.

Several different statutory and regulatory requirements govern performance appraisals and performance-related decisions. For example, quality step-increases and incentive awards are granted under two separate chapters in title 5, United States Code. A single integrated framework for giving performance appraisals for all performance-related purposes is needed to better interrelate the various decisions that are made on the basis of work performance.

The principal changes set forth in sections 4302 (p. 29) and 4303 (p. 30) are fourfold: (1) abolishment of requirements for summary adjective performance ratings and appeals of performance ratings; (2) establishment of the requirement that performance appraisals made under a single authority are to be used as a basis for developing, rewarding, reassigning, promoting, demoting, and retaining or removing employees; (3) elimination of the requirement for the central personnel agency to give prior approval to agency appraisal plans, and extension to agencies of substantial latitude to design and operate performance appraisal systems; and (4) establishment of an altered procedure for demoting or removing employees for unacceptable performance.

Agencies will be required to take action, based on performance appraisals, to: (1) recognize employees whose performance significantly exceeds requirements; (2) help employees whose performance is unacceptable to improve; and (3) remove employees from their positions when their performance becomes unacceptable, after warning and an opportunity for improvement.

The new procedure for demoting or removing employees from the civil service because of unacceptable performance will provide the employee with at least 30 days written advance warning that his or her performance is not acceptable, permit the employee to be represented and to reply to the proposed action, and give the employee an opportunity to improve within a specified time period. As a safeguard against unwarranted actions, the new procedure will require a higher level official to concur if the decision is that performance has not been raised to acceptable performance during the notice period. The employee must then be demoted, reassigned, or separated within 30 days.

When no action is taken because the employee's performance improved during the notice period, and performance continues to be acceptable for one year from the date of the advance warning, the record of the unacceptable performance shall be removed from the employee's official personnel folder. This provision will ensure that when employees improve their performance to an acceptable level and maintain it at that level, they will be able to pursue their future careers with a clean slate.

Employees who are demoted or removed for unacceptable performance may appeal to the Merit Systems Protection Board. The standards under which a hearing is provided and the criteria against which the propriety of the action is tested are the same as those provided for adverse action cases in section 7701.

The new performance appraisal systems envisioned by this title will contribute to the goal of improving the quality of employee performance by establishing that certain personnel actions must be based on performance appraisals assigned under appraisal systems tailored to the workforce and mission of an agency. This will be to the direct benefit of the vast majority of Federal workers who do their jobs well and want to be judged on the basis of their performance. The increased emphasis on meaningful appraisals will impose additional responsibilities on managers, but it will also provide them with a more effective and equitable means of managing their employees.

## Delegation of Personnel Authorities

Section 1104 (p. 15) gives the Office of Personnel Management authority to delegate personnel management functions, including competitive examining, to heads of agencies.

Over the years, various statutes have placed sole authority in the Commission for conducting certain personnel operations or for approving specific agency personnel actions. These requirements often become the basis for delays in hiring, complex administrative procedures, excessive costs, and unnecessary paperwork. In view of other program authorities vested in agency heads, such restraints seem incongruous.

In order to permit agency managers to evaluate job candidates and to take other actions related to job placement or other aspects of the agency head's personnel management responsibilities, the Civil Service Reform Act would vest authority in the President to delegate to the Director of the Office of Personnel Management any and all personnel functions provided in title 5 of the United States Code. The Director in turn would be permitted to redelegate such functions to agency heads, without regard to restrictions, prohibitions, or approval requirements on delegations set forth elsewhere in title 5.

To protect against possible misuse of authority, delegations would be accomplished through performance agreements which set forth the expected standard of performance. Agency performance would be monitored and corrective action taken under periodic audits by the Office of Personnel Management. Agency managers would not have authority to abrogate merit principles. veterans preference, or other generally applicable provisions of law or Executive order. Any prohibited personnel practice violations could be investigated and officials found culpable of such violations could be prosecuted by the Special Counsel before the Merit Systems Protection Board.

As envisioned, the Office of Personnel Management would delegate examining and other personnel management authorities to agencies on an individual basis, in accordance with their abilities and resources. Delegations would be carried out through a written performance agreement between an agency and the Office of Personnel Management. The latter would specify required levels of agency performance; conditions for internal redelegation and

negotiability with employee organizations; reporting, review, and other oversight controls; and grounds for revocation, suspension, or modification of the authority. Over the next several years, the Office of Personnel Management will work with the individual departments and agencies to develop their capacity and willingness to accept responsibility for many of the operational activities now performed by the Civil Service Commission.

Increased delegation will accomplish two significant goals: (1) personnel program activities will be improved since they will be administered at the level where they are best understood and by the line managers most able to determine the specific requirements for their implementation, and (2) the Office of Personnel Management will then be able to devote its skills and resources to assisting the agencies in developing needed new programs and techniques and to refining its own ability to monitor and improve, on a Government-wide basis, the utilization of the Federal workforce.

Shifting the locus of personnel authority to the agency level will provide additional benefits. It will give agencies greater control over meeting their own staffing priorities, through all available means. In a short range and practical sense, it will lead to more timely filling of Federal vacancies. However, in future time it should focus agency responsibility for effective personnel management more cohesively. No longer should top agency managers view the total needs of their personnel management as being partly their concern and partly the responsibility of external sources.

### Title III—Staffing

This title provides increased flexibility in staffing and other personnel functions, modifies veterans preference provisions in examining and retention, establishes a new probationary period for initial appointments to supervisory or managerial positions, extends early retirement authority to reorganization situations, authorizes agencies to train employees threatened with separation due to a reduction in force for placement in another agency, and authorizes agencies to accept the service of unpaid student volunteers.

## Staffing Flexibility

Title II authorizes greater delegation of personnel authorities. Title III goes beyond this to provide additional flexibility in the staffing functions of Federal agencies in several ways. Section 3309(g) (p. 54) replaces the "rule of three" with a "rule of seven" for selections from lists of people qualified for employment. It also grants the Office of Personnel Management authority to establish other procedures for referring names to agency selection officials. These changes will permit agency managers to exercise a more reasonable range of judgment in filling jobs.

The statutory requirements for numerical ratings and the rule of three have had the effect of preventing the Federal competitive service from using the newer and more effective procedures for considering and selecting candidates that are in use today among Federal agencies with independent merit systems and some state and local governments. In administering Federal examinations, we are now required by law to make overly fine distinctions among applicants with virtually identical backgrounds. Personnel measuring devices are not sufficiently precise to insure that individuals with the three highest ratings are always the best qualified for a position. Others with slightly lower ratings might be as well qualified.

## Modifications in Veterans Preference in Examining, Selection, and Retention

H.R. 11280 modifies the presently unlimited lifetime preference for non-disabled veterans in examining, selection and retention. It provides veterans preference to those who need it most, and for the period when such assistance is most needed. In particular, it will strengthen the preference rights available to disabled and recent Vietnam Era Veterans.

The veterans preference provisions discussed in the following do not apply to the Senior Executive Service set forth in title IV of this Act. Veterans preference will not apply to that new Service.

## Veterans Preference in Examining and Appointment

Let me make clear at the outset that H.R. 11280 does not reduce the rights of disabled or other 10 point veterans. As I will explain later, there is actually an increase in their opportunities.

Veterans preference for the non-disabled was designed to give special treatment to veterans applying for Federal jobs, primarily to assist them in returning to civilian life and in catching up for that time spent in military service rather than in academic or civilian employment pursuits which enhance job prospects. With the exception of those with continued disability, veterans should, after a reasonable readjustment period, be able and be expected to compete on an equal basis with other job candidates.

After this readjustment period, however, the present lifetime preference for all veterans, regardless of need, imposes a severe hardship on well qualified candidates and denies the Government the opportunity to give equitable consideration to applicants with special skills who may be the best available candidates for particular positions.

Ironically, preference is now such common coin that it fails to give real advantage to those veterans who really need it. In the last few years many State civil service systems have also recognized the need to modernize veterans preference provisions and have enacted a variety of reforms, especially limitations on the number of times veterans may use their preference and time limits on the military service qualifying the veteran for preference.

As I indicated, title III will make no change in preference for disabled veterans or for spouses, widows, and mothers now entitled to preference. They will retain lifetime preference. Disabled veterans will still "float to the top" of certain registers in the manner now provided by law. In addition, to recognize further the special obligations of this Nation to the needs of disabled veterans, section 3112 (p. 50) creates a statutory authority for the noncompetitive appointment and conversion to career employment of disabled veterans who are 50 percent or more disabled or who take a Veterans Administration prescribed vocational training course.

For non-disabled veterans, section 3303a (p. 51) will generally limit preference to ten years after discharge from military service. A briefer, three year period is proposed for retired enlisted veterans and retired officers below major or equivalent. These time limitations recognize that readjustment to civilian life typically occurs during the early years following separation from military service. Thus, preference will still be granted during the period in which special employment assistance is most needed.

No preference will be granted to non-disabled officers retired at the rank of major, the equivalent, and above. This is appropriate because, with their extensive military experience and training, retired officers at these ranks who are not disabled are unlikely to need special help in securing employment.

In summary, these changes, which are to be effective on October 1, 1980, will focus special hiring assistance on disabled veterans, and will continue to provide preference to most Vietnam era veterans during the critical period when the veteran is adjusting to civilian life.

In addition to the noncompetitive appointment authority for certain disabled veterans, title III contains other changes that will preserve or strengthen the rights of veterans. First, under section 3305 (p. 52) the rights of veterans are increased in that all veterans will be permitted to reopen closed examinations for which there is a list at any time during their eligibility for preference. At present, the right of non-disabled veterans to reopen a closed examination is much more limited.

Second, section 309 (p. 60) will extend agency authority to make Veteran Readjustment Appointments for Vietnam Era Veterans without competitive examinations until September 30, 1980. Unless extended, this authority is due to expire June 30, 1978. In addition, assistance to Vietnam Era Veterans is increased by the repeal of the one year time limitation on eligibility for Veteran Readjustment Appointments, by raising the grade ceiling on these appointments from GS-5 to GS-7, and by removing the 14 years of education limit for disabled veterans.

### Veterans Preference in Reduction in Force

Under the current system for retention in reduction in force, all veterans enjoy absolute retention superiority over all nonveterans despite the fact that the nonveteran may have many more years of service or a record of outstanding performance. Section 305 (p. 56) changes would reduce the adverse impact on nonveterans and focus the advantage on those who most need it by providing lifetime absolute preference in retention for disabled veterans and absolute preference during the first three years of service for non-disabled veterans. It would grant five years of additional length of service credit for retention purposes to non-disabled veterans who are beyond the three-year employment period, thus preserving a relative advantage over nonveterans. Moreover, after three years of employment most veterans would have become career permanent employees and therefore advanced to the highest reduction in force retention group.

### Probationary Period for Supervisors and Managers

Section 3321 (p. 54) establishes a new probationary period for first appointment to a supervisory or managerial position. It provides entitlement to a position of no lower grade or pay than the position occupied prior to the supervisory or managerial assignment for new supervisors who do not successfully complete the probationary period.

Supervisory skill is difficult to predict and often bears no relation to the skills that employees may demonstrate in non-supervisory positions. Some competent individual performers do not in fact perform well in a supervisory role. This provision of title III recognizes that selection methods for supervisory or managerial positions are imperfect.

For new supervisors who do not work out but would be valuable non-supervisory employees, a trial period during which the newly selected supervisor could be removed from the supervisory position with a right to return to a non-supervisory position is a much needed management tool.

It will enable top Federal managers to select candidates for supervisory and managerial positions, so vital to agency effectiveness, without fear of "locking-in" someone who is better as an individual worker. The guaranteed right of return protects the rights of individuals and avoids the stigma of an adverse action.

### Other Changes

Section 308 (p. 59) expands coverage of early retirement eligibility in reduction in force situations to cover also major reorganizations and transfers of function, as determined by the Office of Personnel Management. Section 306 (p. 58) allows agencies under certain conditions to train employees, who are threatened with separation due to a reduction in force, for placement in another agency. Section 3111 (p. 47) authorizes agencies to use the volunteer services of students.

Currently, employees can take advantage of the early retirement provision only when the Civil Service Commission determines that the agency is facing a major reduction in force involving removals of employees. The proposed legislation would expand the coverage of the early retirement provision to situations involving reorganization or transfer of function (as approved by the Office of Personnel Management), which may or may not involve a reduction in force.

The present system of early-out retirements has significantly reduced the disruption faced by agencies in dealing with a reduction-in-force situation. The expanded provisions of this bill should be at least equally effective, facilitating more rapid adjustment of the workforce, benefiting employees who would otherwise face dislocation, and increasing the efficiency and economy of organizational transitions. In addition, they would lessen the adverse impact on employee morale and productivity when faced with potential job dislocation.

With regard to the training authorization, current laws do not permit the expenditure of agency funds to train employees for jobs outside the agency. We propose to allow employees who face separation because of reduction in force to be trained for jobs in other agencies. Thus, the Federal Government will be able to retain employees with proven ability and avoid the cost of severance pay, while minimizing the hardship to employees caused by curtailment, reorganization, or realignment of agency functions.

Section 3111 (p. 47) also authorizes Federal agencies, subject to regulations of the Office of Personnel Management, to accept the volunteer services of students who are enrolled at least half-time in a high school, college, graduate, or professional school. Because of a general statutory prohibition on the use of volunteer services, each agency must initiate a time-consuming process to obtain express statutory authorization in order to provide unpaid Federal work exposure for students. This provision will permit agencies to provide worthwhile educational work opportunities to student volunteers when this does not cause the displacement of Federal workers.

## Title IV—Senior Executive Service

The United States Government is the largest employer in the Nation. Its programs are far-reaching, complex, and widely varied. They must be conducted with sensitivity to conflicting interests and under constant public and media attention, for they affect every citizen. To meet this responsibility requires an executive workforce that is carefully chosen, well-trained, motivated, farsighted, able to respond to events, and to achieve Presidential and Congressional goals.

Nevertheless, no fully effective Government-wide system exists today for selecting, assigning, developing, advancing, rewarding, and managing the men and women who administer the hundreds of Federal programs that are vital to the Nation. The Senior Executive Service is designed to provide such a system. Further, it will achieve the following specific improvements: (1) provide better management of the number and distribution of executive personnel; (2) treat in a more realistic fashion the career–noncareer relationships at the executive levels; (3) offer increased advancement opportunities to career executives; (4) give agency managers greater flexibility in assigning executives where they are most needed; (5) ensure the management competence of those entering the Service; (6) make executives more accountable for their performance and remove those whose performance is not fully satisfactory; (7) simplify the multiplicity of laws and authorities which presently govern the executive levels; (8) establish more efficient procedures for staffing executive positions; (9) provide equitable compensation linked with performance; and (10) increase opportunities for minorities and women to enter the executive levels.

### Control of Number and Distribution of Executive Personnel

The number of supergrade and equivalent positions has grown substantially since 1949. However, comparatively little of this growth has occurred in the so-called "quota" spaces administered by the Civil Service Commission. Most of the increase has taken the form of substantive actions initiated by individual Congressional committees and in the uncontrolled "non-quota" positions. The mass of authorities governing executive positions is so complex that it has prevented both Congress and the President from exercising effective control over either the total number of individuals in the executive cadre or the distribution of executive personnel among agencies and programs. Also, it is too unwieldy to allow for rapid response to changes in agency programs. It is extremely difficult to staff new agencies or programs since special legislation is necessary to provide for any substantial number of executive positions.

Under the Senior Executive Service, individual agency executive personnel requirements as well as Government-wide total strength will be set by a zero-based determination of need, and Congress will be advised biennially of Office of Personnel Management decisions about the executive manpower level. Between reviews there will be provision for adjustments to take care of emergencies, new or expanded programs, and discontinuance of programs.

### Career–Noncareer Relationships at the Executive Levels

The existing system for designating career and noncareer positions falls short of assuring protection against politicization of the career service. Moreover, it is so rigid that it fails to provide agency heads sufficient legitimate flexibility to fill critically important positions with executives of their own choosing.

Managerial positions at the supergrade level are now classified as "career" or "noncareer" based on whether or not the incumbent will be deeply involved in the advocacy of controversial Administration programs, or will participate significantly in the determination of major Administration policies. The fact is, however, that executive positions do not array themselves neatly in these respects. In most cases, the responsibilities of executive positions do not fall at either end of the career/noncareer spectrum.

Under the Senior Executive Service, the designation of career and noncareer will be affixed to persons rather than to positions. Agency heads may fill a majority of positions with either career or noncareer executives. The total number of noncareer appointees Government-wide may not exceed 10 percent of the total Senior Executive Service—a figure reflecting the existing proportion of noncareer (political-type) positions at the higher grade levels. This statutorily-based ceiling of 10 percent on noncareer appointments will provide greater protection against politicization of the higher levels than presently exists under the present system that permits expansion of the noncareer total by administrative action. Very importantly, the Office of Personnel Management must reserve certain types of positions requiring absolute assurance of political impartiality, or the public's perception of political impartiality, for career executives. Such positions would include those in the Internal Revenue Service, investigative, and procurement organizations.

## Career Opportunities

The often artificial distinctions now drawn between career and noncareer positions limit opportunities for career employees to undertake positions of the highest responsibility, including Presidential appointments, without relinquishing their career identification. Under the present system, career employees who enter noncareer positions lose their career identity and then, when Administration leadership changes, leave the Government service at the same rate as noncareer executives who intended to serve only a short time. This represents not only a disincentive to career executives to assume positions of higher responsibility, but also a serious loss to the taxpayer of many experienced and talented Federal executives.

Career executives will be able to serve in the highest level positions in the Senior Executive Service without having to terminate their Federal careers, because they will retain their career status regardless of assignment. Moreover, career executives who accept a Presidential appointment requiring Senate confirmation will continue to be covered by the pay, award, retirement and leave provisions of the Senior Executive Service, and are entitled to placement back into the Service when they leave their Presidential appointments. Thus, trained and experienced career executives would not be lost to the Federal service; they would simply revert in assignment to a "general" or "career reserved" position.

## Assignment Flexibility

The vast majority of career executives have had both their mid-level managerial experience and executive service in the same agency. This deprives both the Government and the employee of the rich benefits in competence and understanding which accrue from experience gained in a variety of agencies and programs.

The current rank-in-position system of classifying jobs, combined with ill-defined yet appealable protections against reduction in rank (which would be abolished under title III), limits reassignment and transfer opportunities for career employees and prevents the best use of executive talent. Furthermore, it fails to give adequate recognition to the impact of the individual on the job. The complicated processes of qualification review and position classification which must take place between an agency and the Civil Service Commission are time-consuming, expensive, and frustrating to officials who are charged with getting a job done.

There will be a strong emphasis in the Senior Executive Service on development and mobility of executives within and among agencies. The Reform Bill gives the Office of Personnel Management a positive duty to encourage and assist career employees in moving among agencies. Fulfilling this responsibility will be eased by eliminating the procedural restraints referred to above and by removing the implication of "fault" in reassignment fostered by the present concept of rank in position.

Together, these features would give agency heads greater latitude to determine which positions are especially crucial to program accomplishment at a particular time and to fill these positions with executives who are best fitted to them, while the 10 percent limitation on noncareer appointees would prevent increases in the politically-oriented component of the Senior Executive Service.

## Managerial Competence

While most current incumbents of executive-level positions are highly capable, there are some who are not performing at an optimum level. One chronic problem is the appointment to managerial positions of highly capable professionals who are ill-prepared to take on their new responsibilities.

In the Senior Executive Service managerial qualifications of all career appointees must be approved by qualifications panels within the Office of Personnel Management composed of members from Government, the private sector, and the academic world. Once career employees have had their managerial qualifications approved by the Office of Personnel Management, relative qualifications for a particular position within the agency will be determined by the agency head. Agencies will be required to have systematic executive development programs to insure that talented employees in key positions below Senior Executive Service levels receive necessary preparation for managerial duties, and that the qualifications of Senior Executive Service members not only remain at a high level, but are further enhanced. Finally, career appointees to the Senior Executive Service will be required to serve a one-year probationary period.

### Accountability

At present, executive performance is rarely evaluated rigorously in terms of program accomplishment or meeting goals in such areas as efficiency, productivity, quality of work or service and cost control.

Executives who are clearly ineffective can be removed, although a considerable effort is normally required to do so. It is virtually impossible, however, to remove an executive whose performance is mediocre. Nor do existing provisions properly permit rewarding executives for outstanding performance.

Executives in the Senior Executive Service will be evaluated regularly and at least annually with special emphasis on the achievement of agreed-upon organizational goals. This will be accomplished by using an agency board to advise the agency head on the proper rating. Executives who consistently perform in a mediocre fashion, as well as those found to be severely deficient, must be removed from the Senior Executive Service.

Although executives will not be entitled to appeal removals on such grounds, they will have rights to regular discontinued service retirement (if they have at least 25 years of service or a combination of age 50 and 20 years of service) or placement in a career position outside the Senior Executive Service with salary savings. Thus, there is a balancing of the Government's need to assure that only top performers will occupy senior positions, while reasonably preserving the economic prospects of the executive who is willing to assume the tenure risks of the Senior Executive Service. These entitlements do not apply to an executive who is removed for misbehavior.

In addition, this title would provide that highly successful executives could receive substantial performance incentive pay. The coupling of required systematic evaluation of managerial performance with the ability to reward effective managers and to remove the incapable will pay high dividends in improved management of Federal programs.

### Multiplicity of Authorities and Laws

More than 60 separate personnel authorities governing different categories of executive positions now exist. Some of these authorities cover several thousand positions. Others cover as few as one. In some cases, these authorities establish self-contained, separate personnel systems (like the Foreign Service). In other cases, they merely exempt certain positions from some of the requirements or conditions of employment of the general personnel system by which executive positions are otherwise managed. Most of these special systems were created because circumstances at the time made it difficult for the agencies to manage their employees under the personnel system that applied generally.

In its coverage of most executive branch agencies and personnel systems, the Senior Executive Service eliminates most of these authorities and laws. Government corporations and intelligence community agencies are excluded and additional Presidential exceptions could be made. Any Presidentially-excepted system could be included later by Presidential action without additional legislation.

### More Efficient Procedures

The present system for establishing and filling executive positions is inefficient. The required justification and analyses are time-consuming for both the Commission and the requesting agency.

Under the Senior Executive Service, the agency would have its quota of executive positions established in advance for a two-year period. Needed adjustments within limits could be readily made. The Office of Personnel Management would no longer classify positions by grade or determine if they are career or noncareer. It would determine if career candidates for initial entry into the Senior Executive Service meet managerial qualifications; the agency head would be responsible for approving qualifications for a particular position and for noncareer appointees. (This applies only to initial Senior Executive Service entry.) For movement within the Service—now 55 percent of all staffing actions—the agency head would have complete approval authority. Moreover, in filling positions from within the Government, prior certification of eligibility for the Service by the Office of Personnel Management would be the rule. Thus, there would be very little case-by-case qualification approval activity in the Office of Personnel Management.

## Compensation

Under the Senior Executive Service, the President would establish at least five executive salary rates. All rates would be in the range between the sixth step of GS-15 and the salary of Executive Level IV. Longevity pay increases would be abolished and annual performance awards substituted instead. Under the proposal, highly able executives could substantially increase (up to 20 percent) their compensation for a particular year through performance awards not subject to the ceiling on salary. The performance awards could be given to no more than 50 percent of the executives in the Senior Executive Service. We estimate that the total cost of awards will average about 5–7 percent of executive payroll.

For the most effective career executive the President could confer a personal rank and incentive award. Up to 15 percent of active executives could be given the personal rank of "Meritorious Executive," which would carry an incentive award of $2,500 for each of five years. No more than 1 percent of active executives could have the rank of "Distinguished Executive," which would carry an incentive award of $5,000 for each of five years.

The sum total of all payments to an individual executive—salary and performance and incentive awards—cannot, in any one year, exceed 95 percent of the salary of Executive Level II. This would provide a current cap of $54,625. For each year in which an executive receives a bonus, his or her retirement annuity would be calculated at 2.5 percent instead of whatever lower percentage he or she would normally be entitled to. The granting of these financial incentives will be subject to guidance by the Office of Personnel Management in order to insure that the distribution of awards is based upon actual distinctions in performance. Any evidence of prohibited political preference is subject to investigation by the Special Counsel of the Merit Systems Protection Board.

## Minorities and Women and Executive Development

Roughly half the top career positions in the Federal Government are held by individuals who entered the Government at junior levels and who have spent their entire careers in the Federal service. Despite this pattern, efforts to establish Government-wide executive development programs have received little support. Many agencies still lack effective programs for preparing incumbent and potential executives to assume assignments of increasing responsibility and complexity. Such programs are especially needed for women and minorities, who, as a group, are seriously underrepresented in top management ranks. The regular career promotion process is not functioning adequately to bring women and minorities into key management positions.

The Senior Executive Service mandates an open, systematic executive development program with special emphasis on identifying minorities and women for development. It is only in this way that an enduring solution to this problem can be achieved.

### Title V—Merit Pay

Title V provides authority to establish a merit pay system for supervisors and managers in grades 13 through 15 of the General Schedule. While part of the annual comparability pay raises may be granted to these employees automatically, the remainder will be used to partly fund merit increases. Within-grade salary increases will be replaced by merit increases which will be awarded only in recognition of superior performance.

Unlike the Senior Executive Service where performance pay is granted only for one year at a time, merit pay increases are actual increases in the employee's base salary and will continue in subsequent years.

The merit pay program will not be installed simultaneously in all agencies and at all pay levels. A great deal of preparatory work must be done in designing agency systems, setting standards of performance, and training individuals in the use of the system. It is our belief that the need to set performance standards is one of the most salutary features of the proposal. For the first time in many cases, managers will be told what is expected of them. We estimate that the system will first be applied in not less than one year. Two to three additional years may be required to fully install it at grades GS-13 through GS-15. On the basis of experience at these levels we may wish to recommend expansion of coverage to other grade levels and perhaps eventually to some non-supervisory personnel.

Although title 5 of the United States Code now requires that "pay distinctions be maintained in keeping with work and performance distinctions," the current method of within-grade pay advancement within the rate range for senior managers and supervisors and the extensive appeals mechanism are not truly supportive of this requirement. Further, the only additional tool for accelerating basic pay within a rate range is through the quality step increase. However, the amount which may be granted is small (one step is equivalent to approximately 3 percent of pay) and restricted (no more than one quality step increase each 52 weeks) relative to similar increases granted to outstanding senior managers in the private sector. Therefore, the manner in which within-grade increase funds are currently expended provides virtually no flexibility to make significant pay distinctions among senior managers and supervisors. Barely acceptable performers now generally experience the same

progression through the pay range as do many exceptional performers.

The new merit pay system would remove the barriers to increased management discretion and reward quality job performance rather than time in grade. It would eliminate a virtually automatic entitlement to pay advancement within the rate range and provide that an employee's pay be advanced on the merits of his or her performance rather than on length of service.

The language of Title V grants broad flexibility in the design of each agency's merit pay plan. There are, however, certain principles which will be generally applied. First, in granting increases the agency may take into account both individual performance and organizational accomplishment. Section 5401 (p. 108) requires that salary determinations take into account factors such as improvements in efficiency, productivity and quality of work or service, cost savings, and timeliness of performance.

The amounts available for merit pay will be determined by the Office of Personnel Management. They will be set so as to equal those estimated amounts which are not being paid through regular step increases, quality step increases, and the annual comparability adjustment. For example, in 1977 perhaps 50 percent of the 7.05 percent comparability increase plus the 2 percent ordinarily used for step increases might have been used for merit pay. This would have created a pool of 5.5 percent for merit pay.

Office of Personnel Management regulations will also address the distribution of merit increases and set maximum levels. It is estimated that a ceiling of 12 percent will be placed on the increase any individual manager may receive in a given year. No employee's basic pay may exceed the top rate for the salary range as a result of a merit increase.

The net effect of these changes is that employees as a group will receive neither more nor less than they presently do, but those individuals performing in a superior fashion will receive higher salary increases.

## Title VI—Research, Demonstration, and Other Programs

This title authorizes the Office of Personnel Management to conduct public management research, and to carry out demonstration projects to test new approaches to personnel management. It also permits the Office to waive specific portions of personnel laws in order to engage in controlled experiments in personnel management. The number of employees who can be affected by such experimental projects will be limited and the views of organized employees will be taken into account before such experiments take place. In addition, title VI includes proposals for improving intergovernmental personnel programs.

### Public Management Research

The Government does not have an organized program of research to give it a factual basis for changes in personnel policies. Similarly, it lacks authority to conduct small-scale experiments on promising ideas. As a result, it is often necessary to make system-wide changes before ideas have been tested in practice.

Although Federal personnel management problems are growing in complexity, the Government invests little in civilian personnel research. In defense agencies, the Government has applied a rational approach to developing and buying major defense systems. Similar testing of new ideas occurs regularly in the physical and biological sciences. Comparable investment in research and experimentation in the management sciences has not been made. As a matter of fact, the Federal Government lacks a specific commitment to management research and a specific authority to support and conduct it.

Title VI would solve this problem by giving the Office of Personnel Management authority to support a public management research program which would be directly related to the management improvement needs of agencies. The Office could begin by making use of research completed or underway in State and local governments, the military services, the private sector, and universities. Beyond this, it

would provide the Office the flexibility needed either to conduct research or contract out research projects to Federal agencies, State and local governments, educational institutions, public interest organizations, and the private sector. Finally, the Office would assume a leadership role in identifying public management research needs, reviewing proposed research projects, coordinating research activities, assessing the value of completed research, and applying research results to the solution of agency problems.

A modest investment of resources toward basic and applied public management research should produce enormous benefits in the form of new approaches, theories, frames of reference, and processes which would make more efficient use of existing individual and organizational resources. Additionally, the research effort would encourage innovation in the design, development, and execution of systems of personnel administration which would improve management of the Government's human resources and thereby improve delivery of service to the public.

### Demonstration Projects

The maintenance of a dynamic personnel system requires the continual development and implementation of modern and progressive concepts, procedures, and work practices to facilitate improved employee performance and efficiency. What is needed is a mechanism to reduce the amount of risk involved by getting as many hard facts about the effect of proposed changes as possible. This proposed demonstration project authority would provide that mechanism.

By providing the Office of Personnel Management with the authority to conduct experimental demonstration projects, policymakers would be able to explore new concepts and approaches to particular aspects of personnel management at less cost and with less risk than whole-system changes would require. Equally important, it would enable the determination of the likely effects and ramifications of proposed policy changes before making commitments to put them into effect system-wide.

Pilot testing provides an opportunity to time-test new concepts, modify them, and as their feasibility is demonstrated, extend them a bit at a time throughout the Federal establishment. To be effective, test agencies need to be exempted during the testing period from a variety of legal constraints, delegations of authority normally retained by a central personnel authority, and variations from existing Federal hiring, retention, pay, discipline, and other authorities.

The research projects are intended to be responsive both to current operational problems and long-range needs. Efforts will be directed at producing results for immediate application and toward expanding the technical base for future applications.

The project plans would include evaluation requirements to measure the results of the experiments. Experiments which test out favorably could be, with appropriate legislation or executive authorization, permanently authorized for test agencies or extended to other agencies.

In summary, this demonstration project authority could solve some of the problems personnel directors face daily in such areas as personnel selection, career development, motivation, personnel retention, training methods, and organizational structures. New and different approaches can be tested and their merits evaluated. The best and most progressive work practices and techniques would be further developed, installed, and used for the most efficient conduct of the Government's business.

In the long run, the authority to conduct research and to carry out demonstration projects to test new concepts, methods, and procedures will provide employees greater protection against ill-conceived personnel system changes which could impact adversely on their well-being. At the same time, managers would not have foisted on them impractical personnel management concepts. The title includes a requirement to publish proposed projects in the Federal Register and to consult or negotiate with unions. This will provide a measure of protection to employees against demonstration projects which could adversely affect employees during or subsequent to the life of the project.

### Intergovernmental Personnel Program Improvements

Title VI also deals with Federal personnel requirements that are now conditions for State and local government participation in Federal grant programs. Currently, State and local governments are burdened by Federal personnel requirements that differ from Federal grant program to grant program, are applied unevenly, and are often inconsistent.

This title establishes a flexible yet uniform approach to Federal requirements by abolishing all statutory personnel requirements except those contained in the Intergovernmental Personnel Act, those prohibiting employment discrimination, and those in the Davis–Bacon and Hatch Acts. Federal agencies would be able to require State and local agencies to have personnel administration systems that meet the simplified and consistent personnel standards prescribed by the Office of Personnel Management.

Title VI improves the intergovernmental mobility program by extending eligibility to participate in mobility assignments to a wider range of Federal agencies and to organizations representing member State or local governments; associations of State or local public officials, and nonprofit organizations offering professional advisory, research, development, or related services to governments or universities concerned with public management. The title also corrects present inequities in the pay and benefits of mobility assignees.

## Conclusion

Our studies have made us realize that the subject of civil service reform touches on the interests of many types of groups and many individuals in American society. They include unions, civil rights organizations, women's groups, veterans' organizations, civil service reform groups, professional associations, public interest organizations, consumer's groups, associations of State and local governments, academicians, and leaders in business and industry. We believe that we heard from them all and know what they think about these subjects.

No single set of proposals could possibly satisfy so many diverse interests. Some groups will support these proposals, while others will oppose parts of the package. We think the proposals are balanced and fair to all of these interests.

But most important, these proposals, taken with the other reform measures we plan and the additional pieces of legislation being developed, will put the Federal civil service back on the road toward better service to the public. I believe it is without question that a soundly structured personnel system, providing for effective management of a carefully selected, well trained, motivated, and fairly treated workforce, is essential to good Government. The net result of the proposals we are here to discuss today will be to achieve these ends, to the benefit of all the people of this Nation.

Mr. Chairman, that concludes my formal statement. I will be glad to answer any questions the Committee might have.

# 10

## U.S. Supreme Court
## *Branti* v. *Finkel*
## (Decided
## March 31, 1980)

STEVENS, J., delivered the opinion for the Court, in which BURGER, C. J., and BRENNAN, WHITE, MARSHALL, and BLACKMUN, JJ., joined. STEWART, J., filed a dissenting opinion, *post*, p. 520. POWELL, J., filed a dissenting opinion, in which REHNQUIST, J., joined and in Part I of which STEWART, J., joined, *post*, p. 521.

*Marc L. Parris* argued the cause for petitioner. With him on the briefs was *Charles Apotheker.*

*David MacRae Wagner* argued the cause and filed a brief for respondents.

MR. JUSTICE STEVENS delivered the opinion of the Court.

The question presented is whether the First and Fourteenth Amendments to the Constitution protect an assistant public defender who is satisfactorily performing his job from discharge solely because of his political beliefs.

Respondents, Aaron Finkel and Alan Tabakman, commenced this action in the United States District Court for the Southern District of New York in order to preserve their positions as assistant public defenders in Rockland County, New York.[1] On January 4, 1978, on the basis of a showing that the petitioner public defender was about to discharge them solely because they were Republicans, the District Court entered a temporary restraining order preserving the status quo. After hearing evidence for eight days, the District Court entered detailed findings of fact and permanently enjoined[2] petitioner from terminating or attempting to terminate respondents' employment "upon the sole grounds of their political beliefs."[3] 457 F. Supp. 1284, 1285 (1978). The Court of Appeals affirmed in an unpublished memorandum opinion, judgment order reported at 598 F. 2d 609 (CA2 1979) (table).

The critical facts can be summarized briefly. The Rockland County Public Defender is appointed by the County Legislature for a term of six years. He in turn appoints nine assistants who serve at his pleasure. The two respondents have served as assistants since their respective appointments in March 1971 and September 1975; they are both Republicans.[4]

Petitioner Branti's predecessor, a Republican, was appointed in 1972 by a Republican-dominated County Legislature. By 1977, control of the legislature had shifted to the Democrats and petitioner, also a Democrat, was appointed to replace the incumbent when his term expired. As soon as petitioner was formally appointed on January 3, 1978, he began executing termination notices for six of the nine assistants then in office. Respondents were among those who were to be terminated. With one possible exception, the nine who were to be appointed or retained were all Democrats and were all selected by Democratic legislators or Democratic town chairmen on a basis that had been determined by the Democratic caucus.[5]

The District Court found that Finkel and Tabakman had been selected for termination solely because they were Republicans and thus did not have the necessary Democratic sponsors:

> The sole grounds for the attempted removal of plaintiffs were the facts that plaintiffs' political beliefs differed from those of the ruling Democratic majority in the County Legislature and that the Democratic majority had determined that Assistant Public Defender appointments were to be made on political bases. [457 F. Supp., at 1293.]

The court rejected petitioner's belated attempt to justify the dismissals on nonpolitical grounds. Noting that both Branti and his predecessor had described respondents as "competent attorneys," the District Court expressly found that both had been "satisfactorily performing their duties as Assistant Public Defenders." *Id.*, at 1292.

Having concluded that respondents had been discharged solely because of their political beliefs, the District Court held that those discharges would be permissible under this Court's decision in *Elrod* v. *Burns*, 427 U. S. 347, only if assistant public defenders are the type of policymaking, confidential employees who may be discharged solely on the basis of their political affiliations. The court concluded that respondents clearly did not fall within that category. Although recognizing that they had broad responsibilities with respect to particular cases that were assigned to them, the court found that respondents had "very limited, if any, responsibility" with respect to the overall operation of the public defender's office. They did not "act as advisors or formulate plans for the implementation of the broad goals of the office" and, although they made decisions in the context of specific cases, "they do not make decisions about the orientation and operation of the office in which they work." 457 F. Supp., at 1291.

The District Court also rejected the argument that the confidential character of respondents' work justified conditioning their employment on political grounds. The court found that they did not occupy any confidential relationship to the policymaking process, and did not have access to confidential documents that influenced policymaking deliberations. Rather, the only confidential information to which they had access was the product of their attorney–client relationship with the office's clients; to the extent that such information was shared with the public defender, it did not relate to the formulation of office policy.

In light of these factual findings, the District Court concluded that petitioner could not terminate respondents' employment as assistant public defenders consistent with the First and Fourteenth Amendments. On appeal, a panel of the Second Circuit affirmed, specifically holding that the District Court's findings of fact were adequately supported by the record. That court also expressed "no doubt" that the District

Court "was correct in concluding that an assistant public defender was neither a policymaker nor a confidential employee." We granted certiorari, 443 U. S. 904, and now affirm.

Petitioner advances two principal arguments for reversal:[6] First, that the holding in *Elrod* v. *Burns* is limited to situations in which government employees are coerced into pledging allegiance to a political party that they would not voluntarily support and does not apply to a simple requirement that an employee be sponsored by the party in power; and, second, that, even if party sponsorship is an unconstitutional condition of continued public employment for clerks, deputies, and janitors, it is an acceptable requirement for an assistant public defender.

# I

In *Elrod* v. *Burns* the Court held that the newly elected Democratic Sheriff of Cook County, Ill., had violated the constitutional rights of certain non-civil-service employees by discharging them "because they did not support and were not members of the Democratic Party and had failed to obtain the sponsorship of one of its leaders." 427 U. S., at 351. That holding was supported by two separate opinions.

Writing for the plurality, MR. JUSTICE BRENNAN identified two separate but interrelated reasons supporting the conclusion that the discharges were prohibited by the First and Fourteenth Amendments. First, he analyzed the impact of a political patronage system[7] on freedom of belief and association. Noting that in order to retain their jobs, the Sheriff's employees were required to pledge their allegiance to the Democratic Party, work for or contribute to the party's candidates, or obtain a Democratic sponsor, he concluded that the inevitable tendency of such a system was to coerce employees into compromising their true beliefs.[8] That conclusion, in his opinion, brought the practice within the rule of cases like *Board of Education* v. *Barnette*, 319 U. S. 624, condemning the use of governmental power to prescribe what the citizenry must accept as orthodox opinion.[9]

Second, apart from the potential impact of patronage dismissals on the formation and expression of opinion, MR. JUSTICE BRENNAN also stated that the practice had the effect of imposing an unconstitutional condition on the receipt of a public benefit and therefore came within the rule of cases like *Perry* v. *Sindermann*, 408 U. S. 593. In support of the holding in *Perry* that even an employee with no contractual right to retain his job cannot be dismissed for engaging in constitutionally protected speech, the Court had stated:

> For at least a quarter-century, this Court has made clear that even though a person has no "right" to a valuable governmental benefit and even though the government may deny him the benefit for any number of reasons, there are some reasons upon which the government may not rely. It may not deny a benefit to a person on a basis that infringes his constitutionally protected interests— especially, his interest in freedom of speech. For if the government could deny a benefit to a person because of his constitutionally protected speech or associations, his exercise of those freedoms would in effect be penalized and inhibited. This would allow the government to "produce a result which [it] could not command directly." *Speiser* v. *Randall*, [357 U. S. 513, 526]. Such interference with constitutional rights is impermissible.

\*   \*   \*   \*   \*

Thus, the respondent's lack of a contractual or tenure 'right' to re-employment for the 1969–1970 academic year is immaterial to his free speech claim. Indeed, twice before, this Court has specifically held that the nonrenewal of a nontenured public school teacher's one-year contract may not be predicated on his exercise of First and Fourteenth Amendment rights. *Shelton* v. *Tucker*, [364 U. S. 479]; *Keyishian* v. *Board of Regents,* [385 U. S. 589]. We reaffirm those holdings here. *Id.*, at 597–598.

If the First Amendment protects a public employee from discharge based on what he has said, it must also protect him from discharge based on what he believes.[10] Under this line of analysis, unless the government can demonstrate "an overriding interest," 427 U. S., at 368, "of vital importance," *id.*, at 362, requiring that a person's private beliefs conform to those of the hiring authority, his beliefs cannot be the sole basis for depriving him of continued public employment.

MR. JUSTICE STEWART'S opinion concurring in the judgment avoided comment on the first branch of MR. JUSTICE BRENNAN'S analysis, but expressly relied on the same passage from *Perry* v. *Sindermann* that is quoted above.

Petitioner argues that *Elrod* v. *Burns* should be read to prohibit only dismissals resulting from an employee's failure to capitulate to political coercion. Thus, he argues that, so long as an employee is not asked to change his political affiliation or to contribute to or work for the party's candidates, he may be dismissed with impunity—even though he would not have been dismissed if he had had the proper political sponsorship and even though the sole reason for dismissing him was to replace him with a person who did have such sponsorship. Such an interpretation would surely emasculate the principles set forth in *Elrod*. While it would perhaps eliminate the more blatant forms of coercion described in *Elrod,* it would not eliminate the coercion of belief that necessarily flows from the knowledge that one must have a sponsor in the dominant party in order to retain one's job.[11] More importantly, petitioner's interpretation would require the Court to repudiate entirely the conclusion of both MR. JUSTICE BRENNAN and MR. JUSTICE STEWART that the First Amendment prohibits the dismissal of a public employee solely because of his private political beliefs.

In sum, there is no requirement that dismissed employees prove that they, or other employees, have been coerced into changing, either actually or ostensibly, their political allegiance. To prevail in this type of an action, it was sufficient, as *Elrod* holds, for respondents to prove that they were discharged "solely for the reason that they were not affiliated with or sponsored by the Democratic Party." 427 U. S., at 350.

# II

Both opinions in *Elrod* recognize that party affiliation may be an acceptable requirement for some types of government employment. Thus, if an employee's private political beliefs would interfere with the discharge of his public duties, his First Amendment rights may be required to yield to the State's vital interest in maintaining governmental effectiveness and efficiency. *Id.,* at 366. In *Elrod,* it was clear that the duties of the employees—the chief deputy of the process division of the sheriff's office, a process server and another employee in that office, and a bailiff and security guard at the Juvenile Court of Cook County—were not of that character, for they were, as MR. JUSTICE STEWART stated, "non-policymaking, nonconfidential" employees. *Id.,* at 375.[12]

As MR. JUSTICE BRENNAN noted in *Elrod,* it is not always easy to determine whether a position is one in which political affiliation is a legitimate factor to be considered. *Id.,* at 367. Under some circumstances, a position may be appropriately considered political even though it is neither confidential nor policymaking in character. As one obvious example, if a State's election laws require that precincts be supervised by two election judges of different parties, a Republican judge could be legitimately discharged solely for changing his party registration. That conclusion would not depend on any finding that the job involved participation in policy decisions or access to confidential information. Rather, it would simply rest on the fact that party membership was essential to the discharge of the employee's governmental responsibilities.

It is equally clear that party affiliation is not necessarily relevant to every policymaking or confidential position. The coach of a state university's football team formulates policy, but no one could seriously claim that Republicans make better coaches than Democrats, or vice versa, no matter which party is in control of the state government. On the other hand, it is equally clear that the Governor of a State may appropriately believe that the official duties of various assistants who help him write speeches, explain his views to the press, or communicate with the legislature cannot be performed effectively unless those persons share his political beliefs and party commitments. In sum, the ultimate inquiry is not whether the label "policymaker" or "confidential" fits a particular position; rather, the question is whether the hiring authority can demonstrate that party affiliation is an appropriate requirement for the effective performance of the public office involved.

Having thus framed the issue, it is manifest that the continued employment of an assistant public defender cannot properly be conditioned upon his allegiance to the political party in control of the county government. The primary, if not the only, responsibility of an assistant public defender is to represent individual citizens in controversy with the State.[13] As we recently observed in commenting on the duties of counsel appointed to represent indigent defendants in federal criminal proceedings:

> [T]he primary office performed by appointed counsel parallels the office of privately retained counsel. Although it is true that appointed counsel serves pursuant to statutory authorization and in furtherance of the federal interest in insuring effective representation of criminal defendants, his duty is not to the public at large, except in that general way. His principal responsibility is to serve the undivided interests of his client. Indeed, an indispensable element of the effective performance of his responsibilities is the ability to act independently of the government and to oppose it in adversary litigation. *Ferri* v. *Ackerman,* [444 U. S. 193, 204].

Thus, whatever policymaking occurs in the public defender's office must relate to the needs of individual clients and not to any partisan political interests. Similarly, although an assistant is bound to obtain access to confidential information arising out of various attorney–client relationships, that information has no bearing whatsoever on partisan political concerns. Under these circumstances, it would undermine, rather than promote, the effective performance of an assistant public defender's office to make his tenure dependent on his allegiance to the dominant political party.[14]

Accordingly, the entry of an injunction against termination of respondents' employment on purely political grounds was appropriate and the judgment of the Court of Appeals is
*Affirmed.*

MR. JUSTICE STEWART, dissenting.

I joined the judgment of the Court in *Elrod* v. *Burns,* 427 U. S. 347, because it is my view that, under the First and Fourteenth Amendments, "a nonpolicymaking, nonconfidential government employee can[not] be discharged . . . from a job that he is satisfactorily performing upon the sole ground of his political beliefs." *Id.,* at 375. That judgment in my opinion does not control the present case for the simple reason that the respondents here clearly are not "nonconfidential" employees.

The respondents in the present case are lawyers, and the employment positions involved are those of assistants in the office of the Rockland County Public Defender. The analogy to a firm of lawyers in the private sector is a close one, and I can think of few occupational relationships more instinct with the necessity of mutual confidence and trust than that kind of professional association.

I believe that the petitioner, upon his appointment as Public Defender, was not constitutionally compelled to enter such a close professional and necessarily confidential association with the respondents if he did not wish to do so.[15]

MR. JUSTICE POWELL, with whom MR. JUSTICE REHNQUIST joins, and with whom MR. JUSTICE STEWART joins as to Part I, dissenting.

The Court today continues the evisceration of patronage practices begun in *Elrod* v. *Burns,*

427 U. S. 347 (1976). With scarcely a glance at almost 200 years of American political tradition, the Court further limits the relevance of political affiliation to the selection and retention of public employees. Many public positions previously filled on the basis of membership in national political parties now must be staffed in accordance with a constitutionalized civil service standard that will affect the employment practices of federal, state, and local governments. Governmental hiring practices long thought to be a matter of legislative and executive discretion now will be subjected to judicial oversight. Today's decision is an exercise of judicial lawmaking that, as THE CHIEF JUSTICE wrote in his *Elrod* dissent, "represents a significant intrusion into the area of legislative and policy concerns." *Id.,* at 375. I dissent.

# I

The Court contends that its holding is compelled by the First Amendment. In reaching this conclusion, the Court largely ignores the substantial governmental interests served by patronage. Patronage is a long-accepted practice[16] that never has been eliminated totally by civil service laws and regulations. The flaw in the Court's opinion lies not only in its application of First Amendment principles, see Parts II–IV, *infra,* but also in its promulgation of a new, and substantially expanded, standard for determining which governmental employees may be retained or dismissed on the basis of political affiliation.[17]

In *Elrod* v. *Burns,* three Members of the Court joined a plurality opinion concluding that nonpolicymaking employees could not be dismissed on the basis of political affiliation. 427 U. S., at 367 (opinion of BRENNAN, J., with whom WHITE and MARSHALL, JJ., joined). Two Members of the Court joined an opinion concurring in the judgment and stating that nonpolicymaking, nonconfidential employees could not be so dismissed. *Id.,* at 375 (opinion of STEWART, J., with whom BLACKMUN, J., joined). Notwithstanding its purported reliance upon the holding of *Elrod, ante,* at 512, n. 6, the Court today ignores the limitations inherent in both views. The Court rejects the limited role for patronage recognized in the plurality opinion by holding that not all policymakers may be dismissed because of political affiliation. *Ante,* at 518–520. And the Court refuses to allow confidential employees to be dismissed for partisan reasons. *Ante,* at 520, n. 14; see *ante,* p. 520 (STEWART, J., dissenting). The broad, new standard is articulated as follows:

> [T]he ultimate inquiry is not whether the label "policymaker" or "confidential" fits a particular position; rather, the question is whether the hiring authority can demonstrate that party affiliation is an appropriate requirement for the effective performance of the public office involved. *Ante,* at 518.

The Court gives three examples to illustrate the standard. Election judges and certain executive assistants may be chosen on the basis of political affiliation; college football coaches may not. *Ibid.*[18] And the Court decides in this case that party affiliation is not an appropriate requirement for selection of the attorneys in a public defender's office because "whatever policymaking occurs in the public defender's office must relate to the needs of individual clients and not to any partisan political interests." *Ante,* at 519.

The standard articulated by the Court is framed in vague and sweeping language certain to create vast uncertainty. Elected and appointed officials at all levels who now receive guidance from civil service laws, no longer will know when political affiliation is an appropriate consideration in filling a position. Legislative bodies will not be certain whether they have the final authority to make the delicate line-drawing decisions embodied in the civil service laws. Prudent individuals requested to accept a public appointment must consider whether their predecessors will threaten to oust them through legal action.

One example at the national level illustrates the nature and magnitude of the problem created by today's holding. The President customarily has considered political affiliation in removing and appointing United States attorneys. Given the critical role that these key law enforcement officials play in the administration of the Department of Justice, both Democratic and Republican Attorneys General have concluded, not surprisingly, that they must have the confidence and support of the United States attorneys. And political affiliation has been used as one indicator of loyalty.[19]

Yet, it would be difficult to say, under the Court's standard, that "partisan" concerns properly are relevant to the performance of the duties of a United States attorney. This Court has noted that " '[t]he office of public prosecutor is one which must be administered with courage and independence.' " *Imbler* v. *Pachtman,* 424 U. S. 409, 423 (1976), quoting *Pearson* v. *Reed,* 6 Cal. App. 2d 277, 287, 44 P. 2d 592, 597 (1935). Nevertheless, I believe that the President must have the right to consider political affiliation when he selects top ranking Department of Justice officials. The President and his Attorney General, not this Court, are charged with the responsibility for enforcing the laws and administering the Department of Justice. The Court's vague, overbroad decision may cast serious doubt on the propriety of dismissing United States attorneys, as well as thousands of other policymaking employees at all levels of government, because of their membership in a national political party.[20]

A constitutional standard that is both uncertain in its application and impervious to legislative change will now control selection and removal of key governmental personnel. Federal judges will now be the final arbiters as to who federal, state, and local governments may employ. In my view, the Court is not justified in removing decisions so essential to responsible and efficient governance from the discretion of legislative and executive officials.

## II

The Court errs not only in its selection of a standard, but more fundamentally in its conclusion that the First Amendment prohibits the use of membership in a national political party as a criterion for the dismissal of public employees.[21] In reaching this conclusion, the Court makes new law from inapplicable precedents. The Court suggests that its decision is mandated by the principle that governmental action may not "prescribe what shall be orthodox in politics, nationalism, religion, or other matters of opinion. . . ." *Board of Education* v. *Barnette*, 319 U. S. 624, 642 (1943). The Court also relies upon the decisions in *Perry* v. *Sindermann*, 408 U. S. 593 (1972), and *Keyishian* v. *Board of Regents*, 385 U. S. 589 (1967). *Ante*, at 514–515; see *Elrod* v. *Burns*, 427 U. S., at 358–359 (opinion of BRENNAN, J.). But the propriety of patronage was neither questioned nor addressed in those cases.

Both *Keyishian* and *Perry* involved faculty members who were dismissed from state educational institutions because of their political views.[22] In *Keyishian,* the Court reviewed a state statute that permitted dismissals of faculty members from state institutions for "treasonable or seditious" utterances or acts. The Court noted that academic freedom is "a special concern of the First Amendment, which does not tolerate laws that cast a pall of orthodoxy over the classroom." 385 U. S., at 603. Because of the ambiguity in the statutory language, the Court held that the law was unconstitutionally vague. The Court also held that membership in the Communist Party could not automatically disqualify a person from holding a faculty position in a state university. *Id.*, at 606. In *Perry,* the Court held that the Board of Regents of a state university system could not discharge a professor in retaliation for his exercise of free speech. 408 U. S., at 598. In neither case did the State suggest that the governmental positions traditionally had been regarded as patronage positions. Thus, the Court correctly held that no substantial state interest justified the infringement of free speech. This case presents a question quite different from that in *Keyishian* and *Perry.*

The constitutionality of appointing or dismissing public employees on the basis of political affiliation depends upon the governmental interests served by patronage. No constitutional violation exists if patronage practices further sufficiently important interests to justify tangential burdening of First Amendment rights. See *Buckley* v. *Valeo*, 424 U. S. 1, 25 (1976). This inquiry cannot be resolved by reference to First Amendment cases in which patronage was neither involved nor discussed. Nor can the question in this case be answered in a principled manner without identifying and weighing the governmental interest served by patronage.

# III

Patronage appointments help build stable political parties by offering rewards to persons who assume the tasks necessary to the continued functioning of political organizations. "As all parties are concerned with power they naturally operate by placing members and supporters into positions of power. Thus there is nothing derogatory in saying that a primary function of parties is patronage." J. Jupp, Political Parties 25–26 (1968). The benefits of patronage to a political organization do not derive merely from filling policymaking positions on the basis of political affiliation. Many, if not most, of the jobs filled by patronage at the local level may not involve policymaking functions.[23] The use of patronage to fill such positions builds party loyalty and avoids "splintered parties and unrestrained factionalism [that might] do significant damage to the fabric of government." *Storer* v. *Brown*, 415 U. S. 724, 736 (1974).

Until today, I would have believed that the importance of political parties was self-evident. Political parties, dependent in many ways upon patronage, serve a variety of substantial governmental interests. A party organization allows political candidates to muster donations of time and money necessary to capture the attention of the electorate. Particularly in a time of growing reliance upon expensive television advertisements, a candidate who is neither independently wealthy nor capable of attracting substantial contributions must rely upon party workers to bring his message to the voters.[24] In contests for less visible offices, a candidate may have no efficient method of appealing to the voters unless he enlists the efforts of persons who seek reward through the patronage system. Insofar as the Court's decision today limits the ability of candidates to present their views to the electorate, our democratic process surely is weakened.[25]

Strong political parties also aid effective governance after election campaigns end. Elected officials depend upon appointees who hold similar views to carry out their policies and administer their programs. Patronage—the right to select key personnel and to reward the party "faithful"—serves the public interest by facilitating the implementation of policies endorsed by the electorate.[26] The Court's opinion casts a shadow over this time-honored element of our system. It appears to recognize that the implementation of policy is a legitimate goal of the patronage system and that some, but not all, policymaking employees may be replaced on the basis of their political affiliation. *Ante,* at 518.[27] But the Court does not recognize that the implementation of policy often depends upon the cooperation of public employees who do not hold policymaking posts. As one commentator has written: "What the Court forgets is that, if government is to work, policy implementation is just as important as policymaking. No matter how wise the chief, he has to have the right Indians to transform his ideas into action, to get the job done."[28] The growth of the civil service system already has limited the ability of elected politicians to effect political change. Public employees immune to public pressure "can resist changes in policy without suffering either the loss of their jobs or a cut in their salary."[29] Such effects are proper when they follow from legislative or executive decisions to withhold some jobs from the patronage system. But the Court tips the balance between patronage and nonpatronage positions, and, in my view, imposes unnecessary constraints upon the ability of responsible officials to govern effectively and to carry out new policies.

Although the Executive and Legislative Branches of Government are independent as a matter of constitutional law, effective government is impossible unless the two Branches cooperate to make and enforce laws. Over the decades of our national history, political parties have furthered—if not assured—a measure of cooperation between the Executive and Legislative Branches. A strong party allows an elected executive to implement his programs and policies by working with legislators of the same political organization. But legislators who owe little to their party tend to act independently of its leadership. The result is a dispersion of political influence that may inhibit a political party from enacting its programs into law.[30] The failure to sustain party discipline, at least at the national level, has been traced to the inability of successful political parties to offer patronage positions to their members or to the supporters of elected officials.[31]

The breakdown of party discipline that handicaps elected officials also limits the ability of the electorate to choose wisely among candidates. Voters with little information about individuals seeking office traditionally have relied upon party affiliation as a guide to choosing among candidates. With the decline in party stability, voters are less able to blame or credit a party for the performance of its elected officials. Our national party system is predicated upon the assumption that political parties sponsor, and are responsible for, the performance of the persons they nominate for office.[32]

In sum, the effect of the Court's decision will be to decrease the accountability and denigrate the role of our national political parties. This decision comes at a time when an increasing number of observers question whether our national political parties can continue to operate effectively.[33] Broad-based political parties supply an essential coherence and flexibility to the American political scene. They serve as coalitions of different interests that combine to seek national goals. The decline of party strength inevitably will enhance the influence of special interest groups whose only concern all too often is how a political candidate votes on a single issue. The quality of political debate, and indeed the capacity of government to function in the national interest, suffer when candidates and officeholders are forced to be more responsive to the narrow concerns of unrepresentative special interest groups than to overarching issues of domestic and foreign policy. The Court ignores the substantial governmental interests served by reasonable patronage. In my view, its decision will seriously hamper the functioning of stable political parties.

## IV

The facts of this case also demonstrate that the Court's decision well may impair the right of local voters to structure their government. Consideration of the form of local government in Rockland County, N. Y., demonstrates the antidemocratic effect of the Court's decision.

The voters of the county elect a legislative body. Among the responsibilities that the voters give to the legislature is the selection of a county public defender. In 1972, when the county voters elected a Republican majority in the legislature, a Republican was selected as Public Defender. The Public Defender retained one respondent and appointed the other as Assistant Public Defenders. Not surprisingly, both respondents are Republicans. In 1976, the voters elected a majority of Democrats to the legislature. The Democratic majority, in turn, selected a Democratic Public Defender who replaced both respondents with Assistant Public Defenders approved by the Democratic legislators. *Ante,* at 509–510, and n. 5.

The voters of Rockland County are free to elect their public defender and assistant public defenders instead of delegating their selection to elected and appointed officials.[34] Certainly the Court's holding today would not preclude the voters, the ultimate "hiring authority," from choosing both public defenders and their assistants by party membership. The voters' choice of public officials on the basis of political affiliation is not yet viewed as an inhibition of

speech; it is democracy. Nor may any incumbent contend seriously that the voters' decision not to re-elect him because of his political views is an impermissible infringement upon his right of free speech or affiliation. In other words, the operation of democratic government depends upon the selection of elected officials on precisely the basis rejected by the Court today.

Although the voters of Rockland County could have elected both the public defender and his assistants, they have given their legislators a representative proxy to appoint the public defender. And they have delegated to the public defender the power to choose his assistants. Presumably the voters have adopted this course in order to facilitate more effective representative government. Of course, the voters could have instituted a civil service system that would preclude the selection of either the public defender or his assistants on the basis of political affiliation. But the continuation of the present system reflects the electorate's decision to select certain public employees on the basis of political affiliation.

The Court's decision today thus limits the ability of the voters of a county to structure their democratic government in the way that they please. Now those voters must elect both the public defender and his assistants if they are to fill governmental positions on a partisan basis.[35] Because voters certainly may elect governmental officials on the basis of party ties, it is difficult to perceive a constitutional reason for prohibiting them from delegating that same authority to legislators and appointed officials.

## V

The benefits of political patronage and the freedom of voters to structure their representative government are substantial governmental interests that justify the selection of the assistant public defenders of Rockland County on the basis of political affiliation. The decision to place certain governmental positions within a civil service system is a sensitive political judgment that should be left to the voters and to elected representatives of the people. But the Court's constitutional holding today displaces political responsibility with judicial fiat. In my view, the First Amendment does not incorporate a national civil service system. I would reverse the judgment of the Court of Appeals.

# Notes

1. Jurisdiction was based on 42 U.S.C. § 1983 and 28 U. S. C. § 1343 (3).

2. Pursuant to Rule 65 (a) (2) of the Federal Rules of Civil Procedure, the plenary trial was consolidated with the hearing on the application for a preliminary injunction.

3. The District Court explained that its ruling required petitioner to retain respondents in their prior positions, with full privileges as employees:

"[C]ompliance with the judgment to be entered herein will require defendant both to permit plaintiffs to work as Assistants and to pay them the normal Assistant's salary. Mere payment of plaintiffs' salary will not constitute full compliance with the judgment entered herein; for plaintiffs' constitutional right, which is upheld herein, is the right not to be dismissed from public employment upon the sole ground of their political beliefs. Defendant cannot infringe that right of plaintiffs with impunity by the mere expedient of paying plaintiffs a sum of money." 457 F. Supp. 1284, 1285–1286, n. 4 (1978).

4. The District Court noted that Finkel had changed his party registration from Republican to Democrat in 1977 in the apparent hope that such action would enhance his chances of being reappointed as an assistant when a new, Democratic public defender was appointed. The court concluded that, despite Finkel's formal change of party registration, the parties had regarded him as a Republican at all relevant times. *Id.*, at 1285, n. 2.

5. "An examination of the selection process that was employed in arriving at the name of each of the nine 1978 appointees shows that the hiring decisions were, for all practical purposes, made by Democratic legislators or chairpersons in accordance with the procedures that had been decided upon by the Democratic caucus, and, with respect to every selection save that of Sanchez, those procedures excluded from consideration candidates who were affiliated with a party other than the Democratic Party. Moreover, the evidence shows that the only reason for which Branti sought to terminate plaintiffs as Assistants was that they were not recommended or sponsored pursuant to the procedures that had been decided upon by the Democratic caucus." *Id.*, at 1288.

6. Petitioner also makes two other arguments. First, he contends that the action should have been dismissed because the evidence showed that he would have discharged respondents in any event due to their lack of competence as public defenders. See *Mt. Healthy City Board of Ed.* v. *Doyle,* 429 U. S. 274. The Court of Appeals correctly held this contention foreclosed by the District Court's findings of fact, which it found to be adequately supported by the record. In view of our settled practice of accepting, absent the most exceptional circumstances, factual determinations in which the district court and the court of appeals have concurred, we decline to review these and other findings of fact petitioner argues were clearly erroneous. See *Graver Mfg. Co.* v. *Linde Co.,* 336 U. S. 271, 275; *United States* v. *Ceccolini,* 435 U. S. 268, 273.

Second, relying on testimony that an assistant's term in office automatically expires when the public defender's term expires, petitioner argues that we should treat this case as involving a "failure to reappoint" rather than a dismissal and, as a result, should apply a less stringent standard. Petitioner argues that because respondents knew the system was a patronage system when they were hired, they did not have a reasonable expectation of being rehired when control of the office shifted to the Democratic Party. A similar waiver argument was rejected in *Elrod* v. *Burns,* 427 U. S. 347, 360, n. 13; see also *id.,* at 380 (POWELL, J., dissenting). After *Elrod,* it is clear that the lack of a reasonable expectation of continued employment is not sufficient to justify a dismissal based solely on an employee's private political beliefs.

Unlike MR. JUSTICE POWELL in dissent, *post,* at 526–532, petitioner does not ask us to reconsider the holding in *Elrod.*

7. MR. JUSTICE BRENNAN noted that many other practices are included within the definition of a patronage system, including placing supporters in government jobs not made available by political discharges, granting supporters lucrative government contracts, and giving favored wards improved public services. In that case, as in this, however, the only practice at issue was the dismissal of public employees for partisan reasons. 427 U. S., at 353; *id,* at 374 (opinion of STEWART, J.). In light of the limited nature of the question presented, we have no occasion to address petitioner's argument that there is a compelling governmental interest in maintaining a political

sponsorship system for filling vacancies in the public defender's office.

8. "An individual who is a member of the out-party maintains affiliation with his own party at the risk of losing his job. He works for the election of his party's candidates and espouses its policies at the same risk. The financial and campaign assistance that he is induced to provide to another party furthers the advancement of that party's policies to the detriment of his party's views and ultimately his own beliefs, and any assessment of his salary is tantamount to coerced belief. See *Buckley* v. *Valeo*, 424 U. S. 1, 19 (1976). Even a pledge of allegiance to another party, however ostensible, only serves to compromise the individual's true beliefs. Since the average public employee is hardly in the financial position to support his party and another, or to lend his time to two parties, the individual's ability to act according to his beliefs and to associate with others of his political persuasion is constrained, and support for his party is diminished." *Id.*, at 355–356.

MR. JUSTICE BRENNAN also indicated that a patronage system may affect freedom of belief more indirectly, by distorting the electoral process. Given the increasingly pervasive character of government employment, he concluded that the power to starve political opposition by commanding partisan support, financial and otherwise, may have a significant impact on the formation and expression of political beliefs.

9. "Regardless of the nature of the inducement, whether it be by the denial of public employment or, as in *Board of Education* v. *Barnette*, 319 U. S. 624 (1943), by the influence of a teacher over students, '[i]f there is any fixed star in our constitutional constellation, it is that no official, high or petty, can prescribe what shall be orthodox in politics, nationalism, religion, or other matters of opinion or force citizens to confess by word or act their faith therein.' *Id.*, at 642." *Id.*, at 356.

10. "The Court recognized in *United Public Workers* v. *Mitchell*, 330 U. S. 75, 100 (1947), that 'Congress may not "enact a regulation providing that no Republican, Jew or Negro shall be appointed to federal office. . . ." ' This principle was reaffirmed in *Wieman* v. *Updegraff*, 344 U. S. 183 (1952), which held that a State could not require its employees to establish their loyalty by extracting an oath denying past affiliation with Communists. And in *Cafeteria Workers* v. *McElroy*, 367 U. S. 886, 898 (1961), the Court recognized again that the government could not deny employment because of previous membership in a particular party." *Id.*, at 357–358.

11. As MR. JUSTICE BRENNAN pointed out in *Elrod*, political sponsorship is often purchased at the price of political contributions or campaign work in addition to a simple declaration of allegiance to the party. *Id.*, at 355. Thus, an employee's realization that he must obtain a sponsor in order to retain his job is very likely to lead to the same type of coercion as that described by the plurality in *Elrod*. While there was apparently no overt political pressure exerted on respondents in this case, the potentially coercive effect of requiring sponsorship was demonstrated by Mr. Finkel's change of party registration in a futile attempt to retain his position. See n. 4, *supra*.

12. The plurality emphasized that patronage dismissals could be justified only if they advanced a governmental, rather than a partisan, interest. 427 U. S., at 362. That standard clearly was not met to the extent that employees were expected to perform extracurricular activities for the party, or were being rewarded for past services to the party. Government funds, which are collected from taxpayers of all parties on a nonpolitical basis, cannot be expended for the benefit of one political party simply because that party has control of the government. The compensation of government employees, like the distribution of other public benefits, must be justified by a governmental purpose.

The Sheriff argued that his employees' political beliefs did have a bearing on the official duties they were required to perform because political loyalty was necessary to the continued efficiency of the office. But after noting the tenuous link between political loyalty and efficiency where process servers and clerks were concerned, the plurality held that any small gain in efficiency did not outweigh the employees' First Amendment rights. *Id.*, at 366.

13. This is in contrast to the broader public responsibilities of an official such as a prosecutor. We express no opinion as to whether the deputy of such an official could be dismissed on grounds of political party affiliation or loyalty. Cf. *Newcomb* v. *Brennan*, 558 F. 2d 825 (CA7 1977), cert. denied, 434 U. S. 968 (dismissal of deputy city attorney).

14. As the District Court observed at the end of its opinion, it is difficult to formulate any justification for tying either the selection or retention of an assistant public defender to his party affiliation:

"Perhaps not squarely presented in this action, but deeply disturbing nonetheless, is the question of the propriety of political considerations entering into the selection of attorneys to serve in the sensitive positions of Assistant Public Defenders. By what rationale can it even be suggested that it is legitimate to consider, in the selection process, the politics of one who is to represent indigent defendants accused of crime? No 'compelling state interest' can be served by insisting that those who represent such defendants publicly profess to be Democrats (or Republicans)." 457 F. Supp., at 1293, n. 13.

In his brief petitioner attempts to justify the discharges in this case on the ground that he needs to have absolute confidence in the loyalty of his subordinates. In his dissenting opinion, MR. JUSTICE STEWART makes the same point, relying on an "analogy to a firm of lawyers in the private sector." *Post,* at 521. We cannot accept the proposition, however, that there cannot be "mutual confidence and trust" between attorneys, whether public defenders or private practitioners, unless they are both of the same political party. To the extent that petitioner lacks confidence in the assistants he has inherited from the prior administration for some reason other than their political affiliations, he is, of course, free to discharge them.

15. Contrary to repeated statements in the Court's opinion, the present case does not involve "private beliefs," but public affiliation with a political party.

16. When Thomas Jefferson became the first Chief Executive to succeed a President of the opposing party, he made substantial use of appointment and removal powers. Andrew Jackson, the next President to follow an antagonistic administration, used patronage extensively when he took office. The use of patronage in the early days of our Republic played an important role in democratizing American politics. *Elrod* v. *Burns,* 427 U. S., at 378–379 (POWELL, J., dissenting). President Lincoln's patronage practices and his reliance upon the newly formed Republican Party enabled him to build support for his national policies during the Civil War. See E. McKitrick, Party Politics and the Union and Confederate War Efforts, in The American Party System 117, 131–133 (W. Chambers & W. Burnham eds. 1967). Subsequent patronage reform efforts were "concerned primarily with the corruption and inefficiency that patronage was thought to induce in civil service and the power that patronage practices were thought to give the 'professional' politicians who relied on them." *Elrod* v. *Burns,* 427 U. S., at 379 (POWELL, J., dissenting). As a result of these efforts, most federal and state civil service employment was placed on a nonpatronage basis. *Ibid.* A significant segment of public employment has remained, however, free from civil service constraints.

17. The Court purports to limit the issue in this case to the dismissal of public employees. See *ante,* at 513, n. 7. Yet the Court also states that "it is difficult to formulate any justification for tying either the selection or retention of an assistant public defender to his party affiliation." *Ante,* at 520, n. 14. If this latter statement is not a holding of the Court, it at least suggests that the Court perceives no constitutional distinction between selection and dismissal of public employees.

18. The rationale for the Court's conclusion that election judges may be partisan appointments is not readily apparent. The Court states that "if a State's election laws require that precincts be supervised by two election judges of different parties, a Republican judge could be legitimately discharged solely for changing his party registration." *Ante,* at 518. If the mere presence of a state law mandating political affiliation as a requirement for public employment were sufficient, then the Legislature of Rockland County could reverse the result of this case merely by passing a law mandating that political affiliation be considered when a public defender chooses his assistants. Moreover, it is not apparent that a State could demonstrate, under the standard approved today, that only a political partisan is qualified to be an impartial election judge.

19. See Lemann, The Case for Political Patronage, The Washington Monthly, Dec. 1977, p. 8.

20. The Court notes that prosecutors hold "broader public responsibilities" than public defenders. *Ante,* at 519, n. 13. The Court does not suggest, however, that breadth of responsibility correlates with the appropriateness of political affiliation as a requirement for public employment. Indeed, such a contention would appear to be inconsistent with the Court's assertion that the "ultimate inquiry is not whether the label 'policymaker'. . . fits a particular position . . . ." *Ante,* at 518.

I do not suggest that the Constitution requires a patronage system. Civil service systems have been designed to eliminate corruption and inefficiency not to protect the political beliefs of public employees. Indeed, merit selection systems often impose restrictions on political activities by public employees. D. Rosenbloom, Federal Service and the Constitution: The Development of the Public Employment Relationship 83–86 (1971); see *CSC* v. *Letter Carriers,* 413 U. S. 548 (1973). Of course, civil service systems further important governmental goals, including continuity in the operation of government. A strength of our system has been the blend of civil service and patronage appointments, subject always to oversight and change by the legislative branches of government.

21. In my *Elrod* dissent, I suggested that public employees who lose positions obtained through their participation in the patronage system have not suffered a loss of First Amendment rights. 427 U. S., at

380–381. Such employees assumed the risks of the system and were benefited, not penalized, by its practical operation. But the Court bases its holding on the First Amendment and, accordingly, I consider the constitutional issue.

22. *Board of Education* v. *Barnette,* 319 U. S. 624 (1943), did not involve public employment. In that case, the Court declared that a state statute compelling each public school student to pledge allegiance to the flag violated the First Amendment. Similarly, *Wieman* v. *Updegraff,* 344 U. S. 183 (1952), *Shelton* v. *Tucker,* 364 U. S. 479 (1960), and *Cafeteria Workers* v. *McElroy,* 367 U. S. 886 (1961), did not concern governmental attempts to hire or dismiss employees pursuant to an established patronage system. The Court also relies upon *United Public Workers* v. *Mitchell,* 330 U. S. 75 (1947). *Ante,* at 515, n. 10. In that case, the Court upheld limitations on the political conduct of public employees that far exceed any burden on First Amendment rights demonstrated in this case.

23. See E. Costikyan, Behind Closed Doors: Politics in the Public Interest 253–254 (1966).

24. Television and radio enable well-financed candidates to go directly into the homes of voters far more effectively than even the most well-organized "political machine." See D. Broder, The Party's Over: The Failure of Politics in America 239–240 (1972).

25. Patronage also attracts persons willing to perform the jobs that enable voters to gain easy access to the electoral process. In some localities, "[t]he parties saw that the polls were open when they should be, and that the voting machines worked." Costikyan, Cities *Can* Work, Saturday Review, Apr. 4, 1970, pp. 19, 20. At a time when the percentage of Americans who vote is declining steadily, see Statistical Abstract of the United States 516 (1979), the citizen who distributes his party's literature, who helps to register voters, or who transports voters to the polls on Election Day performs a valuable public service.

26. In addition, political parties raise funds, recruit potential candidates, train party workers, provide assistance to voters, and act as a liaison between voters and governmental bureaucracies. Assistance to constituents is a common form of patronage. At the local level, political clubhouses traditionally have helped procure municipal services for constituents who often have little or no other access to public officials. M. Tolchin & S. Tolchin, To The Victor. . .: Political Patronage from the Clubhouse to the White House 19 (1971). Party organizations have been a means of upward mobility for newcomers to the United States

and members of minority groups. See *Elrod* v. *Burns,* 427 U. S., at 382, and n. 6 (POWELL, J., dissenting); S. Lubell, The Future of American Politics 76–77 (1952).

27. The reasoning of the *Elrod* plurality clearly permitted vestiges of patronage to continue in order to ensure that "representative government not be undercut by tactics obstructing the implementation of policies of the new administration. . . ." 427 U. S., at 367. But in view of the Court's new holding that some policymaking positions may not be filled on the basis of political affiliation, *ante,* at 518, elected officials may find changes in public policy thwarted by policymaking employees protected from replacement by the Constitution. The official with a hostile or foot-dragging subordinate will now be in a difficult position. In order to replace such a subordinate, he must be prepared to prove that the subordinate's "private political beliefs [will] interfere with the discharge of his public duties." *Ante,* at 517.

28. Peters, A Kind Word for the Spoils System, The Washington Monthly, Sept. 1976, p. 30.

29. Tolchin & Tolchin, *supra* n. 26, at 72–73. See Costikyan, *supra* n. 23, at 353–354.

30. Herbers, The Party's Over for the Political Parties, The New York Times Magazine, Dec. 9, 1979, pp. 158, 175.

31. See Costikyan, *supra* n. 23, at 252–253.

32. In local elections, a candidate's party affiliation may be the most salient information communicated to voters. One study has indicated that affiliation remains the predominant influence on voter choice in low-visibility elections such as contests for positions in the state legislature. See Murray & Vedlitz, Party Voting in Lower-Level Electoral Contests, 59 Soc. Sci. Q. 752, 756 (1979).

33. See, *e. g.,* W. Burnham, The 1976 Election: Has the Crisis Been Adjourned?, in American Politics and Public Policy 1, 19–22 (W. Burnham & M. Weinberg eds. 1978); Broder, *supra* n. 24; Herbers, *supra* n. 30, at 159; Pomper, The Decline of the Party in American Elections, 92 Pol. Sci. Q. 21, 40–41 (1977). See also n. 30, *supra.*

34. In Florida, for example, the local public defender is elected. See Fla. Const., Art. 5, § 18; Fla. Stat. § 27.50 (1979).

35. The Court's description of the policymaking functions of a public defender's office suggests that the public defender may no longer be chosen by the County Legislature on a partisan basis. *Ante,* at 519–520.

# III

## Merit Systems:
## Triumph and Discontent

Whatever the subsequent discontents produced, it cannot be emphasized strongly enough that in at least one major respect the Pendleton Act and the reform movement it fueled represented a victory. It greatly reduced opportunities for lower level party patronage. In a seminal article in the *Public Administration Review* in 1960 (reprinted here), Frank Sorauf paid tribute to the triumph of merit systems. Proclaiming that these systems were well on their way "to full victory" over patronage, he concluded that the "scholars and administrators who for so long fought in the vanguard of the movement now savor a triumph in practical affairs of the sort rarely vouchsafed to intellectuals." While top elected officials might see great value in appointing sympathetic partisans to top policy jobs, patronage in lower level positions fell. In tracing the decline of patronage, Sorauf appropriately cautioned against attributing too much impact to the adoption of a merit-system policy. He also viewed change as emanating from broader forces at work in American politics. Sorauf further understood that the decline of patronage not only changed the way public programs were administered, but also influenced elections and government policy by modifying the character of political parties.

Writing over a decade after Sorauf, Albert Aronson provided further testimony concerning the spread of merit systems in a U.S. Civil Service Commission volume called *Biography of an Ideal* (1974). As Director of the Office of State Merit Systems with the Department of Health, Education and Welfare, Aronson organized its program of personnel standards and technical aid to the states. He was, therefore, well positioned to comprehend personnel developments in state and local government. In the chapter reprinted here, Aronson reached a cautiously optimistic conclusion about the spread of merit systems. He allowed that "there are great differences in the calibre of merit system administration from place to place, and from time to time in a given jurisdiction." Yet on balance he found "the net contribution of most systems in improving the quality of service to the public" to be "cumulatively impressive."

Aronson's article also captured how the federal government used grant programs to put pressure on states and counties to adopt merit procedures. In a selection from her perceptive book, *The Influence of Federal Grants,* Martha Derthick masterfully conveys the dynamics of this process in one state—Massachusetts—as it dealt with public assistance programs. Derthick understood that merit-system regulation could help federal administrators professionalize personnel at the state and local level. (See also the selection by Mosher in section I). Hence, administrators at those levels of government would come to resemble federal officials in skills and attitudes. In turn, the homogenization induced by professionalization would reduce friction that would otherwise impede programs that relied on states and localities to implement federal policy (a form of administration by proxy). As Derthick indicates, however, efforts to foster professionalism through merit-system requirements featured a politics of their own.

### From Patronage to New Concerns

The selections by Sorauf, Aronson, and Derthick should not be construed to mean that low-level personnel patronage has vanished from American political life. Manifestations of it persist in many jurisdictions.[1] In broad historical context, however, this form of patronage has clearly declined.

Solutions, however, frequently spawn a new set of problems. With the victory over low-level patronage substantially won, critics sporadically turned to other targets. Section II focused on the concern that merit systems excessively constrained top executives. Variations on this theme as well as additional concerns have also taken root over the last half century. The selections by Sayre, Savas and Ginsburg, and the National Academy of Public Administration vividly illustrate the dimensions of this critique.

In 1948, Professor Wallace Sayre used the forum provided by a book review in the *Public Administration Review* to argue that goal displacement had occurred in public personnel systems (reprinted here). To wit, certain techniques (such as written tests) had become ends in themselves, rather than servants of broader purposes. In Sayre's view, "Personnel administration. . .has tended to become characterized more by procedure, rule, and technique than by purpose or results." The rules promulgated in the name of establishing merit systems had spawned "a reciprocal system of formal and informal techniques of evasion." These patterns of behavior had precipitated a "crisis in civil service administration." Consequently, he argued that "both ends and means" in public personnel administration "now urgently need fundamental reexamination."

Despite Sayre's insightful critique, the decade of the 1950s did not trigger major criticism of personnel practices let alone significant reform. In the 1960s, however, the civil rights movement and the rapid rise of collective bargaining yielded more ferment. With social institutions generally suffering from diminished credibility, the 1970s witnessed new broadsides against the "pathologies" of merit systems. In words more polemical than those used by Sayre, certain reformers took pains to point out how "meritless" merit systems were. Thus, Ralph Nader sponsored a muckraking volume in the 1970s, *The Spoiled System,* by Robert Vaughn.[2] This book severely criticized many personnel practices of the federal government. Others focused on the local level. The reprinted article by E.S. Savas and Sigmund Ginsburg, who both held high administrative posts in New York City under Mayor Lindsay, provides a fundamental critique of local personnel practices in that city (and by implication, many others). In some respects echoing the themes of Wallace Sayre, the two analysts noted that the personnel rules and systems appropriate for 1883 had become rigid and regressive. They listed twelve counterproductive policies involving written examinations, job security, promotions, transfers, the absence of managerial discretion over salary increases, union power, and other issues. In the case of selection processes, for instance, they charged that existing policies led to an "inverse merit system"—to a system that "discriminates against those applicants who are most qualified according to its own standards." Overall, they concluded that the merit system in New York City had developed "rigor mortis"; it had "been warped and distorted to the point where it can hardly do anything at all."

The ferment of the 1970s helped facilitate passage of the federal Civil Service Reform Act of 1978. Aside from striving to foster greater political responsiveness through a Senior Executive Service, it contained other reforms espoused by critics of civil-service systems. For example, it authorized merit-pay plans for certain federal managers, encouraged more accurate and objective performance appraisals, emphasized the importance of affirmative action, and established new procedures and institutions for labor management.

As the reprinted chapter from the National Academy of Public Administration's (NAPA) *Revitalizing Federal Management* attests, however, the law had not satisfied many critics as of the early 1980s. In its general review of federal management practices, the NAPA report claimed that "when managers and personnel experts all over government were consulted, they simply reaffirmed what is common knowledge—the frustrations with the (personnel) system are general and profound." The report claimed that some 8,814 pages of personnel regulations created significant obstacles for federal managers to surmount in getting work performed. Asserting that the "personnel system doesn't seem to work very well for anybody," NAPA called for a new conceptual framework that, among other things, would allow federal executives and managers to play a more pivotal role in personnel management. The new framework would allow "managerial needs" rather than "procedural concerns" to prevail.

If the 1960s and 1970s brought to the fore new sources of discontent with government personnel systems, the decade also witnessed a growing awareness of the realpolitik of such systems. This sense not only appeared in studies that focused on the relationship between elected officials and the career civil service. Other personnel arenas attracted attention as well. For instance, my own analysis of personnel practices in Oakland, California, attempted to show how generic politics permeated virtually all aspects of personnel management in city hall.[3] I argued that such politics was inevitable and in many respects salutary.

Others, however, adopted a less sanguine view of the politics penetrating certain personnel arenas. In this regard, Jay Shafritz's analysis of the politics of position classification in Philadelphia proved particularly perceptive. The selection from his book, *Position Classification: A Behavioral Analysis for the Public Service*, shows how classification in Philadelphia involved various players jockeying for strategic advantage. Classification decisions emerged as much from processes of conflict, bargaining and compromise as from the application of "proven techniques." Just as Sayre had noted the tendency for merit systems to spawn informal methods for surmounting them, Shafritz concluded that "rigid formal structure encourages the growth of organizational politics, because it is through such politicking that reallocations are achieved." While Shafritz foreswore final judgment on whether such politics was beneficial or deleterious, his book sharply criticized the prevailing methods of position classification.

While Shafritz took the orthodoxies of position classification to task, others turned to different targets. Ironically, some of the changes favored by reformers of the 1960s and 1970s came under fire. Consider, for instance, performance appraisal. The Civil Service Reform Act called for new systems of appraising employee performance so that agencies could "use the results of performance appraisals as a basis for training, rewarding, reassigning, promoting, reducing in grade, retaining, and removing employees." This necessitated that "to the maximum extent feasible" accurate evaluation was to occur "on the basis of objective criteria" (subsection 4302, P.L. 45–454). But as the reprinted article by John Nalbandian illustrates, such appraisal faces many pitfalls. Specifically, those advocating the objective systems frequently fail to take into account the supervisor's reluctance to assess subordinates. Nalbandian also notes the difficulties of measuring some of the dimensions of performance affecting managerial behavior. He argues that "objective" appraisal systems may "define away some activities which establish and maintain the productivity, cohesion, and sociability of a work group." In his view it remains far from clear that objective appraisals enhance managerial capabilities. Failure to take into account the human dynamics of the appraisal process may ultimately lead these systems to fail.

The Civil Service Reform Act also called for heightened emphasis on merit-pay systems, or performance contingent pay. Presumably, federal executives and managers who performed better would receive bigger salary increases. Reformers at other levels of government (e.g., Savas and Ginsburg) also endorsed the practice. Some saw it as a major vehicle for improving public schools. But as James Perry's reprinted article demonstrates, merit pay for public managers is no elixir. He contends that "a mismatch exists between the simplicity inherent in merit pay programs and the complexities of organizations.... This mismatch is at the root of many of merit pay's failures." Perry argues that such pay plans often flounder on their inability to obtain and evaluate information concerning subordinate behavior. He notes that they can provide a disincentive for coordination and cooperation among managers. While Perry acknowledges the value of pay as a motivator under some circumstances, he believes that "requiring a public organization's compensation system to harness pay for motivating short-term managerial performance is not realistic."

Similar concern could be expressed about the growing interest in the ethics of public administrators in the 1980s. Ethics is obviously an appropriate focus for those who formulate, implement, and study public personnel policy. If employees hold themselves to high ethical standards, democracy and administration can more harmoniously coexist; government credibility can more readily thrive. Initiatives to enhance the ethics of civil servants are far from simple to craft effectively, however. While most everyone would agree that ethical behavior by civil servants in a democracy involves respect for the rule of law as well as respect for the sanctity and dignity of the individual, it is not always easy to determine what the ethical course of action is in public agencies. Moreover, the quest to foster ethical administrative behavior often unleashes more and more regulation. Civil servants fill out financial statements, submit to random drug tests, face elaborate restrictions on their interactions with firms that do business with government, and more. These regulations may encourage ethical behavior. But this barrage of regulations can also siphon off attention from larger ethical concerns; in some instances, it discourages able and ethical people from working for government. Hence, efforts to instill ethics can also have a down side.

As the selections from this and previous sections indicate, the institutions, rules, and techniques of public personnel administration have persistently bred discontent. They have fueled an interest in finding alternatives to classic merit systems (see also section VI). But is the picture conveyed too gloomy? Can't one find examples of excellence in human-resource management in the public sector? Don't the systems that come under attack often work well in promoting certain personnel values? The answer to all three questions is easy—"yes, by all means." Unfortunately, students of public personnel administration have not devoted much time to documenting cases involving creative management of human resources within government. The selection by Herbert Kaufman represents a notable exception. In his indisputably classic study of the U.S. Forest Service, Kaufman masterfully demonstrates how an entire configuration of personnel practices led to an internalization of common perceptions, values, and premises of action among employees of that agency. These practices included selecting job applicants who would fit the agency's culture, post-entry training, certain transfer and promotion policies, and the use of such physical symbols as the badge and uniform. Kaufman shows how these practices yielded employees who demonstrated "voluntary conformity" with the rules and norms of the agency.

## Sources of Discontent

The field of public personnel administration needs more contemporary studies like that conducted by Kaufman in the late 1950s. In the meantime, the outbursts of discontent with governmental personnel systems must be placed in proper context. Three forces frequently interact to precipitate displeasure with these systems—competing values, uncertainty, and political culture.

As discussed in section I, five core values vie for attention in the personnel arena—agency competence, merit, political responsiveness, social equity, and employee rights and well-being. Often, the pursuit of certain core values involves trade-offs with others. This means that civil-service systems perennially run the risk of being damned if they do and damned if they don't. In a sense, discontent springs from an inability to have one's cake and eat it too. It emanates from difficulties in forging consensus on the appropriate weight to be assigned particular core values—in defining the optimal mix of achievement. This inability to reach agreement means that reform movements often sow the seeds of new discontent and assume a cyclical pattern.[4] When reform succeeds in promoting certain values (e.g., more political responsiveness), it prompts others to pursue change on behalf of the core values that have become less dominant (such as merit or agency competence).

Uncertainty also breeds discontent. It appears in various guises. First, uncertainty stems from difficulties in calibrating the degree to which core personnel values are being achieved in a given setting. One cannot, for instance, check a handy scoreboard to determine achievement in terms of merit or agency competence. Second, ambiguity often characterizes the means of accomplishing personnel objectives. For instance, the exact impact of a particular pay system on agency competence usually remains murky. The limits to existing theory—to an understanding of cause–effect relations—mean that the prospects for error are substantial in any effort to improve personnel systems. Practices hypothesized to accomplish some objective may do nothing of the sort. The epiphenomena generated may prove surprising and distressing. The complexities of evaluating the effects of reform initiatives on the five core values make learning from past reform efforts difficult. Hence, uncertainty can breed discontent by creating a sense that attempts to improve personnel systems seldom work.

To be sure, ambiguity could under some circumstances ameliorate discontent by giving administrators and elected officials wide latitude to interpret the performance of civil-service systems and efforts to reform them. In the absence of concrete evidence, reformers could define victory politically, claiming that the system performs well or that a particular reform has succeeded. The nation's political culture, however, often tilts the resolution of uncertainty toward skepticism.

The political culture of the United States encourages criticism of public agencies and, by implication, personnel systems. It touts the virtues of private enterprise, of running government like a business. The rhetoric of political campaigns and the tendency of the press to highlight bureaucratic foibles reinforce negative stereotypes of public agencies. While the public expresses more positive views about specific agencies and programs, many adhere to the "grand myth" that inefficiency and ineffectiveness permeate the public sector.[5] Thus, much criticism of public personnel systems probably has less to do with the specifics of their performance than stereotypes about government incapacity. Given a negative cultural bias, people may discount, ignore or disregard evidence of accomplishments by these systems. A skeptical political culture biased toward the techniques of business also means that some personnel reforms take life as much because they cater to these biases as because they stand a chance of promoting core personnel values. Merit pay plans for public managers illustrate this phenomenon. While study after study suggests the limits to motivating public managers via merit pay, the practice remains popular with the public. Among other things, it squares with notions that government ought to be run more like a business.

Thus, some criticism of public personnel systems reflects cultural stereotype, rather than accurate diagnosis. This is not to deny that genuine problems mark the performance of government personnel systems. The selections from Sayre, Savas and Ginsburg, NAPA, Shafritz, Nalbandian, and Perry appropriately point to defects in practices. In considering these selections, however, it is important to realize that identification of problems does not automatically imply that reformers have solutions. Given some core personnel values, the cure may be as bad as the disease. Or it may not be feasible politically to pursue the reform. Efforts to improve public personnel systems also need to be kept in proper perspective. Reform in many respects reflects an effort to develop a better set of problems to work on in the personnel arena. One seldom if ever solves problems once and for all. One can move toward realizing a more optimal mix of personnel values. But trade-offs and shifting preferences mean that today's constructive reform will probably be tomorrow's object of criticism. Progress can and often does occur but its march cannot eradicate discontent.

# Notes

1. In New York, for instance, officials in the City of Albany and New York City continue certain patronage practices. In some jurisdictions party officials have used federal jobs programs for this purpose. In other cases, political leaders have put pressure on private contractors to reward their supporters with jobs.

2. Robert G. Vaughn, *The Spoiled System* (New York: Charter House, 1975).

3. Frank J. Thompson, *Personnel Policy in the City: The Politics of Jobs in Oakland* (Berkeley: University of California Press, 1975).

4. See also David H. Rosenbloom, "A Theory of Public Personnel Reforms," in Frederick S. Lane, ed., *Current Issues in Public Administration,* Third Edition (New York: St. Martin's Press, 1986), pp. 361–374.

5. Charles T. Goodsell, *The Case for Bureaucracy: A Public Administration Polemic* (Chatham, N.J.: Chatham, 1985), p. 150 and Frank J. Thompson, "Managing Within Civil Service Systems," in James L. Perry, ed., *Handbook of Public Administration* (San Francisco: Jossey-Bass, 1989), pp. 359–374.

# 11

# The Silent Revolution in Patronage

*Frank J. Sorauf*
*The Pennsylvania State University*

With little fanfare and only quiet celebration the movement to install merit systems in place of the older patronage is well on its way to full victory. The federal government has almost completely been conquered by one form or another of merit appointment, while the traditional political machines, long the major consumers of patronage, are everywhere else in hurried retreat. And the scholars and administrators who for so long fought in the vanguard of the movement now savor a triumph in practical affairs of the sort rarely vouchsafed to intellectuals.

The case against patronage, based largely on the need for administrative expertise and professionalism, is overwhelming. But only rarely have the opponents of patronage stopped to worry about the effects on the parties and political system of abolishing it.[1] Some scholars of political parties have argued that patronage is important to the political process, but there has never been an attempt to compare the merit system's contribution to good administration with its supposed weakening of the party system in the total balance of effective government.

Such a comparison may not be necessary, however. Patronage is slowly dying out—more from its own political causes than from the campaigns of civil service reformers. However substantial the need of the parties for patronage

fifty or even twenty years ago, the need is vastly less today. On the one hand, the organization, functions, and style of American politics, and the consequent need for patronage, have changed dramatically in the last generation; on the other hand, the nature and usefulness of patronage itself also have changed.[2]

## Uses of Patronage

Patronage is best thought of as an incentive system—a political currency with which to "purchase" political activity and political responses. The chief functions of patronage are:

*Maintaining an active party organization.* Experienced politicos maintain that the coin of patronage is necessary to reward the countless activities of an active party organization. The promise or actual holding of a political appointment, they report, is necessary to induce the canvassing of neighborhoods, mailing and telephoning, campaigning and electioneering, and other activities of the local party organization. Illustratively, many a city hall or county court house rests vacant on election day as its denizens go out to man the party organization.

*Promoting intra-party cohesion.* In the hands of a skillful party leader, patronage may be an instrument of party cohesion, edging defecting partisans back into the discipline of the party hierarchy and welding the differing blocs within the party into a unified whole. In one sense President Eisenhower's historic agreement with Senator Taft in Morningside Heights represents an attempt to enlist the support of the Taft Republicans in 1952 by promising them consideration in the party's appointments.

*Attracting voters and supporters.* The patronage appointment often may be used to convert the recipient (and a large portion of his family and friends) into lifelong and devoted supporters of the appointing party. Gratitude for the job will win his support for the party, it is said, and a desire to retain the job by keeping the party in power will enforce it. In some urban areas of Pennsylvania, experienced party men calculate that a well-placed appointment should net the party between six and eight voters. The same reasoning, of course, lies behind the appointment of representatives of special blocs of voters, such as ethnic, national, or religious groups.

*Financing the party and its candidates.* The cruder and more overt forms of this function of patronage have long been known to the fraternity as "macing" the payroll. In the heyday of patronage in American politics, something close to 5 per cent of the appointee's salary was thought a fair return to the party for its benefice. Patronage, always reward for past activity as well as inducement for the future, may also be used to reward a recent contribution to the party coffers.

*Procuring favorable government action.* Less commonly acknowledged, perhaps for its dubious ethics and legality, is the use of patronage to secure favorable policy or administrative action for the party or its followers. At the local government level it may involve the fixing of a traffic ticket, preference for certain applicants for public assistance, the calculated oversight in a public health inspection, or the use of public equipment to remove snow from private rights-of-way. By exploiting the appointee's dependence on the party, the organization reaps the political advantages of a preferred access to public policy-making.

*Creating party discipline in policy-making.* This last function of patronage redounds less to the advantage of political parties than to presidents and governors who use appointments to build support for their programs in legislatures. Franklin Roosevelt's wily use of the dwindling federal patronage, especially his delaying of appointments until after satisfactory congressional performance, scarcely needs more than mention. A number of governors still have at their disposal a vast array of political jobs to use in coordinating executive and legislative policy and in joining the separated powers of government.

But patronage may certainly be misused in ways that adversely affect the parties and political system. It may build up personal machines or followings that parallel and compete with the regular, formal party organization. Poorly administered, it may cause new resentments and hostilities, create more friction within the party than it eases. Also, patronage seldom can perform all of the six purposes at once since to use it for one purpose is to destroy its effectiveness for another. For example, appointments that solidify and activate local party organization may disturb centralized party unity at a higher level and impair party discipline within both party and legislature.[3]

Just how well patronage has performed the six functions for the parties over the years is a matter for considerable conjecture. Partisans usually claim patronage is the "life-blood" of American politics, and yet even among its most devoted and skillful users, many dissent and some are ambivalent. James Farley, for example, has boasted that he could build a major party without patronage, and yet he dissented from the recommendation of the second Hoover Commission that rural postal carriers be taken from the patronage lists.[4] The scholarly studies of patronage and general political folklore indicate that it is fairly effective in maintaining an active organization and, to a lesser extent, in attracting voters and supporters, but that its value in performing the other functions is highly questionable. Political appointees do contribute money to the party treasuries but hardly enough to run a party today. As for the promotion of party cohesion, the intra-party bickering and bitterness occasioned by the division of the spoils is, to this observer, truly staggering.

## Decline in Usefulness

Regardless of the effectiveness of patronage in the past, it is today undergoing rapid changes, most obviously in its steady shrinkage. One observer has estimated that the federal patronage available to the Eisenhower Administration has "not exceeded a fraction of one percent of the total federal establishment."[5] A precise estimate of the number of jobs still under patronage in city, county, and state administrations throughout the country would be impossible to come by, but all hands agree it is declining.

There do remain states where merit systems have made few inroads into patronage and where large numbers of positions (about 50,000 in Pennsylvania, for example) remain at least technically available for distribution by the victorious. But even in these instances the parties are using a steadily decreasing percentage of the jobs for political purposes because patronage as a political currency has been devalued. Merit systems make their greatest inroads into patronage in the well-paid, specialized positions where the call for expertness and training is greatest. The parties are left the less-desirable, poorly paid positions generally. With continued economic prosperity and high levels of employment the economic rewards of these jobs, hardly princely in most cases, are less appealing than formerly. While low pay and chronic job insecurity plague the patronage jobholder, private employment has become progressively more attractive with rising wage levels, union protections and securities, unemployment compensation, pension plans, and fringe benefits. Viewed by most Americans as a short-term, desperation job alternative, the patronage position has lost considerable value as a political incentive.

Patronage also is losing its respectability. Its ethic—the naked political *quid pro quo*—no longer seems to many a natural and reasonable ingredient of politics. Parties often find that the attempt to clean political house after an election produces public outrage and indignation. The mores of the middle-class and the image of civic virtue instilled by public education extol the unfettered, independent voter rather than the patronage-seeking party-liner. The public-spirited citizen rather than the self-interested party worker is celebrated. And the public no longer tolerates the presence of political mediocrities in public service in the name of party loyalty.

Even the job-seekers themselves no longer accept the political obligations of their appointments as readily as once they did. Briefly, patronage has fallen into public disfavor for appearing to approach an outright political payoff, with the result that its usefulness to the parties has diminished.

## Changes in Parties and Politics

The partial passing of the boss and the political machine has been perhaps the most obvious new development in party behavior. Depending heavily on the motive power of patronage, these machines long dominated big city politics and some county and state strongholds as well. They flourished especially in those urban centers inhabited by large groups of immigrants and minorities—groups not yet integrated into American life, often poor and insecure and bewildered by the traditions of American politics. The machine spoke to them in the simple terms of a job, of sympathy in city hall, and of food and fuel to soften the hardest times.

This is not to suggest that political machines have vanished or even that they will vanish within the next generation. But the machine, and the politics of the underprivileged on which it rests, is surely on the decline. Government and other private agencies have taken over the social welfare functions these organizations once provided. Furthermore, first and second generation groups, traditional recipients of the attentions of the machine, are disappearing, and their children and grandchildren now luxuriate in the prosperity and conformity of the suburbs, though in many cities their place will be taken for a time by immigrants from rural areas of the United States. In sum, rising levels of prosperity, higher educational levels, declining numbers of unassimilated groups, and greater concern by government for the unfortunate all point to a decline of the boss and machine and of the patronage they relied on.

Furthermore, party conflict since the 1930's has reflected social and economic appeals to a greater extent than in the preceding decades. Even though they do not yet approach the ideological fervor of European campaigns, American politics has become more involved with issues and less with the issueless politics of patronage, favor, and preferment. Campaigning, too, has shifted from the door-to-door canvass, local rallies, and controlled blocs of votes to the mass media and advertising agencies. Great, attractive candidates serve as the focus of these national campaigns. As a result the importance of the national party organization is increased—the center of party power shifting away from the local units just as clearly as the center of governmental power is shifting from the states and localities to the national government.

### The New Party Worker

What is emerging, then, is a system of political organization more compatible with the middle-class values of suburbia than those of the ethnic or racial neighborhood of the urban center. Rather than relying on the organized party hierarchy, it depends more and more on the volunteer and *ad hoc* political groups and personal followings. In some states, such as California and Wisconsin, party leaders are converting this fleeting volunteer activity into more permanent clubs and party organization,[6] but the manpower of these changing parties contrasts sharply with the ward or precinct committeeman of the older machines. The new political men are far more likely than their predecessors to be motivated by belief, by loyalty to an attractive candidate (e.g., the Citizens for Eisenhower movement), by a sense of civic duty, or by a more generalized social and sporting enthusiasm. They view their political activity more as avocation than vocation.

The parties also have found fresh resources in the organized power of the interest group. It recruits voters for the favored party or candidate and provides campaign and financial assistance as well. Many a candidate today prizes the contacts and communication channels of the local labor union or chamber of commerce more highly than he does the face-to-face campaign. Voters in many corners of the country can testify that candidates rarely knock on their doors any more. Business and labor are major sources of party funds; the contributions of payrollers no longer suffice. Even the "new style" political leader, in contrast with the classic model of the boss, usually has closer ties to interest groups in the community. He may even have been recruited from one.

For these educated, secure, and even prestiged workers and leaders of the new parties, a political appointment holds little fascination. One sophisticated and experienced politician has written that "Men and women are drawn into politics by a combination of motives; these include power, glory, zeal for contention or success, duty, hate, oblivion, hero worship, curiosity, and enjoyment of the work."[7] Today's political worker may more and more find his reward in the satisfaction of a deeply rooted psychological need, the identification with a purposeful organization or a magnetic leader, the ability to serve an economic or professional interest, the release from the tedium of daily routine, or the triumph of an ideal. His "payoff," instead of a political job, may be endorsement for elective office, membership on a civic commission, access to new and influential elites, or a reception in the White House gardens.

### The New Personnel Needs of the Party

These shifts in organization, functions, and personnel of the parties have meant that the patronage that does remain is not the patronage that the parties might easily use. The parties cry for trained, educated, experienced men of ability and affairs, albeit fewer men than formerly. The vast majority of patronage positions are poorly paid and generally unappealing to the men and women of skills and achievement the parties would like to enlist. Very likely the man placed on a trash collection crew will lack the social and political experience to be useful in today's politics, and his meager pay offers the party scant opportunity for fund-raising. The middle-level job, potentially the most useful to the party in rewarding its more capable partisans, is rarely available for political appointment. These are the specialized, expert positions that are generally the first to be put under a merit system. When they do remain under patronage, their specialized qualifications are the hardest to fill from the rank and file of political job-seekers.

At the top, the party often has highly-placed positions available, at least in small number, to reward its leadership corps. Here, however, the party often fails to persuade its most capable men to give up, even temporarily, their positions in business and the professions for a political appointment. In turn, the party workers who would find the patronage position an attractive alternative to their private employment, lack the executive and administrative experience for the positions. Paul David and Ross Pollock write of these problems in the national government:

> For positions at the higher levels, the party organization has only rarely been successful in convincing the administration that its nominees were sufficiently qualified. The administration, on its part, has had to go out and hunt, cajole, and persuade in order to recruit the kind of talent it wanted. . . . The supply of persons with the requisite competence and availability is simply not large enough in either political party, and there is little evidence to suggest that the supply is on the increase.[8]

As its usefulness to them declines, patronage imposes hard and worrisome choices on the party hierarchies. Often the parties' appointments to the plenitude of unattractive patronage jobs go to men and women with no particular record of service to the party and little promise for future service, or whose appointment will do little to integrate the party organization or build party cohesion. Their chief recommendation is their need for a job, and the party, functioning as employment bureau, hopes only for a little gratitude and possible support at the polls. The better paid, more enticing jobs are losing their incentive power for those partisans qualified to hold them, and the party finds itself haunted by the aggressive availability of unqualified job-hunters.

One is forced to conclude that the classic dependence of party on patronage is being undermined on both sides. Forced by the changing nature of American society and by new political problems and values, the parties are shifting to a new mode of operation that relies less than formerly on the incentives of patronage. Patronage, on the other hand, is declining in both quantity and quality, both in the number of jobs available and in their value to the party.

## Short-Term Adjustments

Since party changes were not simply adjustments to the gradual demise of patronage, a further reduction in the supply of patronage in those states where the supply remains large will hardly alter the long-run development of the party system. It may, however, accelerate change in party operations or produce short-term side effects.

In the first place, patronage has persisted chiefly at the local levels and remains the bulwark of local party organization, a faintly anachronistic bulwark, one might add, in an era of centralized party and government. It is in these state and local party organs, despite their declining vigor and importance, that one finds the most vocal proponents of patronage—even of the remaining federal patronage, much of which is channeled through them. This concentration of patronage in the localities fortifies the local party and permits it to resist discipline or centralization by organs higher in the party structure.[9] Thus fortified, these decentralized pockets of political power also fight party cohesion and responsibility in legislatures and, paradoxically, often nullify the value of executive patronage in achieving legislative discipline.

Inevitably, these local units, as they lose their vitality and their part in major policy-making, become primarily dealers in patronage, converting it from a political tool to a political goal.

When patronage declines there, a major resistance to party centralization and to issue-centered campaigns and candidates will die with it.

Secondly, restrictions on patronage weaken the Democratic party more than the Republicans. Patronage appeals more predictably to lower economic strata, to unskilled and semi-skilled workers, to urban dwellers, and to minority groups—all of the demographic groups which, studies show, support the Democratic party. Patronage as an incentive system comports with the economic needs, the understanding of the relationship between citizen and government, and the somewhat exploitative view of politics more common among lower social and economic groups than among the American middle class. Furthermore, the Democratic party also has greater problems in finding substitutes for it. The personal and financial support of the business community are not often at its disposal. The formation of a genteel party, dedicated to a philosophy of government and based on sociability and civic virtue, falls more easily to the Republicans.

Thirdly, since the appeals of patronage are largely economic, its political value and usefulness are apt to be greatest in the remaining pockets of unemployment and economic hardship, for it is there that private employment fails to provide opportunities superior to patronage positions. In these areas, and in the country as a whole if widespread unemployment returns, patronage might enjoy a brief renaissance as a political incentive.

Finally, patronage has been involved in legislative–executive rivalry. Presidents of the United States, harassed by congressional attempts to control patronage through clearance systems and "senatorial courtesy," have been more willing to surrender it than has the Congress. State governors, however, are not so willing to abandon one of the few weapons they have over unruly legislatures.[10] Since the loss of patronage will certainly affect legislative–executive relations in the states more sharply than in the national government, one is justified in supposing that its further loss will make the task of gubernatorial leadership just that much more difficult.

## In Conclusion

To expect anything but a further contraction of patronage would be naïve. 1. Patronage does not meet the needs of present-day party operations. Activities requiring a large number of party workers—canvassing, mass mailings, rallies—are being replaced by radio and television. Political costs are so high that assessments on public salaries are minuscule beside the party's cost. 2. Patronage no longer is the potent inducement to party activity it once was. Public attitudes are increasingly hostile to patronage and the political style it represents. Employment in the private economy also provides an increasingly attractive alternative to patronage positions. 3. As a result, the incentives once provided by patronage are being replaced in the political system. The persons who can contribute most to campaigns, in skill and funds, seek different payoffs—prestige, power, or personal satisfaction rather than jobs.

Even though the further decline of patronage will certainly not destroy or seriously hamper the parties, it will produce political shocks and pockets of discomfort. It will probably hurt Democrats more than Republicans, will be slower and more crucial in economically distressed areas, and will weaken the influence of governors on legislative action more than the President's influence on Congress.

American political parties have, after all, been getting along without patronage to various extents for some time now, and they have survived. Even many large metropolitan cities, whose patronage needs the scholars emphasize, have managed without it. The political party has its causes and justification deep in the American political process and not in the dispensation of political privileges. Patronage is necessary to a certain type of party operation, but others can be maintained without it. The old machines and local party organizations relied on patronage, but they were rooted in social and economic conditions that are disappearing. As they disappear, so will the parties and patronage they fostered.

Ultimately, the decline of patronage will, among a number of causes, speed the parties to further centralization, to the heightening of their ideological content, to a greater reliance on group participation in politics, to greater nationalization of the candidate image and party campaigning, and to the establishment of some modicum of party discipline.

There is something almost quaint in these days of big parties, big government, and advertising agency politics about a political institution that conjures up images of Boss Tweed, torchlight parades, and ward heelers. As the great day of patronage recedes into history, one is tempted to say that the advancing merit systems will not kill patronage before it withers and dies of its own infirmity and old age.

# Notes

1. One would, however, have to mention three specialists in public administration who have recognized and addressed themselves to the conflicting needs of party and administration. See especially Harvey C. Mansfield's paper on "Political Parties, Patronage, and the Federal Government Service," in the American Assembly volume, *The Federal Government Service: Its Character, Prestige, and Problems* (Columbia University, 1954), pp. 81–112. Also relevant are Richard E. Neustadt's review, "On Patronage, Power, and Politics," 15 *Public Administration Review* 108–114 (Spring, 1955) and James R. Watson, "Is Patronage Obsolete?" 18 *Personnel Administration* 3–9 (July, 1955).

2. Very few studies exist of the actual operation of patronage systems across the country. Among the few are: David H. Kurtzman, *Methods of Controlling Votes in Philadelphia* (published by author, 1935);

Frank J. Sorauf, "State Patronage in a Rural County," 50 *American Political Science Review* 1046–1056 (December, 1956); and H. O. Waldby, *The Patronage System in Oklahoma* (The Transcript Co., 1950). In the absence of specific reports and data, one can only proceed uneasily on a mixture of political folklore, scattered scholarship, professional consensus, and personal judgment.

3. I have questioned the political usefulness of patronage at greater length in "Patronage and Party," 3 *Midwest Journal of Political Science* 115–126 (May, 1959).

4. The claim is in James A. Farley, *Behind the Ballots* (Harcourt, Brace, and Co., 1938), p. 237, and the dissent in the Commission on Organization of the Executive Branch of the Government, *Report on Personnel and Civil Service* (U. S. Government Printing Office, 1955), p. 91.

5. Mansfield, *op cit.* note 1 above, p. 94.

6. The literature on the California political clubs is rather extensive, especially in the nonacademic journals, but the only general work on the volunteer movement in politics of which I am aware is Stephen A. Mitchell's *Elm Street Politics* (Oceana Publications, 1959).

7. Stimson Bullitt, *To Be a Politician* (Doubleday and Co., 1959), p. 42. The reader will, in fact, find all of chapter two a stimulating review of the incentives and motives of politics.

8. Paul T. David and Ross Pollock, *Executives for Government* (The Brookings Institution, 1957), pp. 25, 27.

9. The classic expression of this view is E. E. Schattschneider, *Party Government* (Rinehart and Co., 1942).

10. See Duane Lockhard, *New England State Politics* (Princeton University Press, 1959) for reports of the value of patronage to governors in New England. For instance, he describes patronage as "perhaps the most important of these gubernatorial weapons" in Massachusetts (p. 160).

# 12

## State and Local Personnel Administration

*Albert H. Aronson*

### The Growth of Merit Administration

In the early days of the Republic, there was little in the way of full time employment in State and local governments. In a small scale agrarian society with a moving frontier, governmental functions were limited. In 1790 only five percent of the population lived in cities and villages of over 2500 population. There was a distrust of government stemming from colonial rule, and this was strengthened by the nonconformism of the backwoodsman.

Most State and local officials were elected and served part time. They were almost all paid. In the New England town there was rotation in such offices as the assessor, tax collector, constable, town clerk, treasurer, overseer of the poor, and various other minor offices. The townships in the new northern States followed the New England pattern. County officials were also elected and served part time. They were in close contact with the citizenry at the county seat which was located at a central point within a day's easy reach of the farmer in the county.

Initially the higher State offices were filled largely by persons with a sense of public duty and to a considerable extent the lesser State and local posts, although we can assume some personal patronage. However, within the first quarter of the 19th century, as population increased and

SOURCE: From U.S. Civil Service Commission, *Biography Of An Ideal* (Washington, D.C.: Government Printing Office, 1974).

with it the need for more government services, public employment grew and began to be the object of political patronage in the States and growing cities.

DeToqueville, writing after his visit to the country in 1831, expressed his admiration of its decentralized democracy, but says, "It is not the administrative but the political effects of decentralization that I most admire in America." For example, comparing France and America, he cites the citizens' attitude toward crime as an offense against the people rather than against the authorities and their support of law enforcement as more important in combating crime than the better organized state police in France. He notes the instability of public administration in the U.S. and says of the officials:

> those who engage in the perplexities of political life are persons of very moderate pretensions. The pursuit of wealth diverts men of great talents and strong passions from the pursuit of power; and it frequently happens that a man does not undertake to direct the fortunes of the state until he has shown himself incompetent to conduct his own.

### Spoils and Early Civil Service Legislation

In the succeeding half century, the spoils approach to State and local jobs became entrenched. In some of the larger cities department heads were elected and political machines established the use of public payrolls to gain and perpetuate their power. Large scale immigration and slum conditions gave opportunities to provide some ombudsman services to the poor and profit well thereby.

In the early period there was a disorganized rush on elected officials by a horde of job seekers trying to show their political and job credentials. Varied refinements were added by the political bosses, such as the more systematic apportionment of jobs among city or county precincts without regard to qualifications, and even the sale of public jobs. Unnecessary jobs were created, some as sinecures for the most favored, others, with a peak in number just before an election, for persons who could perform political chores.

After the Civil War, industrial and urban growth required new and expanded public services in which contracts provided opportunities for large-scale graft. Public employees, if not themselves implicated, might avert their eyes, when appointed through the political bosses engaged in the graft and serving at their pleasure.

During the 1870's and 1880's there were, along with robber barons and predatory politicians, some leaders in various States who voiced diverse concerns for ethical standards and honest service to the public. There were movements for regulation of the railroads to correct abuses, for medical and legal professionalism to deal with quackery, and for civil service legislation to improve public administration. If reform was not a strong wind, at least it was in the air.

The New York Civil Service Reform Association was formed in 1877. Within a few years there were perhaps forty similar groups in many States and cities. In 1881 delegates from thirteen associations formed the National Civil Service Reform League.

The effort to establish a merit system in the Federal Government and the subsequent passage of the Pendleton Act in 1883 encouraged similar efforts at State and local levels.

The first State civil service law was enacted in New York in 1883. Theodore Roosevelt, then an assemblyman, played an important part in the State legislature, introducing the bill that Grover Cleveland as governor signed into law. Massachusetts followed in 1884.

For the next two decades, although bills were introduced in several State legislatures, no additional State civil service system was established. There was entrenched opposition, both open and sub rosa.

At the local government level, the first municipalities to adopt a civil service system were Albany in 1884, Buffalo in 1885, and New York City in 1888. Syracuse followed in 1894, Chicago and Evanston in 1895, and Seattle in 1896. A number of smaller cities in New York State also established civil service systems during these years. In Massachusetts, Boston and other cities were placed under civil service in 1885 and succeeding years, with the State commission responsible for administration. Cook County, Illinois, was the first county to establish a civil service system, doing so in 1895.

The coverage of the early civil service systems was limited primarily to clerical employees and in the cities to the police and often full-time firemen.

## Muckraking and Reform

With the turn of the century, municipal reform became an important issue.

Lincoln Steffens' articles in *McClure's Magazine* in 1902–03 (published as "The Shame of the Cities" in 1904) exposed municipal corruption in St. Louis, Minneapolis, Pittsburgh, and Philadelphia and treated attempts at reform in Chicago and New York. Of Tammany he said, "Its grafting system is one in which more individuals share than in any I had studied . . .The leaders and captains have their hold because they take care of their own . . . find jobs, most of them at the city's expense."

Public opinion was aroused by the muckrakers, who exposed corruption and spoils in the cities and abuses in State legislatures. State and local civil service systems were advocated in a number of jurisdictions and some were adopted. At the State level, in 1905 Wisconsin and Illinois enacted laws, in 1907 Colorado, and in 1908 New Jersey. Ohio adopted a general provision for civil service in its constitution in 1912, and this was supplemented by a civil service law in 1913. California and Connecticut also passed laws that year, but the latter law became moribund and was repealed in 1921. Kansas passed a law in 1915, but it became inoperative in 1919 when the legislature refused any appropriation for its administration. In 1920 Maryland enacted a personnel law which for the first time provided for a single administrator rather than a bipartisan commission.

The municipal reform movement resulted in changes in the form of government in many cities. In a number of cities this was accompanied by the adoption of civil service systems during the first two decades of the century. In many cases, however, particularly in the smaller cities, these systems covered only the police or police and fire departments.

Among the cities establishing general civil service systems were San Francisco and Rochester in 1900, Los Angeles and Portland in 1903, Philadelphia in 1906, Pittsburgh and Tacoma in 1907, Des Moines in 1908, Cincinnati, Cleveland, and Newark in 1910, Trenton, Jersey City, Oakland, and Spokane in 1911, Sacramento, Minneapolis, and Detroit in 1913, St. Paul in 1914, San Diego in 1915, St. Louis in 1916, and Baltimore in 1920. In New York and Ohio a number of smaller cities set up civil service commissions, and local coverage in Massachusetts was extended to a number of towns.

Los Angeles County adopted a civil service system in 1913 and Milwaukee County in 1918. Several counties in New Jersey elected to come under the State system, and seventeen of the larger counties in New York came under civil service provisions from 1900 to 1914. Ohio's provisions for county coverage were not put into effect.

### Development of Professional Personnel Administration

Many of the civil service commissions were soon starved for funds. Some were too small to have full-time staff. Some became politically dominated and a front for spoils.

Honesty and zeal went a long way toward progress by eliminating the gross abuses, but it was not a substitute for adequate techniques of personnel management.

Technical developments in the 1920's and 1930's, based upon psychological research and industrial engineering experience, laid the ground for more effective and not merely nonpartisan administration.

Group testing was first effectively used by the Army in World War I. The Army Alpha test was devised for selection, placement, and promotion where large numbers of persons had to be classified efficiently. Its validation as a predictor of performance, particularly for officer candidates, paved the way for the introduction of group mental ability testing in industry and in civil service administration. The Army Beta test, devised for use with illiterates, also had some impact. Faced with political pressures, State and local agencies had relied on academic written tests heavily and were glad to have more objective devices.

Performance tests had also been used for some types of jobs. The work of the Research Division of the U.S. Civil Service Commission in the late 1920's was an important contribution, particularly in the development of standardized performance tests for typists and stenographers and general mental ability tests for public service use. It had a significant influence on State and local merit system administration.

Salary standardization was an early problem. The application of job analysis techniques, developed in industry for greater efficiency, resulted in the establishment of job classification plans. In the public service the emphasis has been on the use of job classification for establishing and administering pay plans. There has been some use, however, for performance rating, training and selection, by identifying necessary knowledges and skills related to specific jobs. The first classification plan was installed in Chicago in 1912, eleven years before the Federal Classification Act was adopted.

State and local salaries were low, but job security and fringe benefits were better than in most businesses. Hours were shorter and there were provisions, not as common in business, for paid vacations.

The first public retirement system in the U.S. was the police pension system in New York City, established in 1857. The first State retirement system for public employees was in Massachusetts in 1911, nine years before passage of the Federal Retirement Act.

The National Assembly of Civil Service Commissions was established in 1906 by the U.S. commissioners and representatives of twenty State and local commissions. In 1918 it became the Civil Service Assembly of the U.S. and Canada, and in 1956 the Public Personnel Association. The Assembly's conferences were a forum for civil service administrators and commissioners, discussing common problems and promoting professional development. It established a service for the exchange of tests and other personnel materials. It published a series of volumes on major personnel subjects and a quarterly, the *Public Personnel Review.* This was combined in 1972 with *Personnel Administration,* the journal of the Society for Personnel Administration. The Society, established in 1937, had largely Federal membership but substantial State, local, and industrial participation and subscriptions. The two organizations consolidated in 1973 to become the International Personnel Management Association.

### The Depression and Public Employment

The initial impact of the great depression, beginning in 1929, was retrenchment. As tax revenues decreased, State and local governments cut programs and jobs. Vacancies were generally frozen and there were some reductions in force. However, there was increasing public demand for relief measures for the unemployed and the destitute. Some rather limited State and local emergency programs were initiated. Under various New Deal programs beginning in 1933, the Federal Government provided aid to States and localities as well as Federal work projects. The programs were regarded as temporary and even in States with civil service systems, the administrative jobs in them were exempted. Grants to States, instituted under the 1935 Social Security Act for continuing social programs, are discussed later.

Turnover in the State and local governments was negligible. All jobs were desirable, and political pressures for those open were fierce. However, now the pressures were exerted on behalf of well qualified as well as the marginal and unqualified persons previously proffered by political machines. But the political and personal priorities were not correlated with abilities, and more often than not, placements were without regard to qualifications.

Some jurisdictions suspended examinations, presumably for reasons of economy. The agencies who held competitive examinations were swamped by applicants. One tendency was to reduce the unmanageable numbers by raising minimum qualifications.

Side by side with the abuses of patronage, there was an influx, in a number of States and cities, of able young university and professional school graduates in a wide variety of jobs. While a large number of these left, particularly after military service in World War II, a gratifying number of outstanding persons remained in or returned to the public service. They provided many State and local governments, especially those under operating merit systems, with a generation of high ability.

### Federal Grants and State–Local Administration

The extension of State merit systems through the Federal grant-in-aid programs has been recognized as a major breakthrough in public personnel administration. Prof. Leonard White, former member of the U.S. Civil Service Commission, stated in the *Public Personnel Review* in July 1945: "The importance of this amendment to the steady improvement of personnel standards in the State and county government cannot be exaggerated."

Federal concern with efficient administration in grant programs necessarily involves attention to personnel administration. This has been manifested in a variety of ways. There may be no formal requirements, but informal discussions of key appointments and unofficial assistance in recruitment. There may be the imposition of minimum professional qualifications for specified jobs and approval of salary rates. Another way is a systems approach, which provides technical assistance and requires that there be a State or locally administered merit system that meets Federal standards.

When the Social Security Act was passed in 1935, it included major new grants to States for several categories of public assistance, unemployment insurance, maternal and child health, and crippled children's programs. In the state of the labor market, as previously indicated, the anticipated hundred thousand jobs in the State and local administrative agencies became the targets for unprecedented pressures.

In the Act, Congress had required that, to be Federally approved, a State plan had to provide for methods of proper and efficient administration. However, any Federal requirement as to the selection, tenure, or compensation of State and local employees was specifically precluded.

Only nine States at the time had civil service systems, and several of them were not functioning effectively. Within the next few years there were reports in a number of States of poor administration in the grant programs—waste, inefficiency, and political use of employees and of welfare recipients.

In 1938, the Social Security Board established a State Technical Advisory Service to give assistance to States, on request, for the improvement of personnel administration in the grant programs. A number of States were aided in installing classification and compensation plans and in establishing single agency merit systems. The results stimulated widespread interest in amending the Federal law to remove the prohibition against Federal requirements in personnel administration.

In 1939 President Roosevelt recommended such amendments, stating:

in some States incompetent and politically dominated personnel has been distinctly harmful. Therefore, I recommend that the States be required, as a condition for the receipt of Federal funds, to establish and maintain a merit system for the selection of personnel. Such a requirement would represent a protection to the States and citizens thereof rather than an encroachment by the Federal Government, since it would automatically promote efficiency and eliminate the necessity for minute Federal scrutiny of State operations.

The amendments were supported by the great majority of State program administrators and by civic organizations such as the League of Women Voters and its State affiliates, the National Civil Service Reform League, and the Junior Chambers of Commerce.

A factor in Congressional action was the clash in some States between incumbent Senators and aspiring Governors, in which the latter had the patronage of Federally aided programs. For example, in one primary campaign the State employees, presumably voluntarily, gave two percent of their salaries to the governor's campaign against the incumbent senator, and left the capital the week before the primary to go to their home counties and extol the virtues of the governor. The Senate did not regard this as the best use of Federal grants, and voted 72 to 2 for the merit system amendments.

Over the years the Congress has enacted or re-enacted merit system provisions for additional or revised programs over thirty times. These extended coverage to new public assistance categories, various public health and hospital planning programs, grants for the aging, and State and local civil defense grants. In addition, several programs were made subject to the merit system requirement by administrative action, the most recent being the occupational health and safety program by the Department of Labor in 1971.

In 1940 the Hatch Political Activities Act, restricting political activities of Federal employees, was amended to apply to State and local employees whose principal employment is in a Federally aided activity. The coverage is broader than that of the merit system standards. The Act covers all Federally aided agencies (except educational institutions), not just those to which the merit system requirement applies. It covers non-elective heads of departments and other employees who may be exempted from the merit system. The U.S. Civil Service Commission has had responsibility for enforcement of the Act.

## Federal–State Merit System Relations

A decade after the enactment of requirements for State merit systems in various Federally funded programs, the Council of State Governments prepared a report for the Hoover Commission on Federal–State Relations. It stated:

National insistence upon State-wide merit systems for particular programs has undoubtedly improved the administration of those programs. Experience with merit systems in grant programs has also influenced a considerable number of States to extend these systems to other departments. In addition, many State civil service agencies have been strengthened and revitalized by the services rendered them by the Technical Advisory Service to States of the Social Security Administration.

. . . national supervision should not be confused with national control. National supervision can be most effective when it allows the States to profit from its superior technical facilities and greater experience. The emphasis in national supervision now rests to a large extent—and properly so—on building up the quality of personnel within State agencies. Merit systems are only the first important step in this process. Additional devices of importance include budgeting and planning aid; information, advice, and technical assistance; conferences and inspections. These devices of cooperation, not coercion, will lead to increasingly effective administrative programs.

In 1955 the Commission on Intergovernmental Relations, established by Congress as counterpart to the second Hoover Commission, reported:

In the case of the merit system requirement which appears in many of the grant-in-aid laws, the national government has not generally made specific rules on the qualifications, tenure, pay, promotion, and other conditions of State personnel. Instead, these details are left to the State wherever it follows the customary practices of a civil service or merit system.

Studies made for the Commission indicate that the results of this approach have been generally satisfactory. The Commission suggests that every effort be made to develop similar general standards in other areas of administration, and in program requirements.

In 1969, the Advisory Committee on Merit System Standards in its report "Progress in Intergovernmental Personnel Relations" commented on the Federal–State relationship as follows:

There is evidence that the Federal–State relationship which now exists in respect to merit systems is a fruitful partnership. Of course, there are problems; as former Secretary Gardner has pointed out, "I do not believe that the relationship of the Federal Government to State and local government and to private groups should ever be a comfortable one. The two parties to the relationship have purposes that overlap but are not identical. Each must play its role and function with integrity in terms of its own purposes."

The Federal role involved the development of national standards under the statutory requirements for merit systems in the grant programs, the review of State plans and of personnel operations in relation to the standards, and the provision of technical assistance. The emphasis has been on the last function.

The original Standards for a Merit System of Personnel Administration were issued in 1939 after consultation with administrators of the State grant programs and of civil service agencies and others in the field of public administration. Revisions in the standards were made in 1948 and 1971 after their extensive review by distinguished advisory committees. A revision was made in 1963 after consultation among the Federal grant programs to strengthen provisions in State laws and rules for equal employment opportunity. The Intergovernmental Personnel Act, discussed later in this chapter, transferred the Federal merit system responsibilities to the U.S. Civil Service Commission and provided that the standards in effect at that time would remain in effect until revised by the Commission.

The Federal statutory provisions are in separate titles, applicable to over 300 State agencies and their affiliated local agencies, in various grant programs. These programs at the Federal level are administered in several departments and their constituent agencies. To provide a coordinated approach prior to the enactment of the Intergovernmental Personnel Act, the State Technical Advisory Service and its successor, the Office of State Merit Systems in the Department of Health, Education, and Welfare, was by interdepartmental contracts given responsibility for policy development, review, and technical assistance functions under the various titles. The sanctions remained with the granting agencies, but the joint interdepartmental approach was lauded as a statesmanlike innovation in Federal–State relations.

Most of the grant programs to which the merit system requirement applied have been State-administered or State-supervised and county administered. The relations with the cities have not been as significant, and most of those involved have had civil service systems covering the relatively few grant-in-aid employees affected. In the case of the counties, only a small number have had civil service systems. The county grant agency employees were placed under State merit systems or under supplemental multi-county merit systems established primarily for welfare, health, and defense employees.

In some States the Federal requirements resulted in the application to localities of State laws that had not been put into effect. For example, the Cleveland Press on January 14, 1942, stated:

> State and county offices engaged in administering public aid . . . now are staffed almost entirely with regular civil service employees. This is a fine reform. It means the elimination . . . of the provisional appointment, made without competitive examination and used often as a means of providing a job for a political favorite. As the State Welfare Department's own announcement of the change emphasizes, this 100 percent adherence to civil service standards exists now for the first time in the State's history.

There have been few Federal–State confrontations in the program. Establishment of the merit system has essentially been by State action with Federal cooperation, not by enforcement. There have been forces for merit in every State, and their efforts are sometimes strengthened when they can cite Federal standards in appropriate situations. There have been several instances when governors, and more when State personnel or program administrators, asked for statements of possible sanctions, sometimes stronger than could be supplied.

The technical services provided to the States and to a more limited extent to local governments changed over the years in response to new problems. It included field consultation on personnel policies and administration, exchange of information on practices, provision of technical manuals and guide materials, and a test service.

Draft rule provisions were found useful to a considerable extent by about thirty States in development of their first rules. The draft suggested in the absence of a civil service system, that a Merit System Council be appointed by the governor or by the participating State program agencies, with a career executive. These councils were typically of high calibre, including college presidents and faculty and professional and business leaders.

Cooperation in salary surveys produced data useful to the States generally. Seminars and institutes of varying types were conducted with a total of over one thousand State staff members participating. In continuing demand has been the institute on selection methods.

The cooperative test service was used at one time or another by all States and was relied on heavily by some. The thousands of tests sent to the States and some local governments over the years, involving over a million objective test items adapted to the jobs in the grant programs, was an essential resource in the light of small merit system staffs. Recently new types of tests were developed for the selection of the disadvantaged for "new careers" jobs.

## Extension of Civil Service

Labor market conditions in the depression drew attention to public service employment, its opportunities, and its abuses. Civil service was a livelier newspaper topic than in the previous two decades. The Commission of Inquiry on Public Service Personnel in 1935 helped focus interest in extension and improvement.

At the State level in 1937 new State civil service laws were enacted in Maine, Michigan, Connecticut, Arkansas, and New Mexico. However, Arkansas repealed its law in 1939 and New Mexico in 1941. In Michigan in 1938 a ripper bill emasculated the system, but a constitutional amendment in 1939 established a strong system. One unique feature was for a guaranteed appropriation of 1 percent of payroll.

In 1939 civil service laws were passed in Alabama, Rhode Island, and Minnesota. Tennessee also adopted a civil service law, but provided that the governor might exempt departments from the provisions for competitive appointments and tenure. He promptly exempted all departments except those receiving Federal grants subject to a merit system condition.

Louisiana passed a civil service law in 1940 which was repealed in 1948, leaving only a system for the Federally aided agencies. In 1952 a constitutional provision established a general civil service system. It provided that the governor make appointments to the Civil Service Commission from a list prepared by the presidents of five universities in the State.

Constitutional provisions played an important part in strengthening the merit system in several instances. We have noted two. Earlier, in California in 1933, severe budget cuts greatly weakened the system, but a 1934 constitutional amendment extended civil service coverage and strengthened its organization so that it became a leader among the States.

Yet a constitutional provision cannot assure proper and efficient administration, any more than a statute. It can be some protection against ripper bills. It may also provide a basis for citizen action in enforcement.

There have been great difficulties in attaining consistent local merit system coverage on a State-wide basis in the few States that require it, such as Ohio and Massachusetts. Sufficient funds have not been generally available to provide adequate service to a large number of small jurisdictions. There may also be pressures against effective administration.

In New York State, the 1894 constitutional provision that competitive examinations be given so far as practicable was interpreted as not to require complete local coverage until a court decision in 1937 rejected the interpretation. A study commission appointed by the legislature later worked out a plan with alternative ways of providing service.

There were no wartime extensions of civil service, but Oregon established a system in 1945. Georgia had established a limited civil service system under a provision that permitted extension. The Atlanta Constitution of March 13, 1950, commented on action for extension, as follows:

> Of more than nine thousand State employees, all but 1,659 are now covered by the merit, or civil-service system. That is reassuring. It was only a few years ago that every State job in Georgia was subect to the whims of politics. There was no security for employees, no insistence upon competence with its consequent benefit to the taxpayer. New administrations came into office and the State employees who had worked for the old ones were fired to make room for the friends and relatives of the victorious faction. It was the spoils system at its worst.
>
> The Federal Government, incidentally, is due much of the credit for the turn to the merit system in Georgia. It refused, and rightly, to allocate Federal funds to the State Departments of Labor, Welfare and Health until civil service systems were effectuated therein. The consequent improvement in working conditions in those departments impressed even the die-hard patronage dispensers who had previously fought every attempt to attract more career workers in State jobs. They came to welcome the relief from the thousands of sinecure seekers who descended on them after every successful campaign. And the merit system spread even into departments where Federal funds were not involved.

In the 1950's and 1960's there was a steady growth in the number of States that adopted State-wide civil service systems. In the latter decade, the number of States with comprehensive State merit systems first came to exceed the number of States with limited systems primarily or exclusively for Federally aided agencies. There were also several States that established a personnel office in the Governor's office or a department of administration, usually to administer classification and pay plans, and sometimes to perform other functions. But these State-wide systems did not extend the competitive service or provide tenure to State employees generally.

Some other States that passed general civil service laws during the 1950's were Kansas, Nevada, New Hampshire, Vermont, Oklahoma, and Kentucky. During the 1960's Alaska, Arizona, Delaware, Idaho, Iowa, New Mexico, and Utah adopted comprehensive merit system laws. The current total of States with such State-wide systems is 33, leaving 17 States where the merit system competitive service is more limited.

There also has been an increase over the years in the establishment of general municipal civil service systems. There are wide variations in legal provisions, organization, and scope of coverage, as well as the quality of administration. In some cases there is the form and not the substance of a merit system.

All of the cities with a population over 250,000, with the exception of Washington, D.C., which receives some services from the U.S. Civil Service Commission, have provisions for a municipal civil service system. Most cities between 100,000 and 250,000 are under a law, charter, or ordinance for such a system. Many smaller cities also have civil service systems. In a substantial number of them, coverage is limited to the police and fire departments. A few cities have two systems, one general and one for police and fire.

There has been less activity in establishment of civil service systems at the county level. There are various systems in the counties of the following States: New York, Ohio, New Jersey, and California. In other States coverage is limited to the larger metropolitan or suburban counties. Massachusetts has civil service coverage of localities, and a few States have combined city–county systems.

### Variations in Administration

"Personnel systems," says the report *Progress in Intergovernmental Personnel Relations*, "vary in their quality from practical validity to procedural paralysis." There are great differences in the calibre of merit system administration from place to place, and from time to time in a given jurisdiction.

While we have, in this chapter, treated some national trends, the history of civil service in each State and locality is unique. There are few if any jurisdictions that have had a consistently level performance. For example, Albany, the first city to adopt a civil service plan, in later years became a prime example of a boss-ridden patronage operation. Los Angeles, which had public scandals in 1938, within a few years under a reform commission and an innovative personnel director developed and maintained an outstanding career service.

There are systems, providing efficient service using the best available science-based techniques; others with a merit tradition that buttresses mediocre administration; some in a never-ending struggle to maintain competitive entrance; others with narrow, red-taped operations; and still others with a mere facade of merit.

It has been said of some systems, "The only thing that's worse than civil service is no civil service." Yet the net contribution of most systems in improving the quality of service to the public is cumulatively impressive.

The earlier civic leaders were concerned with the enactment of a civil service law, later ones with the honesty of its administration; and more recently, concern has centered on the effectiveness of administration and its responsiveness to public service needs.

Sometimes the focus has been on the form of organization rather than the factors in its functioning. The political and administrative climate varies so that in some jurisdictions and at some times the commission, personnel board, or merit system council may be an important strength, in other cases unimportant. A merit-minded governor may make progress by supplanting a mediocre personnel director with an excellent one; another governor may replace an experienced mediocrity by an inexperienced one or by a wheeler-dealer.

The quality of administration depends upon such factors as top executive, legislative, and public support, broad gauged personnel leadership, competent professional staff, and adequate appropriations.

# 13

# Professionalization of Personnel

*Martha Derthick*

An effort to professionalize state and local personnel is characteristic of many grant programs. Federal administrators, usually professionals themselves, wish their counterparts at other levels of government to be professionals as well. Accordingly, they seek to influence the selection and training of state and local employees.

"Professionalism" in the context of the federal public assistance program implies possession of those skills and attitudes characteristic of both the professional public administrator and the professional social worker. State and local personnel are expected to value and to implement those principles that are generally regarded as proper to administrative conduct, such as impartiality in dealing with clients, clarity in the enunciation of policies, and thoroughness and accuracy in record keeping. They are also expected to have the humane attitudes toward the poor characteristic of the social-work profession rather than the punitive attitudes that the profession attributes to laymen, and those who deal with clients are expected to be skilled in the treatment of personal and social "problems."

The federal assistance administrators' effort to professionalize their state and local counterparts has always been conditioned by distrust in Congress. In 1935 the House Ways and Means Committee removed a merit-system requirement

SOURCE: Reprinted by permission of the publishers from *The Influence of Federal Grants: Public Assistance in Massachusetts,* by Martha Derthick. Cambridge, Mass.: Harvard University Press, © 1970 by The President and Fellows of Harvard College.

from the social security bill for fear it would be used to make the states hire professional social workers. Representative Fred M. Vinson of Kentucky insisted that "No damned social workers are going to come into my State to tell our people whom they shall hire."[1] Four years later, when the Social Security Board appealed again for the requirement, Congressman McCormack of Massachusetts reminded Commissioner Altmeyer that "Congress has not, let us say, an antifeeling, but they have a feeling of hesitancy, if not opposition—and I am one of them—toward these fine people who are the social workers of the country." McCormack believed that assistance "should be handled by people of local ability who have knowledge of local conditions and the background and surroundings of the people." Altmeyer sought to reassure Congress by pointing out that in states already having merit systems, the proportion of professionally trained workers was less than 5 percent.[2]

Notwithstanding objections from the Ways and Means Committee (the Senate's contrary views prevailed in conference), Congress in 1939 gave the Social Security Board authority to set personnel standards, perhaps because it was sympathetic to some degree of professionalism in the performance of public administration (on the assumption that it would lead to "efficiency") if not in the performance of social work. Even before this was done, the Board was demanding—on the basis of its authority to require efficient administration—that state plans include minimum standards for education, training, and experience. When the amendment was passed, the Board's power over these matters was much strengthened.

Since that time maintenance and improvement of personnel standards have been a major preoccupation of federal assistance administrators. The effort to professionalize state and local personnel may have been greater in public assistance than in other grant programs, for the gap in professional attainment among governments has been especially wide. A federal survey in 1950 showed that 57 percent of federal assistance employees had two or more years of graduate study in a school of social work, whereas only 4 percent of state and local employees did. Only 1 percent of federal employees lacked bachelor's degrees, whereas 40 percent of state and local employees did. Another survey ten years later showed that the educational levels of state and local employees had not increased significantly, although, because the educational level of federal employees had fallen, the intergovernmental gap had narrowed slightly.[3]

Following adoption of the merit-system amendment in 1939, the Social Security Board issued "Standards for a Merit System of Personnel Administration," a distinct body of rules that required, among other things, the establishment of classification and compensation plans and open competitive examinations. In these matters as in most others, the Board's rules were concerned more with method than with content. The Board required that a merit system be set up, but the precise content of the rules remained largely within the discretion of the states. Whether the federal administration's objective of greater professionalism would in fact be achieved depended heavily on circumstances in each state.

## Professionalism in Massachusetts

The Massachusetts case is a good illustration of the problems that federal administrators might face. Extension of the state's civil service system to all assistance personnel, though achieved between 1940 and 1950 at the expense of great federal effort, did not go far toward enhancing professional quality. For reasons rooted deep in the social structure and political institutions of the state, its civil service system was not well suited to that purpose.

Professionalism is manifested in the possession of certain skills and attitudes but, because these are difficult to measure, a readily measurable surrogate—'amount of formal education'— is often resorted to as an indicator of the degree of professionalism. By this measure, public assistance employees in Massachusetts have been extremely "unprofessional." As of 1960, 42.7 percent of them, the highest percentage in the nation, had no college education at all. Professionalism was not an objective of the state's personnel policy. In 1935, as Congress was passing the Social Security Act—and for much the same reason: to provide security to the poor— the Massachusetts legislature was amending the civil service law to prohibit the imposition of any educational requirements.[4]

Although the civil service system posed one obstacle to professionalism, the extreme localism of the administrative structure posed another. Localism, as Congressman McCormack's remarks suggest, may be conceived of as one alternative to professionalism; they represent competing conceptions of the proper criteria of public employment. According to the localistic conception, the special qualification of the public administrator lies in his knowledge of and attachment to the particular community in which he functions; according to the professional conception, it lies in the possession of more universalized skills and attitudes associated with the occupational function. The system of city and town administration in Massachusetts contributed to the development and maintenance of the localistic conception. Most administrators had long careers in the same city or town, and the localized character of the job was one of its main attractions. The federal personnel survey of 1960 showed that Massachusetts employees were much more likely to remain in the same agency than those in other states. "Median years of social welfare experience with present agency" for employees in Massachusetts was 13.5, compared with 6.6 years in all states and 11.5 years in the second-ranking state, Oklahoma. Attachment to place may also help to explain why turnover among public assistance personnel in Massachusetts has been almost the lowest in the nation—9.5 separations per 100 employees in 1959, compared to a national rate of 21.

The state welfare department was more professionalized than the local staffs. The commissioners either had social-work training themselves (like Tompkins and Ott) or were members of a civic elite sympathetic to the social-work profession (like Rotch). The rest of the state staff was generally better educated than local personnel, though it was by no means completely professionalized. In 1960, 45 percent of the department's field representatives lacked college degrees, whereas 63 percent of the local workers, 68 percent of the local supervisors, and 77 percent of the local directors lacked them.

From the start of federal aid, officials urged the state department to raise personnel standards. The department did not actively resist, but it could not pursue the objective of greater professionalism without meeting resistance from local employees and from the legislature and the Division of Civil Service, both of which traditionally protected the interests of public employees and neither of which wanted public employment to become exclusive.[5] In the face of this resistance, the department tended to be unresponsive to federal pressure. Between 1940 and 1950, as federal merit-system standards were applied to Massachusetts, conflicts broke out repeatedly. The efforts of regional officials to bring about change were hampered not only by resistance within the state, but by a lack of detailed federal requirements that might, with Washington's backing, be insisted upon.

These conflicts were never really settled, and for more than a decade after 1950 they lay dormant. Though the Massachusetts system of recruiting and promoting personnel departed radically from the federal ideal, not until 1964 was it directly and fundamentally challenged. Then, in the wake of the 1962 amendments, the federal administration for the first time specified educational standards for state and local workers. The principal requirement was that caseworkers and casework supervisors appointed after October 1, 1965, have bachelor's degrees. This touched off intense controversy in Massachusetts, where it necessitated modification of the thirty-year-old law against all education requirements.

# The Aftermath of the Merit-System Extension, 1940–1950

In the decade after the merit-system requirement was applied to Massachusetts, problems arose constantly in the state's response to it. Perhaps the most vexing of them grew out of the requirement of a state-wide salary schedule, the "welfare compensation plan." Getting 351 cities and towns quite varied in size and social structure to abide by such a schedule took far more effort than the state's civil service division was willing to invest. Nor did the division satisfy the federal demand for a classification plan. These two matters were the subject of intensive negotiations for much of the decade, and a recurrent source of friction well into the 1960s. (The city of Cambridge, for one, refused to conform to the compensation plan.)

Troublesome as these issues were, they need not have stood in the way of the federal desire for better-qualified personnel. The compensation plan in particular was a response as much to the federal desire for equity as to the desire for professionalism. The intention was to secure equal pay for equal work, and the BPA objected quite as much to local deviations in excess of the salary schedule, which might have attracted high-quality personnel in particular places, as to local failures to meet the schedule. But there were issues that touched more directly on the problem of quality, issues having to do with the conduct of examinations and the setting of entrance requirements.

***Integrity of examinations.*** The first of these issues developed out of the examinations that were given in 1940 to candidates for positions newly covered by civil service. In some ways, it set the pattern for later ones.

Soon after Commissioner Rotch set up a merit system in 1940, civil service examinations were administered to incumbents and other applicants. Even before the results became known, the Massachusetts Association of Relief Officers prepared a bill that would have nullified them by automatically extending civil service coverage to incumbents. Meanwhile, the welfare department filed a bill to validate the commissioner's action and the examinations given under it.

Faced with these alternatives, the legislature temporized. It did not want to act without knowing the results of the examinations. If the proportion of incumbents failing was low—on the order of 10 to 15 percent—the legislature's civil service committee was prepared to act favorably on the department's bill, but if, as was rumored, the percentage of failures was much higher, the committee wanted to take steps to protect the threatened incumbents.

In March 1941, Civil Service Director Ulysses J. Lupien reported to Commissioner Rotch that 70 incumbents out of 255, or 27.5 percent, had failed. Sensitive to the interests of local employees, and even more to the desires of the legislature's committee on civil service, Lupien urged consideration of a blanketing-in provision. His would have been less generous than the Relief Officers': he proposed to cover incumbents as of July 1, 1935, the date of the Social Security Act, rather than those as of April 1940, the date Rotch's merit system went into effect. This would have lowered the percentage of disqualified incumbents from 27.5 to 15. Lupien asked Rotch to recommend this to the Social Security Board, and Rotch obliged. He sent a copy of Lupien's letter to the BPA regional representative, adding his own endorsement: "In view of the fact that the [civil service] committee and many of the legislators are quite concerned about this whole matter, I recommend that the Social Security Board give its approval."[6]

When the Relief Officers' bill began to circulate in the fall of 1940, federal officials in the region and in Washington agreed that is was completely unacceptable. The regional attorney argued in a memorandum to the central office that it would constitute a "clear violation" of Board standards; the general counsel and Jane Hoey concurred; and the regional representative informed Rotch that if the blanketing-in provision were passed, it would "raise a question of Plan conformity."[7] Now, faced with a recommendation from Lupien and Rotch and a recalcitrant legislature, regional officials began

to waver. As they analyzed the situation, relying heavily upon the opinions of Lupien and Rotch, it would be best to accept a blanketing-in provision. It had become clear that a bill validating the commissioner's action was essential if merit system coverage were to stand. The action was being challenged in the courts and Rotch was almost certain to lose. Through negotiations with state civil service and welfare officials, the regional office had succeeded in adding several provisions to the department's bill, including one for the welfare compensation plan, which were very important in the federal view. To the regional office, it appeared that the choice was between accepting a bill that was on the whole essential to federal purposes, although it would be flawed by a blanketing-in provision, and adamant opposition to the provision at the possible cost of losing the whole bill.[8]

Despite the regional office's preference for compromise, the central office stood firm. The legislature's civil service committee made two trips to Washington to talk with Board officials and found that they could not be made to yield. In June 1941, the department's bill, with several federally inspired provisions and without the blanketing-in, was passed.

Even then it was not clear that federal objectives had been secured, for the process of hearing appeals from the examinations had not been completed. One of the distinguishing features of the Massachusetts civil service system is the frequency with which examination results are overturned on appeal.[9] The legislature might not have yielded to the Social Security Board were it not for this possibility of protecting incumbents. Through appeals the number of failures was eventually reduced from 70 to 50. The Board's Washington office prodded the regional office to keep track of appeal results and to make sure that incumbents who failed were actually compelled to give up their jobs. Not until June 1942 was it satisfied on this point.[10]

The struggle over examination results ended with a federal victory, but the circumstances of the struggle illustrated the obstacles that federal officials would face in their effort to improve the quality of state and local personnel: a legislature sensitive to the interests of job seekers, a civil service agency sensitive to the desires of the legislature, and a public welfare agency formally committed to higher personnel standards but unwilling or unable to challenge the civil service division or the legislature. This pattern persisted for a long time, a source of frustration to federal officials whose doctrine was that a "single state agency," the welfare department, should be responsible for meeting federal standards.

*Local registers.* A second issue that developed in the early 1940s concerned the territorial units from which local employees should be recruited. The Massachusetts practice before 1940 represented an extreme of localism. The civil service division announced job openings for a specific place, and only residents of that place were admitted to the examination. This was in conflict with Social Security Board policy, which prohibited such residence requirements. The Board wanted examinations to be open to all residents of the state and the list of eligibles to be a single statewide list.

For two years, regional officials negotiated with state officials in an effort to reconcile Massachusetts practice with federal preferences. They succeeded in getting the civil service division to substitute district examinations for local ones (a district was one of the administrative areas defined by the state welfare department to facilitate supervision of local agencies—there were seven as of 1941); but they failed to get provisions for use of state-wide examinations and registers incorporated in the civil service law. Instead, the legislature merely provided that if the list of eligibles were exhausted for any city or town, the civil service director "might" certify eligibles from a district list.

Federal policy in this matter was not very exacting. Although it prohibited local-residence requirements in the conduct of examinations, it did not prohibit the preferential hiring of local residents. The federal objective was to open up examinations to all competitors and, hopefully, if no local residents were on the register, to

compel hiring from a district or state list. In practice, many Massachusetts communities continued to hire only their own residents. Those that wanted to hire from a district list could do so—such a list was available to them— but the civil service division did not compel them to.

*Provisional appointments.* A third issue concerned the making of provisional appointments—appointees who had not passed a civil service exam—when no list of eligibles was available. Federal policy permitted such appointments but specified that these appointees must meet the same qualifications as others, that the same individual should not receive successive appointments, and that provisionals be terminated after six months. In 1941 the Massachusetts legislature stipulated that assistance employees appointed provisionally must meet minimum qualifications, a measure that was federally inspired. But issues arose in the next decade over whether this law was being observed and over the volume and duration of provisional appointments.

Federal merit-system audits in the mid-1940s showed that well over half of the new appointments were provisional. Examinations were given infrequently (as of the 1960s, social-worker examinations were still given only once a year), with the result that registers were exhausted much of the time. There were numerous cases in which provisional appointments extended far beyond six months and appointees did not meet qualifications.

This situation was one of several that contributed to federal dissatisfaction with Massachusetts and to the intensive effort to bring about improvement in 1948–50. The regional office also dealt with it separately, by taking audit exceptions for the salaries of provisionals who had served more than six months. When this was first done—with respect to junior clerk-typists, junior clerk-stenographers, and junior clerks in Waltham and Springfield—Commissioner Tompkins protested that the regional office was acting arbitrarily. He charged the regional representative, Eleanore Schopke, with impugning the integrity of the civil service division. "It is quite clear to me," he wrote, ". . .that neither chicanery nor connivance is employed for purposes of disposition of the available eligibles in order to continue favorite provisionals in specifically designated positions either in State government or local government." In response to her request for information, Tompkins declared that "the State Division of Civil Service, acting in its broad, general administrative areas, does not necessarily have to explain to any other branch of government its priority of selections for Civil Service Examinations."[11]

The subsequent exchange between the regional office and Tompkins shows federal-state relations at a point of maximum stress. Miss Schopke declined to rebut his allegations but called attention to "one statement. . .with which we are in disagreement":

> You state that you believe no exceptions should be taken unless ". . .there is specific evidence that can be produced by your auditors that positive effort to violate and actual violation of the mandate of the Civil Service Commission took place." On the contrary, we believe that audit exceptions must be taken unless we find that every reasonable effort has been made by the State to meet our Merit System Standards within the requirements of the Civil Service Law. In the absence of sufficient evidence, exceptions have been taken.

Tompkins replied that there was "more than *sufficient evidence*" that " 'every reasonable effort has been made by the State' to meet *your* Merit System Standards." And he added:

> We, too, are desirous to make final determinations and particularly with respect to principles of relationships existing between the Federal jurisdiction of government and the local jurisdiction of government, including the State. If it is to be the continuing principle for the Federal Security Agency to challenge either by implication or directly the good faith and legal administrative action of this Department, the State Division of Civil

Service, and local appointing authorities, insofar as compliance with the Merit System Plan provisions of the Commonwealth are concerned. . .it would appear that this principle of relationship needs serious review at a higher echelon level than that of the Regional Office insofar as operating policy with respect to the Merit System Plan is concerned.[12]

In keeping with his threat, Tompkins appealed over the head of the regional representative to the deputy commissioner of social security in an effort to get the audit exceptions reversed.

Tompkins had the last word in this exchange with Miss Schopke, but there is no evidence that she changed her mind about the audit exceptions. The retention of provisional appointees for more than six months continued to be a subject of frequent, though less angry, negotiation between federal and state officials. In the 1960s it was still the most important single source of audit exceptions.

*Educational qualifications.*   Finally, there was the issue of job qualifications. If the federal administration could impose a high standard, its basic objective of high-quality personnel could be realized, and other issues over the civil service system would diminish in importance.

Admission to the civil service in Massachusetts is not achieved, as for federal service, by an examination that tests general knowledge or the ability to reason. Instead, there are as many examinations as there are job classifications, each designed to test knowledge of the particular body of law or set of facts pertinent to the particular job. This has meant that the content of examinations could be prepared for through cram courses or employment experience that provided exposure to the subject matter. Promotions generally have been based on competitive examinations, but great weight is given to seniority. With respect to assistance personnel, in 1940 federal officials found that jobholders frequently entered welfare offices as clerks, acquired sufficient knowledge to pass an examination for worker, and might then move through the ranks to supervisor or even director. The examination for worker stressed factual knowledge of welfare laws such as a clerk could be expected to require.[13]

Federal officials hoped to reform this system through raising the formal qualifications for workers. The Social Security Board had no specific requirement on this point; it merely said that job specifications for all classes should be "suitable for performance of the duties of the position." Regional officials hoped that, through on-the-scene influence, they might elevate Massachusetts standards. In order to comply with merit-system standards Massachusetts had to have a classification plan that would contain descriptions and minimal qualifications for each job. A federal consultant came from Washington to help in preparing this plan. In cooperation with the state welfare department, the consultant drew up standards for the category of social worker that excluded clerks. To be eligible, a candidate must have done casework or completed four years of college or some combination of the two.

The new standard did not last long. It was drawn up in 1942, and in 1943 Civil Service Director Lupien proposed to change it so that anyone with six years of clerical experience might qualify. Lupien had never agreed that the new standard was desirable. Anything that restricted entrance to the civil service made the division's job of recruitment more difficult, not to mention aggravating its relations with the legislature. He asked Rotch to inquire if a change would mean the withholding of federal funds. Rotch did so, apologetically, telling the regional representative that he was prepared to urge that the standard be maintained.[14]

Rotch's question—he actually asked the regional office how far standards might be lowered without jeopardizing grants—was not of the kind that would elicit a candid reply from the Social Security Board. All the Board would say was that it did not consider "six years of any and all types of clerical experience" as suitable qualifying experience for the class of social worker.[15] Lupien found this answer hard to interpret; his successor in 1945, Thomas J. Greehan, noticed that it contained possibilities. Since the Board would not accept "any and all

types" of clerical experience, Greehan proposed giving credit for only one type of clerical experience, that obtained from work "directly related to social casework." When regional officials objected to his admitting clerks to workers' examinations, he explained that he would not admit those "who have been filing or merely answering the telephone." He would admit only those who had "actually determined eligibility and need, made recommendations, and rendered other services." Regional officials yielded, with much reluctance. They regarded the change as a deviation from Board standards, but they rationalized it on the ground that the Board permitted standards to be relaxed during the war. Inevitably, the federal concession proved impossible to retract even after the end of the war. By 1948 regional officials were mainly concerned with getting the civil service director to abide by his agreement to distinguish among the various clerk-candidates according to their experience. Personnel reviews convinced them that no clerk was barred from the workers' examination who had served six years in any welfare agency.

This did not mean that federal pressure produced no change at all in standards of entrance. Partly as a result of prodding and suggestion from regional officials and "technical assistance" in the form of sample questions, the examinations for social worker changed fundamentally between 1940 and 1960. They ceased to depend on detailed knowledge of state law and began to depend on knowledge of the received wisdom of the social-work profession.[16]

Whatever the effect of these examinations on the process of selection, by the criterion of formal education Massachusetts workers continued to be extremely unprofessionalized. A federal survey in 1962 showed that 30.6 percent of caseworkers hired in the previous year had no college education whatever, a higher percentage than in any other state except Arkansas.[17]

## The College-Degree Requirement

The federal effort at professionalization intensified as the stress on services increased.

On the assumption that ability to rehabilitate the poor could be acquired through training, and only in that way, federal administrators coupled measures for service giving with measures to raise educational levels. One approach was to finance attendance at schools of social work. Another was to require the states to conduct in-service training programs. A third, adopted in the fall of 1964, was to stipulate formal education requirements—the college degree for newly hired caseworkers and casework supervisors.

*The Massachusetts response.*  Even before the degree requirement was imposed, the Massachusetts welfare department had responded to the rising federal pressure for improvements in personnel. In 1962 Commissioner Tompkins persuaded the civil service division to adopt standards for the caseworker category that in effect required a college education. Still, such a requirement was not explicit, and it did not stand in the way of promotions for all those who had obtained workers' jobs under the previous standard. Thus the requirement of a degree for both workers and supervisors had a major impact on Massachusetts.

The federal directive was neither unwelcome nor surprising to Commissioner Ott. He had taken office with two basic aims: to shift assistance administration from local governments to the state and to raise the educational level of workers. To achieve the first goal, he looked for help mainly to private or quasi-public organizations in Massachusetts; to achieve the second, he looked to the federal government. He knew that he would not be able to act unless federal officials "forced" him to.[18]. . .

As of [July 1, 1967], the requirement of college degrees for new caseworkers and casework supervisors was in effect without qualification. Higher personnel standards had been achieved and would not have been achieved in the absence of federal action. Although the legislature had grudgingly responded to the federal directive, it declined to remove the general prohibition against educational requirements. That bill, which depended wholly on support from within the state, was beaten in mid-May, while the federally inspired bill was beginning its tortuous way toward approval.[19]

## Professionalism and State Administration

The imposition of the degree requirement was a major step toward the federal goal of professionalism, and it was soon followed by another, the bill for state administration. For the state welfare commissioner and allied reform groups in Massachusetts, the campaign of 1965 over college degrees was a prelude to that for state administration. The lobbying capacity developed for the first campaign was promptly applied to the second and augmented somewhat (for example, by enlisting participation of assistance recipients), perhaps in order to compensate for not being able this time to use the threat that federal funds would be withheld if the reform were not adopted. Though federal officials were still very closely allied with them in spirit, federal influence was not in this case at the reformers' disposal.

Sponsors of state administration saw it as a way of shifting authority and power from the almost completely unprofessionalized local agencies to the more professionalized state department. More fundamentally, it was a way of undermining localism and thus removing one of the major obstacles to professionalism.[20] If there remained any doubt of the state department's own professionalism, the reform bill helped to put it to rest.[21] The bill required the commissioner and the directors of all the community service centers, about fifty of which were anticipated, to have a master's degree in social work. A deputy commissioner and five assistant commissioners were not subject to the degree requirement or to civil service—a provision that was meant to safeguard the interests of certain incumbent state officials and that caused tension between the reformers (who were practical enough to take care of the state staff) and the federal regional officials (who pressed for maximum civil service coverage, but not too hard before the bill was passed, lest they jeopardize a reform that was very much in the federal interest).

It was hard to say where the service center directors would come from. The requirement of a master's degree in social work excluded virtually all incumbent local personnel, whether directors, supervisors, or workers. In 1966 the state department itself had only twenty public assistance staff members with MSW degrees. The House, which had been so much concerned to protect the jobs and promotional chances of incumbents in 1965, uncharacteristically showed no concern whatever for them now. No doubt this was because the question was not put to it directly. Had an effort been made on the floor to qualify or to remove the requirement for social-work degrees, a majority would surely have supported an amendment; but the local administrators no longer had an alert, committed spokesman on the floor to press for such an amendment (Shea had left in 1967 for a job with the legislature's research council). Both the leadership and the reform lobbyists were exerting strong pressure against any amendments, except a few of their own. The legislature seemed to regard the bill, as did politicians generally, as a measure to shift assistance costs to the state. A majority favored this, for it was manifestly in the interests of their local constituencies, but beyond that, they showed little interest in what was in the bill.[22]

# Notes

1. Altmeyer, 36.
2. *Social Security*, Hearings (1939), 2382, 2394.
3. National Social Welfare Assembly, *Salaries and Working Conditions of Social Welfare Manpower in 1960: A Survey Conducted by the United States Department of Labor, Bureau of Labor Statistics, in Cooperation with the National Social Welfare Assembly, Inc., and the United States Department of Health, Education, and Welfare* (no date), 55; see also U.S. Department of Health, Education, and Welfare, *Public Social Welfare Personnel, 1960* (Washington, 1962).
4. On the civil service system in Massachusetts, see George C. S. Benson, *The Administration of the Civil Service in Massachusetts* (Cambridge, 1935), and League of Women Voters of Massachusetts, *The Merit System in Massachusetts: A Study of Public Personnel Administration in the Commonwealth* (Boston, 1961). Educational data are from the federal survey cited in note 3.
5. The division wanted to maximize the potential supply of recruits so as to facilitate its function of keeping jobs filled; the legislature's interest was in protecting the utility of one source of patronage. Many, probably most, members of the Massachusetts legislature rely heavily on patronage to win support from their constituents. Patronage has taken many forms—special license plates, fixing traffic tickets (until a no-fix law took effect in 1966), appeals from civil service examinations, pay raises, life tenure for particular jobholders, liquor licenses, early admission to institutions, and jobs (in general, not particularly in welfare agencies). The legislature's interest in jobs has been the basis of a symbiotic relationship between it and the Division of Civil Service. Legislators are constantly in and out of the division's offices, which are located on the first floor of the Capitol building, to inquire about job vacancies and the timing and results of examinations. The legislature's Committee on Civil Service usually has acted in close cooperation with the division and depended on it for staff support and advice in the drafting of laws. The division in turn has depended on the legislature to produce detailed laws of its own liking. The division director normally sits with the committee in its meetings. When the division and the legislature resisted the proposals of reformers, it was hard to distinguish the interests of the one from those of the other, or to discern the direction of influence between them.
6. Cmsr to reg PA rep, March 7, 1941, Mass. File 654.2, RO.
7. Reg atty to exec dir Office of General Counsel, Oct. 21, 1940; OGC to reg atty, Oct. 24, 1940; dir BPA to reg PA rep, Oct. 31, 1940; and reg PA rep to cmsr, Dec. 26, 1940; all in Mass. 653, RO.
8. Reg PA rep and pers cons to chf, fld sec, prog opns div, and chf STAS, March 7, 1941, with enclosures, Mass. 653.
9. Each year several hundred people appeal examination marks to the Civil Service Commission, often with the aid of their representative in the legislature. A high proportion of the appeals is granted. See League of Women Voters of Massachusetts, *Merit System*, 40ff.
10. There are major discrepancies between my account of these events and that which appears in Linford, 116ff. Linford states (117n) that through the

appeals process "the percentage of failures was reduced from about 55 to something like 5." It seems clear from the contents of the federal files, especially Mass. 654.2, that this overstates the proportion of initial failures and understates the proportion of eventual failures—and thus very much exaggerates the impact of the appeal process.

11. Cmsr to reg PA rep, March 14, 1950, cmsr's files.

12. Reg PA rep to cmsr, March 27, 1950, and cmsr to reg PA rep, March 28, 1950, cmsr's files.

13. Here, for example, are questions that were used in the late 1930s:

A woman with dependent children can be assisted under the A.D.C. law even if she is not a widow. True or False.

The Pondville Hospital is under the State Department of (1) Mental Health, (2) Public Health, (3) Correction, (4) Education, (5) Public Welfare.

The records of births and deaths in a community is usually referred to as——.

14. Cmsr to reg PA rep, Dec. 23, 1943, Mass. 654.2.

15. Exec dir SSB to cmsr, May 2, 1944, cmsr's files.

16. The following examples are drawn from an examination in 1962:

The case worker's frame of mind at the time of the initial interview must be such that he approaches the client with the attitude that:

(1) care should be taken in handling the interview since most people applying for aid are emotionally unstable persons;

(2) if sympathy is shown it will cause the client to be too dependent on the interviewer and thus cause him to lose his interviewing initiative;

(3) the client is an emotionally healthy person and should be treated as such until proven otherwise;

(4) care should be taken to detect the slightest signs of fraud, since most persons applying for aid are inherently dishonest.

The marks by which a particular professional service is distinguished from other professional services are its field, its objectives, its vocational resources and its characteristic methods of work. Which one of the following five phrases best distinguishes the equipment of the social case worker from that of the lawyer, doctor, teacher or nurse?

(1) A more complete knowledge of the interrelationship of local, state and federal government units;

(2) Knowledge of symptoms and causes in deviations of individual human behavior from accepted standards;

(3) Ability to impart knowledge to others because of more adequate education and broader experience;

(4) Capacity to understand and accept the importance of cultural differences;

(5) The ability to use scientific method and carefully control experiments.

17. U.S. Department of Health, Education, and Welfare, *Analysis of Appointments, Public Assistance Caseworkers and Employment Security Interviewers* (Washington, 1963).

18. Interview, June 7, 1965.

19. Two years later, however, the legislature did give the director of civil service discretionary authority to impose educational requirements.

20. The debates over state administration showed how sharply the attitudes of local administrators differentiated them from the cosmopolitan, professionally oriented people who were pressing for reform. Challenged to yield to state administration, local administrators typically declared in defense of themselves that "we know our people"—in their eyes a uniquely valuable qualification that could not be acquired in a college classroom but only by long residence in the same community. "We are taxpayers and homeowners." Thus they expressed a tangible stake in the local community's welfare. Local administrators and workers reacted strongly against State administration not just because they were attached to their jobs (as the reformers often seemed to think), but because they were attached to jobs in particular places. State administration threatened them with the prospect of reassignments and transfers that might compel them to leave their community of residence or undertake a long daily trip. To the reformers, their localism was incomprehensible and socially undesirable. In the reformers' view, welfare workers should be glad to move from place to place in search of professional advancement. To the professional, the local administrators' self-defenses could only be taken as self-indictments, evidence that local administrators failed to share the professional decision-making criteria of impartiality and objectivity. The claim to "know our people" suggested partiality in administration, for particular persons who were judged by local standards to be deserving and against others who were judged not to be. It suggested also a reliance on intuition rather than objective evidence in the determination of eligibility and other aspects of administration. To claim the virtue of taxpaying status was still more suspect

in the eyes of the professional. It confirmed his belief that local, unprofessional administration was penurious and dominated by a desire to keep people off the rolls and control the tax rate. Senator Cohen replied sarcastically to local administrators on the Senate floor. "They know the people, all right, Mr. President—they know all the *wrong* people," Cohen declared. Apparently he meant that they knew the presumably conservative community leadership better than they knew the poor.

21. The strength of the bill was due in large measure to the conviction of the guiding spirit of reform, the chairman of the MCCY, Dr. Martha M. Eliot, retired from a long career with the Children's Bureau, of which she had been chief between 1951 and 1956. As assistant chief in the 1930s, she had been at the chief's side in testimony on the Social Security Act and, thirty years later, back home in Cambridge, she was still pursuing with utmost firmness the principles that the Children's Bureau had stood for since its founding. Foremost among them was the principle of professionalism.

22. Oddly, the legislature actually strengthened the bill's provisions for professionalism. As originally drafted, the bill would have permitted a waiver of the MSW requirement in the initial appointment of service-center directors. The waiver was dropped in the Senate on the motion of Cohen, acting in response to the reformers. The Public Welfare Administrators' Association did not press for restoration in the House. Its strategy was to defeat the whole bill and substitute one that would increase the state's rule-making and supervisory authority (by extending it to general relief) and provide for 100 percent state financing without calling for state administration. That bill was defeated in both the House and the Senate. In 1968, however, the waiver was restored. The PWAA sought to delete the requirement, and, as a compromise, Senator Cohen agreed to the restoration of the waiver.

# 14

# The Triumph
# of Techniques
# Over Purpose

*Wallace S. Sayre*
*Cornell University*

*A review of* Personnel Administration: A
Point of View and a Method, *by Paul Pigors
and Charles A. Myers. McGraw-Hill Book
Co., 1947.*

## I

The appearance of this book marks an
important milestone in the development of
personnel administration. It is the first successful effort to present, within the difficult
requirements of a personnel textbook designed
for general use, the significant findings and
conclusions of the several groundbreaking
monographs produced during the past fifteen
years by the group known as the "human relations" school. The authors, who are professors
of industrial relations at Massachusetts Institute
of Technology, have themselves been important participants in this human relations
movement. They have now undertaken the task
of relating the concepts and methods of human
relations to the theory and practice of personnel administration.

Pigors and Myers are primarily interested,
as are most members of this group, with the

administrative environment of private industry.
This orientation reduces the initial appeal of
their text for those readers who are absorbed
in the tasks or in the study of public personnel
administration. But the major barrier to the
acceptance and influence which *Personnel
Administration* deserves in the public field will
arise from the wide gulf which divides its point
of view and its method from many of the deep-
seated stereotypes and cherished rituals of civil
service administration. This resistance will be
of minor concern to the authors, since they are
assured of a gratifying influence in their chosen
field of private industry; it is a more serious
matter for the public administration fraternity,
because they are now confronted with nothing
less than the confirmation of Louis Brownlow's
prediction, "a failure of the civil service institution to meet the needs of the peace."[1]

The concepts and the methodology of contemporary public personnel administration are,
of course, the product of the dominant objectives set by, and for, the students and the practitioners of the craft. It is possible to identify
these goals in separate terms, even though they
overlap and have always exerted powerful
reciprocal influences upon each other. For the
purpose of demonstrating the values of the
Pigors-Myers text, it is useful to restate the main
streams in the evolution of the premises and
techniques which now characterize personnel
administration in public agencies.

The earliest of these, and still the source of
the most distinctive public personnel practices,
is the goal of eliminating party patronage from
the management of the civil service. This definition of purpose has been the most enduring, the
most widely understood and embraced, and consequently the most influential article of faith in
the growth of the profession. From this premise
the basic structure of civil service administration
has been derived: central personnel control
agencies, bipartisan commissions, quantitative
techniques, the "rule of three," and the whole
familiar arsenal of devices to neutralize and
divert patronage pressures. On the whole, the

means were once appropriate to the problem. But, as Gordon Clapp observed in this *Review* as early as 1941,[2] the merit system advocates having clearly won the day in most jurisdictions, the question now is what to do with the victory —which of these methods are today appropriate to the new priority objectives? And what are the new objectives?

A second, closely associated purpose was gradually made explicit in the development of the public personnel program. This goal is the guarantee of equal treatment to all applicants for public employment and among all public employees. This is clearly a positive ethic of great appeal in a democratic society, and it has won an increasing emphasis from public personnel specialists. The contribution of this goal to personnel methodology has been substantial. Its main effect has been to move personnel administration, in the words of Gordon Clapp, "into the cold objective atmosphere of tests, scores, weighted indices, and split-digit ranking" so completely that "these technical trappings have become the symbols of the merit system" (p. 291).

Still another stream of influence has contributed to the fulfillment of this tendency. The logic of scientific management, the paramount ideology of articulate business management between the two wars, has also exerted a powerful attraction for the personnel administrators. The impersonal goals of management logic made the precise, quantitative techniques of the efficiency engineer plausible and attractive methods for the "scientific" personnel manager. Job classification, factor analysis, numerical efficiency ratings, formal promotion charts, and all their procedural relatives acquired a new and impressive endorsement—the personnel system could now lay claim to the combined virtues of merit, equality in competition, and scientific management.

Finally, public personnel policies and methods have been measurably affected by the goal of a public career service. Stated in its most positive terms, this objective represents an effort to provide the conditions of work which will attract and hold a public service of optimum talents. In its negative aspects, the goal has been translated into an elaborate system of protectionism. In the area of methodology the negative connotations have slowly but surely won the dominant position. The concept of status and the concept of rights earned by seniority, to use but two examples from a large network, have been molded from precedent to precedent into a personnel jurisprudence in which all but the most expert technicians lose their way.

In sum, the personnel administration produced by the confluence of these four streams of influence represents a triumph of techniques over purpose. This is not an unusual outcome in the field of administration. Nor does the conclusion mean that great historical accomplishments should not be recorded. What it does suggest is that both ends and means now urgently need fundamental reexamination.[3]

Private personnel administration has not escaped similar pressures. In particular, it has responded in its development to "scientific" management and to a modified version of careerism. The resulting complex of concepts and methods makes up a formidable system of quantitative techniques and formal rules in private personnel administration. Here, too, one may conclude that the ends have been made captive by the means.

Personnel administration, then, has tended to become characterized more by procedure, rule, and technique than by purpose or results. In the public field especially, quantitative devices have overshadowed qualitative. Standardization and uniformity have been enshrined as major virtues. Universal (and therefore arbitrary) methods have been preferred to experiment and variety. From the perspective of the clientele (the public, the managers, and the employees), these traits increasingly connote rigidity, bureaucracy, institutionalism;—and they are now beginning to evoke a reciprocal system of formal and informal techniques of evasion. Among personnel people there is an accompanying growth of frustration and a loss of satisfying participation in the real work of the organization.

Personnel administration, seen in this context, mirrors the dilemma of all orthodox administration. The traditional conceptual and methodological apparatus of administration has rested heavily upon the fallacy of an "administrative man" comparable to the synthetic, rational "economic man" of the classical economists. During the past fifteen years this fiction of the "administrative man" (which Elton Mayo so aptly called the "rabble hypothesis") has been steadily undermined not only by the painstaking inquiries of many students of human behavior but even more by the movement of great social forces. In the growth of personnel administration this rise of mature dissent may be traced, in large part at least, from its clearest beginnings in the reflections of John Dewey and Mary Follett upon the nature and structure of authority, in the efforts of Ordway Tead and Henry Metcalf to introduce more democratic precepts into the practice of personnel administration, and in the pioneering Hawthorne studies at Western Electric by Elton Mayo, F. J. Roethlisberger, and others. The efficiency engineer and the logician of management have slowly given way, at least at the level of administrative theory, to the psychologist, the sociologist, and other social scientists.

# II

Dissent from the "rabble hypothesis" of traditional personnel administration is the central virtue of the volume by Pigors and Myers. With imagination and ingenuity they have woven into the familiar fabric of the personnel process the point of view and the basic concepts of human relations. It is difficult to condense into a few sentences the full measure of their accomplishment. Much of it, particularly for those concerned with public personnel, is implicit rather than explicit; that is, it must be translated into the specific terms and context of the public service. Perhaps something of the point of view and the method will be conveyed by the following brief excerpts from their introductory description of "basic variables" in personnel administration:

Experience in personnel administration indicates that the basic elements into which we need insight are (1) technical features, (2) the human element, (3) principles and policies, and (4) the time factor.

*Technical Features.*—Modern management and engineering have brought the techniques of organization and productive enterprise to a high level of efficiency. In fact, progress in this direction has far outrun our capacity for dealing efficiently with people. More than that, the inclination to concentrate on mechanical systems and on the logic of efficiency has often led management to subordinate the individual to technical requirements. In what has been called the "machine age," human beings have too often been looked upon as mere functional entities and adjuncts to machines. . . .

*The Human Element.*—The individual in industry should be studied in two ways. First, the personnel administrator should think about the individual's needs and behavior as determined by his current situation. . . . What demand is the work situation making on him that he is unable to meet? Conversely, what demands is he making on his work situation that are not being satisfied? This approach may be called *person-centered thinking.*

Emphasis on the human element meant a step forward in the sense that management no longer defended the proposition that industrial progress can be achieved by a solution of purely technical problems. . . . A more comprehensive view attempts to balance and relate technical and human factors within an inclusive system.

*Principles and Policies.*—The personnel administrator finds it useful to relate his observation of people and of the mechanical element by means of his understanding of the general principles that apply to human situations. This approach may be called *policy-centered thinking.* Modern management thinks about such principles when formulating and administering policies for large-scale situations. These policies relate general principles to specific situations in such a way as to form a guide to action at all organizational levels. . . . Whatever the scale of relationships, clear and consistent policies enable us to act in a way that reconciles the different requirements made by the mechanical system and by the participating individuals. These policies form the basis for reasonable and consistent behavior.

\*    \*    \*    \*    \*

*The Time Factor.*—In seeking understanding of human and technical elements, as well as of the principles that integrate both, the observer finds that he must also consider various aspects of the time element. How *far back* must we look in order to understand the meaning of what is happening now? What future events are we *moving toward?* What is the *sequence* of key facts? What *developmental* stage has been reached by this person or in this relationship? And how fast is the *pace?*

\*    \*    \*    \*    \*

The practical answer to the question of where to begin is found in the situation and in its stage of development. For this reason, it is essential that a personnel worker be flexible and able to think on his feet (pp. 39–41).

The authors are not altogether successful in their attempt to transmute formal personnel procedures into useful human relations instruments.[4] This relative failure highlights one of the most difficult judgments which the human relations group must now make: to what extent can they accept and work within the present structure and methods of personnel administration? What are the hazards that any such acceptance will adulterate their concepts and inhibit further exploration and growth?

The answer, especially in public personnel administration, would seem to lie in a different perspective on the values and uses of quantitive techniques. It is not the techniques per se which have constructed the straightjacket that now imprisons so much of personnel administration. The basic techniques are, when properly used, of considerable value and of even greater potential promise. The real difficulty lies in the fact that (1) the techniques are usually inadequate for the full purpose they are relied upon to accomplish, yet accomplishment is gradually taken for granted; (2) the techniques are prematurely frozen into regulations and procedures for universal application in greatly varying administrative environments, thus stifling at birth the process of genuine research and technical development; and (3) the techniques gradually obscure the ends they were designed to serve. The contrast between this tendency of personnel specialists toward eager installation and canonization of rudimentary techniques and the stubborn experimentalism of the physical sciences is instructive. Even many of those who might be assumed to be the least susceptible to this tendency—the psychologists, with their strong experimental tradition—reveal their imprisonment within the system by devoting their energies to the refinement of the installed methods of testing skills and personality "traits" rather than to the working out of new techniques and applications in the fields of attitudes, motivation, and group dynamics.

The immediate trends as well as some of the most deeply imbedded concepts of public personnel administration are opposed to the human relations points of view. Although this is not the whole problem, it is a revealing index of the crisis in civil service administration. At a time when the urgency, difficulty, and complexity of governmental performance are daily increasing, at a time when industrial personnel administration is moving toward a recognition of the values of experimental and thorough inquiry into human behavior, tempered in application by informality and flexibility in the human relations of organized effort, the public service becomes steadily more dependent upon a cold, impersonal, rigid quantification of human ability and worth in public employment. Nor is even this the full measure of the inadequacy. The methods relied upon lack the objectivity which is their sole claim to usefulness; they provide merely the appearance, not the substance, of the relevant measurement of ability and merit. The variables of personnel administration are too many and to subtle to be contained within a purely statistical frame of reference. In contrast, a prime virtue of the human relations group is its relative lack of conceit about the immutability of its concepts and techniques.

Some readers may wonder whether this review overlooks the "new trends" in federal personnel administration. These trends need to be more carefully examined than opportunity here affords. However, some tentative observations are in order. During the war years, many useful explorations were made in the direction of personnel policies and methods which would be appropriate and adequate for the great tasks of federal administration. Some of these experiments still endure, but the surrounding climate is not encouraging. With perhaps the sole exception of TVA among the federal agencies, there has been uniformly a net loss of opportunity for the development of agency personnel programs responsive to the special needs of agency assignments and climate. The prewar pattern of uniform rules, designed to impose an artificial appearance of order and objectivity upon the federal establishments, has been restored and strengthened, not relaxed. "Decentralization" has been the main theme of "progress" in the postwar federal personnel program. It is relevant to inquire: what is the substance of the program being decentralized? The ultimate values of decentralization depend upon the quality of the program. The decentralization of work load under strict procedural instructions binding those who do the work is a dubious administrative economy; it certainly does not represent an important new trend in the development of an adequate philosophy and method of personnel administration.

# Notes

1. "Successes and Failures," in Leonard D. White, ed., *Civil Service in Wartime* (University of Chicago Press, 1945), p. 243.

2. "The Rule of Three, It Puzzles Me", 1 *Public Administration Review* 287–93 (Spring, 1941).

3. Those readers who find this judgment overdrawn are urged to examine anew *Better Government Personnel, Report of the Commission of Inquiry on Public Service Personnel;* (McGraw-Hill Book Co., 1935), the *Report of the President's Committee on Administrative Management* (Government Printing Office, 1937), and the accompanying monograph by Floyd W. Reeves and Paul T. David, *Personnel Administration in the Federal Service* (Government Printing Office, 1937); the *Report of the President's Committee on Civil Service Improvement* (H. Doc. No. 118, 77th Cong. 1st Sess.); and J. Donald Kingsley's *Representative Bureaucracy; An Interpretation of the British Civil Service* (Antioch Press, 1944).

4. As a textbook, *Personnel Administration* acquires immeasurable additional value from the case materials included. These provide real-life illustrations for most chapters. The cases are presented with satisfying completeness (190 pages are devoted to 19 cases), and each one is accompanied by a series of searching and provocative questions for discussion.

# 15

# The Civil Service: A Meritless System?

*E. S. Savas & Sigmund G. Ginsburg*

The nation's basic civil service law was written in 1883, following the assassination of President Garfield by a disgruntled job seeker. The goal at the time was both noble and urgent: to assure that the merit principle, rather than the patronage principle, would be used for the selection and promotion of federal employees. Subsequently, in reaction to the excesses of the spoils system which had prevailed for the preceding half-century, a civil service reform movement swept the land, spreading through states, counties, cities, and school systems during the next few decades. Today, the so-called merit system—the name given to the elaborate web of civil service laws, rules, and regulations which embrace the merit principle—covers more than 95 per cent of all permanent federal (civilian) employees, all state and county employees paid by federal funds, most state employees, many county employees (particularly in the Northeastern states), most employees in more than three fourths of America's cities, and almost all full-time policemen and firemen.

However, vast changes in government and society have taken place in the last 50 years, and the rules and regulations appropriate for 1883 have now become rigid and regressive. After 90 years, the stage is set for a new era of civil service reform. Recent court decisions have ruled out civil service examinations which had no demonstrable relation to the job to be performed; scholars and political leaders recognize the many

SOURCE: Reprinted with permission of the authors from: *The Public Interest*, No. 32 (Summer 1973), pp. 70–85. Copyright © 1973 by National Affairs, Inc.

shortcomings of today's civil service systems; and now the general public is stirring as well. The citizen sees that government—and tax collection—is a growth industry. (If we extrapolate the current rate of growth of the governmental work force, by the year 2049 every worker in America will be a government employee!) He sees that job security (tenure) exists for his "servants" but not for him. State and local governments spend as much as the federal government (excluding defense), and the citizen can see *their* work at close hand in his daily life. And what he sees is *not* a merit system—certainly not in the common usage of the word "merit." The low productivity of public employees and the malfunctioning of governmental bureaucracies are becoming apparent to an increasing number of frustrated and indignant taxpayers. The problem shows up all over the country in the form of uncivil servants going through pre-programmed motions while awaiting their pensions. Too often the result is mindless bureaucracies that appear to function for the convenience of their staffs rather than the public whom they are supposed to serve. It is the system itself, however, rather than the hapless politician who heads it or the minions toiling within it that is basically at fault.

## Counterproductive Policies

Imagine a large, multi-divisional organization with an annual budget of 10 billion dollars. Imagine further that the organization has the following personnel policies and practices:

- Most entry positions are filled on the basis of written examinations scored to two or three decimal places.
- There is no scientifically supportable evidence that these examinations are related to subsequent on-the-job performance.
- Once a ranked list of examination scores is established, management must choose one of the top three names on the list regardless of

special qualifications, knowledge, experience, aptitude, or training of other applicants on the list.

• After an employee has spent six months on the job, he is virtually guaranteed the job for life, unless his supervisor files a special report urging that the employee be discharged or at least that the granting of tenure be deferred; it is very unusual for a supervisor to take such action.

• An employee, after acquiring such tenure, can be fired only on grounds of dishonesty or incompetence of a truly gross nature, and cannot be shifted to a less demanding assignment.

• An employee is "milked" of his ability and dedication, while given little significant opportunity for advanced training, personal development, career counseling, mid-career job change, or an enriched job that fully engages his evolving interests; no manager cares about this situation.

• Promotions are generally limited to employees who occupy the next lower position within the same division; qualified employees in other divisions of the organization are discriminated against, as are applicants from outside the organization.

• Promotions are made primarily through written examinations, with no credit given for good performance.

• Salary increases are virtually automatic and, with rare exception, are completely unrelated to the employee's work performance.

• Supervisors belong to unions, sometimes to the same unions as the employees they supervise.

• All personnel practices are regulated by a three-man commission, whose powerful chairman is the Director of Personnel. Managers and supervisors must defer to his judgment on all personnel matters except those involving top-level executives.

• The employee unions have enough political power to influence the decision concerning whether or not the chief executive is permitted to stay on; furthermore, they also influence the appointment of top-level managers.

One does not have to be a management expert to be appalled at this array of counterproductive policies or to predict that the hypothetical organization employing such policies would be laughably ineffective.

Unfortunately, neither the policies nor the organization is hypothetical. The foregoing is an accurate description of the venerable civil service system under which New York City is forced to operate. In summary, the system prohibits good management, frustrates able employees, inhibits productivity, lacks the confidence of the city's taxpayers, and fails to respond to the needs of the citizens. While this bleak picture may not yet be fully representative of all civil service systems in the country, neither is it uncommon. Furthermore, considering that New York often serves as a leading indicator of societal problems, this pattern, if it has not already been reproduced elsewhere, may be soon—unless a groundswell of popular opinion leads to a new wave of reform.

More than half of New York's 9.4-billion-dollar budget is spent on the salaries and fringe benefits of its employees. In the last decade, personnel costs have risen by roughly 150 per cent, while the number of employees has increased by about 75 per cent—to 400,000. (Genghis Khan conquered Asia with an army less than half this size; however, he used certain managerial techniques of reward and punishment which are mercifully denied to today's more circumscribed and more humane chief executive.) Of this number, about a quarter of a million (!) constitute the "competitive class" of civil service—that is, employees who are hired and promoted on the basis of competitive examinations. This is the aspect of the civil service system dealt with here.

In order to understand fully the shortcomings of the current system in New York, it is useful to look in turn at each of its major elements: the jobs themselves, recruitment practices, examinations, selection procedures, promotions, and motivational rewards.

## Jobs, Recruitment, and Examinations

*Jobs.* Very narrow, specialized jobs have gradually emerged, in part because this makes it much easier to produce an examination specific enough to give an appearance of relevance and fairness. Credentialism runs rampant, and prerequisites are sometimes introduced with no discernible value except bureaucratic convenience in the subsequent selection process. As a result, artificial and nonsensical divisions have proliferated, and New York City now has Methods Analysts, Management Analysts, and Quantitative Analysts, as well as Office Appliance Operators, Photostat Operators, Audio-Visual Aid Technicians, Doorstop Maintainers, and Foremen of Thermostat Repairers. When the human cogs in the General Motors assembly line at Lordstown stopped working, it was a clear and obvious revolt against the dehumanizing nature of their activity. Could it be that the human cogs in the municipal machinery stopped functioning long ago, for the same reason, and we are just now indirectly noticing their sullen revolt?

***Recruitment.*** The recruiting process for civil service jobs is similarly arbitrary. The law requires only that advertisements of openings appear in certain specified, obscure places and in formidable terminology: the formal descriptions, in "bureaucratese," of the narrow kinds of specialties mentioned above. The Personnel Department seldom goes far beyond this minimal legal requirement. This means that current employees (and their families) have an advantage over outsiders because they know where to look and how to decode the message. This fact, coupled with job qualifications of questionable value, serves to limit access into the service by other potential applicants.

In fact, this traditional process has been so ineffective that out of exasperation a competing recruiting organization was set up within the Mayor's office, not for dispensing patronage, but for recruiting the kind of professional and technical personnel without which modern government cannot really function. The most capable managers in the entire organization devote much of their effort and ingenuity to subverting and bypassing the regulations in order to hire such recruits from outside the system.

***Examinations.*** About 400 civil service examinations are conducted each year in New York City, at great effort and expense, and about half of them consist primarily of written tests. *Yet not a single case could be found where the validity of a written test—with respect to predicting performance on the job—was ever proven.* That this problem transcends New York's borders is indicated by the following statement by the U.S. District Court in Massachusetts in regard to an examination for police officer:

> The categories of questions sound as though they had been drawn from "Alice in Wonderland." On their face the questions seem no better suited to testing ability to perform a policeman's job than would be crossword puzzles.

Heavy reliance on written examinations at least has the advantage of being "safe." No bureaucrat need be saddled with the difficult task of using his judgment somewhere in the selection process. Exclusive reliance on an "objective" test score creates a situation where no one can be accused of favoritism or overt bias, even though a test may demonstrate inherent discrimination against certain cultural minorities.

At present, candidates who pass an examination are ranked on an eligible list based on their adjusted final average, *carried to as many as three decimal places.* (Adjusted final average is derived from the candidate's scores on the individual tests which comprise an examination: written, practical, technical, oral, etc., plus veteran's preference credit, where applicable.) A manager must appoint one of the top three scorers. Now, no one seriously contends that a person who scores 92.463 on an examination of dubious validity is likely to perform better on the job than someone who scores 92.462, or even 91.462. This scientifically unsupportable custom is just another defense against accusations of bias and should be abandoned. Test scores should be rounded off, thereby creating more ties and giving managers more choice and flexibility in selecting their subordinates from among those candidates with the same score. The potential impact of this change, recently endorsed in New York City by Mayor Lindsay, can be indicated by noting that on the 1968 examination for Fire Lieutenant, 25 men scored between 86 and 87, and 203 scored between 81 and 82.

Another vexing problem with the existing system was described by one frustrated manager:

> The City's unimaginative recruitment mechanism, combined with generally unappetizing work surroundings, makes it virtually impossible to recruit stenographers at the entry level. Accordingly, we keep filling entry-level stenographer positions with candidates who make it through a relatively undemanding stenography test which has been watered down to qualify those with minimal skills. No attempt is ever made to differentiate between candidates on the basis of intelligence, work attitudes, motivation, reading comprehension. Thus, we start with an entry group whose competence has not really been tested—and may well be minimal—and proceed to lock ourselves in by demanding that all candidates for higher level positions be selected from this pool, even though the pool may be drained of some of its best talent over time.

An example of the straitjacket created by this rigid procedure can be found in the agency that needed a mechanical engineer for maintenance of heating, ventilating, and air-conditioning equipment. The experience of the six highest-ranking candidates on the "Mechanical Engineer List" was inappropriate, consisting of machine design, drafting, and the like; the seventh-ranked engineer, however, was ideally suited for the job. Nevertheless, the agency was constrained by civil service rules to hire one of the top three. Only by finally persuading four of the top six to waive their legal claims to the job, thereby elevating Number Seven to Number Three, was the agency able to hire the man with the needed experience. If any one of the four who reluctantly withdrew had joined the other two of the top six in refusing to do so, the agency would have faced the choice of hiring either no one or someone with an inappropriate background, even though a suitable candidate was available only a few meaningless points further down the list.

## Selection Procedures: An Inverse Merit System

The most surprising finding is that the current legally mandated selection procedure, ostensibly designed to hire the most meritorious applicants into city service, appears to be a failure according to that very criterion: *It discriminates against those applicants who are most qualified according to its own standards.* Candidates with low passing grades are actually *more* likely to be hired than those with high passing grades! Furthermore, this perverse result seems to hold true for all skill levels.

This finding emerged from a careful study of three representative (written) examinations, which span a broad gamut of entry-level skills: Railroad Porter, a position which requires minimal education; Clerk, a position which requires some educational attainment; and Professional Trainee, a job which requires a college degree. Each examination showed the same general pattern—roughly speaking, the *lower* the percentile ranking, the *greater* the number of hires drawn from that percentile group! Conversely, the *higher* the percentile, the *fewer* the number of people hired from it.

Corroborating evidence was found by analyzing a 10 per cent sample of those 1970 and 1971 examinations which resulted in actual hiring: In almost half of the examinations analyzed (14 of 30), none of the four highest scorers was appointed; in a third of the examinations no one was appointed from the top 10 per cent; and in two of the 30 examinations, no one was appointed from the upper half of the eligible candidates.

These anomalous and unexpected results are presumably due to the long delay between the closing date for applications and the date of the first appointment. Delays are produced by a combination of administrative procedures and applicant-initiated protests, appeals, and law suits. The sample of examinations revealed that in 1970, the median delay was *seven months* and the maximum (of the sample) was *15 months*. If we assume that the "best" people score highest, then it seems reasonable to assume that many will find jobs elsewhere and that as time goes on a decreasing number of them will still be available when "their number is called." Analysis of the data showed that the greater the delay, the deeper into the lists one had to dig to find people still willing to accept appointment. When the delay was "only" three months, the openings were filled from the top 15 per cent of the list, but when the delay was six months, hires were drawn from the top 37 per cent, and when the delay was 15 months (for the Clerk examination), it was necessary to dip all the way down to 63 per cent in order to fill the vacancies.

One could argue that this finding is true but irrelevant, and that the 6,000th person on the Clerk list, for example, is really not significantly worse than the fifth, both of whom were hired. But if this assertion is accepted, then one is essentially admitting that the entire examination process is virtually useless.

In summary, as far as drawing new recruits into public employment via examination is concerned, the evidence strongly suggests that *New York City's civil service system functions as an inverse merit system* (something the public at large has cynically assumed for years). Although additional verification is needed before this finding can be generalized, at the moment the burden of proof must fall on those who would maintain that New York's civil service really is a merit system in this respect. Indeed, to anyone familiar with both public and private personnel systems, it is quite obvious that large corporations today are much closer to a true merit system than are our governments.

## Promotion and Motivation

With regard to promotions, the civil service can be described more accurately as a seniority system than as a merit system. The rules discourage "lateral entry" into upper-level positions by outsiders. This means that one usually starts at the bottom and works his way up, which sounds fine: All organizations find it beneficial as a general practice to promote from within, and their current employees have a natural and desirable advantage over outsiders. In New York's civil service, however, this practice is carried to an extreme and becomes an exclusionary device that limits competition. One frustrated high-level city official offered a striking example of the problem:

> In an occupational area like computer operations, applying the usual rigid procedures denies us the option of hiring experienced computer programmers, systems analysts, and data processing managers. It would force us to appoint only computer programming trainees and to wait for these to be trained and developed by years of experience. This is patently absurd.

The current promotion procedure is as follows: Vacancies in positions above the lowest level in an agency are generally filled by promotion on the basis of competitive examination from among persons holding tenured positions in the next lower grade *in the same agency*. If the Civil Service Commission concludes that there are not enough people available at the lower grade to fill all the vacancies via promotion examination, it may decide to conduct an open-competitive examination as well. An open-competitive examination is open to individuals in other city agencies, to individuals in other grades within the same agency, and to complete "outsiders."

But this openness is illusory. Assuming that the "outsider" has somehow ferreted out the fact that an open-competitive examination is being conducted, he is still at a significant disadvantage compared to the "insiders" who take the promotion examination. Any "insider" who passes the promotion examination will be offered the vacant position before it is offered to anyone who passes the open-competitive examination. Even if one accepted the validity of the examinations, one can seriously question whether it is always better for the public to promote an "insider" who scores 70 than to hire an "outsider" who scores 99.

A study was made of 10 pairs of written open-competitive and promotion examinations given for such positions as engineer, accountant, stenographer, planner, and so on. For each position the promotion and the open-competitive examinations were almost identical. Though the results are not conclusive, they are suggestive, to say the least: The lowest-ranked "insider" was selected over the highest-ranked "outsider" despite the fact that the latter scored higher than the former in all cases but one; "insiders" who averaged 14 points below "outsiders" were nevertheless chosen before the latter. One can legitimately ask how the public interest is served by this policy.

Damning though such findings may be, the worst feature of the promotion system is that an employee's chance of promotion bears no relation to his performance on the job. It is the promotion examination that counts and not performance, motivation, or special qualifications. Distressing examples of the unfairness that this system produces are legion. For instance, a man responsible for the successful completion of an important health program failed to pass the promotion test for Senior Public Health Sanitarian. To all who were familiar with his excellent work, this result was positive proof that the examination was completely invalid. At the top of the list on that examination was someone who has never been able to supervise people and has been mediocre on the job. The demonstrated inability of such tests to predict supervisory competence remains one of the major weaknesses of the examination system.

Given the nature of the promotion procedures, there are relatively few ways in which an agency head, manager, or supervisor can motivate, reward, or penalize his workers. Yearly salary increases are authorized under union contracts, while cost-of-living and comparability adjustments occur automatically for non-union employees. In principle, an outstanding employee can receive a special salary increase, but in fact the vast majority of employees are never really evaluated for such increases, as few agencies and few positions come under this policy. How long will a highly motivated and competent individual be willing to put forth extra effort when he receives no real reward compared with others who do much less? A sensible individual would conclude that instead of spending extra energy and effort on doing his job well, his time would be better spent studying for promotion examinations, or simply relaxing. Also demoralizing for supervisors is the knowledge that it is almost impossible to penalize or discharge the barely competent or even incompetent permanent employee. The administrative procedures involved, the time lags, the large amount of managerial effort needed "to make a case," all force the manager to live with the problem rather than to solve it.

## Collective Bargaining vs. Civil Service

The single most compelling reason for major reform of public personnel systems—even aside from the mounting evidence of their meritlessness—is the fact that a new system, collective bargaining, has grown up atop the old system, civil service. The enormous growth in membership, power, and militancy of unions of civil servants has resulted in increased protection, wages, and benefits for New York City employees—and in decreased productivity. The ultimate monopoly of power held by municipal unions raises fundamental and disquieting questions about public employee unionism that are not yet resolved.

It is an inescapable fact, however, that union power has produced a second personnel system overlapping and at times conflicting with and negating the civil service system. Job classifications and duties, recruitment, promotion paths, eligibility for advancement, and grievances all fall within the purview of the civil service system, yet all are in fact negotiated, albeit informally, with the municipal unions. Initial selection of employees had remained the one area under the exclusive regulatory authority of the Civil Service Commission, but this, too, is now becoming subject to joint policy determination with the unions.

A strong argument can therefore be made for acknowledging reality and abolishing the civil service system, relying instead on the collective bargaining system. In effect, this has already been done in one area, the municipal hospitals, which have been taken over by the independent Health and Hospitals Corporation. Its employees are no longer civil servants but continue to be represented by a union, and there has been no discernible harm to them or to the body politic. At the very least, a "Blue Ribbon Commission" should be appointed to consider long-term, fundamental reform of New York's civil service system, with particular focus on the overlap between collective bargaining and civil service.

## What Should Be Done?

In trying to prevent itself from doing the wrong things—nepotism, patronage, prejudice, favoritism, corruption—the civil service system has been warped and distorted to the point where it can do hardly anything at all. In an attempt to protect against past abuses, the "merit system" has been perverted and transformed into a closed and meritless seniority system. A true merit system must be constructed anew, one that provides the opportunity for any qualified citizen to gain access non-politically, to be recognized and rewarded for satisfactory performance, and even to be replaced for unsatisfactory service. The improvements that are needed are obvious:

• The principal determinant of promotions should be a performance appraisal and potential assessment system, based upon performance standards and established with union cooperation. Such a system should include an employee's right to review and appeal the appraisal report.

• An individual's salary increase should be a function of his performance. Salary Review Boards with union representation should be established in each agency to set annual guidelines for allocating salary increases in the agency out of a lump-sum annual budget for raises; for example, "standard" performers might get a five per cent raise, "superior" performers a larger one.

• Examinations should be for broad categories of related positions, with "selective certification" used to appoint specialists from within the pool of qualified candidates.

• Written examinations should be employed only where their validity can be demonstrated. Oral examinations should be used more extensively for both selection and promotion. (We are not referring to the kind of "oral examination" now sometimes given—namely, a stilted interview in which competent interviewers are asked to camouflage their reasonable but subjective impressions of the interviewees by asking the exact same questions in the same sequence and giving numerical ratings to the responses. These "oral examinations" are then graded by employees who conscientiously average the interview scores.)

• In selecting new employees, the emphasis should be on evaluation of qualifications, experience, assessment by prior employers, and an oral or practical examination.

• The custom of scoring examinations to several decimal places should be abandoned. Round off the test scores; this will create more ties and give the appointing authority more freedom to use his judgment.

• Positions should be evaluated regularly to weed out rampant credentialism.

• More upper-level positions should be filled at the discretion of management. A good model can be found in the New York Police Department, where the highest rank attainable by examination is captain, and the Commissioner has the authority to assign captains to higher ranks as long as he is satisfied with their performance.

• The system should stop discriminating against "outsiders." Open competitive and promotion examination lists for a given title should be merged into a single ranked list; alternatively, "outstanding" outsiders should be selected before "good" insiders, and so on. Experience in New York City government should be one of the criteria used in evaluating individuals.

• A flexible system of probationary periods should be instituted, with the duration of the period bearing some logical relationship to the job. The granting of tenure should require a positive act, as it does in universities.

• To improve the performance and motivation of employees, training opportunities should be greatly increased. Job counseling and career planning should be introduced, and tuition-refund plans, evening courses, and released-time programs should all be utilized. Job responsibilities should be enlarged ("enriched") commensurate with employee acceptance. The constricted domain of the unfortunate doorstop maintainer might be expanded to include hinges and doorknobs, and in time even simple locks. So far Victor Gotbaum, the municipality's farsighted union leader, has done more for job training and enrichment than anyone on the management side.

The recommendations presented above would tend to make New York City's system more similar to the federal civil service. The federal system 1) makes far greater use of selective certification; 2) more readily accepts outside applicants for middle and upper positions, and evaluates them on the basis of their education and experience rather than by written examination; 3) bases promotions on performance rather than examination; 4) has a much shorter average time span for promotions; 5) identifies talented individuals early, at the time of the entrance examination; 6) encourages movement between government agencies; 7) is more concerned about training and identification of persons with higher potential; and 8) has a one-year probationary period for new appointees, with positive action by supervisors necessary for retention.

People who have served in both consider the federal system vastly superior to the one under which the city operates. However, some of the recommendations we have made would also apply to the federal government: 1) the need for evaluating duties and responsibilities of positions regularly to insure against demanding greater or different qualifications than the job requires; 2) strengthening the performance evaluation and potential assessment system; 3) doing away with automatic raises and tying them more closely to performance; and 4) making it easier to reward good performers and to demote or remove incompetent performers.

## Racial and Ethnic Problems

The managerial virtues of such proposed changes are clear, but would they create an even worse problem of racial and ethnic patronage? In New York today, the civil service system is undergoing strain in part because of the widespread belief that to be successful in certain jobs one must possess traits that the system was designed to ignore: culture, class, neighborhood, and other such euphemisms for race and ethnicity. Hence the color-blind hiring practices which successfully staffed city agencies a half-century ago are not well suited for staffing the new municipal agencies that deal with problem families, drug addicts, and unemployed youths. Nor do they adequately provide the recruits needed by a police department whose job has changed significantly and now requires considerable community cooperation for effective crime control. Cultural rapport is vital for success in both the new agencies and old ones facing new challenges.

Ingenious job descriptions (with the adjective "community" frequently in the titles), public employment programs aimed at reducing unemployment in particular neighborhoods, and carefully targeted recruitment campaigns are being used to get around the color-blind system, but such policies have hardly gone unnoticed. Those groups that are already well represented within the civil service decry the "decline in standards," and attack such hiring programs in the courts and at the bargaining table. They may recognize the irrationality of the system, but they fear that civil service reform and greater managerial flexibility will be used to advance newcomers at their expense.

Those major groups that are not yet proportionally represented, black and Spanish-speaking New Yorkers, recognize the irrationality of the system; they are successfully challenging discriminatory examinations which exclude them, and thereby introducing greater flexibility into the system. At the same time, though, they fear that a reformed civil service will allow supervisors the flexibility to discriminate against them.

We conclude that the civil service system is already enmeshed in all the strains of racial and ethnic politics in the grand New York tradition, and that a reformed system would be embroiled in similar, but hardly worse, fashion. This endemic condition, therefore, offers no grounds for abandoning the civil service changes advocated here, changes that are likely in time to provide improved delivery of public services to all citizens and neighborhoods.

## The Prospects for Reform

How can civil service reform be brought about? At first glance, the picture is not very promising. Elected chief executives are understandably wary of the issue, on two counts. First, an attempt at reform might easily lead to demoralization of the work force, with employee resentment leading to a further drastic decline in government performance, to the chagrin of its head. Second, elected officials fear the voting power of the growing army of civil servants. In New York City, the conventional wisdom runs as follows: There are some 400,000 employees. Each one votes himself and influences several relatives and friends. Hence municipal employees represent a voting bloc of more than a million votes, more than enough to ensure victory or defeat. Therefore, the logic goes, don't do anything that might antagonize the work force—and be sure to treat it especially well in election years.

It is not at all clear, however, that this simplistic arithmetic really applies: At least one seventh of the work force lives out of town and is therefore ineligible to vote in New York's

municipal elections; voter registration, turnout, and bloc voting may be no greater for civil servants than for other groups; many of those influenced by government employees are themselves in public service and should not be counted twice; and other friends who are not on the public payroll might resent the "good deal" that they attribute to the tenured civil servant, and hence would approve of reform.

Furthermore, candid discussions with many public employees reveal support for civil service reform; able and devoted civil servants—and there are many thousands of them—resent it when they see incompetent co-workers receive equal pay and pass promotion examinations, and they are tired of being vilified by the public for the lethargy of such colleagues. They would respond favorably to sensible improvements, for the overwhelming majority want to be effective in their work and to have pride in their organization. Therefore, the irreconcilable opposition to civil service reform probably numbers far, far less than one million, and political leaders should be able to deal with such opposition by mobilizing the many latent forces for reform.

But for too long there has been a mutually convenient conspiracy of silence among civil service employees, their unions, and public officials about the quantity and quality of work performed, the productivity of government agencies, and the level of service delivered to the public. Employees received security, generous fringe benefits and pensions, and constantly improving salaries. (The top civil service salary is now close to $40,000.) The unions acquired members and political power. The public officials' reward was the possibility of reelection or reappointment. However, that era is drawing to a close as taxpayers demand better performance and as alert political leaders sense the popular mood.

The time now seems right for a long-overdue reform of the civil service. The intent of reform should be to adapt the civil service system to changing times and changing needs in order to bring about more efficient and more effective government. Several of the steps recommended by us were accepted in New York and are being implemented. Although the procedures will generally vary from state to state, many of the changes needed in the nation's civil service system can be effected by the direct and indirect authority of the chief executives. Other changes may require enlightened rule-making by appointed civil service commissions. Still others will require action by state legislatures.

Inevitably, there will be opposition to any changes, and the dread spectre of the 19th-century spoils system is already being exhumed and summoned to the battlements. Certainly, safeguards will be needed. But the surest safeguard of all is the fact that current political realities have greatly reduced the threat of the spoils system. Today an elected official can best secure his own reelection by creating and maintaining an efficient and effective organization to deliver governmental services to the public. He cannot do this without a competent work force. Trite though it may sound, the best protection against abuses is an enlightened citizenry, demanding performance and accountability of its government, and aided by a vigilant free press. These conditions exist today in New York, and in other places as well.

The argument for reform is overwhelming. The potential future imperfections of a revitalized personnel system are small and distant compared to the actual weaknesses, large and immediate, of today's illusory merit system. Undoubtedly, the prescription should be applied selectively. Some states and cities are still suffering under a corrupt spoils system and can benefit from the kinds of changes introduced long ago by the *first* wave of civil service reform. By far the most common affliction, however, is the rigor mortis of overdeveloped and regressive civil service systems. If these are reformed, no doubt the time will come again, in another 50 or 100 years, when the disadvantages of the system advocated here will outweigh its advantages. At such time, new reforms—reforms that meet the needs of those new conditions—will again be in order, for no system devised by man works well forever.

# 16

# New Concepts for Personnel Management

*National Academy of Public Administration*

The Federal Personal Manual (FPM) has eight thousand eight hundred and fourteen pages. If regulations generated good personnel management, the Federal government would have the best personnel system in the world.

But instead, when managers and personnel experts all over government were consulted, they simply reaffirmed what is common knowledge—the frustrations with the system are general and profound. Even experienced personnel officers admit that nobody really understands those 8,814 pages. They certainly are not understood by managers, nor do they describe a personnel system which works for them or for their employees in the workplace where a personnel system should really pay off. In sharp contrast to successful personnel systems elsewhere, Federal managers do not feel that the system is designed to meet their needs, but see it as just another set of obstacles they must overcome in doing their jobs.

In fact, the personnel system doesn't seem to work very well for *anybody*. Because of this, the NAPA Panel was asked to make the personnel systems a central priority in its study.

The reactions of various personnel system users can be summarized as follows:

***Executives and line managers*** feel almost totally divorced from what should be one of their most important systems. They regard themselves

SOURCE: *National Academy of Public Administration, Revitalizing Federal Management: Managers and Their Overburdened Systems* (Washington, 1983).

as being required to operate under a system which is imposed on them from outside their own agencies, and they feel that they play almost no role in the development of that system, either governmentwide or within their own agencies. They feel they have little or no voice in how the system functions and thus have no sense of responsibility for whether it works well or poorly. They recognize that 8,814 pages of FPM means that the system rests in the hands of the personnel specialists, many of whom have only a tenuous grip on their own processes. Finally, and most significantly, managers have become passive and indifferent. Lacking any sense of relevance in personnel matters, they seldom feel any reward (or penalty) for how they handle personnel situations, spend far too little time on them, and frequently resent the time they do spend because it seems bureaucratic and unproductive. Yet no decisions made by these managers are more important.

***Personnel specialists*** spend far too much time in the mechanical or procedural elements of the system: interpreting the 8,814 pages of the manual, supplementing them with additional hundreds of pages of procedures within their own agency, and administering the paperwork and reporting which the system demands. They believe that they are left with far too little time to consult and work with line managers or employers in positive personnel work, such as recruitment of high quality people, sound employee evaluation and merit pay determinations, and design of intelligent programs for employee development, training, promotion, and transfer. This preoccupation with process also makes more difficult the exploration of cooperation with unions in creative approaches to positive employee incentives.

***The Office of Personnel Management*** operates approximately 70 percent of all examining operations, directly conducts training programs, administers compensation and fringe benefits programs, and runs the Federal retirement system. It also attempts to keep the manual up to date—often unsuccessfully. It relies heavily on standard procedures, preapprovals of agency plans, and audits of individual positions and even individual actions, as system controls. When it develops personnel policy, it is often not able to obtain sufficiently broad inputs from managers and executives in addition to its network of personnel officers. And, it spends minimal time in personnel research and development activities or in exerting its role as the Federal government's personnel system leadership, a role which was intended as an important element of the Civil Service Reform Act.

## The Present System

The staff studies on which this report is based makes many specific recommendations for reform of the Federal Personnel Manual. But the NAPA Panel strongly believes that "hacking away at the underbrush" is not a feasible solution to the problem of personnel system ineffectiveness. *A more advanced concept of personnel system value and accountability is needed which goes beyond the advances of the Civil Service Reform Act by placing responsibility for effective personnel management squarely in the hands of the manager, and not in the personnel organization.*

At present, accountability is divided and varies by functional areas within personnel management so that no one is fully accountable. For example:

• Only the agency head has the authority to hire, promote, train, and fire employees, but this must be done following specific procedures laid down by OPM and frequently with OPM approvals of plans or individual actions.
• OPM and agency position classifiers usually have the final say in position classification while the line manager is accountable for determining duties, assignments of duties, and work results.
• Delegations to agencies and within agencies for personnel management vary greatly by functional areas (hiring, promoting, training,

separating). Delegation to line managers to act on personnel matters without approval by or formal coordination with others is the rare exception rather than the rule.

These muddied relationships prevail in a government personnel system once highly centralized but in which substantial decentralization took place before and during World War II and again during the Korean War because decentralization was recognized as vital to the success in the war effort. Congress and Presidents have also conceded the need to exempt special government activities from the general civil service: the Tennessee Valley Authority in 1933, the Atomic Energy Commission and the medical functions of the Veterans Administration in 1946, NASA in 1958, the Postal Service in 1970, the U.S. Railway Association in 1973, and the Synthetic Fuels Corporation in 1980. Legislative branch agencies and some security agencies have their own non-civil-service merit systems.

Despite these centrifugal tendencies, there were centralizing forces at work from the 1950's on—notably the recentralization of examining authority in the Civil Service Commission in the 1960's. However, when Congress reconstructed the statutory foundations of the civil service in the Civil Service Reform Act of 1978, it provided authority for the Director of OPM to delegate most of his functions to agency heads.

The basic argument for a centralized, procedurally oriented personnel system is that the Federal government is a single employer, and equity and efficiency demand such a system. However, past decentralizations and exemptions show a clear recognition that the government is *not* a single employer and that flexibility in personnel management delegations to agencies is necessary if they are to administer Federal programs successfully.

On the basis of its overall assessment, the Panel developed several basic assumptions about necessary conditions for further personnel systems reform:

• Effective deregulation is possible only through maximum delegation of authority to agencies with:

> —the relinquishing of detailed controls by the central agency and
> —the decentralization of operations within agencies.

- To carry out this concept, it is essential to hire, develop, and retain the highest quality of executive and managerial leadership—both political and career.

- Executive leadership should be given full responsibility for personnel management and held strictly accountable for actions and results.

- The central personnel agency (the Office of Personnel Management) should provide positive leadership on behalf of the President by:

> —issuing broad guidelines;
> —carrying out far-reaching research and development efforts directly or in cooperation with agencies;
> —monitoring and evaluating personnel management effectiveness within agencies, and, where necessary, withdrawing delegations of authority;
> —actively enforcing sound personnel management through recommending changes to the President and the heads of agencies when it finds system problems in the agencies; and
> —encouraging and assisting agencies to develop strong positive personnel programs.

- The Merit Systems Protection Board will have to be vigorous in its role and competently staffed, particularly in its merit systems review functions.

## A New Conceptual Framework

A new conceptual framework is proposed which is based on consideration of some of the characteristics of successful private sector personnel programs, but, to a surprising degree, it is simply a turnaround of the negative reactions to the Federal personnel system summarized above. In this new framework:

**Federal executives and managers** must take a more direct and active role in personnel management. (Many of their counterparts in highly successful private companies spend on the average of *more than 50 percent of their time* on the development of people.) The Federal system must delegate more "hands-on" authority to these managers and deliberately draw them more into the design of personnel systems and programs, so that the managerial needs will dominate design rather than procedural concerns. Managers must, within established guidelines, take greater control over critical personnel processes, such as recruitment of talent and the classification of positions as to grade and work content, and ultimately must be held accountable for the success or failure of personnel management.

It must be reemphasized that the basic intent of this concept is to shift the center of gravity for personnel program effectiveness away from the professional personnel organization and into the hands of the managers. The focal point for the personnel program is the workplace. Both managers and employees know how complex and interactive this workplace can be, but it is here that the real utilization of an organization's human resources takes place. People are motivated not by systems but by leadership, the value of the job, the chance to contribute and to achieve, and the sense of being needed and rewarded. Federal supervisors, managers and executives cannot afford to be hampered by their own personnel system, nor can they remain indifferent to and unskilled in personnel matters.

**Professional personnel staff** must consult more thoroughly and extensively with agency leadership and line managers to give them professional guidance and assistance and to obtain—in fact demand—clearer signals about what management wants from its personnel programs, and they must monitor programs and personnel operations on management's behalf. This is more of a staff function rather than a line function, and it presumes some shifting of personnel operations (notably recruiting, classification, performance evaluation, and merit pay determinations) into line organizations. But it is also a personnel responsibility of a higher quality and ultimately of far greater value to the organization.

*The Office of Personnel Management* must concentrate less on detailed procedures and focus more on providing direction, leadership, and evaluation. This can be made possible by delegating most operations to the agencies in every feasible way. OPM would continue to design the overall personnel system and give greater emphasis to monitoring and evaluating the conduct of personnel programs throughout the government on behalf of the President. In addition, OPM would continue to guide and review basic compensation and classification systems, and approve certain key individual executive personnel and political appointment actions, as well as labor contracts which are nation- or organizationwide in scope, along with general oversight of labor relations.

Table 1 describes these functional roles and relationships more explicitly in the form of a functional model.

*Recommendations:*

To develop this new concept and partnership, the Panel recommends that:

- OPM and agencies establish and operate under a clear and consistent set of relationships with each other.
- OPM act for the President in developing and guiding a positive personnel program to be carried out by the agencies, and in sponsoring research and development on useful innovations.

OPM adopt broad guidelines which permit agencies to have the flexibility to develop and implement personnel programs responsive to their management needs.

- Agencies select and develop career executives and managers who will be competent and willing to exercise the major personnel management responsibilities recommended in this report.
  - Executives and Line Managers:
    —Take more active roles in personnel, particularly in selection and development of effective employees;

—Help tailor personnel programs to meet their needs;
—Develop a greater sense of personal responsibility for the design and operation of the system;
—Receive rewards based on involvement;
—Be held accountable for effective use of authority delegated to them;
—Participate in developing policies which are approved by the head of their agency or organization.
- Within agencies, personnel offices:
  —Provide staff assistance to top management in the formulation of agency personnel policies and standards;
  —Serve as consultants to executives and line managers, as well as provide staff help in recruiting, training, and other personnel functions.

One of the unfortunate consequences of past personnel practices is that a significant proportion of Federal managers and first line supervisors move into their jobs without adequate training or preparation to exercise their personnel responsibilities. The recommendations of this report call on managers to upgrade their human resources role and would require more direct attention to personnel processes. If real progress is to be made in bringing about the decentralization concept, it is imperative that special efforts be made to train and motivate managers to fulfill their new role. Such special efforts would be warranted if only to repair past neglect, but it becomes an imperative for the future. No significant improvements can be achieved in human resources utilization, personnel program innovation, or reduction of procedural overregulation until managers are properly prepared to accept their more important roles. This need also represents a significant new challenge as well for OPM and the professional personnel staffs in the departments and agencies. They too must "shift gears" and place themselves in more of a service relationship to line leadership than in the past.

Such changes can't be made overnight. The course laid out in this report will require many

## Table 1
## The functional model

Application of concepts that have been successfully applied in industry and in Federal organizations not subject to Civil Service led the Panel to construct a model division of responsibilities against which present relationships can be evaluated. The Panel recognizes that achieving the roles and relationships proposed will take an extended period of time, will have to be phased in, and will involve a learning curve on the part of all participants.

*Central Control and Leadership.* OPM and OMB as staff agencies to the President should exercise the following functions:

| *Function* | *Focal Point* |
|---|---|
| Principles, objectives, and standards for personnel management | OPM |
| Program evaluation | OPM/MSPB/GAO |
| Salary schedules, compensation systems, and fringe benefits | OPM/OMB |
| Control on salary expenditures | OMB |
| Control on numbers of executives | OPM |

*Agency/Department Personnel Management.* Responsibility for all other functions would be shared as outlined below:

| | *OPM* | *Agencies* |
|---|---|---|
| *1. Recruiting and Examining* | OPM delegates recruiting and examining to agencies. Where examining involves "common positions," OPM takes lead in cooperation with interagency groups or the primary employer in the area and monitors process and results. | Agency staff carry out recruiting and examining with line manager involvement. Where OPM has the lead because of "common positions," agency staff and line people participate with OPM in the process. In both situations OPM monitors process and results. |
| *2. Classification* | OPM assigns development of qualification and classification standards to interagency groups or predominant employers. Standards so developed are subject to OPM approval and deal primarily with the "journeyman" level. OPM issues guideline standards for positions above the journeyman level. OPM monitors process and results. | Agencies assign staff and line persons to participate in the development of standards. Each agency adopts guidelines for positions above the full performance (or journeyman) level consistent with its management needs and organizational alignments. Agencies apply the standards, carrying out good classification and position management practices, and constantly evaluate and provide feedback on the classification system and its application. OPM monitors results and reports on them in program evaluation reviews. |
| *3. Merit Protection, Merit Pay, Equal Employment Opportunity, Training, Performance Appraisal, Incentive Awards* | OPM issues broad guidelines and places its emphasis on evaluation. MSPB evaluates Federal merit system against statutory principles. | Agencies implement programs under OPM guidelines and do self-evaluations of subordinate and field organizations. Line managers participate in all developmental, implementation, and evaluation activities. |

*(continued)*

**Table 1** *(continued)*
**The functional model**

| | | |
|---|---|---|
| *4. Labor Management Relations* | OPM provides general guidance and provides data and analysis on FLRA decisions. | Agencies implement program under OPM general guidance. Line managers participate in all LMR activities. |
| *5. Adverse Actions* | OPM provides general guidance and data analysis and guidance. MSPB decides appeals. | Agencies carry out adverse actions with line management involvement and considerable staff advice and support on specific actions. |
| *6. Program Evaluation* | OPM issues evaluation criteria when policy guidance is issued. Prior approvals are kept to minimum required by law. Reporting requirements met through automated systems. Evaluation may be done by OPM or by agencies with reports to or checks by OPM. GAO and MSPB also evaluate programs. OPM enforces standards: withdraws authority, imposes special controls, or reports to agency head or Congress where abuse or misuse of authorities occur or where personnel programs don't measure up to recognized standards. | Agencies reflect evaluation criteria in their programs; develop automated information systems to assist executives and line managers in program evaluation. |

years to bring about. OPM continues to be guarded in stating that "OPM favors delegations if these are consistent with law and OPM's mint and fiduciary responsibilities." But clearly the pace at which this change is implemented could be much greater if OPM and agency leadership can be linked together in a partnership to develop plans for achieving these objectives.

*Recommendations*

• The NAPA Panel recommends that OPM take the lead in planning and promoting a major program to strengthen the personnel role of Federal managers throughout government by implementing the recommendations of this report.

• It also recommends that agency heads adopt the policies of this report which call for greater delegation of authority for personnel matters and that immediate action be initiated to train and motivate all supervisors and managers to prepare them for the assumption of this stronger personnel role.

# 17

# Position Classification: A Behavioral Analysis for the Public Service

*Jay M. Shafritz*

## Introduction

Public personnel programs have perennial problems with the uses and abuses of position classifications—formal job descriptions that organize all jobs in a given organization into classes on the basis of duties and responsibilities for the purpose of delineating authority, establishing chains of command, and providing equitable salary scales. Few public management tools have been as justly and unjustly maligned. While position classifications are almost universally recognized as essential for the administration of a public personnel program, they are frequently denounced as unreasonable constraints on top management, as sappers of employee morale, and for being little more than polite fictions in substance. The definitive history of the United States Civil Service counts position classifications among the "great institutional curses of the federal service at the present time."[1] As with other aspects of traditional public personnel administration, they often represent what Wallace Sayre has termed the "triumph of techniques over purpose."[2] In seeking to thwart the

SOURCE: Reprinted by permission of the author from Jay M. Shafritz, *Position Classification: A Behavioral Analysis for the Public Service* (New York: Praeger Publishers, 1973), pp. 3–9, 44–59. References and footnotes combined and renumbered.

excesses of spoils politics the reform movement instituted many civil service procedures that have inadvertently had the effect of thwarting effective management practices as well. Thus the negative role of the public personnel agency in guarding the merit system has commonly been more influential than the positive role of aiding management in the maintenance of a viable personnel system. This contradictory duality of function in public personnel operations is nowhere more evident than with position classification procedures. While position classifications have received substantial criticism, this has not generated a corresponding revision of established classification principles and practices.

Almost all of the classification procedures currently in practice were catalogued and popularized in 1941 by a landmark study sponsored by the Civil Service Assembly—the former name of the Public Personnel Association. During the subsequent thirty years, position classifications have proved to be one of the few constant factors in a changing world. Most of the current literature in public administration that deals with the subject openly acknowledges its large debt to the 1941 report by the Committee on Position Classification and Pay Plans in the Public Service of the Civil Service Assembly of the United States and Canada.[3] The report, entitled *Position-Classification in the Public Service,* is commonly referred to as the Baruch report after the chairman of the committee, Ismar Baruch. Although Baruch himself recognized in 1941 that position classification was "still a developing art,"[4] Merrill J. Collett, another member of the committee that produced the report, wrote in 1971 that he was "disturbed by the lack of basic change in the field of position classification"[5] in the intervening years.

A variety of factors have inadvertently conspired at this point in time to make many current position classification practices obsolete. The kind of work force that classification plans were originally designed to accommodate no longer exists. The principles of position classification that were established before World War II assumed, in the best scientific management tradition of the time, that work could most efficiently be organized by imitating industrial machinery and creating a system of human interchangeable parts. Thus one person in any given class was considered absolutely equal to any other person in that class.[6] This approach may well have been the most efficient possible system several generations ago. But now, because of advances in the social sciences and radical changes in the nature of the work force, conventional position classification systems are not only obsolete in terms of simply not being as efficient as other modes of organization but also have proved themselves to be counterproductive of the organizational mission. Because of the continual rise in American educational levels, the bulk of the labor force increasingly consists of highly skilled technical and professional employees. Such workers should not be treated as if they were semiskilled laborers, menials, or clerical functionaires; yet position classification systems, designed to meet the needs of these latter employees, are being imposed upon the administrative, professional, and technical employees for reasons that are hardly defensible in light of what is known today about organizing and motivating a work force. The old dichotomy between managers and workers is no longer valid. Workers in the traditional sense are an ever decreasing minority. Replacing the traditional worker as the backbone of production are technical and professional employees. This group is more likely to consider itself part of management than of the oppressed proletariat. It wasn't until the 1960s that this group, which Peter Drucker labels the "knowledge worker,"[7] began to be commonly recognized as the dominant part of the labor force of the future.

Since position classification programs were implemented as part of the civil service reform movement, they were in large measure designed to be control devices even though they are frequently rationalized as being management tools. For example, it has long been thought that the classification process could aid in revealing organizational defects;[8] yet upon closer observation it becomes obvious that it is frequently the classification system itself that creates these defects. As control devices, position classifications are doubly unsuccessful. First, they prevent program managers from having the discretion essential for the optimum success of their mission. Second, they generate an astounding amount of dysfunctional activity whose sole purpose is to get round the control devices. While the controls are frequently and successfully circumvented, the costs of such activity take away resources from the organization's prime goals.

Contributing to the obsolescent status of position classification programs is the fact that other mechanisms are now performing or are capable of performing its primary mission—ensuring "equal pay for equal work." Public employee unions were practically nonexistent when the first classification plans were installed. Today such unions are exceedingly powerful and influential. The trend seems unmistakably toward ever wider unionization of public employees and even greater influence of union representatives in setting personnel policies. Jerry Wurf, president of the American Federation of State, County, and Municipal Employees, AFL-CIO, predicts that, contrary to current practice, unions will eventually represent public employees on all terms of employment including classification and reclassification.[9] This would be an undeniable escalation of the scope of public employee union bargaining;[10] yet there is little doubt that this will eventually come to pass. Once this is accomplished, "equal pay for equal work" will be a matter of labor–management negotiations. Of course not all employees will be covered by employee organizations. For professional and other highly skilled employee groups, there exist new techniques for arriving at equitable salaries. One such technique, the curve approach, "relates salary to the variables of educational attainment, maturity or experience, and relative job performance, making no direct reference to actual position responsibilities."[11] The wide variety of similar techniques, and those that can readily be developed by new research, makes the claim of position classification to be the backbone of an equitable salaries policy less and less tenable.

During the 1950s, while the behavioral movement became increasingly relevant to a variety of social science and administrative disciplines, public personnel administration was left on the sidelines. By 1961 Paul P. Van Riper regretfully described most of the existing writing on public personnel matters as "translations" from other disciplines because public personnel administrators were "creating little new of their own."[12] He found that there was

little in print concerning the American civil service and American public personnel administration which can be termed either exciting or intellectually stimulating in any fundamental sort of way. It is no wonder that the number of college students, at both undergraduate and graduate levels, who are seriously interested in public personnel administration as either a profession or as a field of study and research has undergone a serious decline in the last twenty years.[13]

The serious decline that Van Riper saw in 1961 had become an almost complete rout by 1969. In a survey conducted in preparation for the American Political Science Association's *Biographical Directory,* 7,265 political scientists reported their first-choice field of specialization. In a rank order list of 27 fields of specialization, personnel administration came out in last place. And most of those who do specialize in personnel administration are the older members of the profession. Heinze Eulau considers it a "dying, if not already dead, specialization."[14] A discipline could well afford to be ignored by the academics if its practitioners were actively engaged in research efforts. However, O. Glenn Stahl, writing in 1971, found that research was "still conspicuous by its absence among public personnel agencies."[15] Gerald E. Caiden has accused public personnel administration of being in the doldrums—and with good reason.[16]

While academicians can perhaps afford to be neglectful of advances in personnel administration in general and position classification in particular, the subject is too important to the lives of too many Americans to be ignored, for "More than one out of every six Americans works for a government—federal, state or local."[17] Since position classification is practically universal, the contentment of most of these citizens is dependent to some degree upon the public personnel procedures that govern their working lives. These workers as well as public managers in general have good reason to be unhappy with current practices. With the possible exceptions of performance ratings as customarily administered, more sins in the name of position classification have "been committed against persons and against the effectiveness of administrative operations than in any other function in personnel management."[18] Obviously a problem of such dimensions deserves considerable attention. The present work is an attempt in part to fill in this "attention gap" and in part to generate the kind of interest that will instigate additional work by others. The logical end product of this work and future work by others would be the review of classification principles and practices so that they more positively contribute to the goals of their organizations.

Most textbooks in public administration and public personnel administration contain chapters on position classification, but these are invariably and of necessity superficial examinations that stress the "how to do it" qualities of the classification process and ignore the behavioral implications that these procedures have for management. The source of this information is usually the 1941 Baruch report or secondary sources based upon it. In addition, excellent "how to do it" materials on position classification are published by the U.S. Civil Service Commission,[19] the Public Personnel Association,[20] and the International City Managers' Association.[21]

What is missing is a treatment of position classification that combines the "nuts and bolts" of the classifications process with its behavioral implications. Over the last three decades a tremendous amount of research has been published concerning the relations between man and his organizations.[22] However, the impact of this wealth of information "on both the theory and practices of position classification in the public service has been negligible. . . ."[23]

## Philadelphia as a Case Study

The previous chapters have tended to discuss position classification practices without reference to specific classification programs. Very little case study material dealing with position classification processes is available. This chapter, by presenting a case study of classification practices in one of the nation's largest local jurisdictions, will provide concrete, empirical evidence of the informal procedures that tend to evolve whenever traditional classification practices prevail. There is great utility in seeking to provide a realistic description of position classification practices in a major jurisdiction. While there is nothing new about discussing the informal aspects of an ongoing organization, discussions of bureaucratic realpolitik are conspicuously lacking. According to Albert Somit,

> the public employee who lacks at least an elementary comprehension of the major operational concepts and objectives of administrative realpolitik is professionally handicapped. . . . Scanning the literature of American public administration, anyone familiar with the realities of bureaucratic existence is struck by the almost total absence of any dispassionate analysis of the nature and importance of administrative realpolitik.[24]

Just as police rookies are frequently told by the more experienced patrolmen that they will have to forget everything they learned at the police academy in order to function as real policemen,[25] a young administrator, whether he has a liberal arts background or a Master's in public administration, must suffer through an on-the-job acquisition of administrative realpolitik. "He learns by the punishing effects of violating norms whose existence and whose particular application he discovers by their breach."[26] The material presented below is intended in part to ease this loss of administrative innocence.

It is Philadelphia's Home Rule Charter— adopted in 1951—that to the largest extent determines the city's management style and performance. It provided for an independent Civil Service Commission with a guaranteed financial base.[27] Many of the charter's provisions were created in reaction to the abuses and inefficiencies of the past. It is the opinion of the only historian of the charter movement that the Charter Commission overreacted to the flaws of the previous administrations.

> The Charter was over drafted. Believing that Philadelphians have suffered from the abuse of discretion by its officials, the Charter Commission resolved to produce an instrument that would, if possible, forever forestall further difficulties. To write specific directions into a charter. . . is like putting administrative rules into a government's constitution. Yet the Commission did exactly this.[28]

When specific methods and procedures are frozen into a charter, city officials are frustrated in their efforts to abuse the system, if that is their intent; but at the same time they are equally frustrated in attempts to change the system in order to achieve greater efficiency and thus serve the public interest.

Lincoln Steffens, the famous muckraker of the Progressive era, is noted for writing, after he had visited Philadelphia in 1903, that the city was not only "corrupt and contented" but also "the worst governed city in the country."[29] Prior to the new charter and the reform administration of Mayor Joseph S. Clark in 1952, Philadelphia served as a classic example of corrupt municipal government. Philadelphia's personnel director, Foster B. Roser, has written that

> Philadelphia bore the dubious distinction of having probably the most discredited merit system of any large city in the United States. In spite of all the traditional civil service legal provisions, the system was completely emasculated by political influence and fraud.[30]

The civil service system was completely controlled by committees of the political party in power. Every job required the endorsement of a member of the regular party organization. It was reported by a reputable consulting firm that

> While the Civil Service Commission conforms with the mechanical aspects of the Civil Service Laws and with the rules and Regulations, they are violated in two major respects: the necessity for political endorsement in obtaining appointments and promotions, and the collection of "voluntary contributions" from, and pressure for, political activity by the employees on behalf of the City Committee.[31]

This process ended when a reform mayor armed with the new city charter took office in 1952.[32] In response to the abuses of the former so-called merit system, the new charter contained 22 paragraphs stipulating civil service procedures and provided for a Civil Service Commission, which was to be largely independent of the other branches of the city government.[33]

The commission supervises the activities of the Personnel Department. It does this mainly through the personnel director whom it appoints.[34] It was felt by the framers of the charter that, in not allowing the mayor to appoint the personnel director, the separation of the civil service system from partisan political considerations would be realized. It is the personnel director who administers the civil service regulations under the direction of the commissioners.[35] The commission makes policy by adopting regulations for the management of the system and adopting, subject to the approval of the Administrative Board, the classification and pay plans.[36]

The civil service procedures are critical to the city's management posture because almost all city positions are under civil service jurisdiction. The exemptions allowed are few—essentially confined to department heads, their deputies and secretaries.[37]

When the new charter came into being and the reform administration assumed power in 1952, the previous civil service structure and procedures were almost completely discarded. Existing eligible lists were found to have been dishonestly assembled.[38] Consequently, all employees had to take qualifying examinations if they wished to remain in their current positions. Because the Civil Service Commission felt it necessary to start the whole system anew, it immediately created for itself an immense backlog of work. This caused considerable strain between the Personnel Department and the various operating departments. They needed a variety of personnel services that the Personnel Department, swamped with work as it was, was unable to perform efficiently. In addition, the Personnel Department tended to interpret the charter provisions concerning civil service procedures as strictly as possible. Thus further delays were caused, which the operating departments felt were unwarranted. As a result, the departments complained to the managing director who complained to the mayor who in chorus with the City Council called for the removal of the personnel director and revision of the charter.

The problem was essentially one of definition. Was the Personnel Department primarily an agency to service the operating departments or was it primarily a guardian of the principles of the merit system? This is not an uncommon dilemma with governmental personnel agencies.

> At all levels of government in the United States, the central personnel agency traditionally has a dual role. On the one hand, it has a positive role. . .of aiding management in the selection of qualified employees and maintaining an effective personnel system. On the other hand, it has a negative role of acting as a guardian of the government's personnel system to insure that the personnel program is carried out fairly and impartially and is proof against not only partisan but also personal politics.[39]

Friction continued to develop because the Personnel Department continued to emphasize its negative role. In the first annual report of the new managing director, it was recommended that the personnel director be made part of the mayor's cabinet and thus directly responsible to the mayor. The Personnel Department was found to be "not as responsive as it should be to the requirements of the operating departments."[40] The mayor concurred with the recommendation that the personnel director be included in the cabinet.[41] Some city councilmen were calling for the personnel director's resignation; others merely wanted an investigation of the Personnel Department.[42] Enough pressure was generated by all of the groups unhappy with the performance of the Personnel Department that a study was authorized by the Civil Service Commission. An outside agency was engaged in order to determine how objectively the civil service provisions of the charter had been implemented. The study was made by the Government Consulting Service of the Fels Institute of Local and State Government of the University of Pennsylvania.[43] The report was devastating to the personnel director. It found that he only gave "secondary emphasis to positive personnel management."[44] The report concluded that this "emphasis upon the role of guardian and controller leads the Personnel Department to go beyond and elaborate upon the restrictive personnel provisions of the Charter."[45] As a result, the Civil Service Commission did an about-face. It went from a negative personnel role to a positive one. This trend away from strict constructionism has continued unabated over the years. It accelerated as the original commissioners were removed by the mayor when their terms expired.[46] Now the commission tends to be exceedingly liberal in interpreting its mandate.

It is a matter of opinion whether the commission is liberal in its interpretations out of conviction or out of a strong political allegiance to the mayor. Former Mayor Joseph S. Clark is of the opinion that the present commission is little more than a rubber stamp for the mayor.[47] Even members of the Civil Service Nominating Panel concede that the current commission is much easier for the mayor to control.[48]

An important lesson had been learned. It was not possible to enforce strictly the restrictive provisions of the charter. Therefore, the personnel director had to acquiesce to the operating departments' circumventing the letter of the charter and the Civil Service Regulations by various means. Succeeding personnel directors had before them the example of the first person to occupy their office. He was forced to resign.[49]

Irrespective of a change in role perceptions, there is an institutionalized degree of conflict over personnel policy, with the mayor and the managing director on one side and the personnel director and the Civil Service Commission on the other. The concerns of the two sides are often contradictory. While the managing director's office wants to resolve its personnel problems as quickly and efficiently as possible, the Personnel Department has not forgotten its negative watchdog role. Yet by not barking too often this watchdog maintains its creditability. Consequently, with the Personnel Department as a willing accomplice, informal norms and procedures have been institutionalized that help to overcome the constraints imposed by the classification plan. But, before these informal procedures can be discussed, the formal procedures must be delineated to serve as a point of departure for the analysis. The formal procedures for amending the classification are as follows:

1) Any person who feels that the classification plan needs changing or that any individual position is improperly classified must file a written appeal with the Personnel Director.[50] While individual employees can file their own appeals, in practice the actual paper work is usually done by the departmental personnel officers—that is, if the department is in favor of the proposed change.

2) The Personnel Director is obligated to review all appeals.[51] This means that a personnel technician from the Classification and Pay Division is assigned to do a job audit of the position being appealed.

3) The Classification and Pay Division will submit to the Personnel Director a written report on the audit which will include a recommendation for action.

4) The Personnel Director will schedule the appeal to be heard at the next scheduled meeting of the Civil Service Commission.[52] The meeting is public, and the personnel director is required to notify all parties that might be affected by the appeal of the time and place of the meeting.[53]

5) At the Civil Service Commission meeting the Personnel Director will make his

recommendation for action to the Commissioners. If the concerned employee or his representatives—his departmental officer or his lawyer—or any other interested party is present, they may also present findings.[54]

6) The Personnel Director is required to notify in writing the appellant and the other concerned departments of the final disposition of the appeal.[55]

7) If the amendment is approved by the Civil Service Commission, it is submitted to the Managing Director and the Director of Finance for final approval. If they do not approve of the amendment prior to the next meeting of the Administrative Board, the amendment will be approved or disapproved at that meeting.[56]

8) If the amendment involves the reallocation of a position or the creation of a new position, that position will be considered a vacant position and filled by the normal civil service appointing procedures.[57] An employee whose position is reallocated shall continue in his former class unless he qualifies to be appointed to the new position through normal appointing procedures.[58]

There is no way to avoid any of the above steps, which are required to amend the classification plan. The informal norms and procedures that have been institutionalized can only shorten the time involved and prevent the appeal's being denied at any point in the process. For example, the last step of the amending process requires the approval of the managing director and the director of finance. Frequently, this approval is acquired informally prior to the initiation of any of the other steps. This informal prior approval, while not binding, tends to have a halo effect over the formal process. In such cases, the decisions to be made by the various parties concerned deal not only with the merits of the appeal but also with the implied or expressed wishes of members of the Administrative Board.

The civil service regulations express in great detail all of the formal rules guiding personnel actions. With this convenient guide it is a simple matter to determine whether an observed procedure is part of the formal or the informal system. If an action is not provided for in the regulations, it is not part of the formal merit system. Just as the Supreme Court holds up a law to the Constitution in order to see if the law squares with the Constitution, the researcher can hold personnel procedures up to the civil service regulations in order to see if such practices are in harmony with the regulations. Just as the Supreme Court's interpretations of the law are often reflections of the political and philosophical make-up of the court, the Civil Service Commission's interpretations of the provisions of the regulations and the charter are valid indicators of the political and philosophic make-up of the commission.

Because of the laissez-faire attitudes of recent civil service commissioners, the authority of the commission has gradually been eroded. Thus, the mayor and his administrators have been able to take greater and greater liberties with the regulations. For example, under the regulations, all employees have the right to appeal directly to the Civil Service Commission for a reallocation of their position classification and pay status.[59] Yet it is common knowledge that such an appeal has practically no chance of succeeding without the endorsement of the department concerned. In reality, an employee must appeal to his department for a reallocation. The individual employee retains his right to appeal; but without his department's endorsement his appeal has no practical chance of success. Confronted with a subject's view of his classification status and his department's view of his status, it is only reasonable that the Civil Service Commission will be infinitely more sympathetic to the department, the merits of the situation notwithstanding. Thus the departments have discretion over matters that formerly belonged to the Civil Service Commission. The commission in effect no longer adjudicates these cases directly; it merely sanctions or vetoes decisions already made by the departments. The regulations have not been changed de jure; there has simply been a de facto by-pass.

Because a classification plan is inherently unable to distinguish between levels of performance in similar or identical job titles, informal norms and procedures have evolved that circumvent the letter of the civil service regulations and compensate for the weaknesses of a rigid classification plan. One such norm has already been discussed. An employee doing outstanding work in the opinion of his superiors is more likely to get his department's support on a reclassification appeal. Thus the system is informally capable of rewarding performance on the job by withholding or granting appropriate assistance in classification appeals. The most common situation in which informal norms and procedures circumvent the spirit of the regulations occurs when a department wishes to reward a valued employee. An employee is just as likely to be valued for the outstanding contribution he is making to the organization as for the fact that his personality is appealing to the appropriate individuals.[60] The reasons for the worker's being rewarded are inconsequential to the method by which the reward is achieved. The strategy is invariably the same, since the structure of the process is dictated by the regulations. The goal—the reward—simply put, is more money. As it is impossible simply to grant an employee a raise in salary, because the regulations provide that "pay ranges shall be linked directly to the Classification Plan,"[61] he can only be rewarded by promoting him to a higher-paying classification. The problem then is to justify a new classification.

It is a vital point in the theory of position classification that positions change. Consequently, these changes must be reflected in the classification plan if that plan is going to remain a viable management tool. Such natural changes occur constantly in all levels of municipal employment. The Philadelphia classification plan is maintained by occupational audits and by audits of individual positions undertaken at the request of an employee or department. Therefore, there is nothing unusual in a department requesting that the Personnel Department audit a position that the department concerned feels should be reclassified to a higher level and consequently a higher salary.

Once a department commits itself to assisting a subject in getting reclassified, an elaborate scenario is enacted that revolves around the classification process. The degree of assistance that the department offers its employee is a function of the department's opinion of his value. While a department could offer no assistance for one subject and absolute assistance to another, the actual degree of push that the department offers is usually between the two extreme poles of the continuum. No departmental cooperation is tantamount to no chance at all. The following example concerning John Doe will illustrate absolute assistance. Citing the particulars of an actual case would prove to be extremely embarrassing to the persons involved. It would also violate information given in confidence for disinterested reasons. Therefore, while the illustration used is hypothetical, it is extremely common and can easily be documented.

A departmental head wants to reward John Doe for his outstanding work and/or pleasing personality. If Doe were in a one-position class, it would be possible to ignore the classification process and simply appeal for an amendment to the pay plan on a variety of possible grounds.[62] For example, a subject in a one-position class had an offer of a higher-paying job from another jurisdiction; consequently, he appealed with the support of his department, and the salary was raised for his class in order "to aid in retention."[63] But one-position classes are rare. The more common situation involves promoting a subject out of a class that he shares with others into a higher, already established class or a new class created especially for the occasion.

The first step that a department takes once it decides to push for a promotion through reclassification is informally to sound out the power brokers in the system—namely the managing director's office and the Personnel Department. Because each of these powers has a virtually certain veto over any proposed changes in the classification plan, it is politic to consult with them prior to initiating any formal action. Usually the departmental personnel officer makes these initial contacts; if he is turned down, it is a minor loss of face. If it is felt to be warranted, the department head himself or his deputy or assistant can initiate the contact. While this gives added weight to the request, a refusal is also a greater loss. If the power brokers informally agree to support the appeal, the formal proceedings are initiated.

The departmental personnel officer officially requests in writing that the position of John Doe be audited in order to determine if the position is properly classified. It is at this point that the formal reasons for the reallocation request must be stated. If the request is founded upon actual changes in the duties of the position, the reasons are pretty straightforward and easily stated. However, if, as in John Doe's case, the reason is simply the desire of the department to reward an employee, then reasonable grounds for the reallocation must be fabricated in order to satisfy the formal requirements of the reallocation process. Blatant untruths are never used to justify reallocations; rather, statements are made in such a way that the reasons seem overwhelmingly obvious and reasonable.[64] However, these reasons would hardly be considered sufficient grounds for a reallocation if they were compared to the actual situation. The fact that Doe is newly responsible for the activities of a variety of technical experts may look very impressive on paper; but all that really has changed is an organization chart, which has been redrawn to have the chief of the technicians reporting through Doe to the individual to whom he was formerly responsible. Such fabrications are standard operating procedure. The practice of lying is a common phenomenon in many organizations, and the city of Philadelphia in no way deserves special reprobation for using such an effective management strategy.

> It is often possible to make a change in organization by fictionalizing the basis for change. . . . Organizations are dynamic and need the device of organization fictions to make growth and change possible with a minimum of resistance.[65]

After the formal request for an audit is received, the Classification and Pay Division of the Personnel Department will assign a personnel technician to perform the actual audit. The length of time it takes for the audit procedures to be completed is a function of how cooperative the Personnel Department wishes to be about the reallocation request. The Personnel Department has the option of stalling the procedures for years or dispatching matters within a few weeks. If the department has informally cleared the request at an earlier time, an auditor is quickly sent to interview the individuals concerned with the position. Usually the auditor talks just to the departmental personnel officer, the incumbent, and his immediate superior. These interviewees supply the auditor with all of the information he needs to write a report about the situation upon which the Personnel Department will make its decision to recommend or not to recommend the proposed change to the Civil Service Commission. Because the information given the auditor is often full of misrepresentations, the report that he will later write cannot fail to provide adequate justification for the proposed change. The auditor must officially accept the information given to him as valid even though it may be personally obvious to him that much of the information is false or misleading. A new management trainee, assigned as an auditor in the Classification and Pay Division, asked his supervisor what he should do if he felt that the interviewees were misinforming him. He was told "That's none of your business. Your job is to write down what they tell you."[66] This situation is admitted and accepted by people in the highest levels of the Personnel Department.

Based upon the information given to him, the auditor's report can only come to the conclusions the interviewees arranged for him to reach. Therefore, if prior clearances were obtained, the report will recommend the requested changes. If the recommendation is for a reallocation to an existing class, Doe would need only to qualify on a promotional examination in order to be appointed. However, if no existing class is appropriate for the reallocation, a new class must be established. Once again a personnel technician from the Classification and Pay Division confers with departmental representatives in order to write a class specification appropriate to the new position and satisfactory to the department concerned. The most critical part of this new class specification is the section stating the minimum acceptable training and experience that would qualify an applicant to be admitted to the examination. For example, the management trainee requirement is merely "completion of a bachelor's degree program at a recognized college or university." More advanced class specifications list in addition to degree requirements the length and type of experience required. Usually added to this is an equivalency statement—"or any equivalent combination of acceptable training and experience." Whenever an examination is scheduled for a class, the statement of minimum training and experience is taken verbatim from the class specification and incorporated into the job announcement.[67] In the early days of the middle management system during the 1950s, rather broad equivalencies were accepted so that it was possible for an employee in an administrative series in one department to be promoted to a different career series in another department. This use of equivalencies has grown narrower; thus, while it is still possible for employees to be promoted out of their career series into another department, it is becoming less and less common. As new classes are created, the tendency is to restrict further and further the recruiting base so that only subjects working in the department in which the position exists can be admitted to the examination. For example, the municipally operated Philadelphia General Hospital employs subjects in the administrative analyst series (i.e., Administrative Analyst I, II, III), but new positions above the analysts' level require hospital administrative experience. Consequently, only those analysts currently working in the hospital are eligible for the promotional examination. Administrative analysts in other departments can no longer be promoted into the hospital;[68] they must look to their own

department to create restrictions that will favor their own promotional possibilities. While Philadelphia once favored a great deal of cross-pollination by having its administrators move easily from one department to another, it is becoming more and more to resemble the old New York City system, which "strongly favored career paths which rise more or less vertically, with diagonal movement confined within departments."[69] Philadelphia has not gone as far as New York in requiring that vacancies be filled, wherever "practicable, by promotion from among persons holding positions in a lower grade in the department in which the vacancy exists."[70] However, the same effect is achieved by simply requiring candidates to have experience in the kind of function the department performs.

A considerable amount of bargaining takes place over what kinds of experience will be acceptable equivalents. These decisions are usually made by the Personnel Department in consultation with the department in which the vacancies exist. If a particular department wants to restrict the number of potential eligibles because it has sufficient hopefuls in its own ranks, it is likely to insist upon no equivalencies. If, on the other hand, it does not feel it possesses adequate talent for the new position, it might ask the Personnel Department to accept broad equivalencies and a strictly open competitive examination, which would have the effect of denying its own employees the advantage of being on a promotional list. While these decisions are at the discretion of the personnel director, the wishes of the concerned departments weigh heavily because of the Personnel Department's service function philosophy. It has occurred that bargaining for admission to examinations for new classes was so severe that the Personnel Department, rather than accepting all of the equivalencies that would have been required, chose instead to rewrite the class specification to include all of the unexpected applicants.[71]

Assuming that his department favors Doe's advancement to the new position, the experience and training requirements will probably reflect in remarkable detail Doe's background. The qualifications will be worded as tightly as possible in order to limit to the greatest extent possible the competition that Doe will later have to face on the examination. Civil Service Commission approval of the new class of the reallocation is usually little more than a formality. The commission almost always approves the actions recommended by the Personnel Department, which invariably decides its position on the item at hand before the formal hearing.

As the class specification was tailor made to fit Doe, as the examination for the position is based upon the knowledge, skills, and abilities outlined in the specification, and as the examination was reviewed by Doe's superior, it is unlikely that Doe would have trouble passing the examination. While the chances of Doe's failing the examination are minimal, it is possible, and such things have happened. Regulations do not allow the identification of the candidates' test papers until after they have been scored.[72] Thus the most critical part of the examining process for Doe is the determination of the minimum passing score or passpoint. It is common practice for passpoints in both government and industry to fluctuate, depending upon such factors as the number of applicants and the number of vacancies.[73] The regulations provide the personnel director with considerable discretion in determining the passpoint.

> In determining a minimum passing score, the Director may take into consideration any or all of the following factors which may be pertinent: (a) the minimum competence required for the performance of the duties of the class; (b) the quality of the competitors competing; (c) the difficulty and length of the test; (d) the number of existing and anticipated vacancies to be filled; (e) the recommendations of appointing authorities or other experts; (f) reasonable economy of examining time and expense; (g) the shortage or surplus of qualified competitors; (h) any other pertinent considerations.[74]

In short, the Personnel Department can always find the rationale to establish the passpoint at any level it desires. When there is pressure from a department to ensure that a favored son lands on the eligible list, the Personnel Department tends to set the passpoint low in order to be as sure as possible of passing him. One such examination involving a favored son of the managing director's office had a passpoint of 47 percent.[75] A passpoint of 70 percent would have passed only one of the four contestants. The 47 percent cutoff allowed all four to pass. The departments can just as easily insist upon a high passpoint in order to avoid promoting employees. In one such case, because the managing director's office did not want to promote a management trainee on its staff, it insisted that the passpoint of a promotional examination be set at 70 percent,[76] thus failing the only two candidates when both would have passed had the passpoint been set at 62 percent, for which there was ample precedent.

The operating departments have considerable influence in the examining process. They can effectively influence and determine the kind of examination,[77] its content, and the passpoint to be set for it; thus the departments have the option of allowing the normal examining process to determine promotions or they can intervene and effectively make the decision themselves. Marshall W. Meyer has written that

> bureaucratic regulations can centralize authority in the managerial hierarchy; or rules can remove decisions from the hierarchy, so that the regulations themselves exert authority. A rule that concentrates authority in the managers might be one stating, "Decisions about promotion of employees are made solely by the head of the department." A rule that removes authority from the supervisory structures might state, by contrast, "Promotions are made only on the basis of examination scores." Given a number of examination scores, this rule rather than any person decides who is to be promoted, so one can say that authority is centralized in the regulations.[78]

Philadelphia's civil service regulations certainly centralize authority in themselves; yet Meyer's distinction between authority in the hierarchy or authority in the regulations becomes meaningless when the hierarchy is able to regulate the regulations. Because the departments can influence the promotional examining process in so many ways, the authority that remains with the regulations is essentially procedural and not substantive.

If, after all the effort expounded on behalf of an employee such as Doe, he still fails the examination, his current position is in no way jeopardized by the entire process. The regulations state that, although it is his job that is being reallocated, he will remain in his former job title unless he himself is eligible to be promoted into the new class.[79] In this situation the department has the option of not appointing anyone to the new position or of appointing one of the other eligibles. Because just such a situation does occasionally occur, most employees take every promotional examination for which they can qualify.[80]

If the informal classification processes that have evolved in Philadelphia are examined in light of Herbert Simon's criteria for the performance of the informal structure of an organization,[81] several unfortunate aspects become apparent. In the first chapter, it was stated that the formal structure of an organization functions positively when it encourages the formation of an informal structure along constructive lines. A major intent of this case study of classification procedures has been to determine whether position classification systems (1) encourage the formation of informal structure along constructive lines, (2) set limits on the development of informal relations, and (3) prevent the development of deleterious organization politics. A negative response seems warranted in each of the three instances.

The informal practices that have evolved from the formal structure—the provisions of the charter and the civil service regulations—can hardly be considered constructive when they allow personnel favoritism to play a greater role in determining reallocations than any objective evaluations of merit. While it is true that the informal practices described are generally more efficient in accomplishing their objectives, such efficiency tends to benefit only a small portion of the organization at the expense of the morale of the other segments.

The formal structure does establish some limits on the development of informal relations. The Civil Service Commission rigidly enforces those aspects of the merit system that it considers essential for its concept of integrity. Thus, examinations are administered fairly: it is virtually impossible for anyone to cheat by having answers in advance or changing scores. The authorities can do no more for a favored candidate than to see that all of the examining procedures are in his favor; they cannot manipulate the examination itself.

The same applies to the classification process. The power brokers in the system can only make all circumstances favorable to a reclassification—the actual decision lies with the Civil Service Commission. Yet it is precisely here that there are no limits to the development of informal procedures. All of the vested interests in the system prey upon the Personnel Department by whatever means are at their disposal. The attitude that the Personnel Department can be manipulated to individual advantage is pervasive.

An embarrassing anecdote is illustrative of this situation. A clerical worker had all of the preliminary arrangements made for her to be reallocated to a higher-paying, more professional-sounding position. All that remained was for her to pass the examination written especially for her position. Since the requirements for admission to the examination were tailor made for her, only one other candidate was found eligible for admission. Shortly before the scheduled date of the examination, the candidate found herself in the same crowded elevator as the chairman of the Civil Service Commission. She thereupon explained to the commissioner that she was rather nervous about taking the upcoming exam and that, since it was all arranged for her to be appointed to the position anyway, couldn't she please be allowed to look at the exam in advance? Had this woman assumed that there was anything wrong or unusual about her request, she would certainly not have made it in a crowded elevator. This occurred in 1972. It is indicative of how attitudes toward the Personnel Department have evolved since its strict constructionist stance was abandoned.

The final criterion for our evaluation of the formal structure is whether it prevents the development of deleterious organizational politics. Philadelphia's classification plan, as are many traditional plans, is based upon a rigid set of procedures. This case study has demonstrated that, when such rigidity prevents managers from exercising their discretion in personnel matters, informal norms will be developed to compensate for that rigidity. Irrespective of whether the informal procedures are used to reward personal favorites or genuine merit, the rigid formal structure encourages the growth of organizational politics, because it is through such politicking that reallocations are achieved. Organizational politics tends to be beneficial when merit is rewarded, deleterious when favoritism is rewarded. It is beyond the scope of this study to say which is more common.

## Notes

1. Paul P. Van Riper, *History of the United States Civil Service* (Evanston, Ill.: Row, Peterson, 1958), pp. 557–58.

2. Wallace Sayre, "The Triumph of Techniques over Purpose," *Public Administration Review* 8 (Spring 1948): 134.

3. O. Glenn Stahl, *Public Personnel Administration,* 6th ed. (New York: Harper & Row, 1971), p. 61, a leading textbook on public personnel administration, identifies this as the "still standard work on the subject."

4. Ismar Baruch, *Position-Classification in the Public Service* (Chicago: Civil Service Assembly, 1941), p. xii. This text was reprinted, not revised, by the Public Personnel Association in 1965.

5. Merrill J. Collett, "Re-thinking Position Classification and Management," *Public Personnel Review* 32 (July 1971): 171.

6. It is an elementary observation that once a job requires a significant degree of sophistication, employees vary tremendously in performance; yet public personnel administration has chosen to ignore substantially facts that are equally known by the lowliest file clerks and the highest level executives. Practitioners tend not to believe what is before their eyes when leading authorities in the field say that an impersonal duties description that ignores the variations of incumbency "is a required foundation of personnel management." Quoted phrase from Wallace S. Sayre and Frederick C. Mosher, *An Agenda for Research in Public Personnel Administration* (Washington, D.C.: National Planning Association, 1959), p. 50.

7. Peter F. Drucker, *The New Society: The Anatomy of Industrial Order* (New York: Harper & Row), p. 355. This book was originally published in 1949. Drucker wrote a new Introduction and Epilogue for the 1962 Harper Torchbook edition. In the Epilogue (page 355), he notes that, while this "knowledge worker" was not perceived in 1949, by 1962 it was clearly the "largest and most rapidly growing group in the working population of industrially developed countries, especially the United States."

8. See William E. Mosher and J. Donald Kingsley, *Public Personnel Administration* (New York: Harper & Bros., 1936), p. 381; Norman John Powell, *Personnel Administration in Government* (Englewood Cliffs, N.J.: Prentice-Hall, 1956), pp. 324–25; Elmer V. Williams, "Administrative By-Products of Classification Surveys," *Public Personnel Review* 32 (October 1971): 235–37.

9. Jerry Wurf, "Personnel Opinions," *Public Personnel Review,* 27 (January 1966): 52–53.

10. David T. Stanley maintains that it is only realistic to expect management prerogatives such as job evaluations "to be eroded more and more in the future as strong unions keep trying to expand the scope of collective bargaining." David T. Stanley, "Unions and Government Management: New Relationships in Theory and in Fact," paper presented at the National Conference of the American Society for Public Administration (March 22, 1972), p. 11. Also see Michael Moskow, J. Joseph Doewenberg, and Edward Clifford Koziara, *Collective Bargaining in Public Employment* (New York: Random House, 1970), p. 289.

11. Edward A. Shaw, "The Curve Approach to the Compensation of Scientists," in Paul S. Greenlaw and Robert D. Smith, eds., *Personnel Management: A Management Science Approach* (Scranton, Pa.: International Textbook, 1970), p. 439. Also see Herbert G. Zollitsch and Adolph Langsner, *Wage and Salary Administration* (Cincinnati: South-Western Publishing, 1970); Joseph J. Famularo, ed., *Handbook of Modern Personnel Administration* (New York: McGraw-Hill, 1972), chs. 27–34.

12. Paul P. Van Riper, "Public Personnel Literature: The Last Decade," *Public Personnel Review* 22 (October 1961): 231.

13. *Ibid.*

14. Heinz Eulau, "A Note on the Discipline: Quo Vadimus?" *P.S.: Newsletter of the American Political Science Association* 2 (Winter 1969): 12.

15. Stahl, *op. cit.,* p. 394.

16. For Caiden's plea for a fresh wind, see Gerald E. Caiden, "Public Personnel Administration in the Doldrums?" *Public Personnel Review* 32 (January 1971): 30–35.

17. Frederick G. Mosher, *Democracy and the Public Service* (New York: Oxford University Press, 1968), p. 134.

18. Collett, *op. cit.,* p. 171.

19. *Classification Principles and Policies,* U.S. Civil Service Commission, Personnel Management Series No. 16 (Washington, D.C., 1963).

20. Kenneth Byers, M. Robert Montilla, and Elmer V. Williams, *Elements of Position Classification in Local Government* (Chicago: Public Personnel Association, 1957). The association also published the Baruch report.

21. International City Managers' Association, *Municipal Personnel Administration,* 6th ed. (Chicago: The Association, 1960).

22. The most comprehensive reference guide in this regard is James G. March, ed., *Handbook of Organizations* (Chicago: Rand McNally 1965). Also valuable is Bernard Berelson and Gary A. Steiner, *Human Behavior: An Inventory of Scientific Findings* (New York: Harcourt Brace Jovanovich, 1964).

23. Jay E. Atwood, "Position Synthesis: A Behavioral Approach to Position Classification," *Public Personnel Review* 32 (April 1971): 77. This five-page article is essentially a plea for the application of the findings of the behavioral sciences to the practice of position classification.

24. Albert Somit, "Bureaucratic Realpolitik and the Teaching of Administration," in Claude E. Hawley and Ruth G. Weintraub, eds., *Administrative Questions and Political Answers* (Princeton, N.J.: D. Van Nostrand, 1966), p. 540. While Somit published this article in 1956, his statement concerning the literature of American public administration still holds true today.

25. Arthur Niederhoffer, *Behind the Shield: The Police in Urban Society* (Garden City, N.Y.: Anchor Books, 1969), p. 47.

26. Norton E. Long, "The Administration Organization as a Political System," in Sidney Mailick and Edward H. Van Ness, eds., *Concepts and Issues in Administrative Behavior* (Englewood Cliffs, N.J.: Prentice-Hall, 1962), p. 142.

27. It is required that in every annual operating budget an amount of at least equal to one-half of one percent of the aggregate of all appropriations for compensation to City employees in the civil service shall be appropriated for the work of the Personnel director and the Civil Service Commission. From City of Philadelphia, *Home Rule Charter* (hereafter, *Charter*), section 2-300 (4) (a).

28. Joseph D. Crumlish, *A City Finds Itself: The Philadelphia Home Rule Charter Movement* (Detroit: Wayne State University Press, 1959), p. 92. This is the only comprehensive history of the charter movement. As such, it is excellent. Unfortunately it covers the charter only up to its adoption. There are no similar works on the maintenance and implementation of the charter.

29. Lincoln Steffens, *The Shame of the Cities* (New York: Hill and Wang, 1957), p. 134.

30. Foster B. Roser, "The Philadelphia Story," *Public Personnel Review* 21 (January 1960): 29.

31. Edward N. Hay and Associates, *Report on Philadelphia Civil Service Practices for the Committee of Fifteen* (Philadelphia: November 3, 1948), p. 34. The Committee of Fifteen, legally known as the Special Committee on Finances, was created in 1947 to investigate whether wage demands by city employees were justified. The committee's documentation of the abuse and corruption of city employees did much to aid the charter movement. The committee's final report is a catalogue of the failings of the then existing governmental structure. City of Philadelphia, Special Committee on City Finances, *Philadelphia's Management: An Appraisal by the Committee of Fifteen* (Philadelphia: December 1948).

32. *Charter,* section A-200. While the charter was approved by the voters in April 1951, it did not take effect until January 1952, so that both the charter and the new Mayor would assume power concurrently.

33. *Ibid.,* sections 7-100ff.

34. *Ibid.,* section 3-205.

35. *Ibid.,* section 7-100.

36. *Ibid.,* section 7-400. The charter provides for an Administrative Board consisting of the mayor, the managing director, and the director of finance to govern the administrative details of the city. Reviews of the classification and pay plans by the board presumably ensure that such plans and amendments thereto are financially realistic. See *Charter,* section 3-103, 4-300 (1) (b).

37. *Ibid.,* section 7-301.

38. City of Philadelphia, Personnel Department, *Annual Report: 1952,* p. 7.

39. Edwin Rothman *et al.*, *Philadelphia Government*, 6th ed. (Philadelphia: Pennsylvania Economy League, 1963), p. 343.

40. City of Philadelphia, Managing Director's Office, *Annual Report: 1952*, p. 17.

41. *The Philadelphia Bulletin*, June 4, 1954.

42. *The Philadelphia Inquirer*, August 21, 1953.

43. City of Philadelphia, Civil Service Commission and Personnel Department, *Annual Report: 1954*, p. 7. Dr. Stephen B. Sweeney directed the study.

44. Government Consulting Service, Institute of Local and State Government, University of Pennsylvania, *Report on Philadelphia Personnel Administration*, April 26, 1954, pp. 1–6.

45. *Ibid.*

46. According to *The Philadelphia Bulletin*, May 19, 1969; February 26, 1970; March 9, 1970; and May 20, 1970; the leading local newspaper, they were replaced by men of lesser stature in the community to whom the mayor was politically obligated.

47. Interview with former Mayor Joseph S. Clark, May 9, 1969.

48. *The Philadelphia Bulletin*, May 19, 1969. For the composition and procedures of the panel, see the *Charter*, section 3-1001.

49. Interview with former Mayor Joseph S. Clark, May 9, 1969.

50. City of Philadelphia, Civil Service Commission, *Philadelphia Civil Service Regulations* (hereafter, *Regulations*), sections 5.07, 5.071.

51. *Ibid.*, section 5.074.

52. The Civil Service Commission is required to have meetings at least once a month. *Charter*, section 30804.

53. *Regulations*, sections 5.062, 5.074.

54. If there is a controversy at hand, the meetings tend to function as an adversary proceeding.

The appealing employee and the appointing authority involved shall have the right to be heard publicly and to present evidence, but technical rules of evidence shall not apply.

*Charter*, section 7-201.

55. *Regulations*, section 5.076.

56. *Ibid.*, section 5.077. While the *Charter*, section 4-300 (1) (b), provides that the Administrative Board must approve the classification plan, the Civil Service Regulations allow them to be approved by the managing director and the director of finance only. The mayor is the only other member of the Administrative Board. The regulations do not contradict the charter. A ruling by the city solicitor "has indicated that the Charter requirement is confined to approval of regulations which provide for the preparation, maintenance, and revision of the subjects in Charter, section 4-300 (1) (b), rather than their content." City of Philadelphia, Administrative Board Rule No. 10, *Approval of Civil Service Regulations*, January 4, 1954. This same rule provides that amendments approved by the Civil Service Commission do not require formal Administrative Board approval unless a cabinet officer has an objection.

57. *Regulations*, section 5.09.

58. *Ibid.*, section 5.09.

59. *Ibid.*, sections 5.07, 6.04.

60. A study conducted under the sponsorship of Philadelphia's deputy personnel director found that many middle-management employees felt that advancement after a minimum level depended less on ability "than on who knows and likes you." Quoted phrase from Everett R. Shaw, *A Study of the Management Trainee Program of the City of Philadelphia with Major Emphasis on the Attrition Rate of the Participants of the Program* (March 3, 1967), p. 19.

61. *Regulations*, section 6.02. The formal procedures for amending the pay plan are identical to those employed for amending the classification plan. *Ibid.*, sections 6.04 to 6.046.

62. Pay ranges shall be. . .determined with due regard to ranges of pay for other classes, the relative difficulty and responsibility of work in the several classes, the recruiting experience of the City, and the availability of employees in particular occupational categories, prevailing rates of pay for similar employment in private business in the City and in other governmental jurisdictions, cost of living factors, the financial policies of the City, and other economic considerations.

*Ibid.*, section 6.02.

63. City of Philadelphia, Personnel Department, Classification and Pay Division, Memorandum, January 9, 1967.

64. A similar game plan has been observed in California's state government. See R. Permin Everett and Wade J. Williams, "Line Management's Participation in Classification Decisions," *Public Personnel Review* 24 (January 1963): 30.

65. Robert Dubin, *Human Relations in Administration* (Englewood Cliffs, N.J.: Prentice-Hall, 1951), p. 354, as cited in Dean F. Berry, *The Politics of Personnel Research* (Ann Arbor: University of Michigan Press, 1967), p. 38.

66. This was said to me by my supervisor while I served as a management trainee in the Personnel Department in 1966.

67. *Regulations,* section 5.024.

68. City of Philadelphia, Personnel Department, Classification and Pay Division Memorandum, "New Hospital Administrative Titles," February 13, 1969.

69. William C. Thomas, Jr., "Generalist Versus Specialist: Careers in a Municipal Bureaucracy," *Public Administration Review* 21 (Winter 1961): 8.

70. *McKinney's Consolidated Laws of New York, Annotated,* "Book 9, Civil Service Law" (New York: Edward Thompson, 1958), section 52, as quoted in Thomas, *Ibid.,* p. 8.

71. City of Philadelphia, Personnel Department, Classification and Pay Division, Memorandum, "Broadening of Experience Requirement of Administrative Services Director I Class," June 24, 1969.

72. *Regulations,* sections 9.031 and 9.032.

73. Herbert J. Chruden and Arthur W. Sherman, Jr., *Personnel Management* (3d ed.; Cincinnati: South-Western Publishing, 1968), pp. 187–88.

74. *Regulations,* section 9.062.

75. Civil Service Examination No. C-5107, February 27, 1965.

76. Civil Service Examination No. P-4082, May 1964.

77. For example, if the Personnel Department authorizes an examination to be held on both a promotional and departmental basis, current employes who barely passed the exam would be placed higher than outsiders who achieved perfect scores, and departments would have to offer positions to departmental employees before being allowed to appoint possibly other higher-scoring city employees and outsiders. By determining the kind of examination to be used, the Personnel Department can frequently, for all practical purposes, forecast the final results.

78. Marshall W. Meyer, "The Two Authority Structures of Bureaucratic Organization," *Administrative Science Quarterly* 13 (September 1968): 22.

79. *Regulations,* section 5.091.

80. It has long been observed by the personnel technicians of the Examinations Division that examination announcements are met with a barrage of applications from almost all employees eligible for the examination and a large number of those who are not. This can be accounted for by two factors: (1) it is generally recognized that the examinations are to a great extent a lottery—as much a function of luck and fortune as of native ability, and (2) employees are automatically granted leaves of absence to compete in promotional examinations. *Ibid.,* section 22.13.

81. Herbert A. Simon, *Administrative Behavior* (2d ed.; New York: The Free Press, 1965), p. 149.

# 18

# Performance Appraisal: If Only People Were Not Involved

*John Nalbandian*
*University of Kansas*

Recent developments in performance appraisal technologies facilitate the replacement of subjectivity in the evaluation process with objectivity anchored in job-related behavior and explicit goal statements. While many regard this movement toward "concreteness" as an advance in personnel administration, it has diverted attention from the behavioral foundation underpinning any successful performance appraisal system—the willingness of supervisors to evaluate employees. This article critiques these trends in performance appraisal in light of the supervisor's motivation to assess subordinates and suggests avenues which can be explored to overcome the supervisor's resistance to performance evaluation.

The problems of performance appraisal relate to two attractive and central assumptions of objective appraisal methods:

1. The contribution an employee makes to an organization can be expressed in an objective "performance contract."
2. With emphases on performance results and job-related employee behavior, modern techniques of appraisal significantly enhance the supply of managerial tools.

## Objective Performance Contracts

Subjective appraisal methods lend themselves to favoritism, inefficiency, and conflict in the management of personnel. They permit race, sex, age, friendship, and other non job-related factors to subvert the evaluation process. Modern techniques of evaluation attempt to minimize abuses of both the appraisal function and the employees being evaluated. These new techniques suggest that an employee's contribution to an organization can be explicitly described and that such descriptions allow employees to more clearly understand organizational expectations and evaluative criteria. The method thus promotes confidence in the appraisal process.

The strategies used to develop job-related, explicit performance standards are not employed without cost, however. Performance contracts attempt to reduce the employee's organizational contributions to explicit statements of job-related behavior.[1] Besides the difficulties of arriving at a set of objective expectations and the dysfunctions which may accompany their implementation,[2] the aim itself conflicts with widely accepted notions of employee/employer relationships.[3] Just as employees expect a range of inducements from an employer in return for their services, employers seek a variety of contributions from employees.[4] When realized, expectations of employee loyalty, energy, identity with organizational values, harmony in the work place, and "fitting in," make organizations workable and productive social systems; they provide cohesion and vitality to the order articulated in formal statements enumerating job-related employee contributions.

The relationship between the objective performance contract and this wider version of employer expectations can be seen in Figure 1, which combines two factors associated with the evaluation of employee contributions. The first element relates the evaluative criteria to successful performance of the job. The second identifies the evaluative criteria as explicit or implicit.

**Job-Relatedness of Expectations**

| | High | Low |
|---|---|---|
| Explicit | I<br>quantity and<br>quality of<br>work | II<br>hair length<br>dress code |
| Implicit | III<br>group skills<br>non-designated<br>leadership role<br>values<br>loyalty | IV<br>race<br>sex<br>age<br>lifestyle<br>association |

Locus of Evaluation (label at left between Explicit and Implicit rows)

**Figure 1**

Employer expectations of employees

Theoretically, the matrix captures the totality of potential employer expectations of employees. The trend toward objective performance contracts pointedly attempts to decrease the size of quadrants II and IV which might contain illegal or socially questionable criteria, and enlarge the size of quadrant I. Two strategies may be employed to accomplish this. The first transforms implicit standards into explicit statements. For example, race, sex, and age are often implicitly used in various evaluative functions. By requiring the criteria used in evaluations to be articulated, many can be formally eliminated. As another example, by requiring the criterion "loyalty" to be transformed into explicit statements which define the term, the potential for favoritism and capriciousness in the evaluation process is reduced. The second strategy requires a demonstration that the evaluative criteria are job-related. For example, dress codes and length of hair were once accepted as evaluation factors; now they must be validly justified as job-related. The resulting performance contract (quadrant I) emphasizes *explicit statements* about *job-related behavior* and goals.

While designed to reduce subjectivity and produce benefits, these strategies are not pursued without cost. The first cost relates to behavior affecting production which is difficult to measure. Person A is a productive worker, but likes to talk and disrupts the work of others.

Person B is not very productive, but is excellent at influencing group members to reach compromise solutions when appropriate. Person C has a knack of summarizing discussion and pinpointing key questions which require decision. Person D performs excellent work but in the process creates bad feelings and distrust among others. Person E maintains contacts which exceed the requirements of his/her own job, but as a result provides information and contacts for others in the work group. Person F does satisfactory work but flies off the handle every so often, upsetting the work of others. Person G is willing to confront the supervisor about work group problems when others hesitate.

A second cost is the potential exclusion of factors which may not contribute much to production perhaps, but add considerably to the quality of working life. For example, person A does his/her work but smokes and becomes aggressive when a co-worker requests that he or she stop; further, worker A threatens to appeal a supervisor's request that the employee show more consideration when smoking. Person B organizes a social group which remembers birthdays and other special events. Person C willingly provides transportation when the office work group goes out or an errand is required; Person D does so if the price of gas is shared. Person E does excellent work but gossips off the job and offends members of the work group. Person F is a compassionate figure who lends a friendly ear. None of the characteristics or actions of these people directly affects the production level the way it is usually defined in quadrant I, yet each clearly influences the quality of working life in this hypothetical unit. In short, by attempting to remove *all* criteria which are not related to an individual's production, we also define away some activities which establish and maintain the productivity, cohesion, and sociability of a work group.

The performance contract which falls solely within quadrant I is like a machine without oil: the manager who tries to make this machine work faces a dilemma. If the manager tries to add the oil by informally adjusting the evaluation system to reward those who contribute to the quality of working life and whose implicit contributions increase the productivity of the work unit, charges of hypocrisy are invited. If the manager adheres to the letter of the performance contract, however, he or she will not be able to reward those who are making "unrecognized" yet valuable contributions to the work unit. Fostering attempts in formal appraisal systems to remove subjectivity heightens the tension connected with this dilemma.

### Performance Contracts: A Managerial Tool?

This brings us to the second assumption: objective appraisal systems enhance managerial capabilities. In a recent article on government productivity, Harry Hatry[5] discusses the contributing role of performance appraisal and specifically cites behavioral rating scales and appraisal by objectives as important ingredients in a productivity enhancement program.[6]

While this emphasis on goals, work standards, and behavior related to results should increase productivity,[7] it is quite possible to see objective appraisal systems as more controlling of management than as a managerial tool. To understand this contention one might profitably draw a lesson from the history of position classification. Jay Shafritz[8] notes that part of the appeal of position classification rested on its promised dual purpose. On the one hand it was a managerial tool which might facilitate manpower planning, budgetary estimates, selection processes, and other personnel functions. On the other hand it was a control device, limiting managerial discretion over pay, staffing levels, promotion, and the movement of personnel. The parallel with performance appraisal is worth pursuing. It too is perceived as a managerial tool, helpful in focusing attention on goals and goal-related behavior and in facilitating attempts to link pay to performance. Part of its underlying appeal, however, is that it might also help prevent the mistreatment of personnel by limiting favoritism. While these dual promises are appealing, the lesson of position classification must not be forgotten. Currently many supervisors see position classification not so much as a tool, but as a biased technique which, if anything, places limits on managerially valued discretion. While proponents of behaviorally oriented rating systems admire them as managerial tools, these techniques can just as easily be employed to constrain management.

The inability of performance contracts to capture all the behavior which might improve organizational effectiveness offers employees an opening to perform in accordance with only the criteria upon which they can be formally evaluated. Numerous accounts of employee behavior during job actions—police writing tickets for minor infractions, inspectors citing minimal oversights, etc.—suggest conformity to the letter rather than the spirit of employer expectations and standards. This can lead to organizational paralysis rather than effectiveness.[9]

The determination of how an appraisal technique will function depends only in part on its original purpose. If an agency's work environment is supportive of its employees, an objective appraisal system could be successfully introduced and employed as a managerial tool. But if that environment reflects a distrust of managerial motives, one should expect employees, their agents, and those who oversee personnel actions to exploit the control function that an objective appraisal system affords.

This essay does not endorse those techniques objective appraisal systems are replacing. Rather, the potential for performance evaluation functions to live up to their promise both as developmental tools and accounting devices will go unrealized until more attention is paid to the human dynamics of the evaluation process. Such a discussion can profitably begin by exploring the supervisor's motivation to evaluate employees.[10]

## The Motivation to Evaluate

A supervisor's willingness to evaluate begins with his or her perspective on the appraisal process. Two points stand out. First, supervisors generally believe they know who their effective employees are, even if they cannot articulate the reasoning behind their assessments. For example, if a project had to be completed quickly, the supervisor would select employees he or she "believed" would act most expeditiously. If the task required sensitivity to human needs, the supervisor would select employees he or she "felt" were most capable in that regard. While supervisors may miscalculate in these informal assessments, the key point is that they *believe* they know the capabilities of their employees. Thus, from a motivational standpoint, most supervisors conduct a formal evaluation not because it facilitates the performance of their own job, but because subordinates, superordinates, or perhaps the personnel department has requested or mandated it. In other words, *from the supervisor's perspective,* he or she is being asked to duplicate an assessment already made, and is doing so for somebody else's benefit.

Second, supervisors often associate emotionally discomforting consequences with the interview which is required in most formal evaluation systems.[11] Douglas McGregor[12] described the supervisor's resistance to the excessive responsibility of subjective evaluation procedures. But he did not go far enough. One cannot limit the problem to the technical difficulty of evaluation, the discomfort of "playing God," or the guilt associated with the power to appraise.[13] If these were the main problems, techniques that facilitated a more objective evaluation process might be welcomed. I believe the problem is more closely connected to the supervisor's discomfort regarding the subordinate's reaction to the evaluation.[14]

The great majority of employees tend to see the manager's evaluation as being less favorable than self-estimates.[15] While employees continue to profess a desire to be evaluated,[16] the tendency to overrate themselves produces employee apprehension and disappointment with a formal review process. The experienced supervisor encounters subordinates who will argue, sulk, look bewildered or disappointed, threaten to file grievances, or in some other way react negatively to their appraisal. Recall as well that the supervisor conducts the evaluation in the first place primarily because someone else requires it.

Improvements in evaluation techniques can reduce the likelihood of subjectivity, of error, of halo effects, etc., but they cannot eliminate the idea that "bad news" may be coming. The news may be objectively derived or stem from somebody's judgment, but it is still bad news because it will ultimately affect promotion opportunities, salary levels, job assignment, and perhaps most importantly, the employee's self-esteem and sense of competence.[17] Chris Argyris suggests that there is a widely held proposition among humans that ". . .truth is a good idea and modes of logic and control can be defined to enhance the production of such knowledge. The difficulty is that in real life, the truth is a good idea when it is not threatening."[18] When "truth" affects one's self-esteem, it will almost certainly be regarded as psychologically threatening and produce a psychological defense—thus throwing a monkey wrench into the most objective appraisal system.

In short, the basic impediment to effective performance appraisal is not the technique used, but the motivation of those called upon to evaluate others. Not surprisingly, the steps needed to upgrade the appraisal process have more to do with those using the system than with the system itself.

## Improving the Evaluation Process

There are several elements in a strategy that will help improve performance evaluation. The first is recognizing the role that *trust* plays in implementing an appraisal system.[19] Even where work standards are clear, without organizational trust employees will view performance evaluations with suspicion and defensiveness. Returning to Figure 1, it is virtually impossible to develop an evaluation system that falls exclusively within quadrant I and still expect to have an effective organization. But including quality of working life considerations and implicit performance standards in an assessment process requires confidence that the supervisor's judgment will produce equity rather than exploitation.

Having acknowledged the impact of trust on the implementation of an appraisal system, one should next examine *the supervisor's acceptance of his/her role* as a supervisor and evaluator. Many of the difficulties discussed in this essay could be avoided through the promotion of supervisors who regard evaluations as an integral part of the role they identify with. When the desire to assess, develop, reward, and communicate with employees grows from the supervisor's inner motivation rather than compliance with a mandate or job description, it is much more likely to produce fruitful results.

An organization's promotion policies can go far towards developing a supervisory corps committed to the willing and responsible exercise of supervisory discretion. Unfortunately, inadequate attention to organizational career ladders leads either to the promotion of individuals who have demonstrated superior work but have not necessarily shown supervisory potential, or the promotion of those who have demonstrated supervisory potential but have not necessarily achieved superior production results. David McClelland and David Burnham[20] suggest that these two qualities—line achievement and supervisor success—might reflect distinct motivational profiles, especially as one moves upward in an organizational hierarchy. In most organizations, if a high achiever is rewarded with promotion to a supervisory position, the organization's supervisory capacity might eventually decline if that person has not shown supervisory potential or does not turn out to be an effective supervisor. On the other hand, if the organization promotes those who have demonstrated some supervisory potential, it risks alienating those high achievers who have failed to display supervisory capability. To increase the supervisory capacity of an organization, a method of career progression is necessary which allows high achievers to increase their pay and organizational status without being forced into supervisory positions they would not otherwise seek, or enjoy.

Third, while trust and acceptance of supervisory roles would complement objectivity and strengthen an appraisal system, realization of and sensitivity to the *subjective nature of the supervisor's role* as evaluator should assume a prominent place in the discussion of performance evaluation. As an evaluator of employees, the supervisor exercises a highly visible form of organizational power. The exercise of this power inevitably forces a clash between subjective worlds of the supervisor and subordinate.[21] Both objective and subjective influences shape this inner world. Objectively, both parties must recognize that concerted organizational actions require the exercise of power, but the exercise of power is often abused. The subjective influence, while more subtle, combines with the objective sense regarding the exercise of power and intensifies an ambivalent and often unspoken feeling toward performance appraisal.

Figure 2 suggests that both superior and subordinate unconsciously experience positive and negative drives regarding the use of power. The salient dimension of this subjective world for evaluators is the ambivalence felt, on the one hand, when confronted with the confidence that comes from having an impact on others, from influencing personnel actions, and from having some control over one's own organizational future. Juxtaposed against this positive drive is the burden of responsibility that comes with influencing others, the fear of being unable to live up to the expectations others have of the supervisor to be neutral and to hide the personal preferences which exist within this human being. Similarly, a tense ambivalence characterizes the inner world of the employee subject to the power of evaluation. Almost all organizational members find themselves subordinate to someone, and in these subordinate roles people tend to seek out those who would exercise leadership. We unconsciously long for others to tell us what to do and how we are doing; we desire the comfort of knowing that someone else is watching over us. Simultaneously, we resist the feelings of dependence and helplessness that come from having someone tell us what to do and how we are doing. The subordinate resists "domination" and "submission." The feeling of being a pawn appears alongside the desire to be directed. In short, a complex inner world of evaluation

**Desire to Exercise Power**

| | Positive | Negative |
|---|---|---|
| Superior | I<br>Status<br>Control | II<br>Responsibility<br>Fear of Error |
| Subordinate | III<br>Dependency | IV<br>Submission |

Positions in Hierarchy

**Figure 2**

Unconscious influences on the exercise of power

exists, and the failure of an organization or agency to recognize its existence would detract from even the most objective evaluation system.

Last, *methods of training supervisors in evaluation require rethinking.* While it makes sense to instruct evaluators in the proper use of an appraisal instrument, training someone to give "bad news" demands more skill, imagination, and tolerance than is provided in most performance appraisal training programs. While guidance exists for giving feedback and developing non-defensive climates,[22] the key to the effective training of supervisors is to bring the supervisor together with subordinates and superiors for practice, feedback, and guidance in evaluation. Most training programs for supervisors are deliberately designed to avoid this mix of organizational levels. Traditional supervisory training invites a horizontal slice of an agency's personnel to gather for a prepackaged curriculum thought suitable for (literally) thousands of supervisors. These programs rarely affect supervisory behavior, especially behavior which so deeply reflects the inner world of evaluation. More attention must be given to laying an organizational foundation which supports the training of vertical slices of an agency's personnel—subordinate, superior, superordinate—on problems generated by the participants themselves.[23]

## Summary

While performance appraisal systems which emphasize work objectives and behavioral rating scales hold considerable promise for improving the evaluation process, an incomplete understanding of the human dynamics underlying the appraisal process blunts their attraction. For a technically sound appraisal system to work, four behavioral elements are necessary: trust, acceptance of the appraisal function by those who must do the evaluation, sensitivity to the inner world of performance evaluation, and training designs which recognize the human dynamics of appraisal.

## Notes

1. L. L. Cummings and Donald P. Schwab, *Performance in Organizations: Determinants and Appraisal* (Glenview, Ill.: Scott, Foresman and Company), 1973; Donald E. Klingner, "When the Traditional Job Description Is Not Enough," *Personnel Journal,* Vol. 58 (April 1979), pp. 243–248; Edward E. Lawler, "Performance Appraisal and Pay," *Intergovernmental Personnel Notes,* U.S. Office of Personnel Management (May/June 1979), pp. 19–21; Robert I. Lazer, "The 'Discrimination' Danger in Performance Appraisal," in W. Clay Hamner and Frank L. Schmidt (eds.), *Contemporary Problems in Personnel* (Chicago: St. Claire Press), 1977, pp. 239–245; Robert Pajer, "Performance Appraisal: A Sampler of Systems Worth Knowing About," *Intergovernmental Personnel Notes,* U.S. Office of Personnel Management (May/June 1979), pp. 17–18, 22.

2. John C. Aplin and Peter P. Schoderbek, "How to Measure MBO," *Public Personnel Management,* Vol. 5 (April 1976), pp. 88–95; Peter Blau, *Dynamics of Bureaucracy* (Chicago: University of Chicago Press), 1963; Charles J. Coleman, "Avoiding the Pitfalls in Results Oriented Appraisals," *Personnel,* Vol. 42 (November/December 1965), pp. 24–33; Fred Luthans, "How to Apply MBO," *Public Personnel Management,* Vol. 5 (March/April 1976), pp. 83–87; George S. Odiorne, *Personnel Management by Objectives* (Homewood, Ill.: Richard D. Irwin), 1971; V. G. Ridgway, "Dysfunctional Consequences of Performance Measurements," *Administrative Science Quarterly,* Vol. 1 (September 1956), pp. 240–247.

3. Chester I. Barnard, *The Functions of the Executive* (Cambridge, Mass.: Harvard University Press), 1938; Harry Levinson, "Management by Whose Objectives?" *Harvard Business Review,* Vol. 48 (July/August 1970), pp. 125–134; James G. March

and Herbert A. Simon, *Organizations* (New York: John Wiley and Sons), 1958; Charles R. Milton, *Ethics and Expediency in Personnel Management* (Columbia, S.C.: University of South Carolina Press), 1970; Edgar H. Schein, *Organizational Psychology* (Englewood Cliffs, N.J.: Prentice-Hall), 1965; Herbert A. Simon, *Administrative Behavior* (New York: Free Press), 1957.

4. Barnard, *The Functions of the Executive*.

5. Harry Hatry, "Local Government Uses for Performance Measurement," *Intergovernmental Personnel Notes*, U.S. Office of Personnel Management (May/June 1980), pp. 13–15.

6. Hatry is not alone, of course, in advocating the managerial uses of objective rating methods. See, for example, Cummings and Schwab, *Performance in Organizations: Determinants and Appraisal;* Klingner, "When the Traditional Job Description Is Not Enough"; Pajer, "Performance Appraisal: A Sampler of Systems Worth Knowing About"; Paul H. Thompson and Gene Dalton, "Performance Appraisal: Managers Beware," *Harvard Business Review*, Vol. 48 (January/February 1970), pp. 149–157.

7. Edwin A. Locke, "The Ubiquity of the Technique of Goal Setting in Theories of and Approaches to Employee Motivation," *Academy of Management Review*, Vol. 3 (July 1978), pp. 594–601; Herbert H. Meyer, Emanuel Kay and John R. P. French, Jr., "Split Roles in Performance Appraisal," *Harvard Business Review*, Vol. 43 (January/February 1965), pp. 123–129.

8. Jay M. Shafritz, Walter L. Balk, Albert C. Hyde and David Rosenbloom, *Personnel Management in Government* (New York: Marcel Dekker), 1978, p. 95.

9. Blau, *Dynamics of Bureaucracy;* Ridgway, "Dysfunctional Consequences of Performance Measurements"; William Sauser, Jr., "Evaluating Employee Performance: Needs, Problems, and Possible Solutions," *Public Personnel Management*, Vol. 9 (January/February 1980), pp. 11–18.

10. Ishwar Dayal, "Some Issues in Performance Appraisal," *Personnel Administration*, Vol. 32 (January/February 1969), pp. 27–30; Levinson, "Management by Whose Objectives?" Harry Levinson, "Appraisal of What Performance?" *Harvard Business Review*, Vol. 54 (July/August 1976), pp. 30–46, 160; Douglas McGregor, "An Uneasy Look at Performance Appraisal," *Harvard Business Review*, Vol. 35 (May/June 1957), pp. 89–94.

11. Thomas Decotiis and Andre Petit, "The Performance Appraisal Process: A Model and Some Testable Propositions," *Academy of Management Review*, Vol. 3 (July 1978), pp. 635–646; Winston Oberg, "Make Performance Appraisal Relevant," *Harvard Business Review*, Vol. 50 (January/February 1972), pp. 61–67; Kenneth E. Richards, "A New Concept of Performance Appraisal," *The Journal of Business*, Vol. 32 (July 1959), pp. 229–243.

12. McGregor, "An Uneasy Look at Performance Appraisal."

13. Levinson, "Management by Whose Objectives?"

14. Norman R. R. Maier, *The Appraisal Interview* (New York: John Wiley and Sons), 1958; Oberg, "Make Performance Appraisal Relevant"; Richards, "A New Concept of Performance Appraisal"; Thompson and Dalton, "Performance Appraisal: Managers Beware."

15. Kay Meyer and French Meyer, Jr., "Split Roles in Performance Appraisal."

16. Donald Stone, "An Examination of Six Prevalent Assumptions About Performance Appraisal," *Public Personnel Management*, Vol. 2 (November/December 1973), pp. 408–414.

17. Levinson, "Management by Whose Objectives?"; Levinson, "Appraisal of What Performance?"; McGregor, "An Uneasy Look at Performance Appraisal"; Maier, *The Appraisal Interview*.

18. Chris Argyris, "Making the Undiscussable and Its Undiscussability Discussable," *Public Administration Review*, Vol. 40 (May/June 1980), p. 211.

19. N. Joseph Cayer, *Managing Human Resources: An Introduction to Public Personnel Administration* (New York: St. Martins Press), 1980, p. 135; Jack Gibb, "Defensive Communication," *Journal of Communications*, Vol. 11 (September 1961), pp. 141–148; Dale E. Zand, "Trust and Managerial Problem Solving," *Administrative Science Quarterly*, Vol. 17 (June 1971), pp. 229–238.

20. David C. McClelland and David H. Burnham, "Power Is the Great Motivator," *Harvard Business Review*, Vol. 54 (March/April 1976), pp. 100–110.

21. Eric H. Neilsen and Jan Gypen, "The Subordinate's Predicaments," *Harvard Business Review*, Vol. 57 (September/October 1979), pp. 133–143.

22. Gibb, "Defensive Communications."

23. Neely Gardner, "Action Training and Research: Something Old and Something New," *Public Administration Review*, Vol. 34 (March/April 1974), pp. 106–115.

# 19

# Merit Pay in the Public Sector: The Case for a Failure of Theory

James L. Perry
*Indiana University—Bloomington*

**Abstract**

*Contingent pay has become very popular in response to criticisms of traditional pay policies in government. The new systems, however, have generally failed to increase productivity. Although many scholars have attributed failures of merit pay to poor implementation or weak top management commitment, an alternative explanation is that the theory on which merit pay is based is flawed. It is argued here that merit pay is not appropriate for managerial work, imposes excessive information demands on an organization, and diminishes an organization's ability to coordinate interdependencies.*

## Introduction

Merit pay has had a long history in the U.S. civil service. Graduated pay systems were introduced in the federal civil service shortly after passage of the Pendleton Act (Van Riper, 1958). Step-in-grade systems enjoyed widespread popularity among all levels of government until the 1970s when they came under increasing attack (see, e.g., Patton, 1974; Savas and Ginsburg,

SOURCE: From *Review of Public Personnel Administration*, pp. 57–69, vol. 7 (Fall, 1986). Reprinted by permission.

1973). They were criticized for being automatic and for failing to differentiate employee rewards based upon performance. These shortcomings led to a search for alternatives that resulted in the merit pay provisions of the federal Civil Service Reform Act of 1978 (CSRA) (Hunter and Silverman, 1980; Perry *et al.*, 1982) and similar reforms in a variety of states and localities (Griener *et al.*, 1981).

The CSRA pay reforms were short-lived. In 1984, Congress approved the Performance Management and Recognition Act (also known as the Merit Pay Improvement Act) to correct a litany of problems in the CSRA systems. Among the problems were inadequate funding, pay inequities and ratings manipulation. The 1984 law restored the step-in-grade feature of the old system and instituted a new bonus program to reward performance.

Despite the recent rocky experience with merit pay, there is no indication that it has become less popular with political leaders or the public. The Reagan administration recently has introduced legislation to extend pay-for-performance principles to Grades 1–12 of the General Schedule (*Public Administration Times*, 1986:1). The reported failures of public-sector systems and the undaunted response of politicians to merit-pay experience parallels reactions to the failure of such systems in the private sector. Failures of merit pay in private sector organizations have variously been attributed to a lack of commitment to pay for performance (Patton, 1972; Redling, 1981), problems encountered when implementing the theory (Hamner, 1975), or poor judgments which resulted in applying contingent pay to inappropriate situations (Lawler, 1981; Patton, 1972; Ungson and Steers, 1984).

The prospect that merit pay failures are a sign of problems fundamental to the underlying theory has been explored by only a few scholars. Deci (1975) has argued that money is an ineffective motivator because it relies upon extrinsic rewards and, therefore, stifles intrinsic motivation. The ultimate result of diminished intrinsic motivation is to remove the most powerful and enduring motivators. Meyer (1975) has contended that merit pay damages employee self esteem. He concluded that an incentive system that lowers an employee's self esteem is more destructive than constructive.

In addition to these potential threats to merit pay, which are grounded in alternative theories about its psychology, there is another theoretical basis for questioning the viability of merit pay. Pay-for-individual performance is based on the assumption that organizational performance is the simple additive combination of individuals' separate performances. Yet theorists note that organizations are intricate social environments that cannot be understood as simple aggregations of employees. Therefore, a mismatch exists between the simplicity inherent in merit pay programs and the complexities of organizations (Pearce, in press). This mismatch is at the root of many of merit pay's failures.

This article develops a critique of merit pay theory as it has been applied to government. At the outset, it is important to identify the scope of our theoretical critique. The focus is individually-contingent pay for public managers, what will be called pay-for-individual performance or, simply, merit pay. The critique is not intended to apply to group-contingent pay or to non-managerial employees. The article begins with a brief discussion of the psychological theory that is the rationale for merit pay. An alternative theoretical framework is then presented for understanding the dynamics of pay-for-individual-performance in an organizational context. The predictions of this theoretical framework are discussed in light of research on merit pay in the public sector.

## The Theory Behind Pay-for-Individual-Performance

Lawler (1971; 1981) developed the first and probably most compelling theoretical argument for the motivating potential of individually-contingent compensation. His psychological model of pay is based on Vroom's (1964) cognitive theory of motivation. Lawler (1971) argued that pay acquires a valence or importance as a function of its perceived instrumentality for obtaining other desired outcomes. Pay is probably one of the most powerful rewards that organizations can offer: "Because it is important to most people, pay has the power to influence their membership behavior and their performance" (Lawler, 1981:5).

Because pay can be an attractive reward, it is assumed to motivate members' actions more effectively if it is made contingent on those actions. Using the expectancy theory argument, Lawler (1971; 1981) noted that individually-contingent pay plans tie a presumably valuable reward (pay) directly to an individual's performance and, therefore, should result in a high subjective probability that performance will result in receipt of the valued outcome. Thus, a powerful motivational effect will result when pay is based on individual job performance.

Although research on the effects of pay-for-performance has usually lacked methodological rigor and has concentrated almost exclusively on routine, non-managerial jobs, it generally indicates that contingent pay results in higher performance than non-contingent pay. Reports of improvements in individuals' productivity range from 12.2% (Roethlisberger and Dickson, 1939), to 30% (Locke, *et al.*, 1980), to 39% (Viteles, 1953). Based on a comprehensive review of prior research, Lawler (1971) concluded that individual incentive plans can potentially increase individuals' productivity between 10 to 20 percent.

Not all scholars contend that pay-for-individual-performance results in improved productivity. Research by Deci (1975) and Meyer (1975) is among the most critical. Deci conducted a series of laboratory studies on the effects of external-mediated rewards, such as pay, on subjects' intrinsic motivation. He concluded that contingent pay is undesirable because it reduces intrinsic motivation and leads individuals to develop strategies to achieve rewards with minimum effort. Meyer (1975) argued that most employees have a highly favorable self image, but that the feedback implicit in merit pay awards undercuts this self image. The effect is to damage employee self esteem, a factor important in individual and organizational productivity.

Lawler also acknowledges that merit pay is subject to negative side effects, including the restriction of output and conflict among employees working on interdependent tasks. Bass, Hurder and Ellis (reported in Bass, 1965) found that individual monetary incentives resulted in increased performance by those engaged in a simple task, but *decreased* performance on a more complex one. Bass (1965) suggested that these subjects were already motivated and the addition of financial incentives resulted in a motivational level that was so high that it interfered with performance on the complex task. Similar results are reported by Konovsky and Podsakoff (1984) who found that individual incentives had no impact on performance on an interdependent laboratory task, and that contingent pay actually decreased performance on a task in which subjects' performances were interdependent.

Only one field study has been conducted on the performance consequences of individually-contingent managerial pay. Pearce, Stevenson and Perry (1985) tested the performance effects of the introduction of merit pay for federal managers. The performance measure included four indicators of the productivity of the offices for which these managers were responsible. Productivity measures were available two years before the commencement of merit pay and for the first two years that managers' merit increases were based on these performance measures. They found that office productivity gradually improved over the four-year period, but that the merit pay intervention did not result in a significant change in this trend. Thus, merit pay did not result in improved performance.

The generally favorable reactions merit pay has elicited from senior executives and politicians have impeded its critical assessment. The evidence about the limitations of merit pay presented above hints that its failures represent more than faulty implementation and, in fact, may reflect shortcomings of theories of individual motivation in complex organizations. A

theoretical framework which helps to explain the frequent failures of pay-for-individual-performance is developed below.

# An Alternative Theoretical Perspective

A series of theoretical statements which explain merit pay failure in government organizations is presented in Figure 1. It is necessary to begin with some initial premises or axioms about organizations, managerial behavior and managerial jobs to explain the reasoning behind this set of theoretical linkages. The first premise is that public organizations are systems of cooperative activity which are chartered to act for some common interests. As a system of cooperative activity (Barnard, 1938), a range of participants (e.g., employees, managers, suppliers and clients) contract with the organization, both implicitly and explicitly, to exchange their contributions (e.g., expertise, time, loyalty) for inducements the organization offers (March and Simon, 1958). The inducements an organization offers for members' contributions are likely to vary among categories of participants.

Another premise underlying the theoretical statements is that managerial jobs are characterized by complexity and uncertainty, resulting from the nature of the work performed (Doeringer and Piore, 1971; Mintzberg, 1973; Williamson, 1975). Mintzberg (1973) found that managerial activities were characterized by brevity, variety and discontinuity, indicative of the uncertainty and complexity of managerial work. By their very nature, managerial positions are designed to absorb uncertainty. The scope of managerial work requires a wide range of specific skills that enhances the idiosyncratic nature of managerial jobs. Furthermore, the problems created by uncertainty/complexity cannot be completely mitigated because a manager's rationality is bound by knowledge, skill and time limitations (Simon, 1957).

The premises above are implicit in the theoretical relationships identified in Figure 1.

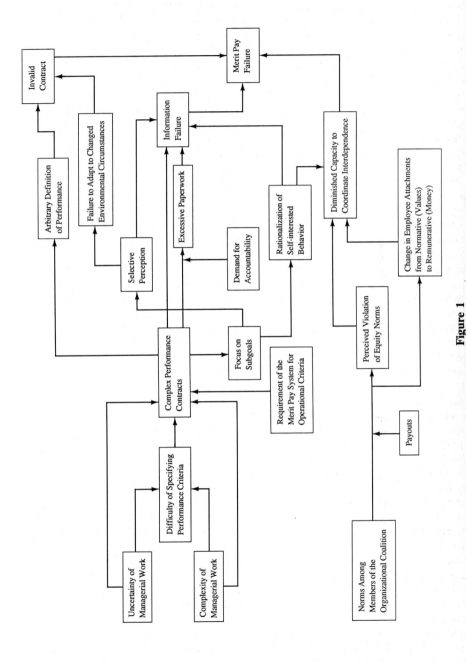

**Figure 1**

A model of the sources of merit pay failure in government organization

The figure indicates that any one of three conditions—invalid contracts, information failure or diminished capacity to coordinate interdependence—are sufficient to produce merit pay failure. These three conditions and how they come about are discussed below.

### Impracticality of Fixed Contracts

Simon (1957) has argued that open-ended employment contracts allow organizations the flexibility to respond to future uncertainty. Open-ended contracts permit employers to call upon the undifferentiated time of employees. Given this flexibility, organizations are ideally situated to respond to uncertainty.

Merit pay involves a significant restriction of an organization's flexibility. The fixed-performance contracts characteristic of merit pay, such as those developed under the Civil Service Reform Act of 1978 (CSRA), are difficult to adapt to changing internal and external circumstances. Williamson (1975) contends that fixed contracts are rigid and completely unsuited for circumstances characterized by uncertainty, a condition that is typical for managerial work, particularly in the public sector. If managerial performance requirements are indeed uncertain, fixed contracts restrict the ability of managers to respond to changes. These contracts can, at best, cover only a portion of desired actions, and, therefore, are artificial representations of the kind of performance that would be most effective for an organization. A related and equally serious liability of fixed contracts is that they discourage deviations from performance agreements even when such deviations may be necessary or appropriate (O'Toole and Churchill, 1982).

Experience in the federal government illustrates the artificiality of fixed contracts. For example, Social Security Administration field offices experienced significant disruptions because of efforts to develop objective performance indicators such as processing time (Pearce and Perry, 1983). Although this is a very specific illustration of the artificiality of fixed-performance contracts, it was not an isolated instance of the difficulty of writing performance contracts under CSRA. The General Accounting Office (United States General Accounting Office, 1984b) found in a two-year study of three agencies that despite the legal requirement that performance appraisals rely on objective criteria, less than half the performance standards contained objective measures.

Despite the very real limitations of fixed contracts, many organizations behave as if these shortcomings can be overcome by establishing elaborate control systems which are used to write comprehensive contracts for their managers. Reports about the consequences of such contracts have largely been anecdotal, but they do not appear to remedy, and perhaps exacerbate, performance management problems. For example, one of the side effects of CSRA-mandated merit pay was an estimated billion dollars for operating costs in the first year (Harron, 1981), partly attributable to supervisory effort in developing elaborate performance agreements. Federal agencies consistently reported excessive paperwork as a result of merit-pay performance appraisals (Perry and Porter, 1980).

Although it may be impossible to predict future states of affairs given uncertainty/complexity and, therefore, to write adequate fixed contracts, it is conceivable that such contracts could be re-written periodically to reflect new circumstances. This strategy also imposes significant costs on managers. The costs of re-writing the contract and re-formulating the pay-for-performance linkage are likely to be prohibitive, particularly if change is rapid. GAO reports (United States General Accounting Office, 1984a) that in 1982 the responsibilities of 20% of federal senior executives changed during the rating period, but a majority (55%) did not have their plans revised. Thus, the contracts of more than 10% of senior executives, and probably a much larger proportion of subordinates reporting to them who were covered by merit pay, were invalid simply because they were not updated.

As an alternative to re-writing the contract, individually-contingent pay programs are frequently adapted to uncertainty by combining subjective and objective measures (Lawler, 1981). This adaptation helps to preserve flexibility, but it has other consequences for pay-for-performance.

For example, Carroll and Schneier (1982) note that the more subjective the rating criterion, the more rater judgment is required not only regarding the degree to which the ratee meets the criterion, but also regarding what the measure actually means. The combination of objective and subjective measures is probably an unreliable solution to the performance measurement problem in government. Public sector performance environments are likely to impose severe strain on a manager's ability to make successful subjective determinations because of real or perceived concerns about politicization (Pagano, 1985).

## Information Failure

Fixed contracts are not only likely to be invalid when applied to managerial work, but the information that is the rationale for fixed-contracts is likely to be a focus for manipulation. The manipulability of information could occur under several circumstances which are inherent in the situation. A supervisor's lack of expertise in a subordinate's job content or difficulty obtaining feedback about a subordinate's performance could permit a subordinate to withhold negative information or pass along positive information, thereby enhancing the subordinate's evaluation. For instance, a subordinate's attempt to beat the appraisal system by seeking an easy contract, reportedly a problem encountered in both federal (O'Toole and Churchill, 1982) and local (Griener, *et al.*, 1981) merit pay systems, is possible when there is unequal information between superior and subordinate. Performance measurement and occupational characteristics of the public sector context (Perry and Porter, 1982) tend to increase the probability of such information asymmetries occurring.

Merit pay exacerbates the tendency of individuals to adhere to subgoals which, in turn, reinforces the problems of information acquisition discussed above. Merit pay tacitly legitimizes self-interested behavior by defining performance in terms of organization subgoals. According to March and Simon (1958), individuals tend to adhere to these subgoals, even when the goals conflict with those of the larger organization, because of selective perception

and rationalization. These processes could produce situations in which a subordinate shirks non-contractual obligations or challenges a superior's interpretation of the contract.

When a manager perceives that it is necessary to deviate from the contract and act in accordance with a broader conception of organizational good, he or she incurs the risk of going unrewarded even when the manager perceives that the spirit of the contract has been satisfied. This appears to be precisely how many public managers have responded. A widespread result of CSRA performance appraisals (Gaertner and Gaertner, 1985; Pearce and Perry, 1983; United States Merit Systems Protection Board, 1981) were systems that employees simultaneously rated "accurate" and "fair," but not "helpful" or conducive to "improved agency effectiveness." Managers acquired a clearer understanding of the criteria on which they were judged, but were not convinced that the criteria were the best ones to promote improved performance or agency effectiveness. One can only infer that one reason the original CSRA merit pay system failed was the decision of many managers to maximize their personal development or agency effectiveness rather than their appraised performance.

Another result of information problems is that supervisors may not closely tie pay to individually-measured performance because they are unable to judge definitively the relative contributions of employees given the limitations of performance appraisals. The difficulty of making definitive judgments about performance is particularly true for managerial jobs. The small numbers of managerial positions (Williamson, 1975) and the uniqueness of managerial jobs increase the power of managers to control the assessments levied by significant others (Thompson, 1967). This phenomenon helps to explain why raters tend to minimize differentials in rated performance and to inflate ratings (see, e.g., Gaertner and Gaertner, 1984), thus limiting the strength of pay-for-performance relationships. The propensity to minimize appraisal differentials is likely to be reinforced because supervisors bear a large part of the cost, in terms of information acquisition and interpersonal conflict, of justifying performance appraisal decisions to their subordinates.

## Reduction of Coordination

Individual performance contracts will diminish coordination by altering patterns of interdependence among organizational members. Coordination problems originate with individual performance contracts and their attention to organizational subgoals. The subgoal focus is a necessary pre-condition for linking pay to performance because of the need to hold managers responsible for results within their control (March and Simon, 1958). The focus on subgoals, however, tends to undermine the organization as a unit of cooperative activity by undermining interdependencies among organizational members.

Thompson (1967) identified three types of interdependence, pooled, sequential, and reciprocal, which, he asserted, represented ascending complexity and coordination requirements. Pooled interdependence is the dependence of each segment of the organization on the others for the well-being of the organization. Sequential interdependence involves situations in which a part of the organization depends upon another for supply of inputs, for disposal of outputs or both. Finally, reciprocal interdependence involves situations in which each unit poses a contingency for the other.

Field and laboratory research have documented the detrimental effects of merit pay upon sequential (Babchuk and Goode, 1951; Whyte, 1955) and reciprocal interdependence (Miller and Hamblin, 1963), the two most complex forms. The detrimental effects of merit pay in the public sector involve pooled interdependence as well. Merit pay undermines pooled interdependence in public organizations in at least two ways: (1) by altering an individual's attachment to the organization and (2) by creating conflicts or inequities among segments of the organization coalition.

Merit pay systems undermine involvement because they treat the manager as a labor contractor and undermine the flexibility of traditional authority relations (Barnard, 1938;

Simon, 1957). Such contracts communicate that the organization is only concerned with the employee's performance as it is reflected in the contract measures. In effect, organizations signal indifference to past contributions and to any extenuating circumstances that may have influenced the recent performance measures. Employees come to focus on the pay delivery and performance measurement system rather than the organization's tasks or mission.

This contention is supported by an assessment of merit pay for federal managers. CSRA required that managerial performance contracts be drawn up before the performance period, and that half of the money made available for raises be tied directly to rated individual managerial performance. Pearce and Porter (1986) reported the effects of this new pay and performance measurement system for federal managers and employees at two agencies. They divided their sample into those who received "outstanding" and "above average" ratings (55%) and those who received "fully successful" (45%) ratings. They found that whereas the organizational commitment of the relatively highly rated managers was stable over the 30-month period, the commitment of the "average" managers dropped significantly after their first merit rating and remained at this reduced level when retested a year later in both of these agencies. Their findings indicate that merit pay significantly reduced the psychological attachments of a large subgroup of satisfactory performers.

Additional evidence of the potential for merit pay to alter pooled dependence is provided by Perry and Pearce (1985) who traced how CSRA has led to a proliferation of new interest groups. The primary purpose of these new groups is the protection of members (e.g., merit pay managers, senior executives) whose employment status was modified by CSRA. The most prominent of these groups, the Senior Executive Association (SEA), sued for restoration of bonuses to original statutory levels after Congress reduced eligibility for bonuses in the summer of 1980 from a maximum of 50 percent of Senior Executive Service (SES) positions to a maximum of 20 percent. The development of SEA and the subsequent suit vividly illustrate how pay-for-performance can alter the focus of employee attachments from the organization's mission to the pay delivery system.

Merit pay also affects pooled interdependence through its influence upon organizational climate (James and Jones, 1974) or atmosphere (Williamson, 1975). Climate and atmosphere are concepts that explain linkages between a specific transaction and attitudes that have broader organizational consequences. The relevance of these concepts to the relationship between merit pay and pooled interdependence arises from the fact that inducements for some members of an organization are primarily remunerative and for others are primarily social or moral. Within government such variations are quite common. Nevertheless, expectations among participants about appropriate rewards for other participants are likely to have significant attitudinal implications. For example, taxpayers may have a great deal of difficulty accepting large contingent financial rewards for government managers because they perceive such rewards as "squandering their taxes."

Attitudes of other groups within the organizational coalition may operate in a pre-emptive fashion by influencing the design of merit pay systems. The result is often a design compromise that radically diminishes the probability for merit pay success. A dramatic illustration of this process occurred during the implementation of CSRA merit pay systems. Congress imposed a cap on merit pay funding because of the political sensitivity of federal pay levels. OPM developed a merit-pay-funding formula which liberally interpreted congressional intent. Simulations of the system indicated that few employees would be worse off and most would be better off (Hunter and Silverman, 1980). Agency and employee reaction to these simulations was favorable, primarily because of OPM's liberal assumptions about the payout formula. However, GAO forced OPM to rescind its formula in favor of one awarding less money shortly before the first payout because the OPM formula did not adhere to the "no-new-money" limitation in the statute. It is important to remember that,

although this particular episode has been labeled an "implementation problem" by many (see, e.g., Pearce and Perry, 1983; Silverman, 1983), the OPM–GAO controversy originated because of statutory language which represented prevailing norms about appropriate reward levels for federal managers.

## Conclusion

This article has presented a theoretical view of why merit pay has failed in many public organizations. It was argued that three conditions, i.e., invalid contracts, information failure, and diminished coordination, prevent contingent pay from contributing to improved organizational performance. The theoretical framework is useful for understanding implementation problems that accompany pay-for-performance. Such problems are, in fact, inherent in this form of motivational program in government programs.

An issue related to this analysis is whether pay-for-group-performance would fare better in light of the theory we have presented. It is quite obvious that some of the limitations of pay-for-performance are common to both individual and group programs, particularly the problem of specifying a performance contract. However, group incentives may affect individual behavior and allocate the costs of information acquisition differently than do individual incentives, thereby producing different outcomes. The relative effectiveness of individual versus group incentives clearly deserves further research.

The present analysis does not refute the instrumental value of pay as a motivator. Pay is undoubtedly a primary consideration in an individual's decision to join an organization and perform on its behalf (Nash and Carroll, 1975; Ellig, 1982; Wallace and Fay, 1983). Although there is evidence that individuals entering public organizations are relatively less motivated by money than their private sector counterparts (Rawls *et al.*, 1975), pay remains a significant factor in employee motivation. An organization's compensation system conveys a variety of signals to current and potential employees, including information about its fairness, the rewards for long-term loyalty and performance, and its labor market competitiveness. All of these factors are relevant to performance in organizations. The arguments in this paper suggest that also requiring a public organization's compensation system to harness pay for motivating short-term managerial performance is not realistic.

## Notes

1. This paper grows out of my collaboration with Jone Pearce. My thanks to her for permitting me to borrow liberally from her ideas. See Pearce, in press.

2. The use of the term *premises* follows Hage (1972). Premises are very general assumptions that help to explain why a particular theoretical relationship occurs.

## References

BABCHUK, N. and W. J. GOODE (1951). "Work Incentives in a Self-Determined Group." *American Sociological Review* 16: 679–687.

BARNARD, C. I. (1938). *The Functions of the Executive.* Cambridge, MA: Harvard University Press.

BASS, B. M. (1965). *Organizational Psychology.* Boston: Allyn and Bacon.

CARROLL, S. J. and C. E. SCHNEIER, JR. (1982). *Performance Appraisal and Review Systems: The Identification, Measurement, and Development of Performance in Organizations.* Glenview, IL: Scott, Foresman.

DECI, E. L. (1975). *Intrinsic Motivation.* New York: Plenum.

DOERINGER, P. and M. PIORE (1971). *Internal Labor Markets and Manpower Analysis.* Boston: D. C. Heath.

ELLIG, B. R. (1982). *Executive Compensation: A Total Pay Perspective.* New York: McGraw-Hill.

GAERTNER, K. H. and G. H. GAERTNER (1984). "Performance Evaluation and Merit Pay: Results in the Environmental Protection Agency and the Mine Safety and Health Administration," pp. 87–111 in P. I. Ingraham and C. Ban (ed.) *Legislating Bureaucratic Change: The Civil Service Reform Act of 1978.* Albany, NY: State University of New York Press.

GAERTNER, K. H. and G. H. GAERTNER (1985). "Performance-Contingent Pay for Federal Managers." *Administration and Society* 17 (May): 7–20.

GRIENER, J. M., H. P. HATRY, M. P. KOSS, A. P. MILLAR and J. P. WOODWARD (1981). *Productivity and Motivation.* Washington, D. C.: The Urban Institute Press.

HAGE J. (1972). *Techniques and Problems in Theory and Construction in Sociology.* New York: John Wiley and Sons.

HAMNER, W. C. (1975). "How to Ruin Motivation with Pay." *Compensation Review* 7 (3): 17–27.

HARRON, M. (1981). "Another View of the Merit Pay System." *Management* 2 (Fall): 18–20.

HUNTER, R. W. and B. R. Silverman (1980). "Merit Pay in the Federal Government." *Personnel Journal* 59 (December): 1003–1007.

JAMES, L. R. and A. P. JONES (1974). "Organizational Climate: A Review of Theory and Research." *Psychological Bulletin* 81 (12): 1096–1112.

KONOVSKY, M. A. and P. M. PODSAKOFF (1984). *Effects of Individual and Group Incentive System and Task Interdependence on Group Productivity.* Academy of Management Meetings, Boston, MA.

LAWLER, E. E., III. (1971). *Pay and Organizational Effectiveness: A Psychological Review.* New York: McGraw-Hill.

LAWLER, E. E., III. (1981). *Pay and Organization Development.* Reading, MA: Addison-Wesley.

LOCKE, E. A., D. B. FEREN, V. M. MCCALEB, K. N. SHAW and A. T. DENNY (1980). "The Relative Effectiveness of Four Methods of Motivating Employee Performance." pp. 363–388 in K. D. Duncan, M. M. Grunsberg and D. Wallis (eds.) *Changes in Working Life.* New York: Wiley.

MARCH, J. G. and H. A. SIMON (1958). *Organizations.* New York: John Wiley and Sons.

MEYER, H. H. (1975). "The Pay for Performance Dilemma." *Organizational Dynamics* 3 (3): 39–50.

MILLER, L. K. and R. L. HAMBLIN (1963). "Interdependence, Differential Rewarding, and Productivity." *American Sociological Review,* 28: 768–778.

MINTZBERG, H. (1973). *The Nature of Managerial Work.* N.Y.: Harper & Row.

NASH, A. N., and S. J. CARROLL JR. (1975). *The Management of Compensation.* Belmont, CA.: Wadsworth.

O'TOOLE, D. E. and J. R. CHURCHILL (1982). "Implementing Pay-for-Performance: Initial Experiences." *Review of Public Personnel Administration* 2 (Summer): 13–28.

PAGANO, M. (1985). "An Exploratory Evaluation of the Civil Service Reform Act's Merit Pay System for the GS 13–15s: A Case Study of the U.S. Department of Health and Human Services," pp. 161–176 in D. H. Rosenbloom (ed.) *Public Personnel Policy: The Politics of Civil Service.* Port Washington, NY: Associated Faculty Press.

PATTON, A. (1974). "Governments' Pay Disincentive." *Business Week* January 14.

PATTON, A. (1972). "Why Incentive Plans Fail." *Harvard Business Review* 50 (3): 58–66.

PEARCE, J. L. (in press). "Why Merit Pay Doesn't Work: Implications for Organization Theory," in Gomez-Mejia and D. B. Balkin (eds.) *Compensation: An Applied Perspective.* Reston, VA: Reston Publishers.

PEARCE, J. L. and J. L. PERRY (1983). "Federal Merit Pay: A Longitudinal Analysis." *Public Administration Review* 43: 315–325.

PEARCE, J. L. and L. W. PORTER (1986). "Employee Responses to Formal Performance Appraisal Feedback." *Journal of Applied Psychology* 71: 211–218.

PEARCE, J. L., W. B. STEVENSON, J. L. PERRY (1985). "Managerial Compensation Based on Organizational Performance: A Time Series Analysis of the Impact of Merit Pay." *Academy of Management Journal* 28 (June): 261–278.

PERRY, J. L., C. HANZLIK and J. L. PEARCE (1982). "Effectiveness of Merit-Pay-Pool Management." *Review of Public Personnel Administration* 2: 5–12.

PERRY, J. L. and J. L. PEARCE (1985). "Civil Service Reform and the Politics of Performance Appraisal," pp. 146–160 in D. H. Rosenbloom (ed.) *Public Personnel Policy: The Politics of Civil Service.* Port Washington, NY: Associated Faculty Press.

PERRY, J. L. and J. L. PEARCE (1983). "Initial Reactions to Federal Merit Pay." *Personnel Journal* 62: 230–237.

PERRY, J. L. and L. W. PORTER (1982). "Factors Affecting the Context for Motivation in Public Organizations." *Academy of Management Review* 7 (January): 89–98.

PERRY, J. L. and L. W. PORTER (1980). *Organizational Assessments of the Civil Service Reform Act.* Washington, D. C.: U. S. Office of Personnel Management.

*Public Administration Times* (1986). "Reagan Recommends Federal Pay Reform." 9 (May 15): 1.

RAWLS, J. R., R. A. ULRICH and O. T. NELSON, Jr. (1975). "A Comparison of Managers Entering or Re-entering the Profit and Nonprofit Sectors."

*Academy of Management Journal* 18 (December): 616–622.

REDLING, E. T. (1981). "Myth vs. Reality: The Relationship Between Top Executive Pay and Corporate Performance." *Compensation Review* Fourth Quarter: 16–24.

ROETHLISBERGER, F. J. and W. DICKSON (1939). *Management and the Worker.* Cambridge, MA: Harvard University Press.

SAVAS, E. S. and S. G. GINSBURG (1973). "The Civil Service: A Meritless System?" *The Public Interest* 32: 70–85.

SILVERMAN, B. R. (1983). "Why the Merit Pay System Failed in the Federal Government." *Personnel Journal* 62 (April): 294–302.

SIMON, H. A. (1957). *Administrative Behavior.* Second Edition. New York: Free Press.

THOMPSON, J. D. (1967). *Organizations in Action.* New York: McGraw-Hill.

United States General Accounting Office (1980). *Postal Service Program Should Provide More Incentive for Improving Performance* (GGD-81-8). Washington, D. C.: U. S. Government Printing Office.

United States General Accounting Office (1984a). *An Assessment of SES Performance Appraisal Systems* (GGD-84-16). Washington, D. C.: U. S. Government Printing Office.

United States General Accounting Office (1984b). *A 2-Year Appraisal of Merit Pay in Three Agencies* (GGD-84-1). Washington, D. C.: U. S. Government Printing Office.

United States Merit Systems Protection Board (1981). *Status Report on Performance Appraisal and Merit Pay Among Mid-Level Employees.* Washington, D. C.: Office of Merit Systems Review and Studies.

UNGSON, G. R. and R. M. STEERS (1984). "Motivation and Politics in Executive Compensation." *Academy of Management Review* 9: 313–323.

VAN RIPER, P. P. (1958). *History of the United States Civil Service.* Evanston, IL: Row, Peterson.

VITELES, M. S. (1953). *Motivation and Morale in Industry.* New York: Norton.

VROOM, V. H. (1964). *Work and Motivation.* New York: Wiley.

WALLACE, M. J., JR. and C. H. FAY (1983). *Compensation Theory and Practice.* Boston: Kent.

WILLIAMSON, O. E. (1975). *Markets and Hierarchies: Analysis and Antitrust Implications.* New York: Free Press.

WHYTE, W. G. (1955). *Money and Motivation.* New York: Harper and Brothers.

# 20

# Developing the Will and Capacity to Conform

*Herbert Kaufman*

## Selecting Men Who Fit

If a man is willing, or even eager, to carry out the preformed decisions of his superiors, but lacks the technical knowledge and the practical skills to do so, the decisions may never be executed at all, and certainly not properly. If he has the knowledge and training, on the other hand, but is vehemently opposed to the decisions he is called upon to execute, the results may be equally disastrous from the point of view of his leaders. It takes both the will and the capacity to conform for a member of an agency to do his job as the leaders of the agency want it done. The Forest Service therefore tries to get people who have both.

The campaign begins with recruiting efforts directed at young men in the last year of high school or the early years of college; pamphlets, films, and speakers supplied by the Forest Service call their attention to the opportunities and attractions of forestry as a career and advise them how to get further information on training and forestry career possibilities. The campaign does not paint an unmixed picture for the potential recruits, however; while it points up the satisfactions of work in forestry, it also indicates the hardships as well. In this respect, it follows the lead of Gifford Pinchot, who,

SOURCE: From *The Forest Ranger*, by Herbert Kaufman. Published for Resources for the Future, Inc., by the Johns Hopkins University Press, 1960. Reprinted by permission.

many years ago, adopted a policy of telling the whole story in plain, unvarnished fashion:

> Young men began to ask about Forestry as a career. Most of these youngsters I discouraged on the ground that if a boy had the stuff in him to make a good forester he would keep at it anyhow. I told him Forestry means hardship and hard work, much responsibility and small pay, which was the cold fact.[1]

Almost half a century later, Pinchot was still pursuing the same policy. Addressing American soldiers in England after World War II, when they were weighing occupational choices before them as they contemplated their return to civilian life, he told them:

> I do not urge any man to take up forestry as a profession. Unless his own love of the woods, his eagerness to work in the woods, drives him to forestry, he had better spend his life in some other way.
>
> For the man who is by nature fitted for forestry, no other profession offers, in my opinion, such promise of usefulness and such opportunity for a happy life. To those of you who are sure beyond question that forestry is the profession for you, I offer my sincere congratulations and my very best wishes.
>
> The national need for the forest and the opening for forestry and foresters was never as great in America as it is today. The risks of the profession are less than they were when forestry in America was new. But the destruction of the forests since those early days, and especially during the war and the aftermath of the war, give to forestry an indispensable usefulness which justifies any man who loves the woods in taking it up.
>
> I end as I began: Unless you are sure, let forestry alone.[2]

Weakly motivated men were thus advised to turn to other pursuits. To a considerable extent those who persisted were self-selected, a rather dedicated group prepared to accept whatever the profession had to offer.

Today, the same practice, a bit modified and softened, but still strikingly candid, obtains. The Service still offers almost as much discouragement as encouragement. For example, potential candidates are told:

Many persons still have only a vague idea of the kind of life the forester really leads. Young men are often attracted to the profession because of the prospect of outdoor work. They are fond of camping in the open and of hunting and fishing.

One who is considering such a career should remember that the forester in his fieldwork sometimes must endure hardships that sportsmen do not encounter. Spending considerable time in the woods as part of one's regular business is quite different from camping out for a few weeks on a vacation.

. . . If he shows outstanding ability, the young forester may find the apprenticeship period a short one, although as the number of foresters increases and competition becomes more intense, the training period may be expected to lengthen.

The young forester is apt to have his headquarters shifted frequently, somewhat like the civil engineer. The places to which he is assigned may not always be the most desirable from the standpoint of personal comfort or convenience, especially for family life. Because of this shifting about, he may be unable for some time to establish a home. On the other hand, if he is an able man, he may ultimately advance to a position that will give him more permanent headquarters and greater opportunity for home life. He must not count himself secure, however, against a change of working field which will necessitate removal to a new place. . . .

Even in the higher positions, whether in Government or private work, the forester may have to spend a good deal of time supervising or inspecting actual field operations. Trips away from his headquarters may be only for a day or so, or they may be for several weeks. In some positions such travel often includes long, hard journeys by horse and pack train. Frequently, it means rough walking, and sometimes days of slow and laborious progress by snowshoe or canoe. Even with the greatest possible extension of good roads, much of the forester's travel for many years to come will necessarily be arduous.[3]

Similarly, in talks before the Society of American Foresters, the professional association of foresters, Forest Service officers have presented the facts with stark candor:

The Forest Service organization presents the form of the traditional pyramid, with necessarily decreasing opportunities for advancement toward the peak. The relatively low rate of turn over, perhaps emphasizes this. . . . There is always a demand for outstanding men to fill responsible positions. Nevertheless, for many years, it has appeared inevitable that the Ranger's job would be the highest position to which many technical foresters entering the Forest Service can advance.[4]

Who, after these warnings, chooses forestry in general as a career, and sets his sights on the Forest Service in particular as an employer? Logically, it would seem to be those who highly value the work itself, and to whom the agency as an organization is attractive. Recruiting publicity tends to deter the impatiently ambitious, the seekers after the easy job and the comfortable and stable life, and the men who grow restless at the thought of positions within the framework of a large organization, with all the administrative burdens and frustrations this entails. To be sure, it is by no means clear that Forest Service publicity is a major factor in the career choices of many foresters, including those in the Service, but it seems safe to assume that at least some of those who enter schools of forestry were exposed to such publicity and were not disheartened by it and doubtless already would have a predisposition to accommodate themselves to the demands made upon members of the Forest Service. Indeed, *all* the men choosing professional forestry as an occupation may be said to have demonstrated by that choice a set of interests and attitudes indicative of a degree of receptivity to the requirements of life in the Forest Service. Some among them, however, will doubtless have made their career selections knowing *specifically* from Forest Service literature what they can expect of the agency and what it will expect of them.

Willingness to conform is in this sense employed as an initial criterion of selection, a standard applied to themselves by the young men crossing the threshold to professional training. All of the Rangers interviewed declare they entered forestry with no illusions about the work. They started with yearnings to work in the field, whatever the hardships, and with profound respect and admiration for the Forest Service and its officers. A couple turned down excellent opportunities elsewhere in order to be associated with the organization and its program. Several had had personal experience through relatives or temporary work that acquainted them beforehand with the nature of the tasks they would be required to perform. In short, they had many of the qualities and attitudes the Service wants in its men, and they were ready even prior to their professional schooling for the demands that would be made upon them later on.

The formal schooling of foresters in the United States concentrates heavily on the technical aspects of the profession—on biology, ecology, silviculture, and forest economics. There are but thirty-eight colleges and universities in the country that offer instruction in forestry at the professional level (twenty-seven of which are accredited by the Society of American Foresters). It is estimated that 90 per cent of the degrees awarded (chiefly the Bachelor of Science in Forestry, but including a substantial number of Masters and a sprinkling of Doctorates) are in general forestry, while the remaining 10 per cent are in special fields like wood technology, range management, wildlife management, forest recreation, and general conservation.[5]

Since so much of the work of a district Ranger is administrative, involving the reconciliation of technical and managerial problems, no one contends a graduate of a forestry school, even if he holds an advanced degree, could step fresh from his college into a Ranger position. On the other hand, foresters have a common set of techncial tools and techniques, a common lore and body of knowledge, so the Forest Service can take for granted many things about the way they would handle property under their jurisdiction. Over 90 per cent of the more than 4,000 professional employees of the Forest Service are foresters; the existence of a widespread consensus on technical matters within the agency is therefore not surprising. In other words, many decisions and actions taken in the field are implanted in these men during their preservice education; appropriate behaviors are in this sense "built into" them. Their receptivity to agency directives is thus produced not only by the constraints upon them, but also by the education and training which results in their wanting to do of their own volition what they are formally required to do. The Rangers interviewed all hold Bachelor's degrees in forestry, and one has a Master's as well, although several of them entered the Service a quarter of a century ago, when college degrees were less usual than they are today. As is true of most forestry students, they all had some field experience, some of it with the Forest Service, gained for the most part during the summer intervals between school years, before they acquired their degrees.

The Forest Service takes pains to induce as many members of this professional reservoir as possible to apply for employment in this agency. All professional positions in the agency are in the classified civil service; recruits enter at the lowest professional ranks by passing the Federal Service Entrance Examination (Forester Option), a written competitive test.[6] Forest Service personnel officers in Washington and in the regions maintain contact with the educational institutions, notifying them of approaching examination dates, reporting on the results of examinations, helping in studies (for example, of academic standing and performance on the tests), and appearing before student bodies both as technical lecturers and recruiters. This provides them with a steady flow of candidates.

Recruiting is not confined to schools of forestry, for the examinations are open to all who have "subject credits. . .equivalent to those required for a Bachelor of Science degree in forestry," but the most intensive efforts are directed at them, and the overwhelming number of candidates and appointees to professional vacancies come from this source.

The percentage of applicants who pass the entrance tests generally depends on the number of vacancies to be filled. Variations in the percentage of applicants who pass the examinations result not from variations in the difficulty of the tests from year to year, but from changes in the passing grade. When the number of vacancies to be filled has been determined, the passing grade is set at a figure that admits about twice the required number of applicants (to allow for declinations). Thus, the ratio of successful to total applicants varies a good deal.[7] In a year of many applicants and few vacancies, the percentage of successful candidates is low; in a year of few applicants and many vacancies, the percentage soars. (Of course, there is never a time when everybody gets through, regardless of the state of the market; there are absolute as well as relative standards.) Before America's entry into the Second World War, when there were more applicants than jobs, the figure was quite low (18 per cent in 1940, for example), but it climbed rapidly (to an estimated 85 per cent) when the postwar industrial demand for foresters far exceeded the supply; it dropped again (to about 40 per cent in 1950) when the demand was temporarily satisfied, and has risen again in recent years (partly because increasing opportunities in private employ have drawn off many potential candidates).[8]

Consequently, it is no longer true, as it was in the past, that the Forest Service gets only the pick of the crop in terms of academic record, particularly since the examination for foresters, like all other options of the Federal Service Entrance Examination, has been changed from a subject-matter test to a test of general mental ability. That is not to say anything is wrong with the examination; this question is irrelevant to the discussion. It does mean, however, that examining practices today place heavier reliance on professional training vis-à-vis test scores for evidence that the men admitted to the Service have the desired technical premises of action "built into" them. Self-selection by career choice, coupled with schooling, do more to assure employee receptivity to agency direction than does testing in a full employment economy.

However, once men are taken into the Forest Service, the members of the agency, who have relied up to this stage on others (the applicants themselves, and their teachers) to provide some of the sought-after propensities in candidates for permanent appointment, take a hand in the process of selection. Under civil service regulations, entrants into the Federal Service must serve a year as probationers before they receive "status" —i.e., procedural protections with respect to discharge or demotion as long as the jobs they occupy remain in existence, and certain preferences with respect to re-employment if their jobs are abolished; during that year, the hiring agency may discharge them at will. Appointing officers (regional foresters for the lower grades of the Forest Service) are thus able to judge the qualifications, attitudes, and personalities of newcomers on the job, and to filter out those who, although they chose forestry as a career and came through the training and the examinations, seem for one reason or another to lack the willingness or the capacity (or both) to conform to the preformed decisions of the bureau leadership. In point of fact, relatively few men are dropped on agency initiative during probation, chiefly because the earlier phases of the selection process turn back most of the men who would not fit. But as many as 10 to 15 per cent withdraw from the organization (some, it is true, at the suggestion of Forest Service line and personnel officers; most, on the other hand, on their own initiative) within the first three years after initial employment. Those who make the grade and stick to the Forest Service are therefore men who know the agency and are not at odds with its goals and methods. They have shown an intrinsic readiness and ability to conform.

## Post-Entry Training

From this point on, the Forest Service undertakes deliberately to intensify both the readiness and the ability: To what the men who survive the screening of the selection process bring with them—have "in" them, one might say—the officers of the agency attempt to add by training.

Some of the training is conducted on a group basis. As young junior foresters—men appointed after passing the entrance examination—come into the Service, they are assembled for orientation courses in their respective regional offices to get an introduction to the history and the mission of the Forest Service, its place in the federal government, the essentials of federal employment, and the nature of the ground-level job and its importance in the execution of Service-wide policies. For several days, the junior foresters stay together, listening to talks by specialists on the staffs of the regional foresters and by selected speakers from outside the Forest Service, and attending discussion and question periods.

In addition, conferences, schools, and training camps are conducted as refresher courses, or to introduce new policies and procedures, or to provide instruction in the handling of special problems and the application of new scientific discoveries for which pre-service training and past experience are not adequate. Some of these are Service-wide, some are regional, but, while Rangers appear at a few of the latter, the ones to which they are most frequently exposed are those at the forest supervisor's level. The training histories of the Rangers studied are by no means identical, but the array of more or less formal courses of practice and instruction which they, considered as a collectivity, have taken is imposing, including as it does general conferences or encampments for review of the whole of the Ranger's job; functional conferences and field studies for wildlife management, timber management, and other phases of Ranger district administration; schools in administrative management; and courses in job instruction, job methods, and job relations for supervisors, developed during World War II and

adapted for use in the Forest Service. And every Ranger attended at least three such formal programs of instruction during his early years in the Service.

But schools and conferences, in spite of the emphasis placed on them in the Forest Service, constitute only a small fraction of the training conducted in the agency. For according to the *Manual:*

> It is the responsibility of each supervising officer to consider annually the training needs of his or her immediate subordinates and to initiate action to provide the opportunity for as much of the needed training as is officially justifiable or practicable.

Allowances for formulation of training plans for each professional employee are included in the financial and workload figures for every level. Training bulletins, film strips, motion pictures, and other materials are provided by personnel officers in Washington and the regions. Training is checked in the course of inspections. Every supervisory officer is continually urged, consciously and deliberately, to train his subordinates. On-the-job training is unquestionably the largest single element in the Service training armory.

Except for new men, most on-the-job training is informal in practice. Extensive plans are drawn up for probationers moving into Ranger districts at sub-Ranger levels. They are instructed at some length by the Rangers, given exercises and formal reading assignments, and conducted on tours of their respective districts. Very soon, however, they are sent into the field on their own, and their work is later checked by the Rangers, who point out specifically what is wrong and why. Assistant Rangers are often asked to draft letters for the signature of the Rangers, who then discuss with them the problems of strategy and authority invariably involved in such written contacts with the public and with higher echelons, explaining each change and the reasons for it. Assistant Rangers are often invited to attend discussions between the Rangers and their clienteles or superiors. In the three to ten years it generally takes a probational forester to reach command of his own district, he is subject—by careful planning, not just by accident—to concentrated training in the form of close supervision. The closeness of supervision is not relaxed, and the breadth of his discretion and the burden of his responsibility are not increased, until he has demonstrated that he knows what his superiors want and that he is capable of doing it.

When a man becomes a Ranger, the intensity of his on-the-job training slacks off a great deal. Still, such training does not cease altogether. Every contact, every request for advice or clearance, and every inspection is an opportunity for still more, much of it chance, but some of it intentional, as officers from higher offices discuss orders, actions, and findings with the Rangers. Whatever the purposes of these procedures, the consequences are to clarify for the Rangers the expectations of their leaders and to impart to them the appropriate way to fulfill those expectations. All training is communication, and, while it is not true that all communication is training, it is clear that far more organizational communication has the effect of training than bears the formal designation. The process thus never stops.

Both technical information about silviculture and agency procedure, on the one hand, and more general information about Forest Service objectives, philosophy, and self-justification, on the other, tend inevitably to become intertwined in all training. But the stress is more heavily on the former than the latter after initial indoctrination. Training is more commonly focused on the "how" of the immediate job rather than the "why" of the Service; it is essentially an effort to inform rather than persuade, to explain rather than arouse enthusiasm for the organization or devotion to its "cause." On occasion, it takes the form of explicating an agency "line," as was the case with a training memorandum from the Chief in 1946 with regard to his proposals for pressing for regulation of cutting on private lands; the memorandum set forth the answers to 55 questions on the subject that members of the Service were presumably to treat as the official service position.[9] More frequently, the

importance of the Forest Service job to the welfare and strength of the nation and its people are pointed up in passing, reaffirming the "faith" of the members of the Service in the work in which they are engaged. On the whole, however, the tone is explanatory, not exhortative. Other modes of influencing behavior may do more to develop the *will* to conform to preformed decisions, although training helps; training builds primarily the *capacity*—the skills, knowledge, and factual premises—that facilitate and encourage adherence.

At the same time, another aspect of training operates as a screening device, selecting for advancement men with the "proper" qualifications *and* motivations. For, in addition to required pre-service and in-service training, they are urged to equip themselves, often on their own time and even at their own expense, to move ahead:

Forest Service managers and executives are given an opportunity to make a continuous study of public administration and administrative management. They are provided with lists of the better study references. From time to time outstanding books and articles are routed to them for study. They are encouraged to enroll in special short-term university courses such as those given in Public Administration at the American, Georgetown, Michigan, Montana, and New York Universities. A few are selected for specialized training in the Intern Management Program sponsored by the Civil Service Commission in Washington, D.C.

To aid men in the more advanced phases of managerial work, special emphasis is placed on group conference participation. Each man is given opportunities to become skilled in conference leadership, in committee work, in panel discussion and in general conference participation. . . . As a result of the conference training, a large percentage of the managers and executives become skilled in the art of conference leadership and as a by-product, become accustomed to public speaking.

Special significance is attached to both public speaking and writing. Occasional courses on these subjects are sponsored officially. In addition, men are encouraged to participate actively in speaking clubs and formal adult courses offered by high schools and colleges...

The Forest Service has learned that the better executives usually participate actively in civic, fraternal, and religious organizations on their personal time... No official stand is taken with respect to such effort but most men do voluntarily take advantage of the opportunities offered for improving their abilities, particularly in the field of public relations.[10]

The education *per se* doubtless does prepare them for the work they will have to do. It does enlarge their capacities to perform their jobs. But those who acquire this training voluntarily, who at some cost to themselves avail themselves of agency-sponsored or -approved programs, indicate by that very fact that they *choose* to fit themselves into the agency pattern in order to advance. It tends to suggest a good deal about their motivations. While, conceivably, men may engage in voluntary training with no aim but to advance themselves, the fact that they do so might be taken as an indication of their tendency to act as the organization wants, to ingratiate themselves with their superiors, regardless of how cynical their attitudes toward the training itself may be. In any event, exposure to the training may well have a more profound effect on them than they realize.

At the very least, then, post-entry training in the Forest Service expands the abilities needed to conform to preformed agency decisions. It also tends to reinforce dedication to the agency and its objectives, although probably less so than some other techniques (discussed below). And, in its voluntary aspects, it helps identify men whose eagerness to advance manifests itself in the will to do what the leaders recommend, let alone direct.[11]

## Building Identification With the Forest Service

In addition to picking and advancing men likely to be receptive to communications from the leaders of the agency, and to "training into" these men the capacity and willingness to adhere to preformed decisions announced by the leadership, the Forest Service enjoys—largely as a result of its deliberate efforts, but partly in consequence of fortuitous circumstances—an environment conducive to an almost automatic tendency to conform to those decisions. That environment is a set of conditions promoting identification[12] of the members of the Forest Service with the well-being of the organization, linking their own positions and welfare and futures with those of the agency, fusing their perspectives with those of their colleagues and superiors. It is a set of conditions that sets them apart from all people "outside" the organization, binds them intimately with other organization members; that "injects into the very nervous systems of the organization members the criteria of decision that the organization wishes to employ," and thereby vastly increases the probability that each of them will "make decisions, by himself, as the organization would like him to decide."[13] Without realizing it, members of the Forest Service thus "internalize" the perceptions, values, and premises of action that prevail in the bureau; unconsciously, very often, they tend to act in the agency-prescribed fashion because that is the way that has become natural to them. Much of what the Service does tends to further this process.

### Transfer and Promotion

For example, transfer of personnel is treated in the Forest Service as a device for "the development, adjustment and broadening of personnel"; consequently, men are deliberately moved a good deal, particularly during their early years in the agency. The Service does not merely wait until vacancies occur; it shifts men to replace each other in what looks like a vast game of musical chairs, but for the serious purpose of giving them a wide range of experience in preparation for advancement to positions that require a broader understanding of national forest administration than can possibly be gained in long assignments at a single duty station. If transfers can be coupled with promotions, the added incentive to move is provided; however, "horizontal transfers [i.e., in the same grade] also may be proposed as a prerequisite to possible future advancement." If an individual declines a proposed transfer, his status in his old post is not prejudiced, for transfers are recommended, not ordered formally, in most cases,[14] and the *Manual* decrees, "There will be a clear-cut determination that the transfer will not work undue hardship either on the transferee in his personal situation or on the receiving or sending unit"; nevertheless, the *Manual* also warns the Service "is forced to insist that those who wish to advance must, at times, waive personal preferences as to location, make inconvenient moves, and serve where most needed..." Hence, when most men are asked to move, they move; it is chiefly old hands with long years of service, no longer interested in rising any higher than they are, who furnish the few declinations. Younger men just starting their careers rarely do, for such an action might impair their futures.

The Rangers studied here have had differing experiences, but all have employment records that reflect the general statements of transfer policy. Of three with more than 20 years in the Forest Service, one was in five locations, one in four, and the third in three within a dozen years; and each moved again at least once later on. As for the younger men, one has served in four places in five years, the other in two places in seven years. Three served in one capacity or another on the staffs of forest supervisors as well as at the district level.

In ten or fifteen years, then, a man in the Forest Service is introduced to many of the problems and practices of national forest administration; he is doubtless "developed, adjusted, and broadened." But the impact of rapid transfer is more profound than training alone; it also builds identifications with the Forest Service as a whole. For during each man's early years, he never has time to sink roots in the communities in which he sojourns so briefly. He gets to know the local people who do the manual work in the woods, but not very well in the short time he spends with them. He barely becomes familiar with an area before he is moved again. Only one thing gives any continuity, any structure, to his

otherwise fluid world: the Service. When he reports to a new area, his superior helps him get installed in his new living quarters, introduces him to the townsfolk who will be his neighbors, acquaints him with all the members of the local work force and fire organization, instructs him in the management of the administrative unit, supervises and evaluates and corrects his work, and prepares him to shoulder heavier responsibilities. Whenever a younger man severs his ties in a location to which he has just become adjusted and takes a new place, an experienced Forest Service officer is there to receive him, support him, guide him. To be sure, there are strains and conflicts and frictions, too. But, in general, it appears from the limited evidence of this study that the men who move rapidly are received sympathetically by those to whom they are detailed, and are taken in hand for a time as the personal as well as the official responsibilities of their immediate supervisors.[15]

Thus, the Forest Service acquires a more or less fraternal aura for its newer members. To be sure, it is the organization that uproots and shifts them in the first place, but the hardships are considerably softened by the visible team of friends and colleagues ready to help them and to make the transitions as smooth and pleasant as possible. Moreover, behind the inconveniences stands the comforting knowledge that transfer is preparation for advancement, that every assignment and detail is recorded, adding to qualifications for promotion when the opportunities arise.[16] The impersonality of the system is reduced, the sense of belonging enhanced— particularly since the frequency of transfers to different locations and administrative levels brings many of the men in each region into personal contact with each other despite the dispersion of the agency.[17] Everywhere, they encounter men with similar interests, similar problems, similar objectives, similar aspirations, similar complaints. They find understanding and appreciation of their problems. Their ties with their fellow-officials are multiplied and deepened. As they become part of the organization, the organization also becomes part of them.

The opportunity for this process of organizational acculturation to have a chance to work its effects on every executive in the Forest Service (i.e., every officer at the Ranger level or higher) is maximized by two practices: One is a firm system of promotion from within for professional positions in national forest administration. The other is a policy of relatively unhurried promotion.

The Forest Service, at least as far as its professional foresters are concerned, constitutes a classic illustration of a career system. The foresters are comparatively safe from the vicissitudes of politics and economics; the merit system has guarded them effectively since the first days of the agency, and reductions in appropriations are absorbed more by the large seasonal work force than by permanent officers. With professional staff thus stabilized, the Service has been able to recruit its new professionals to fill entering, sub-Ranger positions, and to fill virtually every job at the Ranger level and above by advancing someone from a lower grade. Says the *Manual:*

In filling a position, we should avoid or minimize the chance of bringing into the Forest Service persons about whom we know less, because of lack of service and salary records, than we do of our personnel and who might therefore be incorrectly appraised by us as being better qualified than our own personnel.

Without exception, all the Rangers interviewed, though professional foresters, served their "apprenticeships" in sub-Ranger grades; in fact, there are no Rangers now in the Service recruited directly from outside the Service. Furthermore, almost all the officers higher than Ranger in national forest administration have served as Rangers at some time in their careers. To be sure, there is no single set pattern for advancement; there are many alternative ladders, many different routes upward. But they all have one thing in common: vacancies are filled by promotion and transfer, never (for all practical purposes) by lateral entry.[18] There are no "strangers" in the administrative positions in national forest administration, save for the men junior to the Rangers. There are compelling

reasons for this practice; it is a long step indeed from forestry school to the heavy responsibilities of district management. Nevertheless, it means the ethos of the agency is subject to few jarring dissonances from within.

Not only are the higher positions filled by men selected from inside the Service, but men in the lower positions ordinarily occupy them long enough for the process of acculturation to take effect. In part, this is a result of circumstances beyond Forest Service control rather than planning; civil service law requires that employees remain in grade for a year before being promoted, and, in any event, the pyramidal structure of the organization for national forest administration provides fewer openings for advancement than there are men eligible to move ahead. In part, however, it is also deliberate policy; it is estimated by the Service that it will take not less than three years to rise to the command of a Ranger district, and possibly as long as a decade. (One of the Rangers interviewed traversed this distance in less than the minimum, two took three years, one took eight years, and one was twelve in coming up.) The minimum for becoming a forest supervisor is seven or eight years, while seventeen years is a short time to ascend the ladder to regional forester; generally most men in these positions took longer.[19]

As private industry absorbs ever larger percentages of technically trained foresters, and as intensification of forest management creates additional positions in the Forest Service, the rate of advancement tends to become more rapid. Nonetheless, forest officers are exposed for substantial periods to the environment of the agency before they are appointed to executive positions, and they remain always under the surveillance of men who have spent practically their whole adult lives in Forest Service employ. They are absorbed into the organization by a kind of gradual social osmosis, during which they, in turn, absorb many of the prevailing values, assumptions, and customary modes of operation.

Seniority does not automatically bring promotion. Periodically, the regional foresters and assistant regional foresters in each region assemble to review the records of the men under them and determine what their assignments should be. Length of service is a factor in their judgments, to be sure, but it is far outweighed by other elements—principally the evaluation of each man by his immediate superior, by the personnel management division of the regional office, and by the regional forester and his staff (most of whom will have met almost all the professional foresters in their jurisdiction in the course of visits, conferences, inspections, training meetings, and conventions of professional societies and associations, and who also have access to inspection reports, civil service performance ratings, and other appraisals of accomplishment and potential). Some men will be transferred to round out their experience; others will be left where they are to season; still others will be advanced; a number are repeatedly passed over. Some never get beyond the Ranger level, and a few serve out their years without even achieving command of their own districts; some shoot comparatively meteorically through the hierarchy, and many a veteran Ranger has been inspected by a man the Ranger himself trained a few years earlier.

It does not take most men long to learn there are attributes rewarded by the organization, and those who yearn to rise deliberately cultivate those attributes if they can. There is a striving on the part of many to demonstrate they fit into the approved pattern, and even those who profess to be indifferent to promotion cannot help picking up many of the traits of the culture in which they work. For those who fit the pattern naturally, this takes no conscious effort. For others, it takes conscious self-appraisal and adjustment; as one Ranger who failed to advance from his sub-Ranger assignments during his early years put it, "I changed my outlook and reorganized myself and my own line of thinking," and the transformation was followed by promotion. In other words, promotion is a sanction, a reward or a punishment based on excellence on the job, but excellence on the job is in practice measured by the proven predisposition to behave in the organizationally desired fashion rather than just by technical proficiency.[20]

Promotion and transfer are thus far more than methods of staffing. As practiced in the Forest Service, they also foster in each officer

identification with the agency—with its survival and welfare, with its goals, with its procedures, with its members.

## The Use of Symbols

Identification is heightened by the use of symbols. Perhaps the outstanding ones are the uniform and the badge. The whole purpose of uniforms and badges is to identify the members of organizations, to differentiate the wearers from everyone else and to link them with each other. The livery and insignia show at a glance who is "in" an agency and who is not, and establish authority and status at a glance. And they also foster a group spirit and unit, a "we" feeling, a common bond.

In fact, the attitude of the men in the Forest Service toward the uniform varies. Regulations make the wearing of it mandatory in smaller towns, optional for men stationed regularly in larger cities. It is required for appearances in public capacity as spokesmen and representatives of the agency. There is an allowance for the purchase of uniforms. However, some men prefer to wear work clothes most of the time—particularly when dealing with loggers and grazers, before whom they prefer to appear as individuals doing business rather than as authoritative agents of a government bureau—and are regularly admonished by their superiors to get into their "greens."[21] Some wear the uniforms, with pride, whenever they can. Many wear at least part of it most of the time. Yet, although the reactions are mixed, and the observation of the rules somewhat spotty, it is significant that a majority of the officers in the Forest Service expressed a preference for retaining the uniform when polled on the question a few years ago. Despite the unwillingness of many of them in some regions to wear it as regularly as directed, it is a symbol most are not ready to relinquish; the privilege of wearing it still unites them.

The Forest Service insigne—the shield-shaped badge with the agency name and a tree emblazoned on it—is a familiar and respected one the country over. In Washington, the agency uses distinctive wooden plaques rather than the standard signs to identify its offices, while rustic signs bearing its emblem appear on almost all the properties it manages. Indeed, it has been said the adoption of the designation "Service"—now a fairly commonplace term, but a novelty when it was originally selected—instead of the more common "bureau" helped set it in a class by itself, accentuating its self-consciousness and corporate spirit.[22] These are all small things, but they do set the agency apart. Many public servants, asked who their employer is, are likely to name "the government," or perhaps their department. Forest officers will almost invariably respond, "the Forest Service."

The agency symbols, even when they are not enthusiastically supported, keep the members aware of their membership, and encourage them to think in terms of the agency. Consequently, in the course of time, its premises tend to become their own.

### Headquarters Consultation With Field Officers

Identification is further intensified by the Forest Service practice of sounding out field opinion on questions affecting field administration. Social psychologists have indicated that participation in the formulation of organization decisions tends to promote identification.[23] The Forest Service provides many opportunties and channels for such participation.

For instance, the field is sometimes polled formally. As noted earlier, the Washington office requested opinions from the field on whether uniforms should be required, and also on the style of the uniform; the attitudes of members of the Service down to the Ranger district level were obtained, and the policy eventually adopted was based in large part on their reactions. In another case, the Washington staff, anticipating legislation on overtime pay, proposed a tentative stand for the Service to present to the Secretary of Agriculture and Congress; the circular was transmitted to the field with the comment, "As usual we wish, of course, to check with you and have your advice on these—and any other related problems—before making specific recommendations to higher authority." (Reports from the

regional foresters on opinion in their jurisdictions occasionally indicated that the regional foresters did not agree with the judgments of their subordinates, but they dutifully transmitted those judgments just the same. A couple of regional foresters reported comments obliquely critical of the Washington office on the overtime issue, urging headquarters to simplify and stabilize policy.) In a third instance, suggestions for administrative improvement were solicited from the field by Washington; the responses were analyzed, and organized into over a thousand separate recommendations, some minor, others sweeping. Priorities were assigned to the recommendations according to their urgency and the number of times they were mentioned, and projects to put them into practice were instituted. Almost all the proposals, suggestions, and complaints have been acted upon, and work continues on those not yet effectuated. Such massive surveys do not occur every day, but they are made frequently enough, and are supplemented by similar inquiries from the regional offices, to betoken to field men that they are not simply passive instruments manipulated by the agency leaders. Some agency decisions are clearly choices in which they have had a part, even when their personal preferences do not happen to prevail.

Over and above the polling techniques, the Forest Service provides many additional opportunities for field men to make their views known to their superiors. Indeed, these may be even more effective means of encouraging an upward flow of ideas and opinions from the field, for they do not restrict the comments to particular subjects. Thus, as previously noted, few men who are under inspection pass up the chance to ventilate their suggestions and criticisms—both during working hours, and even more so in the informal social hours after the close of business; this practice is not only tolerated, but encouraged and members of the Service insist that their recommendations and complaints *do* get back to the higher levels, sometimes generate action, and do not (unless carried to an extreme) result in injury to the sources for being outspoken. Since Rangers are inspected by supervisors' offices, regional offices, and from time to time as sample districts in their regions by the Washington office, this often permits them to air their convictions quite effectively. The opportunity *can* be abused; the chronic complainer, the "whiner," and the destructive critic are apt to be heavily discounted. But most men are conscious of the possible abuses, and they are able to inject their predilections into the decision-making process with some hope of affecting the final product. It is apparently not just an empty ritual, for Ranger complaints (and complaints from other levels) about excessive paper work and the unwieldiness of the *Forest Service Manual* are generally regarded as the principal factors behind projects to reduce the former and simplify the latter to which the Washington office has devoted much time, energy, and money. In any case, the practice contributes to the general sense of participation. So, too, does the standing official invitation to "inspectees" to file objections to any aspects of inspection reports they consider unfair or inaccurate; many of the men interviewed have registered protests at one time or another, and some have been sustained in their protests.[24]

Forest supervisors and regional offices often seek the advice of Rangers on pending questions quite informally, apart from Service-wide polls and regular inspections. For example, Rangers have been asked about the relative merits of dividing districts as compared with adding to existing staffs and maintaining existing boundaries. If division is chosen, they are consulted about the lines of the new districts, and about the best locations for the new Ranger stations. When projects for national forests are administered from supervisor's offices, the Rangers are drawn into the planning; roads, recreation areas, and other improvements are installed only in consultation with them. A couple of Rangers reported stopping work being done by project crews working out of higher headquarters because the Rangers disapproved of the way the work was being done. In an earlier chapter, mention was made of abandonment by a forest supervisor of plans to spray an area because the Ranger thought the public reaction of his district

would be strongly unfavorable. When adoption of new equipment or practices is contemplated, they are tried out on pilot Ranger districts, and the evaluations by the Rangers play a large part in the decisions to adopt, modify, or reject the machinery or procedures. It would be an exaggeration to say that the Rangers are consulted about *every* decision affecting the management of their districts, but there can be no question that consultation on many matters of concern to them is common enough to lend credibility to the impression that the Rangers participate actively in the formation of administrative policy for national forest administration. Nor do they necessarily wait to be asked for their opinions; they not infrequently take the initiative and urge their ideas upon their supervisors and other superiors.

Conferences for budgetary, policy, or training purposes afford additional opportunities for field officers to impress their concepts on their superiors. When Rangers assemble to work out financial plans with their supervisors and the supervisors' staffs, they come with proposals of their own with regard to their programs for the fiscal period, and they bargain with each other and with their superiors to get as close to their objectives as they can. When district programs are coordinated to mesh with forest policy, forest policy is often adjusted to fit district needs as the Rangers see them. At training conference discussions and seminars, Rangers do not hesitate to point out defects in prevailing policies and to suggest the remedies they favor. Theoretically, all of this could be suppressed. Fiscal and program plans could be arbitrarily decided by the higher offices and simply transmitted to the field for execution. Training conferences could be confined to discussions of how promulgated decisions should be implemented rather than being permitted to range over assessments of the decisions. But this is not the way the Forest Service operates. In part, the leaders may invite participation by field men to ensure the practicability of the decisions the agency reaches; in part they may do it to ensure a minimum of opposition from the field. Whatever the motives behind them, the conferences furnish field men with avenues of access to their leaders, and the field men are encouraged to use them. And they do.

Furthermore, the Rangers are told over and over again that they are the pillars on which the Forest Service rests. According to the *Forest Service Manual* itself:

The Forest Service is dedicated to the principle that resource management begins—and belongs—on the ground. It is logical, therefore, that the ranger district constitutes the backbone of the organization.

And the Chief of the agency, in a speech to the 1958 convention of the National Woolgrowers Association (who have often been critical of Forest Service grazing policy), told the assembled sheep raisers:

The man who is responsible for making the initial decisions for the management of your individual allotments [of grazing privileges] is the district ranger. He lives in your community as a neighbor; his children go to the same schools as yours do. You can be sure that he would not propose livestock reductions that sometimes lead to bitter controversy if he were not thoroughly convinced this action is necessary. . .

We have often heard it said that the rangers and supervisors are good guys but that they are merely doing what they are told to do by some bureaucrat in Washington. It would be utterly impossible for the small staff we have in Washington to be sufficiently familiar with conditions on all of the national forests to make or even to suggest what specific decisions should be made as to the management of individual allotments. Of necessity we have had to delegate responsibility and authority to the men on the ground. We, in Washington, establish general policies and procedures. We make periodic checks and inspections to determine how well the policies and procedures are being carried out, but the responsibility for making the decisions and the authority to carry them out has been delegated to the men on the forests and ranger districts.

Lest it be thought he was trying to evade his own responsibilities, the Chief added:

In the final analysis I am responsible for the action of all the members of the Forest Service. Although we delegate responsibility and authority all the way down the line, I cannot shift the responsibility for the work of the Forest Service to anyone else's shoulders. You might say I 'share' my responsibilities with the regional foresters, forest supervisors, and rangers, but in sharing it I do not escape any of the responsibility for what happens.

Skeptics might argue the speech was a smoke-screen, although it is not so regarded in the Service. But even a skeptic cannot help but be impressed with the fact that the field men are so visible and respected in their communities that the Chief himself—whether engaged in a maneuver to relieve his office of pressure or sincerely depicting the realities of decision-making in his bureau—sometimes takes refuge behind them. It is persuasive evidence that they make important decisions in the Forest Service, and play significant roles in the administration of the agency. The speech was circulated to all the members of the Service on national forests in grazing regions.

Actually, the field men do not seem to need convincing on this point. If anything, it would appear difficult to *alter* their convictions about it. For their day-to-day experience has already persuaded them that all higher headquarters are heavily dependent on them—not only for executing policy pronouncements, but in formulating them as well. Again and again, the researcher is told by officers in the field that they do the bulk of the work even though others sign the papers, and their superiors freely acknowledge this dependency. True, Rangers can complete only a few transactions, and must submit most to higher offices for completion; true, their work is reviewed, and their suggestions often modified or rejected; true, they are inspected, and inspectors check in the woods as well as in the office; true, they are subject to a battery of controls from above. But they know their districts more intimately than any of their superiors. They do the leg work on which Service assessments of the capacity of the land are based. They draw up the plans from which production quotas and targets are derived. They furnish the data for statistical analyses. They plan sales, and make findings and recommendations on which issuance or denial of permits depends. They do the fundamental work for land exchange, though final action depends on a Cabinet-level commission. In short, leadership decisions about what the Forest Service can and should do rest in the last analysis on what the field men tell the leaders. Even the workload calculations so central to budgeting are computed from observations made on sample Ranger districts, and evaluations of equipment come from Ranger experience with each piece of apparatus. The factual premises on which policy decisions are based are furnished in large measure by field officers. They do not have to be told this is the case; they believe it already. Whether or not the Rangers magnify their influence—and it is by no means clear that they do—their belief in their influence is apparently genuine and widespread. That Rangers participate actively and significantly in the running of the Forest Service is taken for granted.

It does not seem likely that all the types and evidences of field participation in agency decisions were deliberately instituted or adduced to create the feeling of identification with job and organization that social psychologists say is linked with a sense of participation. Rather, the various kinds of consultation probably grew out of the nature of resource management problems. But it makes little difference for this study whether the practice was designed to enhance the sense of participation or was simply the incidental fruit of the pursuit of other objectives. The fact is, field officers *do* participate, and to a degree they seem to believe is significant. Thus, they come to identify themselves with the Forest Service and its decisions.

### The Field Man in the Community

People's concepts of themselves and of their places in society reflect to a large extent the way others act toward them and react to them. Each individual's image of himself—his picture of who he is, what he is, where he belongs, how he should behave—is determined partly by the way it appears to him *others* picture him. How others see him, and what they expect, is indicated by cues from the environment:

> An individual identifies himself with and regards as a part of himself the particular constellation of values he learns from his environment. On the basis of this learning the individual defines his own role or status; he learns what group or groups *he* belongs to; what other groups are regarded as "higher" or "lower" than his own; what groups are to be regarded as enemies, antagonists, or competitors; what as allies, helpers, or friends.[25]

The cues that come to Rangers from their environments tend to identify them with the Forest Service. Many of these, of course, come from their superiors, coequals, and subordinates in the organization. Many, however, come from the people outside—from their friends and neighbors, their business associates, their clienteles. When a Ranger takes over a new district, he is generally invited promptly to join local civic and community organizations—partly because his position as manager of large properties automatically makes him a person of some standing in most localities, partly because the Forest Service is always "represented" in such associations. It is with the Rangers that loggers, ranchers, picnickers, and permittees of all kinds do business—both in negotiating agreements with the Forest Service, and when the agreements are supervised. The Rangers are therefore shown considerable deference. The Rangers are cast in the role of law-enforcement officers when trespasses occur; to violators, they often appear, and are treated, as figures of authority. Men engaged for emergency fire fighting see them as fire bosses in full charge of complicated and dangerous operations. They appear before school and college groups, associations of young people (4-H Clubs, Future Farmers of America, etc.), garden clubs, hunting and fishing clubs, and similar groups in fulfillment of their information and education responsibilities (especially for fire prevention purposes). To many local residents, they are employers who provide seasonal employment. In business circles, they appear as executives managing tens—even hundreds—of thousands of acres of valuable land worth millions of dollars and doing thousands of dollars worth of business every year. For most people, in short, they stand for the Forest Service; indeed, they personify the Forest Service. The role is thrust upon them.

Since the way men think of themselves is shaped partly by the way others demonstrate they think of them, and since Rangers are reminded over and over again that they are viewed as representatives and spokesmen of the Forest Service, it stands to reason that they come to identify themselves with the Forest Service. Not only is their role defined for them by the agency; the definition is reinforced by the community. Even the tendency of local populaces to emphasize the personal rather than the official attributes of the Rangers as they are assimilated into localities is counterbalanced to a degree by the rapidity of transfer; from the point of view of the people in a given area, individuals come and go, but there is always the district Ranger of the Forest Service. Eventually, this is how the Rangers see themselves—as parts of the organization rather than simply as individuals.

## Public Relations

In addition to the information and education activities of forest officers in the field, the Forest Service conducts a systematic public relations campaign from its Washington and regional offices. Speakers are sent to meetings, films and film strips are prepared and made available to interested groups, publicity releases are prepared for the mass media of communication, public reports are widely distributed, pamphlets and leaflets about the Service are printed by the Government Printing Office and distributed by the Department of Agriculture and the Superintendent of Documents as part of the government's general information program. The National Advertising Council, as a public service, cooperates with the Forest Service in pressing a campaign against forest fires (using "Smokey Bear" as a symbol). The public relations effort is on a large scale, systematic, and continuous.

Actually, the principal purposes of the public relations program are to acquaint the public with the work of the Forest Service, to make the public fire-conscious and thereby to reduce the incidence of man-caused fires, and, to a lesser extent, to facilitate recruiting of personnel. But the effects are more far-reaching. In the first place, it counters the propaganda of Forest Service critics; by presenting its case as widely as possible, the Service builds grass-roots support for its policies, or, at least, neutralizes the opposition that might develop if the attacks went unanswered. Generally, Congressional attitudes more or less reflect their constituencies' attitudes; this means that Congressmen under pressure from interest groups seeking heavier use of the national forests than the Forest Service deems safe are subjected to counterpressures from the friends the agency has won in their constituencies, and that Congressmen from industrial states having few or no national forests (and who might therefore be indifferent to the forestry program) will often display a friendly concern for the Service. Moreover, the public-relations materials acquaint many users of the national forests with the objectives of the Service, and may reduce somewhat the opposition with which field men must cope.

In the second place, these materials are sent to the members of the agency, providing them with arguments for its programs and policies, reminding them of its purposes and methods, keeping them informed of its problems and the approved solutions, offsetting the effects of criticism and hostile reporting, and reinforcing their dedication to the Service and its activities. The public-relations campaign also creates both inside and outside of the Forest Service an image of the Service as the uncompromising champion of the public interest and welfare, as a defender of public property against spoliation by powerful but selfish special interests, an image that builds up the pride of men associated with it and elevates their personal prestige along with its own.

Public relations is designed to reduce resistance from outside the Service, win support when possible, and counteract centrifugal tendencies that might induce field men to deviate from promulgated policy. It is intended to affect the external forces acting *on* the Rangers while it strengthens *"inside"* them, by heightening their identification with the organization, tendencies toward conforming with agency decisions. It is not always and everywhere completely successful,[26] but it seems to have been quite effective generally.

### The Internalization of Forest Service Perceptions, Values, and Premises of Action

Much that happens to a professional forester in the Forest Service thus tends to tighten the links binding him to the organization. His experiences and his environment gradually infuse into him a view of the world and a hierarchy of preferences coinciding with those of his colleagues. They tie him to his fellows, to the agency. They engender a "militant and corporate spirit," an organized "self-consciousness,"[27] dedication to the organization and its objectives,[28] and a fierce pride in the Service. They practically merge the individual's identity with the identity of the organization; the organization is as much a part of the members as they are of it. At least some of the practices described above were probably initiated with this in mind, but a number were apparently adopted for other reasons and contributed to this result more or less accidentally. Still, whatever the purposes, one outcome of the practices is that field officers (among others) make their administrative decisions in terms of the consequences for the Forest Service, and in terms of criteria the leaders of the Forest Service wish them to employ.

# The Result: Voluntary Conformity

Forest officers are selected in a fashion that winnows out many of the men who probably lack the inherent predisposition to conform to the preformed decisions of the Forest Service, and that guarantees at least a minimum level of technical competence. Their competence is broadened and deepened by post-entry training, both in-service and outside, and by placement, transfer, and promotion policies; the methods of improving technical skill also intensify the predisposition to conform. The predisposition is strengthened by generating identification with the agency (which at the same time adds to understanding of the announced agency objectives). As a consequence, officers of the Forest Service conform to agency decisions not simply because they have to, but because they want to. And they can because they have been equipped to do so.

"Wanting" to conform is used here not to mean an abstract desire to be obedient the way a child wants to be "good" but not to do any of the things that being good means to his parents. Rather, it is employed to mean wishing to do as a matter of personal preference the things that happen to be required. It is in *this* sense Forest Service personnel want to conform. Often, confronted by a situation in the field, there is a course of action they would "instinctively" like to follow, that seems "clearly" to be the "best" and "proper" one; a good deal of the time, this "happens" to be the action prescribed by the Service. That is, they are not consciously "conforming"; they are merely doing what is "right."[29] Inevitably, there is little consciousness on their part of the deliberate search for the appropriate "instincts" by the leaders of the Forest Service, and of the deliberate efforts to cultivate these and weed out others.

Indeed, even when men are overruled—when their "instincts" do not move them in the same directions as their superiors—their adherence to the provisions of the higher decision comes in a sense from inside themselves. They rarely persist in opposition after judgment has been rendered, or engage in administrative sabotage, or carry appeals to higher levels. In part, of course, this obedience is based on the risks of such action.[30] In addition, however, it rests on the widely expressed sentiment that "there's no other way to run a big organization." They value the organization more than they value getting their own way; they therefore carry out directives they opposed, because doing so is "necessary" and "right" —and, though they do not seem to be aware of it, because this feeling is carefully nurtured by the organization.

The thrust toward behaving in accordance with the preformed decisions issued by the Forest Service is thus not imposed on a reluctant and resistant body of men; it is as much internal as external. But the internal forces are not left wholly to chance; although some have developed incidentally, they are also encouraged and even planted.

This completes the inventory of methods by which the Forest Service manages to integrate the organization for national forest administration in spite of the awesome tendencies toward fragmentation to which that organization is heir. But, in order to make the presentation wieldy and clear, the categories of influences on the administrative behavior of district Rangers have been treated as though they were independent of each other. In fact, of course, they cannot be isolated from one another. The interplay among the influences—among the centrifugal and the integrative, the external and the designed and the fortuitous—is the subject of the next, and concluding, chapter. Here, the elements of the organization, heretofore artificially separated for examination, are reassembled and portrayed in their "natural" state.

# Notes

1. G. Pinchot, *Breaking New Ground* (New York: Harcourt, Brace and Co., 1947), p. 64.

2. "From Gifford Pinchot to Students of Forestry at Shrivenham American University," *Journal of Forestry,* Vol. 45, No. 5 (May 1947), p. 353.

3. *Careers in Forestry,* Forest Service, Miscellaneous Publication No. 249, U.S. Department of Agriculture (Revised August, 1955), pp. 3–4.

4. *Proceedings of the Society of American Foresters, 1947* (Washington, D. C.: Society of American Foresters, 1948), p. 45.

5. H. Clepper, "Forestry Education in America," *Journal of Forestry,* Vol. 54, No. 7 (July, 1956),

pp. 455–57; G. D. Marckworth, "Statistics from Schools of Forestry for 1957: Degrees Granted and Enrollments," *Journal of Forestry,* Vol. 56, No. 2 (February, 1958), pp. 129–35. See also, "Colleges and Universities in the United States Offering Instruction in Forestry (November 1, 1957)," compiled by the Society of American Foresters.

6. A few professional foresters come in through examinations for subprofessional positions (Forestry Aid and Fire Control Aid) and become eligible for promotion to professional grades when they complete their period of probation.

7. This is a standard practice in federal entrance-examination scoring.

8. "Traditionally the Forest Service has been able to hire the cream of the graduating class of foresters each year through most of the first half of this century. Graduate foresters competed for federal jobs. Today the Forest Service no longer enjoys an employer's market, indeed this situation has now changed to the point that the Service gets about 20% of the forestry school graduates. Private industry, the state forestry departments and other federal agencies are all in the market for foresters. The result has been a deficiency in foresters for the Forest Service. Beginning in 1954, the Service was unable to fill all vacancies. . . ." W. A. Elkins, *Professional Manpower for the Forest Service* (mimeographed by the Forest Service, 1957). The acute shortage of foresters for the Forest Service was somewhat relieved by the recession of 1958, during which private industry absorbed a smaller proportion of the graduating classes of the schools of forestry than it had for several previous years. But the basic problem—the willingness of industry to pay much better salaries for the ablest young foresters—continues to weaken the competitive recruiting position of the Service in terms of both quality and quantity.

9. Memorandum from the Chief, "Questions on Forest Regulations," April 1, 1946.

10. C. K. Lyman (Assistant Regional Forester, Region Seven), "Managerial Development in the U.S. Forest Service," unpublished manuscript.

11. Of those interviewed, one had taken a Master's degree in forestry and one a course of training in Public Administration at the Littauer School at Harvard. It is probably more than a coincidence that both have moved ahead rapidly and are apparently marked for continued rapid advance.

12. The term "identification" is used here in the sense in which it is employed by H. A. Simon, *Administrative Behavior* (New York: The Macmillan Company, 1947, 1957), p. 205: "A person identifies himself with a group when, in making a decision, he

evaluates the several alternatives of choice in terms of their consequences for the specified group."

13. *Ibid.*, p. 103.

14. One forest supervisor reported he thought he might have been brought up on charges of insubordination if he refused to move. Actually, this seems most unlikely, but this expression of concern by a high-ranking officer suggests how much importance is attached to transfer.

15. And, at times, of their subordinates. One non-professional employee who had served the Forest Service for almost thirty years on one district worked under a total of thirteen Rangers in that period. He took a paternal interest in the young men who supervised him, and the Ranger under whom he was serving at the time of the interviews for this study confessed his great dependence on the older man. "My chief job," the employee said, "is breaking in Rangers," a job he apparently performed proudly, gently, and with affection for those he helped.

16. In many organizations, transfer is employed as a sanction, too. Choice assignments go to the men who fit the organization patterns, undesirable ones to those who depart from the preferred patterns, and to newcomers. (The policeman detailed to the "sticks" is a familiar case in point.) No evidence of this strategy was found in the Forest Service in the course of this study, nor did any of the men interviewed at any level seem to consider this a likely penalty. If it is used at all, it is apparently used sparingly. (However, see footnote 14 above.)

17. Inter-regional transfers are not uncommon, but they are far less frequent than intra-regional shifts.

18. Indeed, every Chief since Gifford Pinchot has come from inside the Service with but one exception, and even he had had extensive Forest Service experience when he was brought back under the New Deal to reorganize the bureau.

19. "The average grade 9 Forester is 41 years old and reached his present grade in 8 years. For GS-11 the same statistic is 44 years of age and 15 years of service to reach it; for GS-12, the age is 48 and elapsed time from entry to present grade is 22 years; and for GS-13, age 50, elapsed time is 23 years." W. A. Elkins, *op. cit.*, p. 5.

20. One regional forester commented: "We would simply like to add a thought or two [here] which we believe has considerable to do with a personnel placement. The first one is that nearly all Forest Service personnel agree that Ranger and Supervisor jobs are the most desirable in the Service because of the great personal satisfaction. In these jobs, the incumbents are line officers in charge of a unit area and can see the accomplishments much more concretely. The second thought is that many of the personnel through their own personal desires to remain Rangers or Supervisors often have considerable effect on what their careers become." Some men, then, prefer to remain in the field rather than advance to positions more remote from the woods. However, from the writer's discussions with forest officers, this would not seem to be the general attitude among men in the earlier stages of their career. Moreover, it appears likely that those who elect to stay in the field do not find onerous the patterns of behavior they are required to observe. Thirdly, as noted above, even those unconcerned about promotion unconsciously adopt the outlook and characteristics of the organizational culture in which they are immersed. Finally, Rangers who demonstrate they cannot or will not observe the requirements of the organization *may* be shifted to positions of less discretion and responsibility. Hence, the preference of some men for field assignments does not by any means nullify the process of organizational acculturation described here.

21. For example, in a report on a General Integrating Inspection of one Ranger district, a forest supervisor wrote in 1957: "Another item believed worthy of comment is the use of the uniform. With an Assistant Ranger position permanently assigned to the District, more stress is needed on the proper use of the uniform. During the past ten years or so many of the field personnel have gone to 'work clothes' and have neglected to wear the 'greens.' This situation should be corrected in accordance with manual guide lines, and the Assistant Rangers in particular should have the proper example set by their immediate superiors."

22. See J. M. Gaus and L. O. Wolcott, *Public Administration and the Department of Agriculture* (Chicago: Public Administration Service, 1940), pp. 265–66.

23. See, for example, G. W. Allport, "The Psychology of Identification," in S. D. Hoslett (ed.), *Human Factors in Management* (New York: Harper & Bros., 1946, First Edition): "We are learning some of the conditions in which reactivity [i.e., "rebellion against authority, . . . disaffection of all sorts"] does decline. . . . Opportunities for consultation on personal problems are, somewhat surprisingly, found to be important. And as members of S.P.S.S.I. [Society for the Psychological Study of Social Issues] have shown, group decision, open discussion, and the retraining of leaders in accordance with democratic standards yield remarkable results. One of Lewin's discoveries in this connection is especially revealing. People who dislike a certain food are resistant to pressure put upon

them in the form of persuasion and request; but when the individual himself as a member of a group votes, after discussion, to alter his food habits, his eagerness to reach his goal is independent of his personal like or dislike. In other words, a person ceases to be reactive and contrary in respect to a desirable course of conduct only when he himself has had a hand in declaring such a course of conduct to be desirable." (P. 259) See also M. Sherif and H. Cantril, *The Psychology of Ego-Involvements* (New York: John Wiley & Sons, 1947), pp. 369–71.

24. The members of the Service are invited to regard inspections as a co-operative rather than an investigatory procedure; they are asked to consider inspections as a means of participating, asked to do so for the explicit reason that this builds identifications. "This attitude towards sharing responsibility," said the Chief in a letter (February 21, 1955) to an Assistant Secretary of Agriculture, "naturally makes each man want to help the man with whom he does the sharing. This mutual-help attitude is reflected in the character and tone of inspections. We always try to recognize good work as well as to point out needed improvement. . . . The attitude is to see how together we can do a better job. I explain this partly because many people do not understand why we customarily state in inspection reports that something 'should' be done rather than say it 'shall' be done. I suppose that with us, should means shall, but we try to avoid the master-and-slave attitude that tends to weaken individual initiative and a sense of joint responsibility." The contents of the letter were reproduced, and circulated in many parts of the Forest Service.

25. M. Sherif and H. Cantril. *op. cit.*, p. 135. See also, R. Linton, *The Study of Man* (New York: D. Appleton-Century Co., 1936), Chapter VIII.

26. According to some observers, there have been "boomerang" effects. Field men who accepted the idealized image of the Forest Service were disillusioned to discover that the leadership sometimes found discretion the better part of valor and adopted strategies calculated to placate some politically powerful users of the national forests.

27. J. M. Gaus and L. O. Wolcott, *loc. cit.*

28. "Many Forest Service men are dedicated in the sense that they will fight for certain courses of action, and against others, almost without regard to the cost in terms of wear and tear upon their own emotional systems or in terms of public criticism and opposition." From a letter to the author from M. Clawson, former head of the Bureau of Land Management.

29. For example, in one region a number of years ago, travel and expense allowances were scaled according to the grades of the personnel involved. Thus, though a superior and a subordinate working together away from their homes might be in close association, the former received a larger reimbursement. Asked whether it might not be reasonable to eliminate, or at least reduce, the rather substantial differential, a subordinate's reply was emphatically negative: "Why, that wouldn't be right," he said. "When I go out cruising timber, say, and I have to spend the night out, I can go to a tourist cabin or a cheap hotel to get a place to sleep, and I can eat in local diners. But the supervisor can't do that. He has to keep up a front. He meets important people, and he can't get along the way I do. Why even the Ranger who works out in the woods with us a lot of the time can't always do the way the rest of us fellows do; it costs him more to do things the way he has to, so why shouldn't he get more?" The fact that other agencies did not draw a distinction by grade did not impress him; the differential seemed "proper" to him and offended neither his sense of abstract equalitarian justice nor of material self-interest. (There were complaints about linking the differential to rank rather than expenses, but few about the appropriateness of some kind of differential. Eventually, however, the differential was abolished for administrative reasons.)

30. Other factors in obedience are discussed in H. A. Simon, D. W. Smithburg, and V. A. Thompson, *Public Administration* (New York: Alfred A. Knopf, 1950), pp. 188–201.

# IV

# Equal Employment Opportunity and Representation

In the century following the Pendleton Act, no single development did more to reshape thinking about public personnel administration than the civil rights movement of the 1960s.[1] The movement rocketed issues of social equity into the center of the personnel-policy sphere. It fueled doubt about whether practices presumed to serve merit ideals in fact did so (written examinations, for example). The upheaval also touched employee rights. The "last-hired first-fired" decision rule embedded in the concept of seniority meant that minorities and women often bore the brunt of retrenchment. The movement questioned whether this was fair. Ferment over civil rights also intersected with issues of political responsiveness. Black mayors coming to power in many cities sought to ensure greater responsiveness to their directives by increasing the degree to which members of their own race occupied key positions in the bureaucracy. Moreover, the extent to which administrative agencies succeeded in hiring more minorities or women often became a barometer by which key groups in the community gauged government concern for their interests. The movement also possessed implications for agency competence. It brought government the benefits of a rich, relatively untapped labor pool thereby enhancing government capacity. Yet by requiring more attention to be focused on the validation of selection processes and special recruitment plans, it frequently added to the financial costs of government as well. In these and countless other ways, the civil rights movement sent waves and ripples through public personnel administration.

Published in 1967, Samuel Krislov's *The Negro in Federal Employment* was a pacesetter in providing conceptual and historical perspective on the issues raised by the civil rights movement. As the selection printed here indicates, Krislov saw the link between broader political questions of representative bureaucracy and of equal employment opportunity. Narrowly defined, the principle of equal employment opportunity insists that individuals not suffer from adverse discrimination in personnel decisions because of such attributes as age, race, sex, religion, or certain physical handicaps. Commitment to representative bureaucracy goes beyond this. It asserts that governments should seek out individuals with certain attributes and qualities for representation in the ranks of administrative agencies.

In considering the quest for social equity, the link between demographic and substantive representation demands scrutiny. Consider, for example, minority representation. Demographic representation refers to the sheer presence of some number of minorities at various levels of the bureaucracy (e.g., 20 percent of the police captains in city X are minority). In contrast, substantive representation requires minority civil servants to act on behalf of their racial group. Demographic representation at times leads to substantive representation. The link between the two forms becomes more likely when minority civil servants deal with issues that have patent ramifications for their counterparts in society. For instance, minority administrators may be especially committed to weeding out discrimination against clients based on race. In many other instances, however, little connection exists between demographic and substantive variants. Agency socialization and incentive structures often homogenize the views of minority and white employees. Moreover, the agency may deal with many issues that do not appear to have particular consequences for the minority community.[2]

Of course, demographic representation looms large in importance even if it does not invariably usher in its substantive counterpart. Demographic representation provides concrete social and economic benefits—adequately paying jobs with reasonable employment security and opportunity for advancement. It may come to symbolize government sensitivity to the minority community. By so doing it can bolster the legitimacy of government authority among minorities and thereby enhance government's capacity to diagnose problems, formulate coherent policy, and implement programs.

While issues of representative bureaucracy frequently underpin discussions of social equity and personnel administration, the official language of government policy tends to emphasize equal employment opportunity. The selection from Krislov provides an excellent overview of the pulling and hauling that characterized the politics of equal employment opportunity from the early 1940s to the passage of the Civil Rights Act of 1964 (the Civil Rights Act). Title VII of the Civil Rights Act, which appears in this volume, constitutes a major watershed for public administration. It defined as "unlawful" any action by an employer to "refuse to hire or to discharge any individual, or otherwise to discriminate against any individual with respect to his compensation, terms, conditions, or privileges of employment, because of such individual's race, color, religion, sex, or national origin...." Title VII also established an enforcement apparatus under the Equal Employment Opportunity Commission (EEOC). While far from a juggernaut, the EEOC clearly possessed more enforcement muscle than its predecessors. Federal lawmakers did not place state and local government under the Civil Rights Act's jurisdiction until 1972; federal agencies did not come under the EEOC's purview until 1978. Nonetheless, the passage of the law in 1964 immediately pushed social equity up the list of priorities for public personnel officials.

## Minorities: *Griggs* Lays the Foundation

Title VII also paved the way for one of the major Supreme Court decisions of the twentieth century, *Griggs* v. *Duke Power Company* (reprinted here). In a unanimous decision[3] with Justice Burger writing for the majority, the court essentially held that certain forms of institutional as well as overt discrimination violated the 1964 Civil Rights Act. Overt discrimination involves a conscious effort by an employer to discriminate against an individual because of race, sex, or other protected attribute. Institutional discrimination, in contrast, entails no conscious effort to discriminate. Rather, it involves the use of credentials, tests, or other selection criteria that have the effect of screening out the legally protected group. In *Griggs* the Supreme Court explicitly asserted that ". . .absence of discriminatory intent does not redeem employment procedures or testing mechanisms that operate as 'built-in headwinds' for minority groups and are unrelated to measuring job capability." The Court ruled that "Congress directed the thrust of the Act to the consequences of employment practices, not simply the motivation." It acknowledged that "diplomas and tests are useful servants" but that Congress "has mandated the commonsense proposition that they are not to become masters of reality." In the wake of the *Griggs* decision, personnel directors working in agencies with inadequate minority representation faced greater pressure to validate their selection mechanisms (i.e., prove that they predicted competence). If the directors failed to do so, they risked being sued by minority advocates.

The *Griggs* decision did not mean that the Supreme Court invariably sided with the most stringent validation standards in cases where minorities failed to obtain representation. Consider, for example, *Washington* v. *Davis* (1976). The case involved a qualifying examination that the District of Columbia's Metropolitan Police Department had administered to applicants for the position of police officer. A disproportionately large number of black applicants had failed the examination. A lower court ruled that the selection process violated the equal protection clause of the Constitution. In overturning the judgment of the lower body, the Supreme Court deconstitutionalized the case claiming that Title VII applied rather than the equal protection clause. The court also found that the District had done enough to validate the test even though the validation procedure related the selection test scores of applicants to their subsequent performance in the police-training program, rather than their actual performance on the job. In deciding against the minority plaintiffs, the court slightly eased pressure on state and local governments by accepting less stringent standards of validation.[4]

The 1970s and 1980s saw the Supreme Court issue several other rulings directly related to affirmative action for racial minorities. Until 1989, these rulings generally reflected continuity in policy. None of the Court decisions represented the bold step toward social equity embodied in *Griggs*. But neither did they feature a significant gutting of this commitment. Two Court decisions help illustrate the balance struck.

In *Firefighters* v. *Stotts* (1984), the Supreme Court reviewed a decision of a federal district court that had enjoined the city of Memphis from applying its last-hired-first-fired seniority policy because of its discriminatory impact. In 1980, the city of Memphis had entered into a consent decree to remedy past discrimination in the Fire Department. Among other things, this decree called for an interim hiring goal whereby the department would annually fill 50 percent of the job vacancies in the department with qualified black applicants. In May 1981, however, a projected budget deficit prompted the city to lay off workers. Subsequently, the federal District Court ruled that, in keeping with its earlier decree, black workers should not be laid off even if they had less seniority than their white coworkers. The federal Court of Appeals for the Sixth District subsequently affirmed the decision. Memphis city officials and the firefighters union appealed the decision to the Supreme Court. In a judgment that reaffirmed the core value of employee rights over social equity, the Court sided with the city and firefighters union. In reaching this decision, the Supreme Court cited Section 703(h) of Title VII, which provides that "it shall not be an unlawful employment practice for an employer to apply different...terms, conditions, or privileges of employment pursuant to a bona fide seniority...system...provided that such differences are not the result of an intention to discriminate because of race."[5]

Racial quotas also attracted considerable attention during the 1980s in part because of the open opposition of the Reagan Administration to their use. Courts had ordered such quotas as a part of remedial actions (i.e., in cases where they found that employers had practiced discrimination in clear violation of the Civil Rights Act). Despite the challenge by the Reagan Administration, the Supreme Court in *United States* v. *Paradise* (1987) reaffirmed the use of this remedy. The case involved a long-standing effort to alleviate the effects of overt racial discrimination in the Alabama Department of Public Safety. Since the early 1970s, the department had dragged its feet in complying with a court order to hire more minorities. By the 1980s, the focus had shifted to the promotion of minorities in the department. After a series of complex moves and countermoves, a district court in 1983 ruled that "for a period of time" at least 50 percent of the promotions to corporal in the Alabama Department of Public Safety had to be awarded to black troopers if qualified black candidates were available. The U.S. Justice Department promptly challenged the ruling on grounds that the "race-conscious relief" ordered by the court violated the Equal Protection Clause of the Fourteenth Amendment to the Constitution. In a five to four ruling, however, the Supreme Court upheld the lower court's decision to order the promotion remedy.[6]

The theme of continuity evident in the years following *Griggs* suddenly became much less applicable in 1989. In June of that year, the Supreme Court announced three decisions, all of which made it more difficult for minorities to press their cause successfully in federal courts.[7] No one decision dealt a death blow to affirmative action. Certainly, none overturned *Griggs*. But taken as a whole, the rulings sent a signal that the Supreme Court would be looking for reasons not to side with minority plaintiffs in equal employment cases. Each ruling garnered the support of the same five justices—Kennedy, O'Connor, Rehnquist, Scalia, and White. Since President Reagan had appointed three of these justices, many observers saw these decisions as heralding Reagan's triumph in bringing his "conservative revolution" to the highest court in the land.

More specifically, two thrusts of the Supreme Court rulings deserve note. First, and most important, the Court made the use of racial targets or quotas as remedies for past discrimination much more open to challenge by white employees who saw themselves as adversely affected.[8] In a case involving the city of Birmingham, Alabama, and the Jefferson County Personnel Board, the Supreme Court affirmed an appeals court ruling that granted white firefighters the right to challenge in court a consent decree entered into by their employer and minority plaintiffs. This decree had sought to remedy past discriminatory practices via a plan that included goals for hiring and promoting blacks as firefighters. By heightening the risk that white employees would drag their employer into court for signing such a decree, the Supreme Court reduced the likelihood that employers would agree to such remedies in the future.

Second, the Supreme Court restricted the grounds on which minority plaintiffs could claim a prima facie case of disparate impact. The *Griggs* decision meant that hiring procedures could be attacked even if the employer did not intend to discriminate against racial minorities. By demonstrating that personnel procedures disproportionately worked against the success of minorities in obtaining certain jobs (i.e., had disparate impact), minority advocates could compel employers either to demonstrate the validity of these procedures or provide a suitable remedy to minorities. Once minority advocates can show disparate impact, the burden of proof shifts to the employer. Hence, to the degree that the Court makes it harder to prove that disparate impact exists, it becomes more costly and difficult for minority plaintiffs to prevail. In *Wards Cove Packing Company* v. *Frank Atonio,* the Supreme Court ruled that disparate impact could *not* be demonstrated purely by statistics showing that minorities held a high percentage of unskilled jobs and a low percentage of skilled ones in the same company. Writing for the majority, Justice White noted that the proper comparison was generally between the racial composition of those holding a particular job and the racial composition of qualified individuals in the relevant labor market. More fundamentally, he emphasized:[9]

> A Title VII plaintiff does not make out a case of disparate impact simply by showing that, 'at the bottom line,' there is racial imbalance in the work force. As a general matter, a plaintiff must demonstrate that it is the application of a specific or particular employment practice that has created the disparate impact under attack.

In this way, the Court shifted more of the burden of proof to minority advocates.

## Women in Government

A second major theme in the quest for social equity during the 1960s, 1970s and 1980s involved the rights of women. If one considers the growing number of females in the workplace, this development hardly seems surprising. In 1950, fewer than 35 percent of American women worked outside of the home. By 1970, this figure had grown to 43 percent and by 1986 to 55 percent. The figures on married women with children provide even more powerful testimony to the feminization of the work force. In 1960, only 19 percent of women with children under age six were in the labor force; by 1987, this figure had grown to 57 percent. These trends show no signs of reversal.[10]

Writing in the mid-1970s, Debra Stewart in an article reprinted here succinctly and perceptively captured many of the issues that concern women employed by government. As Stewart documents, women have succeeded in obtaining substantial numbers of public jobs. The problems that remain have to do with the limited movement of women into top executive positions and the personal price they must pay to accomplish that end. In Stewart's view, role prejudice deeply rooted in the nature of career systems is a major impediment. The pressure for the male career to be the dominant one and for the wife to serve more fully as the "supporter, the comforter, the child rearer, the housekeeper, and the entertainer" remains strong. In her view, "Only women who enjoy the services of a full-time house-husband will start out in the race on equal footing with their male colleagues." In seeking improvement for women, she challenges "the desirability of a change strategy which accepts as given a requirement that women desirous of 'public' success give up family life. . . ." In her view career systems free of role prejudice must recognize "employees as whole people." She suggests several strategies for fostering this including government support for child care.

Policy makers in the courts and legislatures also paid attention to the concerns of women. Many of the most salient court cases, such as *Griggs,* sprang from action by minority plaintiffs. But issues involving the rights of women also attracted attention. In this regard, the Supreme Court's ruling in *Johnson* v. *Transportation Agency* in 1987 stands out sufficiently to justify its selection for this volume. The case stemmed from an affirmative action plan adopted by the Transportation Agency of Santa Clara County, California, in 1978. Among other things, the plan allowed for consideration of gender in making promotions to positions in which women had traditionally been under-represented. The Transportation Agency subsequently announced a vacancy for the pro-motional position of road dispatcher. At the time of the vacancy no woman had ever occupied a dispatcher job or any of the 238 positions in the more general classification series, Skilled Craft Worker, of which this position was a part. Twelve county employees applied for the promotion including Diane Joyce and Paul Johnson. Ultimately the selec-tion process led to seven candidates being certified as eligible for the position including Joyce and Johnson. Although Joyce scored two points lower than Johnson, the Director of the Transportation Agency promoted her. Johnson subsequently sued on grounds that the choice violated his rights under Title VII of the Civil Rights Act. In rejecting the suit, the Supreme Court found that, among other things, the flexible and moderate nature of the agency's affirmative action plan made it permissible to take Joyce's sex into account as one factor in her promotion.

Other policy questions involving women's employment rights also loomed large in the 1980s. Advocates for women became concerned that disparities between male and female salaries would not be addressed if they only strove to ensure that men and women doing the same work received the same pay (i.e., "equal pay for equal work"). Instead they espoused "comparable worth" by arguing that certain occupations dominated by women (e.g., librarians) were undervalued relative to occupations more heavily populated by males. They argued for careful analysis of the tasks and levels of responsibility involved in different occupations so that the pay for "feminine" jobs would become more similar to that of comparable occupations dominated by males. Some state and local jurisdic-tions adopted policies designed to accomplish this end. By the late 1980s, however, federal courts in general and the Supreme Court in particular had not decisively supported com-parable worth as a principle.

The courts did more to fashion policy with respect to sexual harassment. In 1980, the EEOC promulgated guidelines reaffirming that sexual harassment constituted one form of sex discrimination under Title VII of the Civil Rights Act. Behaviors deemed inappropriate in this regard included unwelcome sexual advances, requests for sexual favors, and other verbal or physical conduct of a sexual nature. Drawing on the guidelines, the Supreme Court in *Meritor Savings Bank* v. *Vinson* (1986) set forth three major prin-ciples. First, a female employee could succeed in establishing that a Title VII violation had occurred by proving that harassment based on sex had created a hostile or abusive work environment. She did not necessarily need to show that the environment created an adverse economic impact on her personally. Second, the fact that a woman submitted to the sexual overtures of a supervisor voluntarily was not necessarily a defense for employers under Title VII. In the words of the majority opinion: "The correct inquiry is whether respondent by her conduct indicated that the alleged sexual advances were unwelcome, not whether her actual participation in sexual intercourse was voluntary." Third, employers would not automatically be liable in cases where supervisors sexually harassed employees.[11]

## Retreat or Progress?

Court rulings sympathetic to female and minority rights could well become less common in the 1990s. The Supreme Court rulings of 1989 provide only part of the foundation for this prediction. By the end of his second term, Reagan had appointed approximately half of all the federal lower court judges. Like other presidents, Reagan overwhelmingly appointed judges from his own party. Unlike other presidents, Reagan presided over "the most rigorously and decidedly ideological screening process ever" — one that Attorney General Meese depicted as an effort to "institutionalize the Reagan revolution."[12] These developments could further undercut remedies for past discrimination based on the imposition of gender or racially oriented targets or quotas. These appointments could slowly but steadily vitiate the force of the Supreme Court's decision in *Johnson* v. *Transportation Agency* and even *Griggs.*

Ironically, however, other trends afoot in the 1990s could counteract any tendency to retreat on issues of minority and female rights. *Opportunity 2000,* a federal report published in 1988, argued that a projected labor shortage in the decade of the 1990s would yield a situation where "the opportunity to 'mainstream' affirmative action has never been better." It concluded that employers would probably be driven to hire, retain, and reward minority and female employees out of the basic necessity to meet their needs for human capital. Thus, employers would have new incentives not to see affirmative action "as a zero-sum game in which one person's gain is another person's loss but as a vital human resources process that expands opportunities for everyone."[13]

If this scenario comes to pass, the need for public managers to hone their skills in recruiting and managing a diverse work force will grow. They will have more incentive to become part of the struggle against "unemployment in a sea of opportunity," e.g., the problem of declining labor force participation and deficiencies in basic skills among black males.[14] Special employer initiatives such as training and literacy programs, the elimination of unnecessary job requirements, and mentoring could help address these problems.

The need to recruit and retain capable women through a variety of special initiatives could also become a "competitive necessity" for employers.[15] To some degree echoing the sentiments of Stewart, *Opportunity 2000* concludes:[16]

> Unless employers and employees can find some middle ground between the competing worlds of work and family, someone is bound to pay the price: either the woman herself, in terms of stress, or the employer, in terms of productivity. Either way, both parties lose.

Hence, employer-subsidized day care, flexible work schedules, compressed work weeks, part-time scheduling, job sharing, job finding assistance for dual-career couples, and professional development programs for women may increase in appeal to employers simply because of the need to compete for human resources.

While this scenario possesses considerable plausibility, it is far from assured. It remains up for grabs as to whether public employers will fully address such issues as the under-representation of women and minorities in top policy positions. Many of the proposed initiatives cost money that governments will be hard pressed to find. Moreover, progress by minorities will depend heavily on their obtaining advanced education and skills. In this regard, a report released by the U.S. Office of Personnel Management in the late 1980s notes: "Although the Federal government has traditionally been a large employer of blacks, the increasing skill requirements of Federal jobs could cap the growth of black Federal employment unless black educational preparation, including rates of college graduation, rises."[17] In this regard, the 1980s witnessed a disturbing development—the number of black students enrolled in institutions of higher education fell by 30,000 from its 1980 high. In particular, enrollment of black males declined.[18]

Predicting exactly how interaction between court decisions, labor market forces, economic health, the decisions of elected policy makers, and other variables will affect the fortunes of minorities and women remains guesswork. One thing is far more certain, however. Issues of social equity in one form or another will continue to compete for attention in the personnel arena.

# Notes

1. While this section focuses primarily on women and minorities, the concerns of the elderly, handicapped, and Vietnam veterans also intersect with issues of social equity in the public personnel arena.

2. See, for instance, Frank J. Thompson, "Minority Groups in Public Bureaucracies: Are Passive and Active Representation Linked?" *Administration and Society* 8 (August, 1976), 201–226, and Kenneth J. Meier, *Politics and The Bureaucracy: Policymaking in the Fourth Branch of Government* (Pacific Grove, Cal.: Brooks/Cole, 1987), pp. 180–184.

3. One justice refrained from participation in the case.

4. *Washington* v. *Davis,* 96 S.Ct. 2040 (1976).

5. *Firefighters* v. *Stotts,* 104 S.Ct. 2576 (1984).

6. *United States* v. *Paradise, U.S. Supreme Court Reports,* 94 L.Ed. 2d, 1987, p. 203.

7. Two of the three cases receive attention below. The third case, among other things, narrowed the applicability of the Civil Rights Act of 1866, a law that prohibited racial discrimination in making and enforcing private contracts. See *Brenda Patterson* v. *McLean Credit Union, United States Law Week* 57 (June 13, 1989), pp. 4705–4720.

8. *Martin* v. *Wilks, United States Law Week* 57 (June 13, 1989), pp. 4616–4626. In a related case, the Supreme Court rejected a different kind of quota—one that required prime contractors with the city of Richmond, Virginia, to subcontract at least 30 percent of the dollar amount of each contract for city construction with one or more minority businesses. This rejection of quotas in part rested on the court's conclusion that the record revealed no evidence of prior discrimination by the city in awarding contracts. See *City of Richmond* v. *J.A. Croson Company, United States Law Week* 57 (January 24, 1989), pp. 4132–4158.

9. *Wards Cove Packing Company* v. *Frank Atonio, United States Law Week* 57 (June 6, 1989), p. 4587.

10. U.S. Department of Labor, *Opportunity 2000* (Washington: Government Printing Office, 1988), p. 7; U.S. Bureau of the Census, *Statistical Abstract of the United States, 1988* (Washington, D.C.: Government Printing Office, 1987), pp. 365, 374.

11. *Meritor Savings Bank* v. *Vinson,* 106 S.Ct. 2399 (1986).

12. David M. O'Brien, "The Reagan Judges: His Most Enduring Legacy," in Charles O. Jones, ed., *The Reagan Legacy: Promise and Performance* (Chatham, N.J.: Chatham House, 1988), pp. 60–62.

13. U.S. Department of Labor, *Opportunity 2000*, pp. vii, 176–177.
14. *Ibid.*, pp. 66–67.
15. *Ibid.*, p. 23.
16. *Ibid.*, p. 29.
17. U.S. Office of Personnel Management, *Civil Service 2000* (Washington, 1988), p. 19.
18. *New York Times* (February 5, 1989), pp. 1, 30.

# 21

# The Negro and
# the Federal Service
# in an Era of Change

*Samuel Krislov*

## I

For the Negro, World War II marked a turning point. This period saw the confluence of a number of forces, each of which had been gathering momentum in the immediately preceding years. The scientific historians of the future will find it difficult to disentangle them and to delineate precisely which constituted the determinative forces for progress; conversely, observers with pet theories will find it easy to discover their favorite historical motif in operation. Certainly, however, the growth of Negro economic and political power, the northern migration and urbanization of Negroes, the rise in their educational level, their development of organizational techniques, the absence of competition in the labor market, and the stimulation (by the trauma of Hitlerism) of a keener sense among all Americans of the costs of racism—all played their part. For the Negro subculture of our society, something like Rostow's postulated state of "take-off" was re-enacted. The small, painful advances in the prewar years—here employment of Negroes as elevator operators, there enrollment of a handful at a university or the banding together of a small

SOURCE: From *The Negro in Federal Employment* by Samuel Krislov. Copyright © 1967 by the University of Minnesota. Reprinted by permission. Selection has been retitled and cut, and orginally appeared as Chapter 2, "The Negro and the Federal Service in an Era of Change," pp. 28–45, and Chapter 3, "Representative Bureaucracy and Civil Rights," pp. 46–64.

group into a political organization—paved the way for a major surge when the opportunity was at hand.

Changes in perspective with regard to the civil rights movement are inevitable with the passage of time. But from the vantage point of the mid-1960's, the crucial event looms large and clear—an event that indeed never took place. The planned "March on Washington" in 1941 denoted a new stage in the development of Negro militancy—the scope and substance of demand were of a different order from any earlier effort; a new stage of Negro organization—the mounting of even the threat of the march required preparation and communication to a degree never before attempted; and a new concept of Negro strategy—the discovery was made that public pressure was a weapon available to a minority community. The plan for the march was the prototype of, a rehearsal for, the more dramatic and far-reaching efforts of the 1960's; the effect it had foreshadowed the political gains of later years. The basic ingredients of future strategy—threats of international embarrassment to the United States government and of internal disruption of the domestic establishment—were tried and found potent. In addition, the Negro leadership gained maturity and self-respect and self-knowledge.

It was in January 1941 that A. Philip Randolph, head of the Brotherhood of Sleeping Car Porters, conceived of the march as a way of demonstrating the potential power of the Negro. Faced with the position of the Roosevelt administration, certainly a friendly establishment, that no further economic and social advances for the Negro could be achieved through governmental or political means during the war crisis, Negro leaders nevertheless aggressively demanded governmental protection of the right to equal employment opportunity. To enforce this demand, Randolph came up with the idea of a march on the capital. He pushed his idea for months against the cool indifference and doubts of most of the rather conservative civil rights leaders. To a large extent, as Herbert Garfinkel has shown, support for the march came from the grass roots, forcing reluctant agreement from Negro leaders.[1] Whether the widespread discontent among the Negro masses, which was a reality, could have been organized is, however, problematic. Randolph at various times predicted that 10,000, 50,000, even 100,000 marchers would converge on Washington. But the test of that ability to perform was, as it turned out, not necessary.

Enormous pressures were brought to bear upon Randolph and other Negro leaders to reconsider their plan. The threat it posed for the administration was a multiple one: it suggested a dramatic exposure of racialism in a country fighting a war premised upon opposition to racism; it also threatened consequences in reactions of Negro servicemen and potential draftees, and an inevitable divisiveness in internal politics generally. Eleanor Roosevelt and Fiorello La Guardia were only two of those whose persuasiveness was enlisted in support of the administration's position and whose importunities were hard for Negro leaders to ignore. When the Negroes persisted in the face of pleas, threats, and cajolings, however, the administration itself reconsidered. It had been effectively pressured into doing what its leaders by and large felt was morally desirable but feared would prove politically embarrassing. Now it had been demonstrated that embarrassment was a two-edged blade.

On June 25, a week before the scheduled march, President Roosevelt issued Executive Order 8802 on equal employment. Only the day before, La Guardia had informed the civil rights leaders of the President's willingness to meet their demands and had worked out an agreement with them, including a specific reference to equality in government employment. The order established a Committee on Fair Employment Practice "to provide for the full and equitable participation of all workers in defense industries, without discrimination."

## II

It would be foolish to suggest that this or subsequent orders accomplished all that they purported to seek. No authority was given the Committee on Fair Employment Practice over military personnel at all.[2] As to civilian employment, the President's proclamation did not alter the situation overnight. The primary instrumentality of change with regard to the labor force was not the law of the land but the law of supply and demand. As a shortage of available manpower developed in the wake of increasing production and withdrawal from the labor force of large numbers of able-bodied men, jobs formerly closed opened up to Negroes—in numbers approximating the changeover of a major revolution. At most, laws and regulations were a secondary factor in this change. The bitter opposition of southern congressmen and senators to the fair employment program for government and defense industries suggests that it was thought to have some effect on labor practices generally, but perhaps their vehement protest centered on the governmental agency as a convenient symbol.

The first Committee on Fair Employment Practice was administratively poorly conceived and understaffed.[3] Its triumphs were mainly in airing the problem of discrimination and in moral suasion. Additionally, the Civil Service Commission was induced to add clarifying provisions in its own regulations to further codify the new official stance of the government. The committee, armed with the presidential order and a supplemental letter of September 3, 1941, reached agreement with the commission by which the latter undertook investigations on behalf of the committee.[4] In November 1942 the Civil Service Commission urged all agencies to utilize its new standard form for employment, eliminating photographs.[5] Increasingly too government agencies were forced, because of the wartime shortage of labor, to rely on the Civil Service Commission as a central pool for employees, and hence the commission could place Negroes from its pool in a variety of positions.[6]

The changes in governmental service were remarkable, even against the background of changes in American society generally. Here, after all, legal regulations, when enforced by conscientious administrators, could be more influential than in the nongovernmental sector of employment. On the eve of the war, for the first time, regulations and legislation expressly prohibited racial discrimination in federal employment. As of 1940 civil service regulations explicitly forbade the use of political and religious affiliations as criteria for employment. There was, however, no mention of these being forbidden standards in promotion policy. Nor was there any mention at all of race in either context; when any questions were raised the explanation usually proffered was that the merit system by implication forbade the utilization of such criteria, but logically the same argument should also have made redundant the other two prohibitions. In 1940 Congressman Robert Ramspeck of Georgia, a devoted advocate of the merit system, introduced legislation for a general revision of civil service including provisions forbidding discrimination on grounds of race. The Civil Service Commission and the President hastily acted, only nineteen days before passage of the Ramspeck Act, to promulgate anti-discrimination regulations, obviously to avoid the embarrassment of being forced by another branch of the government to outlaw race prejudice.[7] With the Executive Order of November 7, 1940, reinforced shortly by the Ramspeck Act, racial discrimination became illegal in both employment and promotion policies.

These legal changes helped bring about significant advances in the governmental service. But the general pattern of Negro employment in the less desirable positions that still characterized the economy as a whole prevailed in government too. By and large Negroes found their best opportunities for jobs in positions that whites eschewed, the hand-me-downs of employment.

An analysis made by William Chapman Bradbury in 1952 of figures supplied by the early Committee on Fair Employment Practice showed that Negro employees were concentrated in the temporary war agencies rather than in the older establishments, in less permanent positions, in the more menial roles, and in the Washington, D.C., area rather than in the field. Also, the higher the classification of a Negro, the more likely it was that he held a temporary position or was employed by a strictly wartime agency. More than half of all Negroes in classified service were in temporary positions, and half were in wartime agencies.

The concentration of Negro employment in Washington reflected not only the greater control exercised by high-level officials over the employment structure there but, even more, the general shortage of labor in that district. More detailed scrutiny bears this out rather strikingly. The dramatic rise of Negro service in Washington was not paralleled in the field where the growth was only from some 10 percent of all employees in the prewar period to 11 percent in 1944. Eighty percent of the Negroes in the field were still in the unclassified service, and only 2.6 percent of all clerical and administrative positions in the field were occupied by Negroes.[8]

What was significant, however, was that Negroes in the civil service, at least in Washington, now had sufficient numbers and experience to assert their claims and maintain their role in the after-war period. There was no repetition of the post-World War I situation where Negro gains were wiped out almost overnight. From March 31, 1944, to July 31, 1947, a comparison of figures compiled for a sample group of agencies by the Committee on Fair Employment Practice with figures compiled by the President's Commission on Human Rights showed, there was a slight drop in the percentage of Negroes employed, but the basic pattern remained remarkably stable during those years, both in numbers and in distribution of Negroes in the middle reaches of the bureaucracy.[9]

The wartime committee found it was not easy to implement its theoretical powers. At first, having no field staff, the committee had to utilize the investigative resources of the Civil Service Commission. The commission cooperated freely, and the committee could pursue any investigation further if it chose. But the arrangement was less than ideal. The commission refused to intervene in questions of "working conditions, work assignments, or other matters within the administrative discretion of the several agencies."[10] A Negro could not secure a position allocated to another qualified person even if discrimination had been involved in the appointment, making it of doubtful benefit to the individual to bring a complaint. "In government cases the Committee has *never been allowed* to hold public hearings as in the case of war industries, and thus the sanction of public opinion has not been open to it" (emphasis added), a leading member of the wartime committee staff wrote toward the end of its existence. "As the enforcing agent of the national non-discrimination policy," he suggested somewhat halfheartedly, "Government would perhaps be in an unfortunate position to have to expose its failings to the public."[11] Only three governmental hearings were held, of cases in the Department of Commerce, the Office of Education, and the Newport News Post Office. Nor, by its own admission, did the committee use what power it had to make general recommendations to any great extent.

In all, the Civil Service Commission investigated 1,871 complaints for the committee between October 1941 and March 1946 and found racial discrimination in only 58 instances.[12] (The commission, it should be noted, insisted on defining discrimination solely in terms of violation of its own rules.) The Committee on Fair Employment Practice itself handled 2,048 complaints against the federal government from July 1943 to June 1945, securing adjustments in 23 percent of these cases, compared with adjustments in 39 percent of all cases handled.[13] Perhaps its major function in the government employment area was the inauguration of thorough statistical studies on the extent of racial discrimination.

The modest accomplishments of the Committee on Fair Employment Practice (actually there were two committees of the same name during the wartime period, the first functioning from August 1941 until January 1943, the second beginning its term of office in May 1943[14]) must be viewed in relation to the pressure being exerted in support of the pattern of discriminatory employment. The fair employment program was always a target for congressional criticism. The quest for equality took many guises and alternate forms, in large part as a consequence of that criticism. Originally,

the committee was in the Office of Production Management; later it was moved to the War Manpower Commission. Congress refused to make the agency permanent and in fact ended the committee in 1946 through the so-called Russell Amendment to an appropriations bill. The latter provided that any temporary agency was to be abolished after one year if Congress had not appropriated money for it. The action was clearly aimed at the Committee on Fair Employment Practice and was universally so understood. The following year the amendment was modified to allow the establishment of interdepartmental agencies on a temporary basis, so long as the employees remained on the payrolls of the regular agencies.[15] As a consequence, in later years agencies in the fair employment field were set up as interdepartmental, temporary, executive creations. The exception was President Truman's Fair Employment Board which was set up in 1948 as part of the Civil Service Commission. Not until the Civil Rights Act of 1964 was congressional approval given to a fair employment agency.

The unfriendliness of Congress was an obstacle to the development of equal employment practices, but every President since Roosevelt has maintained such programs. Truman not only set up the Fair Employment Board but also established, in 1952, the President's Committee on Government Contract Compliance, to police the non-discrimination clause in governmental contracts, a provision required by Executive Order 9346 of 1943. A successor Committee on Government Contracts was appointed by President Eisenhower in 1953. After temporizing with a committee authorized merely to receive complaints, Eisenhower also established, on January 18, 1955, a presidential Committee on Government Employment Policy. It had only advisory powers. Many of the characteristic aspects of the fair employment program took form in the Eisenhower years. The separation of the "fair employment officer" from the personnel officer in federal agencies, for example, was an early decision, made under the assumption that a person should not function in a semi-judicial capacity after creating the situation in an executive capacity. (In Truman's administration the agency head had in most instances also been the equal employment officer.) The involvement of Vice President Richard Nixon in one aspect of the program, the Committee on Government Contracts, set another early precedent.

The defeat—until 1964—of fair employment practices as a legislative program at the national level was also mitigated by the gradual development of fair employment commissions at the state level. Although by 1945 a number of states already had statutes prohibiting discrimination —thirteen, according to Theodore Leskes[16]— New York State was the first to set up machinery for enforcement, by establishing in that year a commission. Later in 1945 New Jersey created a Division against Discrimination within the Department of Education. By 1966, 29 states had some rudimentary enforcement legislation.[17] These laws were of diverse effectiveness, scope, and specificity, but their mere existence was evidence of a considerable body of sentiment in favor of nondiscrimination in employment generally and, therefore, had important implications for public employment policy. Certainly it was anomalous for the public sector of employment to follow practices which were condemned as improper by the government in its supervisory capacity.

# III

On March 6, 1961, President Kennedy issued Executive Order 10925 which vested the functions of both the Committee on Government Contracts and the Committee on Government Employment Policy in a new President's Committee on Equal Employment Opportunity. In a move that was calculated to enhance the liberal reputation of Vice President Johnson as well as to secure confidence in the committee, he appointed Johnson permanent chairman. The Secretary of Labor was designated vice chairman.

The order creating the new committee was far more elaborate and constructive than any previous executive order in this field. It gave the committee stronger powers than earlier committees had had, particularly in its requirement that the functions of the committee were not to be merely negative or corrective in nature, but were to be utilized for "positive compliance." The governmental fair employment program transferred to the new committee was concentrated in a separate division. The director for governmental employment throughout the life of the committee was John Hope II, a Negro scholar and administrator whose father had been president and one of the founders of Atlanta University and who, in his own right, had years of experience in the fair employment field.

Much the largest area of activity for the committee was the contract compliance program. Here differences of opinion developed between two committee members, the executive director, John Feild, and Robert Troutman, a businessman and friend of Kennedy's, over voluntary compliance for businesses. Eventually both men were to leave the committee. The governmental program was, however, relatively free of personality clashes and disagreements over approach.

The pronounced emphasis upon the placing of Negroes in high-level positions is said to have started when Robert Kennedy, speaking to businessmen in Birmingham, urged them to employ Negroes and was met by some sarcastic remarks about the character of federal employment in that region. When the then Attorney General investigated he indeed found, according to this story, that the federal government was even more discriminatory than the average business in its employment practices there; he thereupon determined to correct the situation.

It was soon apparent, however, that the mere removal of barriers did not guarantee equal access to jobs. Experience with recruitment under the new federal policy in the South revealed that the earlier pattern of discrimination had itself created social patterns that remained to reinforce unequal employment practices even when a more positive attitude on the part of the administrators in power was evident.

The Kennedy program of conspicuous employment of Negroes at high-grade positions—

at levels previously not truly open to the Negro—was hardly of an apolitical nature. The director of the minorities division of the Democratic National Committee, Louis Martin, himself a Negro and former journalist, worked closely with the White House in this program and vigorously pursued publicity for political advantage. As he frankly stated in an interview, he was consistently looking for appointments with a political impact that statistics, important as they are, could not have. "Hell, I even had a candidate for Secretary of State," he has said.[18] In 1960 he had drawn up a list of some 750 Negroes of ability and set out to try to find employment for them; efforts to place Mexican Americans and other "nonwhites" were also made, but the most conspicuous advances were clearly in Negro employment.

Aiding Mr. Martin in the Kennedy years was Ralph Dungan of the White House staff. He was in charge of filling major staff positions throughout the bureaucracy and was therefore also involved in this effort to symbolize and dramatize the end of discrimination in the federal service. For a brief period of one year Harris Wofford, Jr., acted as White House aid on minority rights. But this did not prove successful. Lee White of the White House staff was also concerned with minority rights and gradually took over more and more of this function in the later years of the Kennedy administration and in the first years of the Johnson administration.[19] Additionally, a sub-Cabinet committee of assistant secretaries met roughly once a month to coordinate activities and compare approaches to problems.

The President's Committee on Equal Employment Opportunity plugged away at compiling the day-to-day statistics and establishing the pattern for routine employment in the bureaucracy, its hand strengthened by dramatic appointments which indicated solidly that a new day had arrived. The annual census of employment which the committee initiated in 1961 provided a factual basis for discussion of the record in different agencies. In addition to the pressure resulting from the committee's routine operation and from the placement efforts of the Democratic party and the White House staff, there were other influences on government agencies, particularly those in the public eye. The very structure of the Equal Employment Opportunity Committee afforded the occasion and reinforcement for such influence. The presence on the committee, for example, of John Macy, chairman of the Civil Service Commission, helped not only in integrating committee activities with those of the commission, but also in allowing the commission to exert informal pressure. For instance, Macy called the attention of the Secretary of Health, Education, and Welfare (at the time, Anthony Celebrezze) to a pattern suggesting discrimination in the Social Security Administration during the first year of the equal employment program. Since Celebrezze was also a member of the committee it was a friendly exchange for informational purposes that led to immediate corrective measures without any formal action on the record at all.

From the beginning the committee's action was aimed at securing positive action and setting up machinery within the various agencies that would take over much of the responsibility for implementation of the program. As was evident as early as Roosevelt's wartime fair employment program, no small organization could police the entire federal establishment. The solution that had been adopted beginning with Eisenhower was the designating within each agency of a deputy employment officer whose function it was to secure, interpret, and adjudge compliance with the equal employment order in his agency. The deputy employment officer was part father confessor, part poster of billboard announcements, part judge, part transmitter of complaints. The function was ill-defined and remains ill-defined to this day. In some agencies the equal employment program is carried out in a separately established division with active participation in recruitment, enforcement, and hearings. In others, it has been merely a formal paper allocation of a responsibility never or seldom exercised.

The handling of individual complaints was regarded as secondary to the committee's over-all responsibility for establishing positive machinery to deal with the problem of discrimination. Complaints, although seriously considered and even elaborately and lavishly documented in some instances, were regarded by the committee as more important as symptoms than for their own sake; a complaint was regarded as indicating where problems had developed in an agency and was to be used as an opening wedge for inquiry into the total picture of the agency's disposition of problems.

# IV

With the strong support the Committee on Equal Employment Opportunity had in the White House during Kennedy's presidency, the committee's record was basically a good one. The growth of Negro employment was sustained throughout the federal service. Indeed the charge of "reverse discrimination" arose in subdued but definite fashion and even received some documentary support. The success of the equal employment opportunity program was undoubtedly due to the efforts of all concerned, hardly to the efforts of the committee alone, which never became noted for aggressiveness of tactics or efficiency. Nevertheless, its record was rather more impressive than that of any previous such establishment.

The committee reported that to November 1963 it had processed 2,243 cases, of 2,699 complaints made, with 36 percent resulting in "corrective action" as compared with 16 percent for the Committee on Government Employment Policy and 23 percent for the wartime Committee on Fair Employment Practice.[20] (Its success with private industry was also notable—72 percent compared with about 20 percent for the President's Committee on Government Contracts.) These figures are perhaps less significant than may appear at first glance since the committee's definition of "corrective action" was always rather generous, including any sort of promotion for the individual or readjustment in his job whether or not instigated by the complaint or the committee findings. Corrective action, in short, might have been purely an artifact of time; in many instances general re-evaluation of a position, which took place irrespective of the complaint of the jobholder, emerged as a favorable statistic in committee reports. In only rare instances did the committee formally find evidence of discrimination, its attitude being that the finding of discrimination was on the whole not a necessary part of its operation. Administrators felt that the label needlessly aroused contention and that more positive results could be achieved by other means. Yet to Negro groups and critics of the committee, the formal finding of discrimination would in itself have been an indication of sincerity and a token of intent. The lack of such candor, the unwillingness to call names, in their eyes indicated doubt and hesitancy on the part of the committee. This difference in outlook was to persist.

The advent of President Johnson's administration did not result in any lessening in prominence of the program. On the contrary there were a series of emphatic statements of support by the President, who, after all, had been the chief architect of the committee's program during his term as Vice President, and energetic backing in action by the White House staff. However, some shift in style became evident with the growth in power on the committee of Hobart Taylor, who had been personally chosen for this post by Johnson. "Hobart is essentially a fixer," one of the more prominent civil rights leaders explained privately. His method was that of a private negotiator seeking to reach a solution for a specific incident, while the logic of the program required the development of broad machinery independent of specific situations. Taylor devoted his attention primarily to the committee's work on contract compliance. His division of time between the committee and his functions in the President's office, together with his approach to routine administration, seemed to be reflected in a general lack of tautness in the organization as a whole.

During the 1964 campaign the Democratic party stressed its achievement and its pledges

*LBF uses appearance of liberalism for votes*

in the field of equal employment, as against the record of a candidate labeled relatively indifferent if not hostile to civil rights. With Goldwater's vote against the Civil Rights Act of 1964 as an ever-present point of contrast, President Johnson again and again made specific references to the intent of his administration to eliminate all signs of discrimination and indicated that "this administration is irrevocably committed" to the achievement of equal employment, not only in the federal service, but throughout the society. Certainly he made it clear that it was unconscionable to have discrimination in the public sector, though its manifestations were to be rooted out everywhere. The choice of Hubert Humphrey, the liberal senator from Minnesota, as vice presidential candidate betokened the same commitment.

President Johnson's representatives on the Democratic National Committee were instrumental in issuing campaign material aimed at the Negro vote—including one pamphlet which listed by name and title the major Negro appointments of the past few years. The party also issued a release (November 23, 1964) summarizing the gains achieved by Negroes in elective offices, concluding that there were 280 Negroes in elective positions in 33 states, all but 10 of whom were Democrats. (The release also gave names, addresses, and phone numbers of such Negroes, presumably for organizational purposes.) The intent of the administration to secure further Negro gains was evidenced by the subsequent choice of Thurgood Marshall as Solicitor General of the United States and other appointments at various levels of high and middling positions throughout the government.

The newly elected Vice President Humphrey was named chairman of the Committee on Equal Employment Opportunity, as Lyndon Johnson had been before him. Apparently, however, Hobart Taylor's influence had already become pervasive with the committee. In any event, the general tenor of operation of the administrative staff was clearly fixed. The Vice President was apparently not too happy with this arrangement and sought some changes. He was probably influenced by the fact that by late 1964 the civil

rights picture had altered and there was now a plethora of organizations in the field. Responsibilities in this field were exercised by the Community Relations Service and such departments as Labor, as well as the President's committee. Most important was the Equal Employment Opportunity Commission, created by Title VII of the Civil Rights Act of 1964. It was given power to prevent discrimination in private employment directly, not merely through government contract provisions. The notion of a superimposed coordinating staff was strongly pressed by the Department of Justice, and the Vice President accepted that recommendation. On February 7, 1965, the White House made public a letter to the Vice President dated February 5, indicating the President's agreement with Humphrey's "recommendation that there be a comparatively simple coordinating mechanism without elaborate staff and organization." Executive Order 11197 which accompanied the letter established the President's Council on Equal Opportunity with the Vice President as chairman, and with representation from no fewer than seventeen agencies actively concerned with civil rights.

The problems of coordination were not small. The Civil Rights Act of 1964 itself presented several problems of interpretation and allocations of responsibility. Section 701b provided "that it shall be the policy of the United States to ensure equal employment opportunity for federal employees without discrimination because of race, color, religion, sex, or national origin, and the President shall utilize his existing authority to effectuate this policy." (This provision was inserted in lieu of a rather broad one suggested by Senator Everett Dirksen of Illinois which would have explicitly prohibited discrimination in public employment generally.[21] Such a provision would have meant not only legislative outlawing of federal discrimination, but assumption by the federal government of direct authority to deal with state and local discrimination as well—a proposal which was to draw support in 1965 but which in 1964 was still seen as premature. The major impetus for enacting this kind of legislation appears to have come from southerners unfriendly to the equal employment program, perhaps with the thought of complicating the program, or more likely with the thought of preventing the passage of the legislation in its entirety.) While Section 709d specifically exempted those already reporting to the President's committee under Executive Order 10925 from the provisions of the bill, it did not provide a clear-cut line of division between the President's committee and the newly created Equal Employment Opportunity Commission.

Nonetheless, the act constituted the first congressional mention of the President's Committee on Equal Employment Opportunity and the executive order, and seemingly gave the program legitimacy, falsely suggesting congressional acceptance of the program. In spring 1964, however, Senator Willis Robertson (Democrat of Virginia) of the Appropriations Committee found an effective weapon against the President's committee, described well by Christopher Pyle and Richard Morgan.[22] The inter-agency aspect of the President's committee had enabled it to operate through existing budgets without having to defend its operations to Congress and account closely for its costs. "Since the program's expenditures were split and buried in the appropriation bills of 18 participating departments and agencies (often under such titles as 'procurement,' 'contract administration,' and 'a study of equal employment opportunity,') the Committee was able to channel well over $3 million into the investigative effort. Close to $1 million was also spent annually by the President's Committee itself out of contributions supplied directly by participating agencies. . . . In contrast the new [Equal Employment Opportunity] Commission fought a battle-royal for its funds this summer before the committees of Congress and came out with only $2.7 million, much of which will have to be spent on costly complaint investigations."[23] Robertson's tactic was to cut from the appropriations bill of each contributing agency a sum equal to its contribution to the committee's expenses. "The cuts were later explained as protests against the excessive use of this indirect method of financing by the Executive branch generally, but a check of the budgets of similar units, such as the Committee on Physical Fitness and the Committee on Employing the Handicapped, shows that the attack was pressed only against the civil rights unit."[24]

The Vice President saw the difficulties involved in requiring the agencies to contribute to the financing of the work of the President's committee when the amounts needed had been cut from their budgets, and he arranged a three-month moratorium with the Appropriations Committee, promising by September 30 either to phase out the President's committee or to seek a direct appropriation for its support from Congress. The determining considerations in the final disposition of the matter are shrouded in the normal mysteries of politics. It is generally agreed that Humphrey, after looking over the situation, decided that the federal program would best be turned over to the Civil Service Commission. However, Pyle and Morgan suggest that it was his intention virtually to the eve of the deadline merely to abolish the President's committee and transfer the contract compliance functions to the President's Council on Equal Opportunity, even though the latter was intended only as a coordinating and not an operating unit.[25] In any event, the Vice President in a letter dated September 24, 1965, recommended to the President the abolition of both the President's Committee on Equal Employment Opportunity and the President's Council on Equal Opportunity and the movement of all their functions into regular departments and the Civil Service Commission. Perhaps his decision to, in effect, withdraw personally was an acknowledgment that the tactics that had proved successful in dealing with the President's committee could also be used against the Council on Equal Employment; more likely it was a result of sheer political pressures and some loss of power by Humphrey.

Pyle and Morgan suggest that this represented a stunning loss of face for the Vice President—he lost two of his major titles—and a setback for the civil rights movement as well. A letter of explanation by the Vice President to the *New Leader* on November 8, 1965,[26] does not dispel the impression that Pyle and Morgan were correct in their analysis, although in this letter and in an earlier press conference the Vice President logically and coherently indicated that he based his major recommendations upon the need to "keep people from getting in each other's way" in dealing with the civil rights question broadly conceived.[27] Some of the arrangements suggest a desire for less zeal and more legalism in dealing with the programs.

The withdrawal of Vice President Humphrey from official connection with the program was viewed with dismay by civil rights organizations generally, and the transfer of the Community Relations Service from the Department of Commerce into the Department of Justice was opposed openly by civil rights leaders. The later resignation of the acting director of the service in opposition to the reorganization and his replacement by the nephew of Roy Wilkins of course had some effect in mitigating this hostility.[28] The most important single development, however, was the transfer of the contract compliance division of the President's committee into the Department of Labor, notoriously a weak department and one with little logical relation to the function it was assigned. Secretary of Labor Wirtz's lack of political leverage, dramatically revealed when he was unable to fire his own undersecretary because of the objections of AFL-CIO head George Meany, added to the implausibility of his being able to be militant in this realm.

In contrast, determination that the "in-house" program of the President's committee should be transferred to the Civil Service Commission was apparently an easy and relatively noncontroversial matter. The Civil Service Commission was credited by Pyle and Morgan with being "apparently eager to set up a tough new program to promote equal opportunity within the federal establishment."[29] Though the *New Leader* writers were skeptical of the Civil Service Commission's ability to pursue the program effectively, there were undoubted advantages in the transfer to the commission, including the possibility of minimizing duplication of channels and establishing more orderly procedures. What was lost was, of course, the advantage of a second structure, for the Civil Service Commission had always had a program of its own, even during the existence of the President's committee.

In ultimate terms, the restoration of the "in-house" program to the Civil Service Commission was inevitable. It is a personnel function which ought to be exercised in the normal civil service manner. The function was of course taken from the Civil Service Commission precisely to dramatize, distinguish, and symbolize the uniqueness of the program, to indicate priorities, and to demonstrate lack of confidence in the commission's zeal in promoting civil rights. The question now is whether the timing was appropriate, whether the program had achieved a sufficient level of maturity in the federal service generally. Only time will tell whether the recent actions of Congress have prematurely or at the appropriate time forced the remerger of these personnel functions. . . .

## Representative Bureaucracy and Civil Rights

Recent Negro efforts to attain greater access to the government service have, then, parallels in past aspirations and achievements of other groups. But the demand of Negroes for a representative share in the bureaucracy reflects a fairly new concept.

Representation in the sense of personification is of course an old idea in political theory. The symbolization or embodiment of the community in the person of the leader, who in turn responsively and conscientiously represents community values, is basic to most political thought of ancient and medieval times, as well as that of the modern era. But the concepts of cross-sectional representativeness and a more or less democratic choice of representatives are both, with a few exceptions, largely post-medieval phenomena.[30] The rather unusual procedures for selection of officials utilized by Athens in the fifth century B.C.—much like those in a lottery—suggest democracy to some modern observers. Generally, though, the first truly modern note on representation is sounded in the writings of Marsilius of Padua and William of Occam, precursors of modern attitudes in this, as in much else. The idea that representatives must be drawn from all elements of society is in any refined sense largely a product of the eighteenth and nineteenth centuries; it was almost unprecedented when asserted by the American colonies. (Actually, this claim was not fully acknowledged in England at least until the reform bills of the nineteenth century.) Indeed, the view that a body of selected representatives should be a microcosmic reproduction of the social and political cleavages in the community is almost, strictly speaking, contemporaneous. By and large, even the great legislative bodies of Western democracy have been a hybrid of elite representation, the best leadership of the community, and representation of the community as a whole.[31]

The application to the bureaucracy of any notion of representativeness seems to have been an exclusive development of the past thirty years or so. J. Donald Kingsley is generally credited with having coined the term "representative bureaucracy" when he utilized that phrase as the title of a book less than a quarter of a century ago. Perhaps even more striking is the fact, borne out in a study of the literature, that to a large extent it was Kingsley who articulated the concept for the first time in an even halfway systematic form.[32]

This late development is hardly surprising. Not only did there have to be acceptance of the idea of representativeness in relation to elective officials before transference of the idea by analogy to other public officials; but there also had to be recognition of the function and importance of the bureaucracy itself before much attention would be given to its composition. This recognition came in large part only after the work of Max Weber focused attention on bureaucratic structures and after the civil service had become regularized and stabilized by the adoption of a merit system. . . .

The perception of the importance of the bureaucracy has of course stimulated unrepresented groups to seek access to it in order to gain influence. The standard of equitable universalistic recruitment also increases pressures. Where there are in theory no barriers, the actual denial of representation in public service becomes even more obviously an affront to dispossessed groups. Such a denial becomes a crude challenge to the loyalty, worth, and power of an unrepresented social group. Consciousness of the growth in size and significance of bureaucracy, emphasis of theorists upon its importance, and even the perception of its relevance as an index of social power all combine to encourage hitherto unheard-from social groups in their demands for appointive, as well as elective, positions in the public service. . . .

# IV

Definition and discussion of "representative bureaucracy" is almost nonexistent. Kingsley contented himself with suggesting that administrative personnel should be drawn from all social classes, and gave little attention to any other consideration. Even a writer like James McCamy, author of several books and articles which at least in part hinge on the concept, has never made an explicit statement of any length on this subject. The most advanced formulation that I could find was in his textbook on American government, in a chapter under the heading "Representative Government: The Executive," where the following statement appears: "It is important for the attitudes of these permanent officials that they be selected to be representative of society."[33]

Presumably everyone regards it as axiomatic that representative bureaucracies like representative legislatures are good things and need no further defense; hence the lack of discussion. It can be suggested, however, that there are a number of discrete concepts of representative bureaucracy and separate justifications for it, and identification of these would seem worthwhile.

Representative bureaucracy may be sought in order to create a microcosm of the community. This concept suggests that the bureaucracy, like the legislature, should be a funnel for divergent points of view and fails if it does not have this Gallup Poll-like quality. Such representativeness has the advantage—already mentioned in this chapter—that social responsibility is thereby shared and diffused, which can lead to general acceptance of governmental programs and policies. Wide distribution of the members of the bureaucracy also operates to secure compliance, since they presumably urge support through broad sectors of the population. A representative bureaucracy, it has also been claimed, is more likely than a bureaucracy dependent on a single class to have employees with diverse skills and talents and with the imagination necessary to deal with problems that emerge; for example, it has been suggested that a representative foreign service is more likely than a monolithic group to apprehend strange points of view in a foreign country.[34] Then too the diffusion of social responsibility not only legitimizes individual policies in the regime generally, but also brings to the representative members of all segments of the society who occupy public positions a broader social point of view than they would otherwise have had; they in turn transmit this socialization experience to others in their social groups.[35] Finally, we may note that a group supports a regime and identifies with it insofar as it has a stake in the system. Such a stake may involve policy considerations but it also involves the group's sharing of honorific status and of societal jobs generally with other groups in the society. Since governmental employment constitutes a larger proportion of the total economy in more complex societies, and since the function of leading the community is a highly valued one, such sharing is an expected concomitant of a democratic—usually technically advanced—society. The degree of such sharing is a good index of concentration of social power and its absence may signal lack of identification with the regime on the part of deprived groups.

Societies only imperfectly achieve this diffusion in their bureaucracies; sometimes unrepresentativeness is by design, sometimes it results from unconscious development. Probably a perfectly representative bureaucracy is unachievable, for it would require uniform distribution of ability throughout the population and uniform interest in government service as well. Furthermore, governmental needs are not in exact proportion to societal needs; the range of talents government demands is narrower than that required for society as a whole. Probably the composition of a governmental structure will always be predominantly clerical and middle class. Kingsley was the first to criticize bureaucracies for their imperfect representativeness, their middle-class predominance. But the very nature of administration, and the technical requirements of organization, are likely to aggravate this type of disproportionate representation. Other types of inequitable recruitment to the public service—along religious, ethnic, caste, and linguistic lines—probably cause more difficulties in the world and are more readily subject to amelioration. Of course insofar as cleavages by religion or language or ethnic background parallel class lines or reinforce each other, they tend to become less manageable. Unfortunately, in most societies, such cleavages do tend to be mutually reinforcing and self-perpetuating, so that the Negro dilemma is in fact not unique but is rather re-enacted with variations throughout the world.

In Western European countries, the main deviations from representative bureaucracy are in the distribution of employees by social class and, secondarily, though quite significantly, by religion. As Chapman notes: "The scanty material available suggests that the majority of officials recruited in each class of the public service come from their corresponding social class and that the remainder come from the social class immediately below. This is of course what would reasonably be expected...Social class in the public service does not work in reverse. The sons of members of the administrative class are to all intents and purposes never found lower down the scale. Unless they can join at their fathers' level they diverge into another profession."[36] The industrial working class and agricultural farm laborers are underrepresented throughout Western Europe. For example, only

10 percent of the Swedish higher officials came from the working class after twenty years of Social Democratic government. Probably parental opposition to education accounts for agricultural underrepresentation in France, Switzerland, Holland, and Denmark. Sometimes occupational and ethnic lines coincide as with the largely agricultural German-speaking population of South Tyrol.[37]

Religion has been a ground for allocation of positions even in the United States. In New York City until very recently the presidencies of the city colleges were by convention allocated along religious lines. But it has been a more important criterion for employment in Europe. In Holland, the Catholic party was traditionally assigned the Ministry of Education and its "colonization," as Chapman calls it, was so successful that a Socialist Prime Minister refused to take over the ministry on the ground that he would be unable to work with the bulk of the bureaucrats there. Similarly the Ministry of the Middle Class in Belgium, the Ministry of Population in France, as well as specific ministries in other countries, have been regarded as Catholic preserves. Control of the Bavarian State Radio has likewise been restricted to Catholics. On the other hand, free thinkers and Free Masons often have gained control of some agencies. In France active participation in Free Masonry is still highly useful for anyone desiring advancement in some branches of the Ministry of the Interior.[38]

A special problem exists where duality of cultural and ethnic lines leads to bilingualism within the society, as in Canada or Belgium. "French-speaking Canadians have insistently brought up another problem—their role in the Federal Civil Service, where the dominant working language is English...'I want my language to be respected in public places, particularly in federal offices'... Some English-speaking Canadians both recognized and regretted this situation. Some even suggested changes, but the mere thought of bilingualism being officially imposed at this level seemed to cause a feeling of apprehension. Thus in Edmonton a civil servant stated—although in a perfectly cordial tone of voice, that 'if you require me after 17 years of service in the Civil Service, to pass and write an examination, to speak French, simply to keep my job, I'm afraid I will have to emigrate to Australia.' "[39]

In Israel where the population has a multi-cultural and multi-ethnic background, there is now general agreement that Hebrew is to be the spoken language, thus reducing tension on what had been a major issue. But a serious problem remains, for the style of thought, type of culture, and manner of decision-taking of Sephardim apparently constitute a barrier similar to the ones the French-Canadians and the Belgian Flemish feel bar them from equal opportunity in their countries. The end result is the same in all three instances: the people of one ethnic-cultural background practically monopolize the upper reaches of the bureaucracy.

Many solutions to the problem of achieving a representative bureaucracy have been attempted by different societies. The most common is requirement of equitable geographic distribution. This may be effected by informal understanding as in the United States—where federal judges, Cabinet officers, and the like are chosen in part to satisfy regional representation—or by specific provision as in Article 101 of the United Nations Charter, which states that "Due regard shall be paid to the importance of recruiting the staff on as wide a geographical basis as possible." For various reasons geographical distribution is generally accepted without controversy as providing a broad-gauge basis for selection of representatives. Due regard to geography very often will also give representation to racial and linguistic elements, and thus contribute to stability.

Another type of solution has been attempted in Lebanon where there is an allocation of political power generally on the basis of the presumed religious distribution of the population. The result has been a limited stability. Since a new distribution based on the changing population lines might upset this stability, there has been no religious census since agreement was reached.[40]

In India there are constitutional quotas, based largely on population, for representation of the "untouchable" caste in both the national service and the local parliaments. Within the limits of the quotas untouchables qualify for positions in terms of their abilities. While the legislative seats are in practice now so apportioned and occupied, the allotment of civil service posts has not worked out quite so simply. Untouchables have qualified for lower-grade positions in greater numbers than there are positions as allocated by their proportion of the population, and they have been distinctly underrepresented in upper-class jobs. There were qualified candidates to fill only 1.3 percent of Class I governmental posts in 1963, although the quota was 12.5 percent; less than half of the allocated positions were filled in Classes II and III.[41] The constitution of the former Malayan Federation provided for a more flexible arrangement, requiring establishment of reasonable quotas "to safeguard the special position of the Malays" in government service, education, and even business.[42] The government of Israel has deliberately solicited Sephardim for many governmental agencies, with a special effort in recent years being made in the Foreign Office. The Post Office and Police departments have by tradition had Sephardi ministers.

Preference to minority groups in access to educational facilities may be either a supplement to or a substitute for governmental employment quotas. In Great Britain bureaucratic reform was possible because of parallel changes in the public school system. Following the example set by the East India Company's school—Haileybury—the public schools made a place for the talented though impecunious. "The public schools merely effected a balance between rationalized organization and traditional power. In fact, the balance represented a compromise—between the reward of intellectual merit, on the one hand, and the reward of hereditary privilege, on the other." [43] In the old Malayan Federation, ethnic quotas for admission to a university were consciously employed in an attempt to avert predominance of the Chinese in the bureaucracy.

# V

In contrast, the American effort to achieve a representative bureaucracy has been more volunteeristic, less rigid in prescribing goals. The American setup constitutes on the whole a novel experiment through emphasis on individual creative action.

This pattern in governmental service provides cues for the Negro youngster who must decide what educational course to pursue. It is difficult for a social group to change its traditional educational and occupational aspirations. Catholics have in recent years engaged in long discussions on the lack of an intellectual tradition in the American church and have concluded its absence is probably traceable to the fact that the Irish and Sicilians who form the backbone of Catholicism in the United States have never emphasized intellectual values.[44] The record of the Jewish community in the United States in overcoming discrimination is often fallaciously contrasted with Negro achievement, overlooking the simple fact that the urban-intellectual values of contemporary Jewry comport well with the current needs of American society, while the values of the Negro community do not. On the other hand, efforts in Israel to change those Jewish social patterns in order to establish a strong agricultural base for the Israeli community have been only mildly successful in spite of tremendous ideological emphasis upon and financial support to that sector of the economy. The social inertia involved in occupational choice can be observed in walking or riding through the streets of any major city in the United States and noting the names on store fronts.

It is not easy for a Negro to seek out the type of training that is currently desired and needed in American society. Visible signs that such efforts will be rewarded are necessary. The Negro press has reported that Negroes still hesitate to go into engineering, where the demand for personnel is high, because they do not believe that they will, at the appropriate juncture in their careers, be regarded as promotable to supervisory positions. They prefer the "free-floating" professions of lawyer, teacher, doctor, and clergyman, in which they seldom face a "promotion" situation; or they go into agencies that have already demonstrated their willingness to make such promotions, i.e., government and welfare organizations.[45] The image of employment in large-scale organizations held by Negroes tends to be fairly accurate, though there is a time lag. Governmental service has always been seen as an attractive employment situation for the Negro, and yet it has also been believed by the Negro community that promotion within it is limited. By giving tangible evidence of the advantages in at least one sector of the economy of increased education as preparation for even more advanced positions, government may encourage the development of skills in the Negro community that is, in fact, the requisite of any real, sustained economic improvement for any underprivileged group.

It can be seen that a truly self-generating cycle has been operating, one that must be broken. Political impotence and the lack of social power are reflected in the absence of prominent office-holders. This absence is noted by the community generally, but especially by Negro youth who see no point in investing financially and psychically in further education. Lack of education is reflected in a paucity of candidates for office. Absence of officeholders means lessened social power. In this cycle, the presence or absence of officeholders is the crucial element, the psychological payoff, the point most amenable to change and most productive of further changes. In a sense it adds another dimension to the concept of "representative bureaucracy"—for the conferral of office demonstrates something about the values and standards of, and opportunities afforded by, the greater community. Bureaucracies, then, constitute a two-way street; their functions of representation are not limited to the mirroring of the community in the administrative process. Bureaucracies by their very structure represent truths about the nature of the societies they administer and the values that dominate them.

In sum, we can distinguish four intertwined meanings of that somewhat vague rubric *representative bureaucracy.* The most obvious is the simple representational notion that all social groups have a right to political participation and to influence. The second can be labeled the functional aspect;[46] the wider the range of talents, types, and regional and family contacts found in a bureaucracy, the more likely it is to be able to fulfill its functions, with respect to both internal efficiency and social setting. Bureaucracies also symbolize values and power realities and are thus representational in both a political and an analytic sense. Therefore, finally, social conduct and future behavior in a society may be channelized and encouraged through the mere constitution of the bureaucracy.

# Notes

1. Herbert Garfinkel, *When Negroes March* (Glencoe, Ill.: Free Press, 1959), pp. 39–41 and 51ff. I have drawn generally from this informative study.

2. *First Report, Fair Employment Practice Committee, July 1943–December 1944* (Washington, D.C.: Government Printing Office, 1945), p. 7; John A. Davis, "Nondiscrimination in the Federal Agencies," *Annals of the American Academy of Political and Social Science,* 244:65–74 (March 1946). In 1944 the committee reached agreement with the War and Navy departments controlling discrimination in war installations.

3. Paul Van Riper, *History of the United States Civil Service* (Evanston, Ill.: Row, Peterson, 1958), p. 438; Davis, "Nondiscrimination in the Federal Agencies," *Annals,* 244:69. At its peak the agency had 53 persons concerned with operations.

4. Davis, "Nondiscrimination in the Federal Agencies," *Annals,* 244:69.

5. Gladys Kammerer, *Impact of War on Federal Personnel Administration, 1939–1945* (Lexington: University of Kentucky Press, 1951), p. 50n.

6. Davis, "Nondiscrimination in the Federal Agencies," *Annals,* 244:70.

7. Van Riper, *History of the United States Civil Service,* pp. 344–347, 438.

8. William Chapman Bradbury, Jr., "Racial Discrimination in the Federal Service" (Ph.D. dissertation, Columbia University, 1952; University Microfilms No. 4557), pp. 40–41.

9. *Ibid.,* pp. 44–48, concludes this from unpublished records of the Committee on Fair Employment Practice now in the National Archives. See especially his tabulation for ten permanent agencies, p. 48.

10. Davis, "Nondiscrimination in the Federal Agencies," *Annals,* 244:67.

11. *Ibid.,* p. 67. *First Report, Fair Employment Practice Committee,* p. 48.

12. *Final Report, Fair Employment Practice Committee, June 28, 1946* (Washington, D.C.: Government Printing Office, 1947), pp. 31–32.

13. Davis, "Nondiscrimination in the Federal Agencies," *Annals,* 244:71–72; *Final Report, Fair Employment Practice Committee,* p. 32. The committee's final report did not give comparable data for the total period of its functioning. Presumably, they would reveal a similar pattern of effectiveness, though at a lower level.

14. Paul Norgren and Samuel Hill, *Toward Fair Employment* (New York: Columbia University Press, 1964), p. 150.

15. U.S. Civil Rights Commission, *Employment* (Washington, D.C.: Government Printing Office, 1961), pp. 19–21.

16. Milton Konvitz and Theodore Leskes, *A Century of Civil Rights* (New York: Columbia University Press, 1961), p. 197.

17. States having anti-discrimination legislation and the enforcing agencies are listed in U.S. Commission on Civil Rights, *Equal Employment Opportunity under the Federal Law* (Washington, D.C.: Government Printing Office, 1966), pp. 6–10.

18. Joseph Kraft, "Washington Insight," *Harper's,* June 1964, p. 112.

19. Harold Fleming, "The Federal Executive and Civil Rights," *Daedalus,* Fall 1965, p. 926.

20. President's Committee on Equal Employment Opportunity, *Report to the President,* November 26, 1963, pp. 105–106.

21. Donald King and Charles Quick, *Legal Aspects of the Civil Rights Movement* (Detroit: Wayne State University Press, 1965), pp. 316–317.

22. "Johnson's Civil Rights Shake-Up," *New Leader,* October 11, 1965, pp. 3–7.

23. *Ibid.,* p. 4.

24. *Ibid.* It is perhaps not irrelevant to note that not until April 1965 was a Negro page ever hired to serve congressmen. See *New York Times,* April 14, 1965, p. 24.

25. *Ibid.*

26. Letter to the editor, *New Leader,* November 8, 1965, p. 33.

27. On the day of the Vice President's letter to the President, Humphrey held a press conference to announce his recommendation. Presidential press secretary Bill Moyers, Attorney General Katzenbach, and Secretary of Labor Wirtz were also present. (Hobart Taylor had a short time earlier been appointed to the Export-Import Bank and therefore was no longer involved in the committee's activities.) White House Press Conference Mimeograph No. 119A.

28. *New York Times,* December 15, 1965, p. 24.

29. *New Leader,* October 11, 1965, p. 5.

30. Francis Coker and Carlton Rodee, "Representation," *Encyclopedia of the Social Sciences.*

31. C. K. Allen, *Democracy and the Individual* (New York: Oxford University Press, 1943), pp. 21–22.

32. J. Donald Kingsley, *Representative Bureaucracy* (Yellow Springs, Ohio: Antioch Press, 1944).

33. James L. McCamy, *American Government* (New York: Harper, 1957), p. 638. See also his *Conduct of the New Diplomacy* (New York: Harper and Row, 1964). But see Van Riper's *History of the United States Civil Service,* pp. 551ff.

34. Richard Johnson, "The Representativeness of the American Foreign Service Officers Corps" (State Department report, undated, mimeographed), pp. 4–5.

35. Samuel A. Stouffer, *Communism, Conformity and Civil Liberties* (New York: Doubleday, 1955).

36. Brian Chapman, *The Profession of Government* (London: Allen and Unwin, 1959), pp. 315–316.

37. *Ibid.,* pp. 315–317.

38. *Ibid.,* pp. 284–286.

39. *A Preliminary Report of the Royal Commission on Bilingualism and Biculturalism* (Ottawa: Queen's Printer, 1965), pp. 73–74.

40. Philip K. Hitti, *A Short History of Lebanon* (New York: St. Martin's Press, 1965), pp. 220–221.

41. See M. N. Srinivas and André Béteille, "The 'Untouchables' of India," *Scientific American,* December 1965, pp. 13–17.

42. Constitution, Federation of Malaya, Articles 40 and 153.

43. Rupert Wilkinson, *Gentlemanly Power* (New York: Oxford University Press, 1964), pp. 22–23 and 10–11.

44. The discussion begun by Monsignor John Tracy Ellis in 1955 was continued by Father Weigel and others. See, for example, John J. Wright, "Catholics and Anti-Intellectualism," *Commonweal,* December 16, 1955, pp. 275–278, and Thomas O'Dea, *American Catholic Dilemma* (New York: Sheed and Ward, 1959).

45. *Negro Press Digest,* April 28, 1964, pp. 4–5.

46. For a discussion of the distinction see my *The Supreme Court in the Political Process* (New York: Macmillan, 1965), p. 30.

# 22

# Title VII of the Civil Rights Act of 1964, As Amended

*U.S. Congress*

## Definitions

***Sec. 701.*** For the purposes of this title—

(a) The term "person" includes one or more individuals, governments, governmental agencies, political subdivisions, labor unions, partnerships, associations, corporations, legal representatives, mutual companies, joint-stock companies, trusts, unincorporated organizations, trustees, trustees in bankruptcy, or receivers. (As amended by P.L. 92–261, eff. March 24, 1972)

(b) The term "employer" means a person engaged in an industry affecting commerce who has fifteen or more employees for each working day in each of twenty or more calendar weeks in the current or preceding calendar year, and any agent of such a person, but such term does not include (1) the United States, a corporation wholly owned by the Government of the United States, an Indian tribe, or any department or agency of the District of Columbia subject by statute to procedures of the competitive service (as defined in section 2102 of title 5 of the United States Code), or (2) a bona fide private membership club (other than a labor organization) which is exempt from taxation under section 501(c) of the Internal Revenue Code of 1954, except that during the first year after the date of enactment of the Equal Employment Opportunity Act of 1972, persons having fewer than twenty-five employees (and their agents) shall not be considered employers. (As amended by P.L. 92–261, eff. March 24, 1972)

(c) The term "employment agency" means any person regularly undertaking with or without compensation to procure employees for an employer or to procure for employees opportunities to work for an employer and includes an agent of such a person. (As amended by P.L. 92–261, eff. March 24, 1972)

(d) The term "labor organization" means a labor organization engaged in an industry affecting commerce, and any agent of such an organization, and includes any organization of any kind, any agency, or employee representation committee, group, association, or plan so engaged in which employees participate and which exists for the purpose, in whole or in part, of dealing with employers concerning grievances, labor disputes, wages, rates of pay, hours, or other terms or conditions of employment, and any conference, general committee, joint or system board, or joint council so engaged which is subordinate to a national or international labor organization.

(e) A labor organization shall be deemed to be engaged in an industry affecting commerce if (1) it maintains or operates a hiring hall or hiring office which procures employees for an employer or procures for employees opportunities to work for an employer, or (2) the number of its members (or, where it is a labor organization composed of other labor organizations or their representatives, if the aggregate number of the members of such labor organization) is (A) twenty-five or more during the first year after the date of enactment of the Equal Employment Opportunity Act of 1972, or (B) fifteen or more thereafter, and such labor organization—

(1) is the certified representative of employees under the provisions of the National Labor Relations Act, as amended, or the Railway Labor Act, as amended;

(2) although not certified, is a national or international labor organization or a local labor organization recognized or acting as the representative of employees of an employer or employers engaged in an industry affecting commerce; or

(3) has chartered a local labor organization or subsidiary body which is representing or

actively seeking to represent employees of employers within the meaning of paragraph (1) or (2); or

(4) has been chartered by a labor organization representing or actively seeking to represent employees within the meaning of paragraph (1) or (2) as the local or subordinate body through which such employees may enjoy membership or become affiliated with such labor organization; or

(5) is a conference, general committee, joint or system board, or joint council subordinate to a national or international labor organization, which includes a labor organization engaged in an industry affecting commerce within the meaning of any of the preceding paragraphs of this subsection. (As amended by P.L. 92–261, eff. March 24, 1972)

(f) The term "employee" means an individual employed by an employer, except that the term "employee" shall not include any person elected to public office in any State or political subdivision of any State by the qualified voters thereof, or any person chosen by such officer to be on such officer's personal staff, or an appointee on the policy making level or an immediate adviser with respect to the exercise of the constitutional or legal powers of the office. The exemption set forth in the preceding sentence shall not include employees subject to the civil service laws of a State government, governmental agency or political subdivision. (As amended by P.L. 92–261, eff. March 24, 1972)

(g) The term "commerce" means trade, traffic, commerce, transportation, transmission, or communication among the several States; or between a State and any place outside thereof; or within the District of Columbia, or a possession of the United States; or between points in the same State but through a point outside thereof.

(h) The term "industry affecting commerce" means any activity, business, or industry in commerce or in which a labor dispute would hinder or obstruct commerce or the free flow of commerce and includes any activity or industry "affecting commerce" within the meaning of the Labor-Management Reporting and Disclosure Act of 1959, and further includes any governmental industry, business, or activity. (As amended by P.L. 92–261, eff. March 24, 1972)

(i) The term "State" includes a State of the United States, the District of Columbia, Puerto Rico, the Virgin Islands, American Samoa, Guam, Wake Island, the Canal Zone, and Outer Continental Shelf lands defined in the Outer Continental Shelf Lands Act.

(j) The term "religion" includes all aspects of religious observance and practice, as well as belief, unless an employer demonstrates that he is unable to reasonably accommodate to an employee's or prospective employee's religious observance or practice without undue hardship on the conduct of the employer's business. (Added by P.L. 92–261, eff. March 24, 1972)

(k) The terms "because of sex" or "on the basis of sex" include, but are not limited to, because of or on the basis of pregnancy, childbirth or related medical conditions; and women affected by pregnancy, childbirth, or related medical conditions shall be treated the same for all employment-related purposes, including receipt of benefits under fringe benefit programs, as other persons not so affected but similar in their ability or inability to work, and nothing in Section 703(h) of this title shall be interpreted to permit otherwise. This subsection shall not require an employer to pay for health insurance benefits for abortion, except where the life of the mother would be endangered if the fetus were carried to term, or except where medical complications have arisen from an abortion: *Provided,* That nothing herein shall preclude an employer from providing abortion benefits or otherwise affect bargaining agreements in regard to abortion. [Section 701(k) was added by P.L. 95–555, effective October 31, 1978, except that employers were given until April 28, 1979, to make necessary adjustments in existing fringe benefit or insurance programs. Also, employers were required to wait until October 31, 1979, or until the expiration of an applicable collective bargaining contract, before they could reduce benefits under a current plan in order to comply with the amendment.]

## Exemption

**Sec. 702.** This title shall not apply to an employer with respect to the employment of aliens outside any State, or to a religious corporation, association, educational institution, or society with respect to the employment of individuals of a particular religion to perform work connected with the carrying on by such corporation, association, educational institution, or society of its activities. (As amended by P.L. 92–261, eff. March 24, 1972)

# Discrimination Because of Race, Color, Religion, Sex, or National Origin

**Sec. 703.** (a) It shall be an unlawful employment practice for an employer—

(1) to fail or refuse to hire or to discharge any individual, or otherwise to discriminate against any individual with respect to his compensation, terms, conditions, or privileges of employment, because of such individual's race, color, religion, sex, or national origin; or

(2) to limit, segregate, or classify his employees or applicants for employment in any way which would deprive or tend to deprive any individual of employment opportunities or otherwise adversely affect his status as an employee, because of such individual's race, color, religion, sex, or national origin. (As amended by P.L. 92–261, eff. March 24, 1972)

(b) It shall be an unlawful employment practice for an employment agency to fail or refuse to refer for employment, or otherwise to discriminate against, any individual because of his race, color, religion, sex, or national origin, or to classify or refer for employment any individual on the basis of his race, color, religion, sex or national origin.

(c) It shall be an unlawful employment practice for a labor organization—

(1) to exclude or to expel from its membership, or otherwise to discriminate against, any individual because of his race, color, religion, sex, or national origin;

(2) to limit, segregate, or classify its membership or applicants for membership or to classify or fail or refuse to refer for employment any individual, in any way which would deprive or tend to deprive any individual of employment opportunites, or would limit such employment opportunities or otherwise adversely affect his status as an employee or as an applicant for employment, because of such individual's race, color, religion, sex, or national origin; or

(3) to cause or attempt to cause an employer to discriminate against an individual in violation of this section. (As amended by P.L. 92–261, eff. March 24, 1972)

(d) It shall be an unlawful employment practice for any employer, labor organization, or joint labor-management committee controlling apprenticeship or other training or retraining, including on-the-job training programs, to discriminate against any individual because of his race, color, religion, sex, or national origin in admission to, or employment in, any program established to provide apprenticeship or other training.

(e) Notwithstanding any other provision of this title, (1) it shall not be an unlawful employment practice for an employer to hire and employ employees, for an employment agency to classify, or refer for employment any individual, for a labor organization to classify its membership or to classify or refer for employment any individual, or for an employer, labor organization, or joint labor-management committee controlling apprenticeship or other training or retraining programs to admit or employ any individual in any such program, on the basis of his religion, sex, or national origin in those certain instances where religion, sex, or national origin is a bona fide occupational qualification reasonably necessary to the normal operation of that particular business or enterprise, and (2) it shall not be an unlawful employment practice for a school, college, university, or other educational institution or institution of learning to hire and employ employees of a particular religion if such school, college, university, or other educational institution or institution of learning is, in whole or in substantial part, owned, supported, controlled, or managed by a particular religion or by a particular religious corporation, association, or society, or if the curriculum of such school, college, university, or other educational institution or institution of learning is directed toward the propagation of a particular religion.

(f) As used in this title, the phrase "unlawful employment practice" shall not be deemed to include any action or measure taken by an employer, labor organization, joint labor-management committee, or employment agency with respect to an individual who is a member of the Communist Party of the United States or of any other organization required to register as a Communist-action or Communist-front organization by final order of the Subversive Activities Control Board pursuant to the Subversive Activities Control Act of 1950.

(g) Notwithstanding any other provision of this title, it shall not be an unlawful employment practice for an employer to fail or refuse to hire and employ any individual for any position, for an employer to discharge an individual from any position, or for an employment agency to fail or refuse to refer any individual for employment in any position, or for a labor organization to fail or refuse to refer any individual for employment in any position, if—

(1) the occupancy of such position, or access to the premises in or upon which any part of the duties of such position is performed or is to be performed, is subject to any requirement imposed in the interest of the national security of the United States under any security program in effect pursuant to or administered under any statute of the United States or any Executive order of the President; and

(2) such individual has not fulfilled or has ceased to fulfill that requirement.

(h) Notwithstanding any other provision of this title, it shall not be an unlawful employment practice for an employer to apply different standards of compensation, of different terms, conditions, or privileges of employment pursuant to a bona fide seniority or merit system, or a system which measures earnings by quantity or quality of production or to employees who work in different locations, provided that such differences are not the result of an intention to discriminate because of race, color, religion, sex, or national origin; nor shall it be an unlawful employment practice for an employer to give and to act upon the results of any professionally developed ability test provided that such test, its administration or action upon the results is not designed, intended, or used to discriminate because of race, color, religion, sex, or national origin. It shall not be an unlawful employment practice under this title for any employer to differentiate upon the basis of sex in determining the amount of the wages or compensation paid to employees of such employer if such differentiation is authorized by the provisions of Section 6(d) of the Fair Labor Standards Act of 1938 as amended (29 USC 206(d)).

(i) Nothing contained in this title shall apply to any business or enterprise on or near an Indian reservation with respect to any publicly announced employment practice of such business or enterprise under which a preferential treatment is given to any individual because he is an Indian living on or near a reservation.

(j) Nothing contained in this title shall be interpreted to require any employer, employment agency, labor organization, or joint labor-management committee subject to this title to grant preferential treatment to any individual or to any group because of the race, color, religion, sex, or national origin of such individual or group on account of an imbalance which may exist with respect to the total number or percentage of persons of any race, color, religion, sex, or national origin employed by any employer, referred or classified for employment by any employment agency or labor organization, admitted to membership or classified by any labor organzation, or admitted to, or employed in, any apprenticeship or other training program, in comparison with the total number or percentage of persons of such race, color, religion, sex or national origin in any community, State, section, or other area, or in the available work force in any community, State, section, or other area.

religion, sex, or national origin when religion, sex, or national origin is a bona fide occupational qualification for employment. (As amended by P.L. 92–261, eff. March 24, 1972)

## Other Unlawful Employment Practices

*Sec. 704.* (a) It shall be an unlawful employment practice for an employer to discriminate against any of his employees or applicants for employment, for an employment agency or joint labor-managment committee controlling apprenticeship or other training or retraining, including on-the-job training programs, to discriminate against any individual, or for a labor organization to discriminate against any member thereof or applicant for membership, because he has opposed any practice made an unlawful employment practice by this title, or because he has made a charge, testified, assisted, or participated in any manner in an investigation, proceeding, or hearing under this title. (As amended by P.L. 92–261, eff. March 24, 1972)

(b) It shall be an unlawful employment practice for an employer, labor organization, employment agency, or joint labor-management committee controlling apprenticeship or other training or retraining, including on-the-job training programs, to print or cause to be printed or published any notice or advertisement relating to employment by such an employer or membership in or any classification or referral for employment by such a labor organization, or relating to any classification or referral for employment by such an employment agency or relating to admission to, or employment in, any program established to provide apprenticeship or other training by such a joint labor-management committee indicating any preference, limitation, specification, or discrimination, based on race, color, religion, sex or national origin, except that such a notice or advertisement may indicate a preference, limitation, specification, or discrimination based on

## Equal Employment Opportunity Commission

*Sec. 705.* (a) There is hereby created a Commission to be known as the Equal Employment Opportunity Commission, which shall be composed of five members, not more than three of whom shall be members of the same political party. Members of the Commission shall be appointed by the President by and with the advice and consent of the Senate for a term of five years. Any individual chosen to fill a vacancy shall be appointed only for the unexpired term of the member whom he shall succeed, and all members of the Commission shall continue to serve until their successors are appointed and qualified, except that no such member of the Commission shall continue to serve (1) for more than sixty days when the Congress is in session unless a nomination to fill such vacancy shall have been submitted to the Senate, or (2) after the adjournment sine die of the session of the Senate in which such nomination was submitted. The President shall designate one member to serve as Chairman of the Commission, and one member to serve as Vice Chairman. The Chairman shall be responsible on behalf of the Commission for the administrative operations of the Commission, and, except as provided in subsection (b), shall appoint, in accordance with the provisions of title 5, United States Code, governing appointments in the competitive service, such officers, agents, attorneys, hearing examiners, and employees as he deems necessary to assist it in the performance of its functions and to fix their compensation in accordance with the provisions of chapter 51 and subchapter III of chapter 53 of title 5, United States Code, relating to classification and General Schedule pay rates:

Provided, That assignment, removal, and compensation of hearing examiners shall be in accordance with sections 3105, 3344, 5362, and 7521 of title 5, United States Code. (As amended by P.L. 92–261, eff. March 24, 1972)

(b)(1) There shall be a General Counsel of the Commission appointed by the President, by and with the advice and consent of the Senate, for a term of four years. The General Counsel shall have responsibility for the conduct of litigation as provided in sections 706 and 707 of this title. The General Counsel shall have such other duties as the Commission may prescribe or as may be provided by law and shall concur with the Chairman of the Commission on the appointment and supervision of regional attorneys. The General Counsel of the Commission on the effective date of this Act shall continue in such position and perform the functions specified in this subsection until a successor is appointed and qualified.

(2) Attorneys appointed under this section may, at the direction of the Commission, appear for and represent the Commission in any case in court, provided that the Attorney General shall conduct all litigation to which the Commission is a party in the Supreme Court pursuant to this title.

(c) A vacancy in the Commission shall not impair the right of the remaining members to exercise all the powers of the Commission and three members thereof shall constitute a quorum. (As amended by P.L. 92–261, eff. March 24, 1972)

(d) The Commission shall have an official seal which shall be judicially noticed.

(e) The Commission shall at the close of each fiscal year report to the Congress and to the President concerning the action it has taken, and the moneys it has disbursed. It shall make such further reports on the cause of and means of eliminating discrimination and such recommendations for further legislation as may appear desirable. (As amended by P.L. 93–608, January 2, 1975.)

(f) The principal office of the Commission shall be in or near the District of Columbia, but it may meet or exercise any or all its powers at any other place. The Commission may establish such regional or State offices as it deems necessary to accomplish the purpose of this title.

(g) The Commission shall have power—

(1) to cooperate with and, with their consent, utilize regional, State, local, and other agencies, both public and private, and individuals;

(2) to pay to witnesses whose depositions are taken or who are summoned before the Commission or any of its agents the same witness and mileage fees as are paid to witnesses in the courts of the United States;

(3) to furnish to persons subject to this title such technical assistance as they may request to further their compliance with this title or an order issued thereunder;

(4) upon the request of (i) any employer, whose employees or some of them, or (ii) any labor organization, whose members or some of them, refuse or threaten to refuse to cooperate in effectuating the provisions of this title, to assist in such effectuation by conciliation or such other remedial action as is provided by this title;

(5) to make such technical studies as are appropriate to effectuate the purposes and policies of this title and to make the results of such studies available to the public;

(6) to intervene in a civil action brought under section 706 by an aggrieved party against a respondent other than a government, governmental agency or political subdivision. (As amended by P.L. No. 92–261, eff. March 24, 1972)

(h) The Commission shall, in any of its educational or promotional activities, cooperate with other departments and agencies in the performance of such educational and promotional activities.

(i) All officers, agents, attorneys and employees of the Commission, including the members of the Commission, shall be subject to the provisions of section 9 of the act of August 2, 1939, as amended (Hatch Act), notwithstanding any exemption contained in such section.

## Prevention of Unlawful Employment Practices

*Sec. 706.* (a) The Commission is empowered, as hereinafter provided, to prevent any person from engaging in any unlawful employment practice as set forth in section 703 or 704 of this title. (As amended by P.L. 92–261, eff. March 24, 1972)

(b) Whenever a charge is filed by or on behalf of a person claiming to be aggrieved, or by a member of the Commission, alleging that an employer, employment agency, labor organization, or joint labor-management committee controlling apprenticeship or other training or retraining, including on-the-job training programs, has engaged in an unlawful employment practice, the Commission shall serve a notice of the charge (including the date, place and circumstances of the alleged unlawful employment practice) on such employer, employment agency, labor organization, or joint labor-management committee (hereinafter referred to as the 'respondent') within ten days and shall make an investigation thereof. Charges shall be in writing under oath or affirmation and shall contain such information and be in such form as the Commission requires. Charges shall not be made public by the Commission. If the Commission determines after such investigation that there is not reasonable cause to believe that the charge is true, it shall dismiss the charge and promptly notify the person claiming to be aggrieved and the respondent of its action. In determining whether reasonable cause exists, the Commission shall accord substantial weight to final findings and orders made by State or local authorities in proceedings commenced under State or local law pursuant to the requirements of subsections (c) and (d). If the Commission determines after such investigation that there is reasonable cause to believe that the charge is true, the Commission shall endeavor to eliminate any such alleged unlawful employment practice by informal methods of conference, conciliation, and persuasion. Nothing said or done during and as a part of such informal endeavors may be made public by the Commission, its officers or employees, or used as evidence in a subsequent proceeding without the written consent of the persons concerned. Any person who makes public information in violation of this subsection shall be fined not more than $1,000 or imprisoned for not more than one year, or both. The Commission shall make its determination on reasonable cause as promptly as possible and, so far as practicable, not later than one hundred and twenty days from the filing of the charge or, where applicable under subsection (c) or (d), from the date upon which the Commission is authorized to take action with respect to the charge. (As amended by P.L. 92–261, eff. Mar. 24, 1972)

(c) In the case of an alleged unlawful employment practice occurring in a State, or political subdivision of a State, which has a State or local law prohibiting the unlawful employment practice alleged and establishing or authorizing a State or local authority to grant or seek relief from such practice or to institute criminal proceedings with respect thereto upon receiving notice thereof, no charge may be filed under subsection (a) by the person aggrieved before the expiration of sixty days after proceedings have been commenced under the State or local law, unless such proceedings have been earlier terminated, provided that such sixty-day period shall be extended to one hundred and twenty days during the first year after the effective date of such State or local law. If any requirement for the commencement of such proceedings is imposed by a State or local authority other than a requirement of the filing of a written and signed statement of the facts upon which the proceeding is based, the proceeding shall be deemed to have been commenced for the purposes of this subsection at the time such statement is sent by registered mail to the appropriate State or local authority.

(d) In the case of any charge filed by a member of the Commission alleging an unlawful employment practice occurring in a State or political subdivision of a State which has a State or local law prohibiting the practice alleged and establishing or authorizing a State or local authority to grant or seek relief from such practice or to institute criminal proceedings with respect thereto upon receiving notice thereof, the Commission shall, before taking any action with respect to such charge, notify the appropriate State or local officials and, upon request, afford them a reasonable time, but not less than sixty days (provided that such sixty-day period shall be extended to one hundred and twenty days during the first year after the effective date of such State or local law), unless a shorter period is requested, to act under such State or local law to remedy the practice alleged.

(e) A charge under this section shall be filed within one hundred and eighty days after the alleged unlawful employment practice occurred and notice of the charge (including the date, place and circumstances of the alleged unlawful employment practice) shall be served upon the person against whom such charge is made within ten days thereafter, except that in the case of an unlawful employment practice with respect to which the person aggrieved has initially instituted proceedings with a State or local agency with authority to grant or seek relief from such practice or to institute criminal proceedings with respect thereto upon receiving notice thereof, such charge shall be filed by or on behalf of the person aggrieved within three hundred days after the alleged unlawful employment practice occurred, or within thirty days after receiving notice that the State or local agency has terminated the proceedings under the State or local law, whichever is earlier, and a copy of such charge shall be filed by the Commission with the State or local agency. (As amended by P.L. 92–261, eff. March 24, 1972)

(f)(1) If within thirty days after a charge is filed with the Commission or within thirty days after expiration of any period of reference under subsection (c) or (d), the Commission has been unable to secure from the respondent a conciliation agreement acceptable to the Commission, the Commission may bring a civil action against any respondent not a government, governmental agency, or political subdivision named in the charge. In the case of a respondent which is a government, governmental agency, or political subdivision, if the Commission has been unable to secure from the respondent a conciliation agreement acceptable to the Commission, the Commission shall take no further action and shall refer the case to the Attorney General who may bring a civil action against such respondent in the appropriate United States district court. The person or persons aggrieved shall have the right to intervene in a civil action brought by the Commission or the Attorney General in a case involving a government, governmental agency, or political subdivision. If a charge filed with the Commission pursuant to subsection (b) is dismissed by the Commission, or if within one hundred and eighty days from the filing of such charge or the expiration of any period of reference under the subsection (c) or (d), whichever is later, the Commission has not filed a civil action under this section or the Attorney General has not filed a civil action in a case involving a government, governmental agency, or political subdivision, or the Commission has not entered into a conciliation agreement to which the person aggrieved is a party, the Commission, or the Attorney General in a case involving a government, governmental agency, or political subdivision, shall so notify the person aggrieved and within ninety days after the giving of such notice a civil action may be brought against the respondent named in the charge (A) by the person claiming to be aggrieved or (B) if such charge was filed by a member of the Commission, by any person whom the charge alleges was aggrieved by the alleged unlawful employment practice. Upon application by the complainant and in such circumstances as the court may deem just, the court may appoint an attorney for such complainant and may authorize the commencement of the action without the payment fees, costs, or security. Upon timely application, the court may, in its discretion, permit the Commission, or the Attorney General in a case involving a government, governmental agency, or political subdivision, to intervene in such civil action upon certification that the case is of general public importance. Upon request, the court may, in its discretion, stay further proceedings for not more than sixty days pending the termination of State or local proceedings described in subsections (c) or (d) of this section or further efforts of the Commission to obtain voluntary compliance.

(2) Whenever a charge is filed with the Commission and the Commission concludes on the basis of a preliminary investigation that prompt judicial action is necessary to carry out the purpose of this Act, the Commission, or the Attorney General in a case involving a government, governmental agency, or political subdivision, may bring an action for appropriate temporary or preliminary relief pending final disposition of such charge. Any temporary restraining order or other order granting preliminary or temporary relief shall be issued in accordance with rule 65 of the Federal Rules of Civil Procedure. It shall be the duty of a court having jurisdiction over proceedings under this section to assign cases for hearing at the earliest practicable date and to cause such cases to be in every way expedited.

(3) Each United States district court and each United States court of a place subject to the jurisdiction of the United States shall have jurisdiction of actions brought under this title. Such an action may be brought in any judicial district in the State in which the unlawful employment practice is alleged to have been committed, in the judicial district in which the employment records relevant to such practice are maintained and administered, or in the judicial district in which the aggrieved person would have worked but for the alleged unlawful employment practice, but if the respondent is not found within any such district, such an action may be brought within the judicial district in which the respondent has his principal office. For purposes of sections 1404 and 1406 of title 28 of the United States Code, the judicial district in which the respondent has his principal office shall in all cases be considered a district in which the action might have been brought.

(4) It shall be the duty of the chief judge of the district (or in his absence, the acting chief judge) in which the case is pending immediately to designate a judge in such district to hear and determine the case. In the event that no judge in the district is available to hear and determine the case, the chief judge of the district, or the acting chief judge, as the case may be, shall certify this fact to the chief judge of the circuit (or in his absence, the acting chief judge) who shall then designate a district or circuit judge of the circuit to hear and determine the case.

(5) It shall be the duty of the judge designated pursuant to this subsection to assign the case for hearing at the earliest practicable date and to cause the case to be in every way expedited. If such judge has not scheduled the case for trial within one hundred and twenty days after issue has been joined that judge may appoint a master pursuant to rule 53 of the Federal Rules of Civil Procedure. (As amended by P.L. 92–261, eff. March 24, 1972)

(g) If the court finds that the respondent has intentionally engaged in or is intentionally engaging in an unlawful employment practice charged in the complaint, the court may enjoin the respondent from engaging in such unlawful employment practice, and order such affirmative action as may be appropriate, which may include, but is not limited to, reinstatement or hiring of employees, with or without back pay (payable by the employer, employment agency, or labor organization, as the case may be, responsible for the unlawful employment practice), or any other equitable relief as the court deems appropriate. Back pay liability shall not accrue from a date more than two years prior to the filing of a charge with the Commission. Interim earnings or amounts earnable with reasonable diligence by the person or persons discriminated against shall operate to reduce the back pay otherwise allowable. No order of the court shall require the admission or reinstatement of an individual as a member of a union, or the hiring, reinstatement, or promotion of an individual as an employee, or the payment to him of any back pay, if such individual was refused admission, suspended, or expelled, or was refused employment or advancement or was suspended or discharged for any reason other than discrimination on account of race, color, religion, sex, or national origin or in violation of section 704(a). (As amended by P.L. 92–261, eff. March 24, 1972)

(h) The provisions of the Act entitled "An Act to amend the Judicial Code and to define and limit the jurisdiction of courts sitting in equity, and for other purposes," approved March 23, 1932 (29 U.S.C. 101–115), shall not apply with respect to civil actions brought under this section. (As amended by P.L. 92–261, eff. March 24, 1972)

(i) In any case in which an employer, employment agency, or labor organization fails to comply with an order of a court issued in a civil action brought under this section the Commission may commence proceedings to compel compliance with such order. (As amended by P.L. 92–261, eff. March 24, 1972)

(j) Any civil action brought under this section and any proceedings brought under subsection (j) shall be subject to appeal as provided in sections 1291 and 1292, title 28, United States Code. (As amended by P.L. 92–261, eff. March 24, 1972)

(k) In any action or proceeding under this title the court may allow the prevailing party, other than the Commission or the United States, a reasonable attorney's fee as part of the costs, and the Commission and the United States shall be liable for costs the same as a private person.

*Sec. 707.* (a) Whenever the Attorney General has reasonable cause to believe that any person or group of persons is engaged in a pattern or practice of resistance to the full enjoyment of any of the rights secured by this title, and that the pattern or practice is of such a nature and is intended to deny the full exercise of the rights herein described, the Attorney General may bring a civil action in the appropriate district court of the United States by filing with it a complaint (1) signed by him (or in his absence the Acting Attorney General), (2) setting forth facts pertaining to such pattern or practice, and (3) requesting such relief, including an application for a permanent or temporary injunction, restraining order or other order against the person or persons responsible for such pattern or practice, as he deems necessary to insure the full enjoyment of the rights herein described.

(b) The district courts of the United States shall have and shall exercise jurisdiction of proceedings instituted pursuant to this section, and in any such proceeding the Attorney General may file with the clerk of such court a request that a court of three judges be convened to hear and determine the case. Such request by the Attorney General shall be accompanied by a certificate that, in his opinion, the case is of general public importance. A copy of the certificate and request for a three-judge court shall be immediately furnished by such clerk to the chief judge of the circuit (or in his absence, the presiding circuit judge of the circuit) in which the case is pending. Upon receipt of such request it shall be the duty of the chief judge of the circuit or the presiding circuit judge, as the case may be, to designate immediately three judges in such circuit, of whom at least one shall be a circuit judge and another of whom shall be a district judge of the court in which the proceeding was instituted, to hear and determine such case, and it shall be the duty of the judges so designated to assign the case for hearing at the earliest practicable date, to participate in the hearing and determination thereof, and to cause the case to be in every way expedited. An appeal from the final judgment of such court will lie to the Supreme Court.

In the event the Attorney General fails to file such a request in any such proceeding, it shall be the duty of the chief judge in the district (or in his absence, the acting chief judge) in which the case is pending immediately to designate a judge in such district to hear and determine the case. In the event that no judge of the district is available to hear and determine the case, the chief judge of the district, or the acting chief judge, as the case may be, shall certify this fact to the chief judge of the circuit (or in his absence, the acting chief judge) who shall then designate a district or circuit judge of the circuit to hear and determine the case.

It shall be the duty of the judge designated pursuant to this section to assign the case for hearing at the earliest practicable date and to cause the case to be in every way expedited.

(c) Effective two years after the date of enactment of the Equal Employment Opportunity Act of 1972, the functions of the Attorney General under this section shall be transferred to the Commission, together with such personnel, property, records, and unexpended balances of appropriations, allocations, and other funds employed, used, held, available, or to be made available in connection with such functions unless the President submits, and neither House of Congress vetoes, a reorganization plan pursuant to chapter 9 of title 5, United States Code, inconsistent with the provisions of this subsection. The Commission shall carry out such functions in accordance with subsections (d) and (e) of this section. (Added by P.L. 92–261, eff. March 24, 1972)

(d) Upon the transfer of functions provided for in subsection (c) of this section, in all suits commenced pursuant to this section prior to the date of such transfer, proceedings shall continue without abatement, all court orders and decrees shall remain in effect, and the Commission shall be substituted as a party for the United States of America, the Attorney General, or the Acting Attorney General, as appropriate. (Added by P.L. 92–261, eff. March 24, 1972)

(e) Subsequent to the date of enactment of the Equal Employment Opportunity Act of 1972, the Commission shall have authority to investigate and act on a charge of a pattern or practice of discrimination, whether filed by or on behalf of a person claiming to be aggrieved or by a member of the Commission. All such actions shall be conducted in accordance with the procedures set forth in section 706 of this Act. (Added by P.L. 92–261, eff. March 24, 1972)

## Effect of State Laws

*Sec. 708.* Nothing in this title shall be deemed to exempt or relieve any person from any liability, duty, penalty, or punishment provided by any present or future law of any State or political subdivision of a State, other than any such law which purports to require or permit the doing of any act which would be an unlawful employment practice under this title.

## Investigations, Inspections, Records, State Agencies

*Sec. 709.* (a) In connection with any investigation of a charge filed under section 706, the Commission or its designated representative shall at all reasonable times have access to, for the purposes of examination, and the right to copy any evidence of any person being investigated or proceeded against that relates to unlawful employment practices covered by this title and is relevant to the charge under investigation.

(b) The Commission may cooperate with State and local agencies charged with the administration of State fair employment practices laws and, with the consent of such agencies, may, for the purpose of carrying out its functions and duties under this title and within the limitation of funds appropriated specifically for such purpose, engage in and contribute to the cost of research and other projects of mutual interest undertaken by such agencies and utilize the services of such agencies and their employees, and, notwithstanding any other provision of law, pay by advance of reimbursement such agencies and their employees for services rendered to assist the Commission in carrying out this title. In furtherance of such cooperative efforts, the Commission may enter into written agreements with such State or local agencies and such agreements may include provisions under which the Commission shall refrain from processing a charge in any cases or class of cases specified in such agreements or under which the Commission shall relieve any person or class of persons in such State or locality from requirements imposed under this section. The Commission shall rescind any such agreement whenever it determines that the agreement no longer serves the interest of effective enforcement of this title. (As amended by P.L. 92–261, eff. March 24, 1972)

(c) Every employer, employment agency, and labor organization subject to this title shall (1) make and keep such records relevant to the determinations of whether unlawful employment practices have been or are being committed, (2) preserve such records for such periods, and (3) make such reports therefrom as the Commission shall prescribe by regulation or order, after public hearing, as reasonable, necessary, or appropriate for the enforcement of this title or the regulations or orders thereunder. The Commission shall, by regulation, require each employer, labor organization, and joint labor-management committee subject to this title which controls an apprenticeship or other training program to maintain such records as are reasonably necessary to carry out the purposes of this title, including, but not limited to, a list of applicants who wish to participate in such program, including the chronological order in which applications were received, and to furnish to the Commission upon request, a detailed description of the manner in which persons are selected to participate in the apprenticeship or other training program. Any employer, employment agency, labor organization, or joint labor-management committee which believes that the application to it of any regulation or order issued under this section would result in undue hardship may apply to the Commission for an exemption from the application of such regulation or order, and, if such application for an exemption is denied, bring a civil action in the United States district court for the district where such records are kept. If the Commission or the court, as the case may be, finds that the application of the regulation or order to the employer, employment agency, or labor organization in question would impose an undue hardship, the Commission or the court, as the case may be, may grant appropriate relief. If any person required to comply with the provisions of this subsection fails or refuses to do so, the United States district court for the district in which such person is found, resides, or transacts business, shall, upon application of the Commission, or the Attorney General in a case involving a governmental agency or political subdivision, have jurisdiction to issue to such person an order requiring him to comply. (As amended by P.L. 92–261, eff. March 24 1972)

(d) In prescribing requirements pursuant to subsection (c) of this section, the Commission shall consult with other interested State and Federal agencies and shall endeavor to coordinate its requirements with those adopted by such agencies. The Commission shall furnish upon request and without cost to any State or local agency charged with the administration of a fair employment practice law information obtained pursuant to subsection (c) of this section from any employer, employment agency, labor organization or joint labor-management committee subject to the jurisdiction of such agency. Such information shall be furnished on condition that it not be made public by the recipient agency prior to the institution of a proceeding under State or local law involving such information. If this condition is violated by a recipient agency, the Commission may decline to honor subsequent requests pursuant to this subsection. (As amended by P.L. 92–261, eff. March 24, 1972)

(e) It shall be unlawful for any officer or employee of the Commission to make public in any manner whatever any information obtained by the Commission pursuant to its authority under this section prior to the institution of any proceeding under this title involving such information. Any officer or employee of the Commission who shall make public in any manner whatever any information in violation of this subsection shall be guilty of a misdemeanor and upon conviction thereof, shall be fined not more than $1,000, or imprisoned not more than one year.

## Investigatory Powers

*Sec. 710.* For the purpose of all hearings and investigations conducted by the Commission or its duly authorized agents or agencies, section 11 of the National Labor Relations Act (49 Stat. 455; 29 U.S.C. 161) shall apply. (As amended by P.L. 92–261, eff. March 24, 1972)

## Notices to Be Posted

*Sec. 711.* (a) Every employer, employment agency and labor organization, as the case may be, shall post and keep posted in conspicuous places upon its premises where notices to employees, applicants for employment and members are customarily posted a notice to be prepared or approved by the Commission setting forth excerpts from, or summaries of, the pertinent provisions of this title and information pertinent to the filing of a complaint.

(b) A willful violation of this section shall be punishable by a fine of not more than $100 for each separate offense.

## Veterans' Preference

*Sec. 712.* Nothing contained in this title shall be construed to repeal or modify any Federal, State, territorial, or local law creating special rights or preference for veterans.

## Rules and Regulations

*Sec. 713.* (a) The Commission shall have authority from time to time to issue, amend, or rescind suitable procedural regulations to carry out the provisions of this title. Regulations issued under this section shall be in conformity with the standards and limitations of the Administrative Procedure Act.

(b) In any action or proceeding based on any alleged unlawful employment practice, no person shall be subject to any liability or punishment for or on account of (1) the commission by such person of an unlawful employment practice if he pleads and proves that the act of omission complained of was in good faith, in conformity with, and in reliance on any written interpretation or opinion of the Commission, or (2) the failure of such person to publish and file any information required by any provision of this title if he pleads and proves that he failed to publish and file such information in good faith, in conformity with the instructions of the Commission issued under this title regarding the filing of such information. Such a defense, if established, shall be a bar to the action or proceeding, notwithstanding that (A) after such act or omission, such interpretation or opinion is modified or rescinded or is determined by judicial authority to be invalid or of no legal effect, or (B) after publishing or filing the description and annual reports, such publication or filing is determined by judicial authority not to be in conformity with the requirements of this title.

## Forcibly Resisting the Commission or Its Representatives

*Sec. 714.* The provisions of sections 111 and 1114, title 18, United States Code, shall apply to officers, agents, and employees of the Commission in the performance of their official duties. Notwithstanding the provisions of sections 111 and 1114 of title 18, United States Code, whoever in violation of the provisions of section 1114 of such title kills a person while engaged in or on account of the performance of his official functions under this Act shall be punished by imprisonment for any term of years or for life. (As amended by P.L. 92–261, eff. March 24, 1972)

## Special Study by Secretary of Labor

*Sec. 715.* There shall be established an Equal Employment Opportunity Coordinating Council (hereinafter referred to in this section as the Council) composed of the Secretary of Labor, the Chairman of the Equal Employment Opportunity Commission, the Attorney General, the Chairman of the United States Civil Service Commission, and the Chairman of the United States Civil Rights Commission, or their respective delegates. The Council shall have the responsibility for developing and implementing agreements, policies and practices designed to maximize effort, promote efficiency, and eliminate conflict, competition, duplication and inconsistency among the operations, functions and jurisdictions of the various departments, agencies and branches of the Federal Government responsible for the implementation and enforcement of equal employment opportunity legislation, orders, and policies. On or before July 1 of each year, the Council shall transmit to the President and to the Congress a report of its activities, together with such recommendations for legislative or administrative changes as it concludes are desirable to further promote the purposes of this section. (As amended by P.L. 92–261, eff. March 24, 1972)

## Effective Date

*Sec. 716.* (a) This title shall become effective one year after the date of its enactment. (The effective date thus is July 2, 1965.)

(b) Notwithstanding subsection (a), sections of this title other than sections 703, 704, 706, and 707 shall become effective immediately.

(c) The President shall, as soon as feasible after the enactment of this title, convene one or more conferences for the purpose of enabling the leaders of groups whose members will be affected by this title to become familiar with the rights afforded and obiligations imposed by its provisions, and for the purpose of making plans which will result in the fair and effective administration of this title when all of its provisions become effective. The President shall invite the participation in such conference or conferences of (1) the members of the President's Committee on Equal Employment Opportunity, (2) the members of the Commission on Civil Rights, (3) representatives of State and local agencies engaged in furthering equal employment opportunity, (4) representatives of private agencies engaged in furthering equal employment opportunity, and (5) representatives of employers, labor organizations, and employment agencies who will be subject to this title.

## Nondiscrimination in Federal Government Employment

*Sec. 717.* (a) All personnel actions affecting employees or applicants for employment (except with regard to aliens employed outside the limits of the United States) in military departments as defined in section 102 of title 5, United States Code in executive agencies as defined in section 105 of title 5, United States Code (including employees and applicants for employment who are paid from nonappropriated funds), in the United States Postal Service and the Postal Rate Commission, in those units of the Government of the District of Columbia having positions in the competitive service, and in those units of the legislative and judicial branches of the Federal Government having positions in the competitive service, and in the Library of Congress shall be made free from any discrimination based on race, color, religion, sex, or national origin. (Added by P.L. 92–261, eff. March 24, 1972)

(b) Except as otherwise provided in this subsection, the Civil Service Commission shall have authority to enforce the provisions of subsection (a) through appropriate remedies, including reinstatement or hiring of employees with or without back pay, as will effectuate the policies of this section, and shall issue such rules, regulations, orders and instructions as it deems necessary and appropriate to carry out its responsibilities under this section. The Civil Service Commission shall—

(1) be responsible for the annual review and approval of a national and regional equal employment opportunity plan which each department and agency and each appropriate unit referred to in subsection (a) of this section shall submit in order to maintain an affirmative program of equal employment opportunity for all such employees and applicants for employment;

(2) be responsible for the review and evaluation of the operation of all agency equal employment opportunity programs, periodically obtaining and publishing (on at least a semi-annual basis) progress reports from each such department, agency, or unit; and

(3) consult with and solicit the recommendations of interested individuals, groups, and organizations relating to equal employment opportunity.

The head of each such department, agency, or unit shall comply with such rules, regulations, orders, and instructions which shall include a provision that an employee or applicant for employment shall be notified of any final action taken on any complaint of discrimination filed by him thereunder. The plan submitted by each department, agency, and unit shall include, but not be limited to—

(1) provision for the establishment of training and education programs designed to provide a maximum opportunity for employees to advance so as to perform at their highest potential; and

(2) a description of the qualifications in terms of training and experience relating to equal employment opportunity for the principal and operating officials of each such department, agency, or unit responsible for carrying out the equal employment opportunity program and of the allocation of personnel and resources proposed by such department, agency, or unit to carry out its equal employment opportunity program.

With respect to employment in the Library of Congress, authorities granted in this subsection to the Civil Service Commission shall be exercised by the Librarian of Congress. (Added by P.L. 92–261, eff. March 24, 1972)

(c) Within thirty days of receipt of notice of final action taken by a department, agency, or unit referred to in subsection 717(a), or by the Civil Service Commission upon an appeal from a decision or order of such department, agency, or unit on a complaint of discrimination based on race, color, religion, sex or national origin, brought pursuant to subsection (a) of this section, Executive Order 11478 or any succeeding executive orders, or after one hundred and eighty days from the filing of the initial charge with the department, agency, or unit or with the Civil Service Commission on appeal from a decision or order of such department, agency, or unit, an employee or applicant for employment, if aggrieved by the final disposition of his complaint, or by the failure to take final action on his complaint, may file a civil action as provided in section 706, in which civil action the head of the department, agency, or unit, as appropriate, shall be the defendant.

(d) The provisions of section 706 (f) through (k), as applicable, shall govern civil actions brought hereunder. (Added by P.L. 92–261, eff. March 24, 1972)

(e) Nothing contained in this Act shall relieve any Government agency or official of its or his primary responsibility to assure nondiscrimination in employment as required by the Constitution and statutes or of its or his responsibilities under Executive Order 11478 relating to equal employment opportunity in the Federal Government. (Added by P.L. 92–261, eff. March 24, 1972)

## Special Provision With Respect to Denial, Termination and Suspension of Government Contracts

*Sec. 718.* No Government contract, or portion thereof, with any employer, shall be denied, withheld, terminated, or suspended, by any agency or officer of the United States under any equal employment opportunity law or order, where such employer has an affirmative action plan which has previously been accepted by the Government for the same facility within the past twelve months without first according such employer full hearing and adjudication under the provisions of title 5, United States Code, section 554, and the following pertinent sections: Provided, That if such employer has deviated substantially from such previously agreed to affirmative action plan, this section shall not apply: Provided further, That for the purposes of this section an affirmative action plan shall be deemed to have been accepted by the Government at the time the appropriate compliance agency has accepted such plan unless within forty-five days thereafter the Office of Federal Contract Compliance has disapproved such plan. (Added by P.L. 92–261, eff. March 24, 1972)

# 23

## Griggs, et al. v.
## Duke Power Co.

*U.S. Supreme Court*

### Opinion of the Court

Mr. Chief Justice Burger delivered the opinion of the Court.

We granted the writ in this case to resolve the question whether an employer is prohibited by the Civil Rights Act of 1964, Title VII, from requiring a high school education or passing of a standardized general intelligence test as a condition of employment in or transfer to jobs when (a) neither standard is shown to be significantly related to successful job performance, (b) both requirements operate to disqualify Negroes at a substantially higher rate than white applicants, and (c) the jobs in question formerly had been filled only by white employees as part of a longstanding practice of giving preference to whites.[1]

Congress provided, in Title VII of the Civil Rights Act of 1964, for class actions for enforcement of provisions of the Act and this proceeding was brought by a group of incumbent Negro employees against Duke Power Company. All the petitioners are employed at the Company's Dan River Steam Station, a power generating facility located at Draper, North Carolina. At the time this action was instituted, the Company had 95 employees at the Dan River Station, 14 of whom were Negroes; 13 of these are petitioners here.

The District Court found that prior to July 2, 1965, the effective date of the Civil Rights Act of 1964, the Company openly discriminated on the basis of race in the hiring and assigning

SOURCE: 401 U.S. 424 (1970). Extraneous material deleted.

of employees at its Dan River plant. The plant was organized into five operating departments: (1) Labor, (2) Coal Handling, (3) Operations, (4) Maintenance, and (5) Laboratory and Test. Negroes were employed only in the Labor Department where the highest paying jobs paid less than the lowest paying jobs in the other four "operating" departments in which only whites were employed.[2] Promotions were normally made within each department on the basis of job seniority. Transferees into a department usually began in the lowest position.

In 1955 the Company instituted a policy of requiring a high school education for initial assignment to any department except Labor, and for transfer from the Coal Handling to any "inside" department (Operations, Maintenance, or Laboratory). When the Company abandoned its policy of restricting Negroes to the Labor Department in 1965, completion of high school also was made a prerequisite to transfer from Labor to any other department. From the time the high school requirement was instituted to the time of trial, however, white employees hired before the time of the high school education requirement continued to perform satisfactorily and achieve promotions in the "operating" departments. Findings on this score are not challenged.

The Company added a further requirement for new employees on July 2, 1965, the date on which Title VII became effective. To qualify for placement in any but the Labor Department it became necessary to register satisfactory scores on two professionally prepared aptitude tests, as well as to have a high school education. Completion of high school alone continued to render employees eligible for transfer to the four desirable departments from which Negroes had been excluded if the incumbent had been employed prior to the time of the new requirement. In September 1965 the Company began to permit incumbent employees who lacked a high school education to qualify for transfer from Labor or Coal Handling to an "inside" job by passing two tests—The Wonderlic Personnel Test, which purports to measure general intelligence, and the Bennett Mechanical Comprehension Test. Neither was directed or intended to measure the ability to learn to perform a particular job or category of jobs. The requisite scores used for both initial hiring and transfer approximated the national median for high school graduates.[3]

The District Court had found that while the Company previously followed a policy of overt racial discrimination in a period prior to the Act, such conduct had ceased. The District Court also concluded that Title VII was intended to be prospective only and, consequently, the impact of prior inequities was beyond the reach of corrective action authorized by the Act.

The Court of Appeals was confronted with a question of first impression, as are we, concerning the meaning of Title VII. After careful analysis a majority of that court concluded that a subjective test of the employer's intent should govern, particularly in a close case, and that in this case there was no showing of a discriminatory purpose in the adoption of the diploma and test requirements. On this basis, the Court of Appeals concluded there was no violation of the Act.

The Court of Appeals reversed the District Court in part, rejecting the holding that residual discrimination arising from prior employment practices was insulated from remedial action.[4] The Court of Appeals noted, however, that the District Court was correct in its conclusion that there was no showing of a racial purpose or invidious intent in the adoption of the high school diploma requirement or general intelligence test and that these standards had been applied fairly to whites and Negroes alike. It held that, in the absence of a discriminatory purpose, use of such requirements was permitted by the Act. In so doing, the Court of Appeals rejected the claim that because these two requirements operated to render ineligible a markedly disproportionate number of Negroes, they were unlawful under Title VII unless shown to be job related.[5] We granted the writ on these claims. 399 U.S. 926.

The objective of Congress in the enactment of Title VII is plain from the language of the statute. It was to achieve equality of employment opportunities and remove barriers that have operated in the past to favor an identifiable group of white employees over other employees. Under the Act, practices, procedures, or tests neutral on their face, and even neutral in terms of intent, cannot be maintained if they operate to "freeze" the status quo of prior discriminatory employment practices.

The Court of Appeals' opinion, and the partial dissent, agreed that, on the record in the present case, "whites register far better on the Company's alternative requirements" than Negroes.[6] 410. 2d 1225, 1239 n. 6. This consequence would appear to be directly traceable to race. Basic intelligence must have the means of articulation to manifest itself fairly in a testing process. Because they are Negroes, petitioners have long received inferior education in segregated schools and this Court expressly recognized these differences in *Gaston County* v. *United States,* 395 U.S. 285 (1969). There, because of the inferior education received by Negroes in North Carolina, this Court barred the institution of a literacy test for voter registration on the ground that the test would abridge the right to vote indirectly on account of race. Congress did not intend by Title VII, however, to guarantee a job to every person regardless of qualifications. In short, the Act does not command that any person be hired simply because he was formerly the subject of discrimination, or because he is a member of a minority group. Discriminatory preference for any group, minority or majority, is precisely and only what Congress has proscribed. What is required by Congress is the removal of artificial, arbitrary, and unnecessary barriers to employment when the barriers operate invidiously to discriminate on the basis of racial or other impermissible classification.

Congress has now provided that tests or criteria for employment or promotion may not provide equality of opportunity merely in the sense of the fabled offer of milk to the stork and the fox. On the contrary, Congress has now required that the posture and condition of the job-seeker be taken into account. It has—to resort again to the fable—provided that the vessel in which the milk is proffered be one all seekers can use. The Act proscribes not only overt discrimination but also practices that are fair in form, but discriminatory in operation. The touchstone is business necessity. If an employment practice which operates to exclude Negroes cannot be shown to be related to job performance, the practice is prohibited.

On the record before us, neither the high school completion requirement nor the general intelligence test is shown to bear a demonstrable relationship to successful performance of the jobs for which it was used. Both were adopted, as the Court of Appeals noted, without meaningful study of their relationship to job-performance ability. Rather, a vice president of the Company testified, the requirements were instituted on the Company's judgment that they generally would improve the overall quality of the work force.

The evidence, however, shows that employees who have not completed high school or taken the tests have continued to perform satisfactorily and make progress in departments for which the high school and test criteria are now used.[7] The promotion record of present employees who would not be able to meet the new criteria thus suggests the possibility that the requirements may not be needed even for the limited purpose of preserving the avowed policy of advancement within the Company. In the context of this case, it is unnecessary to reach the question whether testing requirements that take into account capability for the next succeeding position or related future promotion might be utilized upon a showing that such long-range requirements fulfill a genuine business need. In the present case the Company has made no such showing.

The Court of Appeals held that the Company had adopted the diploma and test requirements without any "intention to discriminate against Negro employees." 420 F. 2d, at 1232. We do not suggest that either the District Court or the Court of Appeals erred in examining the employer's intent; but good intent or absence of discriminatory intent does not redeem employment procedures or testing mechanisms that operate as "built-in headwinds" for minority groups and are unrelated to measuring job capability.

The Company's lack of discriminatory intent is suggested by special efforts to help the undereducated employees through Company financing of two-thirds the cost of tuition for high school training. But Congress directed the thrust of the Act to the *consequences* of employment practices, not simply the motivation. More than that, Congress has placed on the employer the burden of showing that any given requirement must have a manifest relationship to the employment in question.

The facts of this case demonstrate the inadequacy of broad and general testing devices as well as the infirmity of using diplomas or degrees as fixed measures of capability. History is filled with examples of men and women who rendered highly effective performance without the conventional badges of accomplishment in terms of certificates, diplomas, or degrees. Diplomas and tests are useful servants, but Congress has mandated the commonsense proposition that they are not to become masters of reality.

The Company contends that its general intelligence tests are specifically permitted by § 703 (h) of the Act.[8] That section authorizes the use of "any professionally developed ability test" that is not "designed, intended, *or used* to discriminate because of race. . . ." (Emphasis added.)

The Equal Employment Opportunity Commission, having enforcement responsibility, has issued guidelines interpreting § 703 (h) to permit only the use of job-related tests.[9] The administrative interpretation of the Act by the enforcing agency is entitled to great deference. See, e.g., *United States* v. *City of Chicago,* 400 U.S. 8 (1970); *Udall* v. *Tallman,* 380 U.S. 1 (1965); *Power Reactor Co.* v. *Electricians,* 367 U.S. 396 (1961). Since the Act and its legislative history support the Commission's construction, this affords good reason to treat the guidelines as expressing the will of Congress.

Section 703 (h) was not contained in the House version of the Civil Rights Act but was added in the Senate during extended debate. For a period, debate revolved around claims that the bill as proposed would prohibit all testing and force employers to hire unqualified persons simply because they were part of a group formerly subject to job discrimination.[10] Proponents of Title VII sought throughout the debate to assure the critics that the Act would have no effect on job-related tests. Senators Case of New Jersey and Clark of Pennsylvania, co-managers of the bill on the Senate floor, issued a memorandum explaining that the proposed Title VII

> expressly protects the employer's right to insist that any prospective applicant, Negro or white, *must meet the applicable job qualifications.* Indeed, the very purpose of Title VII is to promote hiring on the basis of job qualifications, rather than on the basis of race or color. 110 Cong. Rec. 7247.[11] (Emphasis added.)

Despite these assurances, Senator Tower of Texas introduced an amendment authorizing "professionally developed ability tests." Proponents of Title VII opposed the amendment because, as written, it would permit an employer to give any test,

> whether it was a good test or not, so long as it was professionally designed. Discrimination could actually exist under the guise of compliance with the statute. 110 Cong. Rec. 13504 (remarks of Sen. Case).

The amendment was defeated and two days later Senator Tower offered a substitute amendment which was adopted verbatim and is now the testing provision of § 703 (h). Speaking for the supporters of Title VII, Senator Humphrey, who had vigorously opposed the first amendment, endorsed the substitute amendment, stating:

> Senators on both sides of the aisle who were deeply interested in Title VII have examined the text of this amendment and have found it to be in accord with the intent and purpose of that Title. 110 Cong. Rec. 13724.

The amendment was then adopted.[12] From the sum of the legislative history relevant in this case, the conclusion is inescapable that the EEOC's construction of § 703 (h) to require that employment tests be job related comports with congressional intent.

Nothing in the Act precludes the use of testing or measuring procedures; obviously they are useful. What Congress has forbidden is giving these devices and mechanisms controlling force unless they are demonstrably a reasonable measure of job performance. Congress has not commanded that the less qualified be preferred over the better qualified simply because of minority origins. Far from disparaging job qualifications as such, Congress has made such qualifications the controlling factor, so that race, religion, nationality, and sex become irrelevant. What Congress has commanded is that any tests used must measure the person for the job and not the person in the abstract.

The judgment of the Court of Appeals is, as to that portion of the judgment appealed from, reversed.

Mr. Justice Brennan took no part in the consideration or decision of this case.

# Notes

1. The Act provides:

Sec. 703. (a) It shall be an unlawful employment practice for an employer—. . .

(2) to limit, segregate, or classify his employees in any way which would deprive or tend to deprive any individual of employment opportunities or otherwise adversely affect his status as an employee, because of such individual's race, color, religion, sex, or national origin. . . .

(h) Notwithstanding any other provision of this Title, it shall not be an unlawful employment practice for an employer. . .to give and to act upon the results of any professionally developed ability test provided that such test, its administration or action upon the results is not designed, intended or used to discriminate because of race, color, religion, sex or national origin. . . . 78 Stat. 255, 42 U.S.C. § 2000e-2.

2. A Negro was first assigned to a job in an operating department in August 1966, five months after charges had been filed with the Equal Employment Opportunity Commission. The employee, a high school graduate who had begun in the Labor Department in 1953, was promoted to a job in the Coal Handling Department.

3. The test standards are thus more stringent than the high school requirement, since they would screen out approximately half of all high school graduates.

4. The Court of Appeals ruled that Negroes employed in the Labor Department at a time when there was no high school or test requirement for entrance into the higher paying departments could not now be made subject to those requirements, since whites hired contemporaneously into those departments were never subject to them. The Court of Appeals also required that the seniority rights of those Negroes be measured on a plantwide, rather than a departmental, basis. However, the Court of Appeals denied relief to the Negro employees without a high school education or its equivalent who were hired into the Labor Department after institution of the educational requirement.

5. One member of that court disagreed with this aspect of the decision, maintaining, as do the petitioners in this Court, that Title VII prohibits the use of employment criteria that operate in a racially exclusionary fashion and do not measure skills or abilities necessary to performance of the jobs for which those criteria are used.

6. In North Carolina, 1960 census statistics show that, while 34 percent of white males had completed high school, only 12 percent of Negro males had done so. U.S. Bureau of the Census, *U.S. Census of Population: 1960,* vol. 1, Characteristics of the Population, pt. 35, Table 47.

Similarly, with respect to standardized tests, the EEOC in one case found that use of a battery of tests, including the Wonderlic and Bennett tests used by the Company in the instant case, resulted in 58 percent of whites passing the tests, as compared with only 6 percent of the blacks. Decision of EEOC, CCH Empl. Prac. Guide, ¶ 17,304.53 (Dec. 2, 1966). See also Decision of EEOC 70–552, CCH Empl. Prac. Guide, ¶ 6139 (Feb. 19, 1970).

7. For example, between July 2, 1965, and November 14, 1966, the percentage of white employees who were promoted but who were not high school graduates was nearly identical to the percentage of nongraduates in the entire white work force.

8. Section 703 (h) applies only to tests. It has no applicability to the high school diploma requirement.

9. EEOC Guidelines on Employment Testing Procedures, issued August 24, 1966, provide:

The Commission accordingly interprets "professionally developed ability test" to mean a test which fairly measures the knowledge or skills required by the particular job or class of jobs which the applicant seeks, or which fairly affords the employer a chance to measure the applicant's ability to perform a particular job or class of jobs. The fact that a test was prepared by an individual or organization claiming expertise in test preparation does not, without more, justify its use within the meaning of Title VII.

The EEOC position has been elaborated in the new Guidelines on Employee Selection Procedures, 29 CFR § 1607, 35 Fed. Reg. 12333 (Aug. 1, 1970). These guidelines demand that employers using tests have available "data demonstrating that the test is predictive of or significantly correlated with important elements of work behavior which comprise or are relevant to the job or jobs for which candidates are being evaluated." (*Id.,* at § 1607.4 (c).)

10. The congressional discussion was prompted by the decision of a hearing examiner for the Illinois Fair Employment Commission in *Myart v. Motorola Co.* (The decision is reprinted at 110 Cong. Rec. 5662.) That case suggested that standardized tests on which whites performed better than Negroes could never be used. The decision was taken to mean that such tests could never be justified even if the needs of the business required them. A number of Senators feared that Title VII might produce a similar result. See remarks of Senators Ervin, 110 Cong. Rec. 5614–5616; Smathers, *id.,* at 5999–6000; Holland, *id.,* at 7012–7013; Hill, *id.,* at 8447; Tower, *id.,* at 9024; Talmadge, *id.,* at 9025–9026; Fulbright, *id.,* at 9599–9600; and Ellender, *id.,* at 9600.

11. The Court of Appeals majority, in finding no requirement in Title VII that employment tests be job related, relied in part on a quotation from an earlier Clark-Case interpretative memorandum addressed to the question of the constitutionality of Title VII. The Senators said in that memorandum:

There is no requirement in Title VII that employers abandon bona fide qualification tests where, because of differences in background and education, members of some groups are able to perform better on these tests than members of other groups. An employer may set his qualifications as high as he likes, he may test to determine which applicants have these qualifications, and he may hire, assign, and promote on the basis of test performance. 110 Cong. Rec. 7213.

However, nothing there stated conflicts with the later memorandum dealing specifically with the debate over employer testing, 110 Cong. Rec. 7247 (quoted from in the text above), in which Senators Clark and Case explained that tests which measure "applicable job qualifications" are permissible under Title VII. In the earlier memorandum Clark and Case assured the Senate that employers were not to be prohibited from using tests that determine *qualifications.*

Certainly a reasonable interpretation of what the Senators meant, in light of the subsequent memorandum directed specifically at employer testing, was that nothing in the Act prevents employers from requiring that applicants be fit for the job.

12. Senator Tower's original amendment provided in part that a test would be permissible

"if...in the case of any individual who is seeking employment with such employer, such test is designed to determine or predict whether such individual is suitable or trainable with respect to his employment in the particular business or enterprise involved...." 110 Cong. Rec. 13492.

This language indicates that Senator Tower's aim was simply to make certain that job-related tests would be permitted. The opposition to the amendment was based on its loose wording which the proponents of Title VII feared would be susceptible of misinterpretation. The final amendment, which was acceptable to all sides, could hardly have required less of a job relation than the first.

# 24

# Women in Top Jobs: An Opportunity for Federal Leadership

*Debra W. Stewart*
*North Carolina State University*

The year 1976 finds American women firmly entrenched in the country's labor force. With nine out of ten women having worked during their lifetime and 46 per cent of all American women currently engaged in salaried employment, the female worker is no longer a deviant case.[1] This trend toward large-scale participation is mirrored in the public sector. There females constitute some 41.7 per cent of the white collar work force and, in certain cases, occupy up to 63 per cent of all agency slots.[2] Accordingly, policy objectives, congruent with emerging national needs in this sphere, relate less to mere participation of women in the labor force and more to the character of that participation. Focusing specifically on government as employer, the issue becomes not how many women will be employed in the public service of the future, but rather in what capacity they will be employed.

This article is grounded in the assumption that expansion of employment opportunity for women in American society calls for a focus, not on jobs per se, but rather on job stratification. National occupational data reveals small numbers of women have indeed gained acceptance in the most prestigious occupations: 9.8 per cent of the physicians, 7 per cent of the

lawyers and judges, 9.4 per cent of the full professors, and 2.3 per cent of highest level (GS16–18) federal civil servants.[3] Yet the pattern of mobility parallels that recently identified in Great Britain. There women's entry into top slots has gone from breakthrough in earlier decades to acceptance, but now remains fixed on a plateau.[4] The public policy question is simply: "how might these percentages be increased?" Through an analysis of obstacles to full participation in the upper echelons of private and public bureaucracy, this article aims to bring change direction into sharp relief and, in the process, to illuminate the special leadership role for the federal public service.

## Obstacles to Change

In the plethora of recent works on women in American society three broad explanations for the blockage of female entry into high-level decision-making positions are found: the political, the biological, and the sociological.[5] Each type of explanation contains elements of the others, the sociological in particular having pronounced biological and political dimensions. Nevertheless, these labels do function to locate the core of each explanation as well as to allow for some demarcation of boundary lines. Critical examination of each explanatory model, and its implications, in conjunction with data on public and private sector employment patterns serves to highlight that set of factors best explaining the barrier to movement beyond the current threshold. Only through such isolation of the "problem," will the solution in the form of a change strategy emerge.

## The Political Thesis

In the most extreme form the political thesis posits that men constitute the ruling class of the world and are determined to stay in power. In the words of one author, male-female relations reflect "...the oldest, most rigid class/caste system in existence, the class system based on sex—a system consolidated over thousands of years, lending the archtypal male and female roles an undeserved legitimacy and seeming permanence."[6] This analysis points out that characteristically "feminine" traits are nothing more than the traits of any oppressed class. While emphasizing the historical similarity between the condition of women as an oppressed class in American society and the condition of blacks, this mode of analysis stresses the ubiquitous character of the sexual class system.

To the extent that this thesis is correct, only a rigorously enforced quota system would facilitate the movement of significant numbers of women into top jobs in American society. And yet, if this analysis does capture reality, the possibility of gaining the political clout to make such a quota system effective, even in government employment, is highly problematic. But, before subscribing to an analysis which yields only the alternatives of subjection or revolution, elements of feder   service experience, challenging the politica. thesis, should be brought forward.

While at one level the class/power explanation fits with the picture of women clustering in the low pay and low status jobs, it is contradicted by formal government action endorsing EEO for women, as well as by the pattern of employment variation across agencies within the federal government. With respect to the formal endorsement of EEO, which may go as far as requiring affirmative action, one could simply respond that this is just a move in the symbolic politics game. Such moves are necessary to feign compliance with the formal American "equality of opportunity" ideology. Indeed we know from cross-national studies that formal ideology may account for little in explaining the position of women in modern society.[7] The debate on formal vs. real opportunity is not easily resolved, for it gets into the motivations of EEO rule makers. Fortunately, we need not await such resolution before pronouncing judgment on the political thesis.

The pattern of employment within and across government agencies clearly flies in the face of this class/power analysis. If, in fact, there were a conscious male conspiracy, bent on keeping women in low status jobs, then one would expect to find little variation in opportunity for distaff advancement across agencies. This expectation is, however, not borne out by the data. On the contrary one is struck by the apparent variation in opportunity across agencies. Table 1 illustrates this point.

These agencies are selected for examination because they exhibit substantial variation. While the percentage of women in GS grades 1–6 ranges from an adequate 54.1 per cent in Agriculture, to an expansive 84.1 per cent in HUD, variation in the percentage employed in GS grades 7–12, and 13+ is truly striking. In the middle-range grades, GS 7–12, women account for a high 55.6 per cent in HEW, and a low 9.4 per cent of the total in Transportation. Differences become even more pronounced in grades GS 13 through GS 18. Here, If figures reflect real opportunity, HEW stands out as the agency where women have made greatest strides, with the percentages in grades 14–15–16 appearing as 14.3, 9.2, and 8 respectively. While admittedly there remains room for opportunity expansion in HEW, these percentages seem quite favorable when juxtaposed to the NASA figures of 8 per cent (GS 14), .5 per cent (GS 15), and 0 per cent (GS 16). The point verified by even a cursory glance at Table 1 is that advancement for women has varied by agency. Since men have traditionally been the guardians of the gates in all agencies, the variation calls into question the political thesis itself.

## The Biological Thesis

As distinct from the political thesis, which blames men, the biological thesis blames evolution for the dearth of women in positions of power. The thrust of the "biology is destiny" argument is not simply that certain mental or behavior traits may be sex linked and hence

**Table 1**
**Women as per cent of total employed by grade, within selected federal agencies, 1974[8]**

| Grade(s) | HEW | HUD | Agriculture | NASA | Transportation |
|---|---|---|---|---|---|
| 1–6 | 81.0% | 84.1% | 54.1% | 77.9% | 77.5% |
| | (49,447)* | (4,417) | (14,776) | (3,928) | (7,438) |
| 7–12 | 55.6% | 29.6% | 9.8% | 14.2% | 9.4% |
| | (24,212) | (2,311) | (4,628) | (1,314) | (3,084) |
| 13 | 18.3% | 10.4% | 3.9% | 1.8% | 1.3% |
| | (1,227) | (177) | (212) | (98) | (169) |
| 14 | 14.3% | 6.1% | 3% | .8% | 1.1% |
| | (641) | (66) | (72) | (25) | (53) |
| 15 | 9.2% | 5.2% | 1.1% | .5% | .7% |
| | (268) | (31) | (13) | (9) | (13) |
| 16 | 8% | 1.4% | 1.7% | 0% | 2.1% |
| | (22) | (1) | (3) | (0) | (4) |
| 17 | 5.5% | 0% | 0% | ** | 1.2% |
| | (5) | (0) | (0) | | (1) |
| 18 | 3.8% | 0% | 0% | | 0% |
| | (1) | (0) | (0) | | (0) |

*N = (49,447)
**NASA shows no personnel in 17 and 18 grades in the GS and equivalent pay plan.

physiologically determined, but that presence of some traits and absence of others act directly on the fitness of women for high-level decision-making positions. One variation of this argument fixes on the concept of leadership. Leadership, seen here as the major activity of the high-level decision makers, is not merely associated with an official position, but must be granted to a would-be leader by a follower. Yet, as Lionel Tiger, the major proponent of this position, would argue, it is just this trait, the capacity to compel followership, that women do not have and, furthermore, can not have because of their physiological makeup.[9] Adapting such an argument to organizational life, one would say that underlying regularities in the species explain the paucity of women in top jobs. Women have not laid claim to leadership roles in the bureaucracy chiefly because they are women, and not because of limited opportunity. Should an aggressively enforced affirmative action program put a woman into formal leadership position, male colleagues will, on any issue of great significance, be strongly disposed to form an all-male group and accordingly to exclude the interloper from decision making on that issue.

A second variation of the "biology is destiny" thesis attributes the sparseness of women in positions of power to the functioning female sex hormones. The very facts of menstrual cycle and menopause limit a woman's capacity for leadership because these biological conditions lead inevitably to periodically impaired judgment. Put most practically by Dr. Edgar Berman, physician and advisor to former Vice-President Hubert Humphrey, "If you had an investment in a bank, you wouldn't want the president of your bank making a loan under these raging [female] hormonal influences at that particular period."[10]

To the extent that the "biology destiny" thesis is correct, we may simply be wrong headed in trying to move women up into high-level decision-making positions in American society. Whether the explanation is rooted in an inability to command followership or to control raging hormones, the public policy implication is obvious. No realistic conception of the "public interest" could be served by moving boldly against "nature."

The popular appeal of this kind of argument is unquestionably limited, since it goes against the grain of a fundamentally egalitarian ethos in U.S. political culture. One can as well question the character of research that supports these conclusions.[11] For our purposes, however, it is sufficient to examine this explanation in light of both our own national experience and empirical data on trends in female employment.

As was suggested at the very beginning of this article, the fact that some women have made it into top jobs is indisputable. They are found, albeit in small number, in the most prestigious of occupations. Particularly in the Executive Branch of government where merit weighs heavier toward promotion than family relationships[12] numerous women have held top positions and have unquestionably "commanded" followership.[13] At one level this may constitute prima facie evidence of the fatuousness of the "biology is destiny" explanation. If biological considerations set the limits of possible achievement, how does one explain these loophole women?

Furthermore, to the extent that biological considerations hold sway, one would expect little variation in the general pattern of labor force participation over time. We would expect the life-cycle pattern, conventionally identified with the female labor force, to remain constant, i.e., "taking a job when first out of school, withdrawing from the labor force for marriage and motherhood, and returning to paid work in later years when children are in school or on their own."[14] Yet Labor Department statistics suggest that a dramatic shift has occurred in participation rates among women in the 25 to 34 age bracket. Participation rates of this cohort, traditionally thought most intensely constrained by their biological stage of life, jumped from 34 per cent in 1950 to 52 per cent by 1974.[15] While such a pattern does not directly refute the biological determinant thesis, as far as top jobs are concerned, it does make one skeptical of broad generalizations rooted in biological makeup.

## The Sociological Thesis

From a sociological perspective, the concept of role differentiation holds the key to the difficulties faced by women when entering high-level positions in the organizational world. As formally defined, the term *role* refers to "a position in a social structure, involving a pattern of specific expectations, privileges, responsibilities, including attitudes and behaviors, and codified to some recognizable degree by norms, values, and sanctions."[16]

Using this framework, the thesis holds that while for men role differentiation within the family complements occupational role achievement, it frustrates such "outside" role achievement for women. The role conflict phenomenon is highlighted in discussion of both the functions of the women in the family and the personal qualities deemed necessary for adequate performance.

Motherhood, as distinct from fatherhood, has traditionally been viewed as a full-time job. Women report spending 60 hours a week in their housewife role; even when employed outside the home, women tend to remain responsible for both the mothering and general housekeeping functions.[17] These essentially caring and cleaning functions are best carried out by one who exhibits conventional female traits of understanding, helpfulness, solicitousness, and passivity.

Obviously, the role conflict stems from the fact that top jobs in government and elsewhere demand both a full-time commitment, irrespective of family obligations, and a strength in personality traits diametrically opposed to those cultivated by the mother role. For women, goals set by the occupational role and the family role are at worst mutually exclusive and at best only partially reconcilable. As stated in an earlier study of role contradiction: "the full realization of one role threatens defeat in the other."[18] In short, the major obstacle to enlarging the percentage of women in top government jobs is that society is organized so as to discourage larger numbers of female contestants for those jobs.[19]

Having said all this, one might still raise the question: why must this be? What is it that in fact sustains a pattern of action which results in differential access to top jobs based on sex? Role differentiation, it can be argued, is rooted in gender differentiation which encompasses dimensions of both the political and biological theses elaborated above. It is from the biological fact of sex that gender differences are inferred. To view the woman as passive, solicitous, understanding, and nonachievement oriented is to say nothing of her biology and everything about her gender. Gender as a cultural phenomenon reinforces family and occupational role choices insofar as it sanctions those choices. The political dimension of gender differentiation intrudes with the realization that those attributes commonly associated with the "feminine" are also the attributes generally associated with ruled classes.[20]

Hence, while neither the biological nor political thesis stands on its own, dimensions of each fit when viewed in conjunction with the gender-based analysis of role differentiation. In a recent work, Kenneth Boulding effectively weaves these competing explanations together in the concept of role prejudice.[21] Role prejudice is viewed as a product of a false social learning process by which certain biological or genetic characteristics of individuals come to be associated with certain roles. According to Boulding, role prejudice develops when there are genetic differences in the human population which are visible, but not significant for role performance. The political implication is that such role prejudice translates into discrimination against individuals who strive to achieve outside of their socially defined role set. It is this "role prejudice," a prejudice shared by women and men alike, that accounts for the political reality of few top spots for women.

If the analysis is correct, the question then becomes how to dissolve role prejudice. Is it possible, given the grounding of role prejudice in the psychocultural phenomenon of gender differentiation, that women as a percentage of top job holders in the federal service or elsewhere will ever surpass the single digit mark? In order to answer this question one must probe the attitudinal and the structural supports for role prejudice.

## The Response of the Private Sector: Role Prejudice as Attitude

At first glance the term *role prejudice* suggests a problem of individual attitude. In conventional usage, prejudice suggests an inner tendency to respond unfavorably to persons on the basis of their group membership.[22] This inner tendency is essentially a problem of attitude and hence is susceptible to modification through innovative techniques of organizational development. Accordingly, the response of private industry to the role prejudice phenomenon has been to employ various kinds of awareness training programs in the service of an "integration" objective. Recognizing that career advancement for women is blocked by organizational "scripts" that discourage women from aiming high, concerned private firms are trying to develop new scripts that facilitate female adaptation to the existing career system.[23]

To be sure, this direction promises to improve the organizational climate for women already competing for top slots in American industry. Just as federal equal opportunity legislation mandated the elimination of formal barriers to advancement for women, awareness training programs undermine those informal obstacles to change that stem from individually held sex role stereotypes. Still, given this thrust, the question from an analytical perspective remains: will this combination of legal and organizational development measures facilitate substantial movement beyond current threshold?

Admittedly the data is not yet in to answer this question definitively. Still, there is reason to believe the answer to the question will be no. That negative response emerges from a more probing consideration of the role prejudice concept, a consideration stressing the structural dimension of the role prejudice phenomenon.

From decades of research in the field of social psychology we know that individual attitudes can in fact be modified. Yet role prejudice as it resides in the very structure of the career system may account to a far greater degree for the dearth of women at the top. I would argue that this is indeed the situation we now face in the consideration of equal opportunity for women. Through understanding the symbiotic relationship between gender differentiation and career systems the road for public service action is illuminated.

## The Nature of Career Systems

In advanced industrial societies the career system is biased in favor of the "two-person, single career."[24] This two-person, single career option is played out through an organization which places a combination of formal and informal demands on both members of a married couple, while formally employing only the man. To insure success in this single endeavor the wife role requires meeting fully the stereotype definition of "feminine," e.g., to be the supporter, the comforter, the child rearer, the housekeeper, and the entertainer.[25] Her achievement is vicarious; achievement needs are met either completely or predominantly in her husband's accomplishments.[26]

The two-person, single career pattern that has received the most popular attention is that associated with corporate executives,[27] but the analysis applies equally well to any high-level organizational decision-making position. Since reputation in high-level executive careers is measured against time, and recognition for achievement is frequently a function of age, the supportive role played by the wife is a key element in success.[28] A recent analysis of career executive marriages stresses the importance of this supportive female role by pointing out that the substantially lower divorce rate among executives could be attributed to the dampening effect such separation would have upon a man's career.[29] This two-person, single career

route to success has become so institutionalized that even those observers concerned with the potentially dehumanizing aspects of contemporary bureaucracy eulogize the traditional wife for her shelter-giving qualities.[30]

Those women who do try to achieve non-vicariously within the modern career system tend to start later and may proceed more slowly in large part because they are acting out a single-person rather than two-person career. Most succinctly summed up in a recent study by Hochschild (1975) the essential problem with the career systems of the modern world is that their guiding rules are made to suit men. The traditional family functions as the service agency supporting the organization in which the male career is conducted.[31] Role prejudice resides thus in the very structure of modern careers systems, not merely in the attitudes of individuals towards members of the opposite sex.

If this analysis of role prejudice as inherent in the structure of modern career systems is correct, it casts serious doubt on the feasibility of private industry's integration strategy. The burgeoning literature on private sector opportunity expansion glorifies the aspiring female executive in terms of the extent to which she magnifies her male counterpart.[32] Debate centers largely on the effectiveness of alternative mechanisms for integrating females into the male career system. One analyst assures us that although a time lag is inevitable until women change individual role expectations, amalgamation is clearly down the road.[33] Little attention is paid to the less tractable obstacles blocking the way.

Yet if the analysis presented above accurately describes the bias in modern career systems, "making it" within that system is simply not feasible for most women. Only women who enjoy the services of a full-time house-husband will start out in the race on equal footing with their male colleagues. Even with all other things being equal, structural factors will assign women to a competitive disadvantage in the push for top jobs. Nothing in the career histories of top executives in the United States suggests that the structural characteristics of the modern career system will change in a more favorable direction. On the contrary, if any change has occurred in recent years it has been in the direction of intensification.[34] Hence we must challenge the feasibility of this method for moving beyond the current level of accomplishment. We can as well question on normative grounds the desirability of a change strategy which accepts as given a requirement that women desirous of "public" success give up family life while men continue to enjoy the family life option. This seems to be the practical outcome of the private sector approach.

It is against this backdrop that a new direction for public sector equal opportunity can be set and strategies for implementation considered. The time has come for the public service to bring a new orientation to the very concept of career and accordingly to go beyond the now traditional "modern" career system.

## A Leadership Role for the Federal Service

The federal service historically has taken the initiative in removing formal barriers to female participation in the labor market.[35] Nonetheless, it is now time to probe deeper into the barriers to further advancement. To the extent that the career system blocks further advancement, it is necessary to attack that system directly. Quite naturally questions arise as to the shape of an alternative career system. Here only in broad strokes can the vital dimensions of this ideal be sketched.

The hallmark of a career system free of role prejudice is formal recognition of employees as whole people. In terms of the shape of the alternative career system this suggests that organizations themselves must assume the responsibility for meeting many needs now met by the family-*qua* service agency. Further, it implies that we must develop and institutionalize new models for measuring achievement. Such models should take into account success in broad life experience as well as in "service to the agency" as

narrowly defined. Finally, we must cultivate an organizational ethos that balances the conventional "male" value of competition with the traditional "female" value of cooperation.[36]

Today the federal service could move toward this ideal by acting on any or all of the following: the further development of flexible work schedules and the institutionalization of permanent, part-time, promotion track slots for men and women; the de-emphasis of "freedom of movement" as a criterion for advancement; the exploration of job splitting possibilities for husbands and wives, and the conscious development of career tracks for such couples; the establishment of government career counseling, advertising, and legitimizing these options; and finally, the securing of government support for comprehensive quality child care.

In reaction to this alternative future for the public organization, one might protest that such "reform" strikes at values close to the heart of modern public management—the values of excellence and of productivity.

To recommend the transformation of the modern career system is not to gainsay the importance of excellence, but rather to recognize that excellence as a concept relates to the quality of personnel and not to the organization of work itself. With attention focused on people and the quality of their contribution, one might stress that excellence in this sphere resides neither in numbers of hours worked, nor in the distribution of those hours. Indeed, research suggests that excellence can be achieved under varying conditions.[37] For those who cling to measuring performance by the totality of commitment to a job, it need be stressed that individuals choosing to define personal achievement in that way would remain free to make that choice, just as many ambitious women have done, per force, under today's rules of the game. What this new vision of the public service promises is simply multiple career routes to excellence, within the organizational structure, including one which views the human being as a multifaceted creature.

But what of the more pressing issue of productivity? Few would deny that productivity is on the mind of most public managers today.

Improved productivity management means simply getting more out of all available resources. Thus, on one level at least, little conflict is generated when productivity needs are juxtaposed to important dimensions of the alternative career structure. Some advocates of the alternative career model might even argue that the part-time employment strategy would yield a dividend in enhanced productivity per employee.[38] The least that can be said is that there is no compelling reason for believing in an inverse relationship between productivity and the modification of the work environment suggested above.

## Conclusion

This article began with the posing of a dilemma. Why, when women constitute nearly 40 per cent of America's labor force, have so few women made it to the top? While the political and biological explanations both hold some appeal, the sociological explanation casts the most revealing light on this phenomenon. Specifically, it has been argued that the concept of role prejudice, as it resides not merely in attitudes, but more significantly in the structure of contemporary career systems, holds the key to understanding the dearth of women at the top. To the extent that this analysis is correct, success via the concerned private sector's "integration" approach becomes problematic, while a new direction for public service leadership emerges. That direction implies movement toward the alternative career system ideal, and preliminary steps along that road have been suggested.

Since the federal government has long set the tone for employment practice in the equal opportunity area, the impact of its response to the current dilemma will resonate far beyond the immediate federal employee population.[39] Presently, the impulse for expansion of opportunity for women at the top of government service is strong. This thrust need not flounder on the shoals of organizational myopia. If the history of federal service leadership in an earlier era holds a vision of the future, we might rest confident that it will not.

## Notes

1. "International Women's Year...More Women Focus on a Career," *Monthly Labor Review,* Vol. 98, No. 11 (November 1975), p. 2; and U.S. Department of Labor, Women's Bureau, "Facts on Women Workers" (February 1973).

2. U.S. Civil Service Commission, *Study of Employment of Women in the Federal Government, 1974,* GS and Equivalent Pay Plan. Women occupy 63 per cent of all full-time slots in the Department of HEW.

3. Stuart H. Garfinkle, "Occupations of Women and Black Workers, 1962–74, *Monthly Labor Review,* Vol. 98, No. 11 (November 1975), p. 28; for university professors see "Making Affirmative Action Work in Higher Education," Carnegie Council on Policy Studies in Higher Education (July 1975), p. 26; for federal civil servants, GS 16–18, see U.S. Civil Service Commission, *op. cit.*

4. Michael P. Fogarty, R. Rapoport, and R.N. Rapoport, *Sex, Career, and Family* (Beverly Hills: Sage, 1971), p. 20. Also see Elizabeth Waldman and Beverly J. McEaddy, "Where Women Work—An Analysis by Industry and Occupation," *Monthly Labor Review,* Vol. 97, No. 5 (May 1974), p. 3.

5. For an analysis of similar constraints on women in state legislative politics see Jean J. Kirkpatrick, *Political Women* (New York: Basic Books, 1974), ch. 1.

6. Shulamith Firestone, *The Dialectic of Sex* (New York: William Morrow, 1970), p. 19. Also reflecting this perspective are: Gunnar Myrdal, "A Parallel to the Negro Problem," In *An American Dilemma* (New York: Harper and Row, 1962), Appendix 5; Helen Hacker, "Women Are a Minority Group," *Social Forces,* Vol. 30, No. 1 (October 1959), pp. 60–68; Kirsten Amundsen, *The Silenced Majority* (Englewood Cliffs, N.J.: Prentice-Hall, 1971).

7. Elena Haavio-Mannela and Veronica Stolte-Heiskanen, "The Position of Women in Society: Formal Ideology vs. Everyday Ethic," *Social Science Information,* Vol. VI (December 1967), p. 171.

8. U.S. Civil Service Commission, *op. cit.*

9. Lionel Tiger, *Men in Groups* (New York: Random House, 1969), ch. 4.

10. Nancy L. Ross, *Washington Post,* July 29, 1970, cited by Judith Hole and Ellen Levine, *Rebirth of Feminism* (New York: Quadrangle Books, 1971), p. 174.

11. *Ibid.,* pp. 172–174.

12. Martin Gruberg reports that family relationship has been traditionally a major access route to elected political office for women. Martin Gruberg,

*Women In American Politics* (Oshkosh, Wis.: Academia Press, 1968), p. 121.

13. For an abbreviated review of such women see *ibid.*, pp. 134–144.

14. U.S. Department of Labor, Women's Bureau, *Handbook of Women Workers* (Washington, D.C.: U.S. Government Printing Office, 1969), p. 18.

15. Deborah Pisetizner Klein, "Women in the Labor Force: The Middle Years," *Monthly Labor Review,* Vol. 98, No. 11 (November 1975), p. 11.

16. Jean Lipman-Blumen, "Role De-Differentiation as a System Response to Crisis," *Sociological Inquiry,* Vol. 43, No. 2, p. 106.

17. Kenneth M. Davidson, Ruth Bader Binsburg, and Herma Kay Hill, "Marriage and Family Life," in *Sex-Based Discrimination: Text, Cases, and Materials* (St. Paul, Minn.: West Publishing Company, 1974), p. 188. See also Janice Neepert Hedges and Jeanne K. Barnett, "Working Woman and the Division of Household Tasks," *Monthly Labor Review,* Vol. 95, No. 4 (April 1972), pp. 9–14, which reports results of one study indicating that wives, employed more than 30 hours a week, spend an average of 34 hours a week on household tasks. Women not employed report spending 57 hours a week on household tasks. Husbands' contribution to household jobs averaged to 1.6 hours a day, whether or not their wives worked.

18. Mirra Komarovsky, "Cultural Contradictions in Sex Role," *American Journal of Sociology,* Vol. 52, No. 3 (November 1946), p. 184.

19. Recent research suggests that the domestic role differentiation phenomenon is reified in the response of managers to employees. Managers expect male employees to give top priority to jobs when career demands and family obligations conflict; yet they expect female employees to sacrifice their careers to family responsibilities. See Benson Rosen and Thomas H. Jerdee, "Sex Stereotyping in the Executive Suite," *Harvard Business Review,* Vol. 52, No. 2 (March/April 1974), p. 47.

20. Hacker, *op. cit.*

21. Kenneth Boulding, "Role Prejudice as an Economic Problem," *Monthly Labor Review,* Vol. 97, No. 5 (May 1974), p. 40.

22. See Milton Yinger, "Prejudice," *International Encyclopedia of the Social Sciences* (New York: Macmillan Company, 1968), p. 449.

23. For a discussion of the need for and operation of such programs, see Rosalind Loring and Theodora Wells, *Breakthrough: Women into Management* (New York: Van Nostrand Reinhold, 1972), pp. 57–64; and Dorothy Jongeward and Dru Scott,

*Affirmative Action for Women: A Practical Guide* (Reading Mass: Addison-Wesley, 1973), ch. 7–10.

24. Hanna Papanek, "Men, Women, and Work: Reflections on the Two-Person Career," *American Journal of Sociology,* Vol. 78, No. 4 (January 1973), pp. 852–872. The term "two-person, single career" was coined by Papanek, whose work informed this analysis. The concept of "two-person, single career" needs to be distinguished from the "dual career" in which the husband and wife are each gainfully employed in their own individual careers.

25. *Ibid.,* pp. 856–864.

26. For a recent study of the correlates of vicarious achievement orientations, see Jean Lipman-Blumen, "How Ideology Shapes Women's Lives," *Scientific American,* Vol. 226, No. 1 (January 1972).

27. William H. Whyte (tr.), *The Organization Man* (New York: Anchor Books, 1957), pp. 286–291.

28. For analysis of the same phenomenon in the academic world, see Arlie R. Hochschild, "Inside the Clockwork of Male Careers," in Florence Howe (ed.), *Women and the Power to Change* (New York: McGraw-Hill, 1975), pp. 47–80.

29. Signs by the early 1970s that even the executive divorce rate is on the rise have generated substantial concern among personnel specialists in the private sector. See "The High Cost of Executive Divorce," *Duns Review,* Vol. 98 (October 1971), pp. 52–54.

30. Warren Bennis warns the aspiring executive that "...living in temporary systems...[of the future organization]...augur[s] social strains and tensions.... To be a good wife in this era will be to undertake the profession of providing stability and continuity," "Changing Organizations" in William Scott (ed.), *Organizational Concepts and Analysis* (Belmont, Calif.: Dickenson Publishing Co., 1969), p. 154.

31. Hochschild, *op. cit.,* p. 59.

32. This point is well illustrated in recent issues of the *MBA* magazine. See "The Woman MBA," *MBA,* Vol. 9, No. 2 (February 1975), pp. 25–41; and "The Struggle for Status," *MBA,* Vol. 10, No. 2 (February 1976), pp. 25–40.

33. Victor Fuchs, "Women's Earnings: Recent Trends and Long-Run Prospects," *Monthly Labor Review,* Vol. 97, No. 5 (May 1974), pp. 23–26.

34. "The New Youth Movement," *Dun's Review,* Vol. 98 (August 1971), p. 47. This article reports a trend toward putting younger men in top slots of old line as well as new companies and predicts "In five years or so you will find the top men in business are going to be in their forties."

35. For discussion of specific measures taken, see Samuel Krislov, *Representative Bureaucracy*

(Englewood Cliffs, N.J.: Prentice-Hall, 1974), p. 114.

36. Hochschild, *op. cit.*, p. 28.

37. *Exploitation From 9 to 5: Report of the Twentieth Century Fund Task Force On Women and Employment* (Lexington, Mass.: D.C. Heath and Company, 1975), p. 80.

38. *Ibid.*, p. 79.

39. *Ibid.*, p. 72.

# 25

# Johnson v. Transp. Agency, Santa Clara County, Cal.

*U.S. Supreme Court*

Constance E. Brooks, Washington, D.C., for petitioner.
Steven Woodside, San Jose, Cal., for respondents.

Justice BRENNAN delivered the opinion of the Court.

Respondent, Transportation Agency of Santa Clara County, California, unilaterally promulgated an Affirmative Action Plan applicable, *inter alia,* to promotions of employees. In selecting applicants for the promotional position of road dispatcher, the Agency, pursuant to the Plan, passed over petitioner Paul Johnson, a male employee, and promoted a female employee applicant, Diane Joyce. The question for decision is whether in making the promotion the Agency impermissibly took into account the sex of the applicants in violation of Title VII of the Civil Rights Act of 1964, 42 U.S.C. § 2000e *et seq.*[1] The District Court for the Northern District of California, in an action filed by petitioner following receipt of a right-to-sue letter from the Equal Employment Opportunity Commission (EEOC), held that respondent had violated Title VII. App. to Pet. for Cert. 1a. The Court of Appeals for the Ninth Circuit reversed. 748 F.2d 1308 (1984); modified, 770 F.2d 752 (1985). We granted certiorari, 478 U.S. ——, 106 S.Ct. 3331, 92 L.Ed.2d 737 (1986). We affirm.[2]

## I

### A

[1] In December 1978, the Santa Clara County Transit District Board of Supervisors adopted an Affirmative Action Plan (Plan) for the County Transportation Agency. The Plan implemented a County Affirmative Action Plan, which had been adopted, declared the County, because "mere prohibition of discriminatory practices is not enough to remedy the effects of past practices and to permit attainment of an equitable representation of minorities, women and handicapped persons." App. 31.[3] Relevant to this case, the Agency Plan provides that, in making promotions to positions within a traditionally segregated job classification in which women have been significantly underrepresented, the Agency is authorized to consider as one factor the sex of a qualified applicant.

In reviewing the composition of its work force, the Agency noted in its Plan that women were represented in numbers far less than their proportion of the county labor force in both the Agency as a whole and in five of seven job categories. Specifically, while women constituted 36.4% of the area labor market, they composed only 22.4% of Agency employees. Furthermore, women working at the Agency were concentrated largely in EEOC job categories traditionally held by women: women made up 76% of Office and Clerical Workers, but only 7.1% of Agency Officals and Administrators, 8.6% of Professionals, 9.7% of Technicians, and 22% of Service and Maintenance workers. As for the job classification relevant to this case, none of the 238 Skilled Craft Worker positions was held by a woman. *Id.,* at 49. The Plan noted that this underrepresentation of women in part reflected the fact that women had not traditionally been employed in these positions, and that they had not been strongly motivated to seek training or employment in them "because of the limited opportunities that have existed in the past for them to work in such classifications." *Id.,* at 57. The Plan also observed that, while the proportion of ethnic minorities in the Agency as a whole exceeded the proportion of such minorities in the county work force, a smaller percentage of minority employees held management, professional, and technical positions.[4]

The Agency stated that its Plan was intended to achieve "a statistically measurable yearly improvement in hiring, training and promotion of minorities and women throughout the Agency in all major job classifications where they are underrepresented." *Id.*, at 43. As a benchmark by which to evaluate progress, the Agency stated that its long-term goal was to attain a work force whose composition reflected the proportion of minorities and women in the area labor force. *Id.*, at 54. Thus, for the Skilled Craft category in which the road dispatcher position at issue here was classified, the Agency's aspiration was that eventually about 36% of the jobs would be occupied by women.

The Plan acknowledged that a number of factors might make it unrealistic to rely on the Agency's long-term goals in evaluating the Agency's progress in expanding job opportunities for minorities and women. Among the factors identified were low turnover rates in some classifications, the fact that some jobs involved heavy labor, the small number of positions within some job categories, the limited number of entry positions leading to the Technical and Skilled Craft classifications, and the limited number of minorities and women qualified for positions requiring specialized training and experience. *Id.*, at 56–57. As a result, the Plan counselled that short-range goals be established and annually adjusted to serve as the most realistic guide for actual employment decisions. Among the tasks identified as important in establishing such short-term goals was the acquisition of data "reflecting the ratio of minorities, women and handicapped persons who are working in the local area in major job classifications relating to those utilized by the County Administration," so as to determine the availability of members of such groups who "possess the desired qualifications or potential for placement." *Id.*, at 64. These data on qualified group members, along with predictions of position vacancies, were to serve as the basis for "realistic yearly employment goals for women, minorities and handicapped persons in each EEOC job category and major job classification." *Ibid.*

The Agency's Plan thus set aside no specific number of positions for minorities or women, but authorized the consideration of ethnicity or sex as a factor when evaluating qualified candidates for jobs in which members of such groups were poorly represented. One such job was the road dispatcher position that is the subject of the dispute in this case.

**B**

On December 12, 1979, the Agency announced a vacancy for the promotional position of road dispatcher in the Agency's Roads Division. Dispatchers assign road crews, equipment, and materials, and maintain records pertaining to road maintenance jobs. *Id.*, at 23–24. The position requires at minimum four years of dispatch or road maintenance work experience for Santa Clara County. The EEOC job classification scheme designates a road dispatcher as a Skilled Craft worker.

Twelve County employees applied for the promotion, including Joyce and Johnson. Joyce had worked for the County since 1970, serving as an account clerk until 1975. She had applied for a road dispatcher position in 1974, but was deemed ineligible because she had not served as a road maintenance worker. In 1975, Joyce transferred from a senior account clerk position to a road maintenance worker position, becoming the first woman to fill such a job. Tr. 83–84. During her four years in that position, she occasionally worked out of class as a road dispatcher.

Petitioner Johnson began with the county in 1967 as a road yard clerk, after private employment that included working as a supervisor and dispatcher. He had also unsuccessfully applied for the road dispatcher opening in 1974. In 1977, his clerical position was downgraded, and he sought and received a transfer to the position of road maintenance worker. *Id.*, at 127. He also occasionally worked out of class as a dispatcher while performing that job.

Nine of the applicants, including Joyce and Johnson, were deemed qualified for the job, and were interviewed by a two-person board. Seven of the applicants scored above 70 on this interview, which meant that they were certified as eligible for selection by the appointing authority. The scores awarded ranged from 70 to 80. Johnson was tied for second with score of 75, while Joyce ranked next with a score of 73. A second interview was conducted by three Agency supervisors, who ultimately recommended that Johnson be promoted. Prior to the second interview, Joyce had contacted the County's Affirmative Action Office because she feared that her application might not receive disinterested review.[5] The Office in turn contacted the Agency's Affirmative Action Coordinator, whom the Agency's Plan makes responsible for, *inter alia,* keeping the Director informed of opportunities for the Agency to accomplish its objectives under the Plan. At the time, the Agency employed no women in any Skilled Craft position, and had never employed a woman as a road dispatcher. The Coordinator recommended to the Director of the Agency, James Graebner, that Joyce be promoted.

Graebner, authorized to choose any of the seven persons deemed eligible, thus had the benefit of suggestions by the second interview panel and by the Agency Coordinator in arriving at his decision. After deliberation, Graebner concluded that the promotion should be given to Joyce. As he testified: "I tried to look at the whole picture, the combination of her qualifications and Mr. Johnson's qualifications, their test scores, their expertise, their background, affirmative action matters, things like that...I believe it was a combination of all those." *Id.,* at 68.

The certification form naming Joyce as the person promoted to the dispatcher position stated that both she and Johnson were rated as well-qualified for the job. The evaluation of Joyce read: "Well qualified by virtue of 18 years of past clerical experience including 3½ years at West Yard plus almost 5 years as a [road maintenance worker]." App. 27. The evaluation of Johnson was as follows: "Well qualified applicant; two years of [road maintenance worker] experience plus 11 years of Road Yard Clerk. Has had previous outside Dispatch experience but was 13 years ago." *Ibid.* Graebner testified that he did not regard as significant the fact that Johnson scored 75 and

Joyce 73 when interviewed by the two-person board. Tr. 57–58.

Petitioner Johnson filed a complaint with the EEOC alleging that he had been denied promotion on the basis of sex in violation of Title VII. He received a right-to-sue letter from the agency on March 10, 1981, and on March 20, 1981, filed suit in the United States District Court for the Northern District of California. The District Court found that Johnson was more qualified for the dispatcher position than Joyce, and that the sex of Joyce was the *"determining factor* in her selection." App. to Pet. for Cert. 4a (emphasis in original). The court acknowledged that, since the Agency justified its decision on the basis of its Affirmative Action Plan, the criteria announced in *Steelworkers* v. *Weber,* 443 U.S. 193, 99 S.Ct. 2721, 61 L.Ed.2d 480 (1979), should be applied in evaluating the validity of the plan. App. to Pet. for Cert. 5a. It then found the Agency's Plan invalid on the ground that the evidence did not satisfy *Weber's* criterion that the Plan be temporary. *Id.,* at 6a. The Court of Appeals for the Ninth Circuit reversed, holding that the absence of an express termination date in the Plan was not dispositive, since the Plan repeatedly expressed its objective as the attainment, rather than the maintenance, of a work force mirroring the labor force in the county. 748 F.2d, at 1312, modified, 770 F.2d 752 (1985). The Court of Appeals added that the fact that the Plan established no fixed percentage of positions for minorities or women made it less essential that the Plan contain a relatively explicit deadline. 748 F.2d, at 1312. The Court held further that the Agency's consideration of Joyce's sex in filling the road dispatcher position was lawful. The Agency Plan had been adopted, the court said, to address a conspicuous imbalance in the Agency's work force, and neither unnecessarily trammeled the rights of other employees, nor created an absolute bar to their advancement. *Id.,* at 1313–1314.

## II

[2, 3]   As a preliminary matter, we note that petitioner bears the burden of establishing the

invalidity of the Agency's Plan. Only last term in *Wygant* v. *Jackson Board of Education,* 476 U.S. ——, ——, 106 S.Ct. 1842, 1848, 90 L.Ed.2d 260 (1986), we held that "[t]he ultimate burden remains with the employees to demonstrate the unconstitutionality of an affirmative-action program," and we see no basis for a different rule regarding a plan's alleged violation of Title VII. This case also fits readily within the analytical framework set forth in *McDonnell Douglas Corp.* v. *Green,* 411 U.S. 792, 93 S.Ct. 1817, 36 L.Ed.2d 668 (1973). Once a plaintiff establishes a prima facie case that race or sex has been taken into account in an employer's employment decision, the burden shifts to the employer to articulate a non-discriminatory rationale for its decision. The existence of an affirmative action plan provides such a rationale. If such a plan is articulated as the basis for the employer's decision, the burden shifts to the plaintiff to prove that the employer's justification is pretextual and the plan is invalid. As a practical matter, of course, an employer will generally seek to avoid a charge of pretext by presenting evidence in support of its plan. That does not mean, however, as petitioner suggests, that reliance on an affirmative action plan is to be treated as an affirmative defense requiring the employer to carry the burden of proving the validity of the plan. The burden of proving its invalidity remains on the plaintiff.

The assessment of the legality of the Agency Plan must be guided by our decision in *Weber, supra.*[6] In that case, the Court addressed the question whether the employer violated Title VII by adopting a voluntary affirmative action plan designed to "eliminate manifest racial imbalances in traditionally segregated job categories." *Id.,* 443 U.S., at 197, 99 S.Ct. at 2724. The respondent employee in that case challenged the employer's denial of his application for a position in a newly established craft training program, contending that the employer's selection process impermissibly took into account the race of the applicants. The selection process was guided by an affirmative action plan, which provided that 50% of the new trainees were to be black until the percentage of black skilled craftworkers in the employer's plant approximated the percentage of blacks in the local labor force. Adoption of the plan had been prompted by the fact that only 5 of 273, or 1.83%, of skilled craftworkers at the plant were black, even though the work force in the area was approximately 39% black. Because of the historical exclusion of blacks from craft positions, the employer regarded its former policy of hiring trained outsiders as inadequate to redress the imbalance in its work force.

We upheld the employer's decision to select less senior black applicants over the white respondent, for we found that taking race into account was consistent with Title VII's objective of "break[ing] down old patterns of racial segregation and hierarchy." *Id.,* at 208, 99 S.Ct., at 2730. As we stated:

> It would be ironic indeed if a law triggered by a Nation's concern over centuries of racial injustice and intended to improve the lot of those who had "been excluded from the American dream for so long" constituted the first legislative prohibition of all voluntary, private, race-conscious efforts to abolish traditional patterns of racial segregation and hierarchy. *Id.,* at 204, 99 S.Ct., at 2728 (quoting remarks of Sen. Humphrey, 110 Cong.Rec. 6552 (1964)).[7]

[4]  We noted that the plan did not "unnecessarily trammel the interests of the white employees," since it did not require "the discharge of white workers and their replacement with new black hirees." *Ibid.* Nor did the plan create "an absolute bar to the advancement of white employees," since half of those trained in the new program were to be white. *Ibid.* Finally, we observed that the plan was a temporary measure, not designed to maintain racial balance, but to "eliminate a manifest racial imbalance." *Ibid.* As Justice BLACKMUN's concurrence made clear, *Weber* held that an employer seeking to justify the adoption of a plan need not point to its own prior discriminatory practices, nor even to evidence of an "arguable violation" on its part. *Id.,* at 212, 99 S.Ct., at 2731. Rather, it need point only to a

"conspicuous...imbalance in traditionally segregated job categories." *Id.*, at 209, 99 S.Ct., at 2730. Our decision was grounded in the recognition that voluntary employer action can play a crucial role in furthering Title VII's purpose of eliminating the effects of discrimination in the workplace, and that Title VII should not be read to thwart such efforts. *Id.*, at 204, 99 S.Ct. at 2727–28.[8]

In reviewing the employment decision at issue in this case, we must first examine whether that decision was made pursuant to a plan prompted by concerns similar to those of the employer in *Weber*. Next, we must determine whether the effect of the plan on males and non-minorities is comparable to the effect of the plan in that case.

[5, 6]   The first issue is therefore whether consideration of the sex of applicants for skilled craft jobs was justified by the existence of a "manifest imbalance" that reflected underrepresentation of women in "traditionally segregated job categories." *Id.*, at 197, 99 S.Ct., at 2724. In determining whether an imbalance exists that would justify taking sex or race into account, a comparison of the percentage of minorities or women in the employer's work force with the percentage in the area labor market or general population is appropriate in analyzing jobs that require no special expertise, see *Teamsters* v. *United States,* 431 U.S. 324, 97 S.Ct. 1843, 52 L.Ed.2d 396 (1977) (comparison between percentage of blacks in employer's work force and in general population proper in determining extent of imbalance in truck driving positions), or training programs designed to provide expertise, see *Weber, supra* (comparison between proportion of blacks working at plant and proportion of blacks in area labor force appropriate in calculating imbalance for purpose of establishing preferential admission to craft training program). Where a job requires special training, however, the comparison should be with those in the labor force who possess the relevant qualifications. See *Hazlewood School District* v. *United States,* 433 U.S. 299, 97 S.Ct. 2736, 53 L.Ed.2d 768 (1977) (must compare percentage of blacks in employer's work ranks with percentage of qualified black teachers in area labor force in determining underrepresentation in teaching positions). The requirement that the "manifest imbalance" related to a "traditionally segregated job category" provides assurance both that sex or race will be taken into account in a manner consistent with Title VII's purpose of eliminating the effects of employment discrimination, and that the interests of those employees not benefitting from the plan will not be unduly infringed.

[7]   A manifest imbalance need not be such that it would support a prima facie case against the employer, as suggested in Justice O'CONNOR's concurrence, *post,* since we do not regard as identical the constraints of Title VII and the federal constitution on voluntarily adopted affirmative action plans.[9] Application of the "prima facie" standard in Title VII cases would be inconsistent with *Weber's* focus on statistical imbalance,[10] and could inappropriately create a significant disincentive for employers to adopt an affirmative action plan. See *Weber, supra,* 443 U.S., at 204, 99 S.Ct., at 2727–28 (Title VII intended as a "catalyst" for employer efforts to eliminate vestiges of discrimination). A corporation concerned with maximizing return on investment, for instance, is hardly likely to adopt a plan if in order to do so it must compile evidence that could be used to subject it to a colorable Title VII suit.[11]

[8]   It is clear that the decision to hire Joyce was made pursuant to an Agency plan that directed that sex or race be taken into account for the purpose of remedying underrepresentation. The Agency Plan acknowledged the "limited opportunities that have existed in the past," App. 57, for women to find employment in certain job classifications "where women have not been traditionally employed in significant numbers." *Id.*, at 51.[12] As a result, observed the Plan, women were concentrated in traditionally female jobs in the Agency, and represented a lower percentage in other job classifications than would be expected if such traditional segregation had not occurred. Specifically, 9 of the 10 Para-Professionals and 110 of the 145 Office and Clerical Workers were

women. By contrast, women were only 2 of the 28 Officials and Administrators, 5 of the 58 Professionals, 12 of the 124 Technicians, none of the Skilled Craft Workers, and 1—who was Joyce—of the 110 Road Maintenance Workers. *Id.*, at 51–52. The Plan sought to remedy these imbalances through "hiring, training and promotion of. . .women throughout the Agency in all major job classifications where they are underrepresented." *Id.*, at 43.

As an initial matter, the Agency adopted as a benchmark for measuring progress in eliminating underrepresentation the long-term goal of a work force that mirrored in its major job classifications the percentage of women in the area labor market.[13] Even as it did so, however, the Agency acknowledged that such a figure could not by itself necessarily justify taking into account the sex of applicants for positions in all job categories. For positions requiring specialized training and experience, the Plan observed that the number of minorities and women "who possess the qualifications required for entry into such job classifications is limited." *Id.*, at 56. The Plan therefore directed that annual short-term goals be formulated that would provide a more realistic indication of the degree to which sex should be taken into account in filling particular positions. *Id.*, at 61–64. The Plan stressed that such goals "should not be construed as 'quotas' that must be met," but as reasonable aspirations in correcting the imbalance in the Agency's work force. *Id.*, at 64. These goals were to take into account factors such as "turnover, lay-offs, lateral transfers, new job openings, retirements and availability of minorities, women and handicapped persons in the area work force who possess the desired qualifications or potential for placement." *Ibid.* The Plan specifically directed that, in establishing such goals, the Agency work with the County Planning Department and other sources in attempting to compile data on the percentage of minorities and women in the local labor force that were actually working in the job classifications comprising the Agency work force. *Id.*, at 63–64. From the outset, therefore, the Plan sought annually to develop even more refined measures of the underrepresentation in each job category that required attention.

As the Agency Plan recognized, women were most egregiously underrepresented in the Skilled Craft job category, since *none* of the 238 positions was occupied by a woman. In mid-1980, when Joyce was selected for the road dispatcher position, the Agency was still in the process of refining its short-term goals for Skilled Craft Workers in accordance with the directive of the Plan. This process did not reach fruition until 1982, when the Agency established a short-term goal for that year of three women for the 55 expected openings in that job category—a modest goal of about 6% for that category.

We reject petitioner's argument that, since only the long-term goal was in place for Skilled Craft positions at the time of Joyce's promotion, it was inappropriate for the Director to take into account affirmative action considerations in filling the road dispatcher position. The Agency's Plan emphasized that the long-term goals were not to be taken as guides for actual hiring decisions, but that supervisors were to consider a host of practical factors in seeking to meet affirmative action objectives, including the fact that in some job categories women were not qualified in numbers comparable to their representation in the labor force.

[9]   By contrast, had the Plan simply calculated imbalances in all categories according to the proportion of women in the area labor pool, and then directed that hiring be governed solely by those figures, its validity fairly could be called into question. This is because analysis of a more specialized labor pool normally is necessary in determining underrepresentation in some positions. If a plan failed to take distinctions in qualifications into account in providing guidance for actual employment decisions, it would dictate mere blind hiring by the numbers, for it would hold supervisors to "achievement of a particular percentage of minority employment or membership. . .regardless of circumstances such as economic conditions or the number of qualified minority applicants. . ." *Sheet Metal Workers'* v. *EEOC*, 478 U.S. ——, 106 S.Ct. 3019, 92 L.Ed.2d 344 (1986)

(O'CONNOR, J., concurring in part and dissenting in part).

The Agency's Plan emphatically did *not* authorize such blind hiring. It expressly directed that numerous factors be taken into account in making hiring decisions, including specifically the qualifications of female applicants for particular jobs. Thus, despite the fact that no precise short-term goal was yet in place for the Skilled Craft category in mid-1980, the Agency's management nevertheless had been clearly instructed that they were not to hire solely by reference to statistics. The fact that only the long-term goal had been established for this category posed no danger that personnel decisions would be made by reflexive adherence to a numerical standard.

Furthermore, in considering the candidates for the road dispatcher position in 1980, the Agency hardly needed to rely on a refined short-term goal to realize that it had a significant problem of underrepresentation that required attention. Given the obvious imbalance in the Skilled Craft category, and given the Agency's commitment to eliminating such imbalances, it was plainly not unreasonable for the Agency to determine that it was appropriate to consider as one factor the sex of Ms. Joyce in making its decision.[14] The promotion of Joyce thus satisfies the first requirement enunciated in *Weber,* since it was undertaken to further an affirmative action plan designed to eliminate Agency work force imbalances in traditionally segregated job categories.

We next consider whether the Agency Plan unnecessarily trammeled the rights of male employees or created an absolute bar to their advancement. In contrast to the plan in *Weber,* which provided that 50% of the positions in the craft training program were exclusively for blacks, and to the consent decree upheld last term in *Firefighters* v. *Cleveland,* 478 U.S. ——, 106 S.Ct. 3063, 92 L.Ed.2d 405 (1986), which required the promotion of specific numbers of minorities, the Plan sets aside no positions for women. The Plan expressly states that "[t]he 'goals' established for each Division should not be construed as 'quotas' that must be met." App.

64. Rather, the Plan merely authorizes that consideration be given to affirmative action concerns when evaluating qualified applicants. As the Agency Director testified, the sex of Joyce was but one of numerous factors he took into account in arriving at his decision. Tr. 68. The Plan thus resembles the "Harvard Plan" approvingly noted by Justice POWELL in *University of California Regents* v. *Bakke,* 438 U.S. 265, 316–319, 98 S.Ct. 2733, 2761–63, 57 L.Ed.2d 750 (1978), which considers race along with other criteria in determining admission to the college. As Justice POWELL observed, "In such an admissions program, race or ethnic background may be deemed a 'plus' in a particular applicant's file, yet it does not insulate the individual from comparison with all other candidates for the available seats." *Id.,* at 317, 98 S.Ct., at 2762. Similarly, the Agency Plan requires women to compete with all other qualified applicants. *No* persons are automatically excluded from consideration; *all* are able to have their qualifications weighed against those of other applicants.

In addition, petitioner had no absolute entitlement to the road dispatcher position. Seven of the applicants were classified as qualified and eligible, and the Agency Director was authorized to promote any of the seven. Thus, denial of the promotion unsettled no legitimate firmly rooted expectation on the part of the petitioner. Furthermore, while the petitioner in this case was denied a promotion, he retained his employment with the Agency, at the same salary and with the same seniority, and remained eligible for other promotions.[15]

Finally, the Agency's Plan was intended to *attain* a balanced work force, not to maintain one. The Plan contains ten references to the Agency's desire to "attain" such a balance, but no reference whatsoever to a goal of maintaining it. The Director testified that, while the "broader goal" of affirmative action, defined as "the desire to hire, to promote, to give opportunity and training on an equitable, non-discriminatory basis," is something that is "a permanent part" of "the Agency's operating philosophy," that broader goal "is divorced, if you will, from specific numbers or percentages." Tr. 48–49.

The Agency acknowledged the difficulties that it would confront in remedying the imbalance in its work force, and it anticipated only gradual increases in the representation of minorities and women.[16] It is thus unsurprising that the Plan contains no explicit end date, for the Agency's flexible, case-by-case approach was not expected to yield success in a brief period of time. Express assurance that a program is only temporary may be necessary if the program actually sets aside positions according to specific numbers. See, *e.g., Firefighters, supra,* 478 U.S., at ——, 106 S.Ct., at —— (four-year duration for consent decree providing for promotion of particular number of minorities); *Weber,* 443 U.S., at 199, 99 S.Ct., at 2725 (plan requiring that blacks constitute 50% of new trainees in effect until percentage of employer work force equal to percentage in local labor force). This is necessary both to minimize the effect of the program on other employees, and to ensure that the plan's goals "[are] not being used simply to achieve and maintain...balance, but rather as a benchmark against which" the employer may measure its progress in eliminating the underrepresentation of minorities and women. *Sheet Metal Workers, supra,* 478 U.S., at ——, 106 S.Ct., at 3051. In this case, however, substantial evidence shows that the Agency has sought to take a moderate, gradual approach to eliminating the imbalance in its work force, one which establishes realistic guidance for employment decisions, and which visits minimal intrusion on the legitimate expectations of other employees. Given this fact, as well as the Agency's express commitment to "attain" a balanced work force, there is ample assurance that the Agency does not seek to use its Plan to maintain a permanent racial and sexual balance.

## III

In evaluating the compliance of an affirmative action plan with Title VII's prohibition on discrimination, we must be mindful of "this Court's and Congress' consistent emphasis on

'the value of voluntary efforts to further the objectives of the law.' " *Wygant,* 476 U.S., at ——, 106 S.Ct., at 1855 (O'CONNOR, J., concurring in part and concurring in judgment) (quoting *Bakke, supra,* 438 U.S., at 364, 98 S.Ct., at 2785–86). The Agency in the case before us has undertaken such a voluntary effort, and has done so in full recognition of both the difficulties and the potential for intrusion on males and non-minorities. The Agency has identified a conspicuous imbalance in job categories traditionally segregated by race and sex. It has made clear from the outset, however, that employment decisions may not be justified solely by reference to this imbalance, but must rest on a multitude of practical, realistic factors. It has therefore committed itself to annual adjustment of goals so as to provide a reasonable guide for actual hiring and promotion decisions. The Agency earmarks no positions for anyone; sex is but one of several factors that may be taken into account in evaluating qualified applicants for a position.[17] As both the Plan's language and its manner of operation attest, the Agency has no intention of establishing a work force whose permanent composition is dictated by rigid numerical standards.

We therefore hold that the Agency appropriately took into account as one factor the sex of Diane Joyce in determining that she should be promoted to the road dispatcher position. The decision to do so was made pursuant to an affirmative action plan that represents a moderate, flexible, case-by-case approach to effecting a gradual improvement in the representation of minorities and women in the Agency's work force. Such a plan is fully consistent with Title VII, for it embodies the contribution that voluntary employer action can make in eliminating the vestiges of discrimination in the workplace. Accordingly, the judgment of the Court of Appeals is *Affirmed.*

Justice STEVENS, concurring.

While I join the Court's opinion, I write separately to explain my view of this case's position in our evolving antidiscrimination law and to emphasize that the opinion does not establish the permissible outer limits of voluntary programs undertaken by employers to benefit disadvantaged groups.

# I

Antidiscrimination measures may benefit protected groups in two distinct ways. As a sword, such measures may confer benefits by specifying that a person's membership in a disadvantaged group must be a neutral, irrelevant factor in governmental or private decisionmaking or, alternatively, by compelling decisionmakers to give favorable consideration to disadvantaged group status. As a shield, an antidiscrimination statute can also help a member of a protected class by assuring decisionmakers in some instances that, when they elect for good reasons of their own to grant a preference of some sort to a minority citizen, they will not violate the law. The Court properly holds that the statutory shield allowed respondent to take Diane Joyce's sex into account in promoting her to the road dispatcher position.

Prior to 1978 the Court construed the Civil Rights Act of 1964 as an absolute blanket prohibition against discrimination which neither required nor permitted discriminatory preferences for any group, minority or majority. The Court unambiguously endorsed the neutral approach, first in the context of gender discrimination[18] and then in the context of racial discrimination against a white person.[19] As I explained in my separate opinion in *University of California Regents* v. *Bakke,* 438 U.S. 265, 412–418, 98 S.Ct. 2733, 2810–2813, 57 L.Ed.2d 750 (1978), and as the Court forcefully stated in *McDonald* v. *Santa Fe Trail Transportation Co.,* 427 U.S. 273, 280, 96 S.Ct. 2574, 2578, 49 L.Ed.2d 493 (1976), Congress intended " 'to eliminate all practices which operate to disadvantage the employment opportunities of any group protected by Title VII including Caucasians.' " (citations omitted). If the Court had adhered to that construction of the Act, petitioner would unquestionably prevail in this case. But it has not done so.

In the *Bakke* case in 1978 and again in *Steelworkers* v. *Weber,* 443 U.S. 193, 99 S.Ct. 2721, 61 L.Ed.2d 480 (1979), a majority of the Court interpreted the antidiscriminatory strategy of the statute in a fundamentally different way. The Court held in the *Weber* case that an employer's program designed to increase the number of black craftworkers in an aluminum plant did not violate Title VII.[20] It remains clear that the Act does not *require* any employer to grant preferential treatment on the basis of race or gender, but since 1978 the Court has unambiguously interpreted the statute to *permit* the voluntary adoption of special programs to benefit members of the minority groups for whose protection the statute was enacted. Neither the "same standards" language used in *McDonald,* nor the "color blind" rhetoric used by the Senators and Congressmen who enacted the bill, is now controlling. Thus, as was true in *Runyon* v. *McCrary,* 427 U.S. 160, 189, 96 S.Ct. 2586, 2603, 49 L.Ed.2d 415 (1976) (STEVENS, J., concurring), the only problem for me is whether to adhere to an authoritative construction of the Act that is at odds with my understanding of the actual intent of the authors of the legislation. I conclude without hesitation that I must answer that question in the affirmative, just as I did in *Runyon, Id.,* at 191–192, 96 S.Ct., at 2604–05.

*Bakke* and *Weber* have been decided and are now an important part of the fabric of our law. This consideration is sufficiently compelling for me to adhere to the basic construction of this legislation that the Court adopted in *Bakke* and in *Weber.* There is an undoubted public interest in "stability and orderly development of the law." 427 U.S., at 190, 96 S.Ct., at 2604.[21]

The logic of antidiscrimination legislation requires that judicial contructions of Title VII leave "breathing room" for employer initiatives to benefit members of minority groups. If Title VII had never been enacted, a private employer would be free to hire members of minority groups for any reason that might seem sensible from a business or a social point of view. The Court's opinion in *Weber* reflects the same approach; the opinion relied heavily on legislative history indicating that Congress intended that traditional management prerogatives be left undisturbed to the greatest extent possible. See 443 U.S., at 206–207, 99 S.Ct., at 2728–2729. As we observed Last Term,

> [i]t would be ironic indeed if a law triggered by a Nation's concern over centuries of racial injustice and intended to improve the lot of those who had "been excluded from the American dream for so long" constituted the first legislative prohibition of all voluntary, private, race-conscious efforts to abolish traditional patterns of racial segregation and hierarchy.

*Firefighters* v. *Cleveland,* 478 U.S. ——, ——, 106 S.Ct. 3063, 3072, 92 L.Ed.2d 405 (1986) (citing *Weber,* 443 U.S., at 204, 99 S.Ct., at 2727). In *Firefighters,* we again acknowledged Congress' concern in Title VII to avoid "undue federal interference with managerial discretion." 478 U.S., at ——, 106 S.Ct., at 3074.[22]

As construed in *Weber* and in *Firefighters,* the statute does not absolutely prohibit preferential hiring in favor of minorities; it was merely intended to protect historically disadvantaged groups *against* discrimination and not to hamper managerial efforts to benefit members of disadvantaged groups that are consistent with that paramount purpose. The preference granted by respondent in this case does not violate the statute as so construed; the record amply supports the conclusion that the challenged employment decision served the legitimate purpose of creating diversity in a category of employment that had been almost an exclusive province of males in the past. Respondent's voluntary decision is surely not prohibited by Title VII as construed in *Weber.*

## II

Whether a voluntary decision of the kind made by respondent would ever be prohibited by Title VII is a question we need not answer until it is squarely presented. Given the interpretation of the statute the Court adopted in *Weber,* I see no reason why the employer has any duty, prior to granting a preference to a qualified minority employee, to determine whether his past conduct might constitute an arguable violation of Title VII. Indeed, in some instances the employer may find it more helpful to focus on the future. Instead of retroactively scrutinizing his own or society's possible exclusions of minorities in the past to determine the outer limits of a valid affirmative-action program— or indeed, any particular affirmative-action decision—in many cases the employer will find it more appropriate to consider other legitimate reasons to give preferences to members of underrepresented groups. Statutes enacted for the benefit of minority groups should not block these forward-looking considerations.

> Public and private employers might choose to implement affirmative action for many reasons other than to purge their own past sins of discrimination. The Jackson school board, for example, said it had done so in part to improve the quality of education in Jackson—whether by improving black students' performance or by dispelling for black and white students alike any idea that white supremacy governs our social institutions. Other employers might advance different forward-looking reasons for affirmative action: improving their services to black constituencies, averting racial tension over the allocation of jobs in a community, or increasing the diversity of a work force, to name but a few examples. Or they might adopt affirmative action simply to eliminate from their operations all de facto embodiment of a system of racial caste. All of these reasons aspire to a racially integrated future, but none reduces to "racial balancing for its own sake." Sullivan, The Supreme Court—Comment, Sins of Discrimination: Last Term's Affirmative Action Cases, 100 Harv.L.Rev. 78, 96 (1986).

The Court today does not foreclose other voluntary decisions based in part on a qualified employee's membership in a disadvantaged group. Accordingly, I concur.

Justice O'CONNOR, concurring in the judgment.

In *Steelworkers* v. *Weber,* 443 U.S. 193, 99 S.Ct. 2721, 61 L.Ed.2d 480 (1979), this Court held that § 703(d) of Title VII does not prohibit voluntary affirmative action efforts if the employer sought to remedy a "manifest . . . imbalanc[e] in traditionally segregated job categories." *Id.,* at 197, 99 S.Ct., at 2724. As Justice SCALIA illuminates with excruciating clarity, § 703 has been interpreted by *Weber* and succeeding cases to permit what its language read literally would prohibit. *Post,* at 1465; see also *ante,* at 1457 (STEVENS, J., concurring). Section 703(d) prohibits employment discrimination "against *any individual* because of his race, color, religion, sex, or national origin." 42 U.S.C. § 2000e–2(d) (emphasis added). The *Weber* Court, however, concluded that voluntary affirmative action was permissible in some circumstances because a prohibition of every type of affirmative action would " 'bring about an end completely at variance with the purpose of the statute.' " 443 U.S., at 202, 99 S.Ct., at 2726 (quoting *United States* v. *Public Utilities Comm'n,* 345 U.S. 295, 315, 73 S.Ct. 706, 717, 97 L.Ed. 1020 (1953)). This purpose, according to the Court, was to open employment opportunities for blacks in occupations that had been traditionally closed to them.

None of the parties in this case have suggested that we overrule *Weber* and that question was not raised, briefed, or argued in this Court or in the courts below. If the Court is faithful to its normal prudential restraints and to the principle of *stare decisis* we must address once again the propriety of an affirmative action plan under Title VII in light of our precedents, precedents that have upheld affirmative action in a variety of circumstances. This time the question posed is whether a public employer violates Title VII by promoting a qualified woman rather than a marginally better qualified man when there is a statistical imbalance sufficient to support a claim of a pattern or practice of discrimination against women under Title VII.

I concur in the judgment of the Court in light of our precedents. I write separately, however,

because the Court has chosen to follow an expansive and ill-defined approach to voluntary affirmative action by public employers despite the limitations imposed by the Constitution and by the provisions of Title VII, and because the dissent rejects the Court's precedents and addresses the question of how Title VII should be interpreted as if the Court were writing on a clean slate. The former course of action gives insufficient guidance to courts and litigants; the latter course of action serves as a useful point of academic discussion, but fails to reckon with the reality of the course that the majority of the Court has determined to follow. . . .

Justice WHITE, dissenting.

I agree with Parts I and II of Justice SCALIA's dissenting opinion. Although I do not join Part III, I also would overrule *Weber.* My understanding of *Weber* was, and is, that the employer's plan did not violate Title VII because it was designed to remedy intentional and systematic exclusion of blacks by the employer and the unions from certain job categories. That is how I understood the phrase "traditionally segregated jobs" we used in that case. The Court now interprets it to mean nothing more than a manifest imbalance between one identifiable group and another in an employer's labor force. As so interpreted, that case, as well as today's decision, as Justice SCALIA so well demonstrates, is a perversion of Title VII. I would overrule *Weber* and reverse the judgment below.

Justice SCALIA, with whom THE CHIEF JUSTICE joins, and with whom Justice WHITE joins in Parts I and II, dissenting.

With a clarity which, had it not proven so unavailing, one might well recommend as a model of statutory draftsmanship, Title VII of the Civil Rights Act of 1964 declares:

It shall be an unlawful employment practice for an employer—

(1) to fail or refuse to hire or to discharge any individual, or otherwise to discriminate against any individual with respect to his compensation, terms, conditions, or privileges of employment, because of such individual's race, color, religion, sex, or national origin; or

(2) to limit, segregate, or classify his employees or applicants for employment in any way which would deprive or tend to deprive any individual of employment opportunities or otherwise adversely affect his status as an employee, because of such individual's race, color, religion, sex, or national origin. 42 U.S.C. § 2000e-2(a).

The Court today completes the process of converting this from a guarantee that race or sex will *not* be the basis for employment determinations, to a guarantee that it often *will*. Ever so subtly, without even alluding to the last obstacles preserved by earlier opinions that we now push out of our path, we effectively replace the goal of a discrimination-free society with the quite incompatible goal of proportionate representation by race and by sex in the workplace. Part I of this dissent will describe the nature of the plan that the Court approves, and its effect upon this petitioner. Part II will discuss prior holdings that are tacitly overruled, and prior distinctions that are disregarded. Part III will describe the engine of discrimination we have finally completed.

# I

On October 16, 1979, the County of Santa Clara adopted an Affirmative Action Program (County plan) which sought the "attainment of a County work force whose composition... includes women, disabled persons and ethnic minorities in a ratio in all job categories that reflects their distribution in the Santa Clara County area work force." App. 113. In order to comply with the County plan and various requirements imposed by federal and state agencies, the Transportation Agency adopted, effective December 18, 1978, the Equal Employment Opportunity Affirmative Action Plan (Agency plan or plan) at issue here. Its stated long-range goal was the same as the County plan's: "to attain a work force whose composition in all job levels and major job classifications approximates the distribution of women, minority and handicapped persons in the Santa

Clara County work force." *Id.*, at 54. The plan called for the establishment of a procedure by which Division Directors would review the ethnic and sexual composition of their work forces whenever they sought to fill a vacancy, which procedure was expected to include "a requirement that Division Directors indicate why they did *not* select minorities, women and handicapped persons if such persons were on the list of eligibles considered and if the Division had an underrepresentation of such persons in the job classification being filled." *Id.*, at 75 (emphasis in original).

Several salient features of the plan should be noted. Most importantly, the plan's purpose was assuredly not to remedy prior sex discrimination by the Agency. It could not have been, because there was no prior sex discrimination to remedy. The majority, in cataloguing the Agency's alleged misdeeds, *ante,* at 1448, n. 5, neglects to mention the District Court's finding that the Agency "has not discriminated in the past, and does not discriminate in the present against women in regard to employment opportunities in general and promotions in particular." App. to Pet. for Cert. 13a. This finding was not disturbed by the Ninth Circuit.

Not only was the plan not directed at the results of past sex discrimination by the Agency, but its objective was not to achieve the state of affairs that this Court has dubiously assumed would result from an absence of discrimination—an overall work force "more or less representative of the racial and ethnic composition of the population in the community." *Teamsters* v. *United States,* 431 U.S. 324, 340, n. 20, 97 S.Ct. 1843, 1856, n. 20, 52 L.Ed.2d 396 (1977). Rather, the oft-stated goal was to mirror the racial and sexual composition of the entire county labor force, not merely in the Agency work force as a whole, but in each and every individual job category at the Agency. In a discrimination-free world, it would obviously be a statistical oddity for every job category to match the racial and sexual composition of even that portion of the county work force *qualified* for that job; it would be utterly miraculous for each of them to match, as the plan expected, the composition of the *entire* work force. Quite obviously, the plan did not seek to replicate what a lack of discrimination would produce, but rather imposed racial and sexual tailoring that would, in defiance of normal expectations and laws of probability, give each protected racial and sexual group a governmentally determined "proper" proportion of each job category.

That the plan was not directed at remedying or eliminating the effects of past discrimination is most clearly illustrated by its description of what it regarded as the *"Factors Hindering Goal Attainment"—i.e.,* the existing impediments to the racially and sexually representative work force that it pursued. The plan noted that it would be "difficult," App. 55, to attain its objective of across-the-board statistical parity in at least some job categories, because:

> a. Most of the positions require specialized training and experience. Until recently, relatively few minorities, women and handicapped persons sought entry into these positions. Consequently, the number of persons from these groups in the area labor force who possess the qualifications required for entry into such job classifications is limited.
>
> \*    \*    \*    \*    \*
>
> c. Many of the Agency positions where women are underrepresented involve heavy labor; e.g., Road Maintenance Worker. Consequently, few women seek entry into these positions.
>
> \*    \*    \*    \*    \*
>
> f. Many women are not strongly motivated to seek employment in job classifications where they have not been traditionally employed because of the limited opportunities that have existed in the past for them to work in such classifications. *Id.,* at 56–57.

That is, the qualifications and desires of women may fail to match the Agency's Platonic ideal of a work force. The plan concluded from this, of course, not that the ideal should be reconsidered, but that its attainment could not be immediate. *Id.,* at 58–60. It would, in any event,

be rigorously pursued, by giving "special consideration to Affirmative Action requirements in every individual hiring action pertaining to positions where minorities, women and handicapped persons continue to be underrepresented." *Id.,* at 60.[23]

Finally, the one message that the plan unmistakably communicated was that concrete results were expected, and supervisory personnel would be evaluated on the basis of the affirmative-action numbers they produced. The plan's implementation was expected to "result in a statistically measurable yearly improvement in the hiring, training and promotion of minorities, women and handicapped persons in the major job classifications utilized by the Agency where these groups are underrepresented." *Id.,* at 35. Its Preface declared that "[t]he degree to which each Agency Division *attains the Plan's objectives* will provide a direct measure of that Division Director's personal commitment to the EEO Policy," *ibid.* (emphasis added), and the plan itself repeated that "[t]he degree to which each Division *attains the Agency Affirmative Action employment goals* will provide a measure of that Director's commitment and effectiveness in carrying out the Division's EEO Affirmative Action requirements." *Id.,* at 44 (emphasis added). As noted earlier, supervisors were reminded of the need to give attention to affirmative action in every employment decision, and to explain their reasons for *failing* to hire women and minorities whenever there was an opportunity to do so.

The petitioner in the present case, Paul E. Johnson, had been an employee of the Agency since 1967, coming there from a private company where he had been a road dispatcher for seventeen years. He had first applied for the position of Road Dispatcher at the Agency in 1974, coming in second. Several years later, after a reorganization resulted in a downgrading of his Road Yard Clerk II position, in which Johnson "could see no future," Tr. 1217, he requested and received a voluntary demotion from Road Yard Clerk II to Road Maintenance Worker, to increase his experience and thus improve his chances for future promotion. When the Road Dispatcher job next became vacant, in 1979, he was the leading candidate—and indeed was assigned to work out of class full-time in the vacancy, from September of 1979 until June of 1980. There is no question why he did not get the job.

The fact of discrimination against Johnson is much clearer, and its degree more shocking than the majority and Justice O'CONNOR's concurring opinion would suggest—largely because neither of them recites a single one of the District Court findings that govern this appeal, relying instead upon portions of the transcript which those findings implicitly rejected, and even upon a document (favorably comparing Joyce to Johnson), *ante,* at 1448, that was prepared *after* Joyce was selected. See App. 27–28; Tr. 223–227. It is worth mentioning, for example, the trier of fact's determination that, if the Affirmative Action coordinator had not intervened, "the decision as to whom to pro-mote. . .would have been made by [the Road Operations Division Director]," App. to Pet. for Cert. 12a, who had recommended that Johnson be appointed to the position. *Ibid.*[24] Likewise, the even more extraordinary findings that James Graebner, the Agency Director who made the appointment, "did not inspect the applications and related examination records of either [Paul Johnson] or Diane Joyce before making his deci-sion," *ibid.,* and indeed "did little or nothing to inquire into the results of the interview process and conclusions which [were] described as of critical importance to the selection process." *Id.,* at 3a. In light of these determina-tions, it is impossible to believe (or think that the District Court believed) Graebner's self-serving statements relied upon by the majority and concurrence, such as the assertion that he "tried to look at the whole picture, the com-bination of [Joyce's] qualifications and Mr. Johnson's qualifications, their test scores, their expertise, their background, affirmative action matters, things like that," Tr. 68 (quoted *ante,* at 1448–1449; *ante,* at 1449 (O'CONNOR, J., concurring in judgment)). It was evidently enough for Graebner to know that both can-didates (in the words of Johnson's counsel, to

which Graebner assented) "met the M.Q.'s, the minimum. Both were minimally qualified." Tr. 25. When asked whether he had "any basis," *ibid.,* for determining whether one of the can-didates was more qualified than the other, Graebner candidly answered, "No. . . . As I've said, they both appeared, and my conversations with people tended to corroborate, that they were both capable of performing the work." *Ibid.*

After a two-day trial, the District Court concluded that Diane Joyce's gender was "*the determining factor,*" *id.,* at 4a, in her selection for the position. Specifically, it found that "[b]ased upon the examination results and the departmental interview, [Mr. Johnson] was more qualified for the position of Road Dispatcher than Diane Joyce," *id.,* at 12a; that "[b]ut for [Mr. Johnson's] sex, male, he would have been promoted to the position of Road Dispatcher," *id.,* at 13a; and that "[b]ut for Diane Joyce's sex, female, she would not have been appointed to the position. . . ." *Ibid.* The Ninth Circuit did not reject these factual findings as clearly erroneous, nor could it have done so on the record before us. We are bound by those findings under Federal Rule of Civil Procedure 52(a).

# II

The most significant proposition of law established by today's decision is that racial or sexual discrimination is permitted under Title VII when it is intended to overcome the effect, not of the employer's own discrimination, but of societal attitudes that have limited the entry of certain races, or of a particular sex, into certain jobs. . . .

Today's decision does more, however, than merely reaffirm *Weber,* and more than merely extend it to public actors. It is impossible not to be aware that the practical effect of our holding is to accomplish *de facto* what the law—in language even plainer than that ignored in *Weber,* see 42 U.S.C. § 2000e–2(j)—forbids anyone from accomplishing *de jure:* in many contexts it effectively *requires* employers, public as well as private to engage in intentional discrimination on the basis of race or sex. This Court's prior interpretations of Title VII, especially the decision in *Griggs v. Duke Power Co.,* 401 U.S. 424, 91 S. Ct.849, 28 L.Ed.2d 158 (1971), subject employers to a potential Title VII suit whenever there is a noticeable imbalance in the representation of minorities or women in the employer's work force. Even the employer who is confident of ultimately prevailing in such a suit must contemplate the expense and adverse publicity of a trial, because the extent of the imbalance, and the "job relatedness" of his selection criteria, are questions of fact to be explored through rebuttal and counter-rebuttal of a "prima facie case" consisting of no more than the showing that the employer's selection process "selects those from the protected class at a 'significantly' lesser rate than their counterparts." B. Schlei & P. Grossman, Employment Discrimination Law 91 (2d ed. 1983). If, however, employers are free to discriminate through affirmative action, without fear of "reverse discrimination" suits by their nonminority or male victims, they are offered a threshold defense against Title VII liability premised on numerical disparities. Thus, after today's decision the *failure* to engage in reverse discrimination is economic folly, and arguably a breach of duty to shareholders or taxpayers, wherever the cost of anticipated Title VII litigation exceeds the cost of hiring less capable (though still minimally capable) workers. (This situtation is more likely to obtain, of course, with respect to the least skilled jobs—perversely creating an incentive to discriminate against precisely those members of the nonfavored groups *least* likely to have profited from societal discrimination in the past.) It is predictable, moreover, that this incentive will be greatly magnified by economic pressures brought to bear by government contracting agencies upon employers who refuse to discriminate in the fashion we have now approved. A statute designed to establish a color-blind and gender-blind workplace has thus been converted into a powerful engine of racism and sexism, not merely *permitting* intentional race- and sex-biased

discrimination, but often making it, through operation of the legal system, practically compelled.

It is unlikely that today's result will be displeasing to politically elected officials, to whom it provides the means of quickly accommodating the demands of organized groups to achieve concrete, numerical improvement in the economic status of particular constituencies. Nor will it displease the world of corporate and governmental employers (many of whom have filed briefs as *amici* in the present case, all on the side of Santa Clara) for whom the cost of hiring less qualified workers is often substantially less—and infinitely more predictable—than the cost of litigating Title VII cases and of seeking to convince federal agencies by non-numerical means that no discrimination exists. In fact, the only losers in the process are the Johnsons of the country, for whom Title VII has been not merely repealed but actually inverted. The irony is that these individuals—predominantly unknown, unaffluent, unorganized—suffer this injustice at the hands of a Court fond of thinking itself the champion of the politically impotent. I dissent.

# Notes

1. Section 703(a) of the Act 78 Stat. 255, as amended, 86 Stat. 109, 42 U.S.C. § 2000e-2(a), provides that it "shall be an unlawful employment practice for an employer—

"(1) to fail or refuse to hire or to discharge any individual, or otherwise to discriminate against any individual with respect to his compensation, terms, conditions, or privileges of employment, because of such individual's race, color, religion, sex, or national origin; or

"(2) to limit, segregate, or classify his employees or applicants for employment in any way which would deprive or tend to deprive any individual of employment opportunities or otherwise adversely affect his status as an employee, because of such individual's race, color, religion, sex, or national origin."

2. No constitutional issue was either raised or addressed in the litigation below. See 748 F.2d 1308, 1310, n. 1 (1984). We therefore decide in this case only

the issue of the prohibitory scope of Title VII. Of course, where the issue is properly raised, public employers must justify the adoption and implementation of a voluntary affirmative action plan under the Equal Protection Clause. See *Wygant v. Jackson Board of Education,*—— U.S.——, 106 S.Ct. 1842, 90 L.Ed.2d 260 (1986).

3. The Plan reaffirmed earlier County and Agency efforts to address the issue of employment discrimination, dating back to the County's adoption in 1971 of an Equal Employment Opportunity Policy. App. 37–40.

4. While minorities constituted 19.7% of the county labor force, they represented 7.1% of the Agency's Officials and Administrators, 19% of its Professionals, and 16.9% of its Technicians. *Id.,* at 48.

5. Joyce testified that she had had disagreements with two of the three members of the second interview panel. One had been her first supervisor when she began work as a road maintenance worker. In performing arduous work in this job, she had not been issued coveralls, although her male co-workers had received them. After ruining her pants, she complained to her supervisor, to no avail. After three other similar incidents, ruining clothes on each occasion, she filed a grievance, and was issued four pair of coveralls the next day. Tr. 89–90. Joyce had dealt with a second member of the panel for a year and a half in her capacity as chair of the Roads Operations Safety Committee, where she and he "had several differences of opinion on how safety should be implemented." *Id.,* at 90–91. In addition, Joyce testified that she had informed the person responsible for arranging her second interview that she had a disaster preparedness class on a certain day the following week. By this time about ten days had passed since she had notified this person of her availability, and no date had yet been set for the interview. Within a day or two after this conversation, however, she received a notice setting her interview at a time directly in the middle of her disaster preparedness class. *Id.,* at 94–95. This same panel member had earlier described Joyce as a "rebel-rousing, skirt-wearing person," Tr. 153.

6. The dissent maintains that the obligations of a public employer under Title VII must be identical to its obligations under the Constitution, and that a public employer's adoption of an affirmative action plan therefore should be governed by *Wygant.* This rests on the following logic: Title VI embodies the same constraints as the Constitution; Title VI and Title VII have the same prohibitory scope; therefore, Title VII and the Constitution are coterminous for purposes of this case. The flaw is with the second step of the analysis, for it advances a proposition that we explicitly

considered and rejected in *Weber.* As we noted in that case, Title VI was an exercise of federal power "over a matter in which the Federal Government was already directly involved," since Congress "was legislating to assure federal funds would not be used in an improper manner." 443 U.S., at 206 n. 6, 99 S.Ct., at 2729 n. 6. "Title VII, by contrast, was enacted pursuant to the commerce power to regulate purely private decisionmaking and was not intended to incorporate and particularize the commands of the Fifth and Fourteenth Amendments. Title VII and Title VI, therefore, cannot be read *in pari materia." Ibid.* This point is underscored by Congress' concern that the receipt of any form of financial assistance might render an employer subject to the commands of Title VI rather than Title VII. As a result, Congress added § 604 to Title VI, 42 U.S.C. § 2000d–3, which provides:

"Nothing contained in this subchapter shall be construed to authorize action under this subchapter by any department or agency with respect to any employment practice of any employer, employment agency, or labor organization except where a primary objective of the Federal financial assistance is to provide employment."

The sponsor of this section, Senator Cooper, stated that it was designed to clarify that "it was not intended that [T]itle VI would impinge on [T]itle VII." 110 Cong.Rec. 11615 (1964).

While public employers were not added to the definition of "employer" in Title VII until 1972, there is no evidence that this mere addition to the definitional section of the statute was intended to transform the substantive standard governing employer conduct. Indeed, "Congress expressly indicated the intent that the same Title VII principles be applied to governmental and private employers alike." *Dothard* v. *Rawlinson,* 433 U.S. 321, 332 n. 14, 97 S.Ct. 2720, 2728 n. 14, 53 L.Ed.2d 786 (1977). The fact that a public employer must also satisfy the Constitution does not negate the fact that the *statutory* prohibition with which that employer must contend was not intended to extend as far as that of the Constitution.

7. The dissent maintains that *Weber's* conclusion that Title VII does not prohibit voluntary affirmative action programs "rewrote the statute it purported to construe." *Post,* at 1472. *Weber's* decisive rejection of the argument that the "plain language" of the statute prohibits affirmative action rested on (1) legislative history indicating Congress' clear intention that employers play a major role in eliminating the vestiges of discrimination, 443 U.S., at 201–204, 99 S.Ct., at 2726–28, and (2) the language and legislative history of § 703(j) of the statute, which reflect a strong desire

to preserve managerial prerogatives so that they might be utilized for this purpose. *Id.*, at 204–207, 99 S.Ct. at 2727–29. As Justice BLACKMUN said in his concurrence in *Weber,* "[I]f the Court has misperceived the political will, it has the assurance that because the question is statutory Congress may set a different course if it so chooses." *Id.*, at 216, 99 S.Ct., at 2734. Congress has not amended the statue to reject our construction, nor have any such amendments even been proposed, and we therefore may assume that our interpretation was correct.

The dissent faults the fact that we take note of the absence of Congressional efforts to amend the statute to nullify *Weber.* It suggests that Congressional inaction cannot be regarded as acquiescence under all circumstances, but then draws from that unexceptional point the conclusion that *any* reliance on Congressional failure to act is necessarily a "canard." *Post,* at ——. The fact that inaction may not always provide crystalline revelation, however, should not obscure the fact that it may be probative to varying degrees. *Weber,* for instance, was a widely-publicized decision that addressed a prominent issue of public debate. Legislative inattention thus is not a plausible explanation for Congressional inaction. Furthermore, Congress not only passed no contrary legislation in the wake of *Weber,* but not one legislator even proposed a bill to do so. The barriers of the legislative process therefore also seem a poor explanation for failure to act. By contrast, when Congress has been displeased with our interpretation of Title VII, it has not hesitated to amend the statute to tell us so. For instance, when Congress passed the Pregnancy Discrimination Act of 1978, 42 U.S.C. § 2000e(k), "it unambiguously expressed its disapproval of both the holding and the reasoning of the Court in [*General Electric* v. *Gilbert,* 429 U.S. 125, 97 S.Ct. 401, 50 L.Ed.2d 343 (1976)]." *Newport News Shipbuilding & Dry Dock* v. *EEOC,* 462 U.S. 669, 678, 103 S.Ct. 2622, 2628, 77 L.Ed.2d 89 (1983). Surely, it is appropriate to find some probative value in such radically different Congressional reactions to this Court's interpretations of the same statute.

As one scholar has put it, "When a court says to a legislature: 'You (or your predecessor) meant X,' it almost invites the legislature to answer: 'We did not.' " G. Calabresi, A Common Law for the Age of Statutes 31–32 (1982). Any belief in the notion of a dialogue between the judiciary and the legislature must acknowledge that on occasion an invitation declined is as significant as one accepted.

8. See also *Firefighters* v. *Cleveland,* 478 U.S.— —, ——, 106, S.Ct. 3063, 3072, 92 L.Ed.2d 405 (1986)

("We have on numerous occasions recognized that Congress intended for voluntary compliance to be the preferred means of achieving the objectives of Title VII"); *Alexander* v. *Gardner-Denver,* 415 U.S. 36, 44, 94 S.Ct. 1011, 1017, 39 L.Ed.2d 147 (1974) ("Cooperation and voluntary compliance were selected as the preferred means for achieving [Title VII's] goal"). The dissent's suggestion that an affirmative action program may be adopted only to redress an employer's past discrimination, see *post,* at ——, was rejected in *Steelworkers* v. *Weber,* 443 U.S. 193, 99 S.Ct. 2721, 61 L.Ed.2d 480 (1979), because the prospect of liability created by such an admission would create a significant disincentive for voluntary action. As Justice BLACKMUN's concurrence in that case pointed out, such a standard would "plac[e] voluntary compliance with Title VII in profound jeopardy. The only way for the employer and the union to keep their footing on the 'tightrope' it creates would be to eschew all forms of voluntary affirmative action." 443 U.S., at 210, 99 S.Ct., at 2731. Similary, Justice O'CONNOR has observed in the constitutional context that "[t]he impositon of a requirement that public employers make findings that they have engaged in illegal discrimination before they engage in affirmative action programs would severely undermine public employers' incentive to meet voluntarily their civil rights obligations." *Wygant, supra,* at ——, 106, S.Ct., at 1855 (O'CONNOR, J., concurring in part and concurring in the judgment).

Contrary to the dissent's contention, *post,* at ——, our decisions last term in *Firefighters, supra,* and *Sheet Metal Workers* v. *EEOC,* 478 U.S. ——, 106 S.Ct. 3019, 92 L.Ed.2d 344 (1986), provide no support for a standard more restrictive than that enunciated in *Weber. Firefighters* raised the issue of the conditions under which parties could enter into a consent decree providing for explicit numerical quotas. By contrast, the affirmative action plan in this case sets aside no positions for minorities or women. See *infra,* at —— - ——. In *Sheet Metal Workers,* the issue we addressed was the scope of judicial remedial authority under Title VII, authority that has not been exercised in this case. The dissent's suggestion that employers should be able to do no more voluntarily than courts can order as remedies, *post,* at ——, ignores the fundamental difference between volitional private behavior and the exercise of coercion by the state. Plainly, "Congress' concern that federal courts not impose unwanted obligations on employers and unions," *Firefighters, supra,* 478 U.S., at ——, 106 S.Ct. at 3077, reflects a desire to preserve a relatively large domain for voluntary employer action.

9. See *supra,* n. 6.

10. The difference between the "manifest imbalance" and "prima facie" standards is illuminated by *Weber.* Had the Court in that case been concerned with past discrimination by the employer, it would have focused on discrimination in hiring skilled, not unskilled, workers, since only the scarcity of the former in Kaiser's work force would have made it vulnerable to a Title VII suit. In order to make out a prima facie case on such a claim, a plaintiff would be required to compare the percentage of black skilled workers in the Kaiser work force with the percentage of black skilled craft workers in the area labor market. *Weber* obviously did not make such a comparison. Instead, it focused on the disparity between the percentage of black skilled craft workers in Kaiser's ranks and the percentage of blacks in the area labor force. 443 U.S., at 198–199, 99 S.Ct., at 2724–2725. Such an approach reflected a recognition that the proportion of black craft workers in the local labor force was likely as miniscule as the proportion in Kaiser's work force. The Court realized that the lack of imbalance between these figures would mean that employers in precisely those industries in which discrimination has been most effective would be precluded from adopting training programs to increase the percentage of qualified minorities. Thus, in cases such as *Weber,* where the employment decision at issue involves the selection of unskilled persons for a training program, the "manifest imbalance" standard permits comparison with the general labor force. By contrast, the "prima facie" standard would require comparison with the percentage of minorities or women qualified for the job for which the trainees are being trained, a standard that would have invalidated the plan in *Weber* itself.

11. In some cases, of course, the manifest imbalance may be sufficiently egregious to establish a prima facie case. However, as long as there is a manifest imbalance, an employer may adopt a plan even where the disparity is not so striking, without being required to introduce the non-statistical evidence of past discrimination that would be demanded by the "prima facie" standard. See, *e.g., Teamsters* v. *United States,* 431 U.S. 324, 339, 97 S.Ct. 1843, 1856, 52 L.Ed.2d 396 (1977) (statistics in pattern and practice case supplemented by testimony regarding employment practices). Of course, when there is sufficient evidence to meet the more stringent "prima facie" standard, be it statistical, non-statistical, or a combination of the two, the employer is free to adopt an affirmative action plan.

12. For instance, the description of the Skilled Craft Worker category, in which the road dispatcher position is located, is as follows:

"Occupations in which workers perform jobs which require special manual skill and a thorough and comprehensive knowledge of the process involved in the work which is acquired through on-the-job training and experience or through apprenticeship or other formal training programs. Includes: mechanics and repairmen; electricians; heavy equipment operators, stationary engineers, skilled machining occupations, carpenters, compositors and typesetters and kindred workers." App. 108.

As the Court of Appeals said in its decision below, "A plethora of proof is hardly necessary to show that women are generally underrepresented in such positions and that strong social pressures weigh against their participation." 748 F.2d, at 1313.

13. Because of the employment decision at issue in this case, our discussion henceforth refers primarily to the Plan's provisions to remedy the underrepresentation of women. Our analysis could apply as well, however, to the provisions of the plan pertaining to minorities.

14. In addition, the Agency was mindful of the importance of finally hiring a woman in a job category that had formerly been all-male. The Director testified that, while the promotion of Joyce "made a small dent, for sure, in the numbers," nonetheless "philosophically it made a larger impact in that it probably has encouraged other females and minorities to look at the possibility of so-called 'non-traditional' jobs as areas where they and the agency both have samples of a success story." Tr. 64.

15. Furthermore, from 1978 to 1982 Skilled Craft jobs in the Agency increased from 238 to 349. The Agency's personnel figures indicate that the Agency fully expected most of these positions to be filled by men. Of the 111 new Skilled Craft jobs during this period, 105, or almost 95%, went to men. As previously noted, the Agency's 1982 Plan set a goal of hiring only three women out of the 55 new Skilled Craft positions projected for that year, a figure of about 6%. While this degree of employment expansion by an employer is by no means essential to a plan's validity, it underscores the fact that the Plan in this case in no way significantly restricts the employment prospects of such persons. Illustrative of this is the fact that an additional road dispatcher position was created in 1983, and petitioner was awarded the job. Brief for Respondent Transportation Agency 36, n. 35.

16. As the Agency Plan stated, after noting the limited number of minorities and women qualified in certain categories, as well as other difficulties in remedying underrepresentation:

"As indicated by the above factors, it will be much easier to attain the Agency's employment goals in some job categories than in others. It is particularly evident that it will be extremely difficult to significantly increase the representation of women in technical and skilled craft job classifications where they have traditionally been greatly underrepresented. Similarly, only gradual increases in the representation of women, minorities or handicapped persons in managment and professional positions can realistically be expected due to the low turnover that exists in these positions and the small numbers of persons who can be expected to compete for available openings." App. 58.

17. The dissent predicts that today's decision will loose a flood of "less qualified" minorities and women upon the workforce, as employers seek to forestall possible Title VII liability. *Post,* at ——. The first problem with this projection is that it is by no means certain that employers could in every case necessarily avoid liability for discrimination merely by adopting an affirmative action plan. Indeed, our unwillingness to require an admission of discrimination as the price of adopting a plan has been premised on concern that the potential liability to which such an admission would expose an employer would serve as a disincentive for creating an affirmative action program. See *supra,* n. 6.

A second, and more fundamental, problem with the dissent's speculation is that it ignores the fact that "[i]t is a standard tenet of personnel administration that there is rarely a single, 'best qualified' person for a job. An effective personnel system will bring before the selecting official several fully-qualified candidates who each may possess different attributes which recommend them for selection. Especially where the job is an unexceptional, middle-level craft position, without the need for unique work experience or educational attainment and for which several well-qualified candidates are available, final determinations as to which candidate is 'best qualified' are at best subjective." Brief for American Society for Personnel Administration as *Amicus Curiae* 9.

This case provides an example of precisely this point. Any differences in qualifications between Johnson and Joyce were minimal, to say the least. See *supra,* at 1447–1449. The selection of Joyce thus belies the dissent's contention that the beneficiaries of affirmative action programs will be those employees who are merely not "utterly unqualified." *Post,* at ——.

18. "Discriminatory preference for any group, minority or majority, is precisely and only what Congress has proscribed. What is required by Congress is the removal of artificial, arbitrary, and unnecessary barriers to employment when the barriers operate invidiously to discriminate on the basis of racial or other impermissible classification." *Griggs* v. *Duke Power Co.,* 401 U.S. 424, 431, 91 S.Ct. 849, 853, 28 L.Ed.2d 158 (1971).

19. "Similarly the EEOC, whose interpretations are entitled to great deference, [401 U.S.,] at 433–434, 91 S.Ct., at 854–55, has consistently interpreted Title VII to proscribe racial discrimination in private employment against whites on the same terms as racial discrimination against nonwhites, holding that to proceed otherwise would

'constitute a derogation of the Commission's Congressional mandate to eliminate all practices which operate to disadvantage the employment opportunities of any group protected by Title VII, including Caucasians.' EEOC Decision No. 74–31, 7 FEP Cases 1326, 1328, CCH EEOC Decisions ¶ 6404, p. 4084 (1973)."

"This conclusion is in accord with uncontradicted legislative history to the effect that Title VII was intended to 'cover white men and white women and all Americans,' 110 Cong.Rec. 2578 (1964) (remarks of Rep. Celler), and create an 'obligation not to discriminate against whites.' *id.,* at 7218 (memorandum of Sen. Clark). See also *id.,* at 7213 (memorandum of Sens. Clark and Case); *id.,* at 8912 (remarks of Sen. Williams). We therefore hold today that Title VII prohibits racial discrimination against the white petitioners in this case upon the same standards as would be applicable were they Negroes and Jackson white." *McDonald* v. *Santa Fe Trail Transportation Co.,* 427 U.S. 273, 279–280, 96 S.Ct. 2574, 2578–2579, 49 L.Ed.2d 493 (1976) (footnotes omitted).

20. Toward the end of its opinion, the Court mentioned certain reasons why the plan did not impose a special hardship on white employees or white applicants for employment. *Steelworkers* v. *Weber,* 443 U.S. 193, 208, 99 S.Ct. 2721, 2729, 61 L.Ed.2d 480 (1979). I have never understood those comments to constitute a set of conditions that every race conscious plan must satisfy in order to comply with Title VII.

21. "As Mr. Justice Cardozo remarked, with respect to the routine work of the judiciary: 'The labor of judges would be increased almost to the breaking point if every past decision could be reopened in every case, and one could not lay one's own course of bricks on the secure foundation of the courses laid by others who had gone before him.' Turning to the exceptional case, Mr. Justice Cardozo noted: '[W]hen a rule, after it has been duly tested by experience, has been found to be inconsistent with the sense of justice or with the social welfare, there should be less hestitation in frank avowal and full abandonment.... If judges have

woefully misinterpreted the *mores* of their day, or if the *mores* of their day are no longer those of ours, they ought not to tie, in helpless submission, the hands of their successors.' In this case, those admonitions favor adherence to, rather than departure from, precedent." *Id.*, at 190–192, 96 S.Ct. at 2604–2605. For even while writing in dissent in the *Weber* case, Chief Justice Burger observed that the result reached by the majority was one that he "would be inclined to vote for were I a Member of Congress considering a proposed amendment of Title VII." 443 U.S., at 216, 99 S.Ct., at 2734.

22. As Justice BLACKMUN observed in *Weber,* 443 U.S., at 209, 214–215, 99 S.Ct. at 2732–33 (BLACKMUN, J., concurring):

"Strong considerations of equity support an interpretation of Title VII that would permit private affirmative action to reach where Title VII itself does not. The bargain struck in 1964 with the passage of Title VII guaranteed equal opportunity for white and black alike, but where Title VII provides no remedy for blacks, it should not be construed to foreclose private affirmative action for supplying relief. . . . Absent compelling evidence of legislative intent, I would not interpret Title VII itself as a means of 'locking in' the effects of discrimination for which Title VII provides no remedy."

23. This renders utterly incomprehensible the majority's assertion that "the Agency acknowledged that [its long-term goal] could not by itself necessarily justify taking into account the sex of applicants for positions in all job categories." *Ante,* at 1454.

24. The character of this intervention, and the reasoning behind it, was described by the Agency Director in his testimony at trial:

"Q. How did you happen to become involved in this particular promotional opportunity?

"A. I . . . became aware that there was a difference of opinion between specifically the Road Operations people [Mr. Shields] and the Affirmative Action Director [Mr. Morton] as to the desirability of certain of the individuals to be promoted.

\*       \*       \*       \*       \*

". . . Mr. Shields felt that Mr. Johnson should be appointed to that position.

"Q. Mr. Morton felt that Diane Joyce should be appointed?

"A. Mr. Morton was less interested in the particular individual; he felt that this was an opportunity for us to take a step toward meeting our affirmative action goals, and because there was only one person on the [eligibility] list who was one of the protected groups, he felt that this afforded us an opportunity to meet those goals through the appointment of that member of a protected group." Tr. 16–18.

# V

# Employee Rights and Labor Relations

The core value of employee rights and well-being also commands attention in the personnel arena. Law and culture reinforce the view that by virtue of their status as employees of some organization, people deserve certain rights and benefits. In general terms, formal employee rights increase to the extent that laws and regulations constrain executives from unilaterally exposing subordinates to adverse decisions and circumstances (e.g., unsafe working conditions, firing, demotion). The concept generally assumes that personnel who have invested more of their lives in the agency (i.e., have more seniority) should receive greater protection. Employee well-being is a function of the degree to which subordinates gain psychological gratification and enjoy physical safety and comfort on the job.

Many organizational factors bear on the rights of employees. For example, employee rights expand to the extent that rules limit the reasons for which executives can take adverse actions against subordinates. Thus, laws often constrain public executives from punishing employees for engaging in certain activities off the job such as contributing money to a political campaign. Employee rights also grow as the procedures (e.g., appeals systems) for taking adverse action become more elaborate and place a greater burden of proof on executives. Employee rights loom larger as formal rules require executives or other policy makers to consult or bargain with official representatives of subordinates (e.g., union leaders) over a broader scope of issues.

## Courts and Employee Rights

The last quarter of a century has witnessed increased emphasis on employee rights in public agencies. As in other personnel arenas, the courts have led the way in propelling change. David Rosenbloom ranks among the foremost scholars interpreting and documenting the role of the Supreme Court in expanding freedom of expression, association, and thought among public employees as well as their access to procedural due process.[1] The article from the mid-1970s reprinted here captures his major themes in particularly succinct form. Rosenbloom notes that, historically, the courts had applied the doctrine of privilege to civil servants. This doctrine asserts that because public employees enjoy no right to government employment and choose the work voluntarily, they can claim few constitutional rights that the state *in its capacity as employer* cannot abridge. Rosenbloom traces the demise of this doctrine and asks: what new principle has replaced it? He then shows how the Supreme Court has avoided sweeping and clear rulings; instead, it has opted for an idiographic, case-by-case approach, where rulings about employee rights remain linked to specific circumstances. For human-resource managers and staff, this approach engenders considerable uncertainty. But the overall trend toward greater constitutional protections for public employees unmistakably emerges. He notes that "by affording public employees greater constitutional protection. . .the courts have obviously made adverse actions more difficult to justify."

Did the late 1970s and the 1980s witness the abatement of this approach? Again, Rosenbloom emerges as a major interpreter and answers "no." In an article published in the late 1980s, he concludes that the Supreme Court demonstrated deep division and fragmentation on several issues related to public-employee rights. Yet he sees a general pattern. "The Court has continued the trend, beginning in the 1950s, of affording public employees constitutional protections within the context of their employment." Consistent with the idiographic approach the court has persisted in its emphasis on case-by-case adjudication, which tends to "complicate public personnel administration."[2] Changes in the composition of the Supreme Court could precipitate a major policy shift. Certainly the courts faced the need to deal with new variations on the theme as the 1980s ebbed. For example, they needed to judge how far federal officials could go in forcing subordinates to submit to tests for AIDS and drugs. Even with new Supreme Court justices, however, the complexity of decisions concerning employee rights may well reinforce the idiographic approach.

While Rosenbloom captures the general trend present over the last quarter of a century, he also understands that the 1980s witnessed court decisions that, in some respects, curtailed the protection of employees. In several decisions, the Supreme Court increased the personal liability of public employees for violation of the constitutional or statutory rights of citizens affected by their action. These decisions ripped some holes in the cloak of near absolute immunity from civil suits for damages arising from official performance—the doctrine that had prevailed in the past.[3]

## The Rise of Public Employee Unions

A key dimension of employee rights involves the ability of subordinates to organize into formal groups and bargain with "management." In this regard, the 1960s and 1970s saw a huge transformation in government; public-sector union membership soared. To understand the nature of this transformation, historical perspective is essential. Public employee unions have long been present in the United States. In 1912, intensive lobbying by federal employees, especially postal workers, helped stoke congressional approval of the Lloyd-Lafollette Act. Among other things this law formally freed federal employees from the threat of punishment for joining a union. In 1924, Congress approved the Keiss Act, which established collective bargaining for the printing trade unions in the United States Government Printing Office.[4]

From the early years of the union movement in the public sector to the present, the possibility of employee strikes created anxieties. Indeed, an obscure Massachusetts Governor, Calvin Coolidge, gained national fame by suppressing the Boston police strike of 1919 and declaring: "There is no right to strike against the public safety by anybody, anywhere, anytime" (see the Wurf selection). Anti-strike sentiment reached particular intensity in the period immediately following World War II. In 1947, Congress approved the Taft-Hartley Labor Management Relations Act, which gave government the power to intervene in certain strikes in the private sector and flatly forbade strikes by federal employees. In the midst of this anti-strike and anti-union sentiment, one of the leading figures in public administration in the twentieth century, Leonard D. White, published a remarkably balanced essay called "Strikes in the Public Service" (reprinted here). While acknowledging the damage that public-sector strikes could wreak, he argued that such strikes on occasion serve as a healthy stimulus to top management and could promote the public interest. White suggested that in formulating responses to strikes, government policy makers should focus on the consequences of the activity rather than on the public-versus-private distinction. Not all public-sector strikes brought dire consequences. Some private-sector strikes did. White's careful analysis of the issue at a time when many automatically denounced strikes in the public sector testifies to the independence of thought that characterized his work.

White's essay appeared during the first major growth phase of public-sector unions. From 1897 to 1960, membership in public employee unions increased from approximately 11,000 to just over 900,000. This phase featured slow, steady growth with only three years of modest declines. In contrast, the years from 1961 to 1976 featured "explosive" growth. From just over 900,000 members in 1960, public-sector union membership increased to close to six million by 1976.[5] The proportion of all public employees who belonged to unions grew from 11 percent in 1960 to 40 percent in 1976. In part due to a decline in private-sector union membership, the public sector's share of total union membership rose from 6 percent in 1960 to 27 percent in 1976.[6] This period of unexpected growth partly reflected significant policy changes by federal, state, and local governments.

The explosive period commenced with a major policy shift. For years the AFL-CIO had sought revisions of the Lloyd-Lafollette Act in Congress, revisions that would have granted federal unions rights comparable to those enjoyed by their counterparts in the private sector. On January 17, 1962, President Kennedy effectively bypassed the legislative process when he granted many concessions to unions via Executive Order 10988. From the passive tolerance emphasized by the Lloyd-Lafollette Act, the federal government moved to stress the right of employees to form, join, and assist employee organizations. Specific provisions of this and subsequent executive orders facilitated the organizing and bargaining efforts of federal unions. Executive Order 10988 also precipitated legislative activity at the state and local levels. Some states, such as New York and Wisconsin, had approved fairly comprehensive labor-relations policies prior to 1960. In the 1960s and 1970s, great numbers of other states joined the parade. As the 1980s dawned, thirty-nine states provided a legal framework for collective bargaining covering most of their employees.

A speech by Jerry Wurf during his tenure as President of the American Federation of State, County and Municipal Employees of the AFL-CIO (reprinted here) captures the flavor of the union perspective on developments. In this speech to the United States Conference of Mayors in 1967, Wurf articulated several major themes. He criticized civil-service systems as representing excessive obeisance to unilateralism. He also argued that "traditional distinctions between labor-management relations in the private and public sectors" had become "irrelevant"; the model appropriate for one could substantially be applied to the other. He criticized strike restrictions on public employees as "ineffectual" and as warping "genuine collective bargaining."

Other analysts viewed the rise of employee strength with less equanimity. In the reprinted chapter from their book, *The Unions and the Cities,* Harry H. Wellington and Ralph K. Winter, Jr. set forth the views on "the limits" to collective bargaining in the public sector. They rejected arguments for a "full transplant" of the private-sector model of labor relations to government. In their view, "The public sector is not the private, and its labor problems are different, very different indeed." Wellington and Winter saw forces at work in the private sector that would counteract union assertiveness (e.g., union desire to avoid unemployment by extracting excessive wage concessions). They were less sanguine that these forces would prevail in the public sector. In fact, they feared that a "full transplant" of the private-sector model would often "institutionalize the power of public employee unions in a way that would leave competing groups in the political process at a permanent and substantial disadvantage." They argued that concern over increased taxes would not prove a sufficient counterweight; city officials would tend to concede too much in labor negotiations.

While the work of Wellington and Winter articulated a general vision, the reprinted chapter from Raymond Horton's *Municipal Labor Relations in New York City* perceptively plumbs the intricacies of labor relations during the Wagner and Lindsay years. The relevance of Horton's study transcends his description of the political dynamics of New York City. It perceptively deals with general issues that confront policy makers in many other jurisdictions. Some students of public personnel administration had argued that since government was a monopoly supplier of certain critical services, public negotiators opted for soft bargaining postures, rather than face disruption of critical public services. Horton disagreed. In the selection presented here, he argues that the weakness of New York City officials in the bargaining arena derived less from the city's control over critical services than from ineffective political leadership. Horton saw municipal labor relations as inherently political. Efforts to take politics out of the process were doomed to fail. Horton believed that cities with more effective political leadership would cope effectively with union pressures.

From the vantage point of the early 1970s, the march toward greater public-sector unionism seemed relentless. As one observer noted during this time, public-sector unions "are in a position of strength, with no weakening in sight."[7] Soon, however, union momentum diminished. The period from 1977 to the late 1980s was a period of relative stability rather than growth. By 1987, union membership in the public sector amounted to roughly 6.1 million, about the same as in 1976. The percentage of all public employees unionized declined slightly from approximately 40 percent in 1976 to 36 percent in 1987. As of the early 1980s, about 41 percent of all public educational employees belonged to unions; about 19 percent of all state and local employees (excluding those in education) and roughly 37 percent of all federal civil servants were members. The public sector's share of total union membership continued upward, reaching 36 percent in 1987. (This trend reflected the declining membership of unions in the private sector; in 1987, only 13 percent of private-sector workers belonged to unions.)[8]

During this period of stability the unions did score some policy breakthroughs. The Civil Service Reform Act of 1978 established certain new rights for unions at the federal level, although these rights remained much fewer than those enjoyed by postal workers or employees in many states and localities. In 1977, the Supreme Court ruled that an agency shop was permissible in the public sector (*Abood* v. *Detroit Board of Education*). Under an agency shop, all employees must pay dues to the union once a majority of those voting opt for union representation. For instance, faculty members at the State University of New York must pay a small portion of their respective salaries to the union whether they join it or not. This strengthens unions by protecting them from free riders— those who enjoy benefits obtained by their union but who do not pay dues to support it.

## Union Impact

Ultimately, important questions remain about the impact of the union movement on government activities and decisions. Several analyses have addressed this issue. An early study published by The Brookings Institution examined fifteen cities and four urban counties in reaching the conclusion that unions were changing the way local governments were administered. Among other things, chief executives faced more limits in their discretion to manage. Yet this same study cautioned against assuming that collective bargaining settlements would be excessive or that unions would otherwise cripple local governments.[9] A subsequent analysis emphasized that the growth of unions would spawn diverse impacts with respect to compensation, approaches to service delivery, personnel administration, the authority structure of government, and the nature of politics in a given governmental setting. The precise impacts would depend on a host of variables present in the particular context—those relating to the political system, the social structure, the union, and other factors.[10]

Ultimately, insight into union impact in government depends on the application of sophisticated social science methodologies (preferably longitudinal) and the development of pertinent data sets. It requires vigilant effort to synthesize the findings of empirical inquiries denoting any patterns and explaining any inconsistencies. In this regard, the reprinted article by David T. Methe and James L. Perry sets a standard that future analyses should follow. Published in 1980, the article carefully sketches a conceptual framework for assessing the impacts of collective bargaining as potentially influencing four clusters of variables: (1) inputs—the amount and composition of labor, capital, and other factors of production; (2) activities—the rules and procedures for deploying resources; (3) outputs—the tasks accomplished or resources expended by the city government; and (4) consequences—citizen perceptions of changes in matters of concern. They then analyzed a range of studies focused on municipal governments. While noting the limits to these studies' data and methodologies, Methe and Perry found support for several general propositions. For instance, they concluded that collective bargaining had positively affected the salary and fringe-benefit levels of employees but only marginally and only for certain occupations. They noted that the structure of city government (e.g., city manager, commission, mayor–council) did not appear to influence wage and fringe-benefit concessions. They found that unions had driven up city expenditures, although to a lesser extent in larger cities. In these and other respects, the synthesis sets forth propositions that subsequent researchers must address.

The growing significance of public-sector unionism has clearly affected processes and outcomes in government. Yet, concerns that these unions would become unaccountable juggernauts skewing government priorities, threatening democracy, and vitiating public management are overblown. In a few jurisdictions, this has occurred. But in many others, notably much of the Sun Belt, unions remain weak. Several events sent stern warning signals to public officials about the dangers of conceding "too much" to unions. These included the near financial collapse of New York City in the mid-1970s (see the selection by Horton) and voter resistance to higher taxes as manifested in the approval of Proposition 13 in California in 1978. Officials at times assumed very aggressive postures in dealing with unions. President Reagan's firing of the striking members of the Professional Air Traffic Controllers Association (PATCO) in 1981 had its parallels at other levels of government. To many, Reagan's action implied that one could get tough with unions and either reap political benefits or, at a minimum, pay no serious political costs.

The privatization movement of the 1980s also diverted and constrained union aggressiveness. Turning to the private sector to perform government's work through contract or grant often implies shifting functions from a unionized to a nonunionized setting. (The proportion of private-sector workers who belong to unions fell to roughly 13 percent in 1987, some 60 percent below the historic peak of 36 percent achieved in 1953. Using this indicator, government workers emerge as nearly three times "as organized" as their private-sector counterparts.)[11] Public-sector unions have devoted considerable effort to fighting any shift to private provision of public service. Their leaders sense that if unions prove extremely aggressive and disruptive in seeking benefits, they risk heightening the appeal of privatized strategies that would erode their membership base.

In sum, public-sector unions have enhanced their power in the personnel arena. But policy makers and managers skilled in generic politics typically provide a significant and at times overwhelming counterweight.

# Notes

1. Rosenbloom's most comprehensive treatment of the subject may be found in his *Federal Service and the Constitution* (Ithaca, N.Y.: Cornell University Press, 1971).

2. David Rosenbloom, "Constitutional Law and Public Personnel in the 1980s," *Review of Public Personnel Administration* 8 (Spring, 1988), pp. 50, 62.

3. *Ibid.*, p. 62.

4. Leo Troy and Neil Sheflin, "The Flow and Ebb of U.S. Public Sector Unionism," *Government Union Review* 5 (Spring, 1984), p. 7.

5. *Ibid.*, pp. 28–31.

6. *Ibid.*, pp. 9–11.

7. David T. Stanley, *Managing Local Government Under Union Pressure* (Washington: Brookings Institution, 1972), p. 137.

8. Troy and Sheflin, "The Flow and Ebb...," p. 22; Leo Troy, "Public Sector Unionism: The Rising Power Center of Organized Labor," *Government Union Review* 9 (Summer, 1988), pp. 2–3.

9. Stanley, *Managing Local Government Under Union Pressure.*

10. Raymond D. Horton, David Lewin, and James W. Kuhn, "Some Impacts of Collective Bargaining on Local Government: A Diversity Thesis," in Frederick S. Lane, ed., *Current Issues in Public Administration,* Third Edition (New York: St. Martin's Press, 1986), pp. 406–417.

11. Troy, "Public Sector Unionism . . .," p. 3.

# 26

# Public Personnel Administration and the Constitution: An Emergent Approach

*David H. Rosenbloom*
*University of Vermont*

During the past decade the courts have almost completely transformed the nature of the constitutional position of public employees in the United States. This transformation has largely resulted in an expansion of the constitutional rights and protections afforded public employees in their relationship with government in its role as employer. In the early stages of change, judicial decisions tended to destroy prevailing doctrines without replacing them with much more than a demand that the balance between the rights of public employees and public employers be redressed. It is now possible, however, to identify a consistent line of judicial reasoning that has been emerging and to assess, in a preliminary way, its importance for public personnel administration.

## New Foundations

Historically, the constitutional position of public employees in the United States was governed by what has become known as the doctrine of privilege.[1] Under this line of interpretation it

SOURCE: Reprinted with permission from *Public Administration Review* (January/February, 1975). Copyright © 1975 by The American Society for Public Administration, 1120 G Street, N.W., Suite 500, Washington, D.C. All rights reserved.

was generally accepted that because there was no constitutional right to public employment and because such employment was voluntary rather than compulsory, public employees had few constitutional rights which could not be legitimately abridged by the state in its role as employer. That this doctrine has now been completely discarded is common knowledge. The Supreme Court, for example, has stated, ". . .the Court has fully and finally rejected the wooden distinction between 'rights' and 'privileges' that once seemed to govern the applicability of procedural due process rights."[2] It is easier to note the demise of the doctrine of privilege, however, than to comprehend its replacement.

It is impossible to summarize briefly the content of the line of constitutional interpretation that has superseded the doctrine of privilege. It is still emerging, generally vague, and sometimes contradictory in several of its facets. At its foundation, however, are a new set of assumptions. First, the courts currently approach the constitutional position of public employees from the premise ". . .that a state [or the federal government] cannot condition an individual's privilege of public employment on his nonparticipation in conduct which, under the Constitution, is protected from direct interference by the state."[3] Thus, for example, it is now generally agreed that,

> A citizen's right to engage in protected expression or debate is substantially unaffected by the fact that he is also an employee of the government, and as a general rule, he cannot be deprived of his employment merely because he exercises those rights. This is so because dismissal from government employment, like criminal sanctions or damages, may inhibit the propensity of a citizen to exercise his right to freedom of speech and association.[4]

Perhaps more fundamentally, from the viewpoint of public personnel administration, it is also currently accepted that, ". . .whenever there is a substantial interest, other than employment by the state, involved in the discharge of a public employee, he can be removed neither on arbitrary grounds nor without a procedure calculated to determine whether legitimate grounds do exist."[5] These principles create a new set of facts for public employees, but in the absence of further elaboration by the courts they cannot provide sufficient guidance for a corresponding adjustment of public personnel practice. Although there has been little additional theoretical development of the current constitutional approach, an analysis of judicial decisions over the past five years or so indicates that at least one central strand of thought is running through most of the cases and that it is likely to have a considerable impact on public personnel theory and practice in the years to come.

## The Development of an Idiographic Approach

Analysis of judicial decisions involving the procedural and substantive constitutional rights of public employees indicates that the courts have, with only one major exception, demonstrated a marked reluctance to uphold flat, general, across-the-board special restrictions on their rights. The judiciary has largely demanded, rather, that in applying general personnel regulations and principles to individual employees, public employers address the merits of the specific cases at hand. In other words, while it may sometimes be permissible to take adverse action against public employees in such a fashion that it infringes upon their ordinarily held constitutional rights as citizens, such action cannot be taken in all areas and generally cannot be applied without reference to the specific set of facts in each case.

### A. Procedural Due Process

In terms of procedural due process, the emergent principle is evident in a number of recent cases. Prior to the Supreme Court's decisions in *Roth* v. *Board of Regents* and *Perry* v. *Sindermann* (1972),[6] the lower courts were widely divided on the questions of whether a dismissed or nonrenewed public employee had a constitutional right to a statement of reasons for the adverse action and an opportunity to attempt to rebut them. *Roth* established the rule that although there is no general constitutional right to either a statement of reasons or a hearing, both of these might be constitutionally required in individual instances. This would be the case under any one of four conditions. One is the instance of removal or nonrenewal in retaliation for the exercise of constitutional rights such as freedom of speech or association. A second ground is impairment of reputation. The Court held that:

> The State, in declining to rehire the respondent, did not make any charge against him that might seriously damage his standing and associations in his community. It did not base the nonrenewal of his contract on a charge, for example, that he had been guilty of dishonesty or immorality. Had it done so, this would have been a different case. For "[w]here a person's good name, reputation, honor or integrity is at stake because of what the government is doing to him, notice and an opportunity to be heard are essential." [Citations omitted] . . . In such a case, due process would accord an opportunity to refute the charge before University officials.[7]

Third, and perhaps not fully distinguishable, a public employee would have a right to procedural due process if a dismissal or nonrenewal ". . . imposed on him a stigma or other disability that foreclosed his freedom to take advantage of other employment opportunities."[8]

Finally, if one had a property right or interest in a position, procedural due process would be required before employment could be terminated. But, "To have a property interest in a benefit, a person clearly must have more than an abstract need or desire for it. He must, instead, have a legitimate claim of entitlement to it."[9] In the closely related *Sindermann* case, the Court indicated that such a claim need not necessarily be based on a written contract or statutory protection, but might also be based on ". . . an unwritten 'common law'. . . that certain employees shall have the equivalent of tenure."[10]

In avoiding an across-the-board approach, *Roth* and *Sindermann* make it necessary for public personnel administrators and the courts to determine whether a dismissal or nonrenewal is such that it constitutes an infringement upon liberty, including impairment of reputation or future employment possibilities, or upon property interests. This approach requires a good deal of individual judgment in individual cases. For example, what constitutes a charge that might seriously and adversely affect one's reputation or chances of earning a livelihood in a chosen occupational area? Thus far, it has been held that removals or nonrenewals for fraud,[11] racism,[12] lack of veracity,[13] and, at least in connection with high-level urban employment, absenteeism and gross insubordination[14] can violate procedural due process in the absence of a hearing. It has also been strongly suggested that removal at an advanced age tends to preclude subsequent employment and therefore requires the application of procedural due process.[15] On the other hand, a charge of being "anti-establishment" has been found not to create a sufficient impairment of reputation so as to afford constitutional protection.[16] The point is not to ask whether these holdings are consistent or reasonable, but rather to note that a public employee's right to procedural due process protections in adverse actions, where reasons for the action are supplied, must be evaluated on a multi-dimensional basis including an assessment of the nature of the charge, the type and level of position, and the age of the individual. Under these circumstances it is evident that each case is largely a separate one.

The same individualized tendency prevails with regard to the issue of what constitutes a constitutionally cognizable property interest. In *Sindermann* the length of employment was about ten years. In other cases, 29 and 11 years of employment were found to create enough of a property interest to warrant the application of procedural due process.[17] It has also been held that, ". . . regulations or standards of practice governing nontenured employees which create

an expectation of reemployment"[18] can establish a property interest. On the other hand, eight years of employment on a series of one-year certificates was found to be insufficient to require procedural due process in a nonrenewal.[19]

A final question with regard to procedural due process involves the nature of the protections which must be provided when a hearing is required or held. The law here is ambiguous, and its ambiguity is such that prudent public personnel administrators will probably tend to develop considerably more elaborate hearing procedures than have generally prevailed in the past. Confrontation and cross-examination have been required in some cases,[20] but not in others of a similar nature.[21] The courts are also divided on whether a strict separation of prosecutorial and judicial functions is constitutionally required.[22] There is also a question as to whether hearings can constitutionally be closed to the press and the public.[23] If there is any prevailing precept, it is that the more severe the injury to the individual the greater the procedural protections that must be provided, but, again, this is a factor that must be weighed with reference to the specifics of each case.

### B. Freedom of Expression, Association, and Thought

Recent holdings regarding substantive constitutional rights reveal a similar tendency. Here the major issues have been the extent to which public employees can exercise the rights of freedom of expression, association, and thought. The most important case currently governing public employees' rights to freedom of speech is *Pickering* v. *Illinois* (1968). There the Supreme Court held that although ". . . it cannot be gainsaid that the State has interests as an employer in regulating the speech of its employees that differ significantly from those it possesses in connection with regulation of the speech of the citizenry in general,"[24] the proper test is whether the state's interest in limiting public employees' ". . . opportunities to contribute to public debate is. . . significantly greater than its interest in limiting a similar contribution by any member of the general public."[25] The

Court identified six elements which would generally enable the state to abridge legitimately public employees' freedom of expression. These can be paraphrased as follows:

1. The need for maintaining discipline and harmony in the workforce.
2. The need for confidentiality.
3. The possibility that an employee's position is such that his statements might be hard to counter due to his presumed greater access to factual information.
4. The situation in which an employee's statements impede the proper performance of duties.
5. The case where the statements are so without foundation that the individual's basic capability to perform his duties comes into question.
6. The jeopardizing of a close and personal loyalty and confidence.

In applying *Pickering* the courts have developed a fairly consistent pattern requiring individualized judgment. In addition to the above factors, it has been held that the nature of the remarks or expression,[26] degree of disruption,[27] and likelihood that "...the public will attach special importance to the statements made by someone in a particular position..."[28] must be weighed. In general, only discussions of matters of public concern, as opposed to those primarily of interest to co-workers, are subject to protection under *Pickering*.

There is one major exception to all of this— partisan expression and activity. Without in any way attempting to deny its great importance, however, it should be recognized that the Supreme Court has treated regulations for political neutrality differently than others affecting the constitutional position of public employees. Such regulations were initially upheld in *United Public Workers* v. *Mitchell* (1947).[29] Since that time several federal and state courts have held political neutrality provisions to be unconstitutional.[30] The *Mitchell* decision, for example, was held to have been "...vitiated by the force of subsequent decisions,"[31] and placed "...among other decisions outmoded by the passage of time."[32] However, in *Civil Service*

*Commission* v. *National Association of Letter Carriers* (1973) and *Broadrick* v. *Oklahoma* (1973),[33] a companion case, the Supreme Court decided to "...unhesitatingly reaffirm the Mitchell holding...."[34] The Court argues that such a judgment simply confirmed

> the judgment of history, a judgment made by this country over the last century that it is in the best interest of the country, indeed essential, that federal service should depend upon meritorious performance rather than political service, and that the political influence of federal employees on others and on the electoral process should be limited.[35]

In terms of *Pickering,* therefore, the government had an obviously much greater interest in limiting the partisan activities of its employees than it did in limiting those of its other citizens. Moreover, *Broadrick* indicated that the Court is willing to allow great leeway in terms of the wording of restrictions on the political participation of public employees. In this area, therefore, sweeping restrictions on the constitutional rights of public employees, even loosely worded and without regard to position, are legitimate. Elsewhere this is not the case.

The law regarding public employees' rights of freedom of association and thought falls into the predominant idiographic pattern. Their right to freedom of association was broadly guaranteed by the Supreme Court in *Shelton* v. *Tucker* (1960).[36] The case left open the questions of whether public employees could have membership in subversive organizations, organizations with illegal objectives, and unions. Their right to join the latter was guaranteed in *American Federation of State, County, and Municipal Employees* v. *Woodward* (1969).[37] With regard to the former, it was held in *Elfbrandt* v. *Russell* (1966)[38] that there could be no general answer, but rather that each case had to be judged on the basis of whether a public employee actually supported an organization's illegal aims since "[t]hose who join an organization but do not share its unlawful purposes and who do not participate in its unlawful activities surely pose no threat, either as citizens or as public employees."[39]

Similarly, in terms of freedom of thought, adverse actions based on almost anything more than simple refusal to pledge support for the federal and state constitutions are unconstitutional in the absence of a hearing to determine the beliefs an individual holds and how these can negatively and seriously affect governmental interests. Thus, in *Connell* v. *Higginbotham* (1971), for example, the Supreme Court held that a loyalty oath requiring public employees to swear that they ". . .do not believe in the overthrow of the Government of the United States or of the State of Florida by force or violence"[40] falls ". . .within the ambit of decisions of this Court proscribing summary dismissal from public employment without hearing or inquiry required by due process. . . ."[41] Therefore, exclusion from public employment on the basis of association or thought is to be effectuated for the most part only on a case-by-case basis in which specific factors are taken into account.

### C. Equal Protection

There have also been several cases in the area of equal protection which have required an idiographic approach. In *Baker* v. *City of St. Petersburg* (1968),[42] 12 black policemen contested the constitutionality of police department practices under which all blacks were assigned to a zone that was predominantly black in population. The District Court found that the ". . .assignment of Negro officers to the predominantly Negro Zone 13 was not done for the purpose of discrimination but for the purpose of effective administration."[43] The police department argued that blacks could better identify and communicate with blacks than could whites. The Circuit Court of Appeals, however, reversed on the ground that ". . .a Department's practice of assigning Negroes solely on the basis of race to a Negro enclave offends the equal protection clause of the Fourteenth Amendment."[44] Yet the Court went on to say, "We do not hold that the assignment of a Negro officer to a particular task because he is a Negro can never be justified."[45]

The Supreme Court followed this line of reasoning in *Sugarman* v. *Dougall* (1973), a case involving discrimination against aliens. The Court held that ". . .a flat ban on the employment of aliens in positions that have little, if any, relation to a State's legitimate interest, cannot withstand scrutiny under the Fourteenth Amendment."[46] At the same time, however, "A restriction on the employment of noncitizens, narrowly confined, could have particular relevance to this important state responsibility, for alienage itself is a factor that reasonably could be employed in defining 'political community.' "[47]

Although the Supreme Court chose to treat the issue under due process rather than equal protection, a somewhat similar line of reasoning was adopted concerning mandatory maternity leaves. In *Cleveland Board of Education* v. *LaFleur* (1974), the Court found policies requiring pregnant school teachers to leave their jobs four and five months before the expected date of birth to be unconstitutional because "There is no individualized determination by the teacher's doctor—or the school board's—as to any particular teacher's ability to continue at her job."[48] The Court indicated, however, that mandatory leaves applying only in the last few weeks of pregnancy might present a different set of issues and conclusions.

# Implications for Public Personnel Administration

Public personnel administration in the United States still retains a paradigm that was largely developed by the civil service reform movement. With strict regard to public employment, as opposed to wider political interests, the reformers stood for political neutrality, a higher level of morality, and greater administrative efficiency. Each of these goals has left a significant legacy for contemporary public personnel administration which is likely to undergo modification as a result of the emergence of an idiographic approach to the constitutional status of public employees.

The reformers' emphasis on political neutrality led to the enactment of restrictions on the partisan political activity of public employees in a large number of jurisdictions. It also encouraged the development of a position-oriented public personnel administration which attaches rank and salary to positions rather than individuals and thereby makes it somewhat more difficult to exercise political favoritism. Regulations concerning public employees' membership and belief in subversive organizations and causes are also partially subsumed under the goal of political neutrality. However, the idiographic approach seems certain to foster significant changes in this area.

Although the Supreme Court has left no doubt that, in general, regulations for political neutrality are constitutionally permissible, it has also created a presumption that *nonpartisan* political expression by public employees is constitutionally protected. Under *Pickering* and the cases following it, the latter can only be abridged when a government has demonstrable and compelling interests in so doing. Moreover, exclusion from public employment on the basis of political association or political belief is no longer constitutionally legitimate in the absence of procedural due process protections. These strictures require modification of the position orientation because thinking in terms of "classified," "excepted," "sensitive," and "non-sensitive" positions, and position levels is no longer constitutionally viable or useful with regard to some adverse actions.

While the type of position still retains importance in determining the nature of permissible expression, association, and thought, each public employee has a constitutional right to be heard on the merits of his or her individual case. Broad exclusions, except for partisan activity, can no longer withstand constitutional scrutiny. Therefore, the public service may remain largely nonpartisan, but insofar as the Constitution is concerned, public employees as a group cannot be required to be *apolitical* as well. Moreover, it is possible that the partisan/non-partisan distinction, which is clearly a legacy of reform, may prove untenable under conditions of increasing political activity by public employees[49] and that consequently both public personnel administrators and the judiciary will have to rethink many of the issues involved.

The morality of public employees has also been an important concern of public personnel administration in the post-reform period. Removals or exclusions for "...infamous, dishonest, immoral, or notoriously disgraceful conduct"[50] have not been uncommon. The idiographic approach is also likely to have a considerable impact in this area. The *Roth* decision would require a hearing before a public employee could be removed or not renewed on any of the above grounds. Elsewhere it has been held that "...a finding that an employee has done something immoral or indecent could support a dismissal without further inquiry only if all immoral or indecent acts of an employee have some *ascertainable deleterious* effect on the efficiency of the service."[51] Together, these decisions, and the idiographic approach generally, make it necessary to determine: (1) whether an employee has engaged in an alleged act; (2) whether the act can be considered immoral, indecent, etc., both in general and in connection with injury to the employee's reputation and chances for future employment; and (3) whether the act, even if committed and immoral or indecent, is such that the individual's employment would have a demonstrable adverse affect on legitimate objectives of the public services. These requirements not only make it necessary to treat each case separately, but they also introduce a stringency that makes it very probable that many forms of behavior which once served as a basis for exclusion from the public service for immorality or indecency will prove insufficient for this purpose in the future.[52]

The implications of the idiographic approach for the objective of greater administrative efficiency are less clear. "Efficiency" has been used as a justification for many practices, including some, such as racial and sexual discrimination, that are no longer constitutionally acceptable. Techniques for measuring efficiency, however, are still very crude and it appears that in time the idiographic approach will compel public personnel administrators either to develop better ones or to forfeit a good deal of their authority over public employment to the judiciary. The case-by-case approach to the constitutional status of public employees requires the courts to play a far greater role in overseeing public personnel administration than was previously the case. Indeed, the demise of the doctrine of privilege and the development of the idiographic approach have coincided with a broadening of the "...scope of [judicial] review to include a judicial determination as to whether the administrative findings were capricious, arbitrary or unreasonable, or whether such findings were supported by the record."[53] In order to justify many of their regulations before the courts in the future, therefore, public personnel administrators will be increasingly required to demonstrate how these effectuate efficiency.

More general implications of the idiographic approach for public personnel administration follow from its more limited implications for each of the foregoing areas. In its pursuit of political neutrality, higher morality, and greater efficiency, public personnel administration has developed a very considerable policing function. Even though this has declined somewhat in the face of more recent developmental approaches, a large part of the responsibility of most central personnel agencies in the United States is still to ensure compliance with personnel regulations.

The idiographic approach, however, is likely to make many aspects of policing more difficult and costly. In requiring a case-by-case approach to many questions involving the constitutional position of public employees, by affording public employees greater constitutional protection, and by broadening the scope of judicial review of administrative determinations, the courts have obviously made adverse actions more difficult to justify. Hearings must be more frequently held and their procedures must be more elaborate. Open hearings with counsel, confrontation, and cross-examination will become more common. In practice this will almost inevitably lead to a decline in the coercive power of public employers over their employees. The psychological, economic, and time costs of taking adverse actions will often outweigh the benefits that might be gained by removing an employee. Personnel administration by adversary proceeding is not likely to be efficient or effective. The specter of super- and subordinates facing each other at hearings and in law suits and perhaps then returning to work together seems unattractive from almost all perspectives. As a leading civil service reformer expressed it, "If it were necessary to establish unfitness or indolence,...by such proof as would be accepted in a court of law, sentence would seldom be pronounced, even against notorious delinquents...."[54] Thus, insofar as public personnel administrators desire to regulate the on-the-job behavior of public employees they will have to rely less on policing activities and punishment and turn more toward other means of inducing compliance.[55]

A decline in public personnel administration's policing function may also be forthcoming as a result of the peculiar nature of the hearings required by the idiographic approach. In the past the function of most quasi-judicial administrative hearings involving personnel matters has been to determine factually whether a public employee violated a regulation or failed to perform adequately on the job. Constitutional questions were seldom raised and almost always deferred to the courts. In instances where liberty or property, as defined in *Roth* and *Sindermann*, are involved, however, the idiographic approach requires that hearing officials—often employed by central personnel agencies—no longer assume the validity of personnel regulations. Instead, they must assess the relationship of regulations to legitimate personnel goals and to injury to individual employees. Therefore a constitutional question is quickly raised and the hearing process must become more judgmentally independent than has generally been the case. This not only shifts much of the burden of proof from the public employee to the public employer, but it also creates an important, often internal, check on the policing function of public personnel administration at the hearing stage.

Relatedly, one of the most important effects of the idiographic approach may be to reinforce the on-going process of granting unions a larger role in public personnel administration. In some jurisdictions unions have already secured a right to be present at grievance proceedings and adverse action hearings. They may also be authorized to represent employees regardless of the employees' union membership. Expansion of the requirements of procedural due process and the emergence of new substantive constitutional guarantees on a case-by-case basis obviously point in the direction of increasing union attention to the provision of counsel and other legal services. More significantly, to the extent that unions are interested in the security and freedom of public employees, they may further develop their role as judicial pressure groups by actively seeking out and bringing litigation. Such developments would probably strengthen their bargaining position with regard to public personnel matters of constitutional concern and make public personnel administration a more shared enterprise between management and unions.

In sum, then, an analysis of recent cases involving the constitutional position of public employees indicates that although there is still a good deal of ambiguity in some areas, at least one consistent line of judicial reasoning has emerged. The doctrine of privilege has been replaced by an approach requiring that constitutional questions concerning public employees be decided largely on a case-by-case basis. Although an idiographic approach is natural for the judiciary in applying due process, it requires significant modification of public personnel administrative practice. Political neutrality is becoming more narrowly defined as partisan neutrality. Regulations intended to ensure a high level of morality among public servants will have to be more carefully formulated, applied, and related to other personnel objectives. In order to justify regulations designed to foster greater administrative efficiency, public personnel administrators will have to develop better measurement techniques. More generally, the idiographic approach lessens the utility of public personnel administration's policing function and this will probably be compensated

through the development of other means of securing compliance.

The last two points suggest that while the idiographic approach does require some difficult rethinking of public personnel administrative questions, it may well encourage the development of a more satisfying public personnel administration.[56] A decline in the policing function, the expansion of public employees' constitutional guarantees, and a larger role for unions in the formulation of personnel policy may make public employment a more attractive work environment and more competitive with private employment. Public personnel administration will be more technically satisfying if it becomes grounded on a more conscious effort to separate real from presumed relationships and more cognizant of what is not known about employee and organizational behavior. Finally, the emergent constitutional approach requires public personnel administration to be in greater political and social harmony with contemporary behavior and values.

## Notes

1. For a historical analysis of the constitutional position of federal employees in the United States, see David H. Rosenbloom, *Federal Service and the Constitution* (Ithaca: Cornell University Press, 1971). The "idiographic" approach elaborated upon in this article can be seen as the judiciary's method of applying the doctrine of "substantial interest" discussed in the earlier work.

2. *Roth* v. *Board of Regents*, 33 L. Ed. 2d 548, 557 (1972).

3. *Gilmore* v. *James*, 274 F. Supp. 75, 91 (1967).

4. *Pickering* v. *Board of Education*, 391 U.S. 563, 574 (1968).

5. *Birnbaum* v. *Trussell*, 371 F 2d 672, 678 (1968).

6. *Roth,* cited *supra,* n. 2; *Perry* v. *Sindermann,* 33 L. Ed. 2d 570 (1972).

7. *Roth* v. *Board of Regents,* 33 L. Ed. 2d 548, 558.

8. *Ibid.,* p. 559.

9. *Ibid.,* p. 561.

10. *Perry* v. *Sindermann,* 33 L. Ed. 2d 570, 580.

11. *United States* v. *Rasmussen,* 222 F. Supp. 430 (1963).

12. *Birnbaum* v. *Trussell,* cited *supra,* n. 5.

13. *Hostrop* v. *Board of Junior College District No. 515,* 471 F 2d 488 (1972).

14. *Hunter* v. *Ann Arbor,* 325 F. Supp. 847, 854 (1971).

15. *Olson* v. *Regents,* 301 F. Supp. 1356 (1969).

16. *Lipp* v. *Board of Education,* 470 F 2d 802 (1972).

17. *Johnson* v. *Fraley,* 470 F 2d 179 (1972), and *Lucas* v. *Chapman,* 430 F 2d 945 (1970).

18. *Ferguson* v. *Thomas,* 430 F 2d 852, 856 (1970).

19. *Patrone* v. *Howland Local Schools Board of Education,* 472 F 2d 159 (1972).

20. See, among others, *U.S.* v. *Rasmussen,* cited *supra,* n. 11; *Kelley* v. *Herak,* 252 F. Supp. 289 (1966), subsequently overruled in *Herak* v. *Kelley,* 391 F 2d 216 (1968); *Ahern* v. *Board of Education,* 456 F 2d 339 (1972).

21. See, among others, *Polcover* v. *Secretary of Treasury,* 477 F 2d 1223 (1973), and *Bishop* v. *McKee,* 400 F 2d 87 (1968).

22. See *Camero* v. *United States,* 375 F 2d 777 (1967); *Taylor* v. *New York Transit Authority,* 433 F 2d 665 (1970); *Allen* v. *City of Greensboro,* 452 F 2d 489 (1971); and *Simard* v. *Board of Education,* 473 F 2d 988 (1973).

23. In *Fitzgerald* v. *Hampton,* 467 F 2d 755 (1972), it was held that the Constitution requires that a quasi-judicial administrative proceeding involving personnel matters be open to the press and public, at least under the specific circumstances involved.

24. *Pickering* v. *Illinois,* 391 U.S. 563, 568.

25. *Ibid.*, p. 573.

26. See, among others, *Clark* v. *Holmes,* 474 F 2d 928 (1972); *Childwood* v. *Feaster,* 468 F 2d 359 (1972); *Duke* v. *North Texas State University,* 469 F 2d 829 (1973); and *Goldwasser* v. *Brown,* 417 F 2d 1169 (1969).

27. See *Peale* v. *United States,* 325 F. Supp. 193 (1971); *James* v. *Board of Education,* 461 F 2d 566 (1972); *Rozman* v. *Elliott,* 467 F 2d 1145 (1972); *Russo* v. *Central School District,* 469 F 2d 623 (1972); *Hanover* v. *Northrup,* 325 F. Supp. 170 (1971); and *Donahue* v. *Stauton,* 471 F 2d 75 (1972).

28. *Donovan* v. *Reinbold,* 433 F 2d 738, 743 (1970); see also *Fisher* v. *Walker,* 464 F 2d 1147 (1972).

29. 330 U.S. 75 (1947).

30. *Mancuso* v. *Taft,* 341 F. Supp. 574 (1972); *Hobbes* v. *Thompson,* 448 F 2d 456 (1971); *Fort* v. *Civil Service Commission,* 61 Cal. 2d 331 (1964); *Kinnear* v. *San Francisco,* 61 Cal. 2d 341 (1964); *Minielly* v. *Oregon,* 242 Ore. 490 (1966); and *Bagley* v. *Hospital District,* 421 F 2d 409 (1966). Political

neutrality regulations were upheld in *Northern Virginia Regional Park Authority* v. *Civil Service Commission,* 437 F 2d 1347 (1971) and *Kearney* v. *Macy,* 409 F 2d 847 (1969).

31. *Mancuso* v. *Taft,* 341 F. Supp. 574, 577 (1972).

32. *National Association of Letter Carriers* v. *Civil Service Commission,* 346 F. Supp. 578, 585 (1972).

33. 37 L. Ed. 2d 796, and 37 L. Ed. 2d 830 (1973).

34. 37 L. Ed. 2d 796, 804.

35. *Ibid.*

36. 364 U.S. 479 (1960).

37. 406 F 2d 137 (1969).

38. 384 U.S. 11 (1966).

39. *Ibid.*, p. 17.

40. 403 U.S. 207, 208 (1971).

41. *Ibid.*, pp. 208–209.

42. 400 F 2d 294 (1968).

43. *Ibid.*, p. 296.

44. *Ibid.*, p. 300.

45. *Ibid.*, pp. 300–301.

46. 37 L. Ed. 2d 853, 862 (1973). See also *Jalil* v. *Hampton,* 460 F 2d 923 (1972).

47. 37 L. Ed. 853, 864. In passing it should be noted that this decision brings into question the legitimacy of statutes, such as the Foreign Service Act, which prohibit the employment of citizens whose naturalization did not take place prior to a specific number of years before their application for employment was made.

48. 39 L. Ed. 2d 52, 62. Such issues have generally been treated under equal protection. See *Schattman* v. *Texas,* 459 F 2d 32 (1972); *Cohen* v. *Chesterfield County School Board,* 474 F 2d 395 (1973); *LaFleur* v. *Cleveland Board of Education,* 465 F 2d 1184 (1972); *Buckley* v. *Coyle Public School System,* 475 F 2d 92 (1973); and *Green* v. *Waterford Board of Education,* 473 F 2d 629 (1973).

49. For a discussion of increasing political involvement by federal employees, see D. H. Rosenbloom, "Some Political Implications of the Drift Toward a Liberation of Federal Employees," *Public Administration Review,* Vol. XXXI (July/August 1971), pp. 420–426.

50. U.S. Civil Service Commission Rule V. section 3. See Civil Service Commission, *Civil Service Act, Rules, Statutes, Executive Orders, and Regulations* (Washington, D.C.: U.S. Government Printing Office, 1941), p. 37.

51. *Norton* v. *Macy,* 417 F 2d 1161, 1165 (1969), emphasis added.

52. In *Norton* v. *Macy, supra* n. 51, and *Scott* v. *Macy,* 349 F 2d 182 (1965), it was held that homosexuality was not sufficient grounds for removal in the

absence of a showing that it was adversely related to competence or the efficiency of the federal service. Similarly, it is questionable whether it would still be constitutionally possible to dismiss a policeman for living with an unmarried woman. See *The New York Times,* August 1, 1968, p. 27. There have been too few cases to indicate clearly what forms of "immorality," if any, might still provide the basis for general exclusion from public service.

53. *West* v. *Macy,* 284 F. Supp. 105 (1968).

54. U.S. Civil Service Commission, "Reform of the Civil Service: A Report to the President, December 18, 1971," in Charles E. Norton (ed.), *Orations and Addresses of George William Curtis* (New York: Harper and Bros., 1894), Vol. II, p. 51.

55. For a discussion of compliance in organizations, see Amitai Etzioni, *Complex Organizations* (New York: The Free Press, 1961).

56. For a general discussion of how public personnel administration might be further developed, see D. H. Rosenbloom, "Public Personnel Administration and Politics: Toward a New Public Personnel Administration," *Midwest Review of Public Administration,* Vol. VII (April 1973), pp. 98–110.

# 27

# Strikes in the Public Service

*Leonard D. White*

On June 20, 1947, the House of Representatives voted to override President Truman's veto of the Taft-Hartley Labor-Management Relations Act; three days later the Senate concurred, and the act became law. Section 305 of this legislation prohibits strikes by government employees in all-inclusive terms:[1]

> It shall be unlawful for any individual employed by the United States or any agency thereof including wholly owned government corporations to participate in any strike. Any individual employed by the United States or by any such agency who strikes shall be discharged immediately from his employment, and shall forfeit his civil service status, if any, and shall not be eligible for reemployment for three years by the United States or any such agency.

Less than a year earlier the French Parliament had enacted a comprehensive civil service law that in a single sentence adopted a directly opposite public policy: "Le droit syndical est reconnu aux functionnaires," a sentence that freely granted public employees the common rights of private industrial workers. Between these two extremes stands the public policy of most American jurisdictions—the policy of silence so far as the law is concerned. Obviously, this policy has now been challenged. Clearly, too, some policy is likely to be formulated by legislative bodies large and small in the near future. What should that policy be?

SOURCE: From *Public Personnel Review*, Vol. 10, No. 1, January 1949. Reprinted by permission of the International Personnel Management Association.

A discussion of policy opens up many possibilities. Policy seeks to resolve the question of "ought," rather than the question of law. In most questions of "ought," there is more than one defensible answer. Each depends on a set of values. In this particular policy problem, a number of values are involved, and different weights are assigned to them by different persons, all of whom would perhaps recognize each as valid in part. One such value is *authority*, essential for order and continuity in human institutions. Another is the equally basic value of *freedom*, essential for human integrity and the progressive evolution of institutions. The first speaks primarily in terms of the state, the other in terms of the individual. A permanent balance between these two values has never been reached and doubtless never will be reached in a dynamic society. Both are integral parts of human life; both are involved in achieving a moving equilibrium of agreement on all manner of public issues, including the question of public service strikes.[2]

## The View That Government Is Different

One clearly defined position as to proper public policy is implicit in the Taft-Hartley Act: No one has a right to strike against the government at any time under any circumstances. The term "right" is used here in its moral sense. This view was held in 1947 by a majority of Congress and by majorities in a number of state legislatures; it is also held by many executives and officials, by some leaders of civil service unions, and by large numbers of thoughtful citizens who, on the other hand, do not quarrel with the right of employees in private industry to withhold their labor to secure their ends.

These persons stand on the proposition that government is different from private undertakings. The difference is put in various terms: the state is sovereign and cannot brook defiance by any group within it, least of all by its own employees; the state represents the interests of all persons and groups and cannot yield to the pressure of one; the conditions of employment in the public service are fixed by law, unilaterally, and cannot be made the subject of bargaining and bilateral agreement as in a treaty between sovereign powers; the principal employment decisions are made by legislative bodies, not by executives, and consequently a strike is directed against the ultimate representative assemblies, which by definition cannot and in the general interest ought not to have their free decision foreclosed by force.

Behind these affirmations of the special status of public authorities is the conviction that any action tending to undermine the moral authority of the state is dangerous to the life of the community. Strikes of public employees would reduce the state to the position of an ordinary corporation, and could not fail to diminish its moral authority. In the long run, the consequences would be disastrous and must be avoided, even at some sacrifice of the privileges of government employees.

On a narrower scale, it is argued that the inconveniences and risks to the public caused by strikes of civil service unions would be serious, and upon occasion irreparable. The loss of life and property and the temporary dissolution of normal social restraints during the Boston police strike of 1919 are cited in evidence. Strikes of fire fighters, garbage collectors, and public utility employees would precipitate crises in short order. While it is agreed that not all public employees bear such crucial responsibilities, it is argued that there is no logically defensible line of differentiation between one case and another; the only feasible disposition is therefore to ban all strikes of government employees.

The defense of such a policy is buttressed by pointing to alternative methods of seeking satisfaction for claims or grievances. The conditions of public employment are a matter of public record. If unsatisfactory, they can be attacked through the normal processes of public discussion and political change. The channels of public discussion are open, and the sense of fairness of the community will not long allow unfair conditions to prevail. If the public is indifferent or unconvinced, the dissatisfied employee may conclude that his grievances are less than he imagines; or he may find better conditions of employment elsewhere. In the long run, the consequently less efficient conduct of the services will bring its own remedy.

This general policy position was taken by Governor Thomas E. Dewey when he signed the bill banning strikes in the public service in New York in 1947. In an explanatory memorandum he declared:

The conditions of public and private employment are entirely different. The special characteristics of public employment are as follows:

1. Public service is a public trust not only for elected officials but for all employees. It is a trust in behalf of all people. A trustee cannot strike or falter in the performance of his duties.

2. A public employee has as his employer all the people. The people cannot tolerate an attack upon themselves.

3. The public employee has no employer who may profit from depressed conditions of employment.

4. The conditions of public employment, the rules governing it, and the revenues available to pay for it are all matters of public record.

5. Public employees have the right to improve their conditions through arguments before all the people, before legislative bodies, administrative officials and, of course, by their own ballots on Election Day. These rights are so effective that among all the types of employment over the years public employment has been rated as having the best and most desirable conditions.

. . .Government is not an end in itself. It exists solely to serve the people. The very right of private employees to strike depends on the protection of constitutional government under law. Every liberty enjoyed in this nation exists because it is protected by government which functions uninterruptedly. The paralysis of any portion of government could quickly lead to the paralysis of all society.

Franklin D. Roosevelt took much the same position in 1937 when he pointed out that the process of collective bargaining could not be transplanted into the public service. Collective bargaining, he declared, "has its distinct and insurmountable limitations when applied to public personnel management." The President in the same statement also declared his views on the question of strikes by public employees in the following words:[3]

Since their own services have to do with the functioning of the Government, a strike of public employees manifests nothing less than an intent on their part to prevent or obstruct the operations of government until their demands are satisfied. Such action, looking toward the paralysis of government by those who have sworn to support it, is unthinkable and intolerable.

## The Statutory Silence View

A second policy position can be put in some such terms as these: While strikes in the public service are to be avoided wherever possible, circumstances may exist, and occasionally do, in which a strike is defensible in the public interest itself, and is unavoidable in the interest of employees. As a rule, the advocates of this position are not men who encourage strikes or rush into them heedlessly, nor men who are insensitive to the considerations which have already been noted. Rather, they are men with a keen sense of justice who refuse to submit to what they conceive to be harsh injustice, irremediable by any other means. The underlying, dominant values which these men cherish are justice, the democratic right of consultation, and ultimate freedom of action. They are also deeply moved by humanitarian instincts, outraged in their view by conditions of employment which violate minimum American standards. They are as sincere, and as firm, in their position as are the men who would prohibit all public service strikes under any circumstances. They stand for the historic policy of statutory silence on this issue, leaving matters to the good sense of those concerned.

The advocates of this policy solution deny or minimize the difference between public and private employment. They argue that bad employment conditions may prevail in a government office as well as in commerce or industry. They assert that a government supervisor or official can be, and may be, as arbitrary, high-handed, dictatorial, bad-tempered, and grossly unfair as any factory foreman. They believe that short-sighted officials, elected or appointed, may obstinately refuse to authorize salary scales equivalent to those prevailing in the community, preferring to make a record of tax reduction or debt retirement rather than to meet just demands of government employees. They are not impressed with the degree of public awareness of conditions against which employees complain, or the determination of the voters to correct them, perhaps at the cost of an increase in the tax rate. They assert that bad management lowers morale, reduces efficiency, leads to sabotage, and creates a condition from which the public interest directly suffers. They complain that the ordinary channels of communication are not open to public employees, short of a crisis; and the threat of a strike is the only crisis they can create.

The inconvenience caused by a public service strike, moreover, is not necessarily so great as that which would be involved in a stoppage in some privately managed undertakings. A strike on the nation's railroads, once imposed for forty-eight hours in 1946 and again threatened in 1948, would bring instant disaster to the whole country; in 1947 a stike of coal miners caused creeping paralysis of American production; a strike of milk handlers would be as grave as a strike of almost any group of municipal employees. The relative inconvenience of a strike of street maintenance men, or of public welfare case workers, or of seamen on a government-owned barge line is clearly less.

A strike against government, whether federal, state, or municipal, is conceivable, it is argued further, only under the most extreme provocation. Government employees are a conservative group. They have expectations of continuous employment; great numbers have retirement rights that progressively dictate prudence; all are members of their communities, householders and participants in the hundreds of intimate rituals that bind together a community, proud of their status as public employees, and often bound to it by sentiments of deep attachment. "We don't *want* to strike," is a common expression among them when occasionally a crisis develops. Their union leaders, almost without exception, are as firm on the matter of strikes—or more so—than the rank and file. They know that the risks of defeat are great and believe that the long-run interests of their group are served by persuasion and endurance rather than by violence. The development of a situation in which a strike becomes possible normally signifies a breakdown on the part of management, not impulsive and arrogant action by irresponsible groups of employees. The public interest, it is argued, is well served if the threat of a strike unmasks such management.

In private industry, the capacity of organized employees to resist unsatisfactory conditions of employment and to fight back against stupid or arrogant foremanship has been a strong incentive to better management. The fact that a union can threaten the power position of managers and the profit position of a corporation is a healthy stimulus to top management and every intermediate level. It is argued that government, already occupying a protected, noncompetitive status, should not be shielded from this spur to improved administration.

Finally, those who support the right of strike among government workers contend that the right to withhold labor as a means of securing improvement in conditions of employment is one of the fundamental elements of liberty in the American sense of the term. It is of such deep social significance that it ought not to be curtailed anywhere, at any time, except under the strict compulsion of absolute necessity.

Granting the legal authority of the state to impose such a limitation on this normal freedom of American citizens, it is said that it is unwise and unnecessary to do so. The danger of strikes in the public service, on the record of the last half century, is exceedingly small. It is said that this danger is far too slender to support the curtailment of freedom in this small group; and, worse, such a restriction points ominously to its extension elsewhere.

## The View That Strike Consequence Is Real Criterion

It is possible to take a third position, one that differs from both prohibition and tolerance by silence. It may be argued that the former prohibits too much, the latter too little. Each of these positions draws the line between public and private enterprise; all of one group stand in the field of prohibition and all of the other in the field of freedom. This line, it may be argued, is an arbitrary one. It becomes more and more fictitious every decade. Its real meaning as a guide to action grows less and less, and in the matter of public policy concerning strikes it needs to be abandoned.

The true criterion of distinction should be based on the nature and gravity of the consequences involved in a strike, whether by persons employed by government, by a government corporation, by a public trustee, by a mixed enterprise, by a private corporation affected with a public interest, or by a privately owned and operated industry or enterprise. The rule may be stated in some such terms as these: *A strike that would bring direct, immediate, certain, and serious danger to a primary interest of the community should be prohibited by law, with adequate sanctions, but also with adequate means to secure full public consideration and solution of the issues involved.* In other cases the law should remain silent. The criterion of distinction is therefore the consequence of a strike upon the public interest, not the status of the employer.

By way of illustration, some primary interests of the community are the maintenance of public order and individual security; the protection of property against destruction by fire; the maintenance of such urban utilities as water or electricity. Some secondary (although important) interests are the supervision of children at play in a public park; the inspection of water supplies of interstate carriers; the operation of a publicly owned barge line on the Mississippi River. An interruption of the first class would constitute a direct, immediate, certain, and serious danger to the whole community. An interruption of the second would be inconvenient, would result in some loss, and would be annoying to management and some parts of the public. It would, however, affect something less than a primary interest of the community and would not present a direct, immediate, certain, and serious danger to the public interest.

It follows from the preceding propositions that public policy should prohibit strikes in some instances. Again, by way of example, a strike on the railroads (privately owned and operated), and a strike on the New York City subway system (publicly owned and operated) may be cited; or a strike among hospital attendants (public and private), and a strike among milk handlers in an urban centre (privately managed).

The choice of circumstances under which strikes should be prohibited by law can be guided by the suggested criterion, but the criterion is obviously not automatic. The judgment of responsible public authorities has to be called into play in each particular case or class of cases. The line of division gradually worked out might seem at any point of time to be arbitrary—but not thereby capricious. In all this there is nothing new or unusual. Legislative and executive bodies and courts are constantly called upon, in the exercise of judgment and discretion, to make just this type of distinction. It is by means of "arbitrary" decisions by responsible authorities that security benefits are given to factory employees but not to employees of farmers or eleemosynary institutions; that persons with a stated income pay no income tax while others pay 15 and still others 30 per cent;

that persons with less than a full college course in an accredited institution of higher learning are not allowed to take certain civil service examinations.

That it is legislatively feasible to apply this type of criterion in the prohibition of strikes is indicated by some state legislation of 1947. Thus, the legislature of New Jersey selected public utilities as enterprises, the interruption of which would constitute an immediate danger to the community. Strikes and lockouts were forbidden; authority was given the governor to take over the plant, equipment, and facilities; compulsory arbitration of disputes was imposed; and the order of the Board of Arbitration was made conclusive and binding on all parties to the dispute, subject to severe penalties for nonobservance.[4] Minnesota selected charitable hospitals as institutions, the interruption of which would cause irreparable damage; some are publicly owned and operated, others are private, nonprofit institutions. Strikes and lockouts were prohibited and a court of equity was authorized to enjoin one or the other.[5] Indiana singled out public utility employers, "engaged in the business of rendering electric, gas, water, telephone, or transportation services to the public," making no differentiation between public and private employers. Strikes and lockouts were prohibited in all cases in which the governor believed "that a continuation of the dispute will cause or is likely to cause the interruption of the supply of a service on which the community so affected is so dependent that severe hardship would be inflicted on a substantial number of persons by the cessation of such service."[6] In each of these cases, the legislature abandoned the criterion of public and private and adopted the criterion of direct, immediate, certain, and serious danger to the community in deciding the points at which strikes, normally permissible, should be prohibited.

Congress, too, seems to be moving in this direction, although the absolute prohibition of strikes by federal employees is in contradiction. By section 206 of the Taft-Hartley Act, special provision is made to prevent strikes in "an entire industry or substantial part thereof" engaged in foreign or interstate commerce, or engaged in the production of goods for commerce, an interruption of which would imperil the national health or safety. In such cases the President may appoint a board of inquiry, and after receiving its report he may direct the Attorney General to petition any district court to enjoin a threatened strike or lockout (sec. 208). This legislation is parallel to the provisions of the National Defense Act of 1916 under which President Truman some thirty years later seized the railroads on May 18, 1948, and secured a temporary injunction from Justice Goldsborough against a threatened strike by three railway unions. On July 1, 1948, the injunction was made permanent, and on July 29 it was continued in force to permit the unions to secure a Supreme Court ruling. If the Supreme Court sustains this injunction, there will be a presumption that it will also sustain the special procedure established by the Taft-Hartley Act, the effect of which is to enable the government to specify certain types of private employment in which a strike, otherwise recognized by the silence of the law, is banned.

Public policy stated in the terms of these state laws and this aspect of federal policy leaves a maximum of freedom to citizens in their work relations. It does not, of course, prescribe the internal policy of public employee unions within this area of freedom. As a matter of strategy and tactics, or in devotion to high standards of duty, a civil service union could impose upon itself the obligation not to strike against the government under any circumstances. This is the existing policy of most civil service unions, adopted long before the prohibiting legislation of 1946 and 1947. It will doubtless continue to be the policy of most such unions, where no prohibition presently exists. These self-denying ordinances are not, however, a sure guide to public policy on this issue.

## Need for Better Negotiation Machinery

The policy position suggested in the previous section requires, as an essential element, adequate means to secure full public consideration of, and solution for, the issues involved in a disputed claim or grievance in the civil service. Few, if any, American jurisdictions, federal, state, or local, have yet developed adequate machinery for the joint consideration of claims or for the disposition of grievances. The enactment of the recent crop of "no-strike" legislation will compel consideration of this aspect of employee management, not only in these jurisdictions but elsewhere. Here, it is alleged, is to be found the real answer to potential disturbance in the public service, rather than in the negative policy of mere prohibition.

The principal elements of a constructive public policy to prevent strikes by eliminating their causes can be briefly identified. They include:

1. Maintenance of equitable conditions of employment comparable to those prevailing in progressive private industry.

2. Full disclosure by management of the terms and conditions, and obligations, of employment in the public service.

3. Recognition of the right of employees to organize and to meet with the appropriate public authorities for collective representation and negotiation on conditions of employment, broadly construed.

4. Provision of adequate machinery, in which both employees and management have confidence, to deal with employee grievances, whether individual or collective.

Proper recognition of these propositions will require new or enlarged administrative agencies in most jurisdictions. A central personnel agency to formulate and guide the application of personnel policy and to furnish positive leadership is required. This leadership, in turn, depends upon effective support by chief executives—mayors, managers, governors, commissioners, secretaries, and presidents. In large agencies there is needed an industrial relations staff, and in all a familiarity with progressive industrial-relations procedures.

In jurisdictions as extensive as the federal government, and perhaps in the largest state and metropolitan areas, much would be gained by the establishment of an American equivalent of the Whitley Council system of joint negotiation developed in Great Britain after World War I. These national and departmental joint councils (staff side and official side) have been so successful that they are not only fully accepted by the British government, but have also become an integral part of the normal machinery for the consideration of personnel policy. Experience in the Tennessee Valley Authority with the Joint Trades and Labor Council suggests that the crafts are prepared to give support to joint councils where management is ready to cooperate. The Whitley Council ranges far beyond the crafts, however; they are primarily concerned with the clerical, middle, and top management, and also the scientific, technical, and professional grades. Immense resources are untouched in the American public service for lack of any means of responsible consultation between management and staff on large matters of personnel policy.

## Appropriate Sanctions for No-Strike Areas

The policy position suggested in the third section of this paper also requires adequate sanctions in those cases, in public or private employment, where strikes are deemed inadmissible.

The sanctions provided by contemporary American legislation are severe. Section 305 of the Taft-Hartley Act requires immediate discharge, forfeiture of civil service status, if any, and disbarment from future employment by the United States for three years. Requirement of removal under the Hatch Act has been construed not to jeopardize the right to a hearing (39 Op. Atty. Gen. 462), and it may be presumed that section 305 of the Taft-Hartley Act will be given the same construction. However, if upon hearing the employee is found in fact to have struck, the penalty of discharge is automatic. Forfeiture of civil service status would not in itself necessarily involve loss of accrued retirement funds paid in by the government, but most federal appropriation acts carry a proviso

prohibiting the payment of any sum appropriated as salary or compensation to an employee who strikes against the government. This proviso has been strictly construed by the Comptroller General (26 Comp. Gen. 207 and 26 Comp. Gen. 853). It might mean loss of the government's contribution to the retirement fund. Loss of civil service status clearly includes any seniority rights and reemployment rights.

These penalties apply to the whole range of labor and industrial positions where the right to strike has not hitherto been contested. A carpenter employed on the Alaska Railroad, a bricklayer employed on a construction job by the National Park Service, and a seaman employed by the Inland Waterways Corporation could only construe such restrictions on their personal freedom of action as severe and extraordinary, as contrasted with the recognized rights of carpenters, bricklayers, and seamen generally.

The New York statute provides that any public employee (inclusively defined) who goes out on strike "shall thereby abandon and terminate his appointment or employment and shall no longer hold such position, or be entitled to any of the rights or emoluments thereof, except if appointed or reappointed as hereinafter provided." Reappointment is discretionary, requiring application by the striker and hearing by the official having power to remove him and is subject to two limitations: no increase in compensation upon reappointment or for three years thereafter, and appointment on probation for five years without tenure and at the pleasure of the appointing officer. This type of sanction, permitting administrative action "to let the penalty fit the crime," is superior to the automatic requirements of the Taft-Hartley Act. Under the general provisions of the New York retirement fund, however, an employee dismissed for cause loses the government contribution to his pension, and the civil service law provides that such an employee loses any seniority or promotion rights.

Where strikes are prohibited, it is agreed that some form of sanction is essential. Strikes against government-operated enterprises (the coal mines when seized by the United States) can be enjoined by a court, and contempt of court punished in the discretion of the judge. The United Mine Workers were fined $700,000 in 1947 and $1,400,000 in 1948. But when Mr. John L. Lewis stood in danger of a sentence for contempt of court, the miners voluntarily stayed out of the pits. The experience is instructive.

Among government employees the capacity and the will to resistance are relatively feeble. Sanctions can be proportioned to the need for compulsion. A form of sanction, the incidence of which in the first instance will be automatic, the weight of which will be a real deterrent, and the application of which can be tempered by administrative action to the fault of the employee and to the community's sense of fairness and justice, is appropriate. The details need not be developed here, but it is important to insist that responsible administrative discretion be called into play to modify, so far as may be deemed appropriate, the penalties incurred.

## Conclusion

It remains to state briefly the views of the present writer on this perplexing and contentious issue. They have been forecast in the previous pages but may be restated as a means of bringing the discussion into focus. They may be put in the following propositions:

1. The Taft-Hartley Act, the Condon-Wadlin Act, and similar legislation prohibiting strikes among all classes of public employees are unnecessary and are contrary to sound public policy because they unduly restrict the freedom of a large group of American citizens.

2. Strikes should be prohibited, however, when they endanger a primary public interest directly, immediately, certainly, and seriously, whether they occur in public or private enterprises. In all other cases, the law should remain silent.

3. The prohibition of strikes imposes an obligation to ensure full public consideration and settlement of the issues involved in disputed claims or grievances.

4. In public employment this obligation involves maintenance of equitable conditions of employment, full publicity to conditions of employment, recognition of the right to organize and consult on conditions of employment, and adequate machinery for the settlement of grievances.

5. Where exceptionally the right of strike is forbidden, sanctions should be proportionate to the gravity of the offense and should be reviewed by the administrative authorities.

Conflicts in human relations are not solved merely by prohibition. Nor is prohibition congenial to the American tradition of liberty. Within the limits of the public interest as progressively defined by responsible legislative bodies, freedom of individuals and groups to seek their ends by concerted action, but subject to the control of public opinion, is a precious part of the liberty of citizens in this Republic. The present outbreak of antistrike legislation is the joint product of a wave of postwar reaction and the ambiguous position of a single national organization of public employees. It reflects neither present danger nor future prospects of harm. It is symbolic of a tendency toward curtailment of freedom of group action, as the loyalty tests are symbolic of a limitation of freedom of opinion. These freedoms are too essential to jeopardize.

## Notes

1. Analogous state legislation in 1946 and 1947 may be consulted in the following citations: Indiana, Acts 1947, c. 341 (public utilities only); Michigan, Public Acts 1947, p. 524; Minnesota, Laws 1947, c. 335 (charitable hospitals); Missouri, Laws 1947, p. 351; Nebraska, Laws 1947, c. 178; New Jersey, Acts 1947, Senate 323 (public utilities only); New York, Laws 1947, c. 391; Pennsylvania, Laws 1947, p. 1161; Texas, Laws 1947, c. 135; Virginia, Laws 1946, c. 333; Washington, Laws 1947, c. 287.

2. The Civil Service Assembly has not adopted an official policy on the subject; the views here expressed are purely those of the author.

3. *New York Times,* September 5, 1937, p. 14.

4. New Jersey, Acts 1947, Senate 323.

5. Laws of 1947, c. 335.

6. Indiana, Laws 1947, c. 341.

# 28

# City Hall Labor Policies

*Jerry Wurf*

I am pleased at this opportunity to present the point of view of my international union. Since many of you will be dealing with our locals, this discussion may be especially relevant. Hopefully, it will also be useful.

I shall spare you—and myself—those tedious platitudes concerning the incalculable value of ongoing dialogue and the virtues of communication. Dialogue has frequently been used as a term to describe people talking past each other. Alleged breakdowns in communication are often not that at all, but reflect fundamental disagreements which ought to be forthrightly confronted so that resolution might follow. Resolution of conflict seems improbable if we are all thrashing about in the sticky spider web of jargon.

Further, we ought not to be quite so timid—or apprehensive—about such conflict. It is not invariably verbal, and it does, at least occasionally, reflect diverse interests in a gratifyingly diverse society. It was the accommodation of these diverse interests that so preoccupied James Madison in the *Federalist Papers* as this country went about the business of adopting the Constitution. And it is the accommodation of these diverse interests, rather than their repression, that is the distinctive feature of a democratic society.

Unions of employes constitute a major interest group. Like others, it is not totally without blemish. Few human institutions are. The labor movement in this country has had its

SOURCE: From the 1967 speech at the United States Conference of Mayors. Reprinted by permission of the American Federation of State, County, and Municipal Employees, AFL-CIO.

share of opportunists and scoundrels, its quota of individuals who abused the power conferred by their constituents, and its proportion of short-sightedness and lack of vision.

I need not remind a conference of mayors that we hold no monopoly on such limitations.

On balance, I would suggest that the pressure of labor unions for collective bargaining on the terms and conditions of employment has been both desirable and socially constructive. Despite occasional lapses, there is general consensus on this as it relates to the private sector of our economy.

What seems new—and what appears threatening to some—is the relatively recent introduction of this process into public sector labor relations.

It is now almost half a century since the Boston police strike of 1919. A relatively obscure governor, Calvin Coolidge, was propelled by those events into national prominence and ultimately, the presidency. His terse telegram is by now well known: "There is no right to strike against the public safety by anybody, anywhere, anytime."

This is not the appropriate forum for a seminar in labor history, nor do I entertain any pretensions of expertise in this area. Several aspects of the Boston police strike, however, have painful relevance a half-century later:

(1) The police in that city had had their social club for approximately 13 years. They had lobbied, long and unsuccessfully, for wage increases. Repeated failures induced them to turn to traditional unionism. Their announcement of intention to seek affiliation with the AFL was met by the police commissioner arbitrarily forbidding such affiliation. It was this unilateral prohibition and his obdurate denial of all compromise and mediation proposals which precipitated the strike.

(2) Although the issues were generally known, and were certainly reflected in the press, little genuine effort was made towards settlement by the responsible parties. Boston's mayor deplored police unionism, unhappily conceded

that the dissatisfaction had some foundation, and was exercised at the prospect of a suspension of services. Unfortunately, he had no control, and apparently little influence, over the police commissioner. This gentleman devoted the weeks preceding the strike to bland reassurances that things were under control.

(3) The strike, as most of you know, was broken. All participants were discharged. None was reinstated. It was, however, a Pyrrhic victory—and here our traditional histories are inadequate. The new policemen were hired at precisely the pay schedules demanded by those who had struck and lost.

(4) The action at Boston reflected a growing restiveness among police and firemen throughout the country. The mass dismissal undoubtedly intimidated colleagues in other cities. But if subsequent pay scales are any indication the strike that failed was actually an impressive success. If police were intimidated, their communities were not insensitive to what transpired in the Bay State. Police pay improved significantly in city after city.

Candidly, now, is this not a familiar if not classic pattern?

At the risk of belaboring a point, I call your attention to the ingredients:

A widening gap between compensation in the private and pubic sectors. The failure of public sector pay to keep abreast of a war-induced increase in the cost of living. Refusal to even sit down at the negotiating table. Diffusion of authority between the mayor and the police commissioner—the one reluctantly willing, but unable; the other able, but adamantly unwilling. And, finally, the ruthless discharge of over a thousand men in affirmation of a hollow and unjustifiable principle, followed rapidly by exactly the settlement which could have avoided the strike in the first place.

Wasn't it a philosopher who wryly observed that those who did not learn from history were destined to relive it? Perhaps no better demonstration exists than labor relations in the public service.

Until quite recently, management and workers in this sector appeared trapped in a grotesque minuet, the score for which was written a half-century ago. This was an impossingly formal dance. We have been stumbling through the ritualistic steps with the thoughtlessness of zombies.

A careful reexamination seems long overdue.

We live in a country with undreamed-of wealth, a staggering productive capacity, and the most advanced technology known to man. Yet we pay many public employes at levels which would qualify them for welfare supplements.

We are confronted, across the nation, with chronic shortages of policemen, firemen, teachers, nurses, welfare workers.

In many places recruiting is crippled by tragically inadequate pay scales. In some places, we manage to recruit, but are unable to retain employes as private industry pay and conditions of work exert an understandable and irresistible magnetism.

Many vital public services have been transformed by these factors into employment turnstiles, inducing simultaneously administrative inefficiency and excessive operational costs.

Yet employe efforts to improve wages and working conditions have been regarded as arrogant and unbridled self interest and treated in a manner more appropriate to major insurrections.

This disparity, ironically enough, operates largely at lower levels and in what we term social services. Executive assistants, administrative heads, and top level staff are recruited and retained by salaries in the $15,000–$30,000 bracket. We appear to have little difficulty in rationalizing this. Given market realities and the need for talent, such compensation appears unavoidable. It is at the $4,000–$10,000 level that we balk and resort to pious and passionate declaration of the requirement of a sense of dedication to public service.

We have been governed since the 1930s by a public policy which specifically repudiates unilateralism in labor relations. We declared, by statute, that employes had a right to form organizations of their own and that employers were obligated to bargain in good faith.

Yet this fundamental—and sound—public policy applied only to private industry.

Government officials appeared curiously reluctant to adhere to the rules they imposed upon others.

Government representatives who regularly negotiated directly or indirectly with private sector unions for the construction of schools, highways, hospitals and government office buildings found similar negotiations with their own employes to operate these facilities an unacceptable intrusion.

Officials who in pursuit of their duties unhesitatingly executed contracts involving fiscal commitments far into the future suddenly discovered an implacable inability to negotiate the terms and conditions of employment beyond the current legislative session or administrative term.

In some instances, journalists and others are agitated over what they deem excessive concentrations of political power. But paradoxically, public employes in these same situtations are unable to locate anyone with sufficient authority to even discuss—let alone resolve—their problems.

Denied traditional unionism and collective bargaining, some public employes resorted to lobbying. The postal service is probably the outstanding example. Need I remind this group of the jungle of administrative regulations and laws which for many years prohibited even this? There is a nightmarish quality, in retrospect, to a ruling which provided disciplinary action for a letter carrier who visited Washington on his own time, at his own expense, saw his own congressman, and discussed his own working conditions.

Fortunately, this is no longer true.

But even now, a public employe union barred from or frustrated in genuine collective bargaining which turns to legislators to correct inequities is condemned as irresponsible, denounced for flexing political muscle, and regarded with the jaundice conventionally reserved for extortion.

It would appear that public employe unionism was inappropriate, collective bargaining was illegal, and recourse to normal legislative processes was immoral.

Perhaps the greatest irony of all involved the evolution of the civil service system. No exhaustive review is necessary to suggest that this reform originated in the desire to curb the abuses of patronage and to develop a cadre of qualified and competent public servants who could perform with some degree of security, relatively immune to some of our political vagaries.

It was, at the time, an admirably progressive step, and continues to be a valuable adjunct to the process of running government. The principle of merit employment is not to be discarded lightly.

But the system of civil service, either at the federal, or state and local level, ought not be regarded as sacred and immune from the same evaluation and criticism applied to other human instrumentalities.

Parkinson's Law—that work tends to expand to fill the space alloted to it—has been repeatedly validated. Similarly, another proposition, that bureaucracies will always establish justification not only for their existence but for perpetual expansion, can be demonstrated. I venture to suggest that this applies equally to the corporate world and to government agencies.

Though I might be unhappy with excessive publicity on this score, even some unions are not immune to this virus.

Nor is civil service.

A vast, sprawling bureaucracy with self-validating characteristics has developed over the years. Not surprisingly, it is neither all good nor all bad, but its good features ought not to serve as a shield for its shortcomings.

There is no "irrepressible conflict," to use the phrase associated with the Civil War, between collective bargaining and all aspects of civil service. The incompatibility is far from total, as demonstrated by years of coexistence, sometimes amicable, occasionally strained.

There are, admittedly, some tensions.

The uncompromising objectivity of the system is rendered questionable when, as in one major city, the civil service commissioner is simultaneously the director of the City Department of Labor and wears both hats at the pleasure of the mayor.

Scientifically constructed job classifications and career and salary plans are at best dubious in a free market economy. No one has yet defined that weary cliche—a fair day's work for a fair day's pay. What we are dealing with is nowhere near as precise as it appears, but, rather, rough approximations rationalized by an internal logic.

But the integrity of even this more modest approach is relentlessly undermined by those who accommodate the pressures of the market, but who persist in accomplishing this through under-the-counter deals, thus maintaining the fiction of the plan's validity.

Easily the most significant source of incompatibility, however, is that even under the best circumstances, even with the most dedicated and competent personnel, even in the greatest absence of political pressures, civil service continues to represent unilateralism in labor-management relations in the public service. This is something we have difficulty communicating to executives and commissioners who characteristically respond as if they had been personally attacked.

There is, I submit, a legitimate—and critical —difference between my requesting something of you, but leaving the final determination in your hands, and my insistence that we sit together at the negotiating table as equals.

Collective bargaining is more than simply an additional holiday, or a pay increase, or an improved pension plan, or a grievance procedure. It is, of course, all of these, and their importance can hardly be overestimated. But it is, in its most profound sense, a process.

It is a process which transforms pleading to negotiation. It is a process which permits employes dignity as they participate in the formulation of their terms and conditions of employment. It is a process which embraces the democratic ideal and applies it concretely, specifically, effectively, at the place of work.

Public employes and collective bargaining engaged in sporadic flirtations with each other for decades. It is no longer a flirtation. It is a marriage. And it will endure.

Recent years have witnessed a sharp increase in government employment and a dramatic spurt in public employe unionism.

Total government employment went from 7 million in 1955 to 10.5 million in 1966. Projections suggest it will continue to climb. The latest available estimate puts it at approximately 15 million by 1975. If these statistics are accurate (and there seems no reason for skepticism) government employment will constitute 15 percent of the total labor force by 1970.

Some people—possibly a few in this room— mutter darkly about the uncontrollable expansion of the federal bureaucracy. But most of this recent expansion has occurred at the state and local level. Currently approximately 75 percent of all government employment is here. The federal level has been remarkably stable.

We are, therefore, considering one of the fastest growing sectors in our society.

Most certainly we are considering the fastest growing sector in the American labor movement. More specifically, I am here as a representative of what has been termed, by others, as the fastest growing union in the country.

I say this with considerable pride—but without, I hope, boastfulness.

On the contrary, it is offered with genuine gratitude. All that we are, we owe to you.

You represent our best organizers, our most persuasive reason for existence, our defense against membership apathy and indifference, our perpetual prod to militancy, and our assurance of continued growth.

Some observers glance at the statistics of employment, slide to union membership totals, and conclude that organized labor had crested in the major industries and was turning avariciously towards public employes, hungry for the per capita dues that would flow in upon their capture.

Whether or not this is true (I find discussions of human motivations singularly unrevealing) the important thing is that it is irrelevant. Unions would be unable to sign up a single employe if he were satisfied, if his dignity were not offended, if he were treated with justice. What is important is not the motives of union officials in organizing public employes, but the astonishing rapidity and success of their efforts. Barren ground yields poor crops. But here the ground was fertile beyond belief.

But the statistics of government employment have a far greater significance which merits fuller consideration. They suggest a major transformation in the structure and nature of our society.

Fifty years ago, when Calvin Coolidge sent his telegram, the private and public sectors were discrete. They were separate entities, relatively easy to distinguish one from the other. Even if one adds the necessary qualification that every major form of transportation was heavily subsidized in one form or another, or that government-imposed tariffs provided shelters for our industry, even with all this the world of the private entrepreneur and the world of public enterprise were easily identifiable in 1920.

Governor Coolidge may have been tart or he may have been politically motivated or he may have been sincerely concerned with the public welfare. He at least had some grounds for his position.

Those grounds no longer exist. A massive erosion has occurred. And if we fail to recognize this we run the risk of further irrelevant discussion.

In 1920 needy people, if they received any assistance at all, received it from private philanthropies. In 1967, public welfare is a major activity and a significant and growing budget item. Revealingly enough, government involvement has not obliterated private philanthropic efforts. The two complement each other.

Some public transportation is publicly owned, as in New York City, and some is privately owned, as in Washington, D.C.

Our public school system is staggering under the load of additional students, but private school enrollment climbs correspondingly. State universities are flourishing, but so are their private counterparts and their roles are indistinguishable. Furthermore, federal funds underwrite major construction and research programs at leading private universities as well as at public institutions.

For several decades we have had public housing authorities whose objective was the construction of low income accommodations. Serious consideration is currently being given the possibility of private non-profit corporations to renovate entire areas.

The other side of the coin is the development, at breathtaking government expense, of a communications satellite, which promptly becomes the monopoly of a private consortium.

If our emulation of the Japanese high speed trains succeeds, will the Boston–New York–Washington run be a public or a private triumph? It will be both. A private railroad will operate, presumably for profit, the special trains over special track placed on special roadbeds, all designed at public expense.

The examples could be multiplied endlessly: Aerospace research conducted by private companies with government support and using civilian and military personnel almost interchangeably. Government "think tanks" which compete in brilliance with our most prestigious private universities. Government-generated electric power in the Tennessee Valley and private utilities elsewhere.

The clear demarcation between private and public sectors is gone. With some exceptions, it has vanished beneath a maze of overlapping functions, parallel efforts, incredibly complex relationships.

Magically, all this has occurred without violating our historic apprehension of government. Magically, it has taken place within our democratic framework and, astonishingly, has indeed strengthened it.

If this necessarily brief and admittedly oversimplified summary is valid, then one other thing has occurred.

Traditional distinctions between labor-management relations in the private and public sectors have become irrelevant.

One cannot argue logically about the uniqueness of public service, confronted by public bus drivers in New York City and private bus drivers in Washington performing identical services.

Reasonable men cannot really be expected to accept the thesis that all public services are equally crucial. The parks attendant is performing an important function, but social catastrophe is not imminent in his temporary absence. That decorative secretary in a government agency is really not performing differently from her sister in the private world.

This assertion has simply been repeated so frequently that it has gained unwarranted stature and credibility. I invite you to reflect on it for a moment. In our society, where are the critical functions concentrated? Our farms and factories are private. The facilities which transport their products are private. We are dependent for medical research and care upon a profession which is ferociously private in orientation. In war we rely on private enterprise and stake our national survival on its successful performance.

At the same time, I have no desire to commit a similar error in reverse. Certain public services are undeniably critical, in the same way that some private services are. Our international union, consequently, constitutionally regards its police members somewhat differently than its other members.

I am arguing here for reasonable and thoughtful distinctions and against the kind of wholesale, sloppy, and unsupportable generalizations with which we have been afflicted.

I would be remiss if I concluded without commenting on the vexing issue of public employes and the right to strike.

If there is a uniquely American style it is characterized by a pragmatic approach. We have historically tinkered and "made do," preferring the tentative experiment to complex and abstract theorizing.

Discussions of public employe strikes have displayed a regrettable preoccupation with hypothetical concepts and abstract theories (and spurious ones at that). In discussing the problem of strikes, I would point out that our union constitution recognizes that law enforcement groups cannot be allowed the right to strike. However, the prohibition cannot and must not be applied across the board to all public employees.

Actually, we have a wealth of experience on which to draw.

We know, for example, that public employe strikes have been and are illegal in every jurisdiction which does or does not have a law on the subject.

We know, further, that in some jurisdictions the penalties for violation of the strike prohibition are relatively mild and in others they are extremely harsh.

We know, in addition, that in some places elaborate labor-management machinery has been devised and in others no structure is visible.

But certainly both our knowledge and experience are richer than this.

We also know that public employe strikes have occurred in jurisdictions which proscribed them.

They have occurred where the penalties were mild and where the penalties were severe.

They have occurred where there was special legislation and elaborate machinery and in the absence of both legislation and machinery.

Court injunctions and confiscatory fines have not been demonstrably successful in the private sector. Limited experience suggests that they will be no more successful in the public sector.

Earlier I spoke of collective bargaining as a process. It is a process which occurs among equals. It is a process to which the American labor movement is committed. It is not always neat, not always orderly, not always precise. It is occasionally disruptive and sometimes inconveniences people. To be candid, it is on occasion totally exasperating.

Nevertheless, we have knowingly, consciously, and, I think, wisely chosen this process in preference to the authoritarianism of price and wage controls and centralized, presumably scientific administration of our economic activities.

With all of its faults, with all of its occasional lapses, with all the exasperation it sometimes induces, it has worked admirably in the private sector of our economy.

We are determined that it will have the same opportunity in the public sector. But I refer here to genuine collective bargaining—which, I remind you, occurs among equals.

Strike prohibitions are not simply ineffectual, though they are undeniably that. What is far more serious, they warp this vital process. They bring employes to the bargaining table, but as inferiors. Simultaneously they provide false reassurance to management representatives and induce less than genuine negotiations. Ironically, they create the very tensions, exacerbate the very situations, provoke the very strikes they were allegedly formulated to prevent.

It is time we learned from experience and applied its rich lessons. The democracy of our political life deserves full extension into the labor relations of our public life. Public employes will not have it otherwise.

# 29

# The Limits of Collective Bargaining in Public Employment

*Harry H. Wellington
and Ralph K. Winter, Jr.*

Writing in the March 1969 issue of the *Michigan Law Review,* Mr. Theodore Kheel, the distinguished mediator and arbitrator, placed the weight of his considerable authority behind what is fast becoming the conventional wisdom. In the public sector, as in the private, Mr. Kheel argues, "the most effective technique to produce acceptable terms to resolve disputes is voluntary agreement of the parties, and the best system we have for producing agreements between groups is collective bargaining—even though it involves conflict and the possibility of a work disruption."[1] Clearly for Kheel, as for others, the insistence upon a full extension of collective bargaining—including strikes—to public employment stems from a deep commitment to that way of ordering labor-management affairs in private employment. While such a commitment may not be necessary, a minimal acceptance of collective bargaining is a condition precedent to the Kheel view. Those skeptical of the value of collective bargaining in private employment will hardly press its extension. But even if one accepts collective bargaining in the private sector (as we have said in the Introduction we shall for the purposes of this

SOURCE: From *The Unions and the Cities,* by Harry H. Wellington and Ralph K. Winter, Jr., pp. 7–32. Copyright © 1971 by The Brookings Institution. Reprinted by permission.

book), the claims that support it there do not, in any self-evident way, make the case for its full transplant. The public sector is *not* the private, and its labor problems *are* different, very different indeed.

## The Claims for Collective Bargaining in the Private Sector

Four claims are made for private-sector collective bargaining. First, it is said to be a way to achieve industrial peace. The point was put as early as 1902 by the federal Industrial Commission:

> The chief advantage which comes from the practice of periodically determining the conditions of labor by collective bargaining directly between employers and employees is that thereby each side obtains a better understanding of the actual state of the industry, of the conditions which confront the other side, and of the motives which influence it. Most strikes and lockouts would not occur if each party understood exactly the position of the other.[2]

Second, collective bargaining is a way of achieving industrial democracy, that is, participation by workers in their own governance. It is the industrial counterpart of the contemporary demand for community participation.[3]

Third, unions that bargain collectively with employers represent workers in the political arena as well. And political representation through interest groups is one of the most important types of political representation that the individual can have. Government at all levels acts in large part in response to the demands made upon it by the groups to which its citizens belong.[4]

Fourth, and most important, as a result of a belief in the unequal bargaining power of employers and employees, collective bargaining is claimed to be a needed substitute for individual bargaining.[5] Monopsony—a buyer's

*335*

monopoly,[6] in this case a buyer of labor—is alleged to exist in many situations and to create unfair contracts of labor as a result of individual bargaining. While this, in turn, may not mean that workers as a class and over time get significantly less than they should—because monopsony is surely not a general condition but is alleged to exist only in a number of particular circumstances[7]—it may mean that the terms and conditions of employment for an individual or group of workers at a given period of time and in given circumstances may be unfair. What tends to insure fairness in the aggregate and over the long run is the discipline of the market.[8] But monopsony, if it exists, can work substantial injustice to individuals. Governmental support of collective bargaining represents the nation's response to a belief that such injustice occurs. Fairness between employee and employer in wages, hours, and terms and conditions of employment is thought more likely to be ensured where private ordering takes the collective form.[9]

There are, however, generally recognized social costs resulting from this resort to collectivism.[10] In the private sector these costs are primarily economic, and the question is, given the benefits of collective bargaining as an institution, what is the nature of the economic costs? Economists who have turned their attention to this question are legion, and disagreement among them monumental.[11] The principal concerns are of two intertwined sorts. One is summarized by Professor Albert Rees of Princeton:

If the union is viewed solely in terms of its effect on the economy, it must in my opinion be considered an obstacle to the optimum performance of our economic system. It alters the wage structure in a way that impedes the growth of employment in sectors of the economy where productivity and income are naturally high and that leaves too much labor in low-income sectors of the economy like southern agriculture and the least skilled service trades. It benefits most those workers who would in any case be relatively well off, and while some of this gain may be at the expense of the owners of capital, most of it must be at the expense of consumers and the lower-paid workers. Unions interfere blatantly with the use of the most productive techniques in some industries, and this effect is probably not offset by the stimulus to higher productivity furnished by some other unions.[12]

The other concern is stated in the 1967 Report of the Council of Economic Advisers:

Vigorous competition is essential to price stability in a high employment economy. But competitive forces do not and cannot operate with equal strength in every sector of the economy. In industries where the number of competitors is limited, business firms have a substantial measure of discretion in setting prices. In many sectors of the labor market, unions and managements together have a substantial measure of discretion in setting wages. The responsible exercise of discretionary power over wages and prices can help to maintain general price stability. Its irresponsible use can make full employment and price stability incompatible.[13]

And the claim is that this "discretionary power" too often is exercised "irresponsibly."[14]

Disagreement among economists extends to the quantity as well as to the fact of economic malfunctioning that properly is attributable to collective bargaining.[15] But there is no disagreement that at some point the market disciplines or delimits union power. As we shall see in more detail below, union power is frequently constrained by the fact that consumers react to a relative increase in the price of a product by purchasing less of it. As a result any significant real financial benefit, beyond that justified by an increase in productivity, that accrues to workers through collective bargaining may well cause significant unemployment among union members. Because of this employment-benefit relationship, the economic costs imposed by collective bargaining as it presently exists in the private sector seem inherently limited.[16]

## The Claims for Collective Bargaining in the Public Sector

In the area of public employment the claims upon public policy made by the need for industrial peace, industrial democracy, and effective political representation point toward collective bargaining. This is to say that three of the four arguments that support bargaining in the private sector—to some extent, at least—press for similar arrangements in the public sector.

Government is a growth industry, particularly state and municipal government. While federal employment between 1963 and 1970 increased from 2.5 million to 2.9 million, state and local employment rose from 7.2 to 10.1 million,[17] and the increase continues apace. With size comes bureaucracy, and with bureaucracy comes the sense of isolation of the individual worker. His manhood, like that of his industrial counterpart, seems threatened. Lengthening chains of command necessarily depersonalize the employment relationship and contribute to a sense of powerlessness on the part of the worker. If he is to share in the governance of his employment relationship as he does in the private sector, it must be through the device of representation, which means unionization.[18] Accordingly, just as the increase in the size of economic units in private industry fostered unionism, so the enlarging of governmental bureaucracy has encouraged public employees to look to collective action for a sense of control over their employment destiny. The number of government employees, moreover, makes it plain that those employees are members of an interest group that can organize for political representation as well as for job participation.[19]

The pressures thus generated by size and bureaucracy lead inescapably to disruption—to labor unrest—unless these pressures are recognized and unless existing decision-making procedures are accommodated to them. Peace in government employment too, the argument runs, can best be established by making union recognition and collective bargaining accepted public policy.[20]

Much less clearly analogous to the private model, however, is the unequal bargaining power argument. In the private sector that argument really has two aspects. The first, just adumbrated, is affirmative in nature. Monopsony is believed sometimes to result in unfair individual contracts of employment. The unfairness may be reflected in wages, which are less than they would be if the market were more nearly perfect, or in working arrangements that may lodge arbitrary power in a foreman, that is, power to hire, fire, promote, assign, or discipline without respect to substantive or procedural rules. A persistent assertion, generating much heat, relates to the arbitrary exercise of managerial power in individual cases. This assertion goes far to explain the insistence of unions on the establishment in the labor contract of rules, with an accompanying adjudicatory procedure, to govern industrial life.[21]

Judgments about the fairness of the financial terms of the public employee's individual contract of employment are even harder to make than for private sector workers. The case for the existence of private employer monopsony, disputed as it is, asserts only that some private sector employers in some circumstances have too much bargaining power. In the public sector, the case to be proved is that the governmental employer ever has such power. But even if this case could be proved, market norms are at best attenuated guides to questions of fairness. In employment as in all other areas, governmental decisions are properly political decisions, and economic considerations are but one criterion among many. Questions of fairness do not centrally relate to how much imperfection one sees in the market, but more to how much imperfection one sees in the political process. "Low" pay for teachers may be merely a decision—right or wrong, resulting from the pressure of special interests or from a desire to promote the general welfare—to exchange a reduction in the quality or quantity of teachers for higher welfare payments, a domed stadium, and so on. And the ability to make informed judgments about such political decisions is limited because of the understandable but unfortunate fact that the science of politics has failed to supply either as elegant or as reliable a theoretical model as has its sister discipline.

Nevertheless, employment benefits in the public sector may have improved relatively more slowly than in the private sector during the last three decades. An economy with a persistent inflationary bias probably works to the disadvantage of those who must rely on legislation for wage adjustments.[22] Moreover, while public employment was once attractive for the greater job security and retirement benefits it provided, quite similar protection is now available in many areas of the private sector.[23] On the other hand, to the extent that civil service, or merit, systems exist in public employment and these laws are obeyed, the arbitrary exercise of managerial power is substantially reduced. Where it is reduced, a labor policy that relies on individual employment contracts must seem less unacceptable.

The second, or negative, aspect of the unequal bargaining power argument relates to the social costs of collective bargaining. As has been seen, the social costs of collective bargaining in the private sector are principally economic and seem inherently limited by market forces. In the public sector, however, the costs seem economic only in a very narrow sense and are on the whole political. It further seems that, to the extent union power is delimited by market or other forces in the public sector, these constraints do not come into play nearly as quickly as in the private. An understanding of why this is so requires further comparison between collective bargaining in the two sectors.

## The Private Sector Model

Although the private sector is, of course, extraordinarily diverse, the paradigm is an industry that produces a product that is not particularly essential to those who buy it and for which dissimilar products can be substituted. Within the market or markets for this product, most—but not all—of the producers must bargain with a union representing their employees, and this union is generally the same throughout the industry. A price rise of this product relative to others will result in a decrease in the number of units of the product sold. This in turn will result in a cutback in employment. And an increase in price would be dictated by an increase in labor cost relative to output, at least in most situations.[24] Thus, the union is faced with some sort of rough trade-off between, on the one hand, larger benefits for some employees and unemployment for others, and on the other hand, smaller benefits and more employment. Because unions are political organizations, with a legal duty to represent all employees fairly,[25] and with a treasury that comes from per capita dues, there is pressure on the union to avoid the road that leads to unemployment.[26]

This picture of the restraints that the market imposes on collective bargaining settlements undergoes change as the variables change. On the one hand, to the extent that there are nonunion firms within a product market, the impact of union pressure will be diminished by the ability of consumers to purchase identical products from nonunion and, presumably, less expensive sources. On the other hand, to the extent that union organization of competitors within the product market is complete, there will be no such restraint and the principal barriers to union bargaining goals will be the ability of a number of consumers to react to a price change by turning to dissimilar but nevertheless substitutable products.

Two additional variables must be noted. First, where the demand for an industry's product is rather insensitive to price—that is, relatively inelastic—and where all the firms in a product market are organized, the union need fear less the employment-benefit trade-off, for the employer is less concerned about raising prices in response to increased costs. By hypothesis, a price rise affects unit sales of such an employer only minimally. Second, in an expanding industry, wage settlements that exceed increases in productivity may not reduce union employment. They will reduce expansion, hence the employment effect will be experienced only by workers who do not belong to the union. This means that in the short run the politics of the employment-benefit trade-off do not restrain the union in its bargaining demands.

In both of these cases, however, there are at least two restraints on the union. One is the employer's increased incentive to substitute machines for labor, a factor present in the paradigm and all other cases as well. The other restraint stems from the fact that large selections of the nation are unorganized and highly resistant to unionization.[27] Accordingly, capital will seek nonunion labor, and in this way the market will discipline the organized sector.

The employer, in the paradigm and in all variations of it, is motivated primarily by the necessity to maximize profits (and this is so no matter how political a corporation may seem to be). He therefore is not inclined (absent an increase in demand for his product) to raise prices and thereby suffer a loss in profits, and he is organized to transmit and represent the market pressures described above. Generally he will resist, and resist hard, union demands that exceed increases in productivity, for if he accepts such demands he may be forced to raise prices. Should he be unsuccessful in his resistance too often, and should it or the bargain cost him too much, he can be expected to put his money and energy elsewhere.[28]

What all this means is that the social costs imposed by collective bargaining are economic costs; that usually they are limited by powerful market restraints; and that these restraints are visible to anyone who is able to see the forest for the trees.[29]

## The Public Sector Model: Monetary Issues

The paradigm in the public sector is a municipality with an elected city council and an elected mayor who bargains (through others) with unions representing the employees of the city. He bargains also, of course, with other permanent and ad hoc interest groups making claims upon government (business groups, save-the-park committees, neighborhood groups, and so forth). Indeed, the decisions that are made may be thought of roughly as a result of interactions and accommodations among these interest groups, as influenced by perceptions about the attitudes of the electorate and by the goals and programs of the mayor and his city council.[30]

Decisions that cost the city money are generally paid for from taxes and, less often, by borrowing. Not only are there many types of taxes but also there are several layers of government that may make tax revenue available to the city; federal and state as well as local funds may be employed for some purposes. Formal allocation of money for particular uses is made through the city's budget, which may have within it considerable room for adjustments.[31] Thus, a union will bargain hard for as large a share of the budget as it thinks it possibly can obtain, and even try to force a tax increase if it deems that possible.

In the public sector, too, the market operates. In the long run, the supply of labor is a function of the price paid for labor by the public employer relative to what workers earn elsewhere.[32] This is some assurance that public employees in the aggregate—with or without collective bargaining —are not paid too little. The case for employer monopsony, moreover, may be much weaker in the public sector than it is in the private. First, to the extent that most public employees work in urban areas, as they probably do, there may often be a number of substitutable and competing private and public employers in the labor market. When that is the case, there can be little monopsony power.[33] Second, even if public employers occasionally have monopsony power, governmental policy is determined only in part by economic criteria, and there is no assurance, as there is in the private sector where the profit motive prevails, that the power will be exploited.

As noted, market-imposed unemployment is an important restraint on unions in the private sector. In the public sector, the trade-off between benefits and employment seems much less important. Government does not generally sell a product the demand for which is closely related to price. There usually are not close substitutes for the products and services provided by government and the demand for them is relatively inelastic. Such market conditions are favorable to unions in the private sector because they permit the acquisition of benefits without the penalty of unemployment, subject to the restraint of nonunion competitors, actual or potential. But no such restraint limits the demands of public employee unions. Because much government activity is, and must be, a monopoly, product competition, nonunion or otherwise, does not exert a downward pressure on prices and wages. Nor will the existence of a pool of labor ready to work for a wage below union scale attract new capital and create a new, and competitively less expensive, governmental enterprise.

The fear of unemployment, however, can serve as something of a restraining force in two situations. First, if the cost of labor increases, the city may reduce the quality of the service it furnishes by reducing employment. For example, if teachers' salaries are increased, it may decrease the number of teachers and increase class size. However, the ability of city government to accomplish such a change is limited not only by union pressure but also by the pressure of other affected interested groups in the community.[34] Political considerations, therefore, may cause either no reduction in employment or services, or a reduction in an area other than that in which the union members work. Both the political power exerted by the beneficiaries of the services, who are also voters, and the power of the public employee union as a labor organization then combine to create great pressure on political leaders either to seek new funds or to reduce municipal services of another kind. Second, if labor costs increase, the city, like a private employer, may seek to replace labor with machines. The absence of a profit motive, and a political concern for unemployment, however, may be deterrents in addition to the deterrent of union resistance. The public employer that decides it must limit employment because of unit labor costs will likely find that the politically easiest decision is to restrict new hirings rather than to lay off current employees.

Where pensions are concerned, moreover, major concessions may be politically tempting since there is no immediate impact on the taxpayer or the city budget. Whereas actuarial soundness would be insisted on by a profit-seeking entity like a firm, it may be a secondary concern to politicians whose conduct is determined by relatively short-run considerations. The impact of failing to adhere to actuarial principles will frequently fall upon a different mayor and a different city council. In those circumstances, concessions that condemn a city to future impoverishment may not seem intolerable.

Even if a close relationship between increased economic benefits and unemployment does not exist as a significant deterrent to unions in the public sector, might not the argument be made that in some sense the taxpayer is the public sector's functional equivalent of the consumer? If taxes become too high the taxpayer can move to another community. While it is generally much easier for a consumer to substitute products than for a taxpayer to substitute communities, is it not fair to say that, at the point at which a tax increase will cause so many taxpayers to move that it will produce less total revenue, the market disciplines or restrains union and public employer in the same way and for the same reasons that the market disciplines parties in the private sector? Moreover, does not the analogy to the private sector suggest that it is legitimate in an economic sense for unions to push government to the point of substitutability?

Several factors suggest that the answer to this latter question is at best indeterminate, and that the question of legitimacy must be judged not by economic but by political criteria.

In the first place, there is no theoretical reason—economic or political—to suppose that it is desirable for a governmental entity to liquidate its taxing power, to tax up to the point where another tax increase will produce less revenue because of the number of people it drives to different communities. In the private area, profit maximization is a complex concept, but its approximation generally is both a legal requirement and socially useful as a means of allocating resources.[35] The liquidation of taxing power seems neither imperative nor useful.

Second, consider the complexity of the tax structure and the way in which different kinds of taxes (property, sales, income) fall differently upon a given population. Consider, moreover, that the taxing authority of a particular governmental entity may be limited (a municipality may not have the power to impose an income tax). What is necessarily involved, then, is principally the redistribution of income by government rather than resource allocation,[36] and questions of income redistribution surely are essentially political questions.[37]

For his part, the mayor in our paradigm will be disciplined not by a desire to maximize profits but by a desire—in some cases at least—to do a good job (to implement his programs), and in virtually all cases by a wish either to be reelected or to move to a better elective office. What he gives to the union must be taken from some other interest group or from taxpayers. His is the job of coordinating these competing claims while remaining politically viable. And that coordination will be governed by the relative power of the competing interest groups. Coordination, moreover, is not limited to issues involving the level of taxes and the way in which tax moneys are spent. Nonfinancial issues also require coordination, and here too the outcome turns upon the relative power of interest groups. And relative power is affected importantly by the scope of collective bargaining.

# The Public Sector Model: Nonmonetary Issues

In the private sector, unions have pushed to expand the scope of bargaining in response to the desires of their members for a variety of new benefits (pension rights, supplementary unemployment payments, merit increases). These benefits generally impose a monetary cost on the employer. And because employers are restrained by the market, an expanded bargaining agenda means that, if a union negotiates an agreement over more subjects, it generally trades off more of less for less of more.

From the consumer's point of view this in turn means that the price of the product he purchases is not significantly related to the scope of bargaining. And since unions rarely bargain about the nature of the product produced,[38] the consumer can be relatively indifferent as to how many or how few subjects are covered in any collective argreement.[39] Nor need the consumer be concerned about union demands that would not impose a financial cost on the employer, for example, the design of a grievance procedure. While such demands are not subject to the same kind of trade-off as are financial demands, they are unlikely, if granted, to have any impact on the consumer. Their effect is on the quality of life of the parties to the agreement.

In the public sector the cluster of problems that surround the scope of bargaining are much more troublesome than they are in the private sector. The problems have several dimensions.

First, the trade-off between subjects of bargaining in the public sector is less of a protection to the consumer (public) than it is in the private. Where political leaders view the costs of union demands as essentially budgetary, a trade-off can occur. Thus, a demand for higher teacher salaries and a demand for reduced class size may be treated as part of one package. But where a demand, although it has a budgetary effect, is viewed as involving essentially political costs, trade-offs are more difficult. Our paradigmatic mayor, for example, may be under great pressure to make a large monetary settlement with a teachers' union whether or not it is joined to demands for special training programs for disadvantaged children. Interest groups tend to exert pressure against union demands only when they are directly affected. Otherwise, they are apt to join that large constituency (the general public) that wants to avoid labor trouble. Trade-offs can occur only when several demands are resisted by roughly the same groups. Thus, pure budgetary demands can be traded off when they are opposed by taxpayers. But when the identity of the resisting group changes with each demand, political leaders may find it expedient to strike a balance on each issue individually, rather than as part of a total package, by measuring the political power of each interest group involved against the political power of the constituency pressing for labor peace. To put it another way, as important as financial factors are to a mayor, political factors may be even more important. The market allows the businessman no such discretionary choice.

Where a union demand—such as increasing the disciplinary power of teachers—does not have budgetary consequences, some trade-offs may occur. Granting the demand will impose a political cost on the mayor because it may anger another interest group. But because the resisting group may change with each issue, each issue is apt to be treated individually and not as a part of a total package. And this may not protect the public. Differing from the private sector, nonmonetary demands of public sector unions do have effects that go beyond the parties to the agreement. All of us have a stake in how school children are disciplined. Expansion of the subjects of bargaining in the public sector, therefore, may increase the total quantum of union power in the political process.

Second, public employees do not generally produce a product. They perform a service. The way in which a service is performed may become a subject of bargaining. As a result, the nature of that service may be changed. Some of these services—police protection, teaching, health care—involve questions that are politically, socially, or ideologically sensitive. In part this is because government is involved and alternatives to governmentally provided services are relatively dear. In part, government is involved because of society's perception about the nature of the service and society's need for it. This suggests that decisions affecting the nature of a governmentally provided service are much more likely to be challenged and are more urgent than generally is the case with services that are offered privately.

Third, some of the services government provides are performed by professionals—teachers, social workers, and so forth—who are keenly interested in the underlying philosophy that informs their work. To them, theirs is not merely a job to be done for a salary. They may be educators or other "change agents" of society. And this may mean that these employees are concerned with more than incrementally altering a governmental service or its method of delivery. They may be advocates of bold departures that will radically transform the service itself.

The issue is not a threshold one of whether professional public employees should participate in decisions about the nature of the services they provide. Any properly run governmental agency should be interested in, and heavily reliant upon, the judgment of its professional staff. The issue rather is the method of that participation.

Conclusions about this issue as well as the larger issue of a full transplant of collective bargaining to the public sector may be facilitated by addressing some aspects of the governmental decision-making process—particularly at the municipal level—and the impact of collective bargaining on that process.

## Public Employee Unions and the Political Process

Although the market does not discipline the union in the public sector to the extent that it does in the private, the municipal employment paradigm, nevertheless, would seem to be consistent with what Robert A. Dahl has called the " 'normal' American political process," which is "one in which there is a high probability that an active and legitimate group in the population can make itself heard effectively at some crucial stage in the process of decision," for the union may be seen as little more than an "active and legitimate group in the population."[40] With elections in the background to perform, as Mr. Dahl notes, "the critical role...in maximizing political equality and popular sovereignty,"[41] all seems well, at least theoretically, with collective bargaining and public employment.

But there is trouble even in the house of theory if collective bargaining in the public sector means what it does in the private. The trouble is that if unions are able to withhold labor—to strike—as well as to employ the usual methods of political pressure, they may possess a disproportionate share of effective power in the process of decision. Collective bargaining would then be so effective a pressure as to skew the results of the " 'normal' American political process."

One should straightway make plain that the strike issue is not simply the importance of public services as contrasted with services or products produced in the private sector. This is only part of the issue, and in the past the partial truth has beclouded analysis.[42] The services performed by a private transit authority are neither less nor more important to the public than those that would be performed if the transit authority were owned by a municipality. A railroad or a dock strike may be more damaging to a community than "job action" by police. This is not to say that governmental services are not important. They are, both because the demand for them is inelastic and because their disruption may seriously injure a city's economy and occasionally impair the physical welfare of its citizens. Nevertheless, the importance of governmental services is only a necessary part of, rather than a complete answer to, the question: Why be more concerned about strikes in public employment than in private?

The answer to the question is simply that, because strikes in public employment disrupt important services, a large part of a mayor's political constituency will, in many cases, press for a quick end to the strike with little concern for the cost of settlement. This is particularly so where the cost of settlement is borne by a different and larger political constituency, the citizens of the state or nation. Since interest groups other than public employees, with conflicting claims on municipal government, do not, as a general proposition, have anything approaching the effectiveness of the strike—or at least cannot maintain that relative degree of power over the long run—they may be put at a significant competitive disadvantage in the political process.

The private sector strike is designed to exert economic pressure on the employer by depriving him of revenues. The public employee strike is fundamentally different: its sole purpose is to exert political pressure on municipal officials. They are deprived, not of revenues but of the political support of those who are inconvenienced by a disruption of municipal services. But precisely because the private strike is an economic weapon, it is disciplined by the market and the benefit/unemployment trade-off that imposes. And because the public employee strike is a political weapon, it is subject only to the restraints imposed by the political process and they are on the whole less limiting and less disciplinary than those of the market. If this is the case, it must be said that the political process will be radically altered by wholesale importation of the strike weapon. And because of the deceptive simplicity of the analogy to collective bargaining in the private sector, the alteration may take place without anyone realizing what has happened.

Nor is it an answer that, in some municipalities, interest groups other than unions now have a disproportionate share of political power. This is inescapably true, and we do not condone that situation. Indeed, we would be among the first to advocate reform. However, reform cannot be accomplished by giving another interest group disproportionate power, for the losers would be the weakest groups in the community. In most municipalities, the weakest groups are composed of citizens who many believe are most in need of more power.

Therefore, while the purpose and effect of strikes by public employees may seem in the beginning designed merely to establish collective bargaining or to "catch up" with wages and fringe benefits in the private sector, in the long run strikes may become too effective a means for redistributing income; so effective, indeed, that one might see them as an institutionalized means of obtaining and maintaining a subsidy for union members.[43]

As is often the case when one generalizes, this picture may be considered overdrawn. In order to refine analysis, it will be helpful to distinguish between strikes that occur over monetary issues and strikes involving nonmonetary issues. The generalized picture sketched above is mainly concerned with the former. Because there is usually no substitute for governmental services, the citizen-consumer faced with a strike of teachers, or garbage men, or social workers is likely to be seriously inconvenienced. This in turn places enormous pressure on the mayor, who is apt to find it difficult to look to the long-run balance sheet of the municipality. Most citizens are directly affected by a strike of sanitation workers. Few, however, can decipher a municipal budget or trace the relationship between today's labor settlement and next years's increase in the mill rate. Thus, in the typical case the impact of a settlement is less visible—or can more often be concealed—than the impact of a disruption of services. Moreover, the cost of settlement may fall upon a constituency much larger—the whole state or nation—than that represented by the mayor. And revenue sharing schemes that involve unrestricted funds may further lessen public resistance to generous settlements. It follows that the mayor usually will look to the electorate that is clamoring for a settlement, and in these circumstances the union's fear of a long strike, a major check on its power in the private sector, is not a consideration.[44] In the face of all of these factors other interest groups with priorities different from the union's are apt to be much less successful in their pursuit of scarce tax dollars than is the union with power to withhold services.[45]

With respect to strikes over some nonmonetary issues—decentralization of the governance of schools might be an example—the intensity of concern on the part of well-organized interest groups opposed to the union's position would support the mayor in his resistance to union demands. But even here, if the union rank and file back their leadership, pressures for settlement from the general public, which may be largely indifferent as to the underlying issue, might in time become irresistible.[46]

The strike and its threat, moreover, exacerbate the problems associated with the scope of bargaining in public employment. This seems clear if one attends in slightly more detail to techniques of municipal decision making.

Few students of our cities would object to Herbert Kaufman's observation that:

> Decisions of the municipal government emanate from no single source, but from many centers; conflicts and clashes are referred to no single authority, but are settled at many levels and at many points in the system: no single group can guarantee the success of any proposal it supports, the defeat of every idea it objects to. Not even the central governmental organs of the city—the Mayor, the Board of Estimate, the Council—individually or in combination, even approach mastery in this sense.
>
> Each separate decision center consists of a cluster of interested contestants, with a "core-group" in the middle, invested by the rules with the formal authority to legitimize decisions (that is to promulgate them in binding form) and a constellation of related "satellite groups" seeking to influence the authoritative issuances of the core group.[47]

Nor would many disagree with Nelson W. Polsby when, in discussing community decision making that is concerned with an alternative to a "current state of affairs," he argues that the alternative "must be politically palatable and relatively easy to accomplish; otherwise great amounts of influence have to be brought to bear with great skill and efficiency in order to secure its adoption."[48]

It seems probable that such potential subjects of bargaining as school decentralization and a civilian police review board are, where they do not exist, alternatives to the "current state of affairs," which are not "politically palatable and relatively easy to accomplish." If a teachers' union or a police union were to bargain with the municipal employer over these questions, and were able to use the strike to insist that the proposals not be adopted, how much "skill and efficiency" on the part of the proposals' advocates would be necessary to effect a change? And, to put the shoe on the other foot, if a teachers' union were to insist through collective bargaining (with the strike or its threat) upon major changes in school curriculum, would not that union have to be considerably less skillful and efficient in the normal political process than other advocates of community change? The point is that with respect to some subjects, collective bargaining may be too powerful a lever on municipal decision making, too effective a technique for changing or preventing the change of one small but important part of the "current state of affairs."

Unfortunately, in this area the problem is not merely the strike threat and the strike. In a system where impasse procedures involving third parties are established in order to reduce work stoppages—and this is common in those states that have passed public employment bargaining statutes—third party intervention must be partly responsive to union demands. If the scope of bargaining is open-ended, the neutral party, to be effective, will have to work out accommodations that inevitably advance some of the union's claims some of the time. And the neutral, with his eyes fixed on achieving a settlement, can hardly be concerned with balancing all the items on the community agenda or reflecting the interests of all relevant groups.

## The Theory Summarized

Collective bargaining in public employment, then, seems distinguishable from that in the private sector. To begin with, it imposes on society more than a potential misallocation of resources through restrictions on economic output, the principal cost imposed by private sector unions. Collective bargaining by public employees and the political process cannot be separated. The costs of such bargaining, therefore, cannot be fully measured without taking into account the impact on the allocation of political power in the typical municipality. If one assumes, as here, that municipal political processes should be structured to ensure "a high probability that an active and legitimate group in the population can make itself heard effectively at some crucial stage in the process of decision,"[49] then the issue is how powerful

unions will be in the typical municipal political process if a full transplant of collective bargaining is carried out.

The conclusion is that such a transplant would, in many cases, institutionalize the power of public employee unions in a way that would leave competing groups in the political process at a permanent and substantial disadvantage. There are three reasons for this, and each is related to the type of services typically performed by public employees.

First, some of these services are such that any prolonged disruption would entail an actual danger to health and safety.

Second, the demand for numerous governmental services is relatively inelastic, that is, relatively insensitive to changes in price. Indeed, the lack of close substitutes is typical of many governmental endeavors.[50] And, since at least the time of Marshall's *Principles of Economics,* the elasticity of demand for the final service or product has been considered a major determinant of union power.[51] Because the demand for labor is derived from the demand for the product, inelasticity on the product side tends to reduce the employment-benefit trade-off unions face. This is as much the case in the private as in the public sector. But in the private sector, product inelasticity is not typical. Moreover, there is the further restraint on union power created by the real possibility of nonunion entrants into the product market. In the public sector, inelasticity of demand seems more the rule than the exception, and nonunion rivals are not generally a serious problem.

Consider education. A strike by teachers may never create an immediate danger to public health and welfare. Nevertheless, because the demand for education is relatively inelastic, teachers rarely need fear unemployment as a result of union-induced wage increases, and the threat of an important nonunion rival (competitive private schools) is not to be taken seriously so long as potential consumers of private education must pay taxes to support the public school system.

The final reason for fearing a full transplant is the extent to which the disruption of a government service inconveniences municipal voters. A teachers' strike may not endanger public health or welfare. It may, however, seriously inconvenience parents and other citizens who, as voters, have the power to punish one of the parties—and always the same party, the political leadership—to the dispute. How can anyone any longer doubt the vulnerability of a municipal employer to this sort of pressure? Was it simply a matter of indifference to Mayor Lindsay in September 1969 whether another teachers' strike occurred on the eve of a municipal election? Did the size and the speed of the settlement with the United Federation of Teachers (UFT) suggest nothing about one first-rate politician's estimate of his vulnerability? And are the chickens now coming home to roost because of extravagant concessions on pensions for employees of New York City the result only of mistaken actuarial calculations? Or do they reflect the irrelevance of long-run considerations to politicians vulnerable to the strike and compelled to think in terms of short-run political impact?

Those who disagree on this latter point rely principally on their conviction that anticipation of increased taxes as the result of a large labor settlement will countervail the felt inconvenience of a strike, and that municipalities are not, therefore, overly vulnerable to strikes by public employees. The argument made here, however —that governmental budgets in large cities are so complex that generally the effect of any particular labor settlement on the typical municipal budget is a matter of very low visibility—seems adequately convincing. Concern over possible taxes will not, as a general proposition, significantly deter voters who are inconvenienced by a strike from compelling political leaders to settle quickly. Moreover, municipalities are often subsidized by other political entities—the nation or state—and the cost of a strike settlement may not be borne by those demanding an end to the strike.

All this may seem to suggest that it is the strike weapon—whether the issue be monetary or nonmonetary—that cannot be transplanted to the public sector. This is an oversimplification, however. It is the combination of the strike and the typical municipal political process, including the usual methods for raising revenue. One solution, of course, might well be a ban on strikes, if it could be made effective. But that is not the sole alternative, for there may be ways in which municipal political structures can be changed so as to make cities less vulnerable to strikes and to reduce the potential power of public employee unions to tolerable levels. (The relative merits of these alternatives are weighed in Part IV.)

All this may also seem to suggest a sharper distinction between the public and private sectors than actually exists. The discussion here has dealt with models, one for private collective bargaining, the other for public. Each model is located at the core of its sector. But the difference in the impact of collective bargaining in the two sectors should be seen as a continuum. Thus, for example, it may be that market restraints do not sufficiently discipline strike settlements in some regulated industries or in industries that rely mainly on government contracts. Indeed, collective bargaining in such industries has been under steady and insistent attack.

In the public sector, it may be that in any given municipality—but particularly a small one—at any given time, taxpayer resistance or the determination of municipal government, or both, will substantially offset union power even under existing political structures. These plainly are exceptions, however. They do not invalidate the public-private distinction as an analytical tool, for that distinction rests on the very real differences that exist in the vast bulk of situations, situations exemplified by these models. On the other hand, in part because of a recognition that there are exceptions that in particular cases make the models invalid, we shall argue that the law regulating municipal bargaining must be flexible and tailored to the real needs of a particular municipality. The flexibility issue will be addressed directly, and in some detail, after consideration of the contemporary setting in which public bargaining is now developing.

## Notes

1. "Strikes and Public Employment," 67 *Michigan Law Review* 931, 942 (1969).

2. *Final Report of the Industrial Commission* (Government Printing Office, 1902), p. 844.

3. See, for example, testimony of Louis D. Brandeis before the Commission on Industrial Relations, Jan. 23, 1915, in *Industrial·Relations,* Final Report and Testimony Submitted to Congress by the Commission on Industrial Relations, S. Doc. 415, 64 Cong. 1 sess. (1916), 8, 7657–81.

4. See generally H. Wellington, *Labor and the Legal Process* (Yale University Press, 1968), pp. 215–38.

5. See, for example, *Final Report of the Industrial Commission,* p. 800:

It is quite generally recognized that the growth of great aggregations of capital under the control of single groups of men, which is so prominent a feature of the economic development of recent years, necessitates a corresponding aggregation of workingmen into unions, which may be able also to act as units. It is readily perceived that the position of the single workman, face to face with one of our great modern combinations, such as the United States Steel Corporation, is a position of very great weakness. The workman has one thing to sell—his labor. He has perhaps devoted years to the acquirement of a skill which gives his labor power a relatively high value, so long as he is able to put it to use in combination with certain materials and machinery. A single legal person has, to a very great extent, the control of such machinery, and in particular of such materials. Under such conditions there is little competition for the workman's labor. Control of the means of production gives power to dictate to the workingman upon what terms he shall make use of them.

6. The use of the term *monopsony* is not intended to suggest a labor market with a single employer. Rather, we mean any market condition in which the terms and conditions of employment are generally below those that would exist under perfect competition.

7. There is by no means agreement that monopsony is a signficant factor. For a theoretical discussion, see F. Machlup, *The Political Economy of Monopoly: Business, Labor and Government Policies* (Johns Hopkins Press, 1952), pp. 333–79; for an empirical study, see R. Bunting, *Employer Concentration in Local Labor Markets* (University of North Carolina Press, 1962).

8. See L. Reynolds, *Labor Economics and Labor Relations* (3rd, ed. Prentice-Hall, 1961), pp. 18–19. To the extent that monopsonistic conditions exist at any particular time one would expect them to be transitory. For even if we assume a high degree of labor immobility, a low wage level in a labor market will attract outside employers. Over time, therefore, the benefits of monopsony seem to carry with them the seeds of its destruction. But the time may seem very long in the life of any individual worker.

9. See *Labor Management Relations Act,* § 1, 29 U.S.C. § 151 (1964).

10. The monopsony justification views collective bargaining as a system of countervailing power—that is, the collective power of the workers countervails the bargaining power of employers. See J. Galbraith, *American Capitalism: The Concept of Countervailing Power* (Houghton Mifflin, 1952), pp. 121 ff. Even if the entire line of argument up to this point is accepted, collective bargaining nevertheless seems a crude device for meeting the monopsony problem, since there is no particular reason to think that collective bargaining will be instituted where there is monopsony (or that it is more likely to be instituted there). In some circumstances collective bargaining may even raise wages above a "competitive" level. On the other hand, the collective bargaining approach is no cruder than the law's general response to perceived unfairness in the application of the freedom of contract doctrine. See Wellington, *Labor and the Legal Process,* pp.26–38.

11. Compare, e.g., H. Simons, "Some Reflections on Syndicalism," *Journal of Political Economy* 1–25 (1944), with R. Lester, "Reflections on the Labor Monopoly Issue," 55 *Journal of Political Economy* 513 (1947).

12. A. Rees, *The Economics of Trade Unions* (University of Chicago Press, 1962), pp. 194–95. Also see H. Johnson and P. Mieszkowski, *The Effects of Unionization on the Distribution of Income: A General Equilibrium Approach,* 84 *Quarterly Journal of Economics* 539 (1970).

13. *Economic Report of the President Together With the Annual Report of the Council of Economic Advisers,* January 1967, p. 119.

14. *Ibid.,* pp. 119–34. See generally J. Sheahan, *The Wage-Price Guideposts* (Brookings Institution, 1967).

15. See H. Lewis, *Unionism and Relative Wages in the United States: An Empirical Inquiry* (University of Chicago Press, 1963), and earlier studies discussed therein.

16. See generally J. Dunlop, *Wage Determination Under Trade Unions* (Macmillan, 1944), pp. 28–44; M. Friedman, "Some Comments on the Significance of Labor Unions for Economic Policy," in D. Wright (ed.), *The Impact of the Union,* p. 204 (Harcourt, 1951); Rees, *The Economics of the Trade Unions,* pp. 50–60.

In A. Ross, *Trade Union Wage Policy* (University of California, 1948), the argument is made that the employment effect of a wage bargain is not taken into account by either employers or unions (pp. 76–93).

One reason given in support of this conclusion is the difficulty of knowing what effect a particular wage bargain will have on employment. But the forecasting difficulty inheres in any pricing decision, whether it is raising the price of automobiles or of labor, and it certainly does not render the effect of an increase on the volume purchased an irrelevant consideration. Uncertainty as to the impact of a wage decision on employment does not allow union leaders to be indifferent to the fact that there is an impact. If it did, they would all demand rates of $100 per hour.

Ross's second argument is that there is only a loose connection between wage rates and the volume of employment. It is not clear what he means by this assertion. It may be a rephrasing of the uncertainty argument. Presumably he is not asserting that the demand curve for labor is absolutely vertical; although proof of that phenomenon would entitle him to the professional immortality promised by Professor Stigler (see G. Stigler, *The Theory of Price* [3rd ed., Macmillan, 1966] p. 24), the unsupported assertion hardly merits serious consideration. But if the curve is not vertical, then there is a "close connection" since the volume of employment is by hypothesis affected at every point on a declining curve. Probably he means simply that the curve is relatively inelastic, but that conclusion is neither self-evident, supported by his text, nor a proposition generally accepted on the basis of established studies.

17. U.S. Bureau of the Census, *Public Employment in 1970* (1971), Table 1, and Bureau of the Census, *State Distribution of Public Employment in 1963* (1964), Table 1.

18. See *Final Report of the Industrial Commission*, p. 805; C. Summers, "American Legislation for Union Democracy," 25 *Mod. L. Rev.* 273, 275 (1962).

19. For the "early" history, see S. Spero, *Government as Employer* (Remsen, 1948).

20. See, for example, *Governor's Committee on Public Employee Relations, Final Report* (State of New York, 1966), pp. 9–14.

21. See N. Chamberlain, *The Union Challenge to Management Control* (Harper, 1948), p. 94.

22. This is surely one reason that might explain the widely assumed fact that public employees have fallen behind their private sector counterparts. See J. Stieber, "Collective Bargaining in the Public Sector," in L. Ulman (ed.), *Challenges to Collective Bargaining* (Prentice-Hall, 1967), pp. 65, 69.

23. See G. Taylor, "Public Employment: Strikes or Procedures?" 20 *Industrial and Labor Relations Review* 617, 623–25 (1967).

24. The cost increase may, of course, take some time to work through and appear as a price increase.

See Rees, *The Economics of Trade Unions*, pp. 107–09. In some oligopolistic situations the firm may be able to raise prices after a wage increase without suffering a significant decrease in sales.

25. *Steele v. Louisville & Nashville Railroad Co.*, 323 U.S. 192 (1944).

26. The pressure is sometimes resisted. Indeed, the United Mine Workers has chosen more benefits for less employment. See generally M. Baratz, *The Union and the Coal Industry* (Yale University Press, 1955).

27. See H. Cohany, "Trends and Changes in Union Membership," 89 *Monthly Lab. Rev.* 510–13 (1966); I. Bernstein, "The Growth of American Unions, 1945–1960," 2 *Labor History* 131–57 (1961).

28. And the law would protect him in this. Indeed, it would protect him if he were moved by an antiunion animus as well as by valid economic considerations. See *Textile Workers Union of America v. Darlington Manufacturing Co.*, 380 U.S. 263 (1965).

Of course, where fixed costs are large relative to variable costs, it may be difficult for an employer to extricate himself.

29. This does not mean that collective bargaining in the private sector is free of social costs. It means only that the costs are necessarily limited by the discipline of the market.

30. See generally R. Dahl, *Who Governs? Democracy and Power in an American City* (Yale University Press, 1961). On interest group theory generally, see D. Truman, *The Government Process: Political Interests and Public Opinion* (3d printing; Alfred A. Knopf, 1955).

31. See, for example, W. Sayre and H. Kaufman, *Governing New York City: Politics in the Metropolis* (Russell Sage, 1960), pp. 366–72.

32. See M. Moskow, *Teachers and Unions* (University of Pennsylvania, Wharton School of Finance and Commerce, Industrial Research Unit, 1966), pp. 79–86.

33. This is based on the reasonable but not unchallengeable assumption that the number of significant employers in a labor market is related to the existence of monopsony. See R. Bunting, *Employer Concentration in Local Labor Markets*, pp. 3–14. The greater the number of such employers in a labor market, the greater the departure from the classic case of the monopsony of a single employer. The number of employers would clearly seem to affect their ability to make and enforce a collusive wage agreement.

34. Organized parent groups, for example. Compare the unsuccessful attempt of the New York City Board of Education to reduce the employment of

substitute teachers in the public schools in March 1971. *New York Times,* March 11, 1971, p. 1.

35. See generally R. Dorfman, *Prices and Markets* (Prentice-Hall, 1967).

36. In the private sector what is involved is principally resource allocation rather than income redistribution. Income redistribution occurs to the extent that unions are able to increase wages at the expense of profits, but the extent to which this actually happens would seem to be limited. It also occurs if unions, by limiting employment in the union sector through maintenance of wages above a competitive level, increase the supply of labor in the nonunion sector and thereby depress wages there.

37. In the private sector the political question was answered when the National Labor Relations Act was passed: the benefits of collective bargaining (with the strike) outweigh the social costs.

38. The fact that American unions and management are generally economically oriented is a source of great freedom to us all. If either the unions or management decided to make decisions about the nature of services provided or products manufactured on the basis of their own ideological convictions, we would all, as consumers, be less free. Although unions may misallocate resources, consumers are still generally able to satisfy strong desires for particular products by paying more for them and sacrificing less valued items. This is because unions and management generally make no attempt to adjust to anything but economic considerations. Were it otherwise, and the unions—or management—insisted that no products of a certain kind be manufactured, consumers would have much less choice.

39. The major qualification to these generalizations is that sometimes unions can generate more support from the membership for certain demands than for others (more for the size of the work crew, less for wage increases). Just how extensive this phenomenon is, and how it balances out over time, is difficult to say; however, it would not seem to be of great importance in the overall picture.

40. R. Dahl, *A Preface to Democratic Theory* (University of Chicago Press, 1956), p. 145.

41. *Ibid.,* pp. 124–25.

42. See, for example, Spero, *Government as Employer,* pp. 1–15.

43. Strikes in some areas of the private sector may have this effect, too. See below, p. 32.

44. Contrast the situation in the private sector: "...management cannot normally win the short strike. Management can only win the long strike. Also management frequently tends, in fact, to win the long strike. As a strike lengthens, it commonly bears more heavily on the union and the employees than on management. Strike relief is no substitute for a job. Even regular strike benefits, which few unions can afford, and which usually exhaust the union treasury quite rapidly (with some exceptions), are no substitute for a job." E. Livernash, "The Relation of Power to the Structure and Process of Collective Bargaining," 6 *Journal of Law & Economics* 10, 15 (October 1963).

45. A vivid example was provided by an experience in New Jersey. After a twelve-hour strike by Newark firefighters on July 11, 1969, state urban aid funds, originally authorized for helping the poor, were diverted to salary increases for firemen and police. See *New York Times,* Aug. 7, 1969, p. 25. Moreover, government decision makers other than the mayor (for example, the governor) may have interests different from those of the mayor, interests that manifest themselves in pressures for settlement.

46. Consider also the effect of such strikes on the fabric of society. See, for example, M. Mayer, *The Teachers Strike: New York, 1968* (Harper and Row, 1969).

47. "Metropolitan Leadership," quoted in N. Polsby, *Community Power and Political Theory* (Yale University Press, 1963), pp. 127–28.

48. Polsby, in *ibid.,* p. 135.

49. Dahl, *Preface to Democratic Theory,* p. 145.

50. Sometimes this is so because of the nature of the endeavor—national defense, for example—and sometimes because the existence of the governmental operation necessarily inhibits entry by private entities, as in the case of elementary education.

51. A. Marshall, *Principles of Economics* (8th ed.; Macmillan, 1920), pp. 383–86.

# 30

# Lessons From the Lindsay-Wagner Years

*Raymond D. Horton*

One of the major lessons to be learned from this brief examination of municipal labor relations in New York City is that those who claim to understand the labor relations process have good reason to be humble about the depth of their understanding. The observations that follow are offered with that thought firmly in mind. Still, a critical examination of some important, but rather general, matters seems warranted. What are the lessons that should be learned from the city's recent experience with municipal labor relations, and what are the lessons that should be unlearned?

## The Private Sector-Public Sector Analogy

The first lesson to be learned is that collective bargaining in the government of New York City is not analogous to collective bargaining in the private sector. The modern labor relations system examined here was nurtured and then sustained through almost two decades of experimentation and experience on the assumption that collective bargaining in the public sector would function much like the private sector model. The pioneers of public policy in the 1950s assumed that the basic framework of private sector rules and techniques could be applied in the public

SOURCE: From *Municipal Labor Relations in New York City: Lessons from the Lindsay-Wagner Years,* by Raymond Horton, pp. 117–132. Copyright © 1973 by Praeger. Reprinted by permission of the author. Footnotes renumbered.

sector without interfering too much with the governmental process, particularly since the proponents of municipal collective bargaining foresaw preservation of the traditional law against employee strikes. This assumption proved wrong. What is important now is to understand why the analogy failed.

The dispute over the relevance of the private sector paradigm for the public sector has been intensive. Opponents of the basic analogy have argued from a variety of positions; eventually they came to rely primarily on economic theory for the foundation of their rebuttal.[1] Collective bargaining in the public sector, the argument goes, is not analogous to the private sector because no competitive market exists for public services. Government is a monoply, and government employees monopolize the delivery of government services. Consumers of public services accordingly lack certain protections with respect to the price and availability of government services that are afforded consumers in the normal competition of private markets. If General Motors is struck the consumer can buy a Ford, but if the Fire Department is struck the consumer cannot elsewhere secure fire protection. Thus governments are said to be "soft" bargainers because they always must ensure the continuous supply of "essential" public services. For this reason the strike ban in the public sector is necessary and, in the eyes of some, collective bargaining is undesirable.

This rebuttal to the private sector-public sector analogy is put too broadly. Governments per se are not "soft" bargainers; only certain governments are, and then only with respect to certain groups of public employees. The fact that the government of New York City has proved such an easy target for organized civil servants is explained as much by the absence of strong management in government as by the short-run absence of competitive markets. This point must be recognized before labor relations systems like New York City's can be corrected. No market imperative dictates that the city government must lose in collective bargaining.

The government of a city like New York monopolizes services in a more limited sense than is commonly understood. Not many of the services performed by city employees are so essential that public officials and the public somehow are incapable of rationally resisting certain union demands, even in a strike situation. The public is quite capable of accepting strikes for long periods of time with respect to most government services. The nonessential monopolists among city employees recognize this fact better than anyone else and seldom use the strike as a political tactic.

The essential monopolists among civil servants pose the real strike problem, a point to be examined later. But competitive markets and consumer choice exist even with respect to the most essential of government services. Again, even in a strike situation, alternative labor sources exist to ensure a modicum of service except perhaps with respect to fire protection and subway service. In an even broader vein to argue there is no competitive market of government services ignores the hundreds of other government monopolies that ring New York City and the behavior of tens of thousands of New Yorkers who each year move to other local governments in search of better municipal services. If General Motors conducts its labor relations so that strikes occur too often or if labor costs and poor management push the price of Chevrolets too high and the quality too low, the private consumer can buy a Ford; if New York City cannot handle similar labor relations problems with its employees, many of its consumers can (and do) purchase their government services elsewhere.

There is competition for municipal services in the long run and city officials recognize (or should recognize) this fact. Mayor Lindsay himself once said, "The plight of the cities is on the bargaining table."[2] City officials understand no less clearly than corporate officials the functional consequences that can arise from their failures to deal successfully with issues such as strikes, labor costs, management, and productivity. If directly confronted, probably only a very few public officials in New York City would defend as rational (or functional) from the viewpoint of the city's overall needs the decision to increase police salaries by 15 percent and then the subsequent decision to reduce the number of police personnel by 15 percent. Decisions such as these, however, cumulated over time, help cause consumers of New York City services to move to other cities.

Why, then, do not city officials act more "rationally" in municipal labor relations? Why does the reality of long-run market competition not affect the short-run political behavior of public officials? The answer to these questions is grounded in the particular politics of New York City and of the municipal labor relations process. Again, the problem in New York City is the absence of effective political management. The advocates of collective bargaining in New York City assumed, not illogically, the existence of a strong management group of public officials with whom municipal unions would have to bargain. There is no longer a strong management group in New York City with whom municipal unions deal, only a potpourri of disparate public officials who play managerial roles without either managerial power or perspective.

Many persons long have believed that "real" collective bargaining would not occur so long as civil servants were denied the right to strike. This is not true, at least in New York City. There is no "real" collective bargaining because there is no "real" management with whom organized civil servants deal. As a result, what passes for collective bargaining works well for organized civil servants even in the absence of the legal right to strike. The absence of strong management as much as the presence of monopolists explains the unanticipated consequences of municipal collective bargaining in New York City.

## Abdication and Delegation: The Decline of Public Management

If the absence of strong management distorts the labor relations process, it is important to understand how and why this has occurred. Two factors ensured the management void. The first was the *abdication* of managerial responsibility by potentially influential elected officials; the second was their formal *delegation* of that responsibility to others who were not equipped, by dint of power or perspective, to assert the proper managerial responsibilities of the city government. Abdication by public officials resulted largely (but not entirely, as shall be seen) from personal political considerations; delegation, in turn, simply was the political device by which abdication was carried out. The underlying problem with collective bargaining in New York City, again, is grounded in elemental political considerations. The decline of public management occurred primarily because the city's elected political leaders eventually learned through experience that playing the management role created for them more personal political problems than it solved. Whether or not this was a correct judgment politically is irrelevant for the present. The judgment was made during the 1960s, and the consequences followed quickly.

It is unnecessary at this point to reexamine the many instances of delegation existent in the city's labor relations process. The development of the city's modern labor relations program (discussed in detail in Chapters 3 and 5) showed how closely the concepts of evolution and delegation were linked. Particularly from the time of the first Lindsay administration the basic thrust of labor relations reform in New York City was to parcel out the governmental functions and responsibilities of elected public officials to a wider and wider circle of "governmental" participants. Examples of this phenomenon range from the trivial to the important, the zenith of delegation having been reached in 1972 by the decision to permit compulsory, binding arbitration of labor disputes by tripartite groups or individual arbitrators.

Delegation was accomplished under the assumption that the new participants somehow could stand in the place of the city's elected officials, primarily the mayor. This may have been true in a strict legal sense, but it was not true in terms of political power. As the functional responsibilities of the city government were parceled out, the political power necessary to protect the government's interest in municipal labor relations was lost.

Herein lies the essential difference between the Wagner and Lindsay years. Wagner managed to retain a degree of influence over the labor relations process by not succumbing to the temptations of delegation. This was desirable because it allowed a reasonably coherent view of the city's overall needs in labor relations to be developed and preserved a central political actor strong enough to assert those needs. The Lindsay program made both the conception and reality of management impossible in municipal labor relations. Left to exert the interests of the public and the government after the mayor withdrew from an active role in 1969 was a group of negotiators, fact-finders, mediators, arbitrators, and even union representatives who were distinguished as much by their diverse views of what the needs and responsibilities of the government were in municipal labor relations as by their individual lack of political influence.

If abdication and delegation helped produce a labor relations system that was dysfunctional with respect to the protection of important public and governmental interests, the democratic nature of the system was affected for the same reason. A central tenet of democratic politics is that a control relationship must run from the public to those public officials who make important political decisions. The rationale for this principle is a simple one, steeped in a realistic view of human behavior: public officials will be better motivated to "represent" public interests instead of their own when the control relationship exists. If city officials failed to grasp the subtle way in which abdication and delegation endanger the functional nature of municipal labor relations, they failed almost completely to grasp the not-so-subtle implications abdication and delegation held for political democracy.

The "premodern" labor relations system was far from perfect, but elected officials at least played an influential role in the system. This condition also was present during the Wagner years when the first modern labor relations program was introduced. If something was amiss in city labor relations, the public at least had the opportunity to identify elected public officials who might be sanctioned via the electoral process. Delegation, however, diffuses responsibility to nonelected officials and makes electoral choices both more difficult and less meaningful. The "system" becomes the culprit, not the politician (which is often precisely why politicians create such systems). Indeed, if the system functions poorly enough and is so complex as to defy understanding by the average citizen, the beleaguered political leader may even be viewed sympathetically instead of critically by the public.

The city's legislators bear considerable responsibility for the delegation problem. If mayors took the leadership for programmatic innovation in municipal labor relations, legislators provided little opposition. If the mayor with all his staff could not handle the problem, how, it was thought, could legislative bodies? The city's legislators by the early 1970s managed to sanction and seemingly accept a system wherein they played no meaningful role whatsoever in municipal labor relations, despite the fact that collective bargaining more than any other decision-making process in the city primarily was responsible for the allocation of the city's financial resources. The city's expense budget may once have been the product of a combined executive–legislative process; in the 1960s the budgetary process gradually became more than anything else the product of collective bargaining, a distinctly nonlegislative process. Traditional assumptions in a democratic society about the desirable role of legislative bodies in the budgetary process were simply forgotten. The plaintive appeal by one city councilman in 1972 for at least "some" information about collective bargaining is illustrative of the problem.[3] Not only are legislative officials uninvolved in labor relations decision-making, they are incapable even of playing a legislative oversight role because, very simply, there is little about the process they are permitted to see.

Absent any legislative access to collective bargaining, the only effective democratic control link remaining to the public is provided by the involvement of the mayor. If the mayor actually played the role of public representative *and* possessed enough political influence, this would be enough. But short-run priorities increasingly seem to ensure that the mayor will not play the desired role, that instead mayoral involvement will be delegated to others when the real labor relations conflicts emerge. And as delegation from the mayor to other actors increases, public control over and public representation within the labor relations process decrease. At the critical impasse stage, when the dictates of democracy and the needs of the public are most threatened, the fact-finder, mediator, or arbitrator steps in to assume the role of the mayor. The logic of delegation under a system of compulsory arbitration is complete: The most crucial governmental decision is to be made by the least qualified, least influential, and least "public" official.[4]

## Taking the Politics Out of Politics

The absence of strong political or managerial leadership explains the absence of "real" collective bargaining in New York City. Underlying this, of course, were important political factors that induced abdication and delegation by public officials. However, the particular behavioral response of public officials was made easier than it might otherwise have been by some popular attitudes concerning municipal labor relations and politics. One such attitude was that the labor relations process was too "political." The flight of public officials from serious involvement in municipal labor relations did not simply go unnoticed but was applauded, in part because it was believed that this would reduce the intrusion of politics into municipal labor relations. The concept of delegation fit nicely with this attitude and others. Nobody, of course, wanted governmental abdication, but many persons did want delegation. Few persons seemed to realize how closely the two concepts were linked.

It is not difficult to see why the "politics-is-bad" theory of municipal labor relations emerged so strongly when it did. The view that partisan concerns and "good government" do not mix has a long tradition in New York City. Events such as the 1966 transit strike, which were sustained if not produced by partisan and personal rivalries, led many to conclude that politics in its most baneful sense was at the heart of the city's labor relations problem. Not surprisingly, the corollary view was accepted that the key to reform lay in depoliticizing the labor relations process.

This approach to reform was too simplistic. Municipal labor relations is an inherently political process. The allocation of public money and the fixing of public and managerial policies, two major functions of the labor relations process, are central political acts in any organized society. Whatever the procedures by which labor relations decisions are reached—formal or informal, partisan or nonpartisan—the labor relation process inevitably is political.

Critics of the Wagner program, however, usually used the word *politics* in a narrower sense. Labor relations was too political when labor relations decisions were influenced by considerations having to do with "other" political concerns in the city—party rivalries, city–state tensions, electoral politics, personality conflicts. This view merged with the institutionalist view discussed below: The labor relations process could be immunized from unhealthy, extraneous political concerns by creating a formal institutional setting within which to conduct municipal labor relations. The concrete expression of this view was the labor relations program developed during the first Lindsay administration.

Events during the period between 1966 and 1972, recounted in Chapter 5, clearly show how impossible it is to depoliticize municipal labor relations. The major consequence of the formal program was not to reduce the importance of politics but simply to change the locus of political power over municipal labor relations. Electoral politics and partisan rivalries, hostilities between city and state officials, personality conflicts—all of these remained important determinants of municipal labor relations, perhaps even more so than before.

The assumption that labor relations could ever be depoliticized flew in the face of reality in New York City politics. Given the complex, highly pluralistic nature of the overall political system, no important single area of the city's politics ever can be immunized from "other" political concerns. The stakes involved in municipal labor relations are so high and so related to success in other areas that participants always will employ whatever political resources, strategies, and techniques are available to them.

The key to reform is repoliticization; the opposite tack is impossible and, as experience shows, only tends to increase the political influence of organized civil servants at the expense of public officials. The system functions as it does because of existing power relationships; it will not change until new power relationships develop. Attempts to immunize the labor relations process from politics only serve to perpetuate the existing politics of the system. This is the third important lesson.

## Institutionalism

One of the most enduring phenomena in America is the fascination for institutions of government. When a problem exist, Americans create an institution to solve it.[5] The fourth lesson from the history thus far examined is that institutions sometimes do not solve problems but instead exacerbate them. Sometimes institution-builders do not understand the basic problems; sometimes institution-builders do not understand the institutions they build.

The institutional responses to the perceived problems of municipal labor relations have been many. The problem in the 1950s was that civil servants were being treated as "second-class citizens," an outlook that gave rise to the new institution of municipal collective bargaining. Later, when labor unrest was the problem, another new institution was created, the tripartite OCB. The Office of Labor Relations was a response, in part, to the perceived problem that city negotiators were not "professional" enough. When the problem of finality in labor relations disputes remained in the 1970s, compulsory and binding arbitration of labor disputes was introduced.

The apotheosis of the institutional approach occurred after the welfare strike in 1965 when the reforms suggested by the tripartite panel were accepted by the Lindsay administration. The limited, informal, and highly political nature of Wagner's program no doubt did contribute to the discontent of municipal unions, largely because the program was not working as union leaders hoped it would. The basic problem, however, was political, not structural or institutional; by 1965 organized civil servants simply were too strong politically to be easily contained by *any* formal labor relations program. If labor unrest actually reflected institutional weakness rather than political strength the revolt of civil servants probably would have occurred earlier than it did. Wagner's formal labor relations program changed very little between 1958 and 1965; however, municipal unions changed very much during this period, as Chapter 4 showed. Furthermore, if the problems in the mid-1960s did result primarily from institutional inadequacies, the institutional reforms that were made during the early Lindsay years should have eased the problem. This did not happen, as has been seen.

The major determinant of municipal labor relations throughout the entire period was the growing strength of the city's organized civil servants and the impact this had on the behavior of public officials, not the formal nature of the city's labor relations institutions, laws, and procedures. Failing to recognize this fact, instead attributing labor unrest to the institutional inadequacies of the Wagner program, the architects of the Lindsay program explicitly set out to create a formal program in which civil servants would be more influential and city officials would be less influential. The underlying problem was aggravated both by the perception of the problem and the institutional response to it.

The architects of Wagner's program were only somewhat less institutionally oriented than the architects of the Lindsay program. Wagner's program, after all, accepted most of the institutional practices of private sector collective bargaining. There was, however, a fundamental difference between the institutions accepted by the two mayors. The first labor relations program institutionalized the basic notion that the conduct of labor relations in government should remain the primary responsibility of the elected chief executive. The architects of the Lindsay program a decade later went further, creating an institutional setting within which much of the responsibility would be shared by public officials, union officials, and "neutrals."

## Interest Group "Liberalism"

The primary institutional reform during the Lindsay period was the creation of the tripartite OCB. The OCB, staffed with union and city representatives plus third-party neutrals, was designed to oversee the administration of municipal labor relations and provide "impartial" procedures, forums, and personnel for the resolution of labor relations disputes. With respect to its administrative functions, such as certification and determination of bargaining units, the OCB has performed well. The major problem concerns the intervention of OCB personnel and procedures in the resolution of substantive disputes involving questions central to the management and government of New York City.

The notion that the business is advanced and the public interest served when the most "interested" groups are invited to formal participation in political decision-making is a common one in American politics and in the politics of New York City. One political scientist has described the formal incorporation of private groups in government as "interest-group liberalism."[6] The city's formal labor relations program is a classic example.

New York City provides an attractive setting for such a philosophy of government, in large part because there are so many organized political interest groups with long traditions of active involvement in city politics. The notion of any public interest that transcends in importance the pursuits of any single political interest group is a difficult concept in the dog-eat-dog competition of city politics. The bewildering complexity of the city's informal politics has led many to conclude that order and rational decision-making would be enhanced by formally involving private groups in the formal political decision-making process: the more groups that are involved, the greater the likelihood that government will work.[7] The concept of equilibrium lurking behind this contemporary view of politics is not unlike the concept of equilibrium in classic economics: The "unseen hand" determines the most desirable allocation of resources in a competitive system in which many participants pursue their own narrow goals.[8]

Chapter 6 was devoted to showing what were the functional consequences of the city's labor relations decisions. Whether the labor relations process achieves a "desirable" allocation of public resources is difficult to establish authoritatively, though the opinion expressed in this book is that the allocations are undesirable. Given all that is known about the functioning of other political processes built on essentially similar notions of direct interest-group involvement, it should not be altogether surprising that broad public interests are not adequately protected in municipal labor relations.[9] A common strain in the contemporary critique of bureaucracies is that they too often function only with regard for the specific interests of the specific groups formally and informally represented in the decision-making process.

Tripartitism directly contributed to the dominance of union influence in city labor relations. Tripartitism recognizes no difference between the legitimacy of public officials and interest group representatives. In reaching the decision that city and union should have equal representation within the OCB the assumption was that the interests of the public and of organized civil servants were of the same order. This is, at best, a curious notion, somewhat akin to the city government creating a seven-man arbitration panel of two Wall Street representatives, two city officials, and three fiscal "experts" to determine if the city should have a stock transfer tax.

By stretching (considerably) the meaning of representative democracy a theoretical argument at least can be made for the formal inclusion of municipal unions in the administration of the municipal labor relations process.[10] However, exactly who or what interests the third-party neutrals represent remains unclear. The neutrals were conceived as impartial, nonpolitical actors who, like judges, would recommend or make final decisions between the competing interests of organized civil servants and the city government. The neutrals were specialists, chosen for their expertise in the nuances of labor law and conflict-resolution. How a specialist in private and public sector labor relations can be viewed as particularly well equipped to play such an important role in a political process the decisions of which intersect with so much else in city politics also remains unclear.[11] Functionally, the responsibility probably demands a generalist in city politics, not a specialist in labor relations; democratically, the responsibility clearly demands an elected official, not a private citizen "publicized" only by the fact of mutual acceptability to city and union officials.

## The "Liberalism" of Municipal Labor Relations

New York City's labor relations program usually is described as a "liberal" program. Critics of the existing system usually are branded conservative adherents to bygone days when civil servants stood to government like serf stood to lord. The sixth lesson is that New York City's modern labor relations process is anything but liberal; it represents conservatism writ large.

The semantic hassle presented by the words *liberal* and *conservative* must be confronted. Contemporary society bestows the brands of liberal and conservative largely on the basis of how persons or groups react to specific issues at specific times. Proponents of the notion that the city's labor relations system serves liberal ends point, for example, to improvements in the wages of the "working man," preservation of the "merit" system, protection of individuals from "bureaucratic" arbitrariness. Most would consider these liberal goals, and they are—to a point. A central argument of this book is that "the point" has been passed. No small amount of evidence now supports the contentions that other "working men" pay too high a price to support the wages of civil servants, that organized civil servants are as interested in subverting the merit system as preserving it, that the most arbitrary forms of bureaucratic behavior in New York City government often are performed by organized civil servants themselves.

Narrow, issue-oriented evaluations of liberalism and conservatism score debating points and provide good political rhetoric but shed little light on the deeper meanings of liberalism and conservatism. Two quests historically common to political liberalism serve to usefully distinguish it from political conservatism: popular control of government and the diminution of the power of privileged social and political groups.

No reasonable argument can be made that the municipal labor relations process serves to maintain or extend popular control of government in New York City, a point that has been expressed earlier. Do organized civil servants constitute a privileged group, an establishment group, in the politics of New York City? Organized civil servants think of themselves as insurgents in the city politics, but their behavior again and again belies the thought. The intensely negative reaction of organized civil servants to proposals to decentralize the government of New York City is worth considering. Groups who are secure and satisfied with the existing structure of power can be counted on to oppose such grandiose attempts to change "the system." If the next generation of political reformers decides that the "merit" system, not centralized government, is the bête noire of good government in New York City, no group will oppose reform of the merit system more strongly than municipal unions. The list of examples illustrative of the "established power" thesis is long: the UFT's opposition to school decentralization, the

reaction of the PBA to the Civilian Review Board proposal, DC 37's opposition to the initial plan for a semi-autonomous Health and Hospitals Corporation, to name a few. These and other union reactions to change are explained better by the status of organized civil servants within the existing system than by any passing notions of liberalism and conservatism.

In an historical sense, nothing very startling or surprising has happened to organized civil servants in New York City. Over the course of time they simply have come to dominate a particular process in the city's politics, and they now attempt to use that process to preserve and extend their influence. The reader will recall from Chapters 2 and 3 that organized civil servants once were on the outside looking in at the structure of power in municipal labor relations. The nature of the labor relations process today is testimony to the fact that organized civil servants eventually obtained what they always wanted—hegemony in the personnel system of New York City government. The remedial problem is made difficult from the public's point of view because the labor relations process happened to develop in such a way that public control, the quintessence of political democracy, will not be restored easily.

The conservative nature of the city's labor relations stems partly from the "incorporation" principle discussed in the section above. Incorporating already influential political interest groups into the formal process of government only provides such groups additional leverage with which to oppose changes that they view threatening to their interests. The desirable political system is one that is capable of responding, when necessary, to always changing power relationships, not only in the private sector but within government as well. The political subsystem examined in this book plays a conserving rather than countervailing role.

## Strikes and the Public Interest

No single attitude has had a more pervasive influence on New York City labor relations than the view that public employee strikes are inconsistent with the public interest and should be avoided at all costs. Of course nobody likes strikes, but this does not mean all public employee strikes are intolerable. The seventh important lesson from the Lindsay-Wagner years is that labor peace should not be confused with the public interest.

The recent history of municipal labor relations discloses more than a few instances in which it clearly was in the interest of organized civil servants to strike. The old saw that nobody wins in public employee strikes is not true. Sometimes civil servants win; sometimes, though infrequently, the public does. If it occasionally is in the interest of organized civil servants to strike it must be occasionally in the interest of the public to accept a strike. Of course, strikes, if accepted, must be won. Nothing is worse for the public than to accept a strike and then lose it. This, unfortunately, has happened on several occasions in New York City. To accept the opposite premise, that strikes per se are not in the public interest, is to ignore the reality that other public interests than the continuous supply of services are at stake in municipal labor relations. There certainly are cost limits, for example, beyond which it is not in the public interest to receive a public service.

For public officials (and the public) always to equate labor peace with the public interest represents a kind of public death wish that ensures only that the municipal labor relations process will work better for organized civil servants than for anyone else. The unremitting quest of labor peace, born of a fear of public employee strikes and manifested in repeated efforts to "buy" labor peace by raising the ante a "little" more, in the long run perpetuates a system in which neither labor peace nor the public interest ever can be realized.

The short-run syndrome—"buy labor peace now, worry about the costs later"—puts the city government in a defensive position with respect to the major groups of organized civil servants. The leaders of the major unions are a politically intelligent, highly pragmatic group of individuals. Union leaders quickly learned in the 1960s to play the fear of strikes for all it was worth. Once the public employee strike is dreaded deeply enough, the strike itself becomes unnecessary. The threat of a strike suffices. And the elaborate peacekeeping machinery of the city's labor relations program only compounds the problem. The primary impact of the various appeal procedures—fact-finding, mediation, and arbitration—simply is to offer unions other opportunities beyond the bargaining table to realize their demands. If the peacekeeping machinery, even binding arbitration, does not produce enough, the strikes remains a viable political tactic for unions.

One is forced back once again to the "short run vs. long run" problem discussed earlier in this chapter. The immediate costs in any single bargaining impasse of offering "just a little more" in the hope of avoiding conflict may seem, may indeed be, quite small. But the costs of a single settlement, as has been seen, pyramid throughout the civil service, and the number of different bargaining relationships in which the short-run logic can be applied is large.[12] What may seem rational in the short run becomes irrational over time. The question is not whether the short-run costs of accepting and winning a single strike are greater than the long-run costs of buying it off but whether the short-run costs of accepting and winning a single strike are greater than the cumulative long-run costs of buying it off, as well as many other similar conflicts.

The public in the long run pays for *all* of the costs imposed by the advocates of short-run labor peace. The crux of the entire problem, again, is that public officials, the only transients in the municipal labor relations process and city politics, do not pay the costs. Labor peace may not always be in the interest of the public, but labor peace seems always to be perceived by public officials as in *their* interests. The enduring problem is the dichotomy between the interests of public officials and the interests of the public. The only solution to the basic political problem is to recreate a political alliance between these two groups, one that will enable public officials to benefit rather than lose from representing public interests in municipal labor relations. This is a difficult, though not unattainable, goal.

The seven lessons discussed above really are criticisms of some prevailing assumptions concerning municipal labor relations. Critical examination of both assumptions and counter-assumptions is necessary in order to evaluate what changes, if any, might be worthwhile in the city's labor relations process. Some other general points could have been recorded but were not, because preceding chapters explicitly concerned them: the very real conflicts between the best interests of organized civil servants and the best interests of the public; the importance of the behavior of key individuals in determining the nature of municipal labor relations; the pervasive importance of municipal labor relations for the broader politics of the city.

That the existing labor relations system does not work well is an opinion of the author's. That it could work better than it does is an opinion probably held by most New Yorkers. That the system works well probably is an opinion held only by organized civil servants and some of the persons closely associated with the administration of municipal labor relations. One point on which probably all would agree is that changing the system so that it functions differently will be very difficult. This is a lesson that should not be forgotten.

# Notes

1. A concise review of the major arguments can be found in Harry H. Wellington and Ralph K. Winter, Jr., *The Unions and the Cities* (Washington, D.C.: The Brookings Institution, 1971), pp. 7–32.

2. *New York Times,* January 9, 1971, p. 33.

3. The reference is an attempt by city councilman Carter Burden to obtain support for passage of local legislation compelling the disclosure of the terms of collective bargaining contracts. Both city and union officials opposed the legislation—successfully.

4. The arbitrator is deemed qualified, influential, and public only in the most formal sense. In fact, the arbitrator is a specialist operating in a political arena that demands the skills of a generalist, possesses no political influence other than that conveyed by statute, and is public only in the functional sense that arbitration decisions allocate public resources.

5. The preoccupation with political institutions springs from the success Americans have had in building some of the best and most durable governmental institutions in history. Also, the acceptance of institutions is closely related to the desirable, optimistic opinion many Americans have about the amenability of social problems to solution. Liberalism and institutionalism are linked closely in the United States.

6. Theodore J. Lowi, *The End of Liberalism* (New York: W.W. Norton and Co., 1969). Lowi criticizes sharply the practice of interest group involvement in the formal processes of government, arguing that acceptance of this in the mainstream of U.S. government signals "the end of liberalism."

7. Mayor Lindsay's election in 1965 was welcomed by many in large part because he conveyed the notion that he would diminish the importance of interest group "insiderism" in city politics. Certainly his reaction to the 1966 transit strike was consistent with that theme. Over time, however, Lindsay accepted the propriety of interest group politics in New York City. Indeed, Lindsay more than any other mayor probably was responsible for the explicit incorporation of explicit interest groups into the process of city government.

8. Many of those most critical of the ideology and function of market capitalism continue to argue for politics built on similar notions of equilibrium, though the political interest group rather than the individual is viewed as the essential participant in politics.

9. The list of books and articles playing on the theme that bureaucracies over time become captives of the clientele groups they originally are designed to serve or regulate, particularly the latter, is exhaustive. Particular academic attention has been paid the problem in the federal government. For a series of articles by several of the leading scholars concerned with this problem at the federal level, see Alan A. Altshuler, *The Politics of the Federal Bureaucracy* (New York: Dodd, Mead and Co., 1968).

10. Representative democracy, as traditionally conceived, was built around the notion that elected representatives of the public (or various geographical segments of the public) would do the public's business in government. The contemporary approach to representative democracy is quite different: Representatives of various public interest groups should be involved *with* elected or appointed public representatives in performing the business of government. The contemporary view dilutes the traditional one.

11.  The third-party neutrals employed in the city's labor relations process by and large have been lawyers recruited from private practices. Such persons may be very well equipped to deal with the specific legal or compromise problems in a specific labor relations dispute. The political factors relevant in determining whether or not a particular decision should be recommended, however, are not factors that these persons are particularly well equipped to consider. Of course, the system assumed the public officials would use the third-party recommendations only in an advisory way, retaining for themselves the final decision. Given the almost unanimous acceptance of advisory opinion, the neutrals in effect become the final decision-makers.

12.  The way in which the immediate costs involved in the parity decision with the police multiplied throughout the uniformed services is illustrative. The leaders of civil service unions follow negotiations closely in the city, constantly looking for a union gain in other negotiations that might be applicable in their own bargaining situation.

# 31

# The Impacts of Collective Bargaining on Local Government Services: A Review of Research

*David T. Methé and James L. Perry*
*University of California, Irvine*

The past decade's huge growth in local government expenditures, the near bankruptcy of major American cities, and the rising swell of taxpayer discontent are leading indicators of a continuing urban fiscal crisis. A belief of many local government officials, citizens, and scholars is that collective bargaining is partly, and perhaps substantially, to blame for this fiscal crisis.[1] The specific impacts of local government employee unionization and collective bargaining have been debated for the past decade. This debate has yielded occasionally conflicting and, on some issues, only fragmentary empirical evidence. This paper reviews available evidence as a means of developing generalizations about the impact of unionization and collective bargaining on local services and of identifying future research needs.

This review focuses primarily on three principal impacts of public employee unions and collective bargaining. First, the influence exerted on the inputs used to produce local government services, especially employee wages, is assessed. Has unionization and collective bargaining led

to public employee wage and benefit gains? The second issue that is explored involves the productivity of resource utilization. For example, has collective bargaining led to reductions in labor productivity or adjustments in the productivity of other resources? The third impact involves the effects of unionization and collective bargaining on local government expenditure levels. Have local budgets risen with increasing input costs or have local governments held budgets down by compensating, on other ways, for cost increases attributable to collective bargaining? These and other issues are explored following a brief discussion of the analytic framework used for selecting and organizing the research literature.

## The Analytic Framework

The framework we employ to organize the relevant literature and, thereby, to identify the impacts of unionization and collective bargaining on local government services is a modification of taxonomies developed by Bradford, Malt and Oates and by Burkhead and Hennigan.[2] The taxonomy is presented in Figure 1.

Environmental variables influence each component of the system, but they are most crucial in stimulating the need for a particular service. The environment subsumes the economic conditions of supply and demand that influence inputs and outputs and the political and legal conditions that influence service delivery. Environmental factors might exacerbate or moderate the outgrowth of unionization and collective bargaining.

The input category in Figure 1 represents the various factors used in producing a particular service, including both the amount (e.g., number of employees and/or hours-worked) and composition (e.g., number of full-time workers versus number of part-time workers) of human resources. Public employee unions or collective bargaining might affect managerial decisions about the amount and composition of these

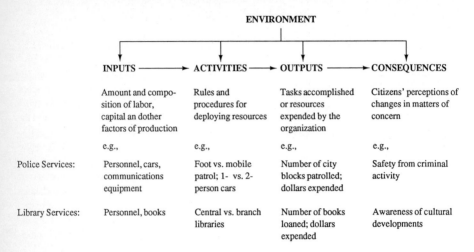

**Figure 1**

A taxonomy for assessing the impacts of collective bargaining on local services

resources. Wages and hours worked are probably the inputs most directly affected by collective bargaining. Impacts upon these inputs are translated, through other policy and strategy decisions, into decisions on the size and composition of the work force.

The activities category in Figure 1 refers to the rules regarding the quality and quantity of services delivered and the procedures for delivering a designated level of service. Since these rules influence the productivity of employees and the efficiency of task accomplishment, and because unions and collective bargaining often influence these rules, it is expected that the productivity of the worker will be affected. The direction of the effect on productivity, either an increase or decrease, will depend upon the type of rule change.

The output category of the taxonomy presented in Figure 1 refers to the tasks accomplished or resources expended by the organization. Since outputs are a result of some combination of inputs and activities, the effects of collective bargaining at other points in the input-output chain might lead to decreases or increases of output.

The consequences category is not a simple derivative of the output component. Consequences of local services involve how citizens perceive matters of concern to them. Despite improvements in how efficiently outputs are produced, environmental factors might hinder a proportionate improvement in the consequences of local services. To the extent that collective bargaining affects outputs directly or how outputs are perceived by citizens, the consequences of local services might be altered.

This input-output taxonomy is used in the next section to classify the impacts of unionization and collective bargaining and to assess the adequacy and coverage of previous research.

## Review of the Literature

Summary information on 20 studies that investigated the impacts of unionization and collective bargaining upon aspects of the delivery of local government services is presented in Table 1. We have selected research on municipal governments that employed large samples from which statistical inferences were drawn.[3] Most of the studies used an *ex post facto* research design and multiple regression analysis. The studies we selected originate predominately from the field of labor economics, but some come from the fields of public administration and organizational behavior.

**Table 1**

**Summary of research on the impacts of unionization and collective bargaining on local government services**

| Study | Scope of Sample | Government Function Studied | Sample Size | Year(s) Data Were Collected | Dependent Variable(s) | Independent Variable(s) | Major Findings |
|---|---|---|---|---|---|---|---|
| Melvin Lurie, "The Effect of Unionization on Wages in the Transit Industry," *Journal of Political Economy*, 69 (December 1961), 558–572. | American Transit Association member organizations | Transit | 250 | 1914–1949 | Basic wage rate per hour Payments per hour for "time not worked" and premium payments Value of fringe benefits | Presence (absence) of a union | 4–10% increase in wages 6–7% increase in non-wage rate earnings 1.5% increase in fringe benefits |
| Orley Ashenfelter, "The Effect of Unionization on Wages in the Public Sector: The Case of Fire Fighters," *Industrial and Labor Relations Review*, 24 (January 1971), 191–202. | Cities with populations of 25,000–100,000 | Fire fighters | 201 | 1961–1966 | Average hourly wage Average annual salary Average weekly duty hours | Presence (absence) of a union | 6–16% increase in average hourly wages 3–9% decrease in average annual duty hours 0–10% increase in average annual salary |

*(continued)*

**Table 1 (continued)**

| Study | Scope of Sample | Government Function Studied | Sample Size | Year(s) Data Were Collected | Dependent Variable(s) | Independent Variable(s) | Major Findings |
|---|---|---|---|---|---|---|---|
| Ronald G. Ehrenberg, "Municipal Government Structures, Unionization, and the Wages of Fire Fighters," *Industrial and Labor Relations Review*, 27 (October 1973), 36–48. | Cities with populations of 25,000–250,000 | Fire fighters | 270 | 1969 | Entrance and maximum annual salary for fire fighters. Average annual salary for all department employees. Fire fighters' annual hours of work. Entrance and maximum hourly wage for fire fighters. Average hourly wage for all department employees | Presence (absence) of a union. Presence (absence) of a written contract | Presence of union has virtually no effect on hours or earnings. In cities with union contracts: 2–18% increase in hourly wages; 2–9% decrease of annual hours; 0–9% increase in annual earnings |
| Roger W. Schmenner, "The Determinants of Municipal Employee Wages," *Review of Economics and Statistics*, 60 (February 1973), 83–90. | 11 large cities (Boston, Providence, New York, Philadelphia, Baltimore, Washington, St. Louis, Denver, New Orleans, San Francisco, and Honolulu) | Police and fire fighters. Teachers. General municipal | 57–80 | 1962–1970 | Minimum police and fire salaries. Average monthly earnings for general employees | Percent employees unionized. Presence (absence) of formal collective bargaining. Work stoppages per employee | High level of unionization increased police-fire salaries 12%; formal collective bargaining decreased police-fire salaries. General municipal employees achieved no salary gains from unionization or bargaining. |

| Study | Scope of Sample | Government Function Studied | Sample Size | Year(s) Data Were Collected | Dependent Variable(s) | Independent Variable(s) | Major Findings |
|---|---|---|---|---|---|---|---|
| James L. Fruend, "Market and Union Influences on Municipal Wages," *Industrial and Labor Relations Review*, 27 (April 1974), 391–404. | Cities with a population over 50,000 | All | 40–80 | 1965–1971 | Percentage change in average weekly earnings, 1965–1971 | Percent unionization of city work force<br>Public sector strike activity | The relationships between wage changes and union power and aggressiveness are negligible |
| Daniel S. Hamermesh, "The Effect of Government Ownership on Union Wages," in Daniel S. Hamermesh (ed.), *Labor in the Public and Non-Profit Sectors* (Princeton, N.J.: Princeton University Press, 1975). PP. 227–263. | Cities with population between 100,000–1,000,000 | Unionized bus drivers<br>Construction trades<br>Random sample of occupations | 23–48 | 1963–1972 | Entry wage of unionized bus drivers relative to manufacturing<br>Wage of government craftsmen relative to that of unionized private craftsmen in the same trade<br>Annual earnings | Presence (absence) of a union | Only in one of three data sets (transit) did the earnings of unionized government employees exceed those of private unionized employees in the same occupation (by 9–12%) |

*(continued)*

**Table 1** (continued)

| Study | Scope of Sample | Government Function Studied | Sample Size | Year(s) Data Were Collected | Dependent Variable(s) | Independent Variable(s) | Major Findings |
|---|---|---|---|---|---|---|---|
| Ronald G. Ehrenberg and Gerald S. Goldstein, "A Model of Public Sector Wage Determination," *Journal of Urban Economics*, 2 (July 1975), 223–245. | Cities with a population over 25,000 | All | 284–478 | 1967 | Average monthly earnings | Percent employees represented by unions or employee associations Geographic factors Occupational factors National union affiliation | 2–16% increase in average monthly earnings Local union/ nonunion wage differentials tended to be larger for each function than the national union/ non-union differentials |
| Thomas A. Kochan and Hoyt N. Wheeler, "Municipal Collective Bargaining: A Model and Analysis of Bargaining Outcomes," *Industrial and Labor Relations Review*, 29 (October 1975), 46–66. | Sample of 380 cities that were known to have engaged in collective bargaining with a local of the International Association of Fire Fighters | Fire fighters | 121 | 1972 | A cumulative index of scores on 53 contract items; progressively higher scores were assigned an item according to the degree it approached union bargaining goals | Union characteristics Management characteristics Degree of multilateral bargaining Environmental characteristics | The legal environment had the greatest effect on the contract index Degree of decision-making power of the management negotiator had a positive association with the contract index |

| Study | Scope of Sample | Government Function Studied | Sample Size | Year(s) Data Were Collected | Dependent Variable(s) | Independent Variable(s) | Major Findings |
|---|---|---|---|---|---|---|---|
| Paul F. Gerhart, "Determinants of Bargaining Outcomes in Local Government Labor Negotiations," *Industrial and Labor Relations Review*, 29 (April 1976), 331–351. | Sample of cities, counties, special districts and school districts of varying (but unspecified) population range | All except teachers and transit | 262 | 1968 | A cumulative index of scores on 158 contract items; progressively higher scores were assigned an item according to the degree it approached union bargaining goals | Statutory bargaining obligation Anti-strike legislation International union affiliation Union political activity Public policy environment (voter sympathy) | Statutory bargaining obligation and public policy environment were related to higher bargaining outcomes Union political activity and international union affiliation had no influence on bargaining outcomes Automatic penalties against strikers lessened union power. |
| David Lewin and John H. Keith, Jr., "Managerial Responses to Perceived Labor Shortages," *Criminology*, 14 (May 1976), 65–93. | Cities with populations over 250,000 | Police | 46–55 | 1971–1972 | Minimum and maximum annual salary for police patrolmen | Presence (absence) of a union | Unionization was related to lower police salaries |

*(continued)*

**Table 1 (continued)**

| Study | Scope of Sample | Government Function Studied | Sample Size | Year(s) Data Were Collected | Dependent Variable(s) | Independent Variable(s) | Major Findings |
|---|---|---|---|---|---|---|---|
| James L. Perry and Charles H. Levine, "An Interorganizational Analysis of Power, Conflict and Settlements in Public Sector Collective Bargaining," *American Political Science Review*, 70 (December 1976), 1185–1201. | New York City | All | 60 | 1968–1972 | A cumulative index of changes of scores on contract items and separate indices for the salary, non-salary cost, and non-cost components of the contract | Union power Relative power | Union power was related to higher amounts of contractual change, greater improvements in non-salary cost items, and greater improvement in noncost items Union power was not related to salary adjustments |
| W. Clayton Hall and Bruce Vanderporten, "Unionization, Monopsony Power and Police Salaries," *Industrial Relations*, 16 (February 1977), 94–100. | Cities with populations over 50,000 | Police | 141 | 1973 | Minimum and maximum annual salary for a police private Average annual salary for all police department personnel | Presence (absence) of a written labor contract Presence (absence) of formal collective negotiations | Existence of a written labor contract was not significant Formal collective negotiations are related to small to moderate pay increases |

| Study | Scope of Sample | Government Function Studied | Sample Size | Year(s) Data Were Collected | Dependent Variable(s) | Independent Variable(s) | Major Findings |
|---|---|---|---|---|---|---|---|
| Richard B. Victor, *The Effects of Unionism on the Wage and Employment Levels of Police and Firefighters* (Santa Monica, Calif.: The Rand Corporation, P-5924, 1977). | Cities with populations over 50,000 | Police and fire fighters | 187–209 | 1975 | Average annual salary Per capita full-time equivalent police and fire fighters | Percentage of the municipal labor force in the function who are union members  Presence (absence) of a recognized union  Presence (absence) of a collective bargaining agreement | The three measures of union power exhibit remarkable internal consistency  7.8–12.3% increase for police wages; 12.1–27.8% increase for fire wages.  Unionism increases fire fighters employment, but not police employment |
| David Shapiro, "Relative Wage Effects of Unions in the Public and Private Sectors," *Industrial and Labor Relations Review*, 31 (January 1978), 193–203. | Males 45–59 years of age | All | 99–1136 | 1971 | Hourly wage rates of blue collar and white collar workers | Whether or not wages are set by collective bargaining | Unionization of white-collar government workers does not result in significant gains in earnings  Unionization of blue-collar workers significantly increases wages |

*(continued)*

**Table 1** *(continued)*

| Study | Scope of Sample | Government Function Studied | Sample Size | Year(s) Data Were Collected | Dependent Variable(s) | Independent Variable(s) | Major Findings |
|---|---|---|---|---|---|---|---|
| Stanley Benecki, "Municipal Expenditure Levels and Collective Bargaining," *Industrial Relations*, 17 (May 1978), 216–230. | Cities with populations over 10,000 | All | 81–347 | 1969–1972 | Expenditure, revenue, debt, and employment levels | Percentage employees represented by unions or employee associations<br>Institutional bargaining variables | Collective bargaining is associated with higher levels of personnel expenditures relative to other expenditures; larger budgets; and lower levels of employment |
| Richard C. Kearney, "The Impacts of Police Unionization on Municipal Budgetary Outcomes." Paper presented at the Annual Meeting of the Midwest Political Science Association, Chicago, April 1978. | Southwestern cities with populations between 10,000 and 250,000 | Police | 109 | 1967–1976 | Police personnel expenditures as a percentage of total police expenditures | Percentage of police employees represented by an organization which conducts formal or informal negotiations<br>Presence (absence) of a collective bargaining contract | Police unions appear to exert a slight impact on budgetary outcomes |

| Study | Scope of Sample | Government Function Studied | Sample Size | Year(s) Data Were Collected | Dependent Variable(s) | Independent Variable(s) | Major Findings |
|---|---|---|---|---|---|---|---|
| Russell L. Smith and William Lyons, "Public Sector Unionization and Municipal Wages: The Case of Fire Fighters." Paper presented at the Annual Meeting of the Midwest Political Science Association, Chicago, April 1978. | Cities with populations over 25,000 in 1960 | Fire fighters | 342–411 | 1960–1970 | Annual salary for entering employees Weekly work hours | Presence (absence) of a local union Presence (absence) of a contract Presence (absence) of a dues checkoff provision | 12% increase in wages 18% reduction in hours Presence of a union was more significant than existence of a contract |
| Philip B. Coulter, "Organizational Effectiveness in the Public Sector: The Example of Municipal Fire Protection," *Administrative Science Quarterly*, 24 (March 1979), 65–81. | Cities with populations over 25,000 | Fire fighters | 324 | 1973 | Expenditures Prevention effectiveness Suppression effectiveness Productivity | Unionization | Unionization was related to higher expenditures, but not to suppression effectiveness or productivity |

*(continued)*

**Table 1** *(continued)*

| Study | Scope of Sample | Government Function Studied | Sample Size | Year(s) Data Were Collected | Dependent Variable(s) | Independent Variable(s) | Major Findings |
|---|---|---|---|---|---|---|---|
| James L. Perry, Harold L. Angle, and Mark E. Pittel, *The Impact of Labor-Management Relations on Productivity and Efficiency in Urban Mass Transit* (Washington, D.C.: U.S. Department of Transportation, Research and Special Programs Administration, Office of University Research, 1979). | Public transit organizations in the Western United States | Transit | 28 | 1977 | Service efficiency (labor productivity, operating expense ratios) Service effectiveness Employee withdrawal (turnover, absenteeism, tardiness) Organizational adaptability | Legal, organizational structure, attitudinal and policy variables | Organizational policies in the collective bargaining agreement significantly influenced service efficiency and employee withdrawal Service effectiveness was not systematically related to the labor-management variables |
| Jean Baderschneider, "Collective Bargaining Pressure on Municipal Fiscal Capacity and Fiscal Effort." Paper presented at the Annual Meeting of the National Academy of Management, Atlanta, August 1979. | Cities with populations over 50,000 in 1975 | All | 289 | 1967 and 1975 | Fiscal capacity (financial capability) Fiscal effort (extent government utilizes its financial capability) | Presence (absence) of collective bargaining legislation covering police and fire fighters | Some support that collective bargaining legislation is associated with ability to pay and substantial support that it is associated with increased fiscal effort |

Several conventions were followed in creating Table 1. First, the studies are listed chronologically to highlight the development of this growing area of research. Second, abbreviated names of variables, rather than the complete variable label, are sometimes used in the table. The independent variables reported in the table are confined primarily to those that measured variations in either unionization or collective bargaining.[4] Finally, the "major findings" column in Table 1 summarizes only the general conclusions of each of the studies.

Even without a detailed examination of each of the studies in Table 1, several generalizations evolve from inspection of the summary information. For example, perusing the column in Table 1 headed "government function studied" reveals that a great deal of research has focused on the uniformed services, i.e., police, fire, and transit. In fact, these functions are examined in a majority of the studies. Research that looks exclusively at other local government functions is an exception. For example, little or no research focuses on recreation, library or social services. Of course, there are good reasons for the predominant emphasis on uniformed services, among them the essential nature of these services, their comparability from city to city, and the availability of adequate data about these services.

A review of Table 1 also indicates that most research on the impacts of collective bargaining relies on data bases drawn from the 1960s and early 1970s. This coincides obviously with the period during which collective bargaining became an important dimension of public management. This period has been characterized as an era of substantial progress for public employee organizations, in terms of both membership growth and bargaining effectiveness.[5] Therefore, any conclusions derived from these studies must recognize the possible confounding influences of this historical period.

A final generalization worth noting concerns the dependent variables most frequently analyzed in this research. Wages, i.e., inputs to local services, have received by far a greater amount of attention from scholars than any other variable. This imbalance of emphasis can probably be attributed to the tradition of relative wage research in economics[6] and to the greater ease of conducting research on wages than on output variables. However, as the chronological progression in the dependent-variable column of Table 1 illustrates, research is increasingly being focused on variables within the output and consequence categories of the taxonomy in Figure 1.

### Inputs

*Wages.* As we noted earlier, the question researchers have most frequently asked about the impact of public sector unionization and collective bargaining concerns employee wage gains. Have municipal employees improved their wages through collective bargaining and, if they have, by how much? The answer to this question seems to be yes—depending upon the occupational group involved—but wage levels overall have risen only marginally because of collective bargaining. Unionized fire fighters have reaped the greatest benefits, with estimates of their hourly wage increases ranging from 2 percent to 28 percent.[7] However, the magnitude of these hourly wage increases is partly attributable to decreases in average duty hours, since annual salaries of fire fighters have been estimated to have increased no more than 12 percent due to collective bargaining.[8]

Other municipal employees have not fared as well as fire fighters, but transit employees are probably a close second with an estimated 9–12 percent wage differential between unionized and non-unionized organizations.[9] The wages of unionized police employees have actually been found to lag behind their non-unionized counterparts in two studies, although two more recent analyses found that police unionization had a positive influence on wages.[10] These contrasting results probably indicate that employees in low-wage police departments organized principally to increase wages, but that their efforts did not achieve instantaneous success.[11]

While the research results are not in complete accord, general municipal employees (e.g., highways, sewerage, sanitation, parks and recreation, and libraries) do not appear to have achieved significant wage gains from unionization. Only Ehrenberg and Goldstein concluded that unionization has had an upward influence on the wages of general municipal employees.[12] Two studies, using more recent samples, found that unionization had no effect on the wages of general municipal employees.[13]

Although the aggregate effects of collective bargaining on local employee wages would appear to be positive, nothing sets the results for public employees apart from their private union counterparts. Scholars have consistently concluded that unionized public employees do no better than unionized private employees.[14] Thus, the observed differences between unionized and nonunionized employees reflect nothing endemic to the public sector, contrary to assertions that have received wide currency.[15]

***Fringe benefits.*** The price of labor might not be the only input that has been affected by unionization and collective bargaining. Although research on employee benefits has been quite limited, there is some indication that employees, by organizing and bargaining collectively, are more likely to improve their benefits and working conditions than they are wages. Four studies that have looked directly at fringe benefits concluded that employees achieved fringe benefit gains through either unionization or collective bargaining.[16] Kochan and Wheeler's finding that collective bargaining has contributed to significant gains in overall bargaining outcomes for fire fighters indicates that significant wage increases for fire fighters have not dampened their success in achieving non-wage gains as well. There is some support, however, for the belief that unions gradually shift their relative priorities between wages and fringe benefits as they become more established. For example, in his study of transit motormen, Lurie concluded that after 1938 transit unions placed a higher priority on securing fringe benefits than they had in the preceding two decades.[17]

***Employment.*** An enduring controversy in economics involves the disemployment effects of unionism.[18] The controversy involves the extent to which bargained increases in wages and other terms of employment will result in reduced levels of employment. This controversy is particularly meaningful to the current predicament of municipal governments. Given the "essential" nature of many municipal services, it seems highly unlikely that increases in the price of labor could be offset by reductions in employment. This does appear to be the case for uniformed services, where the employment levels of police have remained constant and fire fighter employment levels have actually increased despite increases in the price of labor.[19] However, the inelasticity of demand for these occupational groups is not characteristic of all municipal services. Benecki found that unionization significantly reduced overall employment levels, particularly in large cities.[20] These reductions in employment, of course, might result from a variety of sources, among them decisions by the local legislature to decrease the quantity of municipal services in the face of higher labor costs, substitution of new technologies for relatively more expensive labor, or increases in the productivity of existing employees.

***Environmental moderators.*** As we noted in our discussion of the taxonomy, environmental factors affect other variables within each component of the model. Environmental influences are particularly important in assessing the effects of unionization and collective bargaining on local government inputs. Two specific environmental influences, the city government structure and the degree of monopsony power held by the city, seem especially likely to moderate the influences of unionization and collective bargaining on local government inputs.

Three types of city government structure have been studied in assessing the impacts of collective bargaining: city manager, commission, and mayor-council. It is generally believed that a manager or commission type government, because it is more professional, will be able to hold the line against unions more effectively than a mayor-council form of government. However, manager and commission structures do not appear to moderate union influences on wages and fringe benefits.[21] In fact, there is some indication that the wages of union members might actually be higher in the city manager cities, but these wage differentials are probably offset by higher employee productivity.[22]

Another factor that may blunt the power of a union is the monopsony power held by the municipal employer. Monopsony refers to the demand side of the demand-supply equation. It is analogous to a monopoly, but, instead of one supplier, there is only one purchaser of a good or service. Thus, the degree to which a city is the only buyer of particular labor skills in a given geographic area, it exercises monopsony power. With only one exception, research indicates that city monopsony power does dampen union influence.[23] However, Hall and Vanderporten suggest that monopsony power might moderate union influence only under limited circumstances.[24] Hall and Vanderporten found that the ability of geographically isolated cities to wield monopsony power is not sustained when employees have achieved formal bargaining rights. In such cases, bilateral monopoly settlements yielded salaries similar to those reached in cities located in more competitive urban areas. Thus, a strong union might be able to overcome the monopsonistic power of a city.

Other research, while not testing the monopsony issue directly, has looked into differentials in union power associated with city or metropolitan area size. Both Ashenfelter and Ehrenberg found that the union had greater impact upon wages in smaller cities than in larger cities.[25] Gerhart, in assessing aggregate contract outcomes, discovered that unions operating in small SMSAs fared better than unions in jurisdictions outside of SMSAs or than unions in large SMSAs.[26] Surprisingly, contract index scores were lower in large SMSAs. Among his explanations for the relative success of governmental jurisdictions in large SMSAs was that management might be more sophisticated and that the process may be more political, and hence informal, in the largest cities. Both of these would have a tendency to decrease union power relative to management.

Thus, it appears that employer monopsony can have a dampening effect on union power, but only in limited circumstances.

## Activities

While a great deal of heat has been generated in the last several years about collective bargaining and employee productivity, work rules, and policy encroachment, the research to date has shed little light upon these controversies.[27] Although his research was intended to be exploratory rather than conclusive, Stanley's multiple-case study remains the most comprehensive analysis of collective bargaining and municipal activities.[28] His general conclusion was that unions had won victories over working conditions in a narrow sense, but that management maintained firm control over policy determination and operations management.

In the decade since Stanley's research, no one has undertaken to reassess systematically his conclusions. However, two recent studies have looked at various aspects of collective bargaining and work management. Coulter examined the influence of unions on the productivity of fire departments (as measured by the total cost of fires, i.e., expenditures plus property loss, *per capita*).[29] Using a multivariate procedure called discriminant analysis, Coulter concluded that unionism neither decreased nor increased productivity.

Clues to the reasons why unionization or collective bargaining might have no net effect on productivity are provided in a recent study of public mass transit organizations.[30] Collectively-bargained work rules, generally believed to reduce productivity, were found to have both positive and negative effects on labor productivity and operating costs. This finding confirms Stanley's earlier assertion that "some forces tend to offset each other."[31] Overall, however, the transit study concluded that productivity and efficiency could be improved if labor would agree to the relaxation of certain scheduling and guaranteed-minimum work rules, and if both labor and management cooperated in developing work attendance incentives and improving grievance procedures.

## Outputs

Although the research is far from voluminous, we know much more about the impact of collective bargaining on municipal outputs than about its impacts on municipal activities. For instance, widespread consensus surrounds the conclusion that collective bargaining has driven municipal expenditures upward.[32] In the most comprehensive study of the influences of collective bargaining on expenditure patterns, Benecki found that unionization was associated with higher personnel expenditures and higher overall expenditures. These results, however, were not uniform for large and small cities. In the largest cities, unionization was associated with lower levels of governmental activity because of a highly significant and negative relationship between unionization and employment. On the other hand, unionization in the smallest cities was associated with higher levels of governmental activity related to significantly higher personnel expenditures.

A possible reason for this disparity between large and small cities is that larger cities tend to offer a greater quantity and variety of services while smaller cities might offer an irreducible core. The greater quantity and variety offers a source of slack to the larger cities. Benecki speculates that large cities can eliminate peripheral programs and still maintain their core while smaller cities cannot.[33] Thus, large cities are more likely to cut back on output and incur disemployment. Smaller cities are more likely to incur higher levels of expenditures, especially in the personnel sector, and to implement some revenue stopgap, e.g., incurring short-term debt, in order to cope with the aftermaths of unionization and collective bargaining.

The differences between large and small cities might also be accounted for by differences in the development of unionization in the two size classifications.[34] Larger cities exhibit greater unionization, which might reflect longer-standing bargaining relationships. If this is true, then the adjustment mechanism used by smaller cities, that of expenditure adjustment, may represent the short-run impact of bargaining. In the long run, however, employment might be expected to decline in smaller cities just as it has in large cities.

In the fact of expenditure increases, revenues and taxes have risen correspondingly. Schmenner found tax rates positively correlated with police-fire wage settlements.[35] However, when the tax rate was lagged back two years, it was negatively correlated with police-fire wages. Perhaps the most plausible explanation for these temporal differences is that, in the short run, politicians seldom react to negotiated wage increases by increasing taxes. However, local decision makers must ultimately raise taxes as a result of negotiated wage increases. In a similar vein, Baderschneider found that fiscal effort was greater in jurisdictions that were covered by collective bargaining legislation for police and fire fighters.[36]

## Consequences

Like the activities category of the taxonomy, very little research has been directed at discovering how and in what ways unionization and collective bargaining might affect local service effectiveness. Two studies, focusing on fire departments and public transit agencies, have explored simple associations between collective bargaining variables and measures of service effectiveness. Coulter examined the relationship between unionism and fire suppression effectiveness (dollars of property loss per 1000 population).[37] Perry, et al., looked at the associations of a variety of legal, organizational, and policy variables with two measures of transit service effectiveness (revenue passengers per service-area-population and revenue-passengers per revenue vehicle hour).[38] Neither study found any significant relationships between the effectiveness measures and the independent variables.

These results are obviously not sufficient to warrant sweeping conclusions about collective bargaining and the consequences of local services, but they clearly call into question the presumption that bargaining influences significantly the consequences of local services.[39] What might explain the lack of association? One explanation might simply be that the only two services that have been analyzed thus far—fire and transit functions—are not representative of the relationships that exist for most local government functions; analysis of other, non-uniformed services might possibly produce different results. Another explanation is purely methodological. Considering the probably large number of determinants of the effectiveness of any local government service, the influences of collective bargaining might well be indetectable, especially given the crudeness of most measurement methods. Of course, the absence of an association between bargaining and consequences could also indicate that the consequences dimension of the taxonomy is much more complex than the variables that have been studied. For example, if collective bargaining has contributed to redistributions of local government outputs, then any attempt to measure collective bargaining's impacts should probably focus on citywide rather than service-related measures of effectiveness.

## Conclusions

This paper has reviewed empirical research on the impacts of unionization and collective bargaining on local government services. Our conclusions about these impacts are summarized in Table 2. In retrospect, this collection of research findings represents significant strides beyond our knowledge of a few years ago. However, important questions about impacts

within each category in the taxonomy remain to be investigated and answered.

The various studies have shown that unions probably do contribute positively to employee wages. The precise magnitude of this influence is difficult to judge. While more work needs to be done in determining the effect, greater emphasis should be given to non-uniformed employees. More specifically, studies which look at several categories of employees should be conducted. Furthermore, total compensation should be included more frequently in this research. Unionization and collective bargaining probably influence total compensation, but the magnitude is difficult to judge given our existing knowledge.

There is also a need to determine if collective bargaining encourages management to substitute capital for labor and, if so, how much. Furthermore, changes in the occupational composition of the public workforce also need to be assessed. This type of research might shed light on the role unions have played in local government innovation. Better methods for measuring least-cost combinations of capital and labor might first have to be developed.

As public employee unions expand and mature, bargaining emphasis appears to change. Hours, fringe benefits, and work rules may take on greater importance. If this is so, productivity bargaining may become a dominant form of bargaining in the future. It will be crucial to better understand this type of bargaining in order to avoid the pitfalls that Horton uncovered in

### Table 2
### Summary of findings about the impacts of collective bargaining on local services

| | |
|---|---|
| *Inputs:* | Some occupational groups (e.g., fire fighters and transit operators) have achieved significant and substantial gains, other groups (police) have experienced marginal improvements, and some occupational groups have achieved little or no demonstrable improvement in wages or fringes because of collective bargaining. Reductions in employment appear to be most severe in very large cities. |
| *Activities:* | Little of a general nature is known, except that collective bargaining continues to stimulate both positive and negative influences on productivity and work management. |
| *Outputs:* | Collective bargaining has driven municipal expenditures and fiscal effort upward. |
| *Consequences:* | Limited evidence indicates that collective bargaining has had no impact on the effectiveness of local services. |

New York City.[40] Methodologies must also be developed for assessing the productivity-related implications of changes in work rules.

It is with regard to local government outputs and consequences that the most glaring research needs arise. Is it city size alone that is associated with the differential union effect on expenditures or some other variables? Virtually no research has explored unionization's effects on consequences. Only through a more complete understanding of these and other impacts will we be able to sweep away the myths surrounding local government bargaining and replace them with more informed judgments.

# Notes

1. For a sampling of opinion and evidence about the extent to which collective bargaining has affected the fiscal health of local governments, see Harry H. Wellington and Ralph K. Winter, *The Unions and the Cities* (Washington, D.C.: The Brookings Institution, 1971); Arvid Anderson, "Local Government—Bargaining and the Fiscal Crisis: Money, Unions, Politics, and the Public Interest," *Labor Law Journal,* 27 (August 1976), 512–520; Edward M. Gramlich, "The New York City Fiscal Crisis: What Happened and What Is To Be Done?" *American Economic Review,* 66 (May 1976), 415–529; and Robert B. Pennengill and Jogindar S. Uppal, *Can Cities Survive? The Fiscal Plight of American Cities* (New York: St. Martin's Press, 1974).

2. See D. F. Bradford, R. A. Malt, and W. E. Oates, "The Rising Cost of Local Public Services: Some Evidence and Reflections," *National Tax Journal,* 22 (June 1969), 185–202, and Jesse Burkhead and Patrick J. Hennigan, "Productivity Analysis: A Search for Definition and Order," *Public Administration Review,* 38 (January/February 1978), 34–40.

3. These criteria have led to the exclusion of research on teachers as well as single- and multiple-city case studies. A moderate amount of research has focused upon the impacts of collective bargaining in public education. See, for example, W. Clayton Hall and Norman E. Carroll, "The Effect of Teachers' Organization on Salaries and Class Size," *Industrial and Labor Relations Review,* 26 (January 1973), 843–841, and Gary A. Moore, "The Effect of Collective Bargaining on Internal Salary Structures in the

Public Schools," *Industrial and Labor Relations Review,* 29 (April 1976), 352–362. The primary reason for excluding this research is the difference between the institutional contexts of public education and municipal governments. Differences in the composition of their workforces and their legal status threaten the validity of any comparisons.

Case studies tend to be more useful for generating than for testing hypotheses. Although case studies are not included in our review, both single- and multiple-city case studies have been useful for assessing collective bargainings' impacts. See, among others, David Stanley, *Managing Local Government Under Union Pressure* (Washington, D.C.: The Brookings Institution, 1972), and Raymond D. Horton, "Productivity and Productivity Bargaining in Government: A Critical Analysis," *Public Administration Review,* 36 (July/August 1976), 407–414.

4. It should be noted that unionization and collective bargaining are not one and the same. The term *unionization* is usually used to denote the proportion of a work force that belongs to a union, while collective bargaining is used to refer to the formal structure of negotiations between management and labor. However, in this paper the terms are, for the most part, used interchangeably because the measurement of the two concepts in many of the studies does not permit a distinct separation of the effects of each. Many of the studies include collective bargaining as part of the unionization variable or lump collective bargaining together with several factors such as dues checkoff and affiliation with a national union to form a "strength of union" variable. Thus, the distinction between unionization and collective bargaining is valid, but their respective effects cannot be separated given our existing knowledge base.

5. This seems to be the consensus of two recent assessments of the past and future of employee organization and bargaining in the public sector. See John F. Burton, Jr., "The Extent of Collective Bargaining in the Public Sector," and Benjamin Aaron, "Future of Collective Bargaining in the Public Sector," in Benjamin Aaron, Joseph R. Grodin, and James L. Stern (eds.), *Public-Sector Bargaining* (Washington, D.C.: Bureau of National Affairs, 1979), pp. 1–43, 292–315.

6. A substantial amount of economic research has focused on unionism and relative wages since Lewis' pioneering study in the early 1960s. See H. Gregg Lewis, *Unionism and Relative Wages in the United States: An Empirical Inquiry* (Chicago: University of Chicago Press, 1963).

7. The lower of these figures is based upon Ehrenberg's cross-sectional study of fire fighter wages

in 1969, and the higher figure is based upon Smith and Lyon's longitudinal analysis of wage changes between 1960 and 1970. See Ronald G. Ehrenberg, "Municipal Government Structures, Unionization, and the Wages of Fire Fighters," *Industrial and Labor Relations Review,* 27 (October 1973), 36–48, and Russell L. Smith and William Lyons, "Public Sector Unionization and Municipal Wages: The Case of Fire Fighters." Paper presented at the Annual Meeting of the Midwest Political Science Association, Chicago, April 1978.

8. See Orley Ashenfelter, "The Effect of Unionization on Wages in the Public Sector: The Case of Fire Fighters," *Industrial and Labor Relations Review,* 24 (January 1971), 191–202; Ehrenberg, *op. cit.;* and Smith and Lyons, *op. cit.*

9. Daniel S. Hamermesh, "The Effect of Government Ownership on Union Wages," in Daniel S. Hamermesh (ed.), *Labor in the Public and Non-Profit Sectors* (Princeton, N.J.: Princeton University Press, 1975), pp. 227–263.

10. The negative associations between unionization and wages were found by Roger W. Schmenner, "The Determinants of Municipal Employee Wages," *Review of Economics and Statistics,* 60 (February 1973), 83–90, and David Lewin and John H. Keith, Jr., "Managerial Responses to Perceived Labor Shortages," *Criminology,* 14 (May 1976), 65–93. Positive associations were found by W. Clayton Hall and Bruce Vanderporten, "Unionization, Monopsony Power and Police Salaries," *Industrial Relations,* 16 (February 1977), 94–100, and Richard B. Victor, *The Effects of Unionism on the Wage and Employment Levels of Police and Firefighters* (Santa Monica, Calif.: The Rand Corporation, P-5924, 1977).

11. This is the most plausible of the explanations for a negative relationship between police unionism and wages offered by Lewin and Keith, *op. cit.,* p. 76. Another possible explanation, however, is what some researchers term the "simultaneity problem." Simply, this problem involves whether or not several inputs (e.g., wages, fringes, and employment) are determined simultaneously. If several outcomes are determined simultaneously, then ordinary least squares estimates could produce the results found by Lewin and Keith. See Victor, *op. cit.,* p. 7.

12. Ronald G. Ehrenberg and Gerald S. Goldstein, "A Model of Public Sector Wage Determination," *Journal of Urban Economics,* 2 (July 1975), 223–245.

13. See Schmenner, *op. cit.* and James L. Freund, "Market and Union Influences on Municipal Wages," *Industrial and Labor Relations Review,* 27 (April 1974), 391–404. Although the Perry and Levine study included some uniformed employee groups within its sample, it also found no relationship between union power and wage changes. See James L. Perry and Charles H. Levine, "An Interorganizational Analysis of Power, Conflict and Settlements in Public Sector Collective Bargaining," *American Political Science Review,* 70 (December 1976), 1185–1201.

14. See David Shapiro, "Relative Wage Effects of Unions in the Public and Private Sectors," *Industrial and Labor Relations Review,* 31 (January 1978), 193–203, and David Lewin, "Public Sector Labor Relations," *Labor History,* 18 (Winter 1977), 133–144.

15. See, for example, Wellington and Winter, *op. cit.;* and Walter Fogel and David Lewin, "Wage Determination in the Public Sector," *Industrial and Labor Relations Review,* 27 (April 1974), 410–431.

16. See Melvin Lurie, "The Effect of Unionization on Wages in the Transit Industry," *Journal of Political Economy,* 69 (December 1961), 558–572; Thomas A. Kochan and Hoyt N. Wheeler, "Municipal Collective Bargaining: A Model and Analysis of Bargaining Outcomes," *Industrial and Labor Relations Review,* 29 (October 1975), 46–66; Paul F. Gerhart, "Determinants of Bargaining Outcomes in Local Government Labor Negotiations," *Industrial and Labor Relations Review,* 29 (April 1976), 331–351; and Perry and Levine, *op. cit.* None of these studies examined the effects of collective bargaining on particular fringe benefits, such as employee pensions. For a review of research on employer-employee relations and pensions, see Bernard Jump, Jr., "Public Employment, Collective Bargaining, and Employee Wages and Pensions," in John E. Peterson, Catherine Lavigne Spain, and Martharose F. Laffey (eds.), *State and Local Government Finance and Financial Management: A Compendium of Current Research* (Washington, D.C.: Government Finance Research Center, 1978), pp. 74–85.

17. Lurie, *op. cit.* Smith and Lyons, *op. cit.,* also suggest that the union's bargaining emphasis shifts as it becomes more established.

18. For a summary and critique of the classical literature on the wage-employment tradeoff, see Arthur M. Ross, *Trade Union Wage Policy* (Berkeley, Calif.: University of California Press, 1956).

19. See Victor, *op. cit.*

20. Stanley Benecki, "Municipal Expenditure Levels and Collective Bargaining," *Industrial Relations,* 17 (May 1978), 216–230.

21. See Ehrenberg, *op. cit.,* Kochan and Wheeler, *op. cit.* and Gerhart, *op. cit.*

22. Ehrenberg, *op. cit.* and Ehrenberg and Goldstein, *op. cit.*

23. The exception is Schmenner, *op. cit.*

24. Hall and Vanderporten, *op. cit.*

25. Ashenfelter, *op. cit.* and Ehrenberg, *op. cit.*

26. Gerhart, *op. cit.*

27. Several of the studies in Table 1 have investigated activities like work rules, but they have done so only through their inclusion in additive contract indices. See Kochan and Wheeler, *op. cit.*, Gerhart, *op. cit.* and Perry and Levine, *op. cit.*

28. Stanley, *op. cit.*

29. Philip B. Coulter, "Organizational Effectiveness in the Public Sector: The Example of Municipal Fire Protection," *Administrative Science Quarterly,* 24 (March 1979), 65–81.

30. James L. Perry, Harold L. Angle and Mark E. Pittel, *The Impact of Labor-Management Relations on Productivity and Efficiency in Urban Mass Transit* (Washington, D.C.: U.S. Department of Transportation, Research and Special Programs Administration, Office of University Research, 1979).

31. Stanley, *op. cit.*, p. 139.

32. See Benecki, *op. cit.;* Richard C. Kearney, "The Impacts of Police Unionization on Municipal Budgetary Outcomes." Paper presented at the Annual Meeting of the Midwest Political Science Association, Chicago, April 1978; and Coulter, *op. cit.*

33. Benecki, *op. cit.*

34. *Ibid.*

35. Schmenner, *op. cit.*

36. Jean Baderschneider, "Collective Bargaining Pressure on Municipal Fiscal Capacity and Fiscal Effort." Paper presented at the Annual Meeting of the National Academy of Management, Atlanta, August 1979.

37. Coulter, *op. cit.*

38. Perry, Angle, and Pittel, *op. cit.*

39. See, for example, James L. Perry and Carder W. Hunt, "Evaluating the Union-Management Relationship in Government," *Public Administration Review,* 38 (September/October 1978), 431–436.

40. Horton, *op. cit.*

# VI
# Toward 2000

Predictions pose problems for a volume of classics. Aside from the usual difficulties of forecasting policies and practices embedded in extremely complex, constantly changing social systems, volumes of classics to some degree look backward. They seek to come to grips with intellectual and ideological heritage. Yet failure to speculate about the future begs a pivotal question. What issues will preoccupy those concerned with public personnel policy in the 1990s? The answer will in part spring from the constant competition of five core values in the personnel policy arena—agency competence, political responsiveness, merit, social equity, and employee rights and well-being. It will also derive from the degree of progress made in understanding cause–effect relations in human-resource management.

More specifically, however, two issues seem particularly likely to stand out during the 1990s. First, the pervasive emphasis on administration by proxy, especially privatization, will challenge students and practitioners of public personnel administration. Second, there will be increased concern about the human-resource capacity of government— about its ability to attract and retain capable personnel. Much of this concern will focus on the federal government.

Governments have long relied on other levels of government and on private entities (proprietary or nonprofit) to provide resources and help implement public programs. As of the early 1980s, for instance, the federal government administered contracts amounting to $167 billion; these contracts involved some 215,000 firms, which employed more than 30 million workers. The Reagan administration has highlighted the full implications of proxy administration by forcefully arguing for additional privatization.

A pamphlet released in 1988 by the Office of Management and Budget (OMB) captures some of the intellectual underpinnings of this commitment:[1]

> Competition is the driving force behind quality and economy of operations in the private sector. Private sector managers are continually challenged by competitors who may force them out of business if they do not operate in the most efficient manner. The constant competitive pressure forces managers to be innovative and flexible as they promote performance-based management to serve their customers. . . .
>
> Government managers, in normal operations, do not encounter the same pressures for efficiency that private managers do. They have few baselines for comparisons and do not face the constant threat of competition.

The pamphlet then goes on to describe OMB Circular A-76 designed to facilitate the contracting out of government services to private entities. This circular requires that studies be conducted to see whether work should be performed by government or industry. According to the OMB, "This evaluation process alone enhances productivity by challenging government managers to find the most effective and efficient means of doing business at competitive prices." The OMB also claimed that it resulted in conversion to contractor operations about 60 percent of the time.[2]

The Reagan years witnessed steady efforts to accelerate the implementation of the A-76 program. In the fall of 1987, for instance, President Reagan issued Executive Order 12615, which among other things, required officials to identify all government "commercial" activities and develop a schedule to review them for possible private contracting.

The extracts from the OMB pamphlet can best be read as ideology rather than conclusions based on empirically supported theory. For example, serious questions exist about the degree to which contracting appreciably enhances competition in many cases. Government employees even without the threat of contracting often face substantial pressures to perform. Whatever the truth of the OMB assertions, however, they testify to the likelihood that privatization will continue to garner the attention of policy makers and scholars in the 1990s.

The staying power of privatization as a pivotal issue springs from several sources, among others. First, major government programs, such as Medicare and Defense Department weapons procurement, already rely on private vendors. It would require massive and costly restructuring of these programs to do anything other than a privatized approach. Second, the political culture of the United States makes privatization particularly appealing. Americans can essentially reap many of the benefits of big government programs without increasing the size of public bureaucracies. Moreover, privatization fits with the American bias that government administration cannot possibly match the efficiency of the business sector. Third, the erosion of the capacity of the federal work force, another legacy of the Reagan administration, will enhance the allure of privatization. If government cannot attract and retain adequate numbers of highly competent employees, the attractiveness of contracting out government work will grow.

The vast reliance on private contractors means that those concerned with human-resource management in public programs need to expand their focus across the boundaries of government. To be sure, personnel management in governmental agencies continues as the analytic heartland. But understanding the personnel processes of government's private implementing agents is also important. A focus on these processes raises intriguing questions for human-resource specialists. For instance, what personnel regulations should the sponsoring government impose on firms implementing its programs? A clear precedent exists for regulating certain personnel practices of grantees and contractors. As the earlier selections by Aronson and Derthick attest, the professionalization of state and local government personnel in part sprang from merit system requirements promulgated by the federal government under various statutes. In a similar vein, Executive Order 11246 paved the way for the Department of Labor to impose certain affirmative action requirements on private firms contracting with the federal government. These requirements appear to have positively effected the placement of minorities in executive and managerial jobs in those firms.[3]

Drawing on these and related precedents, should government impose more human-resource requirements on grantees and contractors? Or should it deregulate them? The answer to these and similar questions will shape the mix of core personnel values represented in public programs. For instance, the Reagan administration systematically pursued a policy of deregulating private contractors with respect to affirmative action. Among other things, it cut back the staff of the regulatory agency responsible for the program by one-third. It reduced pressures on private firms to establish multiyear goals and timetables for hiring minorities. It referred fewer cases involving contractor non-compliance with affirmative action to the Solicitor General for prosecution.[4]

The implications of privatization for other aspects of public personnel practice also deserve attention. For instance, privatization affords an opportunity for a new variation on an old theme—patronage. Elected officials have in the past sporadically sought to ensure that their supporters received government contracts. Pressuring contractors to employ party stalwarts could become an additional component of such an initiative. In Chicago, for instance, the late Mayor Harold Washington proposed a "Chicago First" program in 1987 whereby his Office of Employment and Training would refer "deserving" job applicants to private companies doing business with the city.[5]

Privatization has also fueled concern about ethics. Firms with a heavy stake in winning government contracts face constant temptations to bribe or otherwise bestow favors on public officials who influence the awarding, administration, and profitability of these contracts. Government administrators occasionally succumb. In rare cases, civil servants accept overt bribes for explicit favors. In other cases, government administrators bestow more subtle favors on contractors for more subtle awards. A contract officer may, for instance, go out of his or her way to give a private firm the benefit of a doubt in hopes of obtaining lucrative employment with that company after resigning from government. These ethical threats spawn more and more rules designed to control public workers' behavior. For instance, civil servants face more requirements to fill out elaborate financial statements and in some cases find their post-government ability to perform certain jobs for private contractors limited by law.

Aside from privatization, issues of competence and capacity will challenge personnel policy makers in the 1990s. In this regard, the federal government had aroused particular concern as the 1980s ebbed. The two selections reprinted here—one from the Volcker Commission and the other from a futuristic report commissioned by the U.S. Office of Personnel Management—capture this mounting sense of a "quiet crisis" in government's human-resource capacity. It may be premature to bestow "classic" status on these selections. But if the diagnoses and prescriptions of these reports prove valid, students and practitioners may well look back from the year 2000 either ruefully noting their prescience in predicting decline or gratefully acknowledging their role as a catalyst for reform.

With funding from such private organizations as the Ford and Rockefeller foundations, Paul Volcker (the widely respected former chairman of the Federal Reserve Board) agreed to head the National Commission on the Public Service (the Commission). The Commission dedicated itself "to placing high on the Nation's Agenda the need to strengthen the effectiveness of the career services of government." In a report released in late March 1989, the Commission warned that "America will be left with a government of the mediocre" if certain steps were not taken.[6] The excerpt reprinted here summarizes the major thrust of the report. Pointing to evidence suggesting erosion in the human resource base of government, the Commission proffered twelve recommendations. Its proposals called for a broad range of action—greater emphasis on ethical standards, depoliticization of the top levels of government, better civic education in the nation's schools, scholarship programs in return for government service, higher pay for civil servants, and more.

Just prior to the release of the Volcker Commission report, the U.S. Office of Personnel Management had parsimoniously pointed to critical dimensions of concern in a publication entitled *Civil Service 2000.* This report typified a spate of analyses that appeared in the late 1980s which projected workforce trends in the 1990s and their implications for employers.[7] As the excerpt reprinted here indicates, *Civil Service 2000* reached essentially the same empirical conclusion as the Volcker Commission, that the federal government faced "a slowly emerging crisis of competence." The report pointed to three critical ingredients of this predicament—increasingly noncompetitive salaries especially in certain regions of the country, declining public esteem for civil servants and government, and the aggravations created by outdated public-management practices. Moreover, the report asserted that certain forces likely to be present in the 1990s would fuel the crisis. Specifically, competition for well-qualified workers will become more intense; a growing share of federal jobs will demand the highest skills and a new retirement system will reduce the incentive federal executives have to remain with the government for long periods. *Civil Service 2000* goes on to urge certain remedies some of which resemble the Volcker Commission proposals as well as the recommendations of earlier reformers (see pertinent materials in sections II and III).

In considering the thrust of *Civil Service 2000,* its intersection with the earlier discussion of privatization deserves special attention. The report fully recognizes that privatization via contracts creates new demands for skilled governmental managers to oversee the contracting process. "These managers must be at least as knowledgeable and capable as the contractors they monitor. . . ." It goes on to bemoan the fact that at present "many Federal contract management jobs are typically low-level, low-paying slots with little prestige or chance for advancement. . . . Unless ways are found to attract and reward top quality Federal managers, the road toward contracting out Federal services is likely to be strewn with embarrassing frauds and expensive failures."

The road to reform will in all probability be bumpy; it may be impassable. For instance, efforts to bring the pay of top-level federal executives more into line with that of the private sector face many obstacles in part because executive salaries are linked to those of members of Congress. In 1989, for instance, public outcry helped kill a significant increase in federal pay endorsed by the Quadrennial Commission,[8] President Reagan and (at least initially) congressional leaders. This increase would have been a significant step forward in attracting and retaining competent top-level executives.

Some analysts see the problem of competence as rooted in much more fundamental phenomena than the perennial public reluctance to pay federal executives competitive rates. For instance, in a speech before the National Academy of Public Administration in fall 1987, Aaron Wildavsky argued that much of what ails the civil service springs from "ideological dissensus within the political stratum, profound disagreements over equality, democracy, and hence the role of government, disagreements that create conflicting expectations that no conceivable cadre of civil servants can meet."[9]

One can, of course, conjure up a more optimistic scenario. The road to reform may be passible. Many state and local governments seem less likely than the federal establishment to face a fundamental problem of competence in the 1990s. Among divided political elites, consensus may nonetheless develop that no one's interests get served by seeing government capacity plummet. Yet even optimists cannot sensibly doubt the pressing challenges facing those involved in the personnel arena in the 1990s. Triumphs and defeats in this sphere will often not be very visible; they will frequently have delayed, sleeper effects. However difficult to monitor and assess, choices in the personnel arena will be important. As in the past, public personnel policy must remain a critical focus for those who seek efficient, effective, equitable, and responsive government.

# Notes

1. U.S. Office of Management and Budget, *Enhancing Governmental Productivity Through Competition* (Washington, 1988), p. 1.

2. *Ibid.*, p. 1.

3. Edward M. Meyers, "Regulation of Federal Contractors' Employment Patterns," *Public Administration Review* 49 (January/February, 1989), pp. 52–60.

4. *Ibid.*, p. 55.

5. Anne Freedman, "Doing Battle with the Patronage Army: Politics, Courts, and Personnel Administration in Chicago," *Public Administration Review* 48 (September/October, 1988), p. 856.

6. A brochure of the National Commission on Public Service and the *Albany Times Union* (March 30, 1989), p. A-4.

7. See also U.S. Department of Labor, *Opportunity 2000* (Washington: Government Printing Office, 1988). New York State government also commissioned studies of this genre.

8. Authorized in 1967, the Quadrennial Commission convenes every four years to study pay levels for members of Congress, federal judges, and top federal executives in order to make new salary recommendations to the president.

9. Aaron Wildavsky, "'Ubiquitous Anomie' or Public Service in an Era of Ideological Dissensus," in *The Campus and the Public Service* (Washington: National Academy of Public Administration, 1988), p. 5.

# 32

## Leadership for America: Rebuilding the Public Service

*The Volcker Commission*

### Summary and Main Conclusions

The central message of this report of the Commission on the Public Service is both simple and profound, both urgent and timeless. In essence, we call for a renewed sense of commitment by all Americans to the highest traditions of the public service—to a public service responsive to the political will of the people and also protective of our constitutional values; to a public service able to cope with complexity and conflict and also able to maintain the highest ethical standards; to a public service attractive to the young and talented from all parts of our society and also capable of earning the respect of all our citizens.

A great nation must demand no less. The multiple challenges thrust upon the Government of the United States as we approach the 21st Century can only reinforce the point. Yet, there is evidence on all sides of an erosion of performance and morale across government in America. Too many of our most talented public servants—those with the skills and dedication that are the hallmarks of an effective career service—are ready to leave. Too few of our brightest young people—those with the imagination and energy that are essential for the future—are willing to join.

SOURCE: National Commission on The Public Service, pp. 1–9, (Volcker Commission, Washington, 1989).

Meanwhile, the need for a strong public service is growing, not lessening. Americans have always expected their national government to guarantee their basic freedoms and provide for the common defense. We continue to expect our government to keep the peace with other nations, resolve differences among our own people, pay the bills for needed services, and honor the people's trust by providing the highest levels of integrity and performance.

At the same time, Americans now live in a stronger, more populous nation, a nation with unprecedented opportunity. But they also live in a world of enormous complexity and awesome risks. Our economy is infinitely more open to international competition, our currency floats in a world-wide market, and we live with complex technologies beyond the understanding of any single human mind. Our diplomacy is much more complicated, and the wise use of our unparalleled military power more difficult. And for all our scientific achievements, we are assaulted daily by new social, environmental, and health issues almost incomprehensible in scope and impact—issues like drugs, AIDS, and global warming.

Faced with these challenges, the simple idea that Americans must draw upon talented and dedicated individuals to serve us in government is uncontestable. America must have a public service that can both value the lessons of experience and appreciate the requirements for change; a public service that both responds to political leadership and respects the law; a public service with the professional skills and the ethical sensitivity America deserves.

Surely, there can be no doubt that moral challenge and personal excitement are inherent in the great enterprise of democratic government. There is work to be done of enormous importance. Individuals can make a difference.

But unfortunately there is growing evidence that these basic truths have been clouded by a sense of frustration inside government and a lack of public trust outside. The resulting erosion in the quality of America's public service is difficult to measure; there are still many examples of excellence among those who carry out the nation's business at home and abroad. Nevertheless, it is evident that public service is neither as attractive as it once was nor as effective in meeting perceived needs. No doubt, opposition to specific policies of government has contributed to a lack of respect for the public servants who struggle to make the policies work. This drives away much of our best talent which can only make the situation worse.

One need not search far to see grounds for concern. Crippled nuclear weapons plants, defense procurement scandals, leaking hazardous waste dumps, near-misses in air traffic control, and the costly collapse of so many savings and loans have multiple causes. But each such story carries some similar refrains about government's inability to recruit and retain a talented work force: the Department of Defense is losing its top procurement specialists to contractors who can pay much more; the Federal Aviation Administration is unable to hold skilled traffic controllers because of stress and working conditions; the Environmental Protection Agency is unable to fill key engineering jobs because the brightest students simply are not interested; the Federal Savings and Loan Insurance Corporation (FSLIC) simply cannot hire and pay able executives.

This erosion has been gradual, almost imperceptible, year by year. But it has occurred nonetheless. Consider the following evidence compiled by the Commission's five task forces on the growing recruitment problem:

- Only 13 percent of the senior executives recently interviewed by the General Accounting Office would recommend that young people start their careers in government, while several recent surveys show that less than half the senior career civil servants would recommend a job in government to their own children.
- Of the 610 engineering students who received bachelors, masters, and doctoral degrees at the Massachusetts Institute of Technology and Stanford University in 1986, and the 600 who graduated from Rensselaer Polytechnic Institute

in 1987, only 29 took jobs in government at any level.

- Half the respondents to a recent survey of federal personnel officers said recruitment of quality personnel had become more difficult over the past five years.
- Three-quarters of the respondents to the Commission's survey of recent Presidential Management Interns—a prestigious program for recruiting the top graduates of America's schools of public affairs—said they would leave government within 10 years.

If these trends continue, America will soon be left with a government of the mediocre, locked into careers of last resort or waiting for a chance to move on to other jobs.

But this need not and should not be. By the choices we make today, we can enter the 21st century with a public service fully equipped to meet the challenges of intense competition abroad and growing complexity at home. The strongest wish of the Commission is that this report can be a step in that process, pointing toward necessary changes, while serving as a catalyst for national debate and further efforts at all levels of government.

America should and can act now to restore the leadership, talent, and performance essential to the strong public service the future demands. To those ends, the Commission believes:

- First, the President and Congress must provide the essential environment for effective leadership and public support.
- Second, educational institutions and the agencies of government must work to enlarge the base of talent available for, and committed to, public service.
- Third, the American people should demand first-class performance and the highest ethical standards, and, by the same token, must be willing to provide what is necessary to attract and retain needed talent.

These three themes—*leadership, talent,* and *performance*—shape this report. They are both wide-ranging and interrelated. They also provide a framework for a concrete agenda for action, directed toward a series of basic goals discussed in further detail in the report that follows. Specifically, to strengthen executive *leadership,* we call upon the President and Congress to:

- Take action now by word and deed to rebuild public trust in government;
- Clear away obstacles to the ability of the President to attract talented appointees from all parts of society;
- Make more room at senior levels of departments and agencies for career executives;
- Provide a framework within which those federal departments and agencies can exercise greater flexibility in managing programs and personnel; and
- Encourage a stronger partnership between presidential appointees and career executives.

To broaden the government's *talent base,* we call upon educational institutions and government to:

- Develop more student awareness of, and educational training for, the challenges of government and public service;
- Develop new channels for spreading the word about government jobs and the rewards of public service;
- Enhance the efforts to recruit top college graduates and those with specific professional skills for government jobs;
- Simplify the hiring process; and
- Increase the representation of minorities in public careers.

To place a greater emphasis on quality and *performance* throughout government, we ask for the public and its leaders to:

- Build a pay system that is both fair and competitive;
- Rebuild the government's chief personnel agency to give it the strength and mandate it needs;
- Set higher goals for government performance and productivity;
- Provide more effective training and executive development; and
- Improve government working conditions.

To further these basic goals, the Commission makes a series of specific recommendations throughout the report (see Appendix I). Twelve key proposals deserve mention here:

*First,* **Presidents, their chief lieutenants, and Congress must articulate early and often the necessary and honorable role that public servants play in the democratic process, at the same time making clear they will demand the highest standards of ethics and performance possible from those who hold the public trust. Members of Congress and their staffs should be covered by similiar standards. Codes of conduct to convey such standards should be simple and straightforward, and should focus on the affirmative values that must guide public servants in the exercise of their responsibilities.**

*Second,* within program guidelines from the President, **cabinet officers and agency heads should be given greater flexibility to administer their organizations, including greater freedom to hire and fire personnel, provided there are appropriate review procedures within the Administration and oversight from Congress.**

*Third,* **the President should highlight the important role of the Office of Personnel Management (OPM) by establishing and maintaining contact with its Director and by ensuring participation by the Director in cabinet level discussions on human resource management issues. The Commission further recommends decentralization of a portion of OPM's operating responsibilities to maximize its role of personnel policy guidance to federal departments and agencies.**

*Fourth,* **the growth in recent years in the number of presidential appointees, whether those subject to Senate confirmation, noncareer senior executives, or personal and confidential assistants, should be curtailed. Although a reduction in the total number of presidential** appointees must be based on a position-by-position assessment, the Commission is confident that a substantial cut is possible, and believes a cut from the current 3,000 to no more than 2,000 is a reasonable target. Every President must have politically and philosophically compatible officials to implement his Administration's program. At the same time, however, experience suggests that excessive numbers of political appointees serving relatively brief periods may undermine the President's ability to govern, insulating the Administration from needed dispassionate advice and institutional memory. The mere size of the political turnover almost guarantees management gaps and discontinuities, while the best of the career professionals will leave government if they do not have challenging opportunities at the sub-cabinet level.

*Fifth,* the President and Congress must ensure that federal managers receive the added training they will need to perform effectively. The education of public servants must not end upon appointment to the civil service. Government must invest more in its executive development programs and develop stronger partnerships with America's colleges and universities.

*Sixth,* the nation should recognize the importance of civic education as a part of social studies and history in the nation's primary and secondary school curricula. Starting with a comprehensive review of current programs, the nation's educators and parents should work toward new curricula and livelier textbooks designed to enhance student understanding of America's civic institutions, relate formal learning about those institutions to the problems students care about, and link classroom learning to extracurricular practice.

*Seventh,* America should take advantage of the natural idealism of its youth by expanding and encouraging national volunteer service, whether through existing programs like ACTION, the Peace Corps, and VISTA, or experiments with initiatives like President Bush's Youth Engaged in Service (YES), and some of the ideas contained in the Democratic Leadership Council's citizen corps proposal.

*Eighth,* the President and Congress should establish a Presidential Public Service Scholarship Program targeted to 1,000 college or college-bound students each year, with careful attention to the recruitment of minority students. Admission to the program might be modeled on appointment to the military service academies—that is, through nomination by members of Congress—and should include tuition and other costs, in return for a commitment to a determined number of years of government service.

*Ninth,* the President should work with Congress to give high priority to restoring the depleted purchasing power of executive, judicial, and legislative salaries by the beginning of a new Congress in 1991, starting with an immediate increase of 25 percent. At the same time, the Commission recommends that Congress enact legislation eliminating speaking honoraria and other income related to their public responsibilities.

*Tenth,* if Congress is unable to act on its own salaries, the Commission recommends that the President make separate recommendations for judges and top level executives and that the Congress promptly act upon them. Needed pay raises for presidential appointees, senior career executives, and judges should no longer be dependent on the ability of Congress to raise its own pay.

*Eleventh,* the President and Congress should give a higher budget priority to civil service pay in the General Schedule pay system. In determining the appropriate increase, the Commission concludes that the current goal of national comparability between public and private pay is simplistic and unworkable, and is neither fair to the civil service nor to the public it serves. **The Commission therefore recommends a new civil service pay-setting process that recognizes the objective fact that pay differs by occupation and by localities characterized by widely different living costs and labor market pressures.**

*Twelfth,* **the President and Congress should establish a permanent independent advisory council, composed of members from the public and private sector, both to monitor the ongoing state of the public service and to make such recommendations for improvements as they think desirable.** The Commission applauds President Bush's pledge of leadership of the public service. Indeed, his recent statements reflect the spirit and concerns that led to the creation of the Commission. However, the problems that make up this "quiet crisis" are many and complex and have been long in the making. Corrective action will not only require presidential leadership and congressional support, but must be part of a coherent and sustained long term strategy. The proposed independent advisory council is designed to ensure that the state of the public service remains high on the national agenda.

This report speaks directly to a number of audiences: to the *American people* about the importance to their civic institutions of talented men and women; to *young people* about the challenges and satisfactions they can find in serving their government; to *candidates for elective office* about the long-term costs of "bureaucrat bashing"; to the *media* about the need not only to hold public servants to high standards but also to recognize those who serve successfully; to *university schools of public affairs* about developing curricula for training of a new generation of government managers; and to *business leaders* about the importance of quality government support to the private sector.

Finally, the report speaks to the *civil service* about its obligations to the highest standards of performance. The Commission fully supports the need for better pay and working conditions in much of government. But **the Commission also recognizes that public support for those improvements is dependent on a commitment by the civil servants themselves to efficiency, responsiveness, and integrity.**

# 33

# Civil Service 2000: Policies for the Future

*U.S. Office of Personnel Management*

## The Coming Crisis

The Federal government faces a slowly emerging crisis of competence. For years, many Federal agencies have been able to hire and retain highly-educated, highly-skilled workforces, even though their wages, incentives and working conditions have not been fully competitive with those offered by private employers. But as labor markets become tighter during the early 1990s, hiring qualified workers will become more difficult. Unless steps are taken now to address the problem, the average qualifications and competence of many segments of the Federal workforce will deteriorate, perhaps so much as to impair the ability of some agencies to function.

Many factors have contributed to the current situation:

• **For many high-skills jobs in expensive regions, Federal compensation is increasingly non-competitive.** The most recent report of the President's Commission on Compensation of Career Federal Executives reported that the gap between top Federal general schedule salaries and comparable private salaries was 24 percent. In high-wage areas such as New York City, the Northeast, and the Pacific Coast, and in high-ranking jobs, the Federal wage disadvantage is even greater.

SOURCE: U.S. Office of Personnel Management, Washington, D.C., 1988.

• **For many years, public esteem for civil servants has been declining and the prestige of government jobs has been falling.** Over the past two decades a succession of political candidates has campaigned against "waste in Washington." These candidates often equated the problems of government with the unresponsiveness or incompetence of civil servants. Gradually, this drumbeat of criticism has transformed traditional public skepticism about the government into a mood of outright disdain and hostility. As public esteem for Federal employment has eroded, fewer of the most talented individuals have entered government service. This has left the government to hire what some have suggested, only half jokingly, is the "best of the desperate."

• **Low pay and low prestige have been exacerbated by outdated management practices and needless aggravations.** The inherent frustrations and constraints of large bureaucracies have been compounded in the Federal government by limited advancement opportunities, needless aggravation, and, often, poor working conditions. Most Federal managers must hire and motivate a workforce in the face of a number of obstacles. Some of these problems are inevitable. For example, because the Federal government is run by Presidential appointees, there is a ceiling on the career advancement opportunities of most top civil servants. And because many employees hold sensitive positions, they are subject to random drug testing, even though they are not suspected of drug use and may find the tests objectionable.

Other annoyances could be avoided, however. Many Federal offices are drab or even seedy. Federal telephones are monitored to check for personal calls. Periodically, thousands of non-essential Federal employees are sent home to await the resolution of another Congressional budget impasse. In addition, Federal workers often see that unproductive employees are retained, while those making extra efforts are not always rewarded. Regardless of the attitudes they bring with them to government, many

Federal workers soon come to believe that energy, initiative and risk-taking are less valued behaviors than "going by the book" and staying out of trouble.

There are a growing number of indicators that these problems have already begun to affect the Federal government's ability to recruit and retain the best. For example, limited (and perhaps not fully comparable) data on test scores suggest that the average for new hires on recent tests stands in the mid-80s, compared to averages in the mid-90s for candidates who took the PACE exam during the 1970s. The number of graduates of schools of public administration entering Federal service has dropped by 25 percent since 1979. The IRS now hires accountants from the 54th percentile of the national CPA examination, compared to candidates from the 86th percentile hired by the Big Eight firms. At some VA hospitals, intensive care beds are unavailable because of a national shortage of nurses. In a 1987 survey of Federal executives, 54 percent of those asked said that they would not encourage young people to consider a career in Federal service.

There are at least three major reasons why the current problem with recruitment and retention of top-quality Federal employees will grow more severe during the 1990s:

• **First, the competition for well-qualified workers will become more intense during the 1990s.** Not only will the rate of growth of the labor force be slowing and the numbers of young people entering the workforce declining, but substantial numbers of those entering the workforce will have lower levels of competence in language, math, and other basic skills. Private employers will undoubtedly respond to this changing labor market with higher entry-level wages, more recruitment and training of nontraditional workers, more flexible benefit packages, and other adjustments. Unless Federal agencies are able to respond in similar ways, some of them will be unable to compete successfully with the private sector, and may find it much harder to recruit and keep good employees.

• **Second, a growing share of Federal jobs will fall into the highest skill, most competitive categories.** The Federal government is already an extensive employer of professional, technical, and other highly skilled workers. The trend toward contracting out of blue-collar jobs and the shift of service delivery mechanisms to state and local governments will increasingly shift the mix of Federal jobs to higher skill levels. Research, program management, procurement, monitoring, and auditing responsibilities are growing, while direct delivery of services is shrinking. As a result, the need for more well-qualified Federal workers will rise throughout the 1990s. The Federal government will not have the option of hiring foreigners, moving jobs overseas, or "dumbing down" the jobs with computers. It will have to hire more qualified people.

• **Finally, the new, portable Federal Employees Retirement System (FERS) will substantially reduce the "golden handcuffs" that now tie senior employees to the Federal government.** The traditional Civil Service Retirement System (CSRS), with its nonportable benefits that are tied to age and length of service, strongly discourages employees with long service records from leaving the government. Less than 3 percent of those with more than 10 years of service leave the government voluntarily each year. Currently about two-thirds of Federal employees are covered by the CSRS system. As these workers retire, their replacements will be covered under the highly portable FERS and Social Security systems. As a result, Federal employees are likely to be much more willing to leave the government in response to better opportunities elsewhere or dissatisfaction with their situations. If Federal pay, benefits and working conditions are perceived to be inferior to those available from private employers, Federal employers may be faced with higher levels of turnover at senior levels, and the challenge of recruiting and keeping senior professional and technical people will grow.

## Policies for the 1990s

Traditionally, Federal service has offered a number of benefits that have made up for its drawbacks. If the pay was limited and the bureaucracy oppressive, the government at least provided more job security, better and earlier retirement, the chance to affect major national policies, and the personal satisfaction of helping to accomplish important national goals. Now many of those rewards are either diminished or eliminated, at a time when fewer new workers are entering the workplace, and fewer of these new entrants seem inclined toward careers in the Federal government. To cope with this changing demographic and employment environment, the Federal government needs to develop better strategies for attracting, hiring, training, motivating, and keeping talented people. Four steps will be most important:

• **Decentralize authority and responsibility for operations and hiring.** In terms of mission, organization, and skills, there is no such thing as "the Federal government." There is only an aggregation of different agencies, each of which has different goals, different structures, and different employee needs. If these highly diverse organizations are to accomplish their objectives during the labor-short 1990s, individual Federal agencies must be given far more flexibility and freedom in personnel matters. Standardized recruitment, testing, competition, classification, and pay should give way to decentralized personnel management, giving agency managers full responsibility not only for their missions, but for the human resources they need to accomplish them.

• **Continue emphasis on the hiring, training, and promotion of women and minorities.** The Federal government was a serious and successful equal opportunity employer many years before such policies were widely accepted in private industry. All employers in the 1990s will be hiring from a pool of workers dominated by women and minorities. If it remains an exemplary employer of these groups, the Federal government can expect to attract and keep more than its "fair share" of the best qualified members of this changing workforce.

• **Substantially increase internal and external education of Federal workers.**

Federal agencies can either "buy" or "make" the skills they need. In other words, they can recruit and hire highly skilled, qualified workers from the national labor market, or they can invest in their current workers and teach them what they need to know. Since many Federal employers will continue to face difficulties in competing for the best-qualified workers, Federal agencies should systematically invest more in their existing workforces. This will not only make the Federal government a more attractive place to work, it will be a cost-effective way to build Federal skills.

• **Upgrade Federal pay and make benefit packages more flexible. In return, demand performance.** In the end, decentralization, recruitment of minorities and women, and training will not matter much unless the Federal government can offer salaries that are comparable with those offered by other employers. Only a few Federal jobs can expect to continue to draw large numbers of eager applicants because of their intrinsic interest or prestige. Some, but not all, Federal jobs should be much more highly paid than they are today. Some, but not all, workers will respond to innovative benefits, such as day care, additional leave, flexible worktimes, or other options. Just as Federal pay and benefits should be set according to private sector standards, so Federal workers should also be held to private sector standards of performance. A small but important part of the task of building a quality workforce is the flexibility to set high standards, and to fire those who do not measure up. . . .

Implementing these strategies will be politically difficult, and the transition will be time-consuming and possibly expensive. But the alternative—watching the quality of the Federal workforce decline until some agencies become too weak to function properly—is even more threatening. . . .

## Contracting Out

There are many ways in which . . . changes could be implemented. At one extreme, decentralization could mean further privatization or contracting out of Federal activities. Private companies that provide specified services can be held accountable for the quality of their products or services, and may be left free to manage and pay their workforces as they see fit, within the limits of Federal laws mandating equal opportunity, and fair play and working conditions.

Although more can be accomplished in this area, not all or even a majority of Federal responsibilities can be taken over by private entrepreneurs. Private companies cannot regulate business, contract for weapons systems, or authorize grants to state and local governments. Moreover, even when Federal services are contracted out, there is a residual requirement for top-quality Federal managers to oversee the contracting process. These managers must be at least as knowledgeable and capable as the contractors they monitor, if they are to ensure that the contractors perform their assignments satisfactorily and cost-effectively. At present, however, many Federal contract management jobs are typically low-level, low-paying slots with little prestige or chance for advancement. Many of the most capable Federal professionals consider the task of contract management to be a step down in their professional careers. Unless ways are found to attract and reward top-quality Federal contract managers, the road toward contracting out Federal services is likely to be strewn with embarrassing frauds and expensive failures.

## Delegated Authority

While most government services cannot be shifted to private contractors, many of the benefits of private management could be achieved simply by decentralizing authority within the current system.

Under such an arrangement, the top managers of each Federal agency might receive complete authority for recruitment, hiring, firing, training, classification, pay, and benefits. They would be free to differentiate their agencies' personnel practices from others in any

way necessary to obtain the people they need to perform their missions. Already, of course, some of this flexibility has already been provided by the Office of Personnel Management to some agencies, and many of them have begun to employ new approaches. . . .

## Emphasize Employment of Women and Minorities

The Federal government has been a leader in recruiting, managing and promoting women and minorities. While during the 1990s many private companies will be struggling to adjust to a labor market dominated by these groups, the Federal government has, in a sense, already reached the future. Both in numbers and policies, the Federal government is on the leading edge of the changing workforce. . . .

This history may be an advantage to Federal agencies that seek to hire new workers in the labor-short 1990s. As an employer with a demonstrated record of unbiased hiring and upward mobility, and with a set of programs designed to enhance the quality of worklife for women and minorities, the Federal government may be perceived as a particularly attractive employer by these groups. Thus, the best qualified women and minorities may be predisposed to accept Federal job offers. Because the Federal government has a greater proportion of women and minorities in top jobs, new recruits are likely to see Federal employers in a more favorable light compared to private companies where advancement opportunities have been more limited.

In order to capitalize on this strength, Federal agencies should seek to maintain their leadership as exemplary employers of women and minorities. One important area of innovation, the experiments with flexible work schedules and extended leave policies, should continue to be pursued aggressively. Few employers have been able to satisfy the desires of two-earner families for more time away from work to care for children and aging family members.

Organizations that are able to offer more flexible work schedules, while still cost-effectively accomplishing their missions, are more likely to have their pick of the available candidates for hard-to-fill jobs.

A second important strategy concerns child care benefits. While a minority of Federal employers will want to provide on-site care facilities, every agency should be seeking to find cost-effective ways to assist parents in providing high-quality child care. The Federal government should not allow itself to lag behind other employers in the development of programs to address this issue if it wishes to hire and keep large numbers of mothers (and fathers) during the 1990s.

It is recognized that children can be significantly helped or hurt by the quality of care they receive before they enter school. This recognition is rapidly being translated both into political pressure for government action and employer initiatives to provide for employees' needs. In seeking to establish a competitive advantage vis-a-vis other employers, Federal agencies are likely to find child care to be a high leverage addition to their benefit offerings. Assistance may be as simple and cheap as referral services, or as expensive as care vouchers or in-building services. By the late 1990s, child care will have become a standard and widely expected employee benefit. If the Federal government can lead rather than follow this trend, (within the context of budgetary realities and fairness to all employees), its ability to recruit talented parents will certainly be enhanced. (Appendix A discusses this issue more fully.)

Finally, the Federal government should consider revising its approach to the hiring of foreign nationals. Just as products, services, and financial capital move ever-more-easily across international boundaries, so also do people. Many of the fastest growing, most profitable companies in America are responding to changes in U.S. and world labor markets by hiring more non-U.S. nationals, not only for low level service jobs but also for technical and professional positions. While the use of such foreign nationals presents many complex educational, cultural and social issues, and is often politically divisive, some greater measure of flexibility in the use of such workers by the Federal government seems justified. In particular, in the health professions and engineering fields, the available workforce is sometimes dominated by non-citizens. In undertaking greater hiring of such workers, complete decentralization of authority is probably not desirable; rather a more cautious approach seems warranted, providing greater flexibility within the constraints of equity for U.S. nationals, national security concerns and other factors.

## Educate for the Future

After graduation from high school or college, most workers (and their employers) assume that there will be little need for further formal education. Historically, this belief has proven to be accurate for Federal as well as private sector employees. Relatively few workers return to school to learn new disciplines; and when faced with a need for new skills, employers have generally hired new workers just out of school or workers from other firms, rather than retraining their existing staff to fill the new vacancies. For example, when the EPA was established in the early 1970s, most of its employees were hired from outside the Federal government.

This historic pattern is likely to be unworkable for many Federal agencies by the year 2000. The disparity between the salaries, prerequisites, and advancement opportunities available to workers in Federal service and those in the private sector is likely to make it increasingly difficult for Federal agencies to hire talented employees with advanced educations, particularly in such high-growth fields as medicine, engineering, and computer science. If the combination of low prestige and unequal pay that has been true in recent years persists, many other types of skilled workers may be in short supply on Federal rosters. The replacement of the immobilizing CSRS system with the portable

FERS retirement program may increase the need to recruit many highly skilled workers.

The obvious solution to these emerging difficulties in hiring the most educated workers is to educate and train those who are already at work in Federal agencies. Where skills are now or prospectively will be in short supply, agencies should be given the broad latitude to invest in new schooling for current employees. Tuition assistance, educational sabbaticals, and even multi-year advanced training programs should be the norm in agencies that face skill shortages. To prevent abuses, most programs should require some cost sharing, and should require participant's commitment to continued Federal employment. . . .

## Establishing a Direction

Many other policy initiatives could be implemented besides the key areas already discussed. For example, the quality of the Federal work environment is often not competitive with private industry. Compared to plush carpets and modern amenities common in industry, government offices appear drab, crowded, and uninspiring. Employees could be given more choice in selection of equipment and office furnishings. Emphasis could be placed more on productivity rather than scheduling. Restrictions could be altered in favor of policies that reward compliance rather than punish non-conformity. The possibilities for revised policies are as varied as the managers that could implement them. . . .

In establishing competitive employment opportunities, there is no single solution or strategy. Some agencies may find that their missions are so exciting, or their work environments so attractive that they need not offer fully competitive salaries. Others may be able to tap non-traditional sources of employees to fill their needs. Still others may need to offer a combination of pay, benefits, and working conditions that rival or exceed those of the best employers in America.

In the 1990s, the effort to attract a share of the most talented Americans to Federal service will grow more challenging. Without reforms, some agencies may find that the quality of the services they can deliver will slowly erode, undermining public faith and support. For others, business as usual carries a genuine risk of failure to fulfill the basic public responsibilities they are charged with. For the Federal government collectively, the time to address these issues is now, before a slow decline or crisis has irrevocably damaged the reputation for competence, honesty and fairness that the Federal civil service still enjoys.